Mastering VMware vSphere® 5.5

Mastering VMware vSphere® 5.5

Nick Marshall

Scott Lowe

with

Forbes Guthrie

Matt Liebowitz

Josh Atwell

SYBEX®
A Wiley Brand

Acquisitions Editor: Mariann Barsolo

Development Editor: Stephanie Barton

Technical Editor: Jason Boche

Production Editor: Dassi Zeidel

Copy Editor: Judy Flynn

Editorial Manager: Pete Gaughan

Production Manager: Tim Tate

Vice President and Executive Group Publisher: Richard Swadley

Associate Publisher: Chris Webb

Book Designers: Maureen Forys, Happenstance Type-O-Rama; Judy Fung

Proofreader: Rebecca Rider

Indexer: Ted Laux

Project Coordinator, Cover: Katherine Crocker

Cover Designer: Ryan Sneed

Cover Image: ©Getty Images, Inc./ ColorBlind Images

Copyright © 2014 by John Wiley & Sons, Inc., Indianapolis, Indiana

Published simultaneously in Canada

ISBN: 978-1-118-66114-7

ISBN: 978-1-118-75023-0 (ebk)

ISBN: 978-1-1188-2503-7 (ebk)

For general information on our other products and services or to obtain technical support, please contact our Customer Care Department within the U.S. at (877) 762-2974, outside the U.S. at (317) 572-3993 or fax (317) 572-4002.

Wiley publishes in a variety of print and electronic formats and by print-on-demand. Some material included with standard print versions of this book may not be included in e-books or in print-on-demand. If this book refers to media such as a CD or DVD that is not included in the version you purchased, you may download this material at http://booksupport.wiley.com. For more information about Wiley products, visit www.wiley.com.

Library of Congress Control Number: 2013948020

10 9 8 7 6 5 4 3 2 1

Dear Reader,

Thank you for choosing *Mastering VMware vSphere 5.5*. This book is part of a family of premium-quality Sybex books, all of which are written by outstanding authors who combine practical experience with a gift for teaching.

Sybex was founded in 1976. More than 30 years later, we're still committed to producing consistently exceptional books. With each of our titles, we're working hard to set a new standard for the industry. From the paper we print on, to the authors we work with, our goal is to bring you the best books available.

I hope you see all that reflected in these pages. I'd be very interested to hear your comments and get your feedback on how we're doing. Feel free to let me know what you think about this or any other Sybex book by sending me an email at contactus@sybex.com. If you think you've found a technical error in this book, please visit http://sybex.custhelp.com. Customer feedback is critical to our efforts at Sybex.

Best regards,

Chris Webb
Associate Publisher
Sybex, an Imprint of Wiley

I dedicate this book to my wife, Natalie. Your support and encouragement is unwavering. I couldn't have completed such a task without you. I also dedicate this book to my mother. Mum, you were taken too soon but you still influence me every day.

—Nick Marshall

This book is dedicated to my Heavenly Father, who gives me lots of good and perfect gifts (James 1:17 NIV). The opportunity to write another book is one of those gifts, but more precious than that is the gift of family: my wife and my truest friend, Crystal; my kids (Summer, Johnny, Mike, Liz, Rhys, Sean, and Cameron); and those who have been brought into my family (Matt, Christopher, and Tim).

—Scott Lowe

Acknowledgments

When Scott Lowe expressed his interest to "collaborate on a writing project," I would never have believed the journey that was to follow. It's been a rollercoaster, but one I have thoroughly enjoyed. While writing a book has been a huge learning curve for me, one thing is certainly clear: You can't underestimate how important those around you really are.

First of all I want to say thank you to Scott. Handing me such a great responsibility is an honor I will never forget. Your generosity is continuously evident to this day, and your reputation in the industry is second to none. Your work in Chapters 1 and 5 are top notch (as usual), and I hope we can work together again in the future.

Second, I want to say thank you to my contributing authors, Forbes, Matt, and Josh. Your ability to hit the ground running and produce quality work was a real blessing for me as I found my feet. Forbes, your advice and efficiency writing Chapter 4 was much appreciated. Matt, your commitment to Chapter 9 while running many other projects is an inspiration. Josh, thank you for stepping up and sharing your skills in Chapter 14; I couldn't have done it without you.

I'd also like to thank my technical editor, Jason Boche. Jason, thank you not just for finding my mistakes, but also for giving me a more detailed understanding on certain things. This book is better thanks to your attention to detail.

The team at Wiley/Sybex has been so supportive throughout this process, and I'm very grateful of their leadership. Mariann Barsolo, thank you for putting up with my never-ending questions; Stephanie Barton and Dassi Zeidel and the rest of the editing team, thank you for all that you did to ensure the quality of this work and also for understanding all my strange Australian spellings.

There have also been a number of people who helped ensure that the project was a success. Duncan Epping, thank you for your words of wisdom when I was starting out. Grant Orchard, thank you for reading my first drafts. Trevor Roberts Jr., thank you for getting me out of a bind when I needed it most. Fausto Ibarra, thank you for reaching out and getting me in touch with the right people. I'd also like to thank the VMware community as a whole. To all the bloggers, speakers, tweeters, and podcasters: Without you all I would never have started down this road.

Finally, I would like to thank VMware—not only does this company provide me employment, but without VMware this book and more importantly this industry, would not be what it is today.

—*Nick Marshall*

There are some things that get easier after you've done them multiple times. Acknowledging all the people whose support makes writing a book possible isn't one of those things.

I'll start by thanking Nick Marshall, my partner in crime for this book and the bearer of the torch for future revisions of *Mastering VMware vSphere*. I'm thrilled to have had the opportunity to work with you, and I'm equally thrilled to know that this book series is as much a labor of love for you as it has been for me. I look forward to seeing future editions.

I'd also like to thank the contributing authors (in no particular order): Forbes Guthrie, Matt Liebowitz, and Josh Atwell. Thank you all for your hard work and your contributions.

As with any technical book, technical accuracy is critical. My thanks go to Jason Boche, who served as the technical editor for this edition. Jason, your oversight helped make sure that we all got the details correct. Thanks for your feedback, corrections, and constructive criticism.

Next, my thanks go to the entire Sybex team: Mariann Barsolo, the acquisitions editor; Stephanie Barton, the developmental editor; Dassi Zeidel, the production editor; Judy Flynn, the copyeditor; Rebecca Rider, the proofreader; Pete Gaughan, the editorial manager; and Neil Edde for his support. I don't know how the book publishing process works with other publishers, but I can say that you guys have made the process as painless as something like this can be. Thanks for everything.

Finally, thanks to my family for all their support. Crystal, I can't express how much your support has meant to me since I started down the book writing path in 2009. Someday I'll figure out how to repay you. Thanks also to my kids, Sean and Cameron, for putting up with deadlines and late nights spent writing at the computer. I really appreciate your support.

—*Scott Lowe*

About the Authors

Nick Marshall is a consultant with over 13 years IT experience and holds multiple advanced IT certifications, including VMware Certified Advanced Professional 5—Datacenter Administrator (VCAP5-DCA), and VMware Certified Advanced Professional 5—Datacenter Design (VCAP5-DCD). Currently working for VMware, he delivers virtualization and cloud solutions to some of the biggest organizations in the Asia-pacific region.

Previously, Nick has worked in a number of roles ranging from computer assembler to infrastructure architect and has gained experience across the board. Nick is particularly proud of his ability to solve business problems with technical solutions.

Outside of his day job, Nick continues to work on his passion for virtualization by helping run the most popular virtualization podcast, *vBrownBag*, and writing on his personal blog, at www.nickmarshall.com.au. You can also find him speaking at industry conferences such as VMUG and PEX. To recognize his contributions to the VMware community, Nick has been awarded the vExpert award for both 2012 and 2013.

Nick lives with his wife, Natalie and son, Ethan in Sydney, Australia.

Scott Lowe is an author, consultant, speaker, and blogger focusing on virtualization, networking, storage, and other enterprise technologies. Scott is currently a technical architect at VMware, focused on software-defined networking (SDN) and network virtualization.

Scott's technical expertise extends into several areas. He holds industry certifications from Cisco, EMC, Microsoft, NetApp, VMware, and others. He also holds the premier VMware Certified Design Expert (VCDX) certification; Scott is VCDX #39. For Scott's leadership in, support of, and involvement with the VMware community, he has been awarded the vExpert designation for all five years since the program's inception (2009, 2010, 2011, 2012, and 2013).

As an author, Scott has contributed to numerous online magazines focused around VMware and related virtualization technologies. He is regularly quoted as a virtualization expert in virtualization news stories. He has five other published books: *Mastering VMware vSphere 4; VMware vSphere 4 Administration Instant Reference* (with Jase McCarty and Matthew Johnson); *VMware vSphere Design* (with Forbes Guthrie and Maish Saidel-Keesing); and *Mastering VMware vSphere 5* and *VMware vSphere Design, 2nd Edition* (both with Forbes Guthrie), all published by Sybex.

As a speaker, Scott has spoken at several virtualization conferences as well as at VMworld every year since 2009. He regularly speaks at VMware user group meetings, locally in the United States as well as worldwide.

Scott is perhaps best known for his acclaimed virtualization blog at http://blog.scottlowe.org, where he regularly posts technical articles on a wide variety of topics. VMware, Microsoft, and other virtualization industry leaders regularly refer to content on his site, and it is regularly voted among the top five virtualization weblogs worldwide. Scott's weblog is one of the oldest virtualization-centric weblogs that is still active; he's been blogging since early 2005.

Scott lives near Denver, Colorado, with his wife, Crystal; his two youngest sons, Sean and Cameron; and—during the school year—his Chinese exchange student, Tim.

About the Contributors

The following individuals also contributed to this book.

Forbes Guthrie (Chapter 4) is an infrastructure architect who specializes in virtualization. He has worked in a variety of technical roles for over 15 years and achieved several industry certifications, including VMware's VMware Certified Professional—Datacenter Virtualization (VCP2/3/4/5-DV), VMware Certified Advanced Professional 5—Datacenter Administrator (VCAP5-DCA), and VMware Certified Advanced Professional 5—Datacenter Design (VCAP5-DCD). His experience spans many industries, and he has worked in Europe, Asia-Pacific, and North America. He holds a bachelor's degree in mathematics and business analysis and is a former captain in the British Army.

Forbes is the lead author of the first (vSphere 4) and second (vSphere 5) edition of the acclaimed book *VMware vSphere Design*, co-authored by Scott Lowe. He also contributed to Scott's book *Mastering VMware vSphere 5*. Forbes has spoken at VMware's own VMworld conference on the subject of design and vSphere 5.

Forbes's blog, www.vReference.com, is well regarded in the virtualization field and is aggregated on VMware's Planet V12n website. He is probably best known for his collection of free reference cards, long revered by those studying for their VMware qualifications. Forbes has been awarded the luminary designation of vExpert by VMware for his contribution to the virtualization community since its inception. His passion and knowledge have also been rewarded with the peer-reviewed top virtualization bloggers listing for the last five years.

Matt Liebowitz (Chapter 9) is an advisory solution architect with EMC Consulting with a focus on virtualizing business-critical applications. He has been a consultant and architect for over 12 years and has been working with VMware's enterprise virtualization products since 2002. Matt is an author of several books on virtualization, is a frequent contributor to the VMware Technology Network (VMTN), and has been an active blogger on virtualization since 2009.

Matt is honored to have been named a VMware vExpert each year since 2010 and also holds numerous industry certifications from both VMware and Microsoft. He maintains a virtualization focused blog at www.thelowercasew.com and is active on Twitter at @mattliebowitz.

When Matt is not out virtualizing the world, he is happily spending time with his wife, Joann, and his two kids, Tyler and Kaitlyn.

Josh Atwell (Chapter 14) is a vArchitect for VCE focusing on VMware and automation solutions on Vblock. Over the last 10+ years he has worked very hard to allow little pieces of code to do his work for him through various automation tools, especially PowerCLI. Josh is highly active in the virtualization community where he has led multiple technology-based user groups such as CIPTUG, VMUG, and UCS Users Group.

Josh holds both the VMware Certified Advanced Professional 5—Datacenter Administrator (VCAP5-DCA), and VMware Certified Advanced Professional 5—Datacenter Design (VCAP5-DCD) certifications and enjoys working with others on preparing for their certification pursuits through the *vBrownBag* podcast. Never known for lacking an opinion, he blogs at vtesseract.com and talks shop on Twitter as @Josh_Atwell. When not helping folks with things that start with *v*, he enjoys spending time with his children and his supportive wife, who has made everything mentioned possible.

Contents at a Glance

Contents

Foreword

Most people out there have a "bucket list," a list of things they hope to see, do, or accomplish at some point in their life. One of the items on my bucket list had always been writing a book. The desire to write a book first emerged in my early teen years and continued well into adulthood. No matter how hard I tried, though, it seemed as if this particular bucket list item wasn't going to get checked off the list. I know this seems like an odd statement to make now, but bear with me as I share the story—a story not everyone knows—about how that all changed.

The story starts in 2008. I'd managed to gain some visibility in the VMware community through my live-blogging of VMworld 2007 and VMworld 2008, and it was in 2008 that I met Chad Sakac. Chad is now a senior vice president at EMC Corporation, but then he was the leader of a small team of folks who later became known as the vSpecialists. At the time, making a connection with Chad was simply making a connection with a fellow virtualization geek. We chatted, traded virtualization stories, talked technology for a while, and that was that. Or so I thought.

Fast-forward to early 2009 when, somewhat out of the blue, I received an email from Chad. He'd been approached to write a book on VMware's upcoming vSphere 4.0 product release, the email stated, but he was unable to do it. Would I be interested in writing the book, he asked, saying he thought I'd be perfect for the task. Would I be interested? What a question to ask! Of course I was interested. So I responded in the affirmative, Chad connected me with his contacts at Wiley/Sybex, contracts were signed, and off I went. Later that year, at VMworld 2009, my first book, *Mastering VMware vSphere 4*, was released and quickly became one of the hottest titles in virtualization. (Chad contributed the chapter about storage in that book, in case you didn't already know.)

The rest, you could say, is history. My second book, *VMware vSphere 4 Administration Instant Reference*, was co-written with Jase McCarty and Matthew Johnson and released later in 2009. The third book, *VMware vSphere Design*, was co-written with Forbes Guthrie and Maish Saidel-Keesing and published in early 2011. *Mastering VMware vSphere 5*, an update to the book that started it all, was released later in 2011. Forbes and I teamed up again for *VMware vSphere Design, 2nd Edition*, which was released in early 2013.

Naturally, Wiley/Sybex had me in the crosshairs when it came time to talk about revising the *Mastering VMware vSphere* series for the vSphere 5.5 release. As much as I've enjoyed writing this series, this time around my mind went back to early 2009, and I thought about the excitement I'd felt when I was unexpectedly presented with the opportunity I'd always wanted. Sure, I could write the revision, but how much better would it be if I could "pay it forward," so to speak, and give someone else in the community the same opportunity I'd been given? The opportunity to write *Mastering VMware vSphere 4* had been generously dropped in my lap; why not do the same for someone else?

The book you're holding right now represents that decision to pay it forward. With the release of *Mastering VMware vSphere 5.5*, I'm officially passing the torch to Nick Marshall. Nick was a great selection to carry the torch. He'd already demonstrated a commitment to the community through his work on the vBrownBag podcast series as well as through his efforts with Alastair Cooke on AutoLab. During the writing of this book, I've been impressed with Nick's knowledge, dedication to quality, and attention to detail. I'm very excited about Nick taking over the series, and I hope you are as well. I further hope that the VMware community offers Nick the same level of support, feedback, and encouragement along his journey as an author as I have received during my journey.

I'm confident that you'll find this book to be every bit as useful, informative, and valuable as previous versions in the series have been. Nick, along with myself and a team of rock star contributors including Forbes Guthrie, Matt Liebowitz, and Josh Atwell, have put forth every effort to make sure that we have comprehensively addressed the new features and functionality in vSphere 5.5. This includes major new features like VSAN and expanded support for networking protocols like LACP. There's too much to mention here, but rest assured that the entire team has worked really hard to make this the authoritative title that you—the community—needs.

vSphere 5.5 represents a new release for VMware, and *Mastering VMware vSphere 5.5* represents a new release for this series. I hope that you enjoy both.

—*Scott Lowe*
VCDX, vExpert

Introduction

Back in 2005 I was trying to convince my boss that we should use GSX Server on our shiny new DL385. To him, it was a hard sell. He didn't understand why on earth we should install two operating systems onto a server, "It'll just slow it down!" he exclaimed. So I went ahead and started experimenting with VMware software on my desktop computer. Luckily at the time I had a workstation capable of running such things.

The times have changed quite a bit since then, and now virtualization—especially server virtualization—is readily embraced in corporate datacenters worldwide. VMware has gone from a relatively small vendor to one of the corporate heavyweights, garnering a commanding share of the server virtualization market with its top-notch virtualization products. Even now, when other companies such as Microsoft and Citrix have jumped into the server virtualization space, it's still VMware that's almost synonymous with virtualization. For all intents and purposes, VMware invented the market.

If you're reading this, though, there's a chance you're just now starting to learn about virtualization. What is virtualization, and why is it important to you?

I define *virtualization* as *the abstraction of one computing resource from another computing resource*. Consider storage virtualization; in this case, you are abstracting servers (one computing resource) from the storage to which they are connected (another computing resource). This holds true for other forms of virtualization, too, like application virtualization (abstracting applications from the operating system). When most information technology professionals think of virtualization, they think of hardware (or server) virtualization: abstracting the operating system from the underlying hardware on which it runs and thus enabling multiple operating systems to run simultaneously on the same physical server. That is the technology on which VMware has built its market share.

Almost single-handedly, VMware's enterprise-grade virtualization solution has revolutionized how organizations manage their datacenters. Before VMware introduced its powerful virtualization solution, organizations bought a new server every time a new application needed to be provisioned. Over time, datacenters became filled with servers that were all using only a fraction of their overall capacity. Even though these servers were underutilized, organizations still had to pay to power them and to dissipate the heat they generated.

Now, using VMware's server virtualization products, organizations can run multiple operating systems and applications on their existing hardware, and new hardware is purchased only when capacity needs dictate. No longer must organizations purchase a new physical server whenever a new application needs to be deployed. By stacking workloads together using virtualization, organizations derive greater value from their hardware investments. They also reduce operational costs by reducing the number of physical servers and associated hardware in the datacenter, in turn decreasing power usage and cooling needs in the datacenter. In some cases these operational cost savings can be quite significant.

But consolidation is only one benefit of virtualization; companies also realize greater workload mobility, increased uptime, streamlined disaster-recovery options, and a bevy of other benefits from adopting virtualization. And virtualization, specifically server virtualization, has created the foundation for a new way of approaching the computing model: cloud computing.

Cloud computing is built on the tenets of broad network access, resource pooling, rapid elasticity, on-demand self-service, and measured service. Virtualization, such as that provided by VMware's products, enables the IT industry to embrace this new operational model of more efficiently providing services to their customers, whether those customers are internal (their employees) or external (partners, end users, or consumers). That ability to efficiently provide services is the reason virtualization is important to you.

This book provides all the information you, as an information technology professional, need to design, deploy, configure, manage, and monitor a dynamic virtualized environment built on VMware's enterprise-class server virtualization product, vSphere 5.5.

What Is Covered in This Book

This book is written with a start-to-finish approach to installing, configuring, managing, and monitoring a virtual environment using the VMware vSphere 5.5 product suite. The book begins by introducing the vSphere product suite and all of its great features. After introducing all of the bells and whistles, the book details an installation of the product and then moves into configuration. This includes configuring vSphere's extensive networking and storage functionality. We wrap up the configuration discussion with chapters on high availability, redundancy, and resource utilization. After completing the installation and configuration, we move into virtual machine creation and management and then into monitoring and troubleshooting. You can read this book from cover to cover to gain an understanding of the vSphere product suite in preparation for a new virtual environment, or you can use it as a reference if you are an IT professional who has begun your virtualization and wants to complement your skills with real-world tips, tricks, and best practices as found in each chapter.

This book, geared toward the aspiring as well as the practicing virtualization professional, provides information to help implement, manage, maintain, and troubleshoot an enterprise virtualization scenario.

Here is a glance at what's in each chapter:

- **Chapter 1: Introducing VMware vSphere 5.5** We begin with a general overview of all the products that make up the vSphere 5.5 product suite. This chapter also covers vSphere licensing and provides some examples of benefits that an organization might see from adopting vSphere as its virtualization solution.

- **Chapter 2: Planning and Installing VMware ESXi** This chapter looks at selecting the physical hardware, choosing your version of VMware ESXi, planning your installation, and actually installing VMware ESXi, both manually and in an unattended fashion.

- **Chapter 3: Installing and Configuring vCenter Server** In this chapter, we dive deep into planning your vCenter Server environment. vCenter Server is a critical management component of vSphere, and so this chapter discusses the proper design, planning, installation, and configuration for vCenter Server.

◆   **Chapter 4: vSphere Update Manager and the vCenter Support Tools**   This chapter describes what is involved in planning, designing, installing and configuring the vSphere Update Manager. You'll use vCenter Update Manager to keep your vSphere environment patched and up-to-date.

◆   **Chapter 5: Creating and Configuring Virtual Networks**   The virtual networking chapter covers the design, management, and optimization of virtual networks, including new features like the vSphere Distributed Switch and other third-party switches. In this chapter we also initiate discussions and provide solutions on how to integrate the virtual networking architecture with the physical network architecture while maintaining network security.

◆   **Chapter 6: Creating and Configuring Storage Devices**   This in-depth chapter provides an extensive overview of the various storage architectures available for vSphere. In this chapter we discuss Fibre Channel, iSCSI, and NAS storage design and optimization techniques as well as storage features like thin provisioning, multipathing, and round-robin load balancing.

◆   **Chapter 7: Ensuring High Availability and Business Continuity**   This exciting chapter covers the hot topics regarding business continuity and disaster recovery. We provide details on building highly available server clusters in virtual machines. In addition, this chapter discusses the use of vSphere High Availability (HA) and vSphere Fault Tolerance (FT) as ways of providing failover for virtual machines running in a vSphere environment. We also discuss backup options using vSphere's Storage APIs.

◆   **Chapter 8: Securing VMware vSphere**   Security is an important part of any implementation, and in this chapter we cover different security management aspects, including managing direct ESXi host access and integrating vSphere with Active Directory. This chapter also covers how to manage user access for environments with multiple levels of system administration and how to employ Windows users and groups in conjunction with the vSphere security model to ease the administrative delegation that comes with enterprise-level deployments.

◆   **Chapter 9: Creating and Managing Virtual Machines**   This chapter introduces the practices and procedures involved in provisioning virtual machines through vCenter Server. In addition, you're introduced to timesaving techniques, virtual machine optimization, and best practices that will ensure simplified management as the number of virtual machines grows larger over time.

◆   **Chapter 10: Using Templates and vApps**   Chapter 10 introduces the idea of templates, a mechanism for more rapidly deploying standardized VM images. We also discuss cloning and the concept of a vApp—a specialized container used by vSphere for the distribution of multi-VM environments. In addition, we discuss the OVF standard used by VMware and other vendors for distributing VMs.

◆   **Chapter 11: Managing Resource Allocation**   In this chapter we provide a comprehensive look at managing resource allocation. From individual virtual machines to resource pools and clusters of ESXi hosts, this chapter explores how resources are consumed in vSphere and addresses the mechanisms you can use—reservations, limits, and shares—to manage and modify that resource allocation.

◆ **Chapter 12: Balancing Resource Utilization**   Resource allocation isn't the same as resource utilization, and this chapter follows up the discussion of resource allocation in Chapter 11 with a look at some of the ways vSphere offers to balance resource utilization. In this chapter, you'll learn about vSphere vMotion, Enhanced vMotion Compatibility, vSphere Distributed Resource Scheduler (DRS), Storage vMotion, and Storage DRS.

◆ **Chapter 13: Monitoring VMware vSphere Performance**   In Chapter 13 we look at some of the native tools in vSphere that give virtual infrastructure administrators the ability to track and troubleshoot performance issues. The chapter focuses on monitoring CPU, memory, disk, and network adapter performance across ESXi hosts, resource pools, and clusters in vCenter Server. In this chapter you'll also learn about vCenter Operations Manager.

◆ **Chapter 14: Automating VMware vSphere**   Many tasks VMware vSphere administrators face are repetitive, and here automation can help. In Chapter 14 we discuss several different ways to bring automation to your vSphere environment, including vCenter Orchestrator and PowerCLI.

◆ **Appendix: The Bottom Line**   This appendix offers solutions to the Master It problems at the end of each chapter.

The Mastering Series

The Mastering series from Sybex provides outstanding instruction for readers with intermediate and advanced skills, in the form of top-notch training and development for those already working in their field and clear, serious education for those aspiring to become pros. Every Mastering book includes the following:

◆ Real-World Scenarios, ranging from case studies to interviews, that show how the tool, technique, or knowledge presented is applied in actual practice

◆ Skill-based instruction, with chapters organized around real tasks rather than abstract concepts or subjects

◆ Self-review test questions, so you can be certain you're equipped to do the job right

The Hardware behind the Book

Starting out, it can seem difficult to build an environment in which you can learn by implementing the exercises and practices detailed in this book. It is possible to build a practice lab with minimal hardware, and we encourage you to follow along with the book. If you're just starting, we recommend building a nested virtual lab on your laptop or desktop computer. Head to www.labguides.com for details on AutoLab, a nested vSphere automation tool. It only needs VMware Workstation or Fusion installed and 8 GB of RAM. Be sure to read Chapter 2 and Chapter 3 before you attempt to construct any type of environment for development purposes.

For the purpose of writing this book, we used the following hardware configuration:

- Three Hewlett Packard DL-385 servers
- Two Hewlett Packard N36L micro servers
- One Qnap 439 Pro II NAS
- One generic 24-port gigabit switch

As you can see, it's not impossible to set yourself up with a nice lab to follow along. But for some, this is not the sort of environment to which they have access. For entry-level NFS and iSCSI testing, a number of vendors, including EMC, HP, and NetApp, offer virtual storage appliances or simulators that you can use to gain some familiarity with shared storage concepts and that specific vendor's products. We encourage you to use these sorts of tools where applicable in your learning process.

Who Should Buy This Book

This book is for IT professionals looking to strengthen their knowledge of constructing and managing a virtual infrastructure on vSphere 5.5. While the book can also be helpful for those new to IT, a strong set of assumptions is made about the target reader:

- A basic understanding of networking architecture
- Experience working in a Microsoft Windows environment
- Experience managing DNS and DHCP
- A basic understanding of how virtualization differs from traditional physical infrastructures
- A basic understanding of hardware and software components in standard x86 and x64 computing

How to Contact the Authors

We welcome feedback from you about this book or about books you'd like to see from us in the future.

You can reach Nick by writing to nick@nickmarshall.com.au, by following him on Twitter (his username is @nickmarshall9), or by visiting his blog at www.nickmarshall.com.au.

You can reach Scott by writing to scott.lowe@scottlowe.org, by following him on Twitter (his username is @scott_lowe), or by visiting his blog at http://blog.scottlowe.org.

Mastering VMware vSphere® 5.5

## Chapter 1

Introducing VMware vSphere 5.5

Now in its fifth generation, VMware vSphere 5.5 builds on previous generations of VMware's enterprise-grade virtualization products. vSphere 5.5 extends fine-grained resource allocation controls to more types of resources, enabling VMware administrators to have even greater control over how resources are allocated to and used by virtual workloads. With dynamic resource controls, high availability, unprecedented fault-tolerance features, distributed resource management, and backup tools included as part of the suite, IT administrators have all the tools they need to run an enterprise environment ranging from a few servers to thousands of servers.

In this chapter, you will learn to

◆ Identify the role of each product in the vSphere product suite

◆ Recognize the interaction and dependencies between the products in the vSphere suite

◆ Understand how vSphere differs from other virtualization products

Exploring VMware vSphere 5.5

The VMware vSphere product suite is a comprehensive collection of products and features that together provide a full array of enterprise virtualization functionality. The vSphere product suite includes the following products and features:

◆ VMware ESXi

◆ VMware vCenter Server

◆ vSphere Update Manager

◆ VMware vSphere Client and vSphere Web Client

◆ VMware vCenter Orchestrator

◆ vSphere Virtual Symmetric Multi-Processing

◆ vSphere vMotion and Storage vMotion

◆ vSphere Distributed Resource Scheduler (DRS)

◆ vSphere Storage DRS

◆ Storage I/O Control and Network I/O Control

◆ Profile-driven storage

- ◆ vSphere High Availability (HA)

- ◆ vSphere Fault Tolerance (FT)

- ◆ vSphere Storage APIs for Data Protection and VMware Data Protection

- ◆ Virtual SAN (VSAN)

- ◆ vSphere Replication

- ◆ Flash Read Cache

Rather than waiting to introduce these products and features in their own chapters, we will introduce each product or feature in the following sections. This will allow us to explain how each one affects the design, installation, and configuration of your virtual infrastructure. After we cover the features and products in the vSphere suite, you'll have a better grasp of how each of them fits into the design and the big picture of virtualization.

Certain products outside the vSphere product suite extend the vSphere product line with new functionality. These additional products include VMware Horizon View, VMware vCloud Director, VMware vCloud Automation Center, and VMware vCenter Site Recovery Manager, just to name a few. VMware even offers bundles of vSphere and these other products in the vCloud Suite to make it easier for users to purchase and consume the products in their environments. However, because of the size and scope of these products, they are not covered in this book.

As of the writing of this book, VMware vSphere 5.5 is the latest release of the VMware vSphere product family. This book covers functionality found in version 5.5. Where possible, we've tried to note differences between vSphere 5.0 or 5.1 and vSphere 5.5. For detailed information on VMware vSphere 5.0, refer to *Mastering VMware vSphere 5*, also published by Sybex (2011). (If you are still running vSphere 4.*x*, Sybex also offers *Mastering VMware vSphere 4* [2009].)

To help simplify navigation and to help you find information on the breadth of products and features in the vSphere product suite, we've prepared Table 1.1, which contains cross-references to where you can find more information about a particular product or feature elsewhere in the book.

TABLE 1.1: Product and feature cross-references

VMWARE VSPHERE PRODUCT OR FEATURE	MORE INFORMATION FOUND IN THIS CHAPTER
VMware ESXi	Installation – Chapter 2
	Networking – Chapter 5
	Storage – Chapter 6
VMware vCenter Server	Installation – Chapter 3
	Networking – Chapter 5
	Storage – Chapter 6
	Security – Chapter 8
vSphere Update Manager	Chapter 4

TABLE 1.1: Product and feature cross-references *(CONTINUED)*

VMWARE VSPHERE PRODUCT OR FEATURE	MORE INFORMATION FOUND IN THIS CHAPTER
vSphere Client and vSphere Web Client	Installation – Chapter 2 (vSphere Client)
	Installation – Chapter 3 (Web Client)
	Usage – Chapter 3
VMware vCenter Orchestrator	Chapter 14
vSphere Virtual Symmetric Multi-Processing	Chapter 9
vSphere vMotion and Storage vMotion	Chapter 12
vSphere Distributed Resource Scheduler	Chapter 12
vSphere Storage DRS	Chapter 12
Storage I/O Control and Network I/O Control	Chapter 11
Profile-driven storage	Chapter 6
vSphere High Availability	Chapter 7
vSphere Fault Tolerance	Chapter 7
vSphere Storage APIs for Data Protection	Chapter 7
VMware Data Protection	Chapter 7
VSAN	Chapter 6
vSphere Replication	Chapter 7
Flash Read Cache	Installation – Chapter 6
	Usage – Chapter 11

First we'll look at the actual products that make up the VMware vSphere product suite, and then we'll examine the major features. Let's start with the products in the suite; in particular, let's start with VMware ESXi.

Examining the Products in the vSphere Suite

In the following sections, we'll describe and review the products found in the vSphere product suite.

VMWARE ESXI

The core of the vSphere product suite is the hypervisor, which is the virtualization layer that serves as the foundation for the rest of the product line. In vSphere 5 and later, including vSphere 5.5, the hypervisor comes in the form of VMware ESXi.

Long-time users of VMware vSphere may recognize this as a shift in the way VMware provides the hypervisor. Prior to vSphere 5, the hypervisor was available in two forms: VMware ESX and VMware ESXi. Although both products shared the same core virtualization engine, supported the same set of virtualization features, leveraged the same licenses, and were considered bare-metal installation hypervisors (also referred to as Type 1 hypervisors; see the sidebar titled "Type 1 and Type 2 Hypervisors"), there were still notable architectural differences. In VMware ESX, VMware used a Linux-derived Service Console to provide an interactive environment through which users could interact with the hypervisor. The Linux-based Service Console also included services found in traditional operating systems, such as a firewall, Simple Network Management Protocol (SNMP) agents, and a web server.

TYPE 1 AND TYPE 2 HYPERVISORS

Hypervisors are generally grouped into two classes: Type 1 hypervisors and Type 2 hypervisors. Type 1 hypervisors run directly on the system hardware and thus are often referred to as *bare-metal* hypervisors. Type 2 hypervisors require a host operating system, and the host operating system provides I/O device support and memory management. VMware ESXi is a Type 1 bare-metal hypervisor. (In earlier versions of vSphere, VMware ESX was also considered a Type 1 bare-metal hypervisor.) Other Type 1 bare-metal hypervisors include KVM (part of the open-source Linux kernel), Microsoft Hyper-V, and products based on the open-source Xen hypervisor like Citrix XenServer and Oracle VM.

VMware ESXi, on the other hand, is the next generation of the VMware virtualization foundation. Unlike VMware ESX, ESXi installs and runs without the Linux-based Service Console. This gives ESXi an ultralight footprint of approximately 70 MB. Despite the lack of the Service Console, ESXi provides all the same virtualization features that VMware ESX supported in earlier versions. Of course, ESXi 5.5 has been enhanced from earlier versions to support even more functionality, as you'll see in this chapter and in future chapters.

The key reason that VMware ESXi is able to support the same extensive set of virtualization functionality as VMware ESX without the Service Console is that the core of the virtualization functionality wasn't (and still isn't) found in the Service Console. It's the *VMkernel* that is the foundation of the virtualization process. It's the VMkernel that manages the virtual machines' (VMs') access to the underlying physical hardware by providing CPU scheduling, memory management, and virtual switch data processing. Figure 1.1 shows the structure of VMware ESXi.

We mentioned earlier that VMware ESXi 5.5 is enhanced over earlier releases. One such area of enhancement is in the configuration limits of what the hypervisor is capable of supporting. Table 1.2 shows the configuration maximums for the last few versions of VMware ESX/ESXi.

TABLE 1.2:   VMware ESXi maximums

COMPONENT	VMWARE ESXI 5.5 MAXIMUM	VMWARE ESXI 5.0 MAXIMUM	VMWARE ESX/ESXI 4.0 MAXIMUM
Number of virtual CPUs per host	4,096	2,048	512
Number of logical CPUs (hyper-threading enabled)	320	160	64
Number of virtual CPUs per core	32	25	20 (increased to 25 in Update 1)
Amount of RAM per host	4TB	2 TB	1 TB

FIGURE 1.1
The VMkernel is the foundation of the virtualization functionality found in VMware ESXi

These are just some of the configuration maximums. Where appropriate, future chapters will include additional values for VMware ESXi maximums for network interface cards (NICs), storage, VMs, and so forth.

Given that VMware ESXi is the foundation of virtualization within the vSphere product suite, you'll see content for VMware ESXi throughout the book. Table 1.1, earlier in this chapter, tells you where you can find more information about specific features of VMware ESXi elsewhere in the book.

VMWARE VCENTER SERVER

Stop for a moment to think about your current network. Does it include Active Directory? There is a good chance it does. Now imagine your network without Active Directory, without the ease of a centralized management database, without the single sign-on capabilities, and without the simplicity of groups. That is what managing VMware ESXi hosts would be like without using VMware vCenter Server. Not a very pleasant thought, is it? Now calm yourself down, take a deep breath, and know that vCenter Server, like Active Directory, is meant to provide a centralized management platform and framework for all ESXi hosts and their respective VMs. vCenter Server allows IT administrators to deploy, manage, monitor, automate, and secure a virtual infrastructure in a centralized fashion. To help provide scalability, vCenter Server leverages a backend database (Microsoft SQL Server and Oracle are both supported, among others) that stores all the data about the hosts and VMs.

In previous versions of VMware vSphere, vCenter Server was a Windows-only application. Version 5.5 of vSphere still offers this Windows-based installation of vCenter Server but also offers a prebuilt vCenter Server Appliance (a virtual appliance, in fact, something you'll learn about in Chapter 10, "Using Templates and vApps") that is based on Linux. Having a Linux-based vCenter Server Appliance is a great alternative for organizations that don't wish to deploy a Windows Server instance just to manage the vSphere environment.

vCenter Server not only provides configuration and management capabilities—which include features such as VM templates, VM customization, rapid provisioning and deployment of VMs, role-based access controls, and fine-grained resource allocation controls—it also provides the tools for the more advanced features of vSphere vMotion, vSphere Distributed Resource Scheduler, vSphere High Availability, and vSphere Fault Tolerance. All of these features are described briefly in this chapter and in more detail in later chapters.

In addition to vSphere vMotion, vSphere Distributed Resource Scheduler, vSphere High Availability, and vSphere Fault Tolerance, using vCenter Server to manage ESXi hosts enables a number of other features:

◆ Enhanced vMotion Compatibility (EVC), which leverages hardware functionality from Intel and AMD to enable greater CPU compatibility between servers grouped into vSphere DRS clusters

◆ Host profiles, which allow administrators to bring greater consistency to host configurations across larger environments and to identify missing or incorrect configurations

◆ Storage I/O Control, which provides cluster-wide quality of service (QoS) controls so that administrators can ensure that critical applications receive sufficient I/O resources even during times of congestion

◆ vSphere Distributed Switches, which provide the foundation for networking settings and third-party virtual switches that span multiple hosts and multiple clusters

◆ Network I/O Control, which allows administrators to flexibly partition physical NIC bandwidth and provide QoS for different types of traffic

◆ vSphere Storage DRS, which enables VMware vSphere to dynamically migrate storage resources to meet demand, much in the same way that DRS balances CPU and memory utilization

vCenter Server plays a central role in any sizable VMware vSphere implementation. In Chapter 3, "Installing and Configuring vCenter Server," we discuss planning and installing vCenter Server as well as look at ways to ensure its availability. Chapter 3 will also examine the differences between the Windows-based version of vCenter Server and the Linux-based vCenter Server virtual appliance. Because of vCenter Server's central role in a VMware vSphere deployment, we'll touch on vCenter Server in almost every chapter throughout the rest of the book. Refer to Table 1.1 previously in this chapter for specific cross-references.

vCenter Server is available in three packages:

◆ vCenter Server Essentials is integrated into the vSphere Essentials kits for small office deployment.

◆ vCenter Server Standard provides all the functionality of vCenter Server, including provisioning, management, monitoring, and automation.

◆ vCenter Server Foundation is like vCenter Server Standard but is limited to managing three ESXi hosts and does not include vCenter Orchestrator or support for linked-mode operation.

You can find more information on licensing and product editions for VMware vSphere in the section "Licensing VMware vSphere."

vSphere Update Manager

vSphere Update Manager is an add-on package for vCenter Server that helps users keep their ESXi hosts and select VMs patched with the latest updates. vSphere Update Manager provides the following functionality:

◆ Scans to identify systems that are not compliant with the latest updates

◆ User-defined rules for identifying out-of-date systems

◆ Automated installation of patches for ESXi hosts

◆ Full integration with other vSphere features like Distributed Resource Scheduler

vSphere Update Manager works with the Windows-based installation of vCenter Server as well as the prepackaged vCenter Server virtual appliance. Refer to Table 1.1 for more information on where vSphere Update Manager is described in this book.

VMware vSphere Web Client and vSphere Client

vCenter Server provides a centralized management framework for VMware ESXi hosts, but it's the vSphere Web Client (and its predecessor, the Windows-based vSphere Client) where vSphere administrators will spend most of their time.

With the release of vSphere 5, VMware shifted its primary administrative interface to a robust new vSphere Web Client. The vSphere Web Client provides a dynamic, web-based user interface for managing a virtual infrastructure and enables vSphere administrators to manage their infrastructure without needing to install the Windows-based vSphere Client on a system. In its initial release, the vSphere Web Client provided a subset of the functionality available to the "full" Windows-based vSphere Client. However, in subsequent releases—including the 5.5 release—the vSphere Web Client has been enhanced and expanded to include almost all the functionality a vSphere administrator needs to manage a vSphere environment. Further, VMware has stated that the vSphere Web Client will eventually replace the Windows-based vSphere Client entirely. For this reason, we'll use screen shots of the vSphere Web Client throughout this book unless it is impossible to do so.

The Windows-based vSphere Client is still available to allow you to manage ESXi hosts, either directly or through an instance of vCenter Server, but VMware's development efforts are focused on the vSphere Web Client. You can install the vSphere Client by browsing to the URL of an ESXi host or vCenter Server and selecting the appropriate installation link (although keep in mind that Internet access might be required in order to download the client in some instances). The vSphere Client provides a rich graphical user interface (GUI) for all day-to-day management tasks and for the advanced configuration of a virtual infrastructure. While you can connect the vSphere Client either directly to an ESXi host or to an instance of vCenter Server, the full set of management capabilities are available only when you are connecting the vSphere Client to vCenter Server.

As we mentioned earlier, the vSphere Web Client is the stated future direction for VMware vSphere's management interface. For that reason, we focus primarily on how to use the vSphere Web Client throughout this book. Tasks in the vSphere Client should be similar, but note that some tasks can be performed only in the vSphere Web Client, not the Windows-based vSphere Client.

VMware vCenter Orchestrator

VMware vCenter Orchestrator is a workflow automation engine that is automatically installed with every instance of vCenter Server. Using vCenter Orchestrator, vSphere administrators can build automated workflows for a wide variety of tasks available within vCenter Server. The automated workflows you build using vCenter Orchestrator range from simple to complex. VMware also makes vCenter Orchestrator plug-ins to extend the functionality to include manipulating Microsoft Active Directory, Cisco's Unified Computing System (UCS), and VMware vCloud Director. This makes vCenter Orchestrator a powerful tool to use in building automated workflows in the virtualized data center.

Now that we've discussed the specific products in the VMware vSphere product suite, we'd like to take a closer look at some of the significant features.

Examining the Features in VMware vSphere

In the following sections, we'll take a closer look at some of the features that are available in the vSphere product suite. We'll start with Virtual SMP.

vSphere Virtual Symmetric Multi-Processing

The vSphere Virtual Symmetric Multi-Processing (vSMP or Virtual SMP) product allows virtual infrastructure administrators to construct VMs with multiple virtual processors. vSphere Virtual SMP is *not* the licensing product that allows ESXi to be installed on servers with multiple processors; it is the technology that allows the use of multiple processors *inside* a VM. Figure

1.2 identifies the differences between multiple processors in the ESXi host system and multiple virtual processors.

FIGURE 1.2
vSphere Virtual
SMP allows VMs
to be created with
more than one
virtual CPU.

With vSphere Virtual SMP, applications that require and can actually use multiple CPUs can be run in VMs configured with multiple virtual CPUs. This allows organizations to virtualize even more applications without negatively impacting performance or being unable to meet service-level agreements (SLAs).

In vSphere 5, VMware expanded this functionality by also allowing users to specify multiple virtual cores per virtual CPU. Using this feature, a user could provision a dual "socket" VM with two cores per "socket" for a total of four virtual cores. This gives users tremendous flexibility in carving up CPU processing power among the VMs.

vSphere vMotion and vSphere Storage vMotion

If you have read anything about VMware, you have most likely read about the extremely useful feature called vMotion. vSphere vMotion, also known as *live migration*, is a feature of ESXi and vCenter Server that allows an administrator to move a running VM from one physical host to another physical host without having to power off the VM. This migration between two physical hosts occurs with no downtime and with no loss of network connectivity to the VM. The ability to manually move a running VM between physical hosts on an as-needed basis is a powerful feature that has a number of use cases in today's datacenters.

Suppose a physical machine has experienced a nonfatal hardware failure and needs to be repaired. Administrators can easily initiate a series of vMotion operations to remove all VMs from an ESXi host that is to undergo scheduled maintenance. After the maintenance is complete and the server is brought back online, administrators can utilize vMotion to return the VMs to the original server.

Alternately, consider a situation in which you are migrating from one set of physical servers to a new set of physical servers. Assuming that the details have been addressed—and we'll discuss the details around vMotion in Chapter 12, "Balancing Resource Utilization"—you can use vMotion to move the VMs from the old servers to the newer servers, making quick work of a server migration with no interruption of service.

Even in normal day-to-day operations, vMotion can be used when multiple VMs on the same host are in contention for the same resource (which ultimately is causing poor performance across all the VMs). vMotion can solve the problem by allowing an administrator to migrate any VMs that are facing contention to another ESXi host with greater availability for the resource in demand. For example, when two VMs are in contention with each other for CPU resources, an administrator can eliminate the contention by using vMotion to move one of the VMs to an ESXi host that has more available CPU resources.

vMotion moves the execution of a VM, relocating the CPU and memory footprint between physical servers but leaving the storage untouched. Storage vMotion builds on the idea and principle of vMotion by providing the ability to leave the CPU and memory footprint untouched on a physical server but migrating a VM's storage while the VM is still running.

Deploying vSphere in your environment generally means that lots of shared storage—Fibre Channel or iSCSI SAN or NFS—is needed. What happens when you need to migrate from an older storage array to a newer storage array? What kind of downtime would be required? Or what about a situation where you need to rebalance utilization of the array, either from a capacity or performance perspective?

vSphere Storage vMotion directly addresses these situations. By providing the ability to move the storage for a running VM between datastores, Storage vMotion enables administrators to address all of these situations without downtime. This feature ensures that outgrowing datastores or moving to a new SAN does not force an outage for the affected VMs and provides administrators with yet another tool to increase their flexibility in responding to changing business needs.

vSphere Distributed Resource Scheduler

vMotion is a manual operation, meaning that an administrator must initiate the vMotion operation. What if VMware vSphere could perform vMotion operations automatically? That is the basic idea behind vSphere Distributed Resource Scheduler (DRS). If you think that vMotion sounds exciting, your anticipation will only grow after learning about DRS. DRS, simply put, leverages vMotion to provide automatic distribution of resource utilization across multiple ESXi hosts that are configured in a cluster.

Given the prevalence of Microsoft Windows Server in today's datacenters, the use of the term *cluster* often draws IT professionals into thoughts of Microsoft Windows Server clusters. Windows Server clusters are often active-passive or active-active-passive clusters. However, ESXi clusters are fundamentally different, operating in an active-active mode to aggregate and combine resources into a shared pool. Although the underlying concept of aggregating physical hardware to serve a common goal is the same, the technology, configuration, and feature sets are quite different between VMware ESXi clusters and Windows Server clusters.

> ### AGGREGATE CAPACITY AND SINGLE HOST CAPACITY
>
> Although we say that a DRS cluster is an implicit aggregation of CPU and memory capacity, it's important to keep in mind that a VM is limited to using the CPU and RAM of a single physical host at any given time. If you have two ESXi servers with 32 GB of RAM each in a DRS cluster, the cluster will correctly report 64 GB of aggregate RAM available, but any given VM will not be able to use more than approximately 32 GB of RAM at a time.

An ESXi cluster is an implicit aggregation of the CPU power and memory of all hosts involved in the cluster. After two or more hosts have been assigned to a cluster, they work in unison to provide CPU and memory to the VMs assigned to the cluster (keeping in mind that any given VM can only use resources from one host; see the sidebar titled "Aggregate Capacity and Single Host Capacity"). The goal of DRS is twofold:

◆ At startup, DRS attempts to place each VM on the host that is best suited to run that VM at that time.

◆ While a VM is running, DRS seeks to provide that VM with the required hardware resources while minimizing the amount of contention for those resources in an effort to maintain balanced utilization levels.

The first part of DRS is often referred to as *intelligent placement*. DRS can automate the placement of each VM as it is powered on within a cluster, placing it on the host in the cluster that it deems to be best suited to run that VM at that moment.

DRS isn't limited to operating only at VM startup, though. DRS also manages the VM's location while it is running. For example, let's say three servers have been configured in an ESXi cluster with DRS enabled. When one of those servers begins to experience a high contention for CPU utilization, DRS detects that the cluster is imbalanced in its resource usage and uses an internal algorithm to determine which VM(s) should be moved in order to create the least imbalanced cluster. For every VM, DRS will simulate a migration to each host and the results will be compared. The migrations that create the least imbalanced cluster will be recommended or automatically performed, depending upon DRS's configuration.

DRS performs these on-the-fly migrations without any downtime or loss of network connectivity to the VMs by leveraging vMotion, the live migration functionality we described earlier. This makes DRS extremely powerful because it allows clusters of ESXi hosts to dynamically rebalance their resource utilization based on the changing demands of the VMs running on that cluster.

FEWER BIGGER SERVERS OR MORE SMALLER SERVERS?

Remember from Table 1.2 that VMware ESXi supports servers with up to 320 logical CPU cores and up to 4TB of RAM. With vSphere DRS, though, you can combine multiple smaller servers for the purpose of managing aggregate capacity. This means that bigger, more-powerful servers might not be better servers for virtualization projects. These larger servers, in general, are significantly more expensive than smaller servers, and using a greater number of smaller servers (often referred to as "scaling out") may provide greater flexibility than a smaller number of larger servers (often referred to as "scaling up"). The key thing to remember is that a bigger server isn't necessarily a better server.

vSphere Storage DRS

vSphere Storage DRS takes the idea of vSphere DRS and applies it to storage. Just as vSphere DRS helps to balance CPU and memory utilization across a cluster of ESXi hosts, Storage DRS helps balance storage capacity and storage performance across a cluster of datastores using mechanisms that echo those used by vSphere DRS.

We described vSphere DRS's feature called intelligent placement, which automates the placement of new VMs based on resource usage within an ESXi cluster. In the same fashion, Storage DRS has an intelligent placement function that automates the placement of VM virtual disks based on storage utilization. Storage DRS does this through the use of datastore clusters. When you create a new VM, you simply point it to a datastore cluster, and Storage DRS automatically places the VM's virtual disks on an appropriate datastore within that datastore cluster.

Likewise, just as vSphere DRS uses vMotion to balance resource utilization dynamically, Storage DRS uses Storage vMotion to rebalance storage utilization based on capacity and/or latency thresholds. Because Storage vMotion operations are typically much more resource intensive than vMotion operations, vSphere provides extensive controls over the thresholds, timing, and other guidelines that will trigger a Storage DRS automatic migration via Storage vMotion.

Storage I/O Control and Network I/O Control

VMware vSphere has always had extensive controls for modifying or controlling the allocation of CPU and memory resources to VMs. What vSphere didn't have prior to the release of vSphere 4.1 was a way to apply these same sort of extensive controls to storage I/O and network I/O. Storage I/O Control and Network I/O Control address that shortcoming.

Storage I/O Control (SIOC) allows vSphere administrators to assign relative priority to storage I/O as well as assign storage I/O limits to VMs. These settings are enforced cluster-wide; when an ESXi host detects storage congestion through an increase of latency beyond a user-configured threshold, it will apply the settings configured for that VM. The result is that VMware administrators can ensure that the VMs that need priority access to storage resources get the resources they need. In vSphere 4.1, Storage I/O Control applied only to VMFS storage; vSphere 5 extended that functionality to NFS datastores.

The same goes for Network I/O Control (NIOC), which provides VMware administrators with more granular controls over how VMs use network bandwidth provided by the physical NICs. As the widespread adoption of 10 Gigabit Ethernet continues, Network I/O Control provides VMware administrators with a way to more reliably ensure that network bandwidth is properly allocated to VMs based on priority and limits.

PROFILE-DRIVEN STORAGE

With profile-driven storage, vSphere administrators are able to use storage capabilities and VM storage profiles to ensure that VMs are residing on storage that is able to provide the necessary levels of capacity, performance, availability, and redundancy. Profile-driven storage is built on two key components:

- Storage capabilities, leveraging vSphere's storage awareness APIs
- VM storage profiles

Storage capabilities are either provided by the storage array itself (if the array is capable of using vSphere's storage awareness APIs) and/or defined by a vSphere administrator. These storage capabilities represent various attributes of the storage solution.

VM storage profiles define the storage requirements for a VM and its virtual disks. You create VM storage profiles by selecting the storage capabilities that must be present for the VM to run. Datastores that have all the capabilities defined in the VM storage profile are compliant with the VM storage profile and represent possible locations where the VM could be stored.

This functionality gives vSphere administrators much greater visibility into storage capabilities and helps ensure that the appropriate functionality for each VM is indeed being provided by the underlying storage.

Refer to Table 1.1 to find out which chapter discusses profile-driven storage in more detail.

vSphere High Availability

In many cases, high availability—or the lack of high availability—is the key argument used against virtualization. The most common form of this argument more or less sounds like this: "Before virtualization, the failure of a physical server affected only one application or workload. After virtualization, the failure of a physical server will affect many more applications or workloads running on that server at the same time. We can't put all our eggs in one basket!"

VMware addresses this concern with another feature present in ESXi clusters called vSphere High Availability (HA). Once again, by nature of the naming conventions (clusters, high availability), many traditional Windows administrators will have preconceived notions about this feature. Those notions, however, are incorrect in that vSphere HA does not function like a high-availability configuration in Windows. The vSphere HA feature provides an automated process for restarting VMs that were running on an ESXi host at a time of server failure (or other qualifying infrastructure failure, as we'll describe in Chapter 7, "Ensuring High Availability and Business Continuity"). Figure 1.3 depicts the VM migration that occurs when an ESXi host that is part of an HA-enabled cluster experiences failure.

FIGURE 1.3
The vSphere HA feature will restart any VMs that were previously running on an ESXi host that experiences server failure.

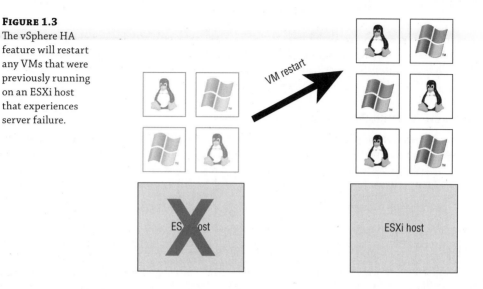

The vSphere HA feature, unlike DRS, does not use the vMotion technology as a means of migrating servers to another host. vMotion applies only to planned migrations, where both the source and destination ESXi host are running and functioning properly. In a vSphere HA failover situation, there is no anticipation of failure; it is not a planned outage, and therefore there is no time to perform a vMotion operation. vSphere HA is intended to minimize unplanned downtime because of the failure of a physical ESXi host or other infrastructure components. We'll go into more detail in Chapter 7 on what kinds of failures vSphere HA helps protect against.

---

vSphere HA Improvements in vSphere 5

vSphere HA received a couple of notable improvements in the vSphere 5.0 release. First, scalability was significantly improved; you could run up to 512 VMs per host (up from 100 in earlier versions) and 3,000 VMs per cluster (up from 1,280 in earlier versions). Second, vSphere HA integrated more closely with the intelligent placement functionality of vSphere DRS, giving vSphere HA greater ability to restart VMs in the event of a host failure. The third and perhaps most significant improvement is the complete rewrite of the underlying architecture for vSphere HA; this entirely new architecture, known as Fault Domain Manager (FDM), eliminated many of the constraints found in earlier versions of VMware vSphere.

By default, vSphere HA does not provide failover in the event of a guest OS failure, although you can configure vSphere HA to monitor VMs and restart them automatically if they fail to respond to an internal heartbeat. This feature is called VM Failure Monitoring, and it uses a combination of internal heartbeats and I/O activity to attempt to detect if the guest OS inside a VM has stopped functioning. If the guest OS has stopped functioning, the VM can be restarted automatically.

With vSphere HA, it's important to understand that there will be an interruption of service. If a physical host fails, vSphere HA restarts the VM, and while the VM is restarting, the applications or services provided by that VM are unavailable. For users who need even higher levels of availability than can be provided using vSphere HA, vSphere Fault Tolerance (FT), which is described in the next section, can help.

vSphere Fault Tolerance

While vSphere HA provides a certain level of availability for VMs in the event of physical host failure, this might not be good enough for some workloads. vSphere Fault Tolerance (FT) might help in these situations.

As we described in the previous section, vSphere HA protects against unplanned physical server failure by providing a way to automatically restart VMs upon physical host failure. This need to restart a VM in the event of a physical host failure means that some downtime—generally less than 3 minutes—is incurred. vSphere FT goes even further and eliminates any downtime in the event of a physical host failure. Using vLockstep technology that is based on VMware's earlier "record and replay" functionality, vSphere FT maintains a mirrored secondary VM on a separate physical host that is kept in lockstep with the primary VM. Everything that occurs on the primary (protected) VM also occurs simultaneously on the secondary (mirrored) VM, so that if the physical host for the primary VM fails, the secondary VM can immediately step in and take over without any loss of connectivity. vSphere FT will also automatically re-create the secondary (mirrored) VM on another host if the physical host for the secondary VM fails, as illustrated in Figure 1.4. This ensures protection for the primary VM at all times.

FIGURE 1.4
vSphere FT provides protection against host failures with no downtime experienced by the VMs.

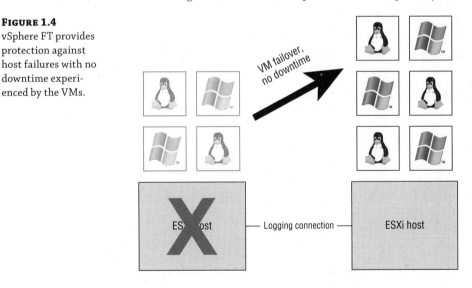

In the event of multiple host failures—say, the hosts running both the primary and secondary VMs failed—vSphere HA will reboot the primary VM on another available server, and vSphere FT will automatically create a new secondary VM. Again, this ensures protection for the primary VM at all times.

vSphere FT can work in conjunction with vMotion. As of vSphere 5.0, vSphere FT is also integrated with vSphere DRS, although this feature does require Enhanced vMotion Compatibility (EVC).

vSphere Storage APIs for Data Protection and VMware Data Protection

One of the most critical aspects to any network, not just a virtualized infrastructure, is a solid backup strategy as defined by a company's disaster recovery and business continuity plan. To help address organizational backup needs, VMware vSphere 5.0 has two key components: the vSphere Storage APIs for Data Protection (VADP) and VMware Data Protection (VDP).

VADP is a set of application programming interfaces (APIs) that backup vendors leverage in order to provide enhanced backup functionality of virtualized environments. VADP enables functionality like file-level backup and restore; support for incremental, differential, and full-image backups; native integration with backup software; and support for multiple storage protocols.

On its own, though, VADP is just a set of interfaces, like a framework for making backups possible. You can't actually back up VMs with VADP. You'll need a VADP-enabled backup application. There are a growing number of third-party backup applications that are designed to work with VADP, and VMware also offers its own backup tool, VMware Data Protection (VDP). VDP leverages VADP and technology based on EMC Avamar to provide a full backup solution for smaller VMware vSphere environments.

Whither VMware Data Recovery?

In vSphere 5.1, VMware phased out its earlier data protection tool, VMware Data Recovery (VDR), in favor of VMware Data Protection. While VDR was provided with vSphere 5.0, VDR is not supported with vSphere 5.1 and later, and VDP should be used instead.

Virtual SAN (VSAN)

VSAN is a major new feature included with vSphere 5.5 and the evolution of work that VMware has been doing for a few years now. Building on top of the work VMware did with the vSphere Storage Appliance (VSA), VSAN lets organizations leverage the storage found in all their individual compute nodes and turn it into—well, a *virtual SAN*.

VSAN requires at least three nodes but will scale to as many as 8 nodes. VSAN also requires solid-state storage in each of the compute nodes; this is done to help improve I/O performance given that most compute nodes have a limited number of physical drive spindles present. (Note that the solid-state storage in the servers used by VSAN is separate from solid-state storage that would be used by vSphere's Flash Read Cache caching functionality. See the section on Flash Read Cache later in this chapter for more details on using solid-state storage for caching.) VSAN pools the storage across the compute nodes, allowing you to create a datastore that spans multiple compute nodes. VSAN employs algorithms to help protect against data loss, such as ensuring that the data exists on multiple participating VSAN nodes at the same time.

More information on VSAN is found in Chapter 6, "Creating and Configuring Storage Devices."

vSphere Replication

vSphere Replication brings data replication, a feature typically found in hardware storage platforms, into vSphere itself. It's been around since vSphere 5.0, when it was only enabled for use in conjunction with VMware Site Recovery Manager (SRM) 5.0. In vSphere 5.1, vSphere Replication was decoupled from SRM and enabled for use even without VMware SRM.

vSphere Replication enables customers to replicate VMs from one vSphere environment to another vSphere environment. Typically, this means from one data center (often referred to as the primary or production data center) to another data center (typically the secondary, backup, or disaster recovery [DR] site). Unlike hardware-based solutions, vSphere Replication operates on a per-VM basis, so it gives customers very granular control over which workloads will be replicated and which workloads won't be replicated.

You can find more information about vSphere Replication in Chapter 7.

Flash Read Cache

Since the release of vSphere 5.0 in 2011, the industry has seen tremendous uptake in the use of solid-state storage (also referred to as flash storage) across a wide variety of use cases. Because solid-state storage can provide massive numbers of I/O operations per second (IOPS) it can handle the increasing I/O demands of virtual workloads. However, solid-state storage is typically more expensive on a per-gigabyte basis than traditional, hard-disk-based storage and therefore is often deployed as a caching mechanism to help speed up frequently accessed data.

Unfortunately, without support in vSphere for managing solid-state storage as a caching mechanism, vSphere architects and administrators have had difficulty fully leveraging solid-state storage in their environments. With the release of vSphere 5.5, VMware addresses that limitation through a feature called *vSphere Flash Read Cache*.

Flash Read Cache brings full support for using solid-state storage as a caching mechanism into vSphere. Using Flash Read Cache, administrators can assign solid-state caching space to VMs much in same manner as VMs are assigned CPU cores, RAM, or network connectivity. vSphere manages how the solid-state caching capacity is allocated and assigned and how it is used by the VMs.

Hardware vendors that provide solid-state storage devices have partnered with VMware to make their products fully support Flash Read Cache.

> ### Real World Scenario
>
> #### REAL WORLD SCENARIO: VMWARE vSPHERE COMPARED TO HYPER-V AND XENSERVER
>
> It's not really possible to compare some virtualization solutions to other virtualization solutions because they are fundamentally different in approach and purpose. Such is the case with VMware ESXi and some of the other virtualization solutions on the market.
>
> To make accurate comparisons between vSphere and other virtualization solutions, you must include only Type 1 ("bare-metal") virtualization solutions. This would include ESXi, of course, and Microsoft Hyper-V and Citrix XenServer. It would not include products such as VMware Server and Microsoft Virtual Server, both of which are Type 2 ("hosted") virtualization products. Even within the Type 1 hypervisors, there are architectural differences that make direct comparisons difficult.
>
> For example, both Microsoft Hyper-V and Citrix XenServer route all the VM I/O through the "parent partition" or "dom0." This typically provides greater hardware compatibility with a wider range of products. In the case of Hyper-V, for example, as soon as Windows Server 2012—the general-purpose operating system running in the parent partition—supports a particular type of hardware, Hyper-V supports it also. Hyper-V "piggybacks" on Windows's hardware drivers and the I/O stack. The same can be said for XenServer, although its "dom0" runs Linux and not Windows.
>
> VMware ESXi, on the other hand, handles I/O within the hypervisor itself. This typically provides greater throughput and lower overhead at the expense of slightly more limited hardware compatibility. In order to add more hardware support or updated drivers, the hypervisor must be updated because the I/O stack and device drivers are in the hypervisor.
>
> This architectural difference is fundamental. Nowhere is this architectural difference more greatly demonstrated than in ESXi, which has a small footprint yet provides a full-featured virtualization solution. Both Citrix XenServer and Microsoft Hyper-V require a full installation of a general-purpose operating system (Windows Server 2012 for Hyper-V, Linux for XenServer) in the parent partition/dom0 in order to operate.
>
> In the end, each of the virtualization products has its own set of advantages and disadvantages, and large organizations may end up using multiple products. For example, VMware vSphere might be best suited in the large corporate datacenter, while Microsoft Hyper-V or Citrix XenServer might be acceptable for test, development, or branch-office deployment. Organizations that don't require VMware vSphere's advanced features like vSphere DRS, vSphere FT, or Storage vMotion may also find that Microsoft Hyper-V or Citrix XenServer is a better fit for their needs.

As you can see, VMware vSphere offers some pretty powerful features that will change the way you view the resources in your datacenter. vSphere also has a wide range of features and functionality. Some of these features, though, might not be applicable to all organizations, which is why VMware has crafted a flexible licensing scheme for organizations of all sizes.

Licensing VMware vSphere

With the introduction of VMware vSphere 4, VMware introduced new licensing tiers and bundles that were intended to provide a good fit for every market segment. That arrangement continued with vSphere 5.0. However, with vSphere 5.1 (and continuing with vSphere 5.5), VMware refined this licensing arrangement with the introduction of the vCloud Suite—a bundling of products including vSphere, vCloud Automation Center, vCenter Site Recovery Manager, vCloud Networking and Security, vCloud Director, and vCenter Operations Management Suite.

While licensing vSphere via the vCloud Suite is likely the preferred way of licensing vSphere moving forward, we don't have the room in this book to discuss all the other products that are included in the vCloud Suite. Instead, we'll focus strictly on vSphere, and we'll explain how the various features that we've discussed so far fit into vSphere's licensing model when vSphere is licensed standalone.

vSphere or vSOM?

VMware sells "standalone" vSphere in one of two ways; as vSphere, with all the various kits and editions, and as vSphere with Operations Management, referred to as vSOM. vSOM is the same as vSphere but adds the vCenter Operations Management Suite. In this section, we are focused on standalone vSphere only, but keep in mind that vSOM would be licensed and packaged in much the same way.

You've already seen how VMware packages and licenses VMware vCenter Server, but here's a quick review:

- ◆ VMware vCenter Server for Essentials, which is bundled with the vSphere Essentials kits (more on the kits in just a moment).

- ◆ VMware vCenter Server Foundation supports the management of up to three vSphere hosts.

- ◆ VMware vCenter Server Standard, which includes all functionality and does not have a preset limit on the number of vSphere hosts it can manage (although normal sizing limits do apply). vCenter Orchestrator is included only in the Standard edition of vCenter Server.

In addition to the three editions of vCenter Server, VMware offers three editions of VMware vSphere:

- ◆ vSphere Standard Edition

- ◆ vSphere Enterprise Edition

- ◆ vSphere Enterprise Plus Edition

No More vRAM and no vCPU Limits

If you've been around the VMware vSphere world for a while, you might recall that VMware introduced the idea of vRAM—the amount of RAM configured for a VM—as a licensing constraint with the release of vSphere 5.0. As of vSphere 5.1, and continuing into vSphere 5.5, VMware no longer uses vRAM entitlements as a licensing mechanism. VMware has removed any licensing limits on the number of vCPUs that can be assigned to a VM.

These three editions are differentiated primarily by the features each edition supports, although there are some capacity limitations with the different editions. Notably missing from the licensing for vSphere 5.5 are limits on vRAM (see the sidebar titled "No More vRAM").

We'll summarize the features that are supported for each edition of VMware vSphere 5.5 in Table 1.3.

TABLE 1.3:   Overview of VMware vSphere product editions

	ESSENTIALS	**ESSENTIALS PLUS**	**STANDARD**	**ENTERPRISE**	**ENTERPRISE PLUS**
vCenter Server compatibility	vCenter Server Essentials	vCenter Server Essentials	vCenter Server Standard	vCenter Server Standard	vCenter Server Standard
vRAM Entitlement	Unlimited	Unlimited	Unlimited	Unlimited	Unlimited
vCPUs per VM	64	64	64	64	64
vMotion		X	X	X	X
High Availability		X	X	X	X
VMware Data Protection		X	X	X	X
vSphere Replication		X	X	X	X
vShield Endpoint		X	X	X	X
vSphere Storage Appliance		X	X	X	X
Fault Tolerance (1 vCPU)			X	X	X
Storage vMotion			X	X	X
Distributed Resource Scheduler and Distributed Power Management				X	X
Storage APIs for Array Integration, Multipathing				X	X

TABLE 1.3: Overview of VMware vSphere product editions *(CONTINUED)*

	ESSENTIALS	ESSENTIALS PLUS	STANDARD	ENTERPRISE	ENTERPRISE PLUS
Big Data Extensions				X	X
Reliable Memory				X	X
Distributed Switch					X
I/O Controls (Network and Storage) and SR-IOV					X
Host Profiles					X
Auto Deploy					X
Policy-driven storage					X
Storage DRS					X
Flash Read Cache					X
App HA					X

Source: "VMware vSphere 5.0 Licensing, Pricing and Packaging" white paper published by VMware, available at `www.vmware.com`*.*

It's important to note that all editions of VMware vSphere 5.5 include support for thin provisioning, vSphere Update Manager, and the vSphere Storage APIs for Data Protection. We did not include them in Table 1.3 because these features are supported in all editions. Because prices change and vary depending on partner, region, and other factors, we have not included any pricing information here.

We did not include VSAN in Table 1.3 because it is licensed separately from vSphere.

On all editions of vSphere, VMware requires at least one year of Support and Subscription (SnS). The only exception is the Essential Kits, as we'll explain in a moment.

In addition to the different editions described previously, VMware offers some bundles, referred to as kits. VMware offers Essentials Kits as well as Acceleration Kits.

Essentials Kits are all-in-one solutions for small environments, supporting up to three vSphere hosts with two CPUs each. To support three hosts with two CPUs each, the Essentials Kits come with six licenses. All these limits are product-enforced. There are three Essentials Kits available:

◆ VMware vSphere Essentials

◆ VMware vSphere Essentials Plus

◆ VMware vSphere Essentials for Retail and Branch Offices

You can't buy these kits on a per-CPU basis; they are bundled solutions for three servers. vSphere Essentials includes one year of subscription; support is optional and available on a per-incident basis. Like other editions, vSphere Essentials Plus requires at least one year of SnS; this must be purchased separately and is not included in the bundle.

The Retail and Branch Offices (RBO) Kits are differentiated from the "normal" Essentials and Essentials Plus Kits only by the licensing guidelines. These kits are licensed per site (10 sites minimum, with a maximum of three hosts per site), and customers can add additional sites as required. Central management of all the sites via vCenter Server Standard is possible, though vCenter Server Standard must be purchased separately. vCenter Server Essentials is included.

VMware also has Acceleration Kits, which combine the different components of the vSphere product suite. There are three Acceleration Kits:

◆ Standard Acceleration Kit: This kit includes one license of vCenter Server Standard plus licenses for vSphere Standard Edition.

◆ Enterprise Acceleration Kit: The Enterprise Acceleration Kit includes one license of vCenter Server Standard and licenses for vSphere Enterprise Edition.

◆ Enterprise Plus Acceleration Kit: This kit includes both licenses for vSphere Enterprise Plus Edition and a single license for vCenter Server Standard.

While the Essentials Kits are bundled and treated as a single unit, the Acceleration Kits merely offer customers an easier way to purchase the necessary licenses in one step.

Now that you have an idea of how VMware licenses vSphere, we'll review why an organization might choose to use vSphere and what benefits that organization could see as a result.

Why Choose vSphere?

Much has been said and written about the total cost of ownership (TCO) and return on investment (ROI) for virtualization projects involving VMware virtualization solutions. Rather than rehashing that material here, we'll instead focus, briefly, on why an organization should choose VMware vSphere as their virtualization platform.

ONLINE TCO CALCULATOR

VMware offers a web-based TCO calculator that helps you calculate the TCO and ROI for a virtualization project using VMware virtualization solutions. This calculator is available online at `www.vmware.com/go/calculator`.

You've already read about the various features that VMware vSphere offers. To help you understand how these features can benefit your organization, we'll apply them to the fictional XYZ Corporation. We'll walk through several different scenarios and look at how vSphere helps in these scenarios:

Scenario 1 XYZ Corporation's IT team has been asked by senior management to rapidly provision six new servers to support a new business initiative. In the past, this meant ordering hardware, waiting on the hardware to arrive, racking and cabling the equipment once it arrived, installing the operating system and patching it with the latest updates, and then installing the application. The time frame for all these steps ranged anywhere from a few days to a few months and was typically a couple of weeks. Now, with VMware vSphere in place, the IT team can use vCenter Server's templates functionality to build a VM, install the operating system, and apply the latest updates, and then rapidly clone—or copy—this VM to create additional VMs. Now their provisioning time is down to hours, likely even minutes. Chapter 10 discusses this functionality in detail.

Scenario 2   Empowered by the IT team's ability to quickly respond to the needs of this new business initiative, XYZ Corporation is moving ahead with deploying updated versions of a line-of-business application. However, the business leaders are a bit concerned about upgrading the current version. Using the snapshot functionality present in ESXi and vCenter Server, the IT team can take a "point-in-time picture" of the VM so that if something goes wrong during the upgrade, it's a simple rollback to the snapshot for recovery. Chapter 9, "Creating and Managing Virtual Machines," discusses snapshots.

Scenario 3   XYZ Corporation is impressed with the IT team and vSphere's functionality and is now interested in expanding its use of virtualization. In order to do so, however, a hardware upgrade is needed on the servers currently running ESXi. The business is worried about the downtime that will be necessary to perform the hardware upgrades. The IT team uses vMotion to move VMs off one host at a time, upgrading each host in turn without incurring any downtime to the company's end users. Chapter 12 discusses vMotion in more depth.

Scenario 4   After the great success it has had virtualizing its infrastructure with vSphere, XYZ Corporation now finds itself in need of a new, larger shared storage array. vSphere's support for Fibre Channel, iSCSI, and NFS gives XYZ room to choose the most cost-effective storage solution available, and the IT team uses Storage vMotion to migrate the VMs without any downtime. Chapter 12 discusses Storage vMotion.

These scenarios begin to provide some idea of the benefits that organizations see when virtualizing with an enterprise-class virtualization solution like VMware vSphere.

WHAT DO I VIRTUALIZE WITH VMWARE VSPHERE?

Virtualization, by its very nature, means that you are going to take multiple operating systems—such as Microsoft Windows, Linux, Solaris, or Novell NetWare—and run them on a single physical server. While VMware vSphere offers broad support for virtualizing a wide range of operating systems, it would be almost impossible for us to discuss how virtualization impacts all the different versions of all the different operating systems that vSphere supports.

Because the majority of organizations that adopt vSphere are primarily virtualizing Microsoft Windows, that operating system will receive the majority of attention when it comes to describing procedures that occur within a virtualized operating system. You will see coverage of tasks for a virtualized installation of Linux as well, but the majority of the coverage will be for Microsoft Windows.

If you are primarily virtualizing something other than Microsoft Windows, VMware provides more in-depth information on all the operating systems it supports and how vSphere interacts with those operating systems on its website at www.vmware.com.

The Bottom Line

Identify the role of each product in the vSphere product suite. The VMware vSphere product suite contains VMware ESXi and vCenter Server. ESXi provides the base virtualization functionality and enables features like Virtual SMP. vCenter Server provides management for ESXi and enables functionality like vMotion, Storage vMotion, vSphere Distributed Resource Scheduler (DRS), vSphere High Availability (HA), and vSphere Fault Tolerance (FT). Storage I/O Control and Network I/O Control provide granular resource controls for VMs. The vStorage APIs for Data Protection (VADP) provide a backup framework that allows for the integration of third-party backup solutions into a vSphere implementation.

Master It Which products are licensed features within the VMware vSphere suite?

Master It Which two features of VMware ESXi and VMware vCenter Server together aim to reduce or eliminate downtime due to unplanned hardware failures?

Master It Name two storage-related features that are new to vSphere 5.5.

Recognize the interaction and dependencies between the products in the vSphere suite. VMware ESXi forms the foundation of the vSphere product suite, but some features require the presence of vCenter Server. Features like vMotion, Storage vMotion, vSphere DRS, vSphere HA, vSphere FT, SIOC, and NIOC require ESXi as well as vCenter Server.

Master It Name three features that are supported only when using vCenter Server along with ESXi.

Master It Name two features that are supported without vCenter Server but with a licensed installation of ESXi.

Understand how vSphere differs from other virtualization products. VMware vSphere's hypervisor, ESXi, uses a Type 1 bare-metal hypervisor that handles I/O directly within the hypervisor. This means that a host operating system, like Windows or Linux, is not required in order for ESXi to function. Although other virtualization solutions are listed as "Type 1 bare-metal hypervisors," most other Type 1 hypervisors on the market today require the presence of a "parent partition" or "dom0" through which all VM I/O must travel.

Master It One of the administrators on your team asked whether he should install Windows Server on the new servers you purchased for ESXi. What should you tell him, and why?

Chapter 2

Planning and Installing VMware ESXi

Now that you've taken a closer look at VMware vSphere and its suite of applications in Chapter 1, "Introducing VMware vSphere 5.5," it's easy to see that VMware ESXi is the foundation of vSphere.

Although the act of installation can be relatively simple, understanding the deployment and configuration options requires planning to ensure a successful, VMware-supported implementation.

In this chapter, you will learn to

◆ Understand ESXi compatibility requirements

◆ Plan an ESXi deployment

◆ Deploy ESXi

◆ Perform post-installation configuration of ESXi

◆ Install the vSphere C# Client

Planning a VMware vSphere Deployment

Deploying VMware vSphere is more than just virtualizing servers. The effects of storage, networking, and security in a vSphere deployment are as equally significant as they are with the physical servers themselves. As a result of this broad impact on numerous facets of your organization's IT, the process of planning the vSphere deployment becomes even more important. Without the appropriate planning for your vSphere implementation, you run the risk of configuration problems, instability, incompatibilities, and diminished financial impact.

Your planning process for a vSphere deployment involves answering a number of questions (please note that this list is far from comprehensive):

◆ What types of servers will I use for the underlying physical hardware?

◆ What kinds of storage will I use, and how will I connect that storage to my servers?

◆ How will the networking be configured?

In some cases, the answers to these questions will determine the answers to other questions. After you have answered these questions, you can then move on to more difficult issues. These center on how the vSphere deployment will impact your staff, your business processes, and your operational procedures. Although still important, we're not going to help you answer those sorts of questions here; instead, let's just focus on the technical issues.

---

vSphere Design Is a Topic on Its Own

The first section of this chapter barely scratches the surface of what is involved in planning and designing a vSphere deployment. vSphere design is significant enough a topic that it warranted its own book: *VMware vSphere Design*, *Second Edition* (Sybex, 2013). If you are interested in a more detailed discussion of design decisions and design impacts, that's the book for you.

In the next few sections, we'll discuss the three major questions that we outlined previously that are a key part of planning your vSphere deployment: compute platform, storage, and network.

Choosing a Server Platform

The first major decision to make when planning to deploy vSphere is choosing a hardware, or "compute," platform. Compared to traditional operating systems like Windows or Linux, ESXi has more stringent hardware restrictions. ESXi won't necessarily support every storage controller or every network adapter chipset available on the market. Although these hardware restrictions do limit the options for deploying a supported virtual infrastructure, they also ensure that the hardware has been tested and will work as expected when used with ESXi. Not every vendor or white-box configuration can play host to ESXi, but the list of supported hardware platforms continues to grow as VMware and hardware vendors test newer models.

You can check for hardware compatibility using the searchable Compatibility Guide available on VMware's website at www.vmware.com/resources/compatibility/. A quick search returns dozens of systems from major vendors such as Hewlett-Packard, Cisco, IBM, and Dell. For example, at the time of this writing, searching the HCG for *HP* returned 202 results, including blades and traditional rack-mount servers supported across several different versions of vSphere 4.1 U3 to 5.1. Within the major vendors like HP, Dell, Cisco, and IBM, it is generally not too difficult to find a tested and supported platform on which to run ESXi, especially their newer models of hardware. When you expand the list to include other vendors, it's clear that there is a substantial base of compatible servers that are supported by vSphere from which to choose.

The Right Server for the Job

Selecting the appropriate server is undoubtedly the first step in ensuring a successful vSphere deployment. In addition, it is the only way to ensure that VMware will provide the necessary support. Remember the discussion from Chapter 1, though—a bigger server isn't necessarily a better server!

Finding a supported server is only the first step. It's also important to find the *right* server—the server that strikes the correct balance of capacity and affordability. Do you use larger servers, such as servers that support up to four or more physical CPUs and 512 GB of RAM? Or would smaller servers, such as servers that support dual physical CPUs and 64 GB of RAM, be a better choice? There is a point of diminishing returns when it comes to adding more physical CPUs and more RAM to a server. Once you pass that point, the servers get more expensive to acquire and support, but the number of VMs the servers can host doesn't increase enough to offset the increase in cost. The challenge, therefore, is finding server models that provide enough expansion for growth and then fitting them with the right amount of resources to meet your needs.

Fortunately, a deeper look into the server models available from a specific vendor, such as HP, reveals server models of all types and sizes (see Figure 2.1), including the following:

FIGURE 2.1
Servers on the HCG come in various sizes and models.

Server Device and Model Information

The detailed lists show actual vendor devices that are either physically tested or are similar to the devices tested by VMware or VMware partners. VMware provides support only for the devices that are listed in this document.
Click on the 'Model' for details.
Click on the 'CPU Series' for details including EVC and Fault Tolerant modes.

Bookmark | Print | Export to CSV

Search Results: Your search for " Systems / Servers" returned **202 results.**   Display: 10

Partner Name	Model	CPU Series	Supported Releases				
HP	ProLiant DL580 G7	Intel Xeon E7-4800 Series	ESX	4.1 U3	4.1 U2	4.1 U1	
			ESXi Installable	4.1 U3	4.1 U2	4.1 U1	
			ESXi Embedded	4.1 U3	4.1 U2	4.1 U1	
			ESXi	5.1	5.0 U2	5.0 U1	5.0
HP	ProLiant DL580 G7	Intel Xeon E7-8800 Series	ESX	4.1 U3	4.1 U2	4.1 U1	
			ESXi Installable	4.1 U3	4.1 U2	4.1 U1	
			ESXi Embedded	4.1 U3	4.1 U2	4.1 U1	
			ESXi	5.1	5.0 U2	5.0 U1	5.0
HP	ProLiant BL20p G2	AMD Opteron 22xx Series	ESX	3.5 U5	3.5 U4	3.5 U3	3.5 U2 ...
			ESXi Installable	3.5 U5	3.5 U4	3.5 U3	3.5 U2 ...
HP	ProLiant BL20p G3	Intel Xeon 70xx Series	ESX	3.5 U5	3.5 U4	3.5 U3	3.5 U2 ...
HP	ProLiant BL20p G4	Intel Xeon 50xx Series	ESX	3.5 U5	3.5 U4	3.5 U3	3.5 U2 ...

♦ Half-height C-class blades, such as the BL460c and BL465c

♦ Full-height C-class blades, such as the BL685c

♦ Dual-socket 1U servers, such as the DL360

♦ Dual-socket 2U servers, such as the DL380 and the DL385

♦ Quad-socket 4U servers, such as the DL580 and DL585

You'll note that Figure 2.1 doesn't show vSphere 5.5 in the list; at the time of this writing, VMware's HCG hadn't yet been updated to include information on vSphere 5.5. However, once VMware updates its HCG to include vSphere 5.5 and vendors complete their testing, you'll be able to easily view compatibility with vSphere 5.5 using VMware's online HCG. Servers are added to the HCG as they are certified, not just at major vSphere releases.

Which server is the right server? The answer to that question depends on many factors. The number of CPU cores is often used as a determining factor, but you should also consider the total number of RAM slots. A higher number of RAM slots means that you can use lower-cost, lower-density RAM modules and still reach high memory configurations. You should also consider server expansion options, such as the number of available Peripheral Component

Interconnect Express (PCIe) buses, expansion slots, and the types of expansion cards supported in the server. Finally, be sure to consider the server form factor; blade servers have advantages and disadvantages when compared to rack-mount servers.

Determining a Storage Architecture

Selecting the right storage solution is the second major decision that you must make before you proceed with your vSphere deployment. The lion's share of advanced features within vSphere—features like vSphere DRS, vSphere HA, and vSphere FT—depend on the presence of a shared storage architecture. While we won't talk in depth on a particular brand of storage hardware, VMware itself has released a feature called virtual SAN (VSAN) with vSphere 5.5, which we'll discuss more in Chapter 6, "Creating and Configuring Storage Devices." As stated, because of the dependency on shared storage, deciding on the correct storage architecture for your vSphere deployment is equally as critical as the choice of the server hardware on which to run ESXi.

THE HCG ISN'T JUST FOR SERVERS

VMware's HCG isn't just for servers. The searchable HCG also provides compatibility information on storage arrays and other storage components. Be sure to use the searchable HCG to verify the compatibility of your host bus adapters (HBAs) and storage arrays to ensure the appropriate level of support from VMware.

VMware also has a Product Interoperability Matrix to assist with software compatibility information; it can be found at the following location:

```
http://partnerweb.vmware.com/comp_guide2/sim/interop_matrix.php
```

Fortunately, vSphere supports a number of storage architectures out of the box and has implemented a modular, plug-in architecture that will make supporting future storage technologies easier. vSphere supports storage based on Fibre Channel and Fibre Channel over Ethernet (FCoE), iSCSI-based storage, and storage accessed via Network File System (NFS). In addition, vSphere supports the use of multiple storage protocols within a single solution so that one portion of the vSphere implementation might run over Fibre Channel while another portion runs over NFS. This provides a great deal of flexibility in choosing your storage solution. Finally, vSphere provides support for software-based initiators as well as hardware initiators (also referred to as host bus adapters or converged network adapters), so this is another option you must consider when selecting your storage solution.

WHAT IS REQUIRED FOR FIBRE CHANNEL OVER ETHERNET SUPPORT?

Fibre Channel over Ethernet (FCoE) is a relatively new storage protocol. However, because FCoE was designed to be compatible with Fibre Channel, it looks, acts, and behaves like Fibre Channel to ESXi. As long as drivers for the FCoE Converged Network Adapter (CNA) are available—and this is where you would go back to the VMware HCG again—support for FCoE should not be an issue.

When determining the correct storage solution, you must consider the following questions:

♦ What type of storage will best integrate with your existing storage or network infrastructure?

♦ Do you have experience or expertise with some types of storage?

♦ Can the storage solution provide the necessary performance to support your environment?

♦ Does the storage solution offer any form of advanced integration with vSphere?

The procedures involved in creating and managing storage devices are discussed in detail in Chapter 6.

Integrating with the Network Infrastructure

The third and final major decision that you need to make during the planning process is how your vSphere deployment will integrate with the existing network infrastructure. In part, this decision is driven by the choice of server hardware and the storage protocol.

For example, an organization selecting a blade form factor may run into limitations on the number of network interface cards (NICs) that can be supported in a given blade model. This affects how the vSphere implementation will integrate with the network. Similarly, organizations choosing to use iSCSI or NFS instead of Fibre Channel will typically have to deploy more NICs in their ESXi hosts to accommodate the additional network traffic or use 10 Gigabit Ethernet. Organizations also need to account for network interfaces for vMotion and vSphere FT.

Until 10 Gigabit Ethernet (10GbE) became common, ESXi hosts in many vSphere deployments had a minimum of 6 NICs and often 8, 10, or even 12 NICs. So, how do you decide how many NICs to use? We'll discuss some of this in greater detail in Chapter 5, "Creating and Configuring Virtual Networks," but here are some general guidelines:

♦ The ESXi management network needs at least one NIC. We strongly recommend adding a second NIC for redundancy. In fact, some features of vSphere, such as vSphere HA, will note warnings if the hosts do not have redundant network connections for the management network.

♦ vMotion needs a NIC. Again, we heartily recommend a second NIC for redundancy. These NICs should be at least Gigabit Ethernet. In some cases, this traffic can be safely combined with ESXi management traffic, so we'll assume that two NICs will handle both ESXi management and vMotion.

♦ vSphere FT, if you will be utilizing that feature, needs a NIC. A second NIC would provide redundancy and is recommended. This should be at least a Gigabit Ethernet NIC, preferably a 10 Gigabit Ethernet NIC.

♦ For deployments using iSCSI or NFS, at least one more NIC, preferably two, is needed. Gigabit Ethernet or 10 Gigabit Ethernet is necessary here. Although you can get by with a single NIC, we strongly recommend at least two.

♦ Finally, at least two NICs are needed for traffic originating from the VMs themselves. Gigabit Ethernet or faster is strongly recommended for VM traffic.

This adds up to eight NICs per server (again, assuming management and vMotion share a pair of NICs). For this sort of deployment, you'll want to ensure that you have enough network ports available, at the appropriate speeds, to accommodate the needs of the vSphere deployment. This is, of course, only a rudimentary discussion of networking design for vSphere and doesn't incorporate any discussion on the use of 10 Gigabit Ethernet, FCoE (which, while a storage protocol, impacts the network design), or what type of virtual switching infrastructure you will use. All of these other factors would affect your networking setup.

How About 10GbE NICs?

Lots of factors go into designing how a vSphere deployment will integrate with the existing network infrastructure. For example, it has been only in the last few years that 10GbE networking has become pervasive in the datacenter. This bandwidth change fundamentally changes how virtual networks are designed.

In one particular case, a company wished to upgrade its existing rack-mount server clusters with six NICs and two Fibre Channel HBAs to two dual-port 10GbE CNAs. Not only physically was there a stark difference from a switch and cabling perspective but the logical configuration was significantly different too. Obviously this allowed for greater bandwidth to each host but it also allowed for more design flexibility.

The final design used VMware Network IO Control (NOIC) and Load-Based Teaming (LBT) to share available bandwidth between the necessary types of traffic but only restricted bandwidth when the network was congested. This resulted in an efficient use of the new bandwidth capability without adding too much configuration complexity. Networking is discussed in more detail in Chapter 5.

With these questions answered, you at least have the basics of a vSphere deployment established. As we mentioned previously, this has been far from a comprehensive or complete discussion on designing a vSphere solution. We do recommend that you find a good resource on vSphere design and consider going through a comprehensive design exercise before actually deploying vSphere.

Deploying VMware ESXi

Once you've established the basics of your vSphere design, you have to decide exactly how you are going to deploy ESXi.

There are three ways to deploy ESXi:

◆ Interactive installation of ESXi

◆ Unattended (scripted) installation of ESXi

◆ Automated provisioning of ESXi

Of these, the simplest is an interactive installation of ESXi. The most complex—but perhaps the most powerful, depending on your needs and your environment—is automated provisioning of ESXi. In the following sections, we'll describe all three of these methods for deploying ESXi in your environment.

Let's start with the simplest method first: interactively installing ESXi.

Installing VMware ESXi Interactively

VMware has done a great job of making the interactive installation of ESXi as simple and straightforward as possible. It takes just minutes to install, so let's walk through the process.

Perform the following steps to interactively install ESXi:

1. Ensure that your server hardware is configured to boot from the CD-ROM drive.

This will vary from manufacturer to manufacturer and will also depend on whether you are installing locally or remotely via an IP-based Keyboard, Video, Mouse (KVM) or other remote management facility.

2. Ensure that VMware ESXi installation media are available to the server.

Again, this will vary based on a local installation (which involves simply inserting the VMware ESXi installation CD into the optical drive) or a remote installation (which typically involves mapping an image of the installation media, known as an ISO image, to a virtual optical drive).

OBTAINING VMWARE ESXI INSTALLATION MEDIA

You can download the installation files from VMware's website at `www.vmware.com/download/`.

---

3. Power on the server.

Once it boots from the installation media, the initial boot menu screen appears, as shown in Figure 2.2.

FIGURE 2.2
The initial ESXi installation routine has options for booting the installer or booting from the local disk.

4. Press Enter to boot the ESXi installer.

The installer will boot the vSphere hypervisor and eventually stop at a welcome message. Press Enter to continue.

5. At the End User License Agreement (EULA) screen, press F11 to accept the EULA and continue with the installation.

6. Next, the installer will display a list of available disks on which you can install or upgrade ESXi.

Potential devices are identified as either local devices or remote devices. Figure 2.3 and Figure 2.4 show two different views of this screen: one with a local device and one with remote devices.

FIGURE 2.3
The installer offers options for both local and remote devices; in this case, only a local device was detected.

FIGURE 2.4
Although local SAS devices are supported, they are listed as remote devices.

RUNNING ESXI AS A VM

You might be able to deduce from the screen shot in Figure 2.3 that we're actually running ESXi 5.5 as a VM. Yes, that's right—you can virtualize ESXi! In this particular case, we're using VMware's desktop virtualization solution for Mac OS X, VMware Fusion, to run an instance of ESXi as a VM. As of this writing, the latest version of VMware Fusion is 5, and it includes ESX Server 5 as an officially supported guest OS.

Storage area network logical unit numbers, or SAN LUNs, are listed as remote, as you can see in Figure 2.4. Local serial attached SCSI (SAS) devices are also listed as remote. Figure 2.4 shows a SAS drive connected to an LSI Logic controller; although this device is physically local to the server on which we are installing ESXi, the installation routine marks it as remote.

If you want to create a boot-from-SAN environment, where each ESXi host boots from a SAN LUN, then you'd select the appropriate SAN LUN here. You can also install directly to your own USB or Secure Digital (SD) device—simply select the appropriate device from the list.

WHICH DESTINATION IS BEST?

Local device, SAN LUN, or USB? Which destination is the best when you're installing ESXi? Those questions truly depend on the overall vSphere design you are implementing, and there is no simple answer. Many variables affect this decision. Are you using an iSCSI SAN and you don't have iSCSI hardware initiators in your servers? That would prevent you from using a boot-from-SAN setup. Are you installing into an environment like Cisco UCS, where booting from SAN is highly recommended? Be sure to consider all the factors when deciding where to install ESXi.

---

7. To get more information about a device, highlight the device and press F1.

The information about the device includes whether it detected an installation of ESXi and what Virtual Machine File System (VMFS) datastores, if any, are present on it, as shown in Figure 2.5. Press Enter to return to the device-selection screen when you have finished reviewing the information for the selected device.

FIGURE 2.5
Checking to see if there are any VMFS datastores on a device can help prevent accidentally overwriting data.

```
                          Disk Details
 * Con Model/Vendor:     EMC        SYMMETRIX
       Full Disk Name:   naa.60000970000192602579533030314143
 ----- LUN ID:           9                                          -----
 Local Target ID:        0
   (n  Capacity:         500.02 GiB
 Remot Path:             /vmfs/devices/disks/naa.600009700001926025
   * LS                  79533030314143                        0 GiB
   * EM  ESX(i) Found:   No                                    0 GiB
   * EM  Datastores:     pod-1-lun-09                          03
 GiB
   * EM                                                        2 GiB
   * EM                     (Enter) OK                         2 GiB

    (Esc) Cancel    (F1) Details    (F5) Refresh    (Enter) Continue
```

8. Use the arrow keys to select the device on which you are going to install ESXi, and press Enter.

9. If the selected device includes a VMFS datastore or an installation of ESXi, you'll be prompted to choose what action you want to take, as illustrated in Figure 2.6. Select the desired action and press Enter.

FIGURE 2.6
You can upgrade or
install ESXi as well
as choose to pre-
serve or overwrite
an existing VMFS
datastore.

```
                           ESXi and VMFS Found

* Cont  The selected storage device contains an installation of
        ESXi and a VMFS datastore.  Choose whether to upgrade
Storag  or install and overwrite the existing ESXi              apacity
------  installation.  Also choose whether to preserve or       -------
Local:  overwrite the existing VMFS datastore.
   (no
Remote  (X) Upgrade ESXi, preserve VMFS datastore
 * LSI  ( ) Install ESXi, preserve VMFS datastore               .90 GiB
 * EMC  ( ) Install ESXi, overwrite VMFS datastore              .00 GiB
 * EMC                                                         0.03
GiB        Use the arrow keys and spacebar to select an option.
 * EMC                                                          .02 GiB

                   (Esc) Cancel        (Enter) OK
  (Es                                                          inue
```

These are the available actions:

◆ Upgrade ESXi, Preserve VMFS Datastore: This option upgrades to ESXi 5.5 and preserves the existing VMFS datastore.

◆ Install ESXi, Preserve VMFS Datastore: This option installs a fresh copy of ESXi 5.5
and preserves the existing VMFS datastore.

◆ Install ESXi, Overwrite VMFS Datastore: This option overwrites the existing VMFS
datastore with a new one and installs a fresh installation of ESXi 5.5.

10. Select the desired keyboard layout and press Enter.

11. Enter (and confirm) a password for the root account. Press Enter when you are ready to
continue with the installation. Be sure to make note of this password—you'll need it later.

12. At the final confirmation screen, press F11 to proceed with the installation of ESXi.

After the installation process begins, it takes only a few minutes to install ESXi onto the
selected storage device.

13. Press Enter to reboot the host at the Installation Complete screen.

After the host reboots, ESXi is installed. ESXi is configured by default to obtain an IP address
via Dynamic Host Configuration Protocol (DHCP). Depending on the network configuration,
you might find that ESXi will not be able to obtain an IP address via DHCP. Later in this chapter,
in the section "Reconfiguring the Management Network," we'll discuss how to correct networking problems after installing ESXi by using the Direct Console User Interface (DCUI).

VMware also provides support for scripted installations of ESXi. As you've already seen,
there isn't a lot of interaction required to install ESXi, but support for scripting the installation of
ESXi reduces the time to deploy even further.

INTERACTIVELY INSTALLING ESXi FROM USB OR ACROSS THE NETWORK

As an alternative to launching the ESXi installer from the installation CD/DVD, you can install ESXi from a USB flash drive or across the network via Preboot Execution Environment (PXE). More details on how to use a USB flash drive or to PXE boot the ESXi installer are found in the *vSphere Installation and Setup Guide*, available from www.vmware.com/go/support-pubs-vsphere. Note that PXE booting the installer is not the same as PXE booting ESXi itself, something that we'll discuss later in the section "Deploying VMware ESXi with vSphere Auto Deploy."

Performing an Unattended Installation of VMware ESXi

ESXi supports the use of an installation script (often referred to as a kickstart, or KS, script) that automates the installation routine. By using an installation script, users can create unattended installation routines that make it easy to quickly deploy multiple instances of ESXi.

ESXi comes with a default installation script on the installation media. Listing 2.1 shows the default installation script.

LISTING 2.1:   ESXi provides a default installation script

```
#
# Sample scripted installation file
#
# Accept the VMware End User License Agreement
vmaccepteula
# Set the root password for the DCUI and Tech Support Mode
rootpw mypassword
# Install on the first local disk available on machine
install --firstdisk --overwritevmfs
# Set the network to DHCP on the first network adapter
network --bootproto=dhcp --device=vmnic0
# A sample post-install script
%post --interpreter=python --ignorefailure=true
import time
stampFile = open('/finished.stamp', mode='w')
stampFile.write( time.asctime() )
```

If you want to use this default install script to install ESXi, you can specify it when booting the VMware ESXi installer by adding the ks=file://etc/vmware/weasel/ks.cfg boot option. We'll show you how to specify that boot option shortly.

Of course, the default installation script is useful only if the settings work for your environment. Otherwise, you'll need to create a custom installation script. The installation script commands are much the same as those supported in previous versions of vSphere. Here's a breakdown of some of the commands supported in the ESXi installation script:

accepteula or vmaccepteula   These commands accept the ESXi license agreement.

install   The install command specifies that this is a fresh installation of ESXi, not an upgrade. You must also specify the following parameters:

> **--firstdisk**   Specifies the disk on which ESXi should be installed. By default, the ESXi installer chooses local disks first, then remote disks, and then USB disks. You can change the order by appending a comma-separated list to the --firstdisk command, like this: --firstdisk=remote,local   This would install to the first available remote disk and then to the first available local disk. Be careful here—you don't want to inadvertently overwrite something (see the next set of commands).

> **--overwritevmfs or --preservevmfs**   These commands specify how the installer will handle existing VMFS datastores. The commands are pretty self-explanatory.

keyboard   This command specifies the keyboard type. It's an optional component in the installation script.

network   This command provides the network configuration for the ESXi host being installed. It is optional but generally recommended. Depending on your configuration, some of the additional parameters are required:

> **--bootproto**   This parameter is set to dhcp for assigning a network address via DHCP or to static for manual assignment of an IP address.

> **--ip**   This sets the IP address and is required with --bootproto=static. The IP address should be specified in standard dotted-decimal format.

> **--gateway**   This command specifies the IP address of the default gateway in standard dotted-decimal format. It's required if you specified --bootproto=static.

> **--netmask**   The network mask, in standard dotted-decimal format, is specified with this command. If you specify --bootproto=static, you must include this value.

> **--hostname**   Specifies the hostname for the installed system.

> **--vlanid**   If you need the system to use a VLAN ID, specify it with this command. Without a VLAN ID specified, the system will respond only to untagged traffic.

> **--addvmportgroup**   This parameter is set to either 0 or 1 and controls whether a default VM Network port group is created. 0 does not create the port group; 1 does create the port group.

reboot   This command is optional and, if specified, will automatically reboot the system at the end of installation. If you add the --noeject parameter, the CD is not ejected.

rootpw   This is a required parameter and sets the root password for the system. If you don't want the root password displayed in the clear, generate an encrypted password and use the --iscrypted parameter.

upgrade   This specifies an upgrade to ESXi 5.5. The upgrade command uses many of the same parameters as install and also supports a parameter for deleting the ESX Service Console VMDK for upgrades from ESX to ESXi. This parameter is the --deletecosvmdk parameter.

This is by no means a comprehensive list of all the commands available in the ESXi installation script, but it does cover the majority of the commands you'll see in use.

Looking back at Listing 2.1, you'll see that the default installation script incorporates a %post section, where additional scripting can be added using either the Python interpreter or the BusyBox interpreter. What you don't see in Listing 2.1 is the %firstboot section, which also allows you to add Python or BusyBox commands for customizing the ESXi installation. This section comes after the installation script commands but before the %post section. Any command supported in the ESXi shell can be executed in the %firstboot section, so commands such as vim-cmd, esxcfg-vswitch, esxcfg-vmknic, and others can be combined in the %firstboot section of the installation script.

A number of commands that were supported in previous versions of vSphere (by ESX or ESXi) are no longer supported in installation scripts for ESXi 5.5, such as these:

◆ autopart (replaced by install, upgrade, or installorupgrade)

◆ auth or authconfig

◆ bootloader

◆ esxlocation

◆ firewall

◆ firewallport

◆ serialnum or vmserialnum

◆ timezone

◆ virtualdisk

◆ zerombr

◆ The --level option of %firstboot

Once you have created the installation script you will use, you need to specify that script as part of the installation routine.

Specifying the location of the installation script as a boot option is not only how you would tell the installer to use the default script but also how you tell the installer to use a custom installation script that you've created. This installation script can be located on a USB flash drive or in a network location accessible via NFS, HTTP, HTTPS, or FTP. Table 2.1 summarizes some of the supported boot options for use with an unattended installation of ESXi.

TABLE 2.1:   Boot options for an unattended ESXi installation

BOOT OPTION	BRIEF DESCRIPTION
ks=*cdrom:/path*	Uses the installation script found at *path* on the CD-ROM. The installer checks all CD-ROM drives until the file matching the specified path is found.
ks=usb	Uses the installation script named ks.cfg found in the root directory of an attached USB device. All USB devices are searched as long as they have a FAT16 or FAT32 file system.

TABLE 2.1: Boot options for an unattended ESXi installation *(CONTINUED)*

BOOT OPTION	BRIEF DESCRIPTION
ks=*usb:/path*	Uses the installation script at the specified *path* on an attached USB device. This allows you to use a different filename or location for the installation script.
ks=*protocol:/ serverpath*	Uses the installation script found at the specified network location. The protocol can be NFS, HTTP, HTTPS, or FTP.
ip=*XX.XX.XX.XX*	Specifies a static IP address for downloading the installation script and the installation media.
nameserver=*XX .XX.XX.XX*	Provides the IP address of a Domain Name System (DNS) server to use for name resolution when downloading the installation script or the installation media.
gateway=*XX.XX.XX .XX*	Provides the network gateway to be used as the default gateway for downloading the installation script and the installation media.
netmask=*XX.XX.XX .XX*	Specifies the network mask for the network interface used to download the installation script or the installation media.
vlanid=*XX*	Configures the network interface to be on the specified VLAN when downloading the installation script or the installation media.

NOT A COMPREHENSIVE LIST OF BOOT OPTIONS

The list found in Table 2.1 includes only some of the more commonly used boot options for performing a scripted installation of ESXi. For the complete list of supported boot options, refer to the *vSphere Installation and Setup Guide*, available from www.vmware.com/go/support-pubs-vsphere.

To use one or more of these boot options during the installation, you'll need to specify them at the boot screen for the ESXi installer. The bottom of the installer boot screen states that you can press Shift+O to edit the boot options.

The following code line is an example that could be used to retrieve the installation script from an HTTP URL; this would be entered at the prompt at the bottom of the installer boot screen:

```
<ENTER: Apply options and boot> <ESC: Cancel>
> runweasel ks=http://192.168.1.1/scripts/ks.cfg ip=192.168.1.200
  netmask=255.255.255.0 gateway=192.168.1.254
```

Using an installation script to install ESXi not only speeds up the installation process but also helps to ensure the consistent configuration of all your ESXi hosts.

The final method for deploying ESXi—using vSphere Auto Deploy—is the most complex, but it also offers administrators a great deal of flexibility.

Deploying VMware ESXi with vSphere Auto Deploy

vSphere Auto Deploy can be configured with one of three different modes:

- Stateless
- Stateless Caching
- Stateful Install

In the Stateless mode, you deploy ESXi using Auto Deploy, but you aren't actually installing ESXi. Instead of actually installing ESXi onto a local disk or a SAN boot LUN, you are building an environment where ESXi is directly loaded into memory on a host as it boots.

In the next mode, Stateless Caching, you deploy ESXi using Auto Deploy just as with Stateless, but the image is cached on the server's local disk or SAN boot LUN. In the event that the Auto Deploy infrastructure is not available, the host boots from a local cache of the image.

The third mode, Stateful Install, is very similar to Stateless Caching except the server's boot order is reversed: local disk first and network second. Unless the server is specifically told to network boot again, the Auto Deploy service is no longer needed. This mode is effectively just a mechanism for network installation.

Auto Deploy uses a set of rules (called *deployment rules*) to control which hosts are assigned a particular ESXi image (called an *image profile*). Deploying a new ESXi image is as simple as modifying the deployment rule to point that physical host to a new image profile and then rebooting with the PXE/network boot option. When the host boots up, it will receive a new image profile.

Sounds easy, right? Maybe not. In theory, it is—but there are several steps you have to accomplish before you're ready to actually deploy ESXi in this fashion:

1. You must set up a vSphere Auto Deploy server. This is the server that stores the image profiles.

2. You must set up and configure a Trivial File Transfer Protocol (TFTP) server on your network.

3. You must configure a DHCP server on your network to pass the correct information to hosts booting up.

4. You must create an image profile using PowerCLI.

5. Still using PowerCLI, you must create a deployment rule that assigns the image profile to a particular subset of hosts.

AUTO DEPLOY DEPENDENCIES

This chapter deals with ESXi host installation methods; however, vSphere Auto Deploy is dependent on Host Profiles, a feature of VMware vCenter. More information about installing vCenter and configuring Host Profiles can be found in Chapter 3, "Installing and Configuring vCenter Server."

Once you've completed these five steps, you're ready to start provisioning hosts with ESXi. When everything is configured and in place, the process looks something like this:

1. When the physical server boots, the server starts a PXE boot sequence. The DHCP server assigns an IP address to the host and provides the IP address of the TFTP server as well as a boot filename to download.

2. The host contacts the TFTP server and downloads the specified filename, which contains the gPXE boot file and a gPXE configuration file.

3. gPXE executes; this causes the host to make an HTTP boot request to the Auto Deploy server. This request includes information about the host, the host hardware, and host network information. This information is written to the server console when gPXE is executing, as you can see in Figure 2.7.

FIGURE 2.7
Host information is echoed to the server console when it performs a network boot.

```
* Booting through VMware AutoDeploy...
*
* Machine attributes:
* . asset=Unknown
* . domain=pods.local
* . hostname=
* . ipv4=10.1.1.250
* . mac=00:25:b5:01:01:1d
* . model=N20-B6620-1
* . oemstring=
* . oemstring=
* . oemstring=
* . oemstring=
* . oemstring=
* . serial=QCI13300011
* . uuid=00000000-0000-0000-0100-000000000004
* . vendor=Cisco Systems Inc
*
* Image Profile: ip-VMware, Inc.-Test-Profile-ba109ee8c801ef0b106b56b1c75aa231
* VC Host: host-178
*
* Bootloader VIB version: 5.0.0-0.0.381646
**********************************************************************
/vmw/cache/a6/b43db2ddd0039debf603013b2acf9d/mboot.c32.71df31a84ca25f89e26a0ff2c
6623d86._
```

4. Based on the information passed to it from gPXE (the host information shown in Figure 2.7), the Auto Deploy server matches the server against a deployment rule and assigns the correct image profile. The Auto Deploy server then streams the assigned ESXi image across the network to the physical host.

When the host has finished executing, you have a system running ESXi. The Auto Deploy server also has the ability to automatically join the ESXi host to vCenter Server and assign a host profile (which we'll discuss in a bit more detail in Chapter 3) for further configuration. As you can see, this system potentially offers administrators tremendous flexibility and power.

Ready to get started with provisioning ESXi hosts using Auto Deploy? Let's start with setting up the vSphere Auto Deploy server.

INSTALLING THE VSPHERE AUTO DEPLOY SERVER

The vSphere Auto Deploy server is where the various ESXi image profiles are stored. The image profile is transferred from this server via HTTP to a physical host when it boots. The image profile is the actual ESXi image, and it comprises multiple VIB files. VIBs are ESXi software packages; these could be drivers, Common Information Management (CIM) providers, or other applications that extend or enhance the ESXi platform. Both VMware and VMware's partners could distribute software as VIBs.

You can install vSphere Auto Deploy on the same system as vCenter Server or on a separate Windows Server–based system (this could certainly be a VM). In addition, the vCenter virtual appliance comes preloaded with the Auto Deploy server installed. If you want to use the vCenter virtual appliance, you need only deploy the appliance and configure the service from the web-based administrative interface. We'll describe the process for deploying the vCenter virtual appliance in more detail in Chapter 3. In this section, we'll walk you through installing the Auto Deploy server on a separate Windows-based system.

Perform the following steps to install the vSphere Auto Deploy server:

1. Make the vCenter Server installation media available to the Windows Server–based system where you will be installing Auto Deploy.

   If this is a VM, you can map the vCenter Server installation ISO to the VM's CD/DVD drive.

2. From the VMware vCenter Installer screen, select VMware Auto Deploy and click Install.

3. Choose the language for the installer and click OK.

   This will launch the vSphere Auto Deploy installation wizard.

4. Click Next at the first screen of the installation wizard.

5. Click Next to acknowledge the VMware patents.

6. Select I Accept The Terms In The License Agreement, and click Next to continue.

7. Click Next to accept the default installation location, the default repository location, and the default maximum repository size.

   If you need to change locations, use either of the Change buttons; if you need to change the repository size, specify a new value in gigabytes (GB).

8. If you are installing on a system separate from vCenter Server, specify the IP address or name of the vCenter Server with which this Auto Deploy server should register.

   You'll also need to provide a username and password. Click Next when you have finished entering this information.

9. Click Next to accept the default Auto Deploy server port.

10. Click Next to accept the Auto Deploy server identifying itself on the network via its IP address (be sure to select the correct address if your server has multiple NICs).

11. Click Install to install the Auto Deploy server.

12. Click Finish to complete the installation.

If you now go back to the vSphere Client (if you haven't installed it yet, skip ahead to the section "Installing the vSphere C# Client" and then come back) and connect to vCenter Server, you'll see a new Auto Deploy icon on the vSphere Client's home page. Click it to see information about the registered Auto Deploy server. Figure 2.8 shows the Auto Deploy screen after we installed and registered an Auto Deploy server with vCenter Server.

FIGURE 2.8

This screen provides information about the Auto Deploy server that is registered with vCenter Server.

That's it for the Auto Deploy server itself; once it's been installed and is up and running, there's very little additional work or configuration required, except configuring TFTP and DHCP on your network to support vSphere Auto Deploy. The next section provides an overview of the required configurations for TFTP and DHCP.

CONFIGURING TFTP AND DHCP FOR AUTO DEPLOY

The exact procedures for configuring TFTP and DHCP are going to vary based on the specific TFTP and DHCP servers you are using on your network. For example, configuring the ISC DHCP server to support vSphere Auto Deploy is dramatically different from configuring the DHCP Server service provided with Windows Server. As a matter of necessity, then, we can provide only high-level information in the following section. Refer to your specific vendor's documentation for details on how the configuration is carried out.

Configuring TFTP

For TFTP, you only need to upload the appropriate TFTP boot files to the TFTP directory. The Download TFTP Boot Zip hyperlink shown in Figure 2.8 provides the necessary files. Simply download the Zip file using that link, unzip the file, and place the contents of the unzipped file in the TFTP directory on the TFTP server.

Configuring DHCP

For DHCP, you need to specify two additional DHCP options:

◆ Option 66, referred to as `next-server` or as Boot Server Host Name, must specify the IP address of the TFTP server.

◆ Option 67, called `boot-filename` or Bootfile Name, should contain the value `undionly .kpxe.vmw-hardwired`.

If you want to identify hosts by IP address in the deployment rules, then you'll need a way to ensure that the host gets the IP address you expect. You can certainly use DHCP reservations to accomplish this, if you like; just be sure that options 66 and 67 apply to the reservation as well.

Once you've configured TFTP and DHCP, you're ready to PXE boot your server, but you still need to create the image profile to deploy ESXi.

CREATING AN IMAGE PROFILE

The process for creating an image profile may seem counterintuitive at first; it did for us. Creating an image profile involves first adding at least one *software depot*. A software depot could be a directory structure of files and folders on an HTTP server, or (more commonly) it could be an offline depot in the form of a Zip file. You can add multiple software depots.

Some software depots will already have one or more image profiles defined, and you can define additional image profiles (usually by cloning an existing image profile). You'll then have the ability to add software packages (in the form of VIBs) to the image profile you've created. Once you've finished adding or removing software packages or drivers from the image profile, you can export the image profile (either to an ISO or as a Zip file for use as an offline depot).

All image profile tasks are accomplished using PowerCLI, so you'll need to ensure that you have a system with PowerCLI installed in order to perform these tasks. We'll describe PowerCLI, along with other automation tools, in more detail in Chapter 14, "Automating VMware vSphere." In the next part of this section, we'll walk you through creating an image profile based on the ESXi 5.5.0 offline depot Zip file available for downloading by registered customers.

Perform the following steps to create an image profile:

1. At a PowerCLI prompt, use the `Connect-VIServer` cmdlet to connect to vCenter Server.

2. Use the `Add-EsxSoftwareDepot` command to add the ESXi 5.5.0 offline depot file:

   ```
   Add-EsxSoftwareDepot C:\vmware-ESXi-5.5.0-XXXXXX-depot.zip
   ```

3. Repeat the `Add-EsxSoftwareDepot` command to add other software depots as necessary. The code listed below adds the online depot file:

   ```
   Add-EsxSoftwareDepot
   https://hostupdate.vmware.com/software/VUM/PRODUCTION/main/vmw-depot-index.xml
   ```

4. Use the `Get-EsxImageProfile` command to list all image profiles in all currently visible depots.

5. To create a new image profile, clone an existing profile (existing profiles are typically read-only) using the `New-EsxImageProfile` command:

   ```
   New-EsxImageProfile -CloneProfile "ESXi-5.5.0-XXXXXX-standard"
   -Name "My_Custom_Profile"
   ```

Once you have an image profile established, you can customize it by adding VIBs or you can export it. You might want to export the image profile because once you exit a PowerCLI session where you've created image profiles, the image profiles will not be available when you start a new session. Exporting the image profile as a Zip file offline depot, you can easily add it back in when you start a new session.

To export an image profile as a Zip file offline depot, run this command:

```
Export-EsxImageProfile -ImageProfile "My_Custom_Profile" -ExportToBundle
-FilePath "C:\path\to\ZIP-file-offline-depot.zip"
```

When you start a new PowerCLI session to work with an image profile, simply add this offline depot with the `Add-EsxSoftwareDepot` command.

The final step is establishing deployment rules that link image profiles to servers in order to provision ESXi to them at boot time. We'll describe how to do this in the next section.

ESTABLISHING DEPLOYMENT RULES

The deployment rules are where the "rubber meets the road" for vSphere Auto Deploy. When you define a deployment rule, you are linking an image profile to one or more hosts. It's at this point that vSphere Auto Deploy will copy all the VIBs defined in the specified image profile up to the Auto Deploy server so that they are accessible from the hosts. Once a deployment rule is in place, you can actually begin provisioning hosts via Auto Deploy (assuming all the other pieces are in place and functioning correctly, of course).

As with image profiles, deployment rules are managed via PowerCLI. You'll use the `New-DeployRule` and `Add-DeployRule` commands to define new deployment rules and add them to the working rule set, respectively.

Perform the following steps to define a new deployment rule:

1. In a PowerCLI session where you've previously connected to vCenter Server and defined an image profile, use the `New-DeployRule` command to define a new deployment rule that matches an image profile to a physical host:

   ```
   New-DeployRule -Name "Img_Rule " -Item "My_Custom_Profile"
   -Pattern "vendor=Cisco", "ipv4=10.1.1.225,10.1.1.250"
   ```

   This rule assigns the image profile named My_Custom_Profile to all hosts with *Cisco* in the vendor string and having either the IP address 10.1.1.225 or 10.1.1.250. You could also specify an IP range like 10.1.1.225-10.1.1.250 (using a hyphen to separate the start and end of the IP address range).

2. Next, create a deployment rule that assigns the ESXi host to a cluster within vCenter Server:

   ```
   New-DeployRule -Name "Default_Cluster" -Item "Cluster-1" -AllHosts
   ```

   This rule puts all hosts into the cluster named Cluster-1 in the vCenter Server with which the Auto Deploy server is registered. (Recall that an Auto Deploy server must be registered with a vCenter Server instance.)

3. Add these rules to the working rule set:

   ```
   Add-DeployRule Img_Rule
   Add-DeployRule Default_Cluster
   ```

   As soon as you add the deployment rules to the working rule set, vSphere Auto Deploy will, if necessary, start uploading VIBs to the Auto Deploy server in order to satisfy the rules you've defined.

4. Verify that these rules have been added to the working rule set with the `Get-DeployRuleSet` command.

Now that a deployment rule is in place, you're ready to provision via Auto Deploy. Boot the physical host that matches the patterns you defined in the deployment rule, and it should follow the boot sequence described at the start of this section. Figure 2.9 shows what it looks like when a host is booting ESXi via vSphere Auto Deploy.

By now, you should be starting to see the flexibility that Auto Deploy offers. If you need to deploy a new ESXi image, you need only define a new image profile (using a new software depot, if necessary), assign that image profile with a deployment rule, and reboot the physical servers. When the servers come up, they will boot the newly assigned ESXi image via PXE.

FIGURE 2.9
Note the differences in the ESXi boot process when using Auto Deploy versus a traditional installation of ESXi.

Of course, there are some additional concerns that you'll need to address should you decide to go this route:

◆ The image profile doesn't contain any ESXi configuration state information, such as virtual switches, security settings, advanced parameters, and so forth. Host profiles are used to store this configuration state information in vCenter Server and pass that configuration information down to a host automatically. You can use a deployment rule to assign a host profile, or you can assign a host profile to a cluster and then use a deployment rule to join hosts to a cluster. We'll describe host profiles in greater detail in Chapter 3.

◆ State information such as log files, generated private keys, and so forth is stored in host memory and is lost during a reboot. Therefore, you must configure additional settings such as setting up syslog for capturing the ESXi logs. Otherwise, this vital operational information is lost every time the host is rebooted. The configuration for capturing this state information can be included in a host profile that is assigned to a host or cluster.

In the Auto Deploy Stateless mode, the ESXi image doesn't contain configuration state and doesn't maintain dynamic state information, and they are therefore considered *stateless ESXi hosts*. All the state information is stored elsewhere instead of on the host itself.

🌐 Real World Scenario

ENSURING AUTO DEPLOY IS AVAILABLE

Author Nick Marshall says, "When working with a customer with vSphere 5.0 Auto Deploy, we had to ensure that all Auto Deploy components were highly available. This meant designing the infrastructure that was responsible for booting and deploying ESXi hosts was more complicated than normal. Services such as PXE and Auto Deploy and the vCenter VMs were all deployed on hosts that were not provisioned using Auto Deploy in a separate management cluster.

As per the Highly Available Auto Deploy best practices in the vSphere documentation, building a separate cluster with a local installation or boot from SAN will ensure there is no chicken-and-egg situation. You need to ensure that in a completely virtualized environment your VMs that provision ESXi hosts with Auto Deploy are not running on the ESXi hosts they need to build."

STATELESS CACHING MODE

Unless your ESXi host hardware does not have any local disks or bootable SAN storage, we would recommend considering one of the two other Auto Deploy modes. These modes offer resiliency for your hosts if at any time the Auto Deploy services become unavailable.

To configure Stateless Caching, follow the previous procedure for Stateless with these additions:

1. Within vCenter, navigate to the Host Profiles section: vCenter ➢ Home ➢ Host Profiles.

2. Create a new host profile or edit the existing one attached to your host.

3. Navigate to System Image Cache Configuration under Advanced Configuration Settings.

4. Select Enable Stateless Caching On The Host.

5. Input the disk configuration details, using the same disk syntax as listed earlier in the section "Performing an Unattended Installation of VMware ESXi." By default it will populate the first available disk, as you can see in Figure 2.10.

6. Click Finish to end the Host Profile Wizard.

7. Next you need to configure the boot order in the host BIOS to boot from the network first, and the local disk second. This procedure will differ depending on your server type.

8. Reboot the host to allow a fresh Auto Deploy image and the new host profile will be attached.

This configuration tells the ESXi host to take the Auto Deploy image loaded in memory and save it to the local disk after a successful boot. If for some reason the network or Auto Deploy server is unavailable when your host reboots, it will fall back and boot the cached copy on its local disk.

FIGURE 2.10
Editing the host profile to allow Stateless Caching on a local disk

STATEFUL MODE

Just like Stateful Caching mode, the Auto Deploy Stateful mode is configured by editing host profiles within vCenter and the boot order settings in the host BIOS.

1. Within vCenter, navigate to the Host Profiles section: vCenter ➤ Home ➤ Host Profiles.

2. Create a new host profile or edit the existing one attached to your host.

3. Navigate to System Image Cache Configuration under Advanced Configuration Settings.

4. Select Enable Stateful Installs On The Host.

5. Input the disk configuration details, using the same disk syntax as listed earlier in the section "Performing an Unattended Installation of VMware ESXi." By default it will populate the first available disk (see Figure 2.10).

6. Click Finish to end the Host Profile Wizard.

7. Next you need to configure the boot order in the host BIOS to boot from the local disk first, and the network second. This procedure will differ depending on your server type.

8. The host will boot into Maintenance mode, and you need to apply the host profile by clicking Remediate Host on the host Summary tab.

9. You will need to provide IP addresses for the host and then reboot the host.

10. Upon this reboot, the host is now running off the local disk like a "normally provisioned" ESXi host.

vSphere Auto Deploy offers some great advantages, especially for environments with lots of ESXi hosts to manage, but it can also add complexity. As mentioned earlier, it all comes down to the design and requirements of your vSphere deployment.

Performing Post-installation Configuration

Whether you are installing from a CD/DVD or performing an unattended installation of ESXi, once the installation is complete, there are several post-installation steps that are necessary or might be necessary, depending on your specific configuration. We'll discuss these tasks in the following sections.

Installing the vSphere C# Client

This might come as a bit of shock for IT professionals who have grown accustomed to managing Microsoft Windows–based servers from the server's console (even via Remote Desktop), but ESXi wasn't designed for you to manage it from the server's console. Instead, you should use the vSphere Client.

In earlier versions, ESXi and vCenter were administered with the C# (pronounced "see sharp") Client. vSphere 5.0 introduced the Web Client. Although the first iteration of the Web Client was not as feature rich as the C# Client, with vSphere 5.1 and 5.5 the tables have turned. To ensure that you can follow which client the instructions are for, we will use the terms *vSphere Client* and *Web Client*.

The vSphere Client is a Windows-only application that allows for connecting directly to an ESXi host or to a vCenter Server installation. The only difference in the tools used is that connecting directly to an ESXi host requires authentication with a user account that exists on that specific host, while connecting to a vCenter Server installation relies on Windows users for authentication. Additionally, some features of the vSphere Client—such as initiating vMotion, for example—are available only when connecting to a vCenter Server installation.

LEARNING A NEW USER INTERFACE

For those who are already used to the vSphere Client, things can feel a little awkward, but learning the new web-based client for vCenter is certainly necessary. While you will be able to perform more traditional tasks in the vSphere Client, the Web Client helps you unlock the full potential when using vSphere 5.5. We'll focus primarily on the vSphere Web Client in this book unless we are directly administering the hosts (as is the case in this chapter) or when using vSphere Client plug-ins that are not currently available in the vSphere Web Client.

You can install either of the vSphere Clients with the vCenter Server installation media. Figure 2.11 shows the VMware vCenter Installer with the vSphere Client option selected.

FIGURE 2.11
You can install the vSphere Client directly from the vCenter Server installation media.

In previous versions of VMware vSphere, one of the easiest installation methods was to simply connect to an ESX/ESXi host or a vCenter Server instance using your web browser.

From there, you clicked a link to download the vSphere Client right from the web page. From vSphere 5.0 onward, the vSphere Client download link for ESXi hosts doesn't point to a local copy of the installation files; it redirects you to a VMware-hosted website to download the files. The vSphere Client download link for vCenter Server 5.5, though, still points to a local copy of the vSphere Client installer.

Because you might not have installed vCenter Server yet—that is the focus of the next chapter, Chapter 3—we'll walk you through installing the vSphere Client from the vCenter Server installation media. Regardless of how you obtain the installer, once the installation wizard starts, the process is the same. It is also worth noting that ESXi cannot be directly managed with the Web Client, so you will probably want to install both clients at some point. Refer to Chapter 3 for details on the Web Client installation.

Perform the following steps to install the vSphere Client from the vCenter Server installation media:

1. Make the vCenter Server installation media available via CD/DVD to the system where you want to install the vSphere Client.

   If you are installing the vSphere Client on a Windows VM, you can mount the vCenter Server installation ISO image as a virtual CD/DVD image. Refer to Chapter 7, "Ensuring High Availability and Business Continuity," for more details if you are unsure how to attach a virtual CD/DVD image.

2. If Autorun doesn't automatically launch the VMware vCenter Installer (shown previously in Figure 2.11), navigate to the CD/DVD and double-click `Autorun.exe`.

3. From the VMware vCenter Installer main screen, click vSphere Client under VMware Product Installers, and then click Install.

4. Select the language for the installer and click OK.

5. Click the Next button on the welcome page of the Virtual Infrastructure Client Wizard.

6. Click Next at the End User Patent Agreement screen.

7. Click the radio button labeled I Accept The Terms In The License Agreement, and then click the Next button.

8. Specify a username and organization name, and then click the Next button.

9. Configure the destination folder, and then click the Next button.

10. Click the Install button to begin the installation.

11. If prompted, select I Have Read And Accept The Terms Of The License Agreement, and then click Install to install the Microsoft .NET Framework, which is a prerequisite for the vSphere Client.

12. When the .NET Framework installation completes (if applicable), click Exit to continue with the rest of the vSphere Client installation.

13. Click the Finish button to complete the installation. Restart the computer if prompted.

64-BIT VS. 32-BIT

Although the vSphere Client can be installed and is supported on 64-bit Windows operating systems, the vSphere Client itself remains a 32-bit application and runs in 32-bit compatibility mode.

Reconfiguring the Management Network

During the installation of ESXi, the installer creates a virtual switch—also known as a *vSwitch*—bound to a physical NIC. The tricky part, depending on your server hardware, is that the installer might select a different physical NIC than the one you need for correct network connectivity. Consider the scenario depicted in Figure 2.12. If, for whatever reason, the ESXi installer doesn't link the correct physical NIC to the vSwitch it creates, then you won't have network connectivity to that host. We'll talk more about why ESXi's network connectivity must be configured with the correct NIC in Chapter 5, but for now just understand that this is a requirement for connectivity. Since you need network connectivity to manage the host from the vSphere Client, how do you fix this?

FIGURE 2.12
Network connectivity won't be established if the ESXi installer links the wrong NIC to the management network.

The simplest fix for this problem is to unplug the network cable from the current Ethernet port in the back of the server and continue trying the remaining ports until the host is accessible, but that's not always possible or desirable. The better way is to use the DCUI to reconfigure the management network so that it is converted the way you need it to be configured.

Perform the following steps to fix the management NIC in ESXi using the DCUI:

1. Access the console of the ESXi host, either physically or via a remote console solution such as an IP-based KVM.

2. On the ESXi home screen, shown in Figure 2.13, press F2 for Customize System/View Logs. If a root password has been set, enter that root password.

3. From the System Customization menu, select Configure Management Network, and press Enter.

4. From the Configure Management Network menu, select Network Adapters, and press Enter.

5. Use the spacebar to toggle which network adapter or adapters will be used for the system's management network, as shown in Figure 2.14. Press Enter when finished.

6. Press Esc to exit the Configure Management Network menu. When prompted to apply changes and restart the management network, press Y.

   After the correct NIC has been assigned to the ESXi management network, the System Customization menu provides a Test Management Network option to verify network connectivity.

7. Press Esc to log out of the System Customization menu and return to the ESXi home screen.

FIGURE 2.13
The ESXi home screen provides options for customizing the system and restarting or shutting down the server.

The other options within the DCUI for troubleshooting management network issues are covered in detail within Chapter 5.

At this point, you should have management network connectivity to the ESXi host, and from
here forward you can use the vSphere Client to perform other configuration tasks, such as configuring time synchronization and name resolution.

Configuring Time Synchronization

Time synchronization in ESXi is an important configuration because the ramifications of
incorrect time run deep. While ensuring that ESXi has the correct time seems trivial, time-
synchronization issues can affect features such as performance charting, SSH key expirations,
NFS access, backup jobs, authentication, and more. After the installation of ESXi or during an
unattended installation of ESXi using an installation script, the host should be configured to
perform time synchronization with a reliable time source. This source could be another server
on your network or a time source located on the Internet. For the sake of managing time synchronization, it is easiest to synchronize all your servers against one reliable internal time
server and then synchronize the internal time server with a reliable Internet time server. ESXi
provides a Network Time Protocol (NTP) implementation to provide this functionality.

The simplest way to configure time synchronization for ESXi involves the vSphere Client.
Perform the following steps to enable NTP using the vSphere Client:

1. Use the vSphere Client to connect directly to the ESXi host (or to a vCenter Server installation, if you have vCenter Server running at this point).

2. Select the hostname from the inventory tree on the left, and then click the Configuration
tab in the details pane on the right.

3. Select Time Configuration from the Software menu.

4. Click the Properties link.

5. In the Time Configuration dialog box, select NTP Client Enabled.

6. Still in the Time Configuration dialog box, click the Options button.

7. Select the NTP Settings option in the left side of the NTP Daemon (ntpd) Options dialog
box, and add one or more NTP servers to the list, as shown in Figure 2.15.

FIGURE 2.15
Specifying NTP servers allows ESXi to automatically keep time synchronized.

8. Check the box marked Restart NTP Service To Apply Changes; then click OK.

9. Click OK to return to the vSphere Client. The Time Configuration area will update to show the new NTP servers.

You'll note that using the vSphere Client to enable NTP this way also automatically enables NTP traffic through the firewall. You can verify this by noting an Open Firewall Ports entry in the Tasks pane or by clicking Security Profile under the Software menu and seeing an entry for NTP Client listed under Outgoing Connections.

WINDOWS AS A RELIABLE TIME SERVER

You can configure an existing Windows server as a reliable time server by performing these steps:

1. Use the Group Policy Object editor to navigate to Administrative Templates ➤ System ➤ Windows Time Service ➤ Time Providers.

2. Select the Enable Windows NTP Server Group Policy option.

3. Navigate to Administrative Templates ➤ System ➤ Windows Time Service.

4. Double-click the Global Configuration Settings option, and select the Enabled radio button.

5. Set the AnnounceFlags option to 4.

6. Click the OK button.

Configuring Name Resolution

Just as we mentioned that time synchronization is important for your vSphere environment, so is name resolution. Although the vSphere dependency on name resolution is less than it was, there is still some functionality that may not work as expected without proper name resolution.

Configuring name resolution is a simple process in the vSphere Client:

1. Use the vSphere Client to connect directly to the ESXi host (or to a vCenter Server installation, if you have vCenter Server running at this point).

2. Select the hostname from the inventory tree on the left, and then click the Configuration tab in the details pane on the right.

3. Select DNS And Routing from the Software menu.

4. Click the Properties link.

5. In the DNS And Routing dialog box, add the IP address(s) of your DNS server(s).

In this chapter we've discussed some of the decisions that you'll have to make as you deploy ESXi in your datacenter, and we've shown you how to deploy these products using both interactive and unattended methods. In the next chapter, we'll show you how to deploy VMware vCenter Server, a key component in your virtualization environment.

The Bottom Line

Understand ESXi compatibility requirements.   Unlike traditional operating systems like Windows or Linux, ESXi has much stricter hardware compatibility requirements. This helps ensure a stable, well-tested product line that is able to support even the most mission-critical applications.

> **Master It**   You have some older servers onto which you'd like to deploy ESXi. They aren't on the Hardware Compatibility Guide. Will they work with ESXi?

Plan an ESXi deployment.   Deploying ESXi will affect many different areas of your organization—not only the server team but also the networking team, the storage team, and the security team. There are many issues to consider, including server hardware, storage hardware, storage protocols or connection types, network topology, and network connections. Failing to plan properly could result in an unstable and unsupported implementation.

> **Master It**   Name three areas of networking that must be considered in a vSphere design.

> **Master It**   What are some of the different types of storage that ESXi can be installed on?

Deploy ESXi.   ESXi can be installed onto any supported and compatible hardware platform. You have three different ways to deploy ESXi: You can install it interactively, you can perform an unattended installation, or you can use vSphere Auto Deploy to provision ESXi as it boots up.

> **Master It**   Your manager asks you to provide him with a copy of the unattended installation script that you will be using when you roll out ESXi using vSphere Auto Deploy. Is this something you can give him?

> **Master It**   Name two advantages and two disadvantages of using vSphere Auto Deploy to provision ESXi hosts.

Perform post-installation configuration of ESXi.   Following the installation of ESXi, some additional configuration steps may be required. For example, if the wrong NIC is assigned to the management network, then the server won't be accessible across the network. You'll also need to configure time synchronization.

> **Master It**   You've installed ESXi on your server, but the welcome web page is inaccessible, and the server doesn't respond to a ping. What could be the problem?

Install the vSphere C# Client. ESXi is managed using the vSphere C# Client, a Windows-only application that provides the functionality to manage the virtualization platform. There are a couple different ways to obtain the vSphere Client installer, including running it directly from the VMware vCenter Installer or by downloading it using a web browser connected to the IP address of a vCenter Server instance.

Master It List two ways by which you can install the vSphere Client.

Chapter 3

Installing and Configuring vCenter Server

In the majority of today's information systems, the client-server architecture is king. This standing is because the client-server architecture can centralize resource management and give end users and client systems simplified access to those resources. Information systems used to exist in a flat, peer-to-peer model, when user accounts were required on every system where resource access was needed and when significant administrative overhead was needed simply to make things work. That is how managing a large infrastructure with many ESXi hosts feels without vCenter Server. vCenter Server brings the advantages of the client-server architecture to the ESXi host and to VM management.

In this chapter, you will learn to

- ◆ Understand the components and role of vCenter Server
- ◆ Plan a vCenter Server deployment
- ◆ Install and configure a vCenter Server database
- ◆ Install and configure the Single Sign-On service
- ◆ Install and configure the Inventory Service
- ◆ Install and configure vCenter Server
- ◆ Install and configure the Web Client service
- ◆ Use vCenter Server's management features

Introducing vCenter Server

As the size of a virtual infrastructure grows, managing the infrastructure from a central location becomes significantly more important. vCenter Server is an application that serves as a centralized management tool for ESXi hosts and their respective VMs. vCenter Server acts as a proxy that performs tasks on the individual ESXi hosts that have been added as members of a vCenter Server installation. As discussed in Chapter 1, "Introducing VMware vSphere 5.5," VMware includes vCenter Server licensing in every kit and every edition of vSphere, underscoring the importance of vCenter Server. Although VMware does offer a few different editions of vCenter Server (vCenter Server Essentials, vCenter Server Foundation, and vCenter Server Standard), we'll focus only on vCenter Server Standard in this book.

While VMware has a number of other products, vCenter is generally the central integration point tying them all together. Software such as vCloud Director, vCloud Automation Center, Site Recovery Manager, and vCenter Operations Manager all depend on an instance of vCenter Server. Not only this, but as you will see, much of the advanced functionality that vSphere offers comes only when vCenter Server is present. Specifically, vCenter Server offers core services in the following areas:

◆ Resource management for ESXi hosts and VMs

◆ Template management

◆ VM deployment

◆ VM management

◆ Scheduled tasks

◆ Statistics and logging

◆ Alarms and event management

◆ ESXi host management

Figure 3.1 outlines the core services available through vCenter Server.

FIGURE 3.1
vCenter Server provides a full spectrum of virtualization management functions.

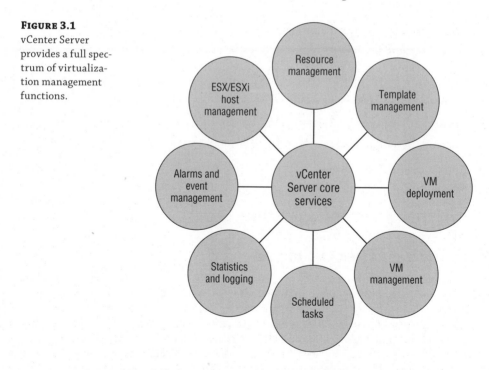

vCenter Server can be installed in one of two different ways: The more traditional approach is an application installed on a Windows server; the newer format is as a Linux-based virtual appliance. You'll learn more about virtual appliances in Chapter 10, "Using Templates and vApps," but for now, suffice it to say that the vCenter Server virtual appliance (which you may see referred to as VCVA or VCSA) offers an option to quickly and easily deploy a full installation of vCenter Server on SuSE Linux.

Because of the breadth of features included in vCenter Server, most of these core services are discussed in later chapters. For example, Chapter 9, "Creating and Managing Virtual Machines," discusses VM deployment, VM management, and template management. Chapter 11, "Managing Resource Allocation," and Chapter 12, "Balancing Resource Utilization," deal with resource management for ESXi hosts and VMs, and Chapter 13, "Monitoring VMware vSphere Performance," discusses alarms. In this chapter, we'll focus primarily on ESXi host management, but we'll also discuss scheduled tasks, statistics and logging, and event management.

There are other key items about vCenter Server that you can't really consider core services. Instead, these underlying features support the core services provided by vCenter Server. In order to help you more fully understand the value of vCenter Server in a vSphere deployment, we need to provide a closer look at the following:

- Centralized user authentication

- Web-based client server

- Inventory system

- Extensible framework

Centralizing User Authentication Using vCenter Single Sign-On

Centralized user authentication is not listed as a core service of vCenter Server, but it is essential to how vCenter Server operates and to reducing the management overhead that vCenter Server brings to a vSphere implementation. In Chapter 2, "Planning and Installing VMware ESXi," we discussed a user's authentication to an ESXi host under the context of a user account created and stored locally on that host. Generally speaking, without vCenter Server you would need a separate user account on each ESXi host for each administrator who needed access to the server. As the number of ESXi hosts and required administrators grows, the number of accounts to manage grows exponentially. There are workarounds for this overhead; one such workaround is integrating your ESXi hosts into Active Directory, a topic we'll discuss in more detail in Chapter 8, "Securing VMware vSphere." In this chapter, we'll assume the use of local accounts, but be aware that using Active Directory integration with your ESXi hosts does change the picture somewhat. In general, though, the centralized user authentication vCenter Server offers is easier to manage than other available methods.

In a virtualized infrastructure with only one or two ESXi hosts, administrative effort is not a major concern. Administering one or two servers would not incur incredible effort on the part of the administrator, and creating user accounts for administrators would not be too much of a burden.

In situations like this, vCenter Server might not be missed from a management perspective, but it will certainly be missed from a feature set viewpoint. In addition to its management capabilities, vCenter Server can perform vMotion, configure vSphere Distributed Resource Scheduler (DRS), establish vSphere High Availability (HA), and use vSphere Fault Tolerance (FT). These features are not accessible using ESXi hosts without vCenter Server. Without vCenter Server, you also lose key functionality such as vSphere Distributed Switches, host profiles, policy-driven storage, and vSphere Update Manager. vCenter Server is a requirement for any enterprise-level virtualization project.

> ### vCenter Server Requirement
>
> Strictly speaking, vCenter Server is not a requirement for a vSphere deployment. You can create and run VMs without it. However, to utilize the advanced features of the vSphere product suite—features such as vSphere Update Manager, vMotion, vSphere DRS, vSphere HA, vSphere Distributed Switches, host profiles, and vSphere FT—vCenter Server must be licensed, installed, and configured accordingly.

But what happens when the environment grows? What happens when there are 10 ESXi hosts and 5 administrators? Now the administrative effort of maintaining all these local accounts on the ESXi hosts becomes a significant burden. If a new account is needed to manage the ESXi hosts, you must create the account on 10 different hosts. If an account password needs to change, you must change it on 10 different hosts. Then add into this equation other VMware components such as vCloud Director or vCenter Orchestrator, with their own possible accounts and passwords.

vCenter—well, more accurately vCenter Single Sign-On (SSO)—addresses this problem. It is a prerequisite for installing vCenter Server; that is, vCenter Server cannot be installed without installing SSO first. We'll explain briefly how SSO works and what other software it interacts with (both VMware and non-VMware).

Prior to vSphere 5.1, when you logged onto vCenter your authentication request was forwarded to either the local security authority on vCenter Server's OS or Active Directory. With SSO, the request can still end up going to Active Directory, but it can also go to a list of locally defined users within SSO itself or to OpenLDAP. Generally speaking, SSO is a more secure way of authenticating to VMware products. Notice we said products and not vSphere? That's because SSO has hooks into vCenter, vCenter Orchestrator (vCO), vCloud Director (vCD), and vCloud Networking and Security (vCNS). Why is this important? It means that SSO can take a single user and provide them with access to everything they need through the virtual infrastructure with a single username and password, and it can do so securely.

The following list outlines the steps taken when a user logs on using the vSphere Web Client (see Figure 3.2).

1. The vSphere Web Client presents a secure web page to log into.

2. The username and password is issued to the SSO server (in the form of a SAML 2.0 token).

3. The SSO server then sends a request to the relevant authentication mechanism (local, AD, or OpenLDAP)

4. Once authentication succeeds, SSO then passes a token to the vSphere Web Client.

5. This token can now be used to authenticate directly with vCenter, vCO, vCNS, or vCD.

As you can see, the authentication procedure can sound more complicated than some more traditional methods; however, all of this ends up being seamless to the end administrator who gets access as they did before.

During the installation of SSO, which we'll detail later in this chapter, you are given three options for the installation type. Depending on the availability requirements of your vCenter Server installation, you may wish to make SSO available from multiple sites or highly available in a cluster. When installing SSO for the first time, the first instance will always be the Primary Node. The SSO installer then allows you to install additional SSO server nodes in the mode that suits your environment.

FIGURE 3.2
The steps taken to issue an authenticated session with the new SSO component.

---

vCENTER SERVER REQUIREMENT

Strictly speaking, vCenter Server is not a requirement for a vSphere deployment. You can create and run VMs without it. However, to utilize the advanced features of the vSphere product suite—features such as vSphere Update Manager, vMotion, vSphere DRS, vSphere HA, vSphere Distributed Switches, host profiles, and vSphere FT—vCenter Server must be licensed, installed, and configured accordingly.

AUTHENTICATION WITH THE vSPHERE CLIENT

Generally speaking, logging onto an ESXi host using the vSphere Client requires an account created and stored locally on that host. Using the same vSphere Client to connect to vCenter Server requires an SSO user account. Keep in mind that SSO and ESXi hosts do not make any attempt to reconcile the user accounts in their respective account databases.

Using the vSphere Client to connect directly to an ESXi host that is currently managed by vCenter Server can cause negative effects in vCenter Server. A successful logon to a managed host results in a pop-up box that warns you of this potential problem.

Using the vSphere Web Client for Administration

With the release of vSphere 5.1, VMware started shipping two different clients to use with vCenter Server. The older, more traditional client is a .NET Windows-only application, while the newer is a server-side installation for administering vSphere from a web browser. While not all browsers are supported, the following browsers are certified and supported with the vSphere Web Client:

◆ Microsoft Internet Explorer, 7, 8, and 9

◆ Mozilla Firefox 3.6 and later

◆ Google Chrome 14 and later

Additionally, to use the vSphere Web Client, you must have Adobe Flash Player version 11.1 or later installed.

WHICH CLIENT TO USE

Now that there are two possible client choices to manage your vCenter Server, you need to decide which client to use day to day. Any new features that are part of the vSphere 5.5 release are not available from the vSphere Client, so that would indicate that the vSphere Web Client is the one to use. But what happens if your storage vendor has a vSphere Client plug-in that has not been updated to work with the vSphere Web Client? Well, in some cases you may not have a choice other than to use the older client, but over time the crossover period will fade away and only the vSphere Web Client will be used. Prior to vSphere 5.5, we would have stated that the vSphere Client was still the one to use, but now that vendors have had time to update things and features are presented only through the vSphere Web Client, it's our opinion that we're on the other side of the curve.

As stated in Chapter 2, previously the vSphere Web Client was not as feature rich as the traditional vSphere Client, but with the release of vSphere 5.5, this has changed. From vSphere 5.1 onward, VMware stated that it was no longer adding features to the .NET vSphere Client: Only the vSphere Web Client would gain new feature capabilities, so it's definitely the one to use.

As you read through the rest of this book, you can assume that unless we specify the vSphere Client, the vSphere Web Client is the default choice and the one you should be using.

Understanding the vCenter Inventory Service

The Inventory Service is tightly integrated with the vSphere Web Client, and in fact, the Inventory Service exists to ensure that the vSphere Web Client performs well. One way to think of the Inventory Service is that it's like a proxy server; it sits between the source (the vCenter Server itself) and the requester (the vSphere Web Client). The Inventory Service reduces traffic to and from the vCenter Server by caching information in its own database.

Not only does the vCenter Inventory Service cache queries and results for the vSphere Web Client, it can also be installed on a separate server to ensure an appropriate level of resources. The reasoning behind this is again solely for performance and scalability benefits.

Real World Scenario

PERFORMANCE OF VSPHERE CLIENT VS. VSPHERE WEB CLIENT

Author Nick Marshall recalls the following experience: "In 2012, I did some work helping a business upgrade from vSphere 4.1 to 5.1. While the environment where this upgrade took place had significant investments in vSphere and the underlying hardware, one administrator was quite unhappy with the performance. As I became more involved in this project, I learned that his frustrations lay with the day-to-day performance of the vSphere Client, not with the actual hosts or 1,000+ VMs.

As I migrated VMs between the two environments, this administrator was expecting to experience the same performance issues that bugged him in their older vSphere 4.1 environment. To his surprise, although the hardware being used was identical and the workloads being managed were the same, the general responsiveness of the newer vSphere Web Client was significantly better than the older client he was used to. The architecture of the newer vSphere Web Client simply performs better at scale than the older vSphere Client."

Providing an Extensible Framework

Just as centralized authentication is not a core vCenter Server service, we don't include vCenter Server's extensible framework as a core service. Rather, this extensible framework provides the foundation for vCenter Server's core services and enables third-party developers to create applications built around vCenter Server. Figure 3.3 shows some of the components that revolve around the core services of vCenter Server.

A key aspect for the success of virtualization is the ability to allow third-party companies to provide additional products that add value, ease, and functionality to existing products. By building vCenter Server in an extensible fashion and providing an application programming interface (API) to it, VMware has shown its interest in allowing third-party software developers to play an integral part in virtualization. The vCenter Server API allows companies to develop custom applications that can take advantage of the virtual infrastructure created in vCenter Server. For example, numerous companies have created backup utilities that work off the exact inventory created inside vCenter Server to allow for advanced backup options of VMs. Storage vendors use the vCenter API to create plug-ins that expose storage details, and other third-party applications use the vCenter Server APIs to provide management, monitoring, life cycle management, or automation functionality.

You can find more information on vCenter Server functionality in Chapter 10, which provides a detailed look at templates along with VM deployment and management, and Chapter 8, which goes deeper into vCenter Server's access controls. Chapter 11 discusses resource management, while Chapter 13 offers an in-depth look at ESXi host and VM monitoring as well as alarms.

You're almost ready to take a closer look at installing, configuring, and managing vCenter Server. First, however, we'll discuss how to choose which version of vCenter Server you should deploy in your environment.

FIGURE 3.3
Other applications can extend vCenter Server's core services to provide additional management functionality.

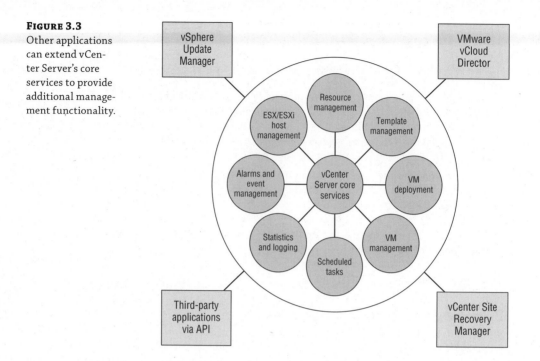

Choosing the Version of vCenter Server

As mentioned in the previous section, vSphere 5.5 vCenter Server comes not only as a Windows-based application but also as a SuSE Linux–based virtual appliance. As a result, one of the primary decisions that you must make as you prepare to deploy vCenter Server is which version you will use. Will you use the Windows Server–based version or the virtual appliance?

There are some advantages and disadvantages to each approach:

◆ If your experience is primarily with Windows Server, you may not be familiar with the Linux underpinnings of the vCenter virtual appliance. This introduces a learning curve that you should consider.

◆ If you need support for Microsoft SQL Server, the Linux-based vCenter virtual appliance won't work; you'll need to deploy the Windows Server–based version of vCenter Server. However, if you are using Oracle, or if you are a small installation without a separate database server, the vCenter Server virtual appliance will work just fine (it has its own embedded database if you don't have or don't need a separate database server).

◆ If you want to use vCenter Heartbeat to protect vCenter Server from downtime, you'll need to use the Windows Server–based version of vCenter Server.

◆ If you need to use linked mode, you must deploy the Windows Server–based version of vCenter Server. The vCenter Server virtual appliance does not support linked mode.

◆ Conversely, if your experience is primarily with Linux, then deploying a Windows Server–based application will require some learning and acclimation for you and/or your staff.

◆ The Linux-based virtual appliance comes preloaded with additional services like Auto Deploy (covered in Chapter 2), Dynamic Host Configuration Protocol (DHCP), Trivial File Transfer Protocol (TFTP), and syslog. If you need these services on your network, you can provide them with a single deployment of the vCenter virtual appliance. With the Windows Server–based version, these services are separate installations or possibly even separate VMs (or, worse yet, separate physical servers!).

◆ Because the vCenter Server virtual appliance naturally runs only as a VM, you are constrained to that particular design decision. If you want or need to run vCenter Server on a physical system, you cannot use the vCenter Server virtual appliance.

As you can see, there are a number of considerations that will affect your decision to deploy vCenter Server as a Windows Server–based installation or as a Linux-based virtual appliance.

AUTHOR NICK MARSHALL'S VIEW ON THE VCENTER VIRTUAL APPLIANCE

Some of the early support limitations around the SuSE Linux–based vCenter Server virtual appliance led people to believe that this solution was more appropriate for smaller installations. This may have been because the virtual appliance was certified to support only 5 hosts and 50 VMs or because deploying a virtual appliance that handles all the various services required would appeal more to a smaller implementation. However, VMware has now certified this solution to support up to 100 hosts and/or 3000 VMs, so the former argument is no longer valid. The way I see it, you should always use the right tool for the job (with proper planning), and the vCenter Server virtual appliance is the right tool for some jobs.

In the next section, we'll discuss some of the planning and design considerations that have to be addressed if you plan to deploy the Windows Server–based version of vCenter Server. Most of these issues apply to the Windows Server–based version of vCenter Server, but some may also apply to the virtual appliance; we'll point those out where applicable.

Planning and Designing a vCenter Server Deployment

vCenter Server is a critical application for managing your virtual infrastructure. Its implementation should be carefully designed and executed to ensure availability and data protection. When discussing the deployment of vCenter Server and its components, the following questions are among the most common questions to ask:

◆ How much hardware do I need to power vCenter Server?

◆ Which database server should I use with vCenter Server?

◆ How do I prepare vCenter Server for disaster recovery?

◆ Should I run vCenter Server in a VM?

A lot of the answers to these questions are dependent on each other, but we have to start somewhere, so we'll start with the first topic: figuring out how much hardware you need for vCenter Server.

Sizing Hardware for vCenter Server

The amount of hardware that vCenter Server requires is directly related to the number of hosts and VMs it will be managing. This planning and design consideration applies only to the Windows Server–based version of vCenter Server; because it is a prepackaged virtual appliance, the virtual hardware of the vCenter Server virtual appliance is predefined and established before it is deployed.

As a starting point, the minimum hardware requirements for the Windows Server–based version of vCenter Server are as follows:

◆ Two 64-bit CPUs or a single dual-core 64-bit CPU.

◆ 2 GHz processor or faster.

◆ 4 GB of RAM or more.

◆ 4 GB of free disk space.

◆ A network adapter (Gigabit Ethernet strongly recommended).

◆ A supported version of Windows (Windows Server 2003, Windows Server 2003 R2, Windows Server 2008, or Windows Server 2008 R2); vCenter Server 5 requires a 64-bit version of Windows.

Keep in mind these are *minimum* system requirements. Large enterprise environments with many ESXi hosts and VMs must scale the vCenter Server system accordingly.

LOCAL DISKS ON VCENTER SERVER

Disk storage allocation is of minimal concern when planning a vCenter Server installation because the data is generally stored in an SQL or Oracle database on a remote server.

In addition, the requirements for the Windows Server–based edition of vCenter Server do not account for running a database server, which vCenter Server requires. Although vCenter Server is the application that performs the management of your ESXi hosts and VMs, vCenter Server uses a database for storing all of its configuration, permissions, statistics, and other data. Figure 3.4 shows the relationship between vCenter Server and the separate database server.

When answering the question of how much hardware vCenter Server requires, you have to address the computer running vCenter Server and the one running the components it depends on, which include the following components:

◆ Database server

◆ Single Sign-On server

- ◆ Inventory server

- ◆ Any other services you wish to co-locate

FIGURE 3.4
vCenter Server acts as a proxy for managing ESXi hosts, but all of the data for vCenter Server is stored in a database.

Although you can run vCenter Server and its dependencies on the same machine, it's usually not recommended because it creates a single point of failure for key aspects of your virtual infrastructure. However, sometimes you don't have a choice, especially in smaller environments when capacity is at a premium. Keep in mind that VMware recommends 10 GB of RAM if vCenter Server, vCenter Single Sign-On, and vCenter Inventory Service are installed on the same machine. This would be the case if you use the Simple Install option when installing vCenter Server.

Throughout this chapter, we'll use the term *separate database server* to refer to a database server application that is separately installed and managed. Although it might reside on the same computer, it is still considered a separate database server because it is managed independently of vCenter Server. You'll also see the term *backend database*, which refers to the actual database that vCenter Server uses on the separate database server.

Without considering the separate database or SSO servers for vCenter Server, VMware suggests a system configured with two CPU cores and 4 GB of RAM to support up to 50 ESXi hosts and 500 powered-on VMs. For environments consisting of up to 300 ESXi hosts and up to 3,000 powered-on VMs, VMware recommends four CPU cores and 8 GB of RAM. Finally, for environments scaling all the way up to 1,000 ESXi hosts and up to 10,000 powered-on VMs, vCenter Server should have 8 CPU cores and 16 GB of RAM.

CPU CORES

Most modern physical servers ship with at least quad-core CPUs. As you can see based on VMware's recommendations, vCenter Server will leverage multiple CPU cores when necessary.

Should you choose to run the separate database server on the same physical computer as vCenter Server, you'll need to consult the documentation for your chosen database server.

Without a doubt, the database server requires additional CPU capacity, RAM, and disk storage just like SSO and the Inventory Service, so you will need to plan accordingly. That brings us to the next topic: choosing which database server to use.

Choosing a Database Server for vCenter Server

In light of the sensitive and critical nature of the data in the vCenter Server databases, VMware supports vCenter Server issues only with backend databases on enterprise-level database servers. Both the Windows Server–based version and the virtual appliance version of vCenter Server use a backend database, so you'll need to decide which one to use either way. vCenter Server officially supports the following database servers:

◆ Microsoft SQL Server 2008 R2 Express (bundled with vCenter Server)

◆ Microsoft SQL Server 2005 (32-bit or 64-bit; SP3 is required, and SP4 is recommended)

◆ Microsoft SQL Server 2008 (32-bit or 64-bit; SP1 is required, and SP2 is recommended)

◆ Microsoft SQL Server 2008 R2

◆ Oracle 10*g* R2 (10.2.0.4 required)

◆ Oracle 11*g* R1 (11.1.0.7 required)

◆ Oracle 11*g* R2 (11.2.0.1 with patch 5 required)

Note that although a database might be supported for use with vCenter Server, that same database might not be supported for other components of vSphere such as vSphere Update Manager or other plug-ins that require database support. For up-to-date compatibility information, refer to the vSphere Compatibility Matrixes available from VMware's website (www .vmware.com). In addition, note that Microsoft SQL Server is supported for use by a Windows Server–based installation of vCenter Server, but it is not supported by the vCenter Server virtual appliance.

For smaller environments, users have the option of using Microsoft SQL Server 2008 Express Edition or, if using the virtual appliance, an embedded database. As of this writing, VMware had not yet published any sizing recommendations regarding the use of the embedded database. As stated in the sidebar "Author Nick Marshall's View on the vCenter Virtual Appliance," the use of the vCenter virtual appliance specifically with the embedded database is probably best suited for smaller environments.

Users should use SQL Server 2008 Express Edition only when their vSphere deployment will be limited in size; otherwise, users should plan on using a separate database server. If you are starting out with a small environment that will work with SQL Server 2008 Express Edition, note that you can upgrade to a full-featured version of SQL Server at a later date. While it is not necessarily an automated or supported migration path, more information on upgrading SQL Server 2008 Express is available on the Microsoft website (www.microsoft.com). Depending on your situation, it might be better to build a new SQL server and then follow the VMware migration plan for relocating vCenter databases.

USING SQL SERVER 2008 EXPRESS EDITION

SQL Server 2008 Express Edition is the minimum database available as a backend to the Windows Server–based version of vCenter Server.

Microsoft SQL Server 2008 Express Edition has physical limitations that include the following:

◆ One CPU maximum

◆ 1 GB maximum of addressable RAM

◆ 4 GB database maximum

Large virtual enterprises will quickly outgrow these SQL Server 2008 Express Edition limitations. Therefore, you might assume that any virtual infrastructures using SQL Server 2008 Express Edition are smaller deployments with little projections, if any, for growth. VMware suggests using SQL Server 2008 Express Edition only for deployments with 5 or fewer hosts and 50 or fewer VMs.

Because the separate database server is independently installed and managed, some additional configuration is required. Later in this chapter, the section "Installing vCenter Server" provides detailed information about working with separate database servers and the specific configuration that is required for each.

So, how does an organization go about choosing which separate database server to use? The process of selection typically reflects what an organization already uses or is licensed to use. Organizations with Oracle may decide to continue to use Oracle for vCenter Server; organizations that are predominantly based on Microsoft SQL Server will likely choose to use SQL Server to support vCenter Server. The choice of which version of vCenter Server—Windows Server–based or virtual appliance—will also affect this decision because the supported databases are different for each version. You should choose the database engine with which you are most familiar and that will support both the current and projected size of the virtual infrastructure.

With regard to the hardware requirements for the database server, the underlying database server will largely determine those requirements. VMware provides some general guidelines around Microsoft SQL Server in the white paper "VirtualCenter Database Performance for Microsoft SQL Server 2005," available on VMware's website at

    www.vmware.com/files/pdf/vc_database_performance.pdf

Although written with VirtualCenter 2.5 in mind, this information applies to newer versions of vCenter Server as well. In a typical configuration with standard logging levels, an SQL Server instance with two CPU cores and 4 GB of RAM allocated to the database application should support all but the very largest or most demanding environments.

If you plan to run the database server and vCenter Server components on the same hardware, you should adjust the hardware requirements accordingly.

Appropriately sizing hardware for vCenter Server and the separate database server is good and necessary. Given the central role that vCenter Server plays in a vSphere environment, though, you must also account for availability.

Planning for vCenter Server Availability

Planning for a vCenter Server deployment is more than just accounting for CPU and memory resources. You must also create a plan for business continuity and disaster recovery. Remember, features such as vSphere vMotion, vSphere Storage vMotion, vSphere DRS, and to a certain extent vSphere HA stop functioning or are significantly impacted when vCenter Server is unavailable. While vCenter Server or any component it depends on is down, you won't be able to clone VMs or deploy new VMs from templates. You also lose centralized authentication and role-based administration of the ESXi hosts. Clearly, there are reasons why you might want vCenter Server to be highly available.

Keep in mind, too, that the heart of the vCenter Server and its components are stored in backend databases. Any good disaster-recovery or business-continuity plan must also include instructions on how to handle data loss or corruption in the backend databases, and the separate database server(s)—if running on a separate physical computer or in a separate VM—should be designed and deployed in a resilient and highly available fashion. This is especially true in larger environments.

There are a few different ways to approach this concern. First, we'll discuss how to protect the vCenter Server components, then the vCenter Server itself, and finally we'll talk about protecting the separate database server.

PROTECTING SINGLE SIGN-ON

Single Sign-On is an integral part of vCenter Server. Without it there is no ability to log in and administer vCenter. Therefore, it is imperative that your protection strategy for the whole of vCenter Server (and it's components) covers vCenter Single Sign-On. There are three methods for ensuring you have an SSO instance available to you with little or no downtime: deploying in a High Availability cluster, deploying to multiple sites, and having a solid backup plan.

During the SSO installation, you have the ability to join an existing deployment and configure a High Availability (HA) cluster. With this configuration, all SSO instances must sit behind a load balancer. Deploying SSO in this way protects you from an outage of the SSO application or server.

The other installation option for SSO is called Multisite. This mode lets you install SSO with multiple physical locations. While this is usually deployed when you need to be able to sign in from multiple locations, it can also be used to facilitate a protection mechanism.

To save the time of redeploying and restoring a backup, if your SSO server is a VM, you can also regularly clone this VM to serve as a recovery point. This, however, is no substitute for a properly configured, company-wide backup solution that covers the SSO deployment.

PROTECTING THE INVENTORY SERVICE

VMware doesn't provide any type of built-in High Availability, but you can always run the Inventory Service on an HA-enabled vSphere cluster (see the section "Running vCenter Server and Its Components as VMs"). While HA is certainly an option for protecting the Inventory Service, unfortunately Fault Tolerance is not because the hardware requirements for this server state the need for two cores, as does SSO.

While the data that the Inventory Service stores is not as important as that in the SSO or vCenter itself, the Inventory Service still needs to be available for vCenter to function and therefore you must consider a plan on how to keep downtime to a minimum. Like SSO, the Inventory Service installs with a backup script within its installation directory. To use this feature, run the following command from the Inventory Service server:

```
vCenter_Server_installation_directory\Infrastructure\Inventory Service\scripts\backup.bat -
file backup_file_name
```

As stated earlier, the data that the Inventory Service holds locally is not as mission critical as the data SSO or vCenter holds. If you were in the position that your Inventory Service needed to be reinstalled and you had no backup to restore, you would only lose the tags metadata (tags are explained later in this chapter).

PROTECTING VCENTER SERVER

First, vCenter Server Heartbeat—a product available from VMware since VirtualCenter/vCenter Server 2.5 to provide high availability with little or no downtime—will be available with support for vCenter Server 5.5 upon release or shortly after the release of vSphere 5.5 (vCenter Server 5.5). Using vCenter Server Heartbeat will automate both the process of keeping the active and passive vCenter Server instances synchronized and the process of failing over from one to another (and back again). The website at www.vmware.com/products/vcenter-server-heartbeat has more information on vCenter Server Heartbeat.

If the vCenter Server computer is a physical server, one way to provide availability is to create a standby vCenter Server system that you can turn on in the event of a failure of the online vCenter Server computer. After failure, you bring the standby server online and attach it to the existing SQL Server database, and then the hosts can be added to the new vCenter Server computer. In this approach, you'll need to find mechanisms to keep the primary and secondary/standby vCenter Server systems synchronized with regard to file system content and configuration settings. The use of the Linux-based virtual appliance might make this approach easier because it is a VM; it therefore can be cloned (a process you'll see in more detail in Chapter 10).

A variation on that approach is to keep the standby vCenter Server system as a VM. You can use physical-to-virtual (P2V) conversion tools to regularly "back up" the physical vCenter Server instance to a standby VM. This method reduces the amount of physical hardware required and leverages the P2V process as a way of keeping the two vCenter Servers synchronized. Obviously, this sort of approach is viable for a Windows Server–based installation on a physical system but not applicable to the virtual appliance version of vCenter Server.

As a last resort for recovering vCenter Server, it's possible to just reinstall the software, point to the existing database, and connect the host systems. Of course, this assumes that the database is housed on a separate system from vCenter Server itself. The installation of vCenter Server is not a time-consuming process. Ultimately, the most important part of the vCenter Server recovery plan is to ensure that the database server is redundant and protected.

PROTECTING THE VCENTER DATABASE

For high availability of the database server supporting vCenter Server, you can configure the backend database on a cluster. Figure 3.5 illustrates using an SQL Server cluster for the backend database. This figure also shows a standby vCenter Server system. Methods used to provide high availability for the database server are in addition to whatever steps you might take to protect vCenter Server itself. Other options might include using SQL log shipping to create a database replica on a separate system. If using clustering or log shipping/database replication is not available or is not within fiscal reach, you should strengthen your database backup strategy to support easy recovery in the event of data loss or corruption. Using the native SQL Server tools, you can create a backup strategy that combines full, differential, and transaction log backups. This strategy allows you to restore data up to the minute when the loss or corruption occurred.

FIGURE 3.5

A good disaster recovery plan for vCenter Server should include a quick means of regaining the user interface as well as ensuring that the data is highly available and protected against damage.

The suggestion of using a VM as a standby system for a physical computer running vCenter Server naturally brings us to the last topic: Should you run vCenter Server in a VM? That's quite a question, and it's one that we'll answer next.

Running vCenter Server and Its Components as VMs

You certainly have the option of skipping a physical server entirely and running vCenter Server and its components as a VM or even multiple VMs. This gives you several advantages, including snapshots, clones, vMotion, vSphere HA, and vSphere DRS.

Snapshots are a feature we'll discuss in detail in Chapter 9. At a high level, snapshot functionality lets you return to a specific point in time for your VM, in this case, your vCenter Server VM. vMotion gives you the portability to move the server from host to host without experiencing server downtime. But what happens when a snapshot is corrupted or the VM is damaged to the point it will not run? With vCenter Server as your VM, you can make regular copies of the virtual disk file and keep a "clone" of the server ready to go in the event of server failure. The clone will have the same system configuration used the last time the virtual disks were copied. Given that the bulk of the data processing by vCenter Server ends up in a backend database running on a different server, this should not be very different. However, remember that the Windows Server–based version of vCenter Server uses an ADAM database to store roles and permissions, so roles and permissions on the clone will "roll back" to the point in time at which the clone was created. Additionally, if you are using the vCenter Server virtual appliance with the embedded database, you could run into issues with snapshots and reverting to snapshots. This might or might not be an issue, but be sure to plan accordingly. Figure 3.6 illustrates the setup of a manual cloning of a vCenter Server VM.

FIGURE 3.6

If vCenter Server is a VM, its virtual disk file can be copied regularly and used as the hard drive for a new VM, effectively providing a point-in-time restore in the event of complete server failure or loss.

vCenter Server VM

Standby vCenter Server VM

Copy virtual disk files

Some organizations may have a "virtualize first" or a "100% virtual" policy; while this may give all the advantages of virtualization, you need to consider other issues in the design of the infrastructure. Having a separate management cluster to host all of the vCenter Server Components, along with any dependencies such as database servers and Active Directory, is fast becoming commonplace. This separate management cluster will ensure that a production workload incident would not negatively impact the manageability of the environment.

SEPARATING MANAGEMENT FROM WORKLOADS

As mentioned, separating the management VMs from the rest of the workload VMs is fast becoming commonplace. The reason behind this is the increased dependency on the virtual infrastructure and its management. VMware itself recommends this design practice in its vCloud Director Architecture Toolkit (vCAT). Think of this design best practice as similar to the way we separate the management network in physical designs. Ensuring that this environment is highly secure and available goes a long way toward decreasing the downtime in the event of a problem.

While delving into design best practices is outside the scope of this book, just as with physical infrastructure design, there are certain things that need to be considered to ensure that your virtual infrastructure is designed to meet business requirements. But like any "best practice," it's a recommendation when there are no requirements that would point you in a different direction. For more information on vSphere design, we recommend you read *VMware vSphere Design* (Sybex, 2013).

By now, you have a good understanding of the importance of vCenter Server in a large enterprise environment and some of the considerations that go into planning for a vCenter Server deployment. You also have a good idea of the components, features, functions, and role of vCenter Server. With this information in mind, let's install vCenter Server. The next section mainly focuses on the installation of the Windows Server–based version of vCenter Server; for information on the vCenter Server virtual appliance, refer to the section "Deploying the vCenter Server Virtual Appliance."

Installing vCenter Server and Its Components

Depending on the size of the environment to be managed, installing vCenter Server can be simple. In small environments, the vCenter Server Installer can install and configure all the necessary components. For larger environments, installing vCenter Server in a scalable and resilient fashion is a bit more involved and requires a few different steps. For example, supporting more than 1,000 ESXi hosts or more than 10,000 VMs requires installing multiple vCenter Server instances in a linked mode group, a scenario that we'll discuss later in this chapter in the section "Installing vCenter Server in a Linked Mode Group." You also know that the majority of vCenter Server deployments needs a separate database server installed and configured to support vCenter Server. The exception would be the very small deployments in which SQL Server 2008 Express Edition is sufficient.

The majority of this discussion is applicable only to installing vCenter Server and its components on a Windows Server–based computer (physical or virtual). However, some tasks—such as the tasks required for preparing separate database servers—are applicable to the use of the vCenter Server virtual appliance as well.

---

vCenter Server Preinstallation Tasks

Before you install vCenter Server, ensure that the computer has been updated with the latest updates, such as Windows Installer 4.5 and all required .NET components, from the Microsoft Windows Update site at the following location:

`www.update.microsoft.com/microsoftupdate/v6/default.aspx`

Depending on the database engine you will use, different configuration steps are required to prepare the database server for vCenter Server, and these steps must be completed before you can actually install vCenter Server. If you are planning on using SQL Server 2008 Express Edition—and you're aware of the limitations of using this edition, as described earlier in the sidebar "Using SQL Server 2008 Express Edition"—you can skip ahead to the section "Installing the vCenter Server Components." Otherwise, let's take a closer look at working with a separate database server and what is required.

Configuring the vCenter Server Backend Database Server

As noted previously, vCenter Server stores the majority of its information in a backend database, usually using a separate database server. It's important to realize that the backend database is a key component to this infrastructure. The backend database server should be designed and deployed accordingly. Without the backend database, you will find yourself rebuilding an entire infrastructure.

---

vCenter Server Business Continuity

Losing the server that runs vCenter Server might result in a small period of downtime; however, losing the backend database to vCenter Server could result in days of downtime and extended periods of rebuilding.

On the backend database server, vCenter Server require specific permissions on their databases. After the database is created and configured appropriately, connecting vCenter Server to it requires that an Open Database Connectivity (ODBC) data source name (DSN) be created on the vCenter Server system. The ODBC DSN should be created under the context of a database user who has full rights and permissions to the database that has been created specifically for storing vCenter Server data.

In the following sections, we'll take a closer look at working with the two possible database servers used in conjunction with vCenter Server: Oracle and Microsoft SQL Server.

WORKING WITH ORACLE DATABASES

Perhaps because Microsoft SQL Server was designed as a Windows-based application, like vCenter Server, working with Oracle as the backend database server involves a bit more effort than using Microsoft SQL Server.

To use Oracle 10*g* or 11*g*, you need to install Oracle and create a database for vCenter Server to use. Although it is supported to run Oracle on the same computer as vCenter Server, it is not a configuration we recommend. Still, in the event that you have valid business reasons for doing so, we'll walk you through the steps for configuring Oracle to support vCenter Server both locally (on the same computer as vCenter Server) and remotely (on a different computer than vCenter Server). If you are deploying the vCenter Server virtual appliance, then only the remote Oracle configuration applies. Both of these sets of instructions assume that you have already created the database you are going to use.

SPECIAL PATCHES NEEDED FOR ORACLE 10G RELEASE 2

For Oracle 10*g* Release 2, you must apply patch 10.2.0.4 to both the client and the Oracle database server in order to support vCenter Server.

PREPARING AN ORACLE DATABASE FOR vCENTER

Perform the following steps to prepare Oracle for vCenter Server if your Oracle database resides on the same computer as vCenter Server:

1. Log into an SQL*Plus session with the system account to create a database user. Run the following SQL command to create a user with the correct permissions:

```
CREATE USER "vpxadmin" PROFILE "DEFAULT" IDENTIFIED BY "vcdbpassword"
DEFAULT TABLESPACE
"VPX" ACCOUNT UNLOCK;
grant connect to VPXADMIN;
grant resource to VPXADMIN;
grant create view to VPXADMIN;
grant create sequence to VPXADMIN;
grant create table to VPXADMIN;
grant create materialized view to VPXADMIN;
grant execute on dbms_lock to VPXADMIN;
grant execute on dbms_job to VPXADMIN;
grant unlimited tablespace to VPXADMIN;
```

   If the RESOURCE role doesn't have CREATE PROCEDURE, CREATE TABLE, and CREATE SEQUENCE privileges assigned, you'll need to grant them to the vCenter Server database user.

2. Run the following SQL command to create the vCenter Server database:

```
CREATE SMALLFILE TABLESPACE "VPX" DATAFILE 'C:\Oracle\ORADATA\VPX\VPX.DBF'
SIZE 1G AUTOEXTEND ON NEXT 10M MAXSIZE UNLIMITED LOGGING EXTENT MANAGEMENT
LOCAL SEGMENT SPACE MANAGEMENT AUTO;
```

   Modify the path to the database as appropriate for your installation.

3. Now you need to assign a user permission to this newly created tablespace. While you are still connected to SQL*Plus, run the following SQL command:

```
CREATE USER vpxAdmin IDENTIFIED BY vpxadmin DEFAULT TABLESPACE vpx;
```

4. Install the Oracle client and the ODBC driver.

5. Modify the tnsnames.ora file to reflect where your Oracle database is located:

```
VC=
(DESCRIPTION=
(ADDRESS_LIST=
(ADDRESS=(PROTOCOL=TCP)(HOST=localhost)(PORT=1521))
)
(CONNECT_DATA=
(SERVICE_NAME=VPX)
)
)
```

   The HOST= value should be set to localhost if you are accessing the Oracle database locally or the name of the remote Oracle database server if you are accessing the database remotely. Specify the remote host as a fully qualified domain name (FQDN), such as esxi-05.lab.local.

6. Create the ODBC DSN. When you are creating the DSN, be sure to specify the service name as listed in TNSNAMES.ORA (in this example, VPX).

7. While logged into SQL*Plus with the system account, run the following SQL command to enable database monitoring via the vCenter Server user:

```
grant select on v_$system_event to VPXADMIN;
grant select on v_$sysmetric_history to VPXADMIN;
grant select on v_$sysstat to VPXADMIN;
grant select on dba_data_files to VPXADMIN;
grant select on v_$loghist to VPXADMIN;
```

8. After you complete the vCenter Server installation, copy the Oracle JDBC driver (ojdbc13.jar) to the tomcat\lib folder under the VMware vCenter Server installation folder.

After the Oracle database is created and configured appropriately and the ODBC DSN is established, you're ready to install vCenter Server.

---

vCenter Server and Oracle

You can find all the downloadable files required to make vCenter Server work with Oracle on Oracle's website at www.oracle.com/technology/software/index.html.

Working with Microsoft SQL Server Databases

In light of the existing widespread deployment of Microsoft SQL Server 2005 and Microsoft SQL Server 2008, it is common to find SQL Server as the backend database for vCenter Server. This is not to say that Oracle does not perform as well or that there is any downside to using Oracle. Microsoft SQL Server just happens to be implemented more commonly than Oracle and therefore is a more common database server for vCenter Server.

If you are considering Microsoft SQL Server as the separate database server for the backend database, keep in mind that the vCenter Server virtual appliance does not support Microsoft SQL Server.

Connecting vCenter Server to a Microsoft SQL Server database, as with the Oracle implementation, requires a few specific configuration tasks, as follows:

◆ vCenter Server supports both Windows and mixed mode authentication. Be aware of which authentication type the SQL Server is using because this setting will affect other portions of the vCenter Server installation.

◆ You must create a new database for vCenter Server. Each vCenter Server—remember that there may be multiple instances of vCenter Server running in a linked mode group—will require its own SQL database.

◆ You must create an SQL login that has dbo (db_owner) access to the databases you created for vCenter Server. If the SQL Server is using Windows authentication, this login must be linked to a domain user account; for mixed mode authentication, the associated domain user account is not required.

◆ You must set the appropriate permissions for this SQL login by mapping the SQL login to the dbo user on the databases created for vCenter Server. In SQL Server 2005/2008, you do this by right-clicking the SQL login, selecting Properties, and then choosing User Mapping.

◆ Not only must the SQL login have dbo privileges on the database created for vCenter Server, it must also be set as the owner of the database. Figure 3.7 shows a new SQL database being created with the owner set to the vCenter Server SQL login.

FIGURE 3.7
The SQL Server 2005/2008 database that vCenter Server uses must be owned by the account vCenter Server uses to connect to the database.

◆ Finally, the SQL login created for use by vCenter Server must also have dbo privileges on the MSDB database but only for the duration of the installation process. This permission can and should be removed after installation is complete to aid in maintaining integrity within the SQL database infrastructure and to adhere to the principle of least privilege security best practices.

If you have an existing SQL Server 2005/2008 database that needs to be used as the backend for vCenter Server, you can use the `sp_changedbowner` stored procedure command to change the database ownership accordingly. For example, the following command would change the database owner to an SQL login named vcdbuser:

```
EXEC sp_changedbowner @loginame='vcdbuser', @map='true'
```

You need to take these steps prior to creating the ODBC DSN to the SQL Server database.

SQL SERVER PERMISSIONS

Not only will most database administrators cringe at the thought of overextending privileges to an SQL Server computer, but also it is not good practice to do so. As a strong security practice, it is best to minimize the permissions of each account that accesses the SQL Server computer. Therefore, in the case of the vCenter Server installation procedure, you will need to grant an SQL Server user account to the db_owner membership on the MSDB database. However, after the installation is complete, this role membership can and should be removed. Normal day-to-day operation of and access to the vCenter Server database does not require this permission. It is a temporary requirement only needed for the installation of vCenter Server.

CONFIGURING THE IDBC DSN

After your database is set up, you can create the ODBC DSN to be used with the vCenter Server installation wizard. SQL Server 2005 and SQL Server 2008 require the use of the SQL Native Client. Because vCenter Server requires SQL Server 2005 or 2008, you're required to use the SQL Native Client. If you do not find the SQL Native Client option while creating the ODBC DSN, you can download it from Microsoft's website or install it from the SQL Server installation media.

After the SQL Native Client has been installed—if it wasn't installed already—then you are ready to create the ODBC DSN that vCenter Server uses to connect to the SQL Server instance hosting its database. This ODBC DSN must be created on the computer where vCenter Server will be installed.

DO I NEED A 32-BIT DATA SOURCE NAME OR A 64-BIT DATA SOURCE NAME?

vCenter Server 5.5 requires a supported 64-bit version of Windows and also requires the use of a 64-bit DSN.

Perform the following steps to create an ODBC DSN to an SQL Server 2005/2008 database:

1. Log onto the computer where vCenter Server will be installed later.

   You need to log on with an account that has administrative permissions on that computer.

2. Open the Data Sources (ODBC) applet from the Administrative Tools menu.

3. Select the System DSN tab.

4. Click the Add button.

5. Select the SQL Native Client from the list of available drivers, and click the Finish button.

   If the SQL Native Client is not in the list, you can download it from Microsoft's website or install it from the SQL Server installation media.

   Go back and install the SQL Native Client; then restart this process.

6. The Create New Data Source To SQL Server dialog box opens. In the Name text box, type the name you want to use to reference the ODBC DSN.

   Make note of this name—this is the name you will give to vCenter Server during installation to establish the database connection.

7. In the Server drop-down list, select the SQL Server 2005/2008 computer where the database was created, or type the name of the computer running SQL Server 2005/2008 that has already been prepared for vCenter Server.

   Be sure that whatever name you enter here can be properly resolved; we generally recommend using the fully qualified domain name.

8. Click the Next button.

9. Choose the correct authentication type, depending upon the configuration of the SQL Server instance.

   If you are using SQL Server authentication, you also need to supply the SQL login and password created earlier for use by vCenter Server. Click Next.

10. If the default database is listed as Master, select the Change The Default Database To check box, and then select the name of the vCenter Server database as the default. Click Next.

11. None of the options on the next screen—including the options for changing the language of the SQL Server system messages, regional settings, and logging options—need to be changed. Click Finish to continue.

12. On the summary screen, click the Test Data Source button to test the ODBC DSN.

    If the tests do not complete successfully, double-check the SQL Server and SQL database configuration outlined previously.

13. Click OK to return to the ODBC Data Source Administrator, which will now have the new System DSN you just created listed.

At this point, you are ready to actually install vCenter Server.

Installing the vCenter Server Components

With the databases in place and configured, you can now install vCenter Server. After you've done that, you can add servers and continue configuring your virtual infrastructure, including adding vCenter Server instances in a linked mode group.

USE THE LATEST VERSION OF VCENTER SERVER

Remember that the latest version of vCenter Server is available for download from www.vmware .com/download. It is often best to install the latest version of the software to ensure the highest levels of compatibility and security. You can also use a newer version of vCenter with older versions of ESXi. vCenter Server 5.5 can manage hosts from version 5.0 and above.

The vCenter Server installation itself takes only a few minutes and is not administratively intensive, assuming you've completed all of the preinstallation tasks. You can start the vCenter Server installation by double-clicking `autorun.exe` inside the vCenter Server installation directory.

The VMware vCenter Installer, shown in Figure 3.8, is the central point for a number of installations:

♦ vCenter Single Sign-On

♦ vCenter Inventory Service

♦ vCenter Server

♦ vSphere Client

♦ vSphere Web Client (Server)

♦ vSphere Update Manager

FIGURE 3.8

The VMware vCenter Installer offers options for installing several different components.

Chapter 4, "vSphere Update Manager and the vCenter Support Tools," provides more detail on vSphere Update Manager and the vCenter Support Tools. You already installed the vSphere Client in Chapter 2. For now, we'll focus just on vCenter Server and its components.

If you will be using Windows authentication with a separate SQL Server database server, there's an important step here before you go any farther. For the vCenter Server services to be able to connect to the SQL database, these services need to run in the context of the domain user account that was granted permission to the database. Be sure that you know the username and password of the account that was granted permission to the backend database before proceeding. You'll also want to be sure that you've created an ODBC DSN with the correct information. You'll need the information for the ODBC DSN as well as the user account when you install vCenter Server. If you are using SQL authentication, you'll need to know the SQL login and password. We'll assume that you will use integrated Windows authentication.

INSTALLING SINGLE SIGN-ON

Earlier in this chapter we explained that vCenter Single Sign-On (SSO) is a prerequisite for vCenter. Not only must it be installed for vCenter to run, it must be running before the vCenter Inventory Service and vCenter Server itself are installed. Use the following steps to install Single Sign-On:

1. From the VMware vCenter Installer, select vCenter Single Sign-On and then click the Install button.

2. After the vCenter Single Sign-On installer has launched, click Next.

3. Select the tick box to accept the end-user license agreement and click Next.

4. Ensure that the prerequisites check is correct and click Next.

5. On the following screen you will be asked to select the deployment mode. The High Availability and Multisite options were explained in the section "Centralizing User Authentication Using vCenter Single Sign-On." For this installation we'll just choose the Primary Node type and click Next.

6. Choose a password for the SSO administrator— the "master SSO password." This account is not linked to any other directory, and is effectively the "root" or "administrator" for this SSO installation.

THE MASTER SSO PASSWORD

When installing SSO for the first time, be sure to remember the account password for the SSO Administrator. The username is always administrator@vsphere.local. This account is needed when installing other VMware components that leverage Single Sign-On.

---

7. On the following screen, you can name the "site" of this installation. Choose an appropriate name, or use the default and click Next.

8. The vCenter Single Sign-On installer will now ask you to accept or change the default HTTPS port that SSO will use and then Click Next.

   Unless there is a conflict in your environment, we would recommend not changing the default port numbers. It can make configuration and troubleshooting more difficult later on.

9. Change the directory for installation if desired and click Next.

10. Finally, review the installation options summary and click Install.

11. Once the installation is complete, click Finish to close the installer.

INSTALLING vCENTER INVENTORY SERVICE

The second prerequisite for vCenter Server installation is the vCenter Inventory Service:

1. From the VMware vCenter Installer, select VMware vCenter Inventory Service and then click the Install button.

2. From the vCenter Inventory Service installer welcome screen, click Next to continue.

3. Select the radio button to accept the end-user license agreement and click Next.

4. Change the directory for installation if desired and click Next.

5. The vCenter Inventory Service installer will now ask you for the FQDN or IP address with a name already in the field. Check or reenter this information and click Next.

6. You will now be asked to select three different ports that the Inventory Service will communicate on. It's best to leave these ports at their preconfigured defaults unless absolutely necessary. Click Next to continue.

7. The JVM Memory screen asks how big your vCenter inventory will be once it's fully configured. Knowing an estimated size is a good idea, but you can always edit this configuration at a later stage using the Tomcat service configuration tool from the Windows Start menu. For now, select Small and click Next to continue.

8. On the Single Sign-On Information screen, you will need to know both the password that you set during SSO installation, the master password, and also any changes made to the default port that SSO is running on. Enter the SSO password and click Next to continue. The installer will verify these details and prompt you to accept the SSO SSL certificate before continuing on to the next screen.

9. Because this is the first installation of vCenter and you have not configured other certificate services, the default security certificates need to be accepted. These can be changed from the default "self-signed" certificates at a later time (covered in Chapter 8). For now, click Install Certificates.

10. Finally, click Install to commence the installation and start the services.

11. Once the installation is complete, click Finish to close the installer.

INSTALLING vCENTER SERVER

After you've logged on as an administrative user to the computer that will run vCenter Server, start the vCenter Server installation process by clicking the link for vCenter Server in the VMware vCenter Installer, shown previously in Figure 3.8. If you have skipped to this section without reading the two prior sections, you will notice that there are a number of prerequisites listed above the Install button. These are mandatory, so make sure to install these first if you have not already done so. If you are running a version of Windows Server that uses User Account Control, you could be prompted to allow the installer to run; if so, select Yes. After you select a language for the installation, you arrive at the installation wizard for vCenter Server.

Perform the following steps to install vCenter Server:

1. From the VMware vCenter Installer, select vCenter Single Sign-On and then click the Install button.

2. Select the appropriate language and click OK.

3. From the installer welcome screen, click Next to continue.

5. Select the radio button to accept the end-user license agreement and click Next.

6. Enter your vCenter Server license key or leave it blank to start a 60-day trial, then click Next.

7. At this point you must select whether to use SQL Server 2008 Express Edition or a separate database server.

   If the environment will be small (a single vCenter Server with fewer than five hosts or fewer than 50 VMs), then using SQL Server 2008 Express is acceptable. For all other deployments, select Use An Existing Supported Database, and select your ODBC DSN from the drop-down list. If you forgot to create the ODBC DSN, you'll need to create it and restart the installation process in order to continue. For the rest of this procedure, we'll assume that you are using an existing supported database. Select the ODBC DSN you created earlier, and click Next.

ODBC TO DB

An ODBC DSN must be defined, and the name must match in order to move past the database configuration page of the installation wizard. Remember to set the appropriate authentication strategy and user permissions for an existing database server. If you receive an error at this point in the installation, revisit the database configuration steps. Remember to set the appropriate database ownership and database roles.

---

8. If you are using SQL authentication, then the next screen prompts for the SQL login and password that have permissions to the SQL database created for vCenter Server. Login information is not required if you are using Windows authentication, so you can just leave these fields blank. If the SQL Server Agent service is not running on the SQL Server computer, you'll receive an error at this step and won't be able to proceed. Make sure the SQL Server Agent service is running. Unless you have specifically configured the database server differently than the default settings, a dialog box pops up warning you about the Full recovery model and the possibility that transaction logs may grow to consume all available disk space.

IMPLICATIONS OF THE SIMPLE RECOVERY MODEL

If your SQL Server database is configured for the Full recovery model, the installer suggests reconfiguring the vCenter Server database into the Simple recovery model. What the warning does not tell you is that doing this means that you will lose the ability to back up transaction logs for the vCenter Server database. If you leave the database set to Full recovery, be sure to work with the database administrator on an automated process to routinely back up and truncate the transaction logs. By having transaction log backups from a database in Full recovery, you have the option to restore to an exact point in time should any type of data corruption occur. If you alter the recovery model as suggested, be sure you are making consistent full backups of the database, but understand that you will be able to recover only to the point of the last full backup because transaction logs will be unavailable.

---

9. The next screen prompts for account information for the vCenter Server services. If you are using Windows authentication with an SQL database, then you should populate the username and password fields with the correct user information. The "correct user" in this context is the domain user account granted permission on the SQL database. If you are using SQL authentication, then the account information is not as important, although you may want to run the vCenter Server services under an account other than the system account (this is a recommended practice for many Windows Server–based applications).

10. If this is the first vCenter Server installation in your environment, then select Create A Standalone VMware vCenter Server Instance. Click Next. We'll cover the other option in the section "Installing vCenter Server in a Linked Mode Group."

11. The next screen provides the option for changing the default TCP and UDP ports on which vCenter Server operates. Unless you have a specific reason to change them, we recommend accepting the defaults. The following ports are listed on this screen:

    ◆ TCP ports 80 and 443 (HTTP and HTTPS)

    ◆ UDP port 902

    ◆ TCP ports 8080 and 8443

    ◆ TCP port 60099

    ◆ TCP ports 389 and 636

12. Once the networking configuration is completed, as with the Inventory Service installer, the vCenter installer will ask about the Java Virtual Machine (JVM) Memory configuration. This is related to how much memory is allocated to JVM and therefore how large the environment is that you intend to support. This setting, as seen in Figure 3.9, can be changed at a later time if you outgrow the setting chosen here. For this installation, leave Small selected and click Next.

FIGURE 3.9
The vCenter Server
installation pro-
gram will optimize
the performance
of vCenter Server
and its components
based on your selec-
tion on this screen.

FIGURE 3.9

The vCenter Server installation program will optimize the performance of vCenter Server and its components based on your selection on this screen.

13. On the Single Sign-On Information screen, you will need to know both the password that you set during SSO installation, the master password, and also any changes made to the default port that SSO is running on. Enter the SSO password and click Next to continue. The installer will verify these details and prompt you to accept the SSO SSL certificate before continuing on to the next screen.

14. Once this installation has connected to an existing Single Sign-On instance, it asks for a vCenter Administrator user or group so that when you log in for the first time, there is an account with access. By default, this is the SSO Administrator account. Click Next to continue.

15. Change the Inventory Service address and port if necessary and click Next to continue.

16. Change the directory for installation if desired and click Next.

17. On the final screen, to start the installation process, click Install.

VCENTER SERVER AND IIS

Despite the fact that vCenter Server is accessible via a web browser, it is not necessary to install Internet Information Services (IIS) on the vCenter Server computer. vCenter Server access via a browser relies on the Tomcat web service that is installed as part of the vCenter Server installation. IIS should be uninstalled because it can cause port conflicts with Tomcat.

After you complete the installation of vCenter Server, browse to vCenter Server's URL (https://<server name> or https://<server ip address>) to open a page that allows you to install the vSphere Client.

The vSphere Web Client connected to vCenter Server should be the primary management tool for managing vCenter. However, if you don't have access to the Web Client Server component, the older vSphere Client can manage vCenter, ESXi hosts, and also their respective VMs.

As we've mentioned on several occasions already, the vSphere Client can connect directly to ESXi hosts under the context of a local user account defined on each ESXi host, or it can connect to a vCenter Server instance under the context of a Windows user account defined in Active Directory or the local SAM (Security Account Manager) of the vCenter Server computer. Using vCenter Server and SSO along with Active Directory user accounts is the recommended deployment scenario.

After you install vCenter Server, a number of new services will be installed to facilitate the operation of vCenter Server:

- VMware Log Browser

- VMware vCenter Inventory Service

- VMware VirtualCenter Management Webservices

- VMware VirtualCenter Server, which is the core of vCenter Server and provides centralized management of ESX/ESXi hosts and VMs

- VMware vSphere Profile-Driven Storage Service

As a vSphere administrator, you should be familiar with the default states of these services. In times of troubleshooting, check the status of the services to see whether they have changed. Keep in mind the dependencies that exist between vCenter Server and other services on the network. For example, if the vCenter Server service is failing to start, be sure to check that the system has access to the SQL Server (or Oracle) database. If vCenter Server cannot access the database because of a lack of connectivity or the database service is not running, then it will not start.

As additional features and extensions are installed, additional services will also be installed to support those features. For example, installing vSphere Update Manager will install an additional service called VMware Update Manager Service. You'll learn more about vSphere Update Manager in Chapter 4. The most important "feature" that you will need to install almost immediately is the vSphere Web Client; let us step you through that process now.

INSTALLING THE vSPHERE WEB CLIENT

In Chapter 2 we explained that there are two different clients that can be used to administer a vCenter Server installation: the old vSphere C# Client and the newer vSphere Web Client. We also guided you through installing the older client. Let us now explain the process to install the vSphere Web Client, and then later in this chapter, we'll explain the differences between these two clients. Here are the steps:

1. From the VMware vCenter Installer, select vSphere Web Client and then click the Install button.

2. Select the appropriate language and click OK.

3. After the installer has launched, click Next.

5. Select the radio button to accept the end-user license agreement and click Next.

6. Change the directory for installation if desired and click Next.

7. You will now be asked to accept or change the HTTP and HTTPS ports that the vSphere Web Client will communicate on. Leave these ports at their preconfigured defaults and click Next.

8. On the following screen you will be asked to register this instance of the vSphere Web Client with your existing SSO installation. Be sure to type in your SSO administrator@ vsphere.local password correctly, and make sure the URL Lookup Service points to the SSO server; then click Next. Click yes if prompted to accept the SSO SSL certificate.

9. Finally, click Install to commence the installation and start the services.

10. Once the installation is complete, click Finish to close the installer.

Now that you've successfully installed all the components to get vCenter Server up and running, you'll probably want to log in and get started. Unless you also wish to know how to deploy either Linked Mode or the virtual appliance version of vCenter, feel free to skip to the section "Exploring vCenter Server."

Installing vCenter Server in a Linked Mode Group

What is a linked mode group, and why might you want to install multiple instances of vCenter Server into such a group? If you need more ESXi hosts or more VMs than a single vCenter Server instance can handle, or if you need more than one instance of vCenter Server, you can install multiple instances of vCenter Server to scale outward or sideways and have those instances share licensing and permission information. These multiple instances of vCenter Server that share information among them are referred to as a *linked mode group*. In a linked mode environment, there are multiple vCenter Server instances, and each of the instances has its own set of hosts, clusters, and VMs.

vCenter Server linked mode uses Microsoft ADAM to replicate the following information between the instances:

◆ Connection information (IP addresses and ports)

◆ Certificates and thumbprints

◆ Licensing information

◆ User roles and permissions

There are a few different reasons why you might need multiple vCenter Server instances running in a linked mode group. With vCenter Server 4.0, one common reason was the size of the environment. With the dramatic increases in capacity incorporated into vCenter Server 4.1 and above, the need for multiple vCenter Server instances due to size will likely decrease. However, you might still use multiple vCenter Server instances. You might prefer to deploy multiple vCenter Server instances in a linked mode group to accommodate organizational or geographic constraints, for example.

Table 3.1 shows the maximum number of hosts or VMs for a single instance of vCenter Server for versions 4.0, 4.1, 5.0, and 5.5. Using a linked mode group is necessary if you need to manage more than the number of ESXi hosts or VMs listed.

TABLE 3.1: Maximum number of hosts or VMs per vCenter Server instance

ITEM	vCENTER SERVER 4.0	vCENTER SERVER 4.1	vCENTER SERVER 5.0 → 5.5
ESXi hosts per vCenter Server instance	200	1,000	1,000
VMs per vCenter Server instance	3,000	10,000	10,000

Before you install additional vCenter Server instances, you must verify the following prerequisites:

◆ All computers that will run vCenter Server in a linked mode group must be members of a domain. The servers can exist in different domains only if a two-way trust relationship exists between the domains.

◆ DNS must be operational. Also, the DNS name of the servers must match the server name.

◆ The servers that will run vCenter Server cannot be domain controllers or terminal servers.

◆ You cannot combine vCenter Server 5 instances in a linked mode group with earlier versions of vCenter Server.

◆ vCenter Server instances in linked mode must be connected to a single SSO server, a two-node SSO cluster, or two nodes in multisite mode.

◆ Windows vCenter is required. Linked mode is not supported with the Linux-based vCenter virtual appliance.

Each vCenter Server instance must have its own backend database, and each database must be configured as outlined earlier with the correct permissions. The databases can all reside on the same database server, or each database can reside on its own database server.

USING MULTIPLE vCENTER SERVER INSTANCES WITH ORACLE

If you are using Oracle, you'll need to make sure that each vCenter Server instance has a different schema owner or uses a dedicated Oracle server for each instance.

After you have met the prerequisites, installing vCenter Server in a linked mode group is straightforward. You follow the steps outlined previously in "Installing vCenter Server" until you get to step 10. In the previous instructions, you installed vCenter Server as a stand-alone instance in step 10. This sets up a master ADAM instance that vCenter Server uses to store its configuration information.

This time, however, at step 10 you simply select the option Join A VMware vCenter Server Group Using Linked Mode To Share Information.

When you select to install into a linked mode group, the next screen also prompts for the name and port number of a remote vCenter Server instance. The new vCenter Server instance uses this information to replicate data from the existing server's ADAM repository.

After you've provided the information to connect to a remote vCenter Server instance, the rest of the installation follows the same steps.

You can also change the linked mode configuration after the installation of vCenter Server. For example, if you install an instance of vCenter Server and then realize you need to create a linked mode group, you can use the vCenter Server Linked Mode Configuration icon on the Start menu to change the configuration.

Perform the following steps to join an existing vCenter Server installation to a linked mode group:

1. Log into the vCenter Server computer as an administrative user, and run vCenter Server Linked Mode Configuration from the Start menu.

2. Click Next at the Welcome To The Installation Wizard For VMware vCenter Server screen.

3. Select Modify Linked Mode Configuration, and click Next.

4. To join an existing linked mode group, select "Join a VMware vCenter Server group using Linked Mode to share information," and click Next. This is shown in Figure 3.10.

FIGURE 3.10
You can join an existing vCenter Server instance to a linked mode group.

5. A warning appears reminding you that you cannot join vCenter Server 5.5 with older versions of vCenter Server. Click OK.

6. Supply the name of the server and the LDAP port. Specify the server name as a fully qualified domain name.

It's generally not necessary to modify the LDAP port unless you know that the other vCenter Server instance is running on a port other than the standard port.

Click Next to continue.

7. Click Continue to proceed.

8. Click Finish.

Using this same process, you can also remove an existing vCenter Server installation from a linked mode group.

After the additional vCenter Server is up and running in the linked mode group, logging in via the vSphere Client displays all the linked vCenter Server instances in the inventory view, as you can see in Figure 3.11.

FIGURE 3.11
In a linked mode environment, the vSphere Client shows all the vCenter Server instances for which a user has permission.

One quick note about linked mode: While the licensing and permissions are shared among all the linked mode group members, each vCenter Server instance is managed separately, and each vCenter Server instance represents a vMotion domain by virtue of each vCenter Server having unique datacenter objects that ultimately represent a vMotion boundary. This means that you can't perform a vMotion migration between vCenter Server instances in a linked mode group. We'll discuss vMotion in detail in Chapter 12.

Installing vCenter Server onto a Windows Server–based computer, though, is only one of the options available for getting vCenter Server running in your environment. For those environments that don't need linked mode support or environments for which you want a full-featured virtual appliance with all the necessary network services, the vCenter Server virtual appliance is a good option. We'll discuss the vCenter Server virtual appliance in the next section.

Deploying the vCenter Server Virtual Appliance

The vCenter Server virtual appliance is a Linux-based VM that comes prepackaged and preinstalled with vCenter Server. Rather than creating a new VM, installing a guest operating system, and then installing vCenter Server, you only need to deploy the virtual appliance. We discussed the vCenter Server virtual appliance earlier in this chapter in the section "Choosing the Version of vCenter Server."

The vCenter Server virtual appliance comes as an Open Virtualization Format (OVF) template. We'll discuss OVF templates in great detail in Chapter 10, but for now we'll simply explain them as an easy way to distribute "prepackaged VMs."

We'll assume that you've already downloaded the files for the vCenter Server virtual appliance from VMware's website at www.vmware.com. You'll need these files before you can proceed with deploying the vCenter Server virtual appliance.

Perform the following steps to deploy the vCenter Server virtual appliance:

1. Launch the vSphere Client (not the vSphere Web Client) and connect to an ESXi host.

   You could connect to a vCenter Server instance using the Web Client, but if you are deploying the vCenter Server virtual appliance, you most likely do not already have a vCenter Server instance up and running.

2. From the File menu, select Deploy OVF Template.

3. At the first screen of the Deploy OVF Template Wizard, click the Browse button to find the OVF file you downloaded for the vCenter Server virtual appliance.

4. After you've selected the OVF file, click Next.

5. Review the details of the vCenter Server virtual appliance, as shown in Figure 3.12. Click Next when you're ready to proceed.

FIGURE 3.12
The vCenter Server virtual appliance comes preinstalled with SuSE Linux 11 and vCenter Server.

6. Supply a display name for the vCenter Server virtual appliance, and click Next.

7. Select a destination datastore, and click Next.

8. Select the disk provisioning type (Thick Provision Lazy Zeroed, Thick Provision Eager Zeroed, or Thin Provision).

Chapter 6, "Creating and Configuring Storage Devices," and Chapter 9 provide more details on the different disk provisioning types. In all likelihood, you'll want to use Thin Provision to help you conserve disk space.

Click Next.

9. Click Finish to start deploying the virtual appliance.

A progress window like the one shown in Figure 3.13 will appear while the vCenter Server virtual appliance is being deployed to the ESXi host.

FIGURE 3.13
This dialog box provides information on the status of the vCenter Server virtual appliance deployment.

10. Once the vCenter Server virtual appliance is fully deployed, go ahead and power it on.

You can use the VM console to watch the virtual appliance boot up. Eventually, it will display a virtual appliance management screen. When booting the vCenter Server virtual appliance it expects a DHCP server to be available on the network. If there is no IP address shown on the management screen, just like Figure 3.14, please follow the next section to assign one. If you do have an IP address, feel free to skip the next section.

FIGURE 3.14
This management screen lets you configure network access to the vCenter Server virtual appliance.

Configuring an IP Address on the vCenter Server Virtual Appliance

The following steps outline how to set a static IP address on the vCenter virtual appliance after it's been booted but no IP address has been allocated. These steps are only necessary to get the virtual appliance on the network. Once complete, all further configuration is performed in the web browser.

1. After the vCenter Server virtual appliance has booted, open the console, select Login, and press Enter.

2. At the login screen, enter the default username and password for the vCenter Server virtual appliance distributed by VMware; the default passwords are `root` and `vmware`.

3. Once logged in, type **/opt/vmware/share/vami/vami_config_net** and press Enter. A prompt-driven network configuration script will start running.

4. Use the menu (**6**) to enter an IP address.

5. Use the menu (**2**) to enter the default gateway.

6. Use the menu (**4**) to enter IP addresses for a primary and secondary DNS servers.

7. Use the menu (**3**) to supply the fully qualified domain name for the virtual appliance.

8. Use the menu (**0**) to review the network configuration, and press (1) to exit if it is correct.

9. Type **exit** and press Enter at the command prompt.

⊕ Real World Scenario

FAILED TO CONNECT TO LOOKUP SERVER – SSL CERTIFICATE ERRORS

On a number of occasions we have installed the vCenter Server virtual appliance and then proceeded to change the IP address after installation. A common problem crops up after changing the IP address. Upon logging into the Web Client, an error is displayed: "`Failed to connect to VMware Lookup Service https://vcsa.lab.local:7444/lookupservice/sdk – SSL certificate verification failed.`"

This error occurs because the self-signed SSL certificates that are generated on the first boot of the vCenter Server virtual appliance are linked to the current IP address. Unless you have replaced the SSL certificates with externally signed certificates, the painless fix is to instruct the vCenter Server virtual appliance to regenerate its certificates upon next boot.

1. Log into the admin interface of the vCenter virtual appliance by going to `https://`*vcsaip*`:5480`.

2. Click the Admin tab.

3. There is an option to "Toggle Certificate Regeneration"; click Enable.

4. Now reboot the vCenter virtual appliance.

5. Log back into the admin interface and click Disable to disable the Certificate Regeneration option.

6. Reboot the vCenter virtual appliance once more.

The vCenter Server virtual appliance has reconfigured its network settings and returned you to the management console. From this point forward, all the configuration is handled via a web browser. As you can see in Figure 3.14, once networking has been established there are three major tasks to getting the virtual appliance up and running:

- Accept the end-user license agreement (EULA).

- Configure the database.

- Start the vCenter Server services.

We'll take a look at each of these steps in the next few sections.

Accepting the End-User License Agreement

To accept the EULA, open a web browser and navigate to port 5480 on the IP address of the vCenter Server virtual appliance, using a URL such as `https://192.168.0.203:5480`, where `192.168.0.203` should be replaced with the IP address assigned to the virtual appliance. You might be prompted with a warning about an invalid certificate; accept the certificate and continue on to the site. You'll eventually reach the login screen for the virtual appliance, as shown in Figure 3.15.

FIGURE 3.15
You must first log into the vCenter Server virtual appliance before you can change any configuration settings.

The default username and password for the vCenter Server virtual appliance distributed by VMware are `root` and `vmware`.

Immediately upon login, you will be presented with a copy of the VMware EULA for the vCenter Server virtual appliance. Review the EULA, and then mark the Accept License Agreement check box and click Next.

VCSA BACKGROUND STARTUP

When you first start up the vCenter Server virtual appliance, you won't be able to do anything prior to accepting the EULA. That's because the services that run through the rest of the configuration process have not started yet. If you view the console of the virtual appliance while clicking accept, you will notice a number of additional services starting in the background.

Once the EULA has been accepted, the wizard asks you to specify what type of configuration you would like. The options presented here are as follows:

Configure With Default Settings   This option is the simplest form of setup where a local database is used for vCenter.

Update From Previous Version   As the name suggests, this configuration option is to be used when upgrading an existing vCenter Server virtual appliance.

Upload Configuration File   If you have a previously configured vCenter Server virtual appliance, you can save the configuration and then upload it during setup to ensure consistency.

Set Custom Configuration   Custom configuration is where you are able to manually specify all aspects of the setup through the rest of the wizard.

Select Set Custom Configuration and click Next to configure the database connection.

Configuring the Database

Like the Windows Server–based version of vCenter Server, the vCenter Server virtual appliance requires a backend database in order to function properly. The virtual appliance supports Oracle and a local embedded database.

To configure the database settings, click the vCenter Server tab on the VMware vCenter Server Appliance web administration screen, and then select Database. From there, you'll have an option to select Embedded or Oracle. As mentioned previously, Microsoft SQL Server is not supported for use with the virtual appliance.

The instructions provided previously for configuring Oracle are still applicable; you need to perform those steps before you configure the database connection. Once the database has been properly configured, you can specify the database name, server, port, username, and password to use when connecting.

When you've configured your database settings accordingly, click Next to move on to the SSO settings.

Setting Up Single Sign-On

Like the database settings in the previous section, the vCenter Server virtual appliance has the ability to use an embedded copy of SSO or utilize an existing external SSO instance. Use the drop-down to select the type of SSO instance.

To complete this form you will need to enter the following information:

◆   Username and password for the vCenter to SSO registration

◆   Account to be allocated as vCenter administrator

◆   The lookup service location URL

Also, if the database is external to the vCenter Server virtual appliance, you need the following information:

◆   DB server

◆   Port

◆ Instance name

◆ Login

◆ Password

◆ DBA login

◆ DBA password

Click Next and we'll finish the wizard by entering any AD information that may be required.

Active Directory Settings

There are only three simple requirements to tie the vCenter Server virtual appliance into an existing Active Directory.

◆ Domain

◆ Administrator user

◆ Administrator password

Click Next to review the configuration.

Starting the vCenter Server Services

After you've accepted the EULA and configured the database SSO and AD, you can start the vCenter Server services on the virtual appliance. This is accomplished by clicking the Start button on the final page of the setup wizard. After a few minutes, the services will start (use the Refresh button to refresh the screen to see that the services are currently shown as Running).

You'll now be able to launch the vSphere Web Client and connect to this instance of the vCenter Server virtual appliance. Remember the default username and password; you'll use those for the vSphere Web Client as well.

Installing or deploying vCenter Server is just the beginning. Before you're ready to start using vCenter Server in earnest, you must become a bit more familiar with the user interface and how to create and manage objects in vCenter Server.

Exploring vCenter Server

As explained, you can access vCenter Server through either the vSphere C# Client or the vSphere Web Client. Previously, the Web Client was not as feature rich compared with the traditional vSphere Client, but in vSphere 5.5, the Web Client is the more feature rich of the two. Therefore, this is the client we will use to demonstrate the majority of features throughout this book. If you are new to vSphere, you should know that VMware has publicly stated its intention to retire the traditional vSphere Client, so it makes sense to use the Web Client and become familiar with how it works. There's a lot to cover, so let's start out at the beginning, logging in.

To run the vSphere Web Client, all that you need is a compatible web browser with Adobe Flash installed. The server that runs the vSphere Web Client has a shortcut in the Start ➢ All Programs ➢ VMware ➢ VMware vSphere Web Client folder, but to access the vCenter Web

Client from another computer, go to the following address: `https://<server.domain`
`.com>:9443/vsphere-client`.

For our vSphere Web Client, this address is `https://vc.lab.local.9443/vsphere-client`.

When you connect to a vCenter Server instance with the vSphere Web Client, you may
receive a security warning message that will be slightly different depending on which web
browser you are using. This security warning appears because the vSphere Web Client uses
HTTP over Secure Sockets Layer (HTTPS) to connect to vCenter Server while the vCenter Server
is using a Secure Sockets Layer (SSL) certificate from an "untrusted" source.

To correct this error, you have the following two options:

◆ You can choose the Do Not Prompt for Security Warnings option (again, the option
depends on your browser). This option tells your browser to ignore that there's an
untrusted certificate.

◆ You can install your own SSL certificate from a trusted certification authority on the vCenter Server. This is certainly recommended, and we will step you through this process in
Chapter 8 when we discuss more around security.

After the vSphere Web Client connects and authenticates to the vSphere Web Client, you will
notice a Getting Started tab that explains the different sections of the user interface. Closing this
reveals the home screen, which is the starting point for the vSphere Web Client.

REMOVING THE GETTING STARTED PAGES

If you prefer not to see the Getting Started pages in the vSphere Client, you can turn them off
either individually or all at once. Individually, you can simply click the close button at the top right
of each one. To turn them all off at once, from the vSphere Web Client Help menu, select Hide All
Getting Started Pages.

What's in the vSphere Web Client Home Screen?

So far, you've seen only the Hosts And Clusters inventory view within the traditional vSphere
Client, but it's very similar in the Web Client. The Hosts And Clusters view is where you manage ESXi hosts, clusters, and VMs. Hosts and VMs you already understand; clusters we'll discuss later in this chapter in the section "Creating and Managing a vCenter Server Inventory." To
see the rest of what vCenter Server has to offer, if you're not already there, click the house icon
on the top of the browser next to the VMware vSphere Web Client name.

As shown in Figure 3.16, the interface is divided into three main areas and there is a search
bar in the upper-right corner.

Navigator (1)   The leftmost column is used for showing inventory and for navigation. It is
the primary item selection tool.

Content Area (2)   Once an item is selected, the larger middle column shows the content or
configuration options for that item.

Search (3)   This bar lets you search for any item and also allows you to save that search for later use.

Global Information (4)   On the right is a column that shows what *has* happened and what *is* happening and brings potential problems to your attention.

FIGURE 3.16
The vSphere Web Client home screen shows the full selection of features within not just vCenter Server but also both other services that hook into the vSphere Web Client.

The home screen lists all the various features that the vSphere Web Client has to offer within the content area in managing ESXi hosts and VMs:

- Under Inventories, the Web Client offers several views, including vCenter, Hosts And Clusters, VMs And Templates, Storage, Networking, and vCenter Orchestrator.

- Under Monitoring, the Web Client has screens for viewing tasks, events, host profiles, storage service classes, and customization specifications.

- Under Administration, there are areas to manage roles, licensing, and the vCenter Solutions Manager.

Many of these features are explored in other areas of the book. For example, networking is discussed in Chapter 5, "Creating and Configuring Virtual Networks," and storage is discussed in Chapter 6. Chapter 10 discusses templates and customization specifications, and Chapter 8 discusses roles and permissions. A large portion of the rest of this chapter is spent just on vCenter Server's inventory views.

From the home screen, you can click any of the icons to navigate to the corresponding area. There may or may not be additional icons here, depending on the plug-ins you have installed. The vSphere Web Client also has another way to navigate quickly and easily, and that's called the *navigator*.

Using the Navigator

The lefthand column of the vSphere Web Client is the Navigator. As stated on the Getting Started tab, the Navigator is an "aggregated view of all objects in the inventory." The top of the navigator shows you exactly where you are in the various screens that vCenter Server provides and also displays a chronological history so you can jump back to a prior screen.

If you click any item in the navigation bar with a "greater than" arrow next to it, the menu slides sideways and displays just the subitems of the selected item (generally this will change the content area too). When you click an item without the arrow, the Navigator menu doesn't change, but it does change the content area. A key point about the vSphere Web Client and vCenter Server is that the menu options and tabs that appear within the application are context sensitive, meaning they change depending on what object is selected or active. You'll learn more about this topic throughout the chapter.

Now that you understand how to navigate using the vSphere Web Client, you're ready to start creating and managing the vCenter Server inventory.

Creating and Managing a vCenter Server Inventory

As a vSphere administrator, you will spend a significant amount of time using the vSphere Web Client. You will spend a great deal of that time working with the various inventory views available in vCenter Server, so it's quite useful to first explain them.

Understanding Inventory Views and Objects

Every vCenter Server has a root object, the datacenter object, which serves as a container for all other objects. Prior to adding an object to the vCenter Server inventory, you must create at least one datacenter object (you can have multiple datacenter objects in a single vCenter Server instance). The objects found within the datacenter object depend on which inventory view is active. The Navigator provides a quick and easy reminder of which inventory view is currently active by displaying the four main inventory trees as tabs at the top. In the Hosts And Clusters view, you will work with ESXi hosts, clusters, resource pools, and VMs. In the VMs And Templates view, you will work with folders, VMs, and templates. In the Storage view, you will work with datastores and datastore clusters; in the Networking view, you'll work with vSphere Standard Switches and vSphere Distributed Switches.

---

vCenter Server Inventory Design

If you are familiar with objects used in Microsoft Windows Active Directory (AD), you may recognize a strong similarity in the best practices of AD design and the design of a vCenter Server inventory. A close parallel can even be drawn between a datacenter object and an organizational unit because both are the building blocks of their respective infrastructures.

You organize the vCenter Server inventory differently in different views. The Hosts And Clusters view is primarily used to determine or control where a VM is executing or how resources are allocated to a VM or group of VMs. You would not, typically, create your logical administrative structure in the Hosts And Clusters inventory view. This would be a good place, though, to provide structure around resource allocation or to group hosts into clusters according to business rules or other guidelines.

In VMs And Templates view, though, the placement of VMs and templates within folders is handled irrespective of the specific host on which that VM is running. This allows you to create a logical structure for VM administration that remains, for the most part, independent of the physical infrastructure upon which those VMs are running. There is one very important tie between the VMs And Templates view and the Hosts And Clusters view: Datacenter objects are shared between them. Datacenter objects span both the Hosts And Clusters view and the VMs And Templates view.

The naming strategy you provide for the objects in vCenter Server should complement existing datacenter design and management. For example, if you have qualified IT staff at each of your three datacenters across the country, then you would most likely create a hierarchical inventory that mirrors that management style. On the other hand, if your IT management was most profoundly set by the various departments in your company, then the datacenter objects might be named after each respective department. In most enterprise environments, the vCenter Server inventory will be a hybrid that involves management by geography, department, server type, and even project title.

The vCenter Server inventory can be structured as needed to support a company's IT management needs. Folders can be created above and below the datacenter object to provide higher or more granular levels of control that can propagate to lower-level child objects. In Chapter 8, we'll discuss the details around vCenter Server permissions and how you can use them in a vCenter Server hierarchy. Figure 3.17 shows a Hosts And Clusters view of a vCenter Server inventory that is based on a geographical management style.

FIGURE 3.17
Users can create folders above the datacenter object to grant permission at a level that can propagate to multiple datacenter objects or to create folders beneath a datacenter to manage the objects within the datacenter object.

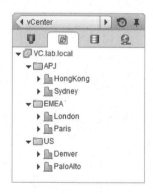

Should a company use more of a departmental approach to IT resource management, then the vCenter Server inventory can be shifted to match that management style. Figure 3.18 reflects a Hosts And Clusters inventory view based on a departmental management style.

FIGURE 3.18
A departmental
vCenter Server
inventory allows
the IT administra-
tor to implement
controls within
each organizational
department.

In most enterprise environments, the vCenter Server inventory will be a hybrid of the different topologies. Perhaps one topology might be a geographical top level, followed by departmental management, followed by project-based resource configuration.

Folders can be used to organize all different object types within vCenter Server. Figure 3.19
shows how you have the ability to create folders designated for the different objects such as
hosts and clusters or VMs and templates.

FIGURE 3.19
Create folders to
organize objects
within the vCenter
Web Client.

These inventory views are mostly separate and independent, although as we pointed out
earlier, they do share datacenter objects. For example, the Hosts And Clusters view may reflect a

physical or geographical focus, while the VMs And Templates view may reflect a departmental or functional focus. Because permissions are granted based on these structures, organizations have the ability to build inventory structures that properly support their administrative structures. Chapter 8 will describe the security model of vCenter Server that will work hand in hand with the management-driven inventory design.

With that basic understanding of vCenter Server inventory views and the hierarchy of inventory objects behind you, it's time for you to actually build out your inventory structure and start creating and adding objects in vCenter Server.

Creating and Adding Inventory Objects

Before you can really build your inventory—in either Hosts And Clusters view or VMs And Templates view—you must get your ESXi hosts into vCenter Server. And before you can get your ESXi hosts into vCenter Server, you need to have a datacenter object.

CREATING A DATACENTER OBJECT

You might have created the datacenter object as part of the Getting Started Wizard, but if you didn't, you must create one now. Don't forget that you can have multiple datacenter objects within a single vCenter Server instance.

Perform the following steps to create a datacenter object:

1. Launch the vSphere Web Client, if it is not already running, and connect to a vCenter Server instance.

2. From the Home screen, select Hosts And Clusters.

3. In the Navigator, right-click the vCenter Server object, and select New Datacenter.

4. Type in a name for the new datacenter object and click OK.

MAKE SURE NAME RESOLUTION IS WORKING

Name resolution—the ability for one computer to match the hostname of another computer to its IP address—is a key component for a number of ESXi functions. We have witnessed a number of problems that were resolved by making sure name resolution was working properly.

We strongly recommend you ensure that name resolution is working in a variety of directions. You will want to do the following:

◆ Ensure that the vCenter Server computer can resolve the hostnames of each and every ESXi host added to the inventory.

◆ Ensure that each and every ESXi host can resolve the hostname of the vCenter Server computer by which it is being managed.

◆ Ensure that each and every ESXi host can resolve the hostnames of the other ESXi hosts in the inventory, especially if those hosts might be combined into a vSphere HA cluster.

For the most scalable and reliable solution, ensure that your Domain Name System (DNS) infrastructure is robust and functional, and make sure the vCenter Server computer and all ESXi hosts are configured to use DNS for name resolution. You'll save yourself a lot of trouble later by investing a little bit of effort in this area now.

Once you create at least one datacenter object, you're ready to add your ESXi hosts to the vCenter Server inventory, as described in the next section.

ADDING ESXi HOSTS

In order for vCenter Server to manage an ESXi host, you must first add the ESXi host to vCenter Server. The process of adding an ESXi host to vCenter Server automatically installs a vCenter agent on the ESXi host through which vCenter Server communicates and manages the host.

Note that vCenter Server 5.5 does support adding and managing ESX/ESXi 4.*x* hosts to the inventory. We'll only describe adding ESXi 5.5 hosts to vCenter Server, but the process is nearly identical for other versions.

Perform the following steps to add an ESXi host to vCenter Server:

1. Launch the vSphere Web Client, if it is not already running, and connect to a vCenter Server instance.

2. From the Navigator, select vCenter ➤ Hosts And Clusters, or simply click the Hosts And Clusters icon from the home screen.

3. In the Navigator, right-click the datacenter object, and select Add Host.

4. In the Add Host Wizard, supply the IP address or fully qualified hostname and user account information for the host being added to vCenter Server. This will typically be the root account.

   Although you supply the root password when adding the host to the vCenter Server inventory, vCenter Server uses the root credentials only long enough to establish a different set of credentials for its own use moving forward. This means that you can change the root password without worrying about breaking the communication and authentication between vCenter Server and your ESXi hosts. In fact, regularly changing the root password is considered a security best practice.

5. When prompted to decide whether to trust the host and an SHA1 fingerprint is displayed, click Yes.

   Strictly speaking, security best practices dictate that you should verify the SHA1 fingerprint before accepting it as valid. ESXi provides the SHA1 fingerprint in the View Support Information screen at the console.

6. The next screen displays a summary of the ESXi host being added, along with information on any VMs currently hosted on that server. Click Next.

7. Figure 3.20 shows the next screen, where you need to assign a license to the host being added.

   The option to add the host in evaluation mode is also available.

   Choose evaluation mode, or assign a license; then click Next.

8. The next screen offers the option to enable lockdown mode. Lockdown mode ensures that the management of the host occurs via vCenter Server, not through the vSphere Client connected directly to the ESXi host. Click Next.

9. Click Finish at the summary screen.

10. Repeat this process for all the ESXi hosts you want to manage using this instance of vCenter Server.

FIGURE 3.20
Licenses can be assigned to an ESXi host as they are added to vCenter Server or at a later time.

Now compare the tabs in the content area in the middle of the vSphere Web Client for the vCenter Server, datacenter, and host objects. You can see that the tabs presented to you look the same, but if you select them, their subsections change depending on the object selected in the inventory tree. This is yet another example of how vCenter Server's user interface is context sensitive and changes the options available to the user depending on what is selected.

You can add hosts to vCenter Server and manage them as separate, individual entities, but you might prefer to group these hosts together into a cluster, another key object in the vCenter Server inventory. We'll describe clusters in the next section.

CREATING A CLUSTER

We've made a few references to clusters here and there, and now it's time to take a closer look at them. Clusters are administrative groupings of ESXi hosts. Once you have grouped hosts into a cluster, you have the ability to enable some of vSphere's most useful features. vSphere High Availability (HA), vSphere Distributed Resource Scheduler (DRS), and vSphere Fault Tolerance (FT) all work only with clusters. We'll describe these features in later chapters; Chapter 7, "Ensuring High Availability and Business Continuity," discusses vSphere HA and vSphere FT, while Chapter 12 discusses vSphere DRS.

Perform the following steps to create a cluster:

1. Launch the vSphere Web Client, if it is not already running, and connect to a vCenter Server instance.

2. Right-click a datacenter object in Hosts And Clusters view.

3. Select New Cluster. This opens the New Cluster Wizard.

4. Supply a name for the cluster.

   Don't select Turn ON vSphere DRS or Turn ON vSphere HA; we'll explore these options later in the book (Chapter 12 and Chapter 7, respectively).

   Click Next.

5. Leave EVC set to Disable (the default), and click Next.

6. Don't select Turn On for vCloud Distributed Storage; again, we'll explain this in Chapter 5.

7. Click OK.

Once the cluster is created, adding hosts to it is a matter of simply dragging the ESXi host object onto the cluster object within the Navigator; vCenter Server will add the host to the cluster. You may be prompted about resource pools; refer to Chapter 11 for more information on what resource pools are and how they work.

Adding ESXi hosts to vCenter Server enables you to manage them with vCenter Server. You'll explore some of vCenter Server's management features in the next section.

Exploring vCenter Server's Management Features

After your ESXi hosts are managed by vCenter Server, you can take advantage of some of vCenter Server's management features:

◆ Basic host management tasks in Hosts And Clusters view

◆ Basic host configuration

◆ Scheduled tasks

◆ Events

◆ Host profiles

◆ Tags

In the next few sections, you'll examine each of these areas in a bit more detail.

Understanding Basic Host Management

A great deal of the day-to-day management tasks for ESXi hosts in vCenter Server occur in the Hosts And Clusters view. From this area, the context (right-click) menu for an ESXi host shows some of the options available:

◆ Enter Maintenance Mode

◆ Reboot

◆ Shutdown

◆ Disconnect

◆ New Virtual Machine

- ◆ Deploy OVF Template
- ◆ New Datastore

The All vCenter Actions submenu has even more options:

- ◆ New vApp
- ◆ New Resource Pool
- ◆ Add Networking
- ◆ Enter Standby Mode
- ◆ Rescan Storage
- ◆ Export System Logs
- ◆ Host Profiles
- ◆ Remove From Inventory

The majority of these options are described in later chapters. Chapter 9 describes creating VMs, and Chapter 11 discusses resource pools. Chapter 8 covers permissions, and Chapter 13 discusses alarms and reports. The remaining actions—shutting down, rebooting, powering on, standing by, disconnecting, and removing from vCenter Server—are self-explanatory and do not need any additional explanation.

Additional commands may appear on this context menu as extensions or are installed into vCenter Server depending on the ESXi host's configuration. For example, after you install vSphere Update Manager, several new commands appear on the context menu for an ESXi host. In addition, ESXi hosts in a cluster enabled for vSphere HA would have additional options. You'll learn more about vSphere HA in Chapter 7.

In addition to the context menu, the tabs across the middle content area of the vSphere Web Client also provide some host-management features. Figure 3.21 shows some of the tabs.

FIGURE 3.21
When a host is selected in the inventory view, the tabs across the top also provide host-management features.

Within each of these tabs are subsections that further divide the settings into appropriate areas. For the most part, these tabs correspond closely to the commands on the context menu. Here are the tabs and subsections that are displayed when a host is selected in the inventory view, along with a brief description of what each does:

Summary   The Summary tab gathers and displays information about the underlying physical hardware, the storage devices that are configured and accessible, the networks that are configured and accessible, and the status of certain features such as vMotion and vSphere

FT. The content within this tab is somewhat configurable. You can drag the different boxes around, change their size, and expand categories to reveal more information. There are no subsections of the Summary tab, but it does provide links to commonly performed host-management tasks.

Monitor The Monitor tab displays all the monitoring information available about the selected host and breaks it down into a number of subsections.

> **Issues** The All Issues subsection lists any current configuration problems with the selected host; this could be any number of things, from a cluster configuration to a network issue. The triggered alarms area relates to alarms on this host that have not been acknowledged or reset.
>
> **Performance** The Performance subsection displays performance information for the host, such as overall CPU utilization, memory utilization, disk I/O, and network throughput. We'll discuss this area in more detail in Chapter 13.
>
> **Storage Reports** The Storage Reports subsection brings together a number of important storage-related pieces of information. For each VM on the selected host, the Storage Views section shows the current multipathing status, the amount of disk space used, the amount of snapshot space used, and the current number of disks.
>
> **Tasks** All tasks related to the selected host are displayed here. The Tasks subsection shows all tasks, the target object, which account initiated the task, which vCenter Server was involved, and the result of the task.
>
> **Events** Similar to the Tasks subsection, the Events subsection lists all events related to the selected host, such as, for example, a triggered alarm. If a host is using almost its entire RAM or if a host's CPU utilization is very high, you may see some triggered alarms.
>
> **Hardware Status** The Hardware Status subsection displays sensor information on hardware components such as fans, CPU temperature, power supplies, network interface cards (NICs) and NIC firmware, and more.
>
> **Log Browser** The Log Browser allows the logs to be retrieved from the host and displayed for analysis. Any one of the host logs, such as the fdm log or the vmkernel log, can be selected and then viewed once the log bundle has been requested from the host. There are also advanced filters to assist with log analysis.

Manage The Manage tab is where you will make configuration changes to the host. Tasks such as configuring storage, configuring the network, changing security settings, configuring hardware, and so forth are all performed here.

Before we show you some of vCenter Server's other management features, we want to walk you through the Manage tab in detail. This is where you'll perform almost all of the ESXi host-configuration tasks and where you're likely to spend a fair amount of time, at least in the beginning.

Examining Basic Host Configuration

You've already seen the Configuration tab of an ESXi host, when in Chapter 2 we showed you how to configure NTP time synchronization. Now we want to spend a bit more time on it; however, in the Web Client, the Settings subsection is in the Host ➤ Manage tab. You'll be visiting this area quite often throughout this book. In Chapter 5, you'll use the Manage tab for networking configuration, and in Chapter 6 you'll use the Manage tab for storage configuration.

SETTINGS SUBSECTION

Figure 3.22 shows the commands available on the Manage tab for an ESXi host that has just been added to vCenter Server.

FIGURE 3.22
The Manage tab of an ESXi host offers a number of different commands to view or modify the host's configuration.

There are a lot of options here, so allow us to quickly run through these options and provide a brief explanation of each.

Default VM Compatibility   When a VM is created, by default it has a certain level of features available to it, and with each new revision of vSphere, new features are added. This causes backward compatibility issues when you want to migrate VMs from a newer environment to an older one. While we explain more about VM compatibility in Chapter 9, this is the area where you can set the default level when a VM is created.

VM Startup/Shutdown   If you want VMs to start up or shut down automatically with the ESXi host, you configure those settings in this area. You can also define the startup order of VMs that are set to start up with the host.

Agent VM Settings   Agent VMs add specific supporting functionality to the virtual environment. Although they are VMs, they are considered part of the infrastructure. For example, vShield Edge and vShield Endpoint both use agent VMs to help supply their functionality.

Swap File Location   This area is where you will configure the location of the swapfiles for running VMs on the host. By default, the swapfile is stored in the same directory as the VM itself. When an ESXi host is in a cluster, the cluster setting overrides the per-host configuration.

Licensing   This command allows you to view the currently licensed features as well as to assign or change the license for the selected ESXi host.

Host Profile   While there is a Host Profiles area accessible from the Home screen, this area lets you attach a host profile as well. See the section "Working with Host Profiles" later in this chapter.

Time Configuration   From here, you can configure time synchronization via NTP for the selected ESXi host. You saw this area within the vSphere Client in Chapter 2.

Authentication Services   We'll discuss this in more detail in Chapter 8, but this area allows you to configure how ESXi hosts authenticate users.

Power Management   If you want to use Distributed Power Management (DPM), you'll need to configure the ESXi hosts appropriately. This area is where that configuration occurs.

Advanced System Settings   The Advanced System Settings area provides direct access to detailed configuration settings on the selected ESXi host. In the majority of instances, this is not an area you'll visit on a regular basis, but it is helpful to know where it is in the event you need to change a setting.

System Resource Allocation   The System Resource Allocation area allows you to fine-tune the resource allocation for the selected ESXi host.

Security Profile   This area allows you to configure which daemons (services) should run on the host.

System Swap   Within this section, you can disable or specify which datastore should be used for host swapfiles. We will explain host swapping and how it differs from VM swapping in Chapter 11.

Processors   In this section, vCenter Server provides details about the processors in the selected ESXi host as well as the ability to enable or disable hyperthreading on that ESXi host.

Memory   This area shows you the amount of memory installed in an ESXi; this only provides information about the memory in the host, how much is allocated to the system (ESXi), and how much is allocated to VMs; there are no options to configure.

Graphics   Within the Graphics section, you can see what type of GPU is in the system and how much memory it has. In Chapter 9 you can read about use cases for sharing the GPU of an ESXi host to the guest VMs in certain circumstances.

Power Management   The Power Management area in the Hardware section differs from the area under the System section above it. This section allows you to set various power-management policies on the selected ESXi host.

vFlash Resource Management   Solid State Drive (SSD)–backed datastores can be allocated to the vFlash resource type in this section. You can then further allocate this resource in the Cache Configuration below.

Cache Configuration   This area allows you to specify or view the amount of space on Solid State Drive (SSD)–backed datastores, or vFlash, that can be used for swapping. Swapping to

SSD as opposed to traditional disks is much faster, and this area allows you to control which SSD-backed datastores may be used for swapping.

NETWORKING SUBSECTION

The following areas are available in the Networking subsection of the Manage tab:

Virtual Switches   In Chapter 5, we'll explore the functionality found in this area. You'll configure network connectivity to both standard and distributed virtual switches in here and within the Network view.

Virtual Adapters   The Virtual Adapters area is where you can configure different network interfaces to the ESXi host to use for Management, vMotion, and Fault Tolerance, for example.

Physical Adapters   The Network Adapters area in the Hardware section of the Configuration tab provides read-only information on the network adapters that are installed in the selected ESXi host.

TCP/IP Configuration   In this area, you can view and change the DNS and routing configuration for the selected ESXi host.

Advanced   In this area, you can view advanced options such as IPv6 configuration.

STORAGE SUBSECTION

The following areas are available in the Storage subsection of the Manage tab.

Storage Adapters   This area provides information on the various storage adapters installed in the ESXi host as well as information on storage resources connected to those adapters.

Storage Devices   The Storage Devices area shows storage LUN and device mapping along with their relative paths to the host. Devices in here generally have a datastore on top of them that can be viewed in the Storage view. This is more of a logical view of storage, whereas the Storage Adapter area described earlier is more physical in nature.

As you can see, vCenter Server provides all the tools that most administrators will need to manage ESXi hosts. Although these host-management tools are visible in the Hosts And Clusters view, several of vCenter Server's other management features are found in the multiple views.

Using Scheduled Tasks

Earlier in this chapter we explained how the vSphere Web Client often displayed the UI depending on the context of the item selected. Scheduled Tasks is a feature that's available from many areas, including vCenter.

From the Navigator, select Manage ➤ Scheduled Tasks to display the Scheduled Tasks area of vCenter Server.

From here, you can create jobs to run based on a defined logic. You can schedule the following list of tasks:

◆   Change the power state of a VM.

◆   Clone a VM.

◆   Deploy a VM from a template.

◆ Move a VM with vMotion.

◆ Move a VM's virtual disks with Storage vMotion.

◆ Create a VM.

◆ Make a snapshot of a VM.

◆ Add a host.

◆ Change the power settings for a cluster.

◆ Change resource settings for a resource pool or VM.

◆ Check compliance for a profile.

As you can see, vCenter Server supports quite a list of tasks you can schedule to run automatically. Because the information required for each scheduled task varies, the wizards are different for each of the tasks. Let's take a look at one task that you might find quite useful to schedule: adding a host.

Why might you want to schedule a task to add a host? Perhaps you know that you will be adding a host to vCenter Server but you want to add it after hours. You can schedule a task to add the host to vCenter Server at a later time, although keep in mind that the host must be reachable and responding when the task is created.

Perform the following steps to create a scheduled task to add a host to vCenter Server:

1. Launch the vSphere Web Client, if it is not already running, and connect to a vCenter Server instance.

2. After you connect to vCenter Server, navigate to the Scheduled Tasks area of the Hosts And Clusters view by selecting a cluster and then choosing Manage ➢ Scheduled Tasks. This example would also work by selecting a datacenter instead of a cluster.

3. Select Schedule A New Task from within the content area.

4. From the list of tasks to schedule, select Add Host.

5. The Add Host Wizard starts.

6. Supply the hostname, username, and password to connect to the host, just as if you were adding the host manually.

7. When prompted to accept the host's SHA1 fingerprint, click Yes.

8. The next three or four steps in the wizard—three steps for ESX, four steps for ESXi—are the same as adding the host manually. Click Next after each step until you come to the point of scheduling the task.

9. Supply a task name and task description, and click the Change button. The Configure Scheduler pop-up is fairly self-explanatory, but you can run the task now, after startup,

or at a later time of your choosing. There's also an option for setting a recurring schedule, but for adding a host, the recurring option doesn't really make sense. Click OK once your scheduler is configured.

10. Specify that you want to receive email notification of the scheduled task when it completes by supplying an email address. Note that vCenter Server must be configured with the name of an SMTP server it can use.

Scheduling the addition of an ESXi host is of fairly limited value. However, the ability to schedule tasks such as powering off a group of VMs, moving their virtual disks to a new datastore, and then powering them back on again is quite useful.

Using Events Console in vCenter Server

The Events view in vCenter Server brings together all the events that have been logged by vCenter Server. Figure 3.23 shows the Events view with an event selected.

FIGURE 3.23
The Events view lets you view event details, search events, and export events (highlighted).

You can view the details of an event by simply clicking it in the list. Any text highlighted in blue is a hyperlink; clicking that text will take you to that object in vCenter Server. You can search through the events using the search box in the upper-right corner of the vSphere Web Client content window, and just on the right below the event list is a button to export the events to a text file. Figure 3.24 shows the dialog box for exporting events.

FIGURE 3.24
Users have a number of options when exporting events out of vCenter Server to a CSV file.

Working with Host Profiles

Host profiles are a powerful feature of vCenter Server. As you'll see in upcoming chapters, there can be a bit of configuration involved in setting up an ESXi host. Although vCenter Server and the vSphere Web Client make it easy to perform these configuration tasks, it's easy to overlook something. Additionally, making all these changes manually for multiple hosts can be time consuming and even more error prone. That's where host profiles can help.

A host profile is essentially a collection of all the various configuration settings for an ESXi host. This includes settings such as NIC assignments, virtual switches, storage configuration, date and time, and more. By attaching a host profile to an ESXi host, you can then compare the compliance of that host with the settings outlined in the host profile. If the host is compliant, then you know its settings are the same as the settings in the host profile. If the host is not compliant, then you can enforce the settings in the host profile to make it compliant. This provides administrators with a way not only to verify consistent settings across ESXi hosts but also to quickly and easily apply settings to new ESXi hosts.

To work with host profiles, select the Home button and then click the Host Profiles icon. Figure 3.25 shows the Host Profiles view in vCenter Server, where a host profile has been created but not yet attached to any hosts.

FIGURE 3.25
Host profiles provide a mechanism for checking and enforcing compliance with a specific configuration.

As you can see in Figure 3.25, there are a number of toolbar buttons across the top of the window, just below the Objects tab. These buttons allow you to perform the following tasks:

◆ Extract a profile from a host.

◆ Import a host profile.

◆ Rename the selected host profile.

◆ Edit the host profile settings.

◆ Copy settings from a host.

◆ Duplicate a host profile.

◆ Attach/detach host profiles from hosts or clusters.

To create a new profile, you must either create one from an existing host or import a profile that was already created somewhere else. Creating a new profile from an existing host requires only that you select the reference host for the new profile. vCenter Server will then compile the host profile based on that host's configuration.

After you create a profile, you can edit the profile to fine-tune the settings contained in it. For example, you might need to change the IP addresses of the DNS servers found in the profile because they've changed since the profile was created.

Perform the following steps to edit the DNS server settings in a host profile:

1. If the vSphere Web Client isn't already running, launch it and connect to a vCenter Server instance.

2. From the home screen, select Host Profiles.

3. Right-click the host profile to be edited, and select Edit Settings.

4. From the tree menu on the left side of the Edit Host Profile window, navigate to Networking Configuration ➢ Netstack Instance ➢ DNS Configuration.

Figure 3.26 shows this area.

FIGURE 3.26
To make changes to a number of ESXi hosts at the same time, put the settings into a host profile, and attach the profile to the hosts.

   5. Change the values shown in the host profile.

   6. Click Next and then Finish to save the changes to the host profile.

Although this procedure describes only how to change DNS settings, the steps for changing other settings within a host profile are much the same. This allows you to quickly create a host profile based on a reference host but then customize the host profile until it represents the correct "golden configuration" for your hosts.

Host profiles don't do anything until they are attached to ESXi hosts. Click the Attach/Detach A Host Profile To Hosts And Clusters button just below the Objects tab in the vSphere Web Client to open a dialog box that allows you to select one or more ESXi hosts to which the host profile should be attached.

After a host profile has been attached to an ESXi host, checking for compliance is as simple as right-clicking that host on the Hosts And Clusters tab and selecting Host Profile ➢ Check Compliance from the context menu.

If an ESXi host is found noncompliant with the settings in a host profile, you can then place the host in maintenance mode and apply the host profile. When you apply the host profile, the settings found in the host profile are enforced on that ESXi host to bring it into compliance. Note that some settings require a reboot to take effect.

To truly understand the power of host profiles, consider a group of ESXi hosts in a cluster. We haven't discussed clusters yet, but as you'll see elsewhere in the book—especially in Chapter 5 and Chapter 6—ESXi hosts in a cluster need to have consistent settings. Without a host profile, you would have to manually review and configure these settings on each host in the cluster. With a host profile that captures the settings, adding a new host to the cluster is a simple two-step process:

   1. Add the host to vCenter Server and to the cluster.

   2. Attach the host profile and apply it.

That's it. The host profile will enforce all the settings on this new host that are required to bring it into compliance with the settings on the rest of the servers in the cluster. This is a huge advantage for larger organizations that need to quickly deploy new ESXi hosts.

Host profiles are also hugely important when using vSphere Auto Deploy to create a stateless environment. In stateless environments using Auto Deploy, configuration settings aren't persistent between reboots. To keep your stateless ESXi hosts properly configured, you'll want to use host profiles to apply the proper settings so that the host retains a consistent configuration over time, even when it's rebooted.

As explained, host profiles really start to become beneficial when your environment has a large number of ESXi host to keep things consistent and manageable. However, host profiles are not the only feature included with vSphere that assists with management; a relatively recent addition to help with this is tags.

Tags

Nearly every item within a vCenter inventory can have a label and metadata added to it by the way of tags. Tags let you group related items together using categories, and they help sort and manage your vCenter objects. Tags can be both exclusive and inclusive, which gives you great flexibility when you design your metadata structure. Let us explain how this might be useful with an example. Say that you want to know which VMs belong to the engineering team, but also which VMs are production, test, or development. In the section "Understanding Inventory Views and Objects" earlier in this chapter, we explained how you could use folders to organize objects for management and security. The problem with folders is that a VM can reside in only one folder; taking this example, you cannot put a VM in both the Engineering folder and the Production folder. With tags, this problem is solved. While you can specify that only a single tag can be applied to a certain object at any one time, you can also specify multiple tags against a single object. We'll now show you how to create some tags and how they could be used.

Each tag must belong to a category (and only a single category), and because of this requirement you must create a category before or at the same time you create any tags. Here are the steps:

1. If the vSphere Web Client isn't already running, launch it and connect to a vCenter Server instance.

2. From the home screen within the Navigator, select Tags.

3. Click the New Tag icon to open the New Tag pop-up.

4. Enter the name of the tag and a description.

5. Change the category to New Category and the window will expand to show more fields.

6. Select the vCenter server, and give the category a name and a description.

7. Decide if this category should allow a single tag or multiple tags per object, and then select what object type(s) are associated with this category, as shown in Figure 3.27.

8. Click OK to save the new tag and category.

FIGURE 3.27
You are able to create both tags and tag categories from the New Tag dialog box.

Tags let you define custom identification or information options for nearly every object type within vCenter, including the following:

- Clusters
- Datacenters
- Datastores
- Distributed Switches
- Folders
- Hosts
- Networks
- Resource pools
- vApps
- Virtual machines

TAGS FLOW THROUGH INTO OTHER VMWARE PRODUCTS

Custom tags within vCenter are used not just within this one product. VMware also exposes your custom tags within its API and allows other VMware (or non-VMware) software to utilize this metadata. One such use of this data lies within vCenter Operations Manager. While it is technically a separate product, it has deep integration with vSphere and vCenter. The tags that are created within the vSphere Web Client can also be used for creating monitored applications or groups of VMs within vCenter Operations Manager.

After you create this tag, you can attach the tag to an object. After the tag is added, it appears in the Tags section of the content area Summary tab. You can use the Assign Tag option in the right-click menu to add tags to various objects, as shown in Figure 3.28.

With the tags clearly defined for various objects, you can then search based on that data. Figure 3.29 shows a custom search for all objects whose tag contains the text *Production*, *Engineering*, and *Windows*.

Using tags to build metadata around your ESXi hosts, VMs, and other objects is quite powerful, and the integration with the vSphere Web Client's search functionality makes large inventories much more manageable.

At this point, you have installed vCenter Server, added at least one ESXi host, and explored some of vCenter Server's features for managing settings on ESXi hosts. Now we'll cover how to manage some of the settings for vCenter Server itself.

FIGURE 3.28
You can add metadata to objects by creating and assigning tags.

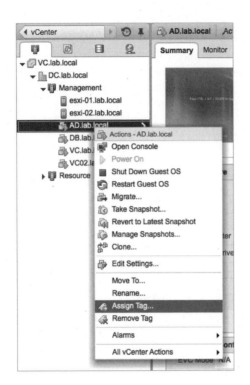

FIGURE 3.29
After you've defined a category and a tag, you can use it as search criteria for quickly finding objects with similar tags.

Search for: Simple Search

| Everything ▼ | that satisfy | all ▼ | of the following criteria: |

Everything Tag Name ▼	is ▼	Production	Remove
Everything Tag Name ▼	is ▼	Engineering	Remove
Everything Tag Name ▼	is ▼	Windows	Remove

Add new criteria...

| Search | Save... | Add another object type |

Search results: Saturday, April 06, 2013 12:03:55 AM

🗂 Virtual Machines

Actions ▾   Show quick filters 🔍 Filter

Name	1 ▲ State	Status	Provisioned Space	Used Space	Host CPU (MHz)
🗂 AD.lab.local	Powered On	⊘ Normal	48.09 GB	8.57 GB	12

1 Objects

Managing vCenter Server Settings

To make it easier for vSphere administrators to find and change the settings that affect the behavior or operation of a vCenter Server instance, VMware centralized these settings into a single area within the vSphere Web Client user interface. This Settings area is found on the Manage tab when a vCenter Server is selected in the vSphere Web Client Navigator. From here you can configure vCenter Server after installation with options that are not provided during installation. The Administration menu contains the following items:

◆ General

◆ Licensing

◆ Message Of The Day

◆ Advanced Settings

The vCenter Server Settings area lets you change the settings that control how vCenter Server operates, as you'll see in the next section.

General vCenter Server Settings

The General vCenter Server Settings area contains 10 vCenter Server settings:

◆ Statistics

◆ Runtime Settings

◆ User Directory

◆ Mail

◆ SNMP Receivers

◆ Ports

◆ Timeout Settings

◆ Logging Settings

◆ Database

◆ SSL Settings

When you have vCenter Server instances running in a linked mode group, be sure to select the correct vCenter Server instance within the Navigator.

Each of these settings controls a specific area of interaction or operation for vCenter Server, which we briefly discuss next:

Statistics On the Statistics page, shown in Figure 3.30, you can configure the collection intervals and the system resources for accumulating statistical performance data in vCenter Server. In addition, it provides a database-sizing calculator that can estimate the size of a vCenter Server database based on the configuration of statistics intervals. By default, the following four collection intervals are available:

◆ Past day: 5 minutes per sample at statistics level 1

◆ Past week: 30 minutes per sample at statistics level 1

◆ Past month: 2 hours per sample at statistics level 1

◆ Past year: 1 day per sample at statistics level 1

FIGURE 3.30
You can customize
statistics collection
intervals to support
broad or detailed
logging.

By selecting an interval and clicking the dropdown list, you can customize the interval configuration. You can set the interval, how long to keep the sample, and what statistics level (level 1 through level 4) vCenter Server will use.

There are four Statistics Collection levels defined in the user interface:

Level 1 Has the basic metrics for average usage of CPU, memory, disk, and network. It also includes data about system uptime, system heartbeat, and DRS metrics. Statistics for devices are not included.

Level 2 Includes all the average, summation, and rollup metrics for CPU, memory, disk, and network. It also includes system uptime, system heartbeat, and DRS metrics. Maximum and minimum rollup types as well as statistics for devices are not included.

Level 3 Includes all metrics for all counter groups, including devices, except for mini-mum and maximum rollups.

Level 4 Includes all metrics that vCenter Server supports.

DATABASE ESTIMATES

By editing the statistics collection configuration, you can see the estimated database size change accordingly. For example, when you reduce the 1-day collection interval to 1 minute as opposed to 5 minutes, the database size jumps from an estimated 14.32 GB to an estimated 26.55 GB. Similarly, if the collection samples taken once per day are kept for 5 years instead of 1 year, the database size jumps from an estimated 14.32 GB to an estimated 29.82 GB. The collection intervals and retention durations should be set to a level required by your company's audit policy.

Runtime Settings The Runtime Settings area lets you configure the vCenter Server unique ID, the IP address used by vCenter Server, and the server name of the computer running vCenter Server. The unique ID will be populated by default, and changing it requires a restart of the vCenter Server service. These settings would normally require changing only when running multiple vCenter Server instances in the same environment.

User Directory   On this page you can set the user directory (usually Active Directory) time-out value, a limit for the number of users and groups returned in a query against the user directory database, and the validation period (in minutes) for synchronizing users and groups used by vCenter Server.

Mail   The Mail page might be the most commonly customized page because its configuration is crucial to the sending of alarm results, as you'll see in Chapter 13. The mail SMTP server name or IP address and the sender account will determine the server and the account from which alarm results will be sent.

SNMP Receivers   The SNMP Receivers configuration page is where you would configure vCenter Server for integration with a Systems Network Management Protocol (SNMP) management system. The receiver URL should be the name or IP address of the server with the appropriate SNMP trap receiver. The SNMP port, if not configured away from the default, should be set at 162, and the community string should be configured appropriately (Public is the default). vCenter Server supports up to four receiver URLs.

Ports   The Ports page is used to configure the HTTP and HTTPS ports used by vCenter Server.

Timeout Settings   This area, the Timeout Settings area, is where you configure client connection timeouts. The settings by default allow for a 30-second time-out for normal operations or 120 seconds for long operations.

Logging Settings   The Logging Settings area customizes the level of detail accumulated in vCenter Server logs. The logging options include the following:

- None (Disable Logging)
- Errors (Errors Only)
- Warning (Errors And Warnings)
- Information (Normal Logging)
- Verbose (Verbose)
- Trivia (Trivia)

By default, vCenter Server stores its logs at C:\Documents and Settings\All Users\ Application Data\VMware\VMware VirtualCenter\Logs (on Windows Server 2003) or C:\ ProgramData\VMware\VMware VirtualCenter\Logs (on Windows Server 2008 and Windows Server 2008 R2).

Database   The Database page lets you configure the maximum number of connections to the backend database, and to limit the growth of the vCenter Server database, you can configure a retention policy. vCenter Server offers options for limiting the length of time that both tasks and events are retained in the backend database.

SSL Settings   On this page you can configure a certificate validity check between vCenter Server and the vSphere Client. If enabled, both systems will check the trust of the SSL certificate presented by the remote host when performing tasks such as adding a host to inventory or establishing a remote console to a VM. We'll discuss more on SSL certificates in Chapter 8.

Licensing

The Licensing configuration area of the vCenter Server Settings dialog box, shown in Figure 3.31, provides the parameters for how this specific vCenter Server instance is licensed. The options include using an evaluation mode or assigning a license key to this instance of vCenter Server.

FIGURE 3.31
Licensing vCenter Server is managed through the vCenter Server Settings dialog box.

When an evaluation of vSphere and vCenter Server is no longer required and the appropriate licenses have been purchased, you must deselect the evaluation option and add a license key. Evaluation licenses are only valid for 60 days after installation.

Message of the Day

As the name suggests, you can edit the message of the day (MOTD) from this area. The MOTD is displayed to users each time they log into vCenter Server. This provides an excellent means of distributing information regarding maintenance schedules or other important information.

Advanced Settings

The Advanced Settings area provides for an extensible configuration interface. These settings should be changed only under specific circumstances, usually at VMware's direction.

vSphere Web Client Administration

As we explained when outlining the home screen of the vSphere Web Client, there are three distinct areas: Inventories, Monitoring, and Administration. So far we've explained a number of features of the Inventories and Monitoring areas, but we also need to briefly touch on the third category of features, Administration.

There are three areas under the Administration banner, Roles, Licensing, and vCenter Solutions Manager. There is some overlap between these areas and those that come under Inventories.

Roles

The Roles option from the Administration menu is available only when the view is set to Administration and the Roles tab is selected. This menu works like a context menu where you can add, edit, rename, or remove roles based on what object is selected. While you set up the roles and accounts within this area, you apply those roles for permissions against vCenter objects within the various inventory views. Chapter 8 describes vCenter Server's roles in detail.

Licensing

In the previous section we explained how you would go about setting a license for a specific vCenter Server through the inventories vCenter view. There are also licensing options when you select individual hosts in the Hosts And Clusters view. However, the Licensing area of the vSphere Web Client home screen gives you a broad view of all your licenses within the environment and to which component those licenses are allocated.

Within Licensing, you can also report on your license usage over time and export this data. Depending on how complex your environment and license agreement is with VMware, you will seldom use this area, or only dedicated licensing staff will look at this section. Standard (Perpetual) licenses or VSPP licensing agreements are all managed through the overall licensing area.

vCenter Solutions Manager

As extensions are added to vCenter Server—such as vSphere Update Manager or vSphere Auto Deploy—additional icons, tabs, and features may appear throughout the vSphere Web Client. The extensions themselves that enable these new features are managed through this vCenter Solutions Manager area.

The next chapter, Chapter 4, discusses one such extension to vCenter Server, and that is vSphere Update Manager.

Log Browser

The Log Browser feature doesn't come under the Administration banner on the vSphere Web Client home screen (because it's only listed in the Navigator), but just like the Licensing section, this feature gives you an aerial view of all logs within your environment. We explained previously, in the section "Understanding Basic Host Management," that within the various objects, you can check their individual logs. This command allows you to view, browse, search, and export the logs from vCenter Server and/or one or more ESXi hosts. When you select the Log Browser from the Navigator on the home screen, you can select which object you wish to see the log entries for and the dialog box shown in Figure 3.32 appears.

Perform the following tasks to export system logs out of vCenter Server:

1. With the vSphere Web Client running and connected to a vCenter Server instance, from the home screen, select Log Browser.

2. Select the vCenter Server from the Select An Object dialog box and click OK.

3. Expand the tree and select the datacenter, cluster, or host objects whose logs you want to export.

4. Select the log(s) you want to export. By default, vpxd is selected. Use the drop-down to select the desired log.

5. Click the Actions menu on the top of the content area and select Export.

6. If you want to include all logs, select VMsupport bundle. Click Export.

7. A new browser window will pop up to specify a local path to save the logs.

FIGURE 3.32
You can view logs from vCenter Server or ESXi hosts easily from the Log Browser on the home screen.

MORE OPTIONS FOR EXPORTING LOGS

On the File menu there is also an Export ➤ Export System Logs option. If you select the vCenter Server object and then choose this menu item, you'll get the same dialog box as if you'd selected Administration ➤ Export System Logs. If, however, you select an ESXi host or a VM, the dialog box changes to show you log export options that are specific to the currently selected inventory object.

In the location you selected, vCenter Server will download `hostname_vmsupport.tgz`; if you decompress that file, you'll find the system logs for the vCenter Server computer. Figure 3.33 shows some log files exported from vCenter Server.

FIGURE 3.33
These logs are for vCenter Server, a single ESXi host, and the computer running the vSphere Client.

We'll continue to explore vCenter Server's functionality in the coming chapters. The next chapter, Chapter 4, explores the functionality added to vCenter Server by the vSphere Update Manager extension.

The Bottom Line

Understand the components and role of vCenter Server. vCenter Server plays a central role in the management of ESXi hosts and VMs. Key features such as vMotion, Storage vMotion, vSphere DRS, vSphere HA, and vSphere FT are all enabled and made possible by vCenter Server. vCenter Server provides scalable authentication and role-based administration based on integration with Active Directory.

Master It Specifically with regard to authentication, what are three key advantages of using vCenter Server?

Plan a vCenter Server deployment. Planning a vCenter Server deployment includes selecting a backend database engine, choosing an authentication method, sizing the hardware appropriately, and providing a sufficient level of high availability and business continuity. You must also decide whether you will run vCenter Server as a VM or on a physical system. Finally, you must decide whether you will use the Windows Server–based version of vCenter Server or deploy the vCenter Server virtual appliance.

Master It What are some of the advantages and disadvantages of running vCenter Server as a VM?

Master It What are some of the advantages and disadvantages of using the vCenter Server virtual appliance?

Install and configure a vCenter Server database.   vCenter Server supports several enterprise-grade database engines, including Oracle and Microsoft SQL Server. Depending on the database in use, there are specific configuration steps and specific permissions that must be applied in order for vCenter Server to work properly.

>**Master It**   Why is it important to protect the database engine used to support vCenter Server?

Install and configure the Single Sign-On service.   SSO is a major change for the security model of vCenter Server. It allows the vSphere Web Client to present multiple solutions interfaces within a single console provided the authenticated user has access.

>**Master It**   After installing vCenter 5.5 and all the appropriate components, an administrator cannot log into the vCenter Server Web Client with his local credentials and gain access to vCenter. What could be missing from the configuration of SSO?

Install and configure the Inventory Service.   The vCenter Inventory Service is a caching service that sits between the vCenter database and the vSphere Web Client used to reduce the load on the database and the vCenter Server itself.

>**Master It**   A corrupt Inventory database has been discovered in your vCenter server infrastructure and needs to be restored from backup. What data will be lost between when the backup was taken and when the corruption occurred?

Install and configure vCenter Server.   vCenter Server is installed using the VMware vCenter Installer. You can install vCenter Server as a stand-alone instance or join a linked mode group for greater scalability. vCenter Server will use a predefined ODBC DSN to communicate with the separate database server.

>**Master It**   When preparing to install vCenter Server, are there any concerns about which Windows account should be used during the installation?

Install and configure the Web Client Server.   The vSphere Web Client is the next generation of the vSphere client from VMware. Instead of installing a client on every machine used to administer vCenter, simply point a web browser to the Web Server Client Server from any machine.

>**Master It**   You have multiple vCenter Server instances within your environment that you wish to manage with the vCenter Web Client. Do you need to install a separate Web Client service for each vCenter server?

Use vCenter Server's management features.   vCenter Server provides a wide range of management features for ESXi hosts and VMs. These features include scheduled tasks, host profiles for consistent configurations, tags for metadata, and event logging.

>**Master It**   Your manager has asked you to show him all of the VMs and hosts that belong to the accounts department but is not interested in seeing the test servers. What tools in vCenter Server will help you in this task?

Chapter 4

vSphere Update Manager and the vCenter Support Tools

Software patches are an unfortunate fact of life in today's IT departments. Most organizations recognize that software updates are necessary to correct problems or flaws and to add new features. Fortunately, VMware offers a tool to help centralize, automate, and manage these patches for vSphere. This tool is called vSphere Update Manager (VUM). The remainder of the vCenter Support Tools assist in centrally deploying and managing hosts.

In this chapter you will learn to

- ◆ Install VUM and integrate it with the vSphere Client

- ◆ Determine which hosts or VMs need to be patched or upgraded

- ◆ Use VUM to upgrade VM hardware or VMware Tools

- ◆ Apply patches to ESXi hosts and older ESX hosts

- ◆ Upgrade hosts and coordinate large-scale datacenter upgrades

- ◆ Utilize alternative approaches to VUM updates when required

- ◆ Install logging collectors

- ◆ Configure hosts for centralized logging

vSphere Update Manager

VUM is a tool designed to help VMware administrators automate and streamline the process of applying updates, which could be patches or upgrades, to their vSphere environment. VUM is fully integrated within vCenter Server and offers the ability to scan and remediate ESXi hosts, host extensions (such as EMC's Powerpath/VE multipathing software), older ESX and ESXi hosts (circa 4.0, 4.1, 5.0, and 5.1), and virtual appliances. VUM can also upgrade VMware Tools and upgrade VM hardware. And VUM is the vehicle used to install and update the Cisco Nexus 1000V third-party distributed virtual switch.

VUM's Host Patching Capabilities in vSphere 5.5

As we have already covered in the previous chapters, vSphere 5 has only the ESXi variant of the hypervisor. With ESX being retired, VUM 5 can migrate ESX 4.*x* hosts across to ESXi. Unfortunately, because of the size allocated for the /boot partition in ESX 3.*x*, these hosts have no migration path to ESXi 5.*x*. Any ESX 4.*x* hosts that had previously been upgraded from ESX 3.*x* will not have the required minimum 350 MB of space in the /boot partition. In these cases a fresh install is required, so you'll need to consider how you want to migrate their settings. If you are licensed for vSphere at the Enterprise Plus level, you should check out the Host Profiles feature because that could help in the migration.

Despite "vanilla" ESX being replaced wholesale with ESXi in vSphere 5.0, VUM 5.5 still supports the great patching capabilities for legacy ESX/ESXi 4.*x* hosts. So in this chapter there will often be callouts to ESX or ESX/ESXi; most of the rest of this book is bereft of such references, but these are here purposefully. Companies will work in a mixed mode of hosts during their migration to vSphere 5, and many will keep older ESX hosts for some time, so this capability of VUM is worth remembering.

VUM integrates itself tightly with vSphere's inherent cluster features. It can use the Distributed Resource Scheduler (DRS) for nondisruptive updating of ESX/ESXi hosts by moving its VMs between hosts in the cluster and avoiding downtime. It can coordinate itself with the cluster's Distributed Power Management (DPM), High Availability (HA), and Fault Tolerance (FT) settings to ensure that they don't prevent VUM from updating at any stage. With vSphere 5, the cluster can even calculate if it can remediate multiple hosts at once while still appeasing its cluster constraints, thus speeding up the overall patching process.

VUM and the vSphere Web Client

As vSphere 5 has matured, the Web Client has become the primary user and administrator client. The older Windows-only C#-based vSphere Client is still available in 5.5, but essentially all the new features are accessible only in the Web Client. There are very few reasons why an administrator needs the vSphere Client installed. VUM is one of those reasons because it remains heavily tied to the incumbent.

Since the release of 5.5 (and Update 1 to 5.1), VUM has included a small Web Client plug-in that enables rudimentary capabilities. It allows baselines to be attached to objects and scans to be initiated, and it displays compliance levels. The Web Client can't administer VUM, configure or make changes to it, or remediate objects—for that you have to go back to the Windows Client. But the Web Client is useful. It's far more visible to the average user. How compliant the object is with your baseline is now front and center on the summary page. Users now realize how up-to-date their VMs are and can see the hosts on which their VMs run.

The Web Client's VUM abilities are limited, and the vSphere Client can do it all, but we'll use the Web Client to demonstrate anything that can be done in both tools. The workflow for these tasks is very similar, so it should be straightforward to follow along in either. In general, because you'll spend most of your time in the Web Client, it seems appropriate to favor that tool where possible.

In the vSphere Client, VUM uses two views: the administrative view, where you can configure VUM settings and manage baselines, and a compliance view, where you can scan and remediate vSphere objects. When applying updates to VMs, VUM can apply snapshots to them to enable rollback in the event of problems. It can identify when hardware upgrades and VMware Tools are needed and combine them into a single, actionable task.

To help keep your vSphere environment patched and up-to-date, VUM utilizes your company's Internet connection to download information about available updates, the products to which those updates apply, and the actual updates themselves. Based on rules and policies defined and applied by the VMware administrator using the vSphere Client, VUM will then apply updates to hosts and VMs. You can schedule update installations and even apply automated updates to VMs that are powered off or suspended.

UPGRADING, PATCHING, AND UPDATING WITHOUT DISCOMBOBULATION

Several common terms sometimes lead to confusion. *Upgrading* refers to the process of bringing the object to a new version, which often includes new features and capabilities. For example, for hosts, this can mean moving from 4.1 to 5.0 or, when the next minor version is available, from 5.1 to 5.5. VM hardware, virtual appliances, and host extensions all tend to be associated with upgrades because they are usually rip-and-replace-type software changes.

The term *patching* is usually reserved for applying remedial software changes to individual host components. This will normally change the host's build number but not its version number. Often these are rolled up into host *updates*, so expect ESXi 5.5 to receive 5.5 Update 1 before you see another 5.*x* version change. However, and certainly somewhat confusingly, the term *updates* is often used to explain the generic process of both patching and upgrading. So applying updates might include host patches (some of which might be rolled into a host update) and various upgrades.

Regardless of the terminology used, it is useful to think about updating in terms of how routine it is—in fact, this is the way this chapter splits it up. Routine updates would include host patches, host updates, and upgrading a VM's VMware Tools. These are the sort of remediation tasks you could expect to perform on, say, a monthly basis because many guest OS patches are, and should be, more trivial to test and apply. Nonroutine updates are the upgrades to hosts and VM hardware. These updates will often change the functionality of the object, so they need to be tested in your environment to make sure they are fully "sociable" and to understand how best to take advantage of the new capabilities that the upgrades are likely to bring.

The one gray area is upgrading host extensions and virtual appliances, because they need to be evaluated on a case-by-case basis. Some of their upgrades will be simple improvements; others can bring significant changes to the way they work. You need to evaluate each extension and appliance upgrade and decide for yourself how much testing is required before you deploy it.

Putting VUM to work in your vSphere deployment involves installing and configuring VUM, setting up baselines, scanning hosts and VMs, and applying patches.

Installing vSphere Update Manager

VUM installs from the vCenter Server DVD installation media and requires that a vCenter Server instance be already installed. You will find that installing VUM is much like installing vCenter Server, which you saw in the previous chapter.

You perform the following high-level steps to install VUM:

1. Configure VUM's database.

2. Create an Open Database Connectivity (ODBC) data source name (DSN) for VUM.

3. Install VUM.

4. (Optional) Install the Update Manager Download Service (UMDS) if desired.

5. Install the VUM plug-in for the vSphere Client.

VUM has a one-to-one relationship with vCenter. That is, for every vCenter instance you need a separate VUM install, and each VUM can provide update services to only one vCenter. The one exception to this is that you can share the job of downloading patches between multiple VUMs (and therefore multiple vCenters) with the use of an optional component known as Update Manager Download Services (UMDS), which is discussed in the section "Installing the Update Manager Download Service (Optional)."

If you have multiple vCenters that are connected via linked mode, you can use VUM, but a separate instance is still required for each vCenter. All the installation, configuration, permissions, update scanning, and remediation are done on a per-VUM basis because they operate independently.

As discussed previously, with vSphere 5.5 there are now two deployment options for vCenter: the conventional Windows installation and the newer Linux-based prebuilt vCenter Server Appliance (vCSA). VUM can happily connect to either installation; however, for obvious reasons, your choice helps to shape your deployment model. If you have a Windows-based vCenter, you can either install VUM on the same server instance or use a separate Windows install. However, because the vCSA is Linux based, if you are opting for this you will have to install VUM on its own Windows install because there is no VUM service available on the vCSA yet.

Defining the Requirements

VUM requires access to a dedicated vCenter instance, so your vSphere licensing must include vCenter. This therefore excludes the free stand-alone ESXi hypervisor version currently available.

The VUM server should have 2 GB of RAM at a minimum, and if it's installed on the same server as vCenter itself, there should be at least 4 GB. We discuss various database options in the next section, but you should avoid installing VUM on the same database as vCenter (it can be on the same server; it just should not be on the same database).

Even though VUM is a 32-bit application, it can only be installed on a 64-bit version of Windows. During the install, you receive a warning if you attempt to put the download repository on a drive with less than 120 GB of free space. Additionally, you cannot install VUM on a server that is also a domain controller.

AVOID INSTALLING VUM ON A VM THAT SITS ON A HOST THAT IT REMEDIATES

Be wary of installing VUM on a VM running on a host in a cluster that it is responsible for remediating. If DRS is disabled on the cluster at any stage, or the cluster has a problem migrating this VUM VM to another host, then to prevent VUM from shutting itself down, the remediation will fail.

Table 4.1 shows the default ports that need to be opened if any of your components are separated by a firewall.

TABLE 4.1: Firewall requirements for VUM

PORT	SOURCE	DESTINATION	PROTOCOL	DESCRIPTION
80	VUM	vCenter	TCP	Inter VUM–vCenter communications
80, 443	VUM	Internet	TCP	Retrieving updates and metadata
902	VUM	Hosts	TCP	Pushing upgrade files
8084	Client plug-in	VUM	TCP	SOAP listening
9084	Hosts	VUM	TCP	HTTP service for patch downloads
9087	Client plug-in	VUM	TCP	Uploading upgrade files

Configuring VUM's Database

Like vCenter Server, VUM requires its own database. Where vCenter Server uses the database to store configuration and performance statistics, VUM uses a database to store patch metadata.

SUPPORTED DATABASE SERVERS

VUM's database support is similar to that of vCenter Server but not identical. In general, most versions of SQL Server 2005, 2008, and 2012 and Oracle 10*g*/11*g* are supported by VUM. For the most up-to-date database compatibility matrix, refer to the latest *vSphere compatibility matrixes*, available from VMware's website.

For small installations (up to 5 hosts and 50 VMs), VUM can use an instance of SQL Server 2008 R2 Express Edition (SQL Express). SQL Express is included on the VMware vCenter media, and the VUM installation will automatically install and configure the SQL Express instance appropriately. No additional work is required outside of the installation routine. However, as you learned in Chapter 3, "Installing and Configuring vCenter Server," SQL Express does have some limitations, so plan accordingly. If you do plan on using SQL Express, you can skip ahead to the section "Installing VUM."

If you decide against using SQL Express, you must now make another decision: Where do you put the VUM database? Although it is possible for VUM to use the same database as vCenter Server, it is strongly recommended that you use a separate database, even if you keep both databases on the same database server. When you move beyond 100 hosts or 1,000 VMs, you should be sure to use separate database servers for both the vCenter Server database and the VUM database as well as separate servers for vCenter Server and the VUM server software. Other factors, such as high availability or capacity, may also affect this decision. Aside from knowing which database server you'll use, the decision to use a single computer versus multiple computers won't affect the procedures described in this section.

In either case, there are specific configuration steps that you'll need to follow, just as you did when installing vCenter Server. You'll need to create and configure the database, assign ownership, and grant permissions to the MSDB database. Be sure to complete these steps before trying to install VUM because this information is required during installation.

Perform the following steps to create and configure a Microsoft SQL Server 2005/2008/2012 database for use with VUM:

1. Launch the SQL Server Management Studio application. When prompted to connect to a server, connect to a supported database server. Select Database Engine as the server type.

2. From the Object Explorer on the left side, expand the server node at the top level.

3. Right-click the Databases node and select New Database.

4. In the New Database window, specify a database name. Use a name that is easy to identify, such as VUM or vSphereUM.

5. Set the owner of the new database.

   Unless you are running the separate database on the same computer as VUM, you will need to set the owner of the database to an SQL login; integrated Windows authentication is not supported with a remote database.

   Figure 4.1 shows a new database being created with an SQL login set as the owner.

6. For ideal performance, set the location of the database and log files so they are on different physical disks or VMDKs than the operating system and the patch repository. Scroll along to the right of the large pane to set the locations.

   Figure 4.2 shows the database and log files stored on a separate drive from the operating system.

7. After the settings are configured, click OK to create the new database.

As with the vCenter Server database, the login that VUM will use to connect to the database server must have dbo permissions on the new database as well as on the MSDB database.

FIGURE 4.1
Set the owner of the database correctly when you create the database.

FIGURE 4.2
Place the database and log files for VUM on different physical drives than the operating system and patch repository.

Creating the Open Database Connectivity Data Source Name

After you configure the separate database server, you must create an ODBC DSN to connect to the backend database. You'll need to have the ODBC DSN created before you start VUM installation, and because VUM is a 32-bit application, the ODBC DSN must be a 32-bit DSN. This is true even though VUM installs only on a 64-bit version of Windows.

Perform the following steps to create an ODBC DSN for the VUM database:

1. Run the 32-bit ODBC Data Source Administrator application found at `%systemroot%\SysWOW64\odbcad32.exe`.

   The 32-bit ODBC Data Source Administrator application looks identical to the 64-bit version. If you're unsure which one you launched, exit and restart to be sure that you have the correct version.

IS THERE ANY WAY TO TELL THE DIFFERENCE?

There is a way to tell the difference between the 64-bit and 32-bit versions of the ODBC Data Source Administrator application: The 64-bit and 32-bit system DSNs are not shared between the two applications. So, if you see your vCenter Server DSN listed on the System DSN tab, you're running the 64-bit version of the tool (because vCenter Server requires a 64-bit DSN).

---

2. Select the System DSN tab.

3. Click the Add button.

4. From the list of available drivers, select the correct driver for the database server you're using.

   As with vCenter Server, you will need to ensure that the correct ODBC driver is installed for the database server hosting the VUM database. SQL Server 2005, 2008, and 2012 all have their own optimized SQL Server Native Client. Make sure the appropriate Native Client is installed.

5. On the first screen of the Create A New Data Source Wizard, fill in the name of the DSN, a description, and the name of the server to which this DSN will connect.

   Be sure to make a note of the DSN name; you'll need this information later. Click Next when you're finished.

6. On the next screen you need to supply an authentication type and credentials to connect to the separate database server. Select With SQL Server Authentication Using A Login ID And Password Entered By The User, and specify an SQL login and password that are valid on the database server and that have the appropriate permissions assigned to the VUM and MSDB databases. Click Next.

   Windows Integrated Authentication is an option only if you have installed the database server component locally on the same server as VUM. It is advised that you use SQL Server Authentication in all cases, even if the database is local, because it makes moving the database easier in the future should your environment grow and require scaling beyond a local instance.

7. Change the default database to the one you created in Figure 4.1 and click Next.

8. Click Finish.

9. In the ODBC Microsoft SQL Server Setup dialog box, click the Test Data Source connection to verify the settings.

   If the results say the tests completed successfully, click OK twice to return to the ODBC Data Source Administrator window. If not, go back and double-check the settings and change them as needed.

With the database created and the ODBC connection defined, you're now ready to proceed with the installation of VUM.

Installing VUM

Now that you have met all the prerequisites—at least one instance of vCenter Server running and accessible across the network, a separate database running and configured appropriately, and an ODBC DSN defined to connect to the preconfigured database—you can start the VUM installation. Before you begin, make sure that you have made a note of the ODBC DSN you defined previously and the SQL login and password configured for access to the database. You'll need these pieces of information during the installation.

Perform the following steps to install VUM:

1. Mount the vCenter Server DVD in the server.

   The VMware vCenter Installer runs automatically; if it does not, simply double-click the DVD drive in My Computer to invoke AutoPlay.

2. Select vSphere Update Manager and click Install.

3. Choose the correct language for the installation, and click OK.

4. On the Welcome To The InstallShield Wizard For VMware vSphere Update Manager screen, click Next to start the installation.

5. Click Next to continue past the end-user patent agreement.

6. Accept the terms in the license agreement, and click Next.

7. The Support Information screen clarifies that VUM 5.5 supports upgrades from ESX/ESXi 4.*x* upward. Leave the check box Download Updates From Default Sources Immediately After Installation ticked, unless the VUM server does not have access to the Internet or you want to postpone a large Internet download until a more convenient time. Click Next.

8. Fill out the next screen with the correct IP address or hostname, HTTP port, username, and password for the vCenter Server instance to which this VUM server will be associated. If you have created a service account to use for VUM, enter it here. Click Next when the information is complete.

9. Select to either install an SQL 2008 Express instance or to use an existing database instance. If you are using a supported separate database server, select the correct DSN from the list, and click Next.

As described previously, using a supported database instance requires that you have already created the database and ODBC DSN. If you haven't created the ODBC DSN yet, you'll need to exit the installation, create the DSN, and restart the installation.

10. The next screen prompts you for user credentials to connect to the database specified in the DSN and configured for use by VUM. Supply the username and password for the SQL login you created before starting the installation, as shown in Figure 4.3.

FIGURE 4.3
Supply the correct username and password for the VUM database.

11. If the SQL Server database is set to the Full recovery model (the default), a dialog box pops up warning you about the need for regular backups.

Click OK to dismiss the dialog box and continue with the installation, but be sure to arrange for regular backups of the database. Otherwise, the database transaction logs could grow to consume all available space.

12. Unless there is a need to change the default port settings, leave the default settings, as shown in Figure 4.4. If there is a proxy server that controls access to the Internet, click the check box labeled Yes, I Have Internet Connection And I Want To Configure Proxy Settings Now. Otherwise, if there isn't a proxy or if you don't know the correct proxy configuration, leave the box deselected, and click Next.

CONFIGURING PROXY SETTINGS DURING INSTALLATION

If you forget to select the box to configure proxy settings during installation, fear not! All is not lost. After you install VUM, you can use the vSphere Client to set the proxy settings accordingly. Just be aware that VUM's first attempt to download patch information will fail because it can't access the Internet.

13. VUM downloads patches and patch metadata from the Internet and stores them locally for use in remediating hosts and guests.

The next screen allows you to specify where to install VUM as well as where to store the patches, as shown in Figure 4.5. Use the Change button to modify the location of the patches to a location with sufficient storage capacity.

FIGURE 4.4
The VUM installation provides the option to configure proxy settings. If there is no proxy, leave the box deselected.

FIGURE 4.5
The default settings for VUM place the application files and the patch repository on the system drive.

In Figure 4.6, you can see where a drive different from the system drive has been selected to store the downloaded patches.

FIGURE 4.6
During installation, you can tell VUM to store the downloaded patches on a drive other than the system drive.

14. If you select a drive or partition with less than 120 GB, a dialog box will pop up warning you to be sure you have sufficient space to download the appropriate patches. It's very reasonable to initially use a smaller disk footprint than 120 GB and grow the disk over time. Just remember to manage this space appropriately because patches will download automatically over time. Click OK to proceed.

15. Click Install to install VUM.

16. Click Finish when the installation is complete.

Installing the Update Manager Download Service (Optional)

An optional step in the deployment of VUM is to install the Update Manager Download Service (UMDS). UMDS provides a centralized download repository. Installing UMDS is especially useful in two situations. First, UMDS is beneficial when you have multiple VUM servers; using UMDS prevents consuming more bandwidth than necessary because the updates need to be downloaded only once. Instead of each VUM server downloading a full copy, multiple VUM servers can leverage the centralized UMDS repository. Second, UMDS is beneficial in environments where the VUM servers do not have direct Internet access. Internet access is required to download the updates and update metadata, so you can use UMDS to download and distribute the information to the individual VUM servers.

To install UMDS on a server, browse the vCenter DVD installation media. UMDS, like VUM, can be installed only on 64-bit servers. From the root of the DVD there is a umds folder. Within that folder run the executable VMware-UMDS.exe.

UMDS is a command-line tool. By default the UMDS tool is installed in C:\Program Files (x86)\VMware\Infrastructure\Update Manager.

You can configure many options in UMDS, but to start using it, you need to configure the following three settings:

1. Specify the updates to download using the -S switch.

2. Download the updates with the -D switch.

3. Export the updates and metadata with the -E switch.

Full details of all the command's switch options are available from the built-in help, by running vmware-umds -H. Figure 4.7 shows the UMDS utility being run from the command prompt. Along with the basic switches that can be seen in Figure 4.7, the full help file provides all the arguments and provides a series of examples of common usage tasks.

FIGURE 4.7

You must configure the UMDS utility at the command prompt.

There are two different designs for using UMDS:

◆   The VUM server does not have network connectivity to the UMDS server. In this case you need to move the downloaded patches and metadata to a removable media drive and physically transfer the data via old-fashioned "sneakernet."

◆   The VUM server can connect to the UMDS server. Although the VUM server may not be allowed to connect directly to the Internet, if it can hit the UMDS, then it can effectively use it as a web proxy. You need to configure a web server on the UMDS server, such as IIS or Apache. Then the VUM server can connect to the UMDS server and download its patches. This is also typically the approach you would take if you wanted to use UMDS as a centralized download server for several VUM instances.

At this point VUM is installed, but you have no way to manage it. In order to manage VUM, you must install the vSphere Client and the VUM plug-in for vCenter Server, as we discuss in the next section.

Installing the vSphere Update Manager Plug-in

The tools to manage and configure VUM are implemented as a vCenter Server plug-in and are completely integrated into vCenter Server and the vSphere Client. However, to access these tools, you must first install and register the plug-in in the vSphere Client. This enables the vSphere Client to manage and configure VUM by adding an Update Manager tab and some extra context menu commands to objects in the vSphere Client. vSphere Client plug-ins are managed on a per-client basis; that is, each installation of the vSphere Client needs to have the plug-in installed in order to access the VUM administration tools.

Perform the following steps to install the VUM plug-in for each instance of the vSphere Client:

1.   Launch the vSphere Client if it isn't already running and connect to the vCenter Server instance that has VUM associated with it.

2. From the vSphere Client's Plug-ins menu, select Manage Plug-ins.

3. Find the vSphere Update Manager extension, and click the blue Download And Install link, as shown in Figure 4.8.

FIGURE 4.8
Installing the vSphere Client plug-in is done from within the vSphere Client.

4. Run through the installation of the vSphere Update Manager extension, selecting the language, agreeing to the license terms, and completing the installation.

5. After the installation is complete, the status of the plug-in is listed as Enabled. Click Close to return to the vSphere Client.

The VUM plug-in is now installed into this instance of the vSphere Client. Remember that the VUM plug-in is per instance of the vSphere Client, so you need to repeat this process on each installation of the vSphere Client. If you have the vSphere Client installed on your desktop workstation and your laptop, you'll need to install the plug-in on both systems as well. After that is done, you are ready to configure VUM for your environment.

VSPHERE WEB CLIENT PLUG-IN

The plug-in for the vSphere Web Client is integrated automatically during a VUM 5.5 installation. Users need only log out and back into the Web Client to see the new VUM details.

Reconfiguring the VUM or UMDS Installation with the Update Manager Utility

When you install VUM or UMDS on a server, a small reconfiguration utility is silently installed. This tool, the Update Manager Utility, allows you change some of the fundamental installation settings without the need to reinstall either VUM or UMDS.

The settings that the tool allows you to change are these:

◆ Proxy settings

◆ Database username and password

◆ vCenter Server IP address

◆ SSL certificate (provides a set of instructions to follow)

Perform the following steps to run the Update Manager Utility:

1. Stop the Update Manager service on the server.

2. Browse to the utility's directory. By default this is: `C:\Program Files (x86)\VMware\Infrastructure\Update Manager`.

3. Run the executable `VMwareUpdateManagerUtility.exe`.

The utility is a simple GUI tool that steps through these VUM/UMDS settings.

Upgrading VUM from a Previous Version

It is possible to upgrade VUM from any VUM installation that is version 4.0 or above. When the VUM 5.5 installation starts, it will recognize the previous version and offer to upgrade it. You can choose to delete the previously downloaded patches and start afresh or keep the existing downloads and potentially save some bandwidth. Remember that like the install itself, the account that VUM uses to connect to the database will need dbo permissions on the MSDB database during the upgrade procedure. You will not be able to change the patch repository's location using an upgrade.

VUM 5.5 is installable only on 64-bit versions of Windows. If you have a 4.*x* VUM install on 32-bit Windows, you need to migrate the data to a new 64-bit server first. There is a special tool on the vCenter 5.0 installation DVD in the `datamigration` folder to help you back up and restore the installation to a new 64 bit machine. You are then able to upgrade it from 5.0 to 5.5.

Configuring vSphere Update Manager

After you have installed and registered the plug-in with the vSphere Client, a new Update Manager icon appears on the vSphere Client home page. Additionally, in the Hosts And Clusters or VMs And Templates inventory view, a new tab labeled Update Manager appears on objects in the vSphere Client. From this Update Manager tab, you can scan for patches, create and attach baselines, stage patches to hosts, and remediate hosts and guests.

Clicking the Update Manager icon at the vSphere Client home page takes you to the main VUM administration screen. Figure 4.9 shows that this area is divided into seven main sections: Baselines And Groups, Configuration, Events, Notifications, Patch Repository, ESXi Images, and VA Upgrades. Initially, as in many other areas of the vSphere Client, you will also see a leading Getting Started tab.

FIGURE 4.9
The tabs in the Update Manager Administration area within the vSphere Client

These seven tabs make up the major areas of configuration for VUM, so let's take a closer look at each section:

Baselines And Groups   Baselines are a key part of how VUM works. To keep ESX/ESXi hosts and VMs updated, VUM uses *baselines*.

VUM uses several different types of baselines. First, baselines are divided into host baselines, designed to update ESX/ESXi hosts, and VM/VA baselines, which are designed to update VMs and virtual appliances.

IMPORTANCE OF BASELINES

As vSphere becomes more central to an organization's infrastructure, baselines become increasingly important. Host baselines provide a stable platform for ever intertwined components. Many datacenter tools take advantage of vSphere APIs, such as the storage arrays via vSphere APIs for Array Integration (VAAI) and backup tools via vSphere APIs for Data Protection (VADP), and interact with vCenter and the hosts in a nontrivial way. Keeping all hosts at the same build level is crucial to maintaining a reliable environment. Additionally, keeping your VMs at a standardized hardware level with the same VMware Tools guest drivers minimizes the variances that can create support issues and troubleshooting headaches.

Baselines are further subdivided into patch baselines, upgrade baselines, and host extension baselines. Patch baselines define lists of patches to be applied to an ESX/ESXi host; upgrade baselines define how to upgrade an ESX/ESXi host, the VM's hardware, VMware Tools, or a virtual appliance. There's also another type of baseline for hosts, known as host extension baselines; these are used to manage the extensions installed onto your ESX/ESXi hosts.

Finally, patch baselines are divided again into dynamic baselines and fixed baselines. Dynamic baselines can change over time—for example, all security host patches since a certain date. But fixed baselines remain constant—for example, a specific host patch that you want to ensure is applied to your hosts.

WHEN SHOULD YOU USE FIXED BASELINES OR DYNAMIC BASELINES?

Fixed baselines are best used to apply a specific fix to a group of hosts. For example, let's say that VMware released a specific fix for ESX/ESXi and you wanted to be sure that it was installed on all your hosts. By creating a fixed baseline that included just that patch and attaching that baseline to your hosts, you could ensure that your hosts had that specific fix installed. Another use for fixed baselines is to establish the approved set of patches that you have tested and are now ready to deploy to the environment as a whole.

Dynamic baselines, on the other hand, are best used to keep systems current with the latest sets of patches. Because these baselines evolve over time, attaching them to your hosts can help you understand just how current your systems are (or aren't!).

Configuration   The bulk of the configuration of VUM is performed on the Configuration tab. From here, users can configure the full range of VUM settings, including network connectivity, download settings, download schedule, notification check schedule, VM settings, ESX/ESXi host settings, and vApp settings. These are some of the various options that you can configure:

Network Connectivity   Under Network Connectivity, you can change the ports on which VUM communicates. In general, there is no need to change these ports, and you should leave them at the defaults.

Download Settings   The Download Settings area allows you to configure what types of patches VUM will download and store. You can add custom URLs to download third-party patches by adding sources, as shown in Figure 4.10.

FIGURE 4.10
Select patch sources so that VUM downloads only certain types of patches.

This is also the area in the settings where you can point to a web server configured on a UMDS instance if you are centralizing your downloads. You set VUM to use a download server by choosing the Use A Shared Repository radio button. You can also import offline patch bundles, distributed as zip files, to add collections of VMware or third-party patches and updates.

The Download Settings area is also where you would set the proxy configuration, if a proxy server is present on your network. VUM needs access to the Internet in order to download the patches and patch metadata, so if a proxy server controls Internet access, you must configure the proxy settings here in order for VUM to work.

Download Schedule   The Download Schedule area allows you to control the timing and frequency of patch downloads. Click the Edit Download Schedule link in the upper-right corner of this area to open the Schedule Update Download Wizard, which allows you to specify the schedule for patch downloads as well as gives you the opportunity to configure email notifications.

> ### EMAIL NOTIFICATIONS REQUIRE SMTP SERVER CONFIGURATION
>
> To receive any email notifications that you might configure in the Schedule Update Download Wizard, you must also configure the SMTP server in the vCenter Server settings, accessible from the Administration menu of the vSphere Client.

Notification Check Schedule   VUM regularly checks for notifications about patch recalls, patch fixes, and other alerts. The schedule for checking for these notifications is configured in this area. As in the Download Schedule area, you can click the Edit Notifications link in the upper-right corner of the window to edit the schedule VUM uses to check for notifications.

VM Settings   Under VM Settings, vSphere administrators configure whether to use VM snapshots when applying upgrades to VMs. As you'll see in Chapter 7, "Ensuring High Availability and Business Continuity," snapshots provide the ability to capture a VM's state at a given point and then roll back to that captured state if so desired. Having the ability, via a snapshot, to undo the installation of a driver from a VMware Tools upgrade can be incredibly valuable. Be careful not to keep the snapshot for an unnecessary length of time because it can affect the VM's performance and, more important, can cause storage issues because it can grow and fill your datastore unexpectedly.

Figure 4.11 shows the default settings that enable snapshots.

FIGURE 4.11
By default, VM snapshots are enabled for use with VUM.

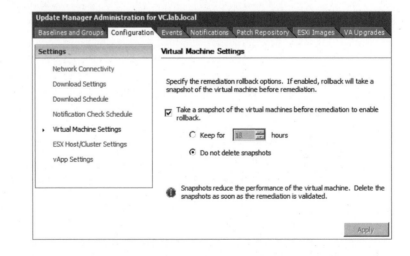

ESX Host/Cluster Settings   The ESX Host/Cluster Settings area provides controls for fine-tuning how VUM handles maintenance mode operations. Before an ESX/ESXi host is patched or upgraded, it is first placed into maintenance mode. When the ESX/ESXi host is part of a cluster that has VMware Distributed Resource Scheduler (DRS) enabled, this will also trigger automatic vMotions of VMs to other hosts in the cluster. These settings allow you to control what happens if a host fails to go into maintenance mode and how many times VUM retries the maintenance mode operation. The default settings specify that VUM will retry three times to place a host in maintenance mode.

You can configure whether VUM will disable certain cluster features in order to perform remediation. Otherwise, VUM may not perform updates on the hosts with these features enabled. The features that VUM can control are Distributed Power Management (DPM), High Availability Admission Control, and Fault Tolerance (FT). You can opt to let the cluster determine if more than one host can be updated at once while safely maintaining compliance with the rest of the cluster settings. If so, then multiple hosts can be patched or upgraded at once.

Last, you can select whether to patch any PXE-booted ESXi 5.*x* hosts.

PATCHING STATELESS PXE-BOOTED SERVERS

When you patch a PXE-booted server, those changes won't survive the host's next reboot because it will revert to the network image. You should apply these patches to the image itself for them to remain persistent.

So why apply them to the hosts?

VUM can apply live install patches, which do not require a host reboot. This means that you can quickly apply a patch to a fleet of PXE-booted ESXi hosts without needing to reboot them, or without needing to update and test the images, in order to pick up an important patch.

---

vApp Settings   The vApp Settings allow you to control whether VUM's smart reboot feature is enabled for vApps. vApps are teams, if you will, of VMs. Consider a multitier application that consists of a frontend web server, a middleware server, and a backend database server. These three different VMs and their respective guest OSes could be combined into a vApp. The smart reboot feature simply restarts the different VMs within the vApp in a way that accommodates inter-VM dependencies. For example, if the database server has to be patched and rebooted, then it is quite likely that the web server and the middleware server will also need to be rebooted, and they shouldn't be restarted until after the database server is back up and available again. The default setting is to leverage smart reboot.

Events   The Events tab lists the VUM-specific events logged. As shown in Figure 4.12, the Events tab lists actions taken by administrators as well as automatic actions taken by VUM. Administrators can sort the list of events by clicking the column headers, but there is no functionality to help users filter out only the events they want to see. There is also no way to export events from here.

FIGURE 4.12
The Events tab lists events logged by VUM during operation and can be a good source of information for troubleshooting.

However, you can also find the events listed in the holistic Management ➤ Events area of the vSphere Client home page (or via the Ctrl+Shift+E keyboard shortcut), and that area does include some filtering functionality as well as the ability to export the events. The Export Events button, shown in Figure 4.13 in the upper-left corner, allows you to export events to a file. (The functionality of the Management ➤ Events area of vCenter Server was discussed in detail in Chapter 3.)

FIGURE 4.13
Events from VUM Manager are included in the Management area of vCenter Server, where information can be exported or filtered.

Notifications This tab displays any notifications gathered by VUM regarding patch recalls, patch fixes, and other alerts issued by VMware.

For example, if VMware recalled a patch, VUM would mark the patch as recalled. This prevents you from installing the recalled patch. A notification that the patch was recalled would be displayed in the Notifications area. Similarly, if a patch is fixed, VUM would update the new patch and include a notification that the patch has been updated.

Patch Repository The Patch Repository tab shows all the patches that are currently in VUM's patch repository. From here, you can also view the details of any specific patch by right-clicking the patch and selecting Show Patch Detail or by double-clicking a patch. Figure 4.14 shows the additional information displayed about a patch when you select Show Patch Detail from the context menu (right click).

This particular item shown in Figure 4.14 is the Virtual Ethernet Module for the Cisco Nexus 1000V.

The Import Patches link in the upper-right corner of the Patch Repository tab allows you to upload patches directly into the repository. Importing patches here is the same as importing them on the Configuration ➤ Download Settings page.

ESXi Images This is the area where you will upload ISO files for upgrading ESX/ESXi. These ISO files are the same images used to create the CD installation media for a base ESXi install. You can find more information on this task in the section "Upgrading Hosts With vSphere Update Manager."

VA Upgrades The VA Upgrades tab lists any suitable virtual appliance upgrades. You can view different versions, see a log of all the changes that have been made since the previous version, and accept any required licensing agreements. For a virtual appliance to be upgradable via VUM, it must have been built with VMware's own free Studio package (at least version 2.0 must have been used).

FIGURE 4.14
The Patch Repository tab also offers more detailed information about each of the items in the repository.

Creating Baselines

VMware provides a few baselines with VUM when it's installed. The following baselines are present upon installation:

- Two dynamic host patch baselines named Critical Host Patches and Non-Critical Host Patches
- A dynamic baseline for upgrading VMware Tools to match the host
- A dynamic baseline for upgrading VM hardware to match the host
- A dynamic VA upgrade baseline named VA Upgrade To Latest

Although these baselines provide a good starting point, many users will need to create additional baselines that better reflect their organizations' specific patching policy or procedures. For example, organizations may want to ensure that ESX/ESXi hosts are kept fully patched with regard to security patches but not necessarily critical nonsecurity patches. This can be accomplished by creating a custom dynamic baseline.

Perform the following steps to create a new dynamic host patch baseline for security-related ESX/ESXi host patches:

1. Launch the vSphere Client, and connect to the vCenter Server instance with which VUM is registered.

2. In the vSphere Client, navigate to the Update Manager Administration area via the vCenter home page, and click the Baselines And Groups tab.

3. Just under the tab bar, you need to select the correct baseline type, Hosts or VMs/VAs. In this case, click the Hosts button.

4. Click the Create link in the area to the right of the list of baselines (not the Create link for Baseline Groups on the far right). This launches the New Baseline Wizard.

5. Supply a name and description for the new baseline, and select Host Patch as the baseline type. Click Next.

6. Select Dynamic, and click Next.

7. On the next screen you define the criteria for the patches to be included in this baseline. Select the correct criteria for the baseline you are defining, and then click Next.

   Figure 4.15 shows a sample selection set—in this case, all security-related patches.

FIGURE 4.15
Dynamic baselines contain a set of criteria that determine which patches are included in the baseline and which are not.

8. Select any patches that match the selection criteria but that you want to exclude from the baseline.

   Use the up/down arrows to move patches out of or into the exclusion list in the lower pane, respectively. In this case, don't exclude any patches and just click Next.

9. Now you have the option to permanently include any patches that are available but that were not automatically included by the selection criteria.

   Once again, use the up/down arrows to remove patches or add patches to be included, respectively. Don't add any additional patches; just click Next.

10. Click Finish to create the baseline.

You can now use this baseline to determine which ESX/ESXi hosts are not compliant with the latest security patches by attaching it to one or more hosts, a procedure you'll learn later in this chapter in the section "Routine Updates."

Groups, or baseline groups, are simply combinations of nonconflicting baselines. You might use a baseline group to combine multiple dynamic patch baselines, like the baseline group shown in Figure 4.16. In that example, a baseline group is defined that includes the built-in Critical Host Patches and Non-Critical Host Patches baselines. By attaching this baseline group to your ESX/ESXi hosts, you would be able to ensure that your hosts had all available patches installed.

FIGURE 4.16

Combining multiple dynamic baselines into a baseline group provides greater flexibility in managing patches.

You can also use baseline groups to combine different types of baselines. Each baseline group can include one of each type of upgrade baseline. For a host baseline group, there is only one type of upgrade baseline—a host upgrade. For VM/VA upgrade baselines, there are multiple types: VA Upgrades, VM Hardware Upgrades, and VM Tools Upgrades. When you are working with a host baseline group, you also have the option of adding a host extension baseline into the baseline group. This ability to combine different types of baselines together into a baseline group simplifies the application of multiple baselines to objects in your vCenter Server hierarchy.

Another use for baseline groups would be to combine a dynamic patch policy and a fixed patch policy into a baseline group. For example, there might be a specific fix for your ESX/ESXi hosts, and you want to ensure that all your hosts have all the critical patches—easily handled by the built-in Critical Host Patches dynamic baseline—as well as the specific fix. To do this, create a fixed baseline for the specific patch you want included, and then combine it in a baseline group with the built-in Critical Host Patches dynamic baseline.

Figure 4.17 shows an example of a host baseline group that combines different types of host baselines. In this example, a baseline group is used to combine a host upgrade baseline and dynamic patch baselines. This would allow you to upgrade an ESX/ESXi host and then ensure that the host has all the applicable updates for the new version.

FIGURE 4.17

Use baseline groups to combine host upgrade and dynamic host patch baselines.

Perform the following steps to create a host baseline group combining multiple host baselines:

1. Launch the vSphere Client if it isn't already running, and connect to the vCenter Server instance with which VUM is registered.

2. Navigate to the Update Manager Administration area, and make sure the Baselines And Groups tab is selected.

3. In the upper-right corner of the Update Manager Administration area, click the Create link to create a new baseline group. This starts the New Baseline Group Wizard.

4. Select Host Baseline Group as the baseline type and create a name for the new baseline group. Click Next.

5. Because we haven't yet discussed how to create a host upgrade baseline, you probably don't have an upgrade baseline listed. Instead, for this procedure, you will combine a dynamic and a fixed-host patch baseline. Select None and click Next to skip attaching an upgrade baseline to this host baseline group.

6. Place a check mark next to each individual baseline to include in this baseline group, as shown in Figure 4.18, and click Next.

FIGURE 4.18
A baseline group combines multiple individual baselines for a more comprehensive patching capability.

7. If you want to include a host extension baseline, select the desired host extension baseline and click Next. Otherwise, just click Next to proceed without adding a host extension baseline.

8. On the summary screen, review the settings, and click Finish to create the new baseline group.

The new baseline group you just created is now included in the list of baseline groups, and you can attach it to ESX/ESXi hosts or clusters to identify which of them are not compliant with the baseline.

You'll see more about host upgrade baselines in the section "Upgrading Hosts with vSphere Update Manager."

Having examined the different areas present within VUM, let's now take a look at actually using VUM to patch hosts and VMs.

Routine Updates

VUM uses the term *remediation* to refer to the process of applying patches and upgrades to a vSphere object. As described in the previous section, VUM uses baselines to create lists of patches based on certain criteria. By attaching a baseline to a host or VM and performing a scan, VUM can determine whether that object is compliant or noncompliant with the baseline. Compliance with the baseline means that the host or VM has all the patches included in the baseline currently installed and is up-to-date; noncompliance means that one or more patches are missing and the target is not up-to-date.

After noncompliance with one or more baselines or baseline groups has been determined, the vSphere administrator can remediate—or *patch*—the hosts or VMs. Optionally, the administrator can stage patches to ESX/ESXi hosts before remediation.

The first step in this process is actually creating the baselines that you will attach to your ESX/ESXi hosts or VMs. How to create a host patch baseline was covered earlier, so you have already seen this process. The next step is attaching a baseline to—or detaching a baseline from—ESX/ESXi hosts or VMs. Let's take a closer look at how to attach and detach baselines.

Attaching and Detaching Baselines or Baseline Groups

Before you patch a host or guest, you must determine whether an ESX/ESXi host or VM is compliant or noncompliant with one or more baselines or baseline groups. Defining a baseline or baseline group alone is not enough. To determine compliance, you must first attach the baseline or baseline group to a host or VM. After it is attached, the baseline or baseline group becomes the "measuring stick" that VUM uses to determine compliance. Attaching and detaching baselines is performed in one of vCenter's inventory views. To attach or detach a baseline or baseline groups for ESX/ESXi hosts, you need to be in the Hosts And Clusters view; for VMs, you need to be in the VMs And Templates view. In both cases, you'll use the Update Manager tab to attach or detach baselines or baseline groups.

In both views, baselines and baseline groups can be attached to a variety of objects. In the Hosts And Clusters view, baselines and baseline groups can be attached to datacenters, clusters, or individual ESX/ESXi hosts. In the VMs And Templates view, baselines and baseline groups can be attached to datacenters, folders, or specific VMs. Because of the hierarchical nature of the vCenter Server inventory, a baseline attached at a higher level will automatically apply to eligible child objects as well. You may also find yourself applying different baselines or baseline groups at different levels of the hierarchy; for example, there may be a specific baseline that applies to all hosts in the environment but another baseline that applies only to a specific subset of hosts.

Let's look at attaching a baseline to a specific ESX/ESXi host. The process is much the same, if not identical, for attaching a baseline to a datacenter, cluster, folder, or VM.

Perform the following steps to attach a baseline or baseline group to an ESX/ESXi host:

1. Launch the vSphere Web Client in your web browser of choice.

   This instance of vCenter Server should have an instance of VUM associated with it.

   Because VUM is integrated with and depends on vCenter Server, you cannot manage, attach, or detach VUM baselines when connected directly to an ESX/ESXi host with the Windows vSphere Client.

2. On the Web Client's home screen, select Hosts And Clusters.

3. In the inventory tree on the left, select the ESX/ESXi host to which you want to attach a baseline or baseline group.

4. In the central panel, select the Monitor tab, followed by the Update Manager subtab. Unlike the Windows vSphere Client, the Web Client lists all applicable baselines and baseline groups, even those not attached.

5. Click the Attach link in the upper-right corner; this link opens the Attach Baseline Or Group dialog box, shown in Figure 4.19.

FIGURE 4.19
The Attach Baseline
Or Group dialog box

host1.lab.local - Attach Baseline or Group	? ▸▸
Individual Baselines	

Name	Type
▾ **Patch Baselines**	
☐ Lab Baseline - Security only host patches	Host Patch
☑ Lab Baseline - Fix for specific issue XYZ	Host Patch
Extension Baselines	
Upgrade Baselines	

Baseline Groups

Name	Type
▾ ☑ Lab Baseline Group	
Critical Host Patches (Predefined)	Host Patch
Non-Critical Host Patches (Predefined)	Host Patch
▸ ☐ Lab Baseline Group - test123	

OK   Cancel

6. Select the baselines and/or baseline groups that you want to attach to this ESX/ESXi host, and then click OK.

The steps for attaching a baseline or baseline group to a VM with a guest OS installed are similar, but let's walk through the process anyway. A very useful baseline to point out is named VMware Tools Upgrade To Match Host. This baseline is a default baseline that is defined upon installation of VUM, and its purpose is to help you identify which VMs have guest OSes running outdated versions of VMware Tools. As you'll see in Chapter 7, using VMware Tools is an important piece of optimizing your guest OSes to run in a virtualized environment, and it's great that VUM can help identify which VMs have guest OSes with an outdated version of VMware Tools installed.

Perform the following steps to attach a baseline to a datacenter so that it applies to all the objects under the datacenter:

1. Launch the vSphere Web Client if it is not already running.

2. Switch to the VMs And Templates inventory view from the Web Client's home screen.

3. Select a datacenter object from the inventory on the left.

4. From the contents pane in the middle, click the Monitor tab followed by the Update Manager tab.

5. Click the Attach button in the top right-hand corner of the Update Manager tab's panel. This opens the Attach Baseline Or Group dialog box.

6. Click to select the VMware Tools Upgrade To Match Host upgrade baseline, and then click OK.

In the event that you need to detach a baseline from an object, highlight the baseline in question, and use the Detach button just above the left corner of the list. Figure 4.20 shows the Detach button about half-way down on the left. This link is visible only when a baseline is highlighted.

FIGURE 4.20

Detaching baselines

Clicking the Detach link then takes you to a screen that also allows you to detach the baseline from other objects to which it is attached. Figure 4.21 shows how VUM allows you to detach the selected baseline or baseline group from other objects at the same time (it does not allow you to detach baselines from objects that have inherited the baseline, only those that have been explicitly attached to each child object—if an object has inherited the baseline, then this can be detached only at the point it was applied).

FIGURE 4.21
When you're detaching a baseline or baseline group, VUM offers the option to detach it from other objects at the same time.

In much the same way as simply defining a baseline or baseline group wasn't enough, simply attaching a baseline or baseline group to an ESX/ESXi host or VM isn't enough to determine compliance or noncompliance. To determine compliance or noncompliance with a baseline or baseline group, you need to perform a scan.

Performing a Scan

The next step after attaching a baseline is to perform a scan. The purpose of a scan is to determine the compliance, or noncompliance, of an object with the baseline. If the object being scanned matches what's defined in the baseline, then the object—be it an ESX/ESXi host, VM, or virtual appliance instance—is compliant. If something is missing from the object, then it's noncompliant.

While the process of scanning these objects within vCenter Server is essentially the same, there are enough differences in the processes and requirements to make it worthwhile to examine each one.

SCANNING VMs

You might perform any of three different types of scans against a VM and virtual appliances using VUM:

◆   Scan the installed version of VMware Tools to see if it's the latest version.

◆   Scan the VM hardware to see if it's the latest version.

◆   Scan a virtual appliance to see if a new version is available and if it can be upgraded.

The process for actually conducting a scan is identical in all three instances except for the check box that indicates what type of scan you'd like to perform, as shown in Figure 4.22.

FIGURE 4.22
Different types of scans are initiated depending on the check boxes selected at the start of the scan.

What differs among these three types of scans are the requirements needed to perform a scan:

Scanning for VMware Tools Upgrades   If you scan a VM for VMware Tools upgrades and that VM does not have VMware Tools installed, the scan will succeed but VUM will report the VM as Incompatible. To get a Compliant or Non-Compliant report, some version of the VMware Tools needs to already be running within the guest OS installed in the VM. Other than that requirement, VUM has no other restrictions. VUM can scan both online and offline VMs and templates.

Scanning for VM Hardware Upgrades   Scanning for VM hardware upgrades requires that the latest version of VMware Tools be installed in the VM first. This, of course, means that a guest OS is installed in the VM. You can perform VM hardware upgrade scans on both online as well as offline VMs and templates.

Scanning Virtual Appliances   Scanning virtual appliances for virtual appliance upgrades can be performed only on virtual appliances created with VMware Studio 2.0 or later. In addition, because of the nature of virtual appliances as prepackaged installations of a guest OS and applications, it's generally not recommended to scan virtual appliances for VMware Tools upgrades or VM hardware upgrades. Virtual appliances are generally distributed in such a way that if the developer of the virtual appliance wants to update VMware Tools or the VM hardware, they will create a new version of the appliance and distribute the entire appliance.

UNMANAGED VMWARE TOOLS

Creators of virtual appliances have the option of installing operating system specific packages (OSPs) for VMware Tools. Because installing VMware Tools through the vSphere Client is mutually exclusive to using the OSP VMware Tools, the OSP VMware Tools will report Unmanaged as the status in the vSphere Client. In addition, scans of virtual appliances for VMware Tools upgrades will report the virtual appliance as Incompatible. It's not something to be concerned about because it allows the virtual appliance creators to use the native operating system packaging tools to more effectively manage the driver updates.

SCANNING ESX/ESXI HOSTS

As with VMs, the requirements for being able to scan an ESX/ESXi host vary depending on the type of scan VUM is performing. In all cases, the ESX/ESXi hosts need to be online and reachable via the network from the VUM server. VUM 5.5 can scan 4.0 and above hosts for updates to patches and extensions or for potential upgrades.

Let's look at the steps involved to perform a scan. Keep in mind that performing a scan on a VM and performing a scan on a virtual appliance are extremely similar processes.

Perform the following steps to initiate a scan of an ESX/ESXi host for patches, extensions, or upgrades after a baseline is attached:

1. Launch the vSphere Web Client if it is not already running.

2. Go to the Hosts And Clusters inventory view from the Web Client's home screen.

3. Select an ESX/ESXi host from the inventory tree on the left.

4. From the contents pane on the right, click the Update Manager tab sitting under the Monitor tab.

5. Click the Scan link in the upper-right corner.

6. Select whether you want to scan for patches and extensions, upgrades, or both, and then click Scan.

When the scan is complete, the Update Manager tab will update to show whether the object is compliant or noncompliant. Compliance is measured on a per-baseline basis. In Figure 4.23, you can see that the selected ESXi host is compliant with the Critical Host Patches baseline but not the Non-Critical Host Patches baseline. This means the host is compliant overall. If a host is noncompliant with at least one attached baseline, the host is considered noncompliant.

FIGURE 4.23
When multiple baselines are attached to an object, compliance is reflected on a per-baseline basis.

When you are viewing the Update Manager tab for an object that contains other objects, such as a datacenter, cluster, or folder, then compliance might be mixed. That is, some objects might be compliant, while other objects might be noncompliant. Figure 4.24 shows a datacenter with mixed compliance reports. In this particular case, you're looking at a compliance report for VMware Tools upgrades to match the host. The compliance report shows objects that are compliant (VMware Tools is up-to-date), noncompliant (VMware Tools is outdated), and incompatible (VMware Tools cannot be installed for some reason).

FIGURE 4.24
VUM can show partial compliance when viewing objects that contain other objects.

VMware Tools Upgrade to Match Host (Predefined)	VM Upgrade
VM Hardware Upgrade to Match Host (Predefined)	VM Upgrade
VA Upgrade to Latest (Predefined)	VA Upgrade
Lab Baseline - ESXi 5.5 Upgrade	Host Upgrade
Lab Baseline - Security only host patches	Host Patch
Lab Baseline - Fix for specific issue XYZ	Host Patch

Non-Compliant (2) **Incompatible (2)** Unknown (0) Compliant (3)

Object	Upgrades	VMware Tools upgrade on power cycle
vMA	1	No
TTYLinux	1	No

VUM can report an object as Incompatible for a number of reasons. In this particular case, VUM is reporting two objects as Incompatible when scanning for VMware Tools. Taking a closer look at Figure 4.24, you can see that these two objects are a VM named TTYLinux and a virtual appliance named vMA. The VM is reported as Incompatible because this is a fresh VM with no guest OS installed yet, and the vMA is reporting Incompatible because it is a virtual appliance running the OSP VMware Tools, which is not intended to be managed by the vSphere Client.

Depending on the type of scan you are performing, scans can be fairly quick. Scanning a large group of VMs for VMware Tools upgrades or VM hardware upgrades may also be fairly quick. Scanning a large group of hosts for patches, on the other hand, might be more time consuming and more resource intensive. Combining several tasks at the same time can also slow down scans while they run concurrently. You can consult VMware's latest copy of the vSphere Configuration Maximums document for version 5.5, which lists the maximum number of concurrent VUM operations possible.

After the scanning is complete and compliance is established, you are ready to fix the non-compliant systems. Before we discuss remediation, let's first look at staging patches to ESX/ESXi hosts.

Staging Patches

If the target of remediation—that is, the object within vCenter Server that you are trying to remediate and make compliant with a baseline—is an ESX/ESXi host, an additional option exists. VUM offers the option of staging patches to ESX/ESXi hosts. Staging a patch to an ESX/ESXi host copies the files across to the host to speed up the actual time of remediation. Staging is not a required step; you can update hosts without staging the updates first, if you prefer. VUM won't stage patches to a PXE-booted ESXi host such as a host provisioned via standard Auto Deploy (although it will stage patches to hosts using *stateful* Auto Deploy).

Staging host patches is particularly useful for companies whose VUM-connected hosts are spread across slow WAN links. This can substantially reduce the outage required on such sites, especially if the WAN link is particularly slow or the patches themselves are very large. Hosts do not need to be in maintenance mode while patches are being staged, but they do during the remediation phase. Staging patches reduces the maintenance mode period associated with remediation. Staging patches also allows the uploads to be scheduled for a time when heavy

WAN utilization is more appropriate, allowing the administrator to remediate the host at a more agreeable time.

At this stage you need to switch back to the Windows vSphere Client. Perform the following steps to stage patches to an ESX/ESXi host using VUM:

1. Launch the vSphere Client if it is not already running, and connect to a vCenter Server instance.

2. Navigate to the Hosts And Clusters view by selecting View ➤ Inventory ➤ Hosts And Clusters, by using the Ctrl+Shift+H keyboard shortcut, or by using the navigation bar.

3. From the inventory list on the left, select an ESX/ESXi host.

4. From the contents pane on the right, scroll through the tabs and select the Update Manager tab.

5. Click the Stage button in the bottom-right corner of the contents pane, or right-click the host and select Stage Patches. Either method activates the Stage Wizard.

6. Select the baselines for the patches you want to be staged, and click Next to proceed.

7. The next screen allows you to deselect any specific patches you do not want to be staged. If you want all the patches to be staged, leave them all selected, and click Next.

8. Click Finish at the summary screen to start the staging process.

After the staging process is complete, the Tasks pane at the bottom of the vSphere Client reflects this, as shown in Figure 4.25.

FIGURE 4.25
The vSphere Client reflects when the process of staging patches is complete.

Recent Tasks			
Name	Target	Status	
Stage	host1.lab.local	✔	Completed
Stage patches to entity	host1.lab.local	✔	Completed

Tasks Alarms

After you stage patches to the ESX/ESXi hosts, you can begin the task of remediating immediately or defer to a later or more appropriate time window.

Remediating Hosts

After you have attached a baseline to a host, scanned the host for compliance, and optionally staged the updates to the host, you're ready to remediate, or update, the ESX/ESXi host.

REMEDIATION

The term *remediation* is simply VMware parlance to mean the process of applying patches or upgrades to an object to bring it up to a compliant level.

Perform the following steps to patch an ESX/ESXi host:

1. Launch the vSphere Client if it is not already running, and connect to a vCenter Server instance.

2. Switch to the Hosts And Clusters view by using the navigation bar, by using the Ctrl+Shift+H keyboard shortcut, or by selecting View ➤ Inventory ➤ Hosts And Clusters.

3. Select an ESX/ESXi host from the inventory tree on the left.

4. From the contents pane on the right, select the Update Manager tab. You might need to scroll through the available tabs to see the Update Manager tab.

5. In the lower-right corner of the window, click the Remediate button. You can also right-click the ESX/ESXi host and select Remediate from the context menu.

6. The Remediate dialog box opens, as shown in Figure 4.26. From here, select the baselines or baseline groups that you want to apply. Click Next.

FIGURE 4.26
The Remediate dialog box allows you to select the baselines or baseline groups against which you would like to remediate an ESX/ESXi host.

7. Deselect any patches or extensions that you don't want applied to the ESX/ESXi host.

   This allows you to customize the exact list of patches. Click Next after you've deselected any patches to exclude.

8. Specify a name and description for the remediation task. Also, choose whether you want the remediation to occur immediately or whether it should run at a specific time.

   Figure 4.27 shows these options.

FIGURE 4.27
When remediating
a host, you need to
specify a name for
the remediation
task and a schedule
for the task.

9. The Host Remediation Options page gives you the option to modify the default settings for how VUM should handle a host's VMs if it has to enter maintenance mode. It also lets you patch PXE-booted ESXi hosts but warns you that those changes will be lost on the next power cycle. Figure 4.28 shows the options available during this stage. Make any changes required and click Next.

FIGURE 4.28
Host remediation
options available if
the host has to enter
maintenance mode

10. If the host is a member of a cluster, you can choose whether to disable any of the cluster settings for DPM, HA, and FT, if you think they may interfere with the remediation process. VUM version 5 now has the option to remediate several hosts at once if the cluster has sufficient compute resources to meet the other cluster controls. In Figure 4.29 you can see the full gamut of cluster options.

FIGURE 4.29
Cluster options during host remediation

11. Review the summary screen, and click Finish if everything is correct. If there are any errors, use the Back button to double-check and change the settings.

If you selected to have the remediation occur immediately, which is the default setting, VUM initiates a task request with vCenter Server. You'll see this task, as well as some related tasks, in the Tasks pane at the bottom of the vSphere Client.

If necessary, VUM automatically puts the ESX/ESXi host into maintenance mode. If the host is a member of a DRS-enabled cluster, putting the host into maintenance mode will, in turn, initiate a series of vMotion operations to migrate all VMs to other hosts in the cluster. It's common to see the remediation task pause for an extended time at the 22% point. This is normal and it often takes around 15 minutes to complete the migrations before progressing further. After the patching is complete, VUM automatically reboots the host, if it is required, and then takes the host out of maintenance mode.

KEEPING HOSTS PATCHED IS IMPORTANT

Keeping your ESX/ESXi hosts patched is important. We all know this, but too often VMware administrators forget to incorporate this key task into their operations.

VUM makes keeping your hosts patched much easier, but you still need to actually do it! Be sure to take the time to establish a regular schedule for applying host updates and take advantage of VUM's integration with vMotion, vCenter Server, and VMware Distributed Resource Scheduler (DRS) to avoid downtime for your end users during the patching process.

Upgrading VMware Tools

VUM can scan and remediate not only ESX/ESXi hosts but also the VMware Tools package running inside your VMs. VMware Tools is an important part of your virtualized infrastructure. The basic idea behind VMware Tools is to provide a set of virtualization-optimized drivers for all the guest OSes that VMware supports with VMware vSphere. These virtualization-optimized drivers help provide the highest levels of performance for guest OSes running on VMware vSphere, and it's considered a best practice to keep VMware Tools up-to-date whenever possible. (You can find a more thorough discussion of VMware Tools in Chapter 9, "Creating and Managing Virtual Machines.")

To help with that task, VUM comes with a prebuilt upgrade baseline named VMware Tools Upgrade To Match Host. This baseline can't be modified or deleted from within the vSphere Client, and its sole purpose is to help vSphere administrators identify VMs that are not running a version of VMware Tools that is appropriate for the host on which it is currently running.

In general, follow the same order of operations for remediating VMware Tools as you did for ESX/ESXi hosts:

1. Attach the baselines to the VMs you want to scan and remediate.

2. Scan the VMs for compliance with the attached baseline.

3. Remediate VMware Tools inside the VMs if it is noncompliant.

The procedure for attaching a baseline was described in the section "Attaching and Detaching Baselines or Baseline Groups," and the process of performing a scan for compliance with a baseline was described in the section "Performing a Scan."

If you have attached a baseline to a VM and scanned VMware Tools on that VM for compliance, the next step is actually remediating VMware Tools inside the VM.

Perform the following steps to remediate VMware Tools:

1. Launch the vSphere Client if it is not already running, and connect to an instance of vCenter Server.

2. Using the menu, navigate to the VMs And Templates area by selecting View ➢ Inventory ➢ VMs And Templates. You can also use the navigation bar or the Ctrl+Shift+V keyboard shortcut.

3. Right-click the VM that you want to remediate, and select Remediate from the context menu. To remediate several VMs, select an object farther up the hierarchy. This displays the Remediate dialog box.

4. In the Remediate dialog box, select the VMware Tools Upgrade To Match Host baseline, and then click Next.

5. Provide a name for the remediation task, and select a schedule for the task. Different schedules are possible for powered-on VMs, powered-off VMs, and suspended VMs, as shown in Figure 4.30.

6. Select an appropriate schedule for each of the different classes of VMs, and then click Next.

7. If you want to take a snapshot of the VM, supply a name for the snapshot and a description.

You may also specify a maximum age for the snapshot and whether to snapshot the VM's memory. The default settings, as shown in Figure 4.31, are Do Not Delete Snapshots and Take A Snapshot Of The Virtual Machines Before Remediation To Enable Rollback.

FIGURE 4.30
VUM supports different schedules for remediating powered-on VMs, powered-off VMs, and suspended VMs.

FIGURE 4.31
VUM integrates with vCenter Server's snapshot functionality to allow remediation operations to be rolled back in the event of a problem.

8. Review the information in the summary screen. If anything is incorrect, use the Back button to double-check and change the settings. Otherwise, click Finish to start the remediation.

A reboot of the guest OS is often required after the VMware Tools upgrade is complete, although this varies from guest OS to guest OS. Windows guests with a version of VMware Tools prior to 5.1 will require a reboot, so plan accordingly. vSphere 5.1 introduced the "zero downtime" tools upgrade, which is designed to minimize guest reboots after the tools have been updated. Updates to certain device drivers still mean a reboot is necessary, but the incidence has been significantly reduced. The Knowledge Base article at http://kb.vmware.com /kb/2015163 details the circumstances that still require a reboot.

Where multiple VMs are joined together in a vApp, VUM and vCenter Server will coordinate restarting the VMs within the vApp to satisfy inter-VM dependencies unless you turned off Smart Reboot in the VUM configuration.

When you are dealing with VMs brought into a VMware vSphere environment from previous versions of VMware Infrastructure, you must be sure to first upgrade VMware Tools to the latest version and then deal with upgrading VM hardware. This process is explained at the end of the section "Upgrading Hosts with vSphere Update Manager." By upgrading the VMware Tools first, you ensure that the appropriate drivers are already loaded into the guest OS when you upgrade the VM hardware.

Upgrading Virtual Appliances and Host Extensions

Once again, you follow the same overall procedure to upgrade virtual appliances and host extensions in VUM as you did with VMware Tools in the previous section:

1. Attach the baseline.

2. Scan for compliance.

3. Remediate.

However, it is worth noting that both virtual appliances and host extensions are less likely to be upgraded quite so routinely. When upgraded, they are replaced wholesale, and their settings are migrated across to the new version.

Virtual appliances and host extensions often come from third-party hardware or software providers. Each vendor will make its own decisions regarding what changes to functionality are included in these upgrades. For some, you may find that the upgrade includes merely minor bug fixes and no change in the way the appliance or extension works. Another upgrade might bring significant changes to how it operates.

For this reason, it is prudent to treat each upgrade to a virtual appliance or host extension as something that needs to be tested thoroughly before running a wide-scale upgrade.

Now let's look at the last major piece of VUM's functionality: upgrading vSphere hosts.

Upgrading Hosts with vSphere Update Manager

Upgrading vSphere ESXi 5.x to the newest versions when they become available, and upgrading legacy vSphere 4.x ESX and ESXi hosts to ESXi 5.5, is principally a three-stage process. Although ESX and ESXi are fundamentally very different hypervisors, VUM can seamlessly upgrade either variant to ESXi 5.5. In fact, while running the Upgrade Wizard, which we'll step through later in this chapter, if you blink, you won't even spot the difference.

Perform the following steps to upgrade a host server with VUM 5.5:

1. Import an ESXi image and create a host upgrade baseline.

2. Upgrade the host by remediating with the upgrade baseline.

3. Upgrade the VMs' VMware Tools and hardware.

Strictly speaking, the last point is not part of the host upgrade procedure. However, most of the time when you upgrade VMs' hardware, it is immediately following a host upgrade (at least you should be upgrading them at that time!).

Importing an ESXi Image and Creating the Host Upgrade Baseline

Previous versions of vSphere used Update Bundles to upgrade hosts. These offline bundle Zip files are still used by vSphere to patch hosts and third-party software but not for host upgrades. In VUM 5.5, all host upgrades use the same image file that is used to install ESXi.

Perform the following steps to import the ISO file into VUM and create the baseline:

1. Launch the vSphere Client if it is not already running, and connect to a vCenter Server instance.

2. Navigate to the Update Manager Administration area by using the navigation bar or by selecting View ➢ Solutions And Applications ➢ Update Manager.

3. Click the ESXi Images tab.

4. Click the blue Import ESXi Image link in the top-right corner of this tab.

5. Use the Browse button, shown in Figure 4.32, to select the new ESXi ISO file. Click Next.

FIGURE 4.32
Select the ESXi image to use for the host upgrade.

6. Monitor the progress of the file upload, as shown in Figure 4.33; this might take a few minutes to complete. Once the file import is complete, verify the summary information and click Next.

FIGURE 4.33
ESXi image import

7. Take this opportunity to let the wizard create a host upgrade baseline for you by leaving the check box selected. Give the baseline a name and appropriate description and click Finish. Figure 4.34 shows an image uploaded into the list of imported images. When an image is selected, the lower pane lists all the software packages included in the image and their version number.

Upgrading a Host

After you've created a host upgrade baseline, you can use this baseline to upgrade an ESX/ESXi host following the same basic sequence of steps outlined previously to remediate other vSphere objects:

1. Attach the baseline to the ESX/ESXi hosts that you want to upgrade. Refer to the previous section "Attaching and Detaching Baselines or Baseline Groups" for a review of how to attach a baseline to an ESX/ESXi host or several hosts.

2. Scan the ESX/ESXi hosts for compliance with the baseline. Don't forget to select to scan for upgrades when presented with the scan options.

3. Remediate the host.

BACK UP YOUR HOST CONFIGURATION AS REQUIRED

Unlike with previous host upgrade methods, VUM no longer supports rollbacks after a problematic upgrade. Before you start the upgrade, make sure you have sufficient information about the state of the host to restore or rebuild it if necessary.

FIGURE 4.34
All the packages
contained in the
imported ESXi
image are shown.

The Remediate Wizard is similar to the process discussed in the section "Remediating Hosts" (Figure 4.25 through Figure 4.29), but there are enough differences to warrant reviewing the process.

Perform the following steps to upgrade an ESX/ESXi host with a VUM host upgrade baseline:

1. Launch the vSphere Client if it is not already running, and connect to a vCenter Server instance.

2. Switch to the Hosts And Clusters view by using the navigation bar, by using the Ctrl+Shift+H keyboard shortcut, or by selecting View ➢ Inventory ➢ Hosts And Clusters.

3. Select the ESX/ESXi host from the inventory tree on the left.

4. From the contents pane on the right, select the Update Manager tab. You might need to scroll through the available tabs to see the Update Manager tab.

5. In the lower-right corner of the window, click the Remediate button. You can also right-click the ESX/ESXi host and select Remediate from the context menu.

6. The Remediate dialog box opens (Figure 4.35). From here, ensure that the Upgrade Baselines radio button is selected in the Baseline Groups And Types frame, then choose the baseline that you want to apply. Click Next.

7. Select the check box to accept the license terms, and then click Next.

8. If you are upgrading the hosts from vSphere 4, the next screen gives you the option to explicitly ignore any third-party software on the host that might prevent a host upgrade, as shown in Figure 4.36. Either select the check box or leave it unchecked and click Next.

FIGURE 4.35
Select the correct upgrade baseline in the right pane if multiple versions are listed.

FIGURE 4.36
Upgrades can ignore third-party software on legacy hosts.

9. Specify a name, description, and a schedule for the remediation task, and then click Next.

10. Choose how the host's VMs should react to the host entering maintenance mode, and click Next.

11. The next page gives you the same cluster options shown in Figure 4.29. You can control how the host's cluster should conform to its own DPM, HA, and FT settings and whether to allow multiple hosts to be upgraded at the same time if the cluster has sufficient resources. Select the options required and click Next.

12. Review the summary, and use the Back button if any settings need to be changed. Click Finish when the settings are correct.

VUM then proceeds with the host upgrade at the scheduled time (Immediately is the default setting in the wizard). The upgrade will be an unattended upgrade, and at the end of the upgrade the host will automatically reboot.

Surprisingly enough, considering the inherent differences between ESX and ESXi, VMware has done a great job of hiding the complex differences during this upgrade procedure. In fact, unless you know which type of host you selected to upgrade beforehand, the only way you can tell during the Remediate Wizard process is by the host version discreetly listed in the lower pane shown in Figure 4.35.

After upgrading all the hosts in a cluster, you should consider upgrading VMware Tools on the VMs and then their virtual hardware version. Upgrading a VM's hardware can prevent that VM from running on older hosts, which is why you should ensure that all the hosts in the same cluster are upgraded first. Otherwise, you can restrict the efficiency of fundamental cluster operations such as DRS and HA.

Keeping in mind that you should upgrade VMware Tools on the VMs first, discussed in the section "Upgrading VMware Tools," let's look at how to upgrade the virtual hardware.

Upgrading VM Hardware

So far, the idea of VM hardware hasn't been discussed, but the topic is covered in Chapter 9. For now, suffice it to say that VMs brought into a VMware vSphere environment from previous versions of ESX/ESXi will have outdated VM hardware. You'll see outdated hardware most often after you upgrade a host. In order to use all the latest functionality of VMware vSphere with these VMs, you will have to upgrade the VM hardware. To help with this process, VUM lets you scan for and remediate VMs with out-of-date VM hardware.

VUM already comes with a VM upgrade baseline that addresses this: the VM Hardware Upgrade To Match Host baseline. This baseline is predefined and can't be changed or deleted from within the vSphere Client. The purpose of this baseline is to determine whether a VM's hardware is current. vSphere 5.5 VMs use hardware version 10 by default. Hardware version 9 is the version used by vSphere 5.1, and version 8 was used by 5.0.

To upgrade the virtual VM version, you again follow the same general sequence:

1. Attach the baseline.

2. Perform a scan.

3. Remediate.

To attach the baseline, follow the same procedures outlined in the section "Attaching and Detaching Baselines or Baseline Groups." Performing a scan is much the same as well; be sure you select the VM Hardware upgrade option when initiating a scan so VUM will detect outdated VM hardware. Even if the correct baseline is attached, outdated VM hardware won't be detected during a scan unless you select this box.

PLANNING FOR DOWNTIME

Remediation of VMs found to be noncompliant—for example, found to have outdated VM hardware—is again much like the other forms of remediation that have already been discussed. The important thing to note is that VM hardware upgrades are done while the VM is powered off. This means you must plan for downtime in the environment to remediate this issue.

VUM performs VM hardware upgrades only when the VM is powered off. It's also important to note that VUM might not be able to conduct an orderly shutdown of the guest OS to do the VM hardware upgrade. To avoid an unexpected shutdown of the guest OS when VUM powers off the VM, specify a schedule in the dialog box shown previously in Figure 4.30 that provides you with enough time to perform an orderly shutdown of the guest OS first.

Depending on which guest OS and which VMware Tools version is running inside the VM, the user may see prompts for "new hardware" after the VM hardware upgrade is complete. If you've followed the recommendations and the latest version of VMware Tools is installed, then all the necessary drivers should already be present, and the "new hardware" should work without any real issues.

Real World Scenario

KEEP A RECORD OF YOUR VM'S IP ADDRESSES

The most common problem faced with upgrading VM hardware is losing the VM's IP address. This occurs if VMware Tools has not been upgraded properly before you start the hardware upgrade process. Normally the new version of VMware Tools can record the VM's IP settings, and if a new VM hardware upgrade changes the network card's driver, VMware Tools can migrate the IP settings across automatically. However, VMware Tools can drop the settings for several reasons; for example, it does not recognize an issue with VMware Tools before it proceeds with the hardware upgrade, you may not have allowed for enough reboots after the VMware Tools upgrade, there may be OS issues caused by the new drivers, and so forth.

While this shouldn't happen, it is seen often enough that a quick plan B is in order. One simple approach, prior to initiating the remediation step, is to list all the VMs to be upgraded in the VMs And Templates view. Right-click one of the columns, and add the IP address to the view. Then from the File menu, select Export List To A Spreadsheet. This way, should one or more VMs lose their IP settings in the upgrade, you have a quick reference you can pull up. It's not foolproof, but this 30-second action might just save you some time trawling through DNS records if things go awry.

Although you might find virtual appliances with old versions of virtual hardware, it's advisable to treat these as special cases and wait for the software vendors to include the hardware upgrade in the next version. Virtual appliances are custom built and tuned by the vendors for their purpose. They are often released with older hardware so they are compatible with as many versions of vSphere as possible. If a new version of VM hardware is available that would benefit the vendor's appliance, the vendor will likely provide a new version of its appliance to take advantage of the new hardware version.

By combining some of the different features of VUM, you can greatly simplify the process of upgrading your virtualized infrastructure to the latest version of VMware vSphere through an orchestrated upgrade.

Performing an Orchestrated Upgrade

A specific use case for baseline groups is the *orchestrated upgrade*. For an orchestrated upgrade, you run a host baseline group and a VM/VA baseline group sequentially to help automate the process of moving an organization's environment fully into VMware vSphere 5.5. Quite simply, it upgrades your hosts and then your VMs in one job.

Consider this sequence of events:

1. You create a host baseline group that combines a host upgrade baseline with a dynamic host patch baseline to apply the latest updates.

2. You create a VM baseline group that combines two different VM upgrade baselines—the VMware Tools upgrade baseline and the VM hardware upgrade baseline.

3. You schedule the host baseline group to execute, followed at some point by the VM baseline group.

4. The host baseline group upgrades the hosts from ESX/ESXi 4.*x* and ESXi 5.0/5.1 to ESXi 5.5 and installs all applicable patches and updates.

5. The VM baseline group upgrades VMware Tools and then upgrades the VM hardware to version 10.

When these two baseline groups have completed, all the hosts and VMs affected by the baselines will be upgraded and patched. Most, if not all, of the tedious tasks surrounding the VMware Tools and VM hardware upgrade have been automated. Congratulations! You've just simplified and automated the upgrade path for your virtual environment.

Investigating Alternative Update Options

In most circumstances, using the VUM tools in the vSphere Client is the easiest and most efficient method of keeping your hosts, VMs, and virtual appliances patched and at the latest, greatest level. However, there are sometimes circumstances where you want to look beyond the standard tools and investigate the alternatives. As you'll learn, vSphere can be updated in several other ways.

Using vSphere Update Manager PowerCLI

vSphere takes advantage of Microsoft's PowerShell scripting environment with the PowerCLI extensions that are discussed in Chapter 14, "Automating VMware vSphere."

Without getting ahead of ourselves, it's worth noting the PowerCLI tools that are available to script many of VUM's functions. The VUM PowerCLI cmdlets cover the most common tasks, like working with baselines and scanning, staging, and remediating vSphere objects. Figure 4.37 shows the list of cmdlets currently available.

FIGURE 4.37
VUM PowerCLI
cmdlets available

To use the VUM PowerCLI, you need to first install the vSphere PowerCLI and then download and install the Update Manager PowerCLI package. You can get more information about this package from VMware's own "VMware vSphere Update Manager PowerCLI Installation and Administration Guide" for VUM 5.5.

Upgrading and Patching without vSphere Update Manager

You can maintain your vSphere environment, keeping the elements patched and upgraded, without resorting to the use of VUM. Also, you may want to use VUM for certain updating tasks but take an alternative approach for others. For example, you might not want to use VUM in the following situations:

◆ You are using the free stand-alone vSphere ESXi hypervisor, which does not come with vCenter Server. Without a licensed vCenter Server, you can't use VUM.

◆ You have only a small environment with one or two small host servers. To maximize the use of your server hardware for VMs, you don't want the infrastructure overhead of another application and another database running.

◆ You rely heavily on scripting to manage your environment, and you would like to take advantage of tools that don't need PowerShell, such as the PowerCLI toolset that VMware offers.

◆ You don't want to use VUM for host upgrades because you choose to always run fresh host rebuilds when required.

◆ You already have kick-start scripts, PowerShell post-install scripts, host profiles, and EDA/UDA tools, or you want to set up an Auto Deploy server to control the installation and upgrading of your hosts.

So, what alternatives are available?

Upgrading and Patching Hosts To upgrade your legacy ESX or ESXi hosts to vSphere 5.5, you have two non-VUM options. You can run through an interactive install from the ESXi 5.5 ISO media, choosing an in-place upgrade. Or you can run a kick-start scripted upgrade along with the same ESXi 5.5 media to perform an unattended upgrade. No command-line utility can upgrade an older ESX or ESXi host to 5.5.

For upgrades from ESXi 5.0 or 5.1 to newer versions, you can likewise use an interactive or unattended upgrade. If you have used VMware's Auto Deploy technology to roll out vSphere, then you will be able to leverage this tool to upgrade or patch it to the latest updates. ESXi 5.x hosts can also be patched and upgraded with the vCLI command-line `esxcli software vib` tool.

The `esxupdate` and `vihostupdate` tools are no longer supported for ESXi 5.x updates.

Upgrading VMs Without VUM, upgrading VM hardware can only be done via the vSphere Client. If the hosts are connected to vCenter, then your connected client can manually upgrade the hardware. You must shut down the VMs yourself and initialize each upgrade. Even without vCenter you can still upgrade each VM by connecting your client straight at the host. Similarly, VMware Tools can be upgraded in each guest OS manually from within the VM's console. You must mount VMware Tools from your vSphere Client.

The `vmware-vmupgrade.exe` tool should not be used to upgrade VMs anymore.

vCenter Support Tools

In addition to VUM, the vCenter Windows installation DVD and the vCSA include a handful of other useful support tools. Figure 4.38 shows the installable Support Tools options available from the DVD.

ESXi Dump Collector

The ESXi Dump Collector is a centralized service that can receive and store memory dumps from ESXi servers should they crash unexpectedly. These memory dumps occur when an ESXi host suffers what is known as a purple screen of death (PSOD), analogous to the Windows blue screen of death (BSOD) or a Linux kernel panic. The kernel grabs the contents of memory and *dumps* them to nonvolatile disk storage before the server reboots. This allows VMware support services to investigate the cause of the PSOD and hopefully recommend an action to prevent the issue from occurring again.

FIGURE 4.38
vCenter Support
Tool options on DVD

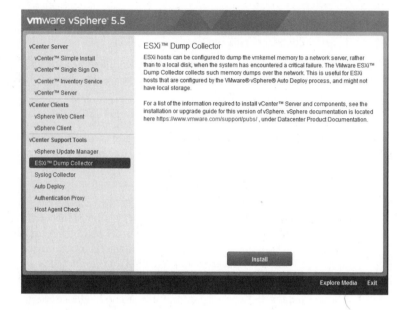

Ordinarily these dumps are sent to the host's local storage in a separate partition not normally mounted to the running filesystem, known as vmkDiagnostic. If the host has been deployed to a USB key/SD card, or via Auto Deploy, then a core dump partition isn't available. For these hosts, it is important to redirect these dumps to a central dump collector. Even if your hosts are not installed or deployed in this way, it can be beneficial, particularly in larger environments, to manage this potentially valuable data in one place.

ESXi Dump Collector on vCSA

The ESXi Dump Collector is installed and already running by default on vCSA instances. Figure 4.39 shows the service enabled.

Here are the steps to check the service status, or to restart or stop it:

1. Log into the console of the vCSA with the root account.

2. The list of services and their status is available on the first screen in the bottom left. If you have navigated away from this screen, it can be found under the vCenter Server tab, and then the Summary subtab.

Only one configuration option is available on the vCSA's ESXi Dump Collector. You can change the amount of storage reserved for all dumps. Core dumps can be anywhere from

100 MB to 300 MB, so size this space appropriately depending on how many hosts are configured, how frequently you might expect them to PSOD, and how long you need to retain the information. If you have a large environment, are experiencing frequent PSODs, or have to keep troubleshooting data for extended periods, then you should consider increasing this level. Figure 4.40 is the console's service configuration tab.

FIGURE 4.39
vCSA services running by default

FIGURE 4.40
vCSA Services tab

Follow these steps to increase the size reserved for core dumps:

1. Log into the console of the vCSA with the root account.

2. Under the vCenter Server tab, click the Services subtab.

3. The first service option allows you to change the default 2 GB repository.

ESXi DUMP COLLECTOR ON A WINDOWS SERVER

If you are using a Windows-based vCenter Server, you can also install the ESXi Dump Collector on a Windows server. This can be the same server as vCenter or a separate server. To install ESXi Dump Collector on Windows, follow these steps:

1. Mount the vCenter Server DVD on the Windows server.

2. If the Autorun splash screen does not appear, manually run the setup wizard from the root of the DVD.

3. Select the appropriate language for the install.

4. Accept the end-user license agreement.

5. Select where to install the application and where the dumps should be stored. As with any volatile data, it is advisable to move the dump repository off the C: drive. Figure 4.41 shows the dump repository moved to the D: drive. This screen of the wizard also allows you to increase (or decrease) the maximum amount of storage that the tool can use to keep core dumps.

FIGURE 4.41
Move the dump repository off the C: drive if possible.

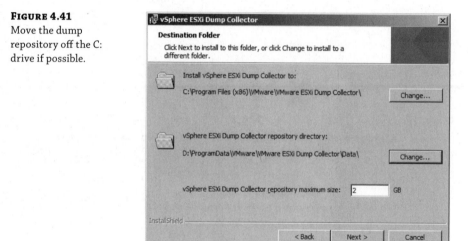

6. The setup type screen allows the installer to register the Dump Collector instance with a vCenter Server instance. Select VMware vCenter Server Installation and click Next.

7. If you selected to integrate the install with a vCenter instance, as described in the previous step, you will now enter the vCenter details and appropriate account credentials. After you click Next, the installer will ask you to verify the server's SSL certificate. Click Yes to accept the certificate.

8. Accept the default port of 6500 and click Next.

9. The next screen allows you to choose how the Dump Collector should be addressed by the hosts on the network. You can pick between hostname or IP address. Using the hostname has the advantage that it is easily recognizable by administrators during troubleshooting, but it relies on name resolution. If a host that has a kernel panic might be running the only contactable DNS VM, then using a straight IP address would be a better option. If the Windows server has multiple IP addresses, you need to pick the address that the hosts can route to. The Dump Collector service will only bind to IPv4 addresses.

10. Click Install.

11. Click Finish to complete the installation.

12. If you selected to integrate the installation with a vCenter installation, log into the vSphere Client and check that it is registered. In the Client's home screen, under Administration, click the VMware ESXi Dump Collector icon. You should see the Dump Collector's details and port number.

DOES THE DUMP COLLECTOR SUPPORT MY DISTRIBUTED SWITCHES?

The vSphere 5.5 Dump Collector (or any 5.*x* collector) will happily receive dumps regardless of which switches the hosts use. However, ESXi 5.0 hosts don't support sending dumps to a centralized Dump Collector if their VMkernel default gateway (on the management network IP, usually vmk0) is connected to a distributed switch. This can be a native virtual distributed switch (vDS) or a third-party switch such as the Cisco 1000v. This was particularly troublesome before being resolved with ESXi 5.1 because the larger enterprises that were probably licensed and using vDS connections for converged network cabling and/or Auto Deploy provisioning were also the most likely candidates to want to use the Dump Collector feature.

If you have existing ESXi 5.0 hosts that use distributed switches, then there are a number of options available. You can upgrade the hosts to at least 5.1, you can move your management connection off the distributed switch to a standard host-based vSwitch, or you can point the core dumps to a local disk.

CONFIGURING ESXi HOSTS TO REDIRECT THEIR CORE DUMPS

The primary method to configure hosts to redirect their core dumps to your newly minted ESX Dump Collector is to use the `esxcli` command-line tool:

1. Log into your host via SSH, via the local ESXi shell, or using a vMA or vCLI installation (vMA or vCLI usage requires additional context switches to identify the host).

2. Review the existing Dump Collector configuration:
   ```
   esxcli system coredump network get
   ```

3. Configure the host's dump redirection settings (management VMkernel interface and collector's IP and port):
   ```
   esxcli system coredump network set -v vmk0 -i 192.168.199.5 -o 6500
   ```

4. Turn on dump redirection:

```
esxcli system coredump network set -e true
```

5. Confirm that the settings are configured correctly:

```
esxcli system coredump network get
```

Figure 4.42 shows the process in a console session.

FIGURE 4.42

Configuring a host
to redirect dumps
to a Dump Collector

Hosts can also be configured for a centralized dump collector via the Host Profiles feature. The recommended approach is to configure one host via the command line, use it as a reference host, and then apply that configuration to the remaining hosts.

It is possible to set the configuration directly by editing a host profile, selecting Network Configuration and then Network Coredump Settings, and selecting the Enabled check box. From here, specify the NIC, server IP, and port details. This is shown in Figure 4.43.

FIGURE 4.43

Configuring a host
to a Dump Collector
via its host profile

TESTING THE ESXI DUMP COLLECTOR

You should check that each host is configured correctly and can communicate with the Dump Collector.

1. Log into your host via SSH, via the local ESXi shell, or using a vMA or vCLI installation (vMA or vCLI usage requires additional context switches to identify the host).

2. Send a test dump to the collector:

   ```
   esxcli system coredump network check
   ```

3. Connect to the Dump Collector server and check that a new dump file is present (check that the date/time stamp of the file aligns to your test). On a vCSA, the dumps are put in /var/log/vmware/netdumps/. On a Windows-based dump collector, they will be in whatever directory you set on the wizard screen shown in Figure 4.41; by default this is %ProgramData%\VMware\VMware ESXi Dump Collector\Data\. In both cases the dumps are organized into directories named after the sending hosts' IP address.

Syslog Collector

An ESXi host will by default save its log files locally. Just as with the ESXi Dump Collector we discussed, it can be beneficial to store all your hosts' logs to a centralized service. This is particularly important for hosts deployed without a persistent scratch partition, such as a stateless host provisioned via Auto Deploy, because those logs are stored in a ramdisk-based partition and are therefore lost on reboots.

There is a wide range of third-party syslog server applications, but vSphere comes with a tool specifically for the task. It is available both on the vCSA and as a Windows installable tool.

SYSLOG COLLECTOR ON VCSA

A Syslog Collector service is installed and by default running on the vCSA. Figure 4.39 shows this service already running. There are no additional configuration steps necessary to enable the central collector; just configure the hosts to send their logs to this collector.

SYSLOG COLLECTOR ON A WINDOWS SERVER

As you saw earlier in Figure 4.38, the Windows-based version of the Syslog Collector can be installed directly from the Autorun DVD splash screen. This syslog server component can be installed on the vCenter Server instance itself or on another Windows server. To install the Syslog Collector on Windows, follow these steps:

1. Mount the vCenter Server DVD on the Windows server.

2. If the Autorun splash screen does not appear, manually run the setup wizard from the root of the DVD.

3. Select the appropriate language for the install.

4. Accept the end user license agreement.

5. Select where to install the application and where the logs should be stored. As with any volatile data, it's advisable to move the syslog repository off the C: drive. As we showed earlier in Figure 4.41 of the Dump Collector install, move the store off to another drive if

possible. This screen in the Syslog Collector Install Wizard also allows you to change the size of log files before they get rotated (default of 2 MB) and the number of logs to keep (default of eight logs). Unless you have specific logging requirements and need to keep logs for extended periods, the existing values should suffice.

6. The setup type screen allows the installer to register the Syslog Collector instance with a vCenter server. Select VMware vCenter Server Installation and click Next.

7. If you selected to integrate the install with a vCenter instance, as described in the previous step, you will now enter the vCenter details and appropriate account credentials. After you click Next, the installer will ask you to verify the server's SSL certificate. Click Yes to accept the certificate.

8. Accept the default port settings and click Next.

9. The next screen allows you to choose how the Syslog Collector should be addressed by the hosts on the network. You can pick between hostname or IP address. Using the hostname has the advantage that it is easily recognizable by administrators during troubleshooting, but it relies on name resolution. If the Windows server has multiple IP addresses, then you need to pick one that the hosts can route to. Like the Dump Collector service, the Syslog Collector service will only bind to IPv4 addresses.

10. Click Install.

11. Click Finish to complete the installation.

12. If you selected to integrate the installation with a vCenter installation, log into the vSphere Client and check that it is registered. In the Client's home screen, under Administration, click the Network Syslog Collector icon. Figure 4.44 shows a configured Syslog Collector with a couple of hosts already connected to it.

FIGURE 4.44
The Network Syslog Collector registered in vCenter

CONFIGURING ESXI HOSTS TO REDIRECT TO A SYSLOG COLLECTOR

There are several ways to configure your ESXi hosts to redirect their logs to a Syslog Collector. The easiest way to configure a host is directly from the vSphere Web Client:

1. Log into the vSphere Web Client, and from the home screen, select Hosts And Clusters.

2. Select the host you want to configure for the Syslog Collector.

3. In the main object pane, select the Manage tab, followed by the Settings subtab.

4. Under Settings, select Advanced System Settings.

5. In the Filter box in the top-right corner of the Advanced System Settings page, type **syslog.global**. Figure 4.45 shows the global syslog settings.

FIGURE 4.45
Setting host syslog settings in the vSphere Web Client

6. Five options are available. The important setting to redirect logs to a Syslog Collector is `syslog.global.logHost`. You can stipulate the protocol (UDP, TCP, or SSL) and the port number, but a resolvable hostname or IP address will suffice. To change this setting, highlight the row and click the edit icon (a pencil) above.

Another popular way to set the syslog configuration setting is via the host's command line. Two commands are required: one to set the configuration and another to enable (reload). Figure 4.46 shows a typical setup.

FIGURE 4.46

Setting host syslog settings via the host's command line

A third option for setting the host's syslog settings is to capture and propagate them through the Host Profile feature. The easiest way to do this is to configure the first host via its advanced settings in the vSphere Web Client and then use that as a reference host to apply the settings to other hosts.

However the hosts are configured for the Syslog Collector, their firewall needs the appropriate ports opened so they can communicate with the Collector. To do this, as seen in Figure 4.47, take the following action:

1. In the vSphere Web Client, select the host.

2. Select the Manage tab, then the Settings subtab.

3. Under System, select Security Profile from the left-hand menu and click the Edit button in the top right.

4. Scroll down the list of named services until you find the syslog entry and select the check box.

(Optional) You can also restrict the IP address or IP range.

FIGURE 4.47

Opening up the firewall ports to communicate with the Syslog Collector

REVIEWING THE LOGS

You can connect the directory on the Syslog Collector and check that it is receiving logs from the host. The directory is shown in the vSphere Client Syslog Collector's overview, which appeared earlier in Figure 4.44. This overview shows a list of hosts that are connecting. When you browse to the directory, you gain access to the logs themselves (they are not available from the client itself).

VCENTER LOG INSIGHT

At the time of vSphere 5.5's release, VMware introduced a new product called Log Insight. This is a separately licensed tool that competes with other third-party log collection and analysis tools. Log Insight can replace the Syslog Collector tool and provides a much richer searching and cross-host correlation analysis. If you find that the included vCenter Log Collector is not sufficient for your internal support needs, then VCenter Log Insight is a tool you may wish to investigate.

Other vCenter Support Tools

In addition to VUM, the ESXi Dump Collector, and the Syslog Collector; several other vCenter Support Tools are shown in Figure 4.38. Each of these tools have already been discussed in previous chapters as it was pertinent to the deployment of ESXi or vCenter.

Auto Deploy   Auto Deploy is a tool to provision ESXi hosts from a central deployment source. Auto Deploy was covered in Chapter 2, "Planning and Installing VMware ESXi."

Authentication Proxy   The Authentication Proxy allows hosts to join an Active Directory domain without needing to include domain credentials in deployment tools such as Auto Deploy depots or scripted install files. Authentication Proxy was covered in Chapter 2.

Host Agent Check   The Host Agent Check tool is a pre-upgrade solution that checks that hosts connected to vCenter are suitable to be connected to vCenter 5.5. This verification prevents host issues after a vCenter upgrade. Host AgentCheck was covered in Chapter 3.

Now you're ready to start taking advantage of the new networking functionality available in VMware vSphere in Chapter 5.

The Bottom Line

Install VUM and integrate it with the vSphere Client.   vSphere Update Manager (VUM) is installed from the VMware vCenter installation media and requires that vCenter Server has already been installed. Like vCenter Server, VUM requires the use of a backend database server. Finally, you must install a plug-in into the vSphere Client in order to access, manage, and configure VUM.

Master It   You have VUM installed, and you've configured it from the vSphere Client on your laptop. One of the other administrators on your team is saying that she can't access or configure VUM and that there must be something wrong with the installation. What is the most likely cause of the problem?

Determine which ESX/ESXi hosts or VMs need to be patched or upgraded. Baselines are the "measuring sticks" whereby VUM knows whether an ESX/ESXi host or VM instance is up-to-date. VUM compares the ESX/ESXi hosts or VMs to the baselines to determine whether they need to be patched and, if so, what patches need to be applied. VUM also uses baselines to determine which ESX/ESXi hosts need to be upgraded to the latest version or which VMs need to have their VM hardware upgraded. VUM comes with some predefined baselines and allows administrators to create additional baselines specific to their environments. Baselines can be fixed—the contents remain constant—or they can be dynamic, where the contents of the baseline change over time. Baseline groups allow administrators to combine baselines and apply them together.

> **Master It** In addition to ensuring that all your ESX/ESXi hosts have the latest critical and security patches installed, you need to ensure that all your ESX/ESXi hosts have another specific patch installed. This additional patch is noncritical and therefore doesn't get included in the critical patch dynamic baseline. How do you work around this problem?

Use VUM to upgrade VM hardware or VMware Tools. VUM can detect VMs with outdated VM hardware versions and guest OSes that have outdated versions of VMware Tools installed. VUM comes with predefined baselines that enable this functionality. In addition, VUM has the ability to upgrade VM hardware versions and upgrade VMware Tools inside guest OSes to ensure that everything is kept up-to-date. This functionality is especially helpful after upgrading your ESX/ESXi hosts to version 5.5 from a previous version.

> **Master It** You've just finished upgrading your virtual infrastructure to VMware vSphere. What two additional tasks should you complete?

Apply patches to ESX/ESXi hosts. Like other complex software products, VMware ESX and VMware ESXi need software patches applied from time to time. These patches might be bug fixes or security fixes. To keep your ESX/ESXi hosts up-to-date with the latest patches, VUM can apply patches to your hosts on a schedule of your choosing. In addition, to reduce downtime during the patching process or perhaps to simplify the deployment of patches to remote offices, VUM can stage patches to ESX/ESXi hosts before the patches are applied.

> **Master It** How can you avoid VM downtime when applying patches (for example, remediating) to your ESX/ESXi hosts?

Upgrade hosts and coordinate large-scale datacenter upgrades. Upgrading hosts manually, each with dozens of VMs on them, is burdensome and doesn't scale well once you have more than a handful to deal with. Short outage windows, host reboots, and VM downtime mean that coordinating upgrades can involve complex planning and careful execution.

> **Master It** Which VUM functionality can simplify the process of upgrading vSphere across a large number of hosts and their VMs?

Utilize alternative approaches to VUM updates when required. VUM presents the simplest and most efficient method to upgrade your vSphere hosts. However, sometimes VUM may not be available. For example, VUM is reliant on vCenter, so if the host isn't connected to a licensed vCenter, then an alternate method to upgrade the host must be used.

> **Master It** Without using VUM, how else can you upgrade an existing host?

Install logging collectors.   vSphere includes two different logging tools for the ESXi hosts. The ESXi Dump Collector takes kernel dumps from the hosts, and the Syslog Collector can centrally store the host's log files.

Master It   You have just started a new job as the vSphere administrator at a company. The company hasn't previously centralized the hosts' logs and you decide you want to collect them, and so you want to install the vSphere Syslog Collector tool and the ESXi Dump Collector tool as well. How do you install them on the company's vCSA instance?

Configure hosts for centralized logging.   To make use of the ESXi Dump Collector or the Syslog Collector tools, you must configure each host to point to the centralized loggers.

Master It   List the ways you can configure your hosts for centralized logging.

Chapter 5

Creating and Configuring Virtual Networks

Eventually, it all comes back to the network. Having servers running VMware ESXi with VMs stored on a highly redundant Fibre Channel SAN is great, but they are ultimately useless if the VMs cannot communicate across the network. What good is the ability to run 10 production systems on a single host at less cost if those production systems aren't available? Clearly, virtual networking within ESXi is a key area for every vSphere administrator to understand fully.

In this chapter, you will learn to

◆ Identify the components of virtual networking

◆ Create virtual switches and distributed virtual switches

◆ Create and manage NIC teaming, VLANs, and private VLANs

◆ Examine the options for third-party virtual switches in your environment

◆ Configure virtual switch security policies

Putting Together a Virtual Network

Designing and building virtual networks with ESXi and vCenter Server bears some similarities to designing and building physical networks, but there are enough significant differences that an overview of components and terminology is warranted. So, we'll take a moment here to define the various components involved in a virtual network, and then we'll discuss some of the factors that affect the design of a virtual network:

vSphere Standard Switch A software-based switch that resides in the VMkernel and provides traffic management for VMs. Users must manage vSphere Standard Switches independently on each ESXi host. You'll see us use the term *vSwitch* to refer to both a vSphere Standard Switch as well as a virtual switch in general.

vSphere Distributed Switch A software-based switch that resides in the VMkernel and provides traffic management for VMs and the VMkernel. Distributed vSwitches are shared by and managed across entire clusters of ESXi hosts. You might see *vSphere Distributed Switch* abbreviated as *VDS*; we'll use *VDS*, *vSphere Distributed Switch*, or just *distributed switch* in this book.

Port/Port Group   A logical object on a vSwitch that provides specialized services for the VMkernel or VMs. A virtual switch can contain a VMkernel port or a VM port group. On a vSphere Distributed Switch, these are called distributed port groups.

VMkernel Port   A specialized virtual switch port type that is configured with an IP address to allow hypervisor management traffic, vMotion, iSCSI storage access, network attached storage (NAS) or Network File System (NFS) access, and vSphere Fault Tolerance (FT) logging. A VMkernel port is also referred to as a *vmknic*.

NO MORE SERVICE CONSOLE PORTS

Because vSphere 5.5, like vSphere 5.0 and 5.1 before it, does not include VMware ESX with a traditional Linux-based Service Console, pure vSphere 5.*x* environments will not use a Service Console port (or *vswif*). Instead, the functionality of a Service Console port in ESX 4.*x* and earlier is handled by a VMkernel port in vSphere 5.*x*.

VM Port Group   A group of virtual switch ports that share a common configuration and allow VMs to access other VMs or the physical network.

Virtual LAN   A logical LAN configured on a virtual or physical switch that provides efficient traffic segmentation, broadcast control, security, and efficient bandwidth utilization by providing traffic only to the ports configured for that particular virtual LAN (VLAN).

Trunk Port (Trunking)   A port on a physical switch that listens for and knows how to pass traffic for multiple VLANs. It does this by maintaining the 802.1q VLAN tags for traffic moving through the trunk port to the connected device(s). Trunk ports are typically used for switch-to-switch connections to allow VLANs to pass freely between switches. Virtual switches support VLANs, and using VLAN trunks allows the VLANs to pass freely into the virtual switches.

TRUNKING VS. LINK AGGREGATION?

You might, depending on your networking vendor, also see use of the term *trunk* to describe an aggregation of multiple individual links into a single logical link. In this book, we use *trunk* only to describe a connection that passes multiple VLAN tags, and we'll use the term *NIC teaming* or *link aggregation* to refer to the practice of bonding multiple individual links together.

Access Port   A port on a physical switch that passes traffic for only a single VLAN. Unlike a trunk port, which maintains the VLAN identification for traffic moving through the port, an access port strips away the VLAN information for traffic moving through the port.

Network Interface Card Team   The aggregation of physical network interface cards (NICs) to form a single logical communication channel. Different types of NIC teams provide varying levels of traffic load balancing and fault tolerance.

vmxnet Adapter   A virtualized network adapter operating inside a guest operating system (guest OS). The vmxnet adapter is a high-performance, 1 Gbps virtual network adapter that operates only if VMware Tools have been installed. The vmxnet adapter is sometimes referred to as a *paravirtualized* driver. The vmxnet adapter is identified as Flexible in the VM properties.

vlance Adapter   A virtualized network adapter operating inside a guest OS. The vlance adapter is a 10/100 Mbps network adapter that is widely compatible with a range of operating systems and is the default adapter used until the VMware Tools installation is completed.

e1000 Adapter   A virtualized network adapter that emulates the Intel e1000 network adapter. The Intel e1000 is a 1 Gbps network adapter. The e1000 network adapter is the most common in 64-bit VMs.

Now that you have a better understanding of the components involved and the terminology that you'll see in this chapter, we'll discuss how these components work together to form a virtual network in support of VMs and ESXi hosts.

Your answers to the following questions will, in large part, determine the design of your virtual networking:

- Do you have or need a dedicated network for management traffic, such as for the management of physical switches?

- Do you have or need a dedicated network for vMotion traffic?

- Do you have an IP storage network? Is this IP storage network a dedicated network? Are you running iSCSI or NAS/NFS?

- How many NICs are standard in your ESXi host design?

- Do the NICs in your hosts run 1 Gb Ethernet or 10 Gb Ethernet?

- Do you need extremely high levels of fault tolerance for VMs?

- Is the existing physical network composed of VLANs?

- Do you want to extend the use of VLANs into the virtual switches?

As a precursor to setting up a virtual networking architecture, you need to identify and document the physical network components and the security needs of the network. It's also important to understand the architecture of the existing physical network, because that also greatly influences the design of the virtual network. If the physical network can't support the use of VLANs, for example, then the virtual network's design has to account for that limitation.

Throughout this chapter, as we discuss the various components of a virtual network in more detail, we'll also provide guidance on how the various components fit into an overall virtual network design. A successful virtual network combines the physical network, NICs, and vSwitches, as shown in Figure 5.1.

FIGURE 5.1
Successful virtual networking is a blend of virtual and physical network adapters and switches.

Because the virtual network implementation makes VMs accessible, it is essential that the virtual network be configured in a manner that supports reliable and efficient communication around the different network infrastructure components.

Working with vSphere Standard Switches

The networking architecture of ESXi revolves around creating and configuring virtual switches. These virtual switches are either vSphere Standard Switches or vSphere Distributed Switches. First we'll discuss vSphere Standard Switches, hereafter called vSwitches; we'll discuss vSphere Distributed Switches next.

You create and manage vSwitches through the vSphere Web Client or through the vSphere CLI using the esxcli command, but they operate within the VMkernel. Virtual switches provide the connectivity to provide communication as follows:

◆ Between VMs within an ESXi host

◆ Between VMs on different ESXi hosts

♦ Between VMs and physical machines on the network

♦ For VMkernel access to networks for vMotion, iSCSI, NFS, or Fault Tolerance logging (and management on ESXi)

Take a look at Figure 5.2, which shows the vSphere Web Client depicting a vSwitch on an ESXi host.

FIGURE 5.2
Virtual switches alone can't provide connectivity; they need ports or port groups and uplinks.

In this figure, the vSwitch isn't depicted alone; it also requires ports or port groups and uplinks. Without uplinks, a virtual switch can't communicate with the upstream network; without ports or port groups, a vSwitch can't provide connectivity for the VMkernel or the VMs. It is for this reason that most of our discussion about virtual switches centers on ports, port groups, and uplinks.

First, though, let's take a closer look at vSwitches and how they are similar to yet different from physical switches in the network.

Comparing Virtual Switches and Physical Switches

Virtual switches in ESXi are constructed by and operate in the VMkernel. Virtual switches (referred to in the general sense as vSwitches) are not managed switches and do not provide all the advanced features that many new physical switches provide. You cannot, for example, telnet into a vSwitch to modify settings. There is no command-line interface (CLI) for a vSwitch, apart from the vSphere CLI commands such as esxcli. Even so, a vSwitch operates like a physical switch in some ways. Like its physical counterpart, a vSwitch functions at layer 2, maintains MAC address tables, forwards frames to other switch ports based on the MAC address, supports VLAN configurations, can trunk VLANs using IEEE 802.1q VLAN tags, and can establish port channels. Similar to physical switches, vSwitches are configured with a specific number of ports.

Despite these similarities, vSwitches do have some differences from physical switches. A vSwitch does not support the use of dynamic negotiation protocols for establishing 802.1q trunks or port channels, such as Dynamic Trunking Protocol (DTP) or Link Aggregation Control Protocol (LACP). A vSwitch cannot be connected to another vSwitch, thereby eliminating a potential loop configuration. Because there is no possibility of looping, the vSwitches do not run Spanning Tree Protocol (STP). Looping can be a common network problem, so this is a real benefit of vSwitches.

SPANNING TREE PROTOCOL

In physical switches, Spanning Tree Protocol (STP) offers redundancy for paths and prevents loops in the network topology by locking redundant paths in a standby state. Only when a path is no longer available will STP activate the standby path.

It is possible to link vSwitches together using a VM with layer 2 bridging software and multiple virtual NICs, but this is not an accidental configuration and would require some effort to establish.

vSwitches and physical switches have some other differences:

♦   A vSwitch authoritatively knows the MAC addresses of the VMs connected to it, so there is no need to learn MAC addresses from the network.

♦   Traffic received by a vSwitch on one uplink is never forwarded out another uplink. This is yet another reason why vSwitches do not run STP.

♦   A vSwitch does not need to perform Internet Group Management Protocol (IGMP) snooping because it knows the multicast interests of the VMs attached to it.

As you can see from this list of differences, you simply can't use virtual switches in the same way you can use physical switches. You can't use a virtual switch as a transit path between two physical switches, for example, because traffic received on one uplink won't be forwarded out another uplink.

With this basic understanding of how vSwitches work, let's now take a closer look at ports and port groups.

Understanding Ports and Port Groups

As described previously in this chapter, a vSwitch allows several different types of communication, including communication to and from the VMkernel and between VMs. To help distinguish between these different types of communication, ESXi uses ports and port groups. A vSwitch without any ports or port groups is like a physical switch that has no physical ports; there is no way to connect anything to the switch, and it is, therefore, useless.

Port groups differentiate between the types of traffic passing through a vSwitch, and they also operate as a boundary for communication and/or security policy configuration. Figure 5.3 and Figure 5.4 show the two different types of ports and port groups that you can configure on a vSwitch:

♦   VMkernel port

♦   VM port group

FIGURE 5.3
Virtual switches
can contain two
connection types:
VMkernel port and
VM port group.

FIGURE 5.4
You can create vir-
tual switches with
both connection
types on the same
switch.

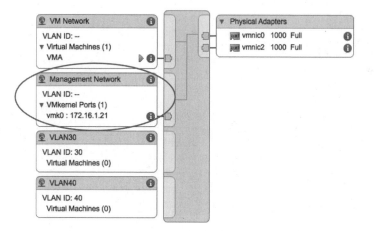

Because a vSwitch cannot be used in any way without at least one port or port group, you'll see that the vSphere Web Client combines the creation of new vSwitches with the creation of new ports or port groups.

As shown in Figure 5.2, though, ports and port groups are only part of the overall solution. The uplinks are the other part of the solution that you need to consider because they provide external network connectivity to the vSwitches.

Understanding Uplinks

Although a vSwitch allows communication between VMs connected to the vSwitch, it cannot communicate with the physical network without uplinks. Just as a physical switch must be connected to other switches to communicate across the network, vSwitches must be connected to the ESXi host's physical NICs as uplinks to communicate with the rest of the network.

Unlike ports and port groups, uplinks aren't required for a vSwitch to function. Physical systems connected to an isolated physical switch with no uplinks to other physical switches in the network can still communicate with each other—just not with any other systems that are not connected to the same isolated switch. Similarly, VMs connected to a vSwitch without any uplinks can communicate with each other but not with VMs on other vSwitches or physical systems.

This sort of configuration is known as an *internal-only* vSwitch. It can be useful to allow VMs to communicate only with each other. VMs that communicate through an internal-only vSwitch do not pass any traffic through a physical adapter on the ESXi host. As shown in Figure 5.5, communication between VMs connected to an internal-only vSwitch takes place entirely in the software and happens at the speed at which the VMkernel can perform the task, whatever that may be.

FIGURE 5.5
VMs communicating through an internal-only vSwitch do not pass any traffic through a physical adapter.

No Uplink, No vMotion

VMs connected to an internal-only vSwitch are not vMotion capable. However, if the VM is disconnected from the internal-only vSwitch, a warning will be provided, but vMotion will succeed if all other requirements have been met. The requirements for vMotion are covered in Chapter 12, "Balancing Resource Utilization."

For VMs to communicate with resources beyond the VMs hosted on the local ESXi host, a vSwitch must be configured to use at least one physical network adapter, or uplink. A vSwitch can be bound to a single network adapter or bound to two or more network adapters.

A vSwitch bound to at least one physical network adapter allows VMs to establish communication with physical servers on the network or with VMs on other ESXi hosts. That's assuming, of course, that the VMs on the other ESXi hosts are connected to a vSwitch that is bound to at least one physical network adapter. Just like a physical network, a virtual network requires connectivity from end to end. Figure 5.6 shows the communication path for VMs connected to a vSwitch bound to a physical network adapter. In the diagram, when vm1 on pod-1-blade-5 needs to communicate with vm2 on pod-1-blade-8, the traffic from the VM passes through vSwitch0 (via a VM port group) to the physical network adapter to which the vSwitch is bound. From the physical network adapter, the traffic will reach the physical switch (PhySw1). The physical switch (PhySw1) passes the traffic to the second physical switch (PhySw2), which will pass the traffic through the physical network adapter associated with the vSwitch on pod-1-blade-8. In the last stage of the communication, the vSwitch will pass the traffic to the destination virtual machine vm2.

FIGURE 5.6

A vSwitch with a single network adapter allows VMs to communicate with physical servers and other VMs on the network.

The vSwitch associated with a physical network adapter provides VMs with the amount of bandwidth the physical adapter is configured to support. All the VMs will share this bandwidth when communicating with physical machines or VMs on other ESXi hosts. In this way, a vSwitch is once again similar to a physical switch. For example, a vSwitch bound to a network adapter with a 1 Gbps maximum speed will provide up to 1 Gbps of bandwidth for the VMs connected to it; similarly, a physical switch with a 1 Gbps uplink to another physical switch provides up to 1 Gbps of bandwidth between the two switches for systems attached to the physical switches.

A vSwitch can also be bound to multiple physical network adapters. In this configuration, the vSwitch is sometimes referred to as a *NIC team*, but in this book we'll use the term *NIC team* or *NIC teaming* to refer specifically to the grouping of network connections, not to refer to a vSwitch with multiple uplinks.

UPLINK LIMITS

Although a single vSwitch can be associated with multiple physical adapters as in a NIC team, a single physical adapter cannot be associated with multiple vSwitches. ESXi hosts can have up to 32 e1000 network adapters, 32 Broadcom TG3 Gigabit Ethernet network ports, or 16 Broadcom BN32 Gigabit Ethernet network ports. ESXi hosts support up to 8 10 Gigabit Ethernet adapters.

Figure 5.7 and Figure 5.8 show a vSwitch bound to multiple physical network adapters. A vSwitch can have a maximum of 32 uplinks. In other words, a single vSwitch can use up to 32 physical network adapters to send and receive traffic from the physical switches. Binding multiple physical NICs to a vSwitch offers the advantage of redundancy and load distribution. In the section "Configuring NIC Teaming," you'll dig deeper into the configuration and workings of this sort of vSwitch configuration.

FIGURE 5.7
A vSwitch using NIC teaming has multiple available adapters for data transfer. NIC teaming offers redundancy and load distribution.

So, we've examined vSwitches, ports and port groups, and uplinks, and you should have a basic understanding of how these pieces begin to fit together to build a virtual network. The next step is to delve deeper into the configuration of the various types of ports and port groups, because they are so essential to virtual networking. We'll start with a discussion on management networking.

Configuring Management Networking

Management traffic is a special type of network traffic that runs across a *VMkernel port*. VMkernel ports provide network access for the VMkernel's TCP/IP stack, which is separate and independent from the network traffic generated by VMs. The ESXi management network, however, is treated a bit differently than "regular" VMkernel traffic in two ways:

◆ First, the ESXi management network is automatically created when you install ESXi. In order for the ESXi host to be reachable across the network, it must have a management network configured and working. So, the ESXi installer automatically sets up an ESXi management network.

◆ Second, the Direct Console User Interface (DCUI)—the user interface that exists when you're working at the physical console of a server running ESXi—provides a mechanism for configuring or reconfiguring the management network but not any other forms of networking on that host.

FIGURE 5.8
Virtual switches using NIC teaming are identified by the multiple physical network adapters assigned to the vSwitch.

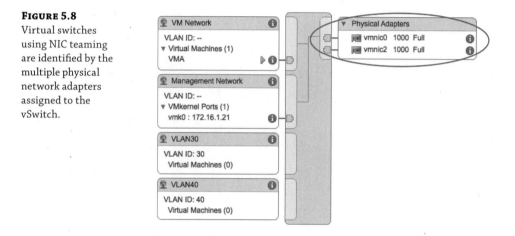

Although the vSphere Web Client offers an option to enable management traffic when configuring networking, as you can see in Figure 5.9, it's unlikely that you'll use this option very often. After all, for you to configure management networking from within the vSphere Web Client, the ESXi host must already have functional management networking in place (vCenter Server communicates with ESXi over the management network). You might use this option if you were creating additional management interfaces. To do this, you would use the procedure described later (in the section "Configuring VMkernel Networking") to create VMkernel ports with the vSphere Web Client, simply enabling Management Traffic in the Enable Services section while creating the VMkernel port.

FIGURE 5.9
The vSphere Client offers a way to enable management networking when configuring networking.

In the event that the ESXi host is unreachable—and therefore cannot be configured using the vSphere Client—you'll need to use the DCUI to configure the management network.

Perform the following steps to configure the ESXi management network using the DCUI:

1. At the server's physical console or using a remote console utility such as the HP iLO, press F2 to enter the System Customization menu.

   If prompted to log in, enter the appropriate credentials.

2. Use the arrow keys to highlight the Configure Management Network option, as shown in Figure 5.10, and press Enter.

FIGURE 5.10
To configure ESXi's equivalent of the Service Console port, use the Configure Management Network option in the System Customization menu.

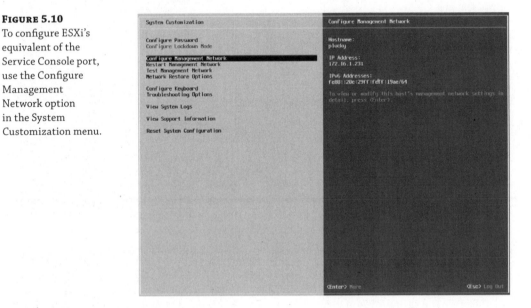

3. From the Configure Management Network menu, select the appropriate option for configuring ESXi management networking, as shown in Figure 5.11.

   You cannot create additional management network interfaces from here; you can only modify the existing management network interface.

4. When finished, follow the screen prompts to exit the management networking configuration.

   If prompted to restart the management networking, select Yes; otherwise, restart the management networking from the System Customization menu, as shown in Figure 5.12.

In looking at Figure 5.10 and Figure 5.12, you'll also see options for testing the management network, which lets you verify that the management network is configured correctly. This is invaluable if you are unsure of the VLAN ID or network adapters that you should use.

We also want to point out the Network Restore Options screen, shown in Figure 5.13. This screen lets you restore the network configuration to defaults, restore a vSphere Standard Switch, or even restore a vSphere Distributed Switch—all very handy options if you are troubleshooting management network connectivity to your ESXi host.

FIGURE 5.11

From the Configure Management Network menu, users can modify assigned network adapters, change the VLAN ID, or alter the IP configuration.

FIGURE 5.12

The Restart Management Network option restarts ESXi's management networking and applies any changes that were made.

FIGURE 5.13
Use the Network
Restore Options
screen to manage
network connectiv-
ity to an ESXi host.

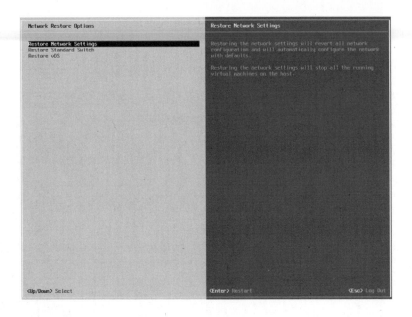

Let's move our discussion of VMkernel networking away from just management traffic and take a closer look at the other types of VMkernel traffic, as well as how to create and configure VMkernel ports.

Configuring VMkernel Networking

VMkernel networking carries management traffic, but it also carries all other forms of traffic that originate with the ESXi host itself (i.e., any traffic that isn't generated by VMs running on that ESXi host). As shown in Figure 5.14 and Figure 5.15, VMkernel ports are used for management, vMotion, iSCSI, NAS/NFS access, and vSphere FT—basically, all types of traffic that are generated by the hypervisor itself. In Chapter 6, "Creating and Configuring Storage Devices." we detail the iSCSI and NAS/NFS configurations; in Chapter 12, we provide details of the vMotion process and how vSphere FT works. These discussions provide insight into the traffic flow between VMkernel and storage devices (iSCSI/NFS) or other ESXi hosts (for vMotion or vSphere FT). At this point, you should be concerned only with configuring VMkernel networking.

A VMkernel port actually comprises two different components: a port group on a vSwitch and a VMkernel network interface, also known as a *vmknic*. Creating a VMkernel port using the vSphere Web Client combines the task of creating the port group and the VMkernel NIC.

Perform the following steps to add a VMkernel port to an existing vSwitch using the vSphere Web Client:

1. If not already connected, open a supported web browser and log in to a vCenter Server instance. For example, if your vCenter Server instance is called "vcenter," then you'll connect to https://vcenter.domain.name:9443/vsphere-client and then log in with appropriate credentials.

2. From the vSphere Web Client home page, select vCenter from the navigation list on the left.

3. From the Inventory Lists area, select Hosts, then click the ESXi host on which you'd like to add the new VMkernel port.

FIGURE 5.14
A VMkernel port is associated with an interface and assigned an IP address for accessing iSCSI or NFS storage devices or for performing vMotion with other ESXi hosts.

FIGURE 5.15
The network labels for VMkernel ports should be as descriptive as possible.

Virtual adapters							
Device	Network Label	Switch	IP Address	TCP/IP Stack	vMotion Traffic	FT Logging	Manageme
vmk0	Management Network	vSwitch0	172.16.1.21	Default	Disabled	Disabled	Enabled
vmk1	vMotion	vSwitch0	172.16.100.21	Default	Enabled	Disabled	Disabled
vmk2	FT	vSwitch0	172.16.200.21	Default	Disabled	Enabled	Disabled
vmk3	VirtualSAN	vSwitch0	172.16.150.21	Default	Disabled	Disabled	Disabled

4. Select the Manage tab, and click the Networking button.

5. Click Virtual Adapters.

6. Click the Add Host Networking icon. This starts the Add Networking wizard.

7. Select VMkernel Network Adapter, and then click Next.

8. Because you're adding a VMkernel port to an existing vSwitch, make sure Select An Existing Standard Switch is selected, then click Browse to select the virtual switch to which the new VMkernel port should be added. Click OK in the Select Switch dialog box, and click Next to continue.

9. Type the name of the port in the Network Label text box.

10. If necessary, specify the VLAN ID for the VMkernel port.

11. Select whether this VMkernel port will be enabled for IPv4, IPv6, or both.

12. Select the TCP/IP stack that this VMkernel port should use. Unless you have already created a custom TCP/IP stack, Default will be the only option listed here. We discuss TCP/IP stacks later in this chapter in the section titled "Configuring TCP/IP Stacks."

13. Select the various functions that will be enabled on this VMkernel port, and then click Next. For a VMkernel port that will be used only for iSCSI or NAS/NFS traffic, all the Enable Services check boxes should be deselected, as shown in Figure 5.16. For a VMkernel port that will act as an additional management interface, only Management Traffic should be selected.

FIGURE 5.16
VMkernel ports can carry IP-based storage traffic, vMotion traffic, Fault Tolerance logging traffic, management traffic, or Virtual SAN traffic.

14. For IPv4 (applicable if you selected IPv4 or IPv4 And IPv6 for IP Settings in the previous step), you may elect to either obtain the configuration automatically (via DHCP) or supply a static configuration. If you opt to use a static configuration, ensure that the IP address is a valid IP address for the network to which the physical NIC is connected.

> **DEFAULT GATEWAY AND DNS SERVERS AREN'T EDITABLE**
>
> Note that the default gateway and DNS server addresses are controlled by the TCP/IP stack configuration and can't be changed here. To change these settings, you'll need to edit the TCP/IP stack settings, as described in the section titled "Configuring TCP/IP Stacks."

15. For IPv6 (applicable if you selected IPv6 or IPv4 And IPv6 for IP Settings earlier), you can choose to obtain configuration automatically via DHCPv6, obtain your configuration automatically via Router Advertisement, and/or assign one or more IPv6 addresses. Use the green plus symbol to add an IPv6 address that is appropriate for the network to which this VMkernel interface will be connected.

16. Click Next to review the configuration summary, and then click Finish.

After you complete these steps, you can use the `esxcli` command—either from an instance of the vSphere Management Assistant or from a system with the vSphere CLI installed—to show the new VMkernel port and the new VMkernel NIC that was created:

```
esxcli --server=<vCenter hostname or IP> --vihost=<ESXi hostname or IP>
--username=<vCenter admin user> network ip interface list
```

DIFFERENT COMMAND-LINE OPTIONS

vSphere 5.5 still provides the `vicfg-*` tools, such as `vicfg-vswitch` and `vicfg-vmknic`. However, most command-line functionality is being collapsed into `esxcli` moving forward, so it's a good idea to try to stick with `esxcli` wherever possible.

To help illustrate the different parts—the VMkernel port and the VMkernel NIC, or vmknic—that are created during this process, let's again walk through the steps for creating a VMkernel port using the vSphere Management Assistant.

Perform the following steps to create a VMkernel port on an existing vSwitch using the command line:

1. Using `PuTTY.exe` (Windows) or a terminal window (Linux or Mac OS X), establish an SSH session to the vSphere Management Assistant.

2. Enter the following command to add a port group named VMkernel to vSwitch0:

```
esxcli --server=<vCenter host name> --vihost=<ESXi host name>
--username=<vCenter administrative user> network vswitch standard
portgroup add --portgroup-name=VMkernel --vswitch-name=vSwitch0
```

3. Use the `esxcli` command to list the port groups on vSwitch0. Note that the port group exists, but nothing has been connected to it (the Active Clients column shows 0).

```
esxcli --server=<vCenter host name> --vihost=<ESXi host name>
--username=<vCenter administrative user> network vswitch standard
portgroup list
```

4. Enter the following command to create the VMkernel port and attach it to the port group created in step 2:

```
esxcli --server=<vCenter host name> --vihost=<ESXi host name>
--username=<vCenter administrative user> network ip interface add
--portgroup-name=VMkernel --interface-name=vmk4
```

5. Use this command to assign an IP address and subnet mask to the VMkernel port created in the previous step:

```
esxcli --server=<vCenter host name> --vihost=<ESXi host name>
--username=<vCenter administrative user> network ip interface ipv4 set
```

```
--interface-name=vmk4 --type=static --ipv4=192.168.1.100
--netmask=255.255.255.0
```

6. Repeat the command from step 3 again, noting now how the Active Clients column has incremented to 1.

This indicates that a vmknic has been connected to a virtual port on the port group. Figure 5.17 shows the output of the esxcli command after completing step 5.

FIGURE 5.17

Using the CLI helps drive home the fact that the port group and the VMkernel port are separate objects.

Aside from the default ports required for the management network, no VMkernel ports are created during the installation of ESXi, so all the nonmanagement VMkernel ports that may be required in your environment will need to be created, either using the vSphere Web Client or via CLI using the vSphere CLI or the vSphere Management Assistant.

In addition to adding VMkernel ports, you might need to edit a VMkernel port, or even remove a VMkernel port. Both of these tasks can be done in the same place you added a VMkernel port: the Networking section of the Manage tab for an ESXi host.

To edit a VMkernel port, select the desired VMkernel port from the list and click the Edit Settings icon (it looks like a pencil). This will bring up the Edit Settings dialog box, where you can change the services for which this port is enabled, change the MTU, and modify the IPv4 and/or IPv6 settings. Of particular interest here is the Analyze Impact section, shown in Figure 5.18, which helps point out dependencies on the VMkernel port in order to prevent unwanted side effects that might result from modifying the VMkernel port's configuration.

To delete a VMkernel port, select the desired VMkernel port from the list and click the Remove Selected Virtual Network Adapter (it looks like a red *X*). In the resulting confirmation dialog box, you'll see the option to analyze the impact (same as with modifying a VMkernel port). Click OK to remove the VMkernel port.

Before we move on to discussing how to configure VM networking, let's look at one more area related to host networking. Next, we'll introduce a feature new to vSphere 5.5: multiple TCP/IP stacks.

FIGURE 5.18
The Analyze Impact
section shows
administrators
dependencies on
VMkernel ports.

Configuring TCP/IP Stacks

Prior to the release of vSphere 5.5, all VMkernel interfaces shared a single instance of a TCP/IP stack. As a result, this means they all shared the same routing table and same DNS configuration. This created some interesting challenges in certain environments; for example, what if you needed a default gateway for your management network but you also needed a default gateway for your NFS traffic? The only workaround was to use a single default gateway and then populate the routing table with static routes. Clearly, this is not a very scalable solution.

With the release of vSphere 5.5, you can now create multiple TCP/IP stacks. Each stack has its own routing table and own DNS configuration.

Let's take a look at how to create TCP/IP stacks. Once we have at least one additional TCP/IP stack created, we will show you how to assign a VMkernel interface to a specific TCP/IP stack.

CREATING A TCP/IP STACK

In this release, creating new TCP/IP stack instances can only be done from the command line using the esxcli command.

To create a new TCP/IP stack, use this command:

```
esxcli --server=<vCenter host name> --vihost=<ESXi host name>
--username=<vCenter administrative user> network ip netstack add
--netstack=<Name of new TCP/IP stack>
```

For example, if you wanted to create a separate TCP/IP stack for your NFS traffic, the command might look something like this:

```
esxcli --server=vcenter.v12nlab.net --vihost=esxi-01.v12nlab.net
--username=root network ip netstack add --netstack=nfsStack
```

You can get a list of all the configured TCP/IP stacks with a very similar `esxcli` command:

```
esxcli --server=<vCenter host name> --vihost=<ESXi host name>
--username=<vCenter administrative user> network ip netstack list
```

Once the new TCP/IP stack is created, you can, if you wish, continue to configure the stack using the `esxcli` command. However, you will probably find it easier to use the vSphere Web Client to do the actual configuration of the new TCP/IP stack, as we describe in the next section.

CONFIGURING TCP/IP STACK SETTINGS

You've actually seen references to the TCP/IP stacks already at least once (when creating a VMkernel interface), but the actual settings for the TCP/IP stacks are found in the same place where you create and configure other host networking settings: in the Networking section of the Manage tab for an ESXi host object, as shown in Figure 5.19.

FIGURE 5.19
TCP/IP stack settings are located with other host networking configuration options.

In Figure 5.19 you can see the new TCP/IP stack, named nfsStack, that we created in previous section. To edit the settings for that stack, you'll simply select it from the list and click the Edit TCP/IP Stack Configuration icon (it looks like a pencil above the list of TCP/IP stacks). That brings up the Edit TCP/IP Stack Configuration dialog box, shown in Figure 5.20.

FIGURE 5.20
Each TCP/IP stack can have its own DNS configuration, routing information, and other advanced settings.

In the Edit TCP/IP Stack Configuration dialog box, make the changes you need to make to the name, DNS configuration, routing, or other advanced settings. Once you're finished, click OK.

One final task regarding TCP/IP stacks remains: assigning interfaces to a TCP/IP stack. Until you actually assign an interface—specifically referring to VMkernel interfaces here—to a TCP/IP stack you've created, the VMkernel interface will use the default system stack and won't be able to use any of the custom settings you've configured.

Assigning Ports to a TCP/IP Stack

Unfortunately, you can assign VMkernel ports to a TCP/IP stack only at the time of creation. In other words, once a VMkernel port has been created, you can't change the TCP/IP stack to which it has been assigned. You must delete the VMkernel port and then re-create it, assigning it to the desired TCP/IP stack. We described how to create and delete VMkernel ports earlier, so we won't go through those tasks again here.

You'll note that it's in step 12 of creating a VMkernel port that you have the option of selecting a specific TCP/IP stack to which to bind this VMkernel port. This is illustrated in Figure 5.21, where you can see the system default stack as well as the custom nfsStack we created earlier listed.

FIGURE 5.21
VMkernel ports can be assigned to a TCP/IP stack only at the time of creation.

One very important thing to note: In this release, using custom TCP/IP stacks isn't supported for use with vMotion, Fault Tolerance logging, management traffic, or Virtual SAN traffic. When you select a custom TCP/IP stack, you'll see that the check boxes to enable these services automatically disable themselves. At this time, you'll only be able to use custom TCP/IP stacks for IP-based storage, like iSCSI and NFS.

It's now time to shift our focus from host networking to VM networking.

Configuring VM Networking

The second type of port group to discuss is the VM port group, which is responsible for all VM networking. The VM port group is quite different from a VMkernel port. With VMkernel networking, there is a one-to-one relationship with an interface: Each VMkernel NIC, or vmknic, requires a matching VMkernel port group on a vSwitch. In addition, these interfaces require IP addresses that are used for management or VMkernel network access.

A VM port group, on the other hand, does not have a one-to-one relationship, and it does not require an IP address. For a moment, forget about vSwitches and consider standard physical switches. When you install or add an unmanaged physical switch into your network environment, that physical switch does not require an IP address: You simply install the switches and plug in the appropriate uplinks that will connect them to the rest of the network.

A vSwitch created with a VM port group is really no different. A vSwitch with a VM port group acts just like an additional unmanaged physical switch. You need only plug in the appropriate uplinks—physical network adapters, in this case—that will connect that vSwitch to the rest of the network. As with an unmanaged physical switch, an IP address does not need to be configured for a VM port group to combine the ports of a vSwitch with those of a physical switch. Figure 5.22 shows the switch-to-switch connection between a vSwitch and a physical switch.

FIGURE 5.22
A vSwitch with a VM port group uses an associated physical network adapter to establish a switch-to-switch connection with a physical switch.

Perform the following steps to create a vSwitch with a VM port group using the vSphere Web Client:

1. Use the vSphere Web Client to establish a connection to a vCenter Server instance.

2. From the vSphere Web Client home page, click vCenter from the Inventories section, then select Hosts from the inventory lists on the left.

3. Select the ESXi host on which you'd like to add a vSwitch, then click Manage, and finally, select the Networking section.

4. Click the Add Host Networking icon (a small globe with a plus sign) to start the Add Networking wizard.

5. Select the Virtual Machine Port Group For A Standard Switch radio button, and click Next.

6. Because you are creating a new vSwitch, select the New Standard Switch radio button. Click Next.

7. Click the green plus icon to add physical network adapters to the new vSwitch you are creating. From the Add Physical Adapters To The Switch dialog box, select the NIC or NICs connected to the switch that can carry the appropriate traffic for your VMs.

8. Click OK when you're done selecting physical network adapters. This returns you to the Create A Standard Switch screen, where you can click Next to continue.

9. Type the name of the VM port group in the Network Label text box.

10. Specify a VLAN ID, if necessary, and click Next.

11. Click Next to review the virtual switch configuration, and then click Finish.

If you are a command-line junkie, you can create a VM port group from the vSphere CLI as well. You can probably guess the commands that are involved from the previous examples, but we'll walk you through the process anyway.

Perform the following steps to create a vSwitch with a VM port group using the command line:

1. Using PuTTY.exe (Windows) or a terminal window (Linux or Mac OS X), establish an SSH session to a running instance of the vSphere Management Assistant.

2. Enter the following command to add a virtual switch named vSwitch1:

```
esxcli --server=<vCenter host name> --vihost=<ESXi host name>
--username=<vCenter administrative user> network vswitch standard add
--vswitch-name=vSwitch1
```

3. Enter the following command to bind the physical NIC vmnic1 to vSwitch1:

```
esxcli --server=<vCenter host name> --vihost=<ESXi host name>
--username=<vCenter administrative user> network vswitch standard
uplink add --vswitch-name=vSwitch1 --uplink-name=vmnic1
```

By binding a physical NIC to the vSwitch, you provide network connectivity to the rest of the network for VMs connected to this vSwitch. Again, remember that you can assign any given physical NIC to only one vSwitch at a time (but a vSwitch may have multiple physical NICs bound at the same time).

4. Enter the following command to create a VM port group named ProductionLAN on vSwitch1:

```
esxcli --server=<vCenter host name> --vihost=<ESXi host name>
--username=<vCenter administrative user> network vswitch standard
portgroup add --vswitch-name=vSwitch1 --portgroup-name=ProductionLAN
```

Of the different connection types—VMkernel ports and VM port groups—vSphere administrators will spend most of their time creating, modifying, managing, and removing VM port groups.

PORTS AND PORT GROUPS ON A VIRTUAL SWITCH

A vSwitch can consist of multiple connection types, or each connection type can be created in its own vSwitch.

Configuring VLANs

Several times so far we've referenced the use of the VLAN ID when configuring a VMkernel port and a VM port group. As defined previously in this chapter, a virtual LAN (VLAN) is a logical LAN that provides efficient segmentation, security, and broadcast control while allowing traffic to share the same physical LAN segments or same physical switches. Figure 5.23 shows a typical VLAN configuration across physical switches.

FIGURE 5.23
Virtual LANs provide secure traffic segmentation without the cost of additional hardware.

VLANs utilize the IEEE 802.1q standard for *tagging*, or marking, traffic as belonging to a particular VLAN. The VLAN tag, also known as the VLAN ID, is a numeric value between 1 and 4094, and it uniquely identifies that VLAN across the network. Physical switches such as the ones depicted in Figure 5.23 must be configured with ports to trunk the VLANs across the switches. These ports are known as *trunk* (or *trunking*) ports. Ports not configured to trunk VLANs are known as *access* ports and can carry traffic only for a single VLAN at a time.

USING VLAN ID 4095

Normally the VLAN ID will range from 1 to 4094. In a vSphere environment, however, a VLAN ID of 4095 is also valid. Using this VLAN ID with ESXi causes the VLAN tagging information to be passed through the vSwitch all the way up to the guest OS. This is called *virtual guest tagging (VGT)* and is useful only for guest OSes that support and understand VLAN tags.

VLANs are an important part of ESXi networking because of the impact they have on the number of vSwitches and uplinks that are required. Consider this configuration:

♦ The management network needs access to the network segment carrying management traffic.

♦ Other VMkernel ports, depending upon their purpose, may need access to an isolated vMotion segment or the network segment carrying iSCSI and NAS/NFS traffic.

♦ VM port groups need access to whatever network segments are applicable for the VMs running on the ESXi hosts.

Without VLANs, this configuration would require three or more separate vSwitches, each bound to a different physical adapter, and each physical adapter would need to be physically connected to the correct network segment, as illustrated in Figure 5.24.

FIGURE 5.24
Supporting multiple networks without VLANs can increase the number of vSwitches, uplinks, and cabling that is required.

Add in an IP-based storage network and a few more VM networks that need to be supported and the number of required vSwitches and uplinks quickly grows. And this doesn't even take uplink redundancy, for example NIC teaming, into account!

VLANs are the answer to this dilemma. Figure 5.25 shows the same network as in Figure 5.24, but with VLANs this time.

While the reduction from Figure 5.24 to Figure 5.25 is only a single vSwitch and a single uplink, you can easily add more VM networks to the configuration in Figure 5.25 by simply adding another port group with another VLAN ID. Blade servers provide an excellent example of when VLANs offer tremendous benefit. Because of the small form factor of the blade casing, blade servers have historically offered limited expansion slots for physical network adapters. VLANs allow these blade servers to support more networks than they would be able to otherwise.

NO VLAN NEEDED

Virtual switches in the VMkernel do not need VLANs if an ESXi host has enough physical network adapters to connect to each of the different network segments. However, VLANs provide added flexibility in adapting to future network changes, so the use of VLANs where possible is recommended.

As shown in Figure 5.25, VLANs are handled by configuring different port groups within a vSwitch. The relationship between VLANs and port groups is not a one-to-one relationship;

a port group can be associated with only one VLAN at a time, but multiple port groups can be associated with a single VLAN. Later in this chapter when we discuss security settings (in the section "Configuring Virtual Switch Security"), you'll see some examples of when you might have multiple port groups associated with a single VLAN.

FIGURE 5.25
VLANs can reduce the number of vSwitches, uplinks, and cabling required.

To make VLANs work properly with a port group, the uplinks for that vSwitch must be connected to a physical switch port configured as a trunk port. A trunk port understands how to pass traffic from multiple VLANs simultaneously while also preserving the VLAN IDs on the traffic. Figure 5.26 shows a snippet of configuration from a Cisco Catalyst 3560G switch for a couple of ports configured as trunk ports.

FIGURE 5.26
The physical switch ports must be configured as trunk ports in order to pass the VLAN information to the ESXi hosts for the port groups to use.

```
!
interface GigabitEthernet0/6
 switchport trunk encapsulation dot1q
 switchport trunk native vlan 999
 switchport mode trunk
 spanning-tree portfast trunk
!
interface GigabitEthernet0/7
 switchport trunk encapsulation dot1q
 switchport trunk native vlan 999
 switchport mode trunk
 spanning-tree portfast trunk
!
```

The configuration for switches from other manufacturers will vary, of course, so be sure to check with your particular switch manufacturer for specific details on how to configure a trunk port.

THE NATIVE VLAN

In Figure 5.26, you might notice the `switchport trunk native vlan 999` command. The default native VLAN (also known as the untagged VLAN) on most switches is VLAN ID 1. If you need to pass traffic on VLAN 1 to the ESXi hosts, you should designate another VLAN as the native VLAN using this command (or its equivalent). We recommend creating a dummy VLAN, like 999, and setting that as the native VLAN. This ensures that all VLANs will be tagged with the VLAN ID as they pass into the ESXi hosts. Keep in mind this might affect behaviors like PXE booting, which generally requires untagged traffic.

When the physical switch ports are correctly configured as trunk ports, the physical switch passes the VLAN tags up to the ESXi server, where the vSwitch tries to direct the traffic to a port group with that VLAN ID assigned. If there is no port group configured with that VLAN ID, the traffic is discarded.

Perform the following steps to configure a VM port group using VLAN ID 30:

1. Use the vSphere Web Client to establish a connection to a vCenter Server instance.

2. Navigate to the ESXi host to which you want to add the VM port group, click the Manage tab, and then select Networking.

3. Make sure Virtual Switches is selected on the left side, then select the vSwitch where the new port group should be created.

4. Click the Add Host Networking icon (looks like a globe with a plus sign in the corner) to start the Add Networking wizard.

5. Select the Virtual Machine Port Group For A Standard Switch radio button, then click Next.

6. Make sure the Select An Existing Standard Switch radio button is selected and, if necessary, use the Browse button to choose which virtual switch will host the new VM port group. Click Next.

7. Type the name of the VM port group in the Network Label text box.

   Embedding the VLAN ID and a brief description into the name of the port group is strongly recommended, so typing something like **VLANXXX-NetworkDescription** would be appropriate, where *XXX* represents the VLAN ID.

8. Type **30** in the VLAN ID (Optional) text box, as shown in Figure 5.27.

FIGURE 5.27
You must specify the correct VLAN ID in order for a port group to receive traffic intended for a particular VLAN.

You will want to substitute a value that is correct for your network here.

9. Click Next to review the vSwitch configuration, and then click Finish.

As you've probably gathered by now, you can also use the `esxcli` command from the vSphere CLI to create or modify the VLAN settings for ports or port groups. We won't go through the steps here because the commands are extremely similar to what we've shown you already.

Although VLANs reduce the costs of constructing multiple logical subnets, keep in mind that they do not address traffic constraints. Although VLANs logically separate network segments, all the traffic still runs on the same physical network underneath. For bandwidth-intensive network operations, the disadvantage of the shared physical network might outweigh the scalability and cost savings of a VLAN.

CONTROLLING THE VLANS PASSED ACROSS A VLAN TRUNK

You might see the `switchport trunk allowed vlan` command in some Cisco switch configurations as well. This command allows you to control what VLANs are passed across the VLAN trunk to the device at the other end of the link—in this case, an ESXi host. You will need to ensure that all the VLANs that are defined on the vSwitches are also included in the `switchport trunk allowed vlan` command or those VLANs not included in the command won't work.

Configuring NIC Teaming

We know that in order for a vSwitch and its associated ports or port groups to communicate with other ESXi hosts or with physical systems, the vSwitch must have at least one uplink. An *uplink* is a physical network adapter that is bound to the vSwitch and connected to a physical network switch. With the uplink connected to the physical network, there is connectivity for the VMkernel and the VMs connected to that vSwitch. But what happens when that physical network adapter fails, when the cable connecting that uplink to the physical network fails, or the upstream physical switch to which that uplink is connected fails? With a single uplink, network connectivity to the entire vSwitch and all of its ports or port groups is lost. This is where NIC teaming comes in.

NIC teaming involves connecting multiple physical network adapters to a single vSwitch. NIC teaming provides redundancy and load balancing of network communications to the VMkernel and VMs.

Figure 5.28 illustrates NIC teaming conceptually. Both of the vSwitches have two uplinks, and each of the uplinks connects to a different physical switch. Note that NIC teaming supports all the different connection types, so it can be used with ESXi management networking, VMkernel networking, and networking for VMs.

FIGURE 5.28
Virtual switches with multiple uplinks offer redundancy and load balancing.

Figure 5.29 shows what NIC teaming looks like from within the vSphere Web Client. In this example, the vSwitch is configured with an association to multiple physical network adapters (uplinks). As mentioned previously, the ESXi host can have a maximum of 32 uplinks; these uplinks can be spread across multiple vSwitches or all tossed into a NIC team on one vSwitch. Remember that you can connect a physical NIC to only one vSwitch at a time.

FIGURE 5.29
The vSphere Web
Client shows when
multiple physical
network adapters
are associated to a
vSwitch using NIC
teaming.

Building a functional NIC team requires that all uplinks be connected to physical switches in the same broadcast domain. If VLANs are used, then all the switches should be configured for VLAN trunking, and the appropriate subset of VLANs must be allowed across the VLAN trunk. In a Cisco switch, this is typically controlled with the `switchport trunk allowed vlan` statement.

In Figure 5.30, the NIC team for vSwitch0 will work, because both of the physical switches share VLAN 100 and are therefore in the same broadcast domain. The NIC team for vSwitch1, however, will not work because the physical network adapters do not share a common broadcast domain.

FIGURE 5.30
All the physical
network adapters
in a NIC team must
belong to the same
layer 2 broadcast
domain.

CONSTRUCTING NIC TEAMS

NIC teams should be built on physical network adapters located on separate bus architectures. For example, if an ESXi host contains two onboard network adapters and a PCI Express–based quad-port network adapter, a NIC team should be constructed using one onboard network adapter and one network adapter on the PCI bus. This design eliminates a single point of failure.

Perform the following steps to create a NIC team with an existing vSwitch using the vSphere Web Client:

1. Use the vSphere Web Client to establish a connection to a vCenter Server instance.

2. Navigate to the Networking section of the Manage tab for the ESXi host where you want to create the NIC team. We prefer to use the inventory lists rather than the hierarchy tree, but either method is fine.

3. Make sure Virtual Switches is selected on the left, then select the virtual switch that will be assigned a NIC team and click the Manage The Physical Adapters Connected To The Selected Virtual Switch icon (it looks like a NIC with a wrench).

4. In the Manage Physical Network Adapters dialog box, click the green Add Adapters icon.

5. From the Add Physical Adapters To the Switch dialog box, select the appropriate adapter (or adapters) from the list, as shown in Figure 5.31.

FIGURE 5.31
Create a NIC team by adding network adapters that belong to the same layer 2 broadcast domain as the original adapter.

PUTTING NEW ADAPTERS INTO A DIFFERENT FAILOVER GROUP

The Add Physical Adapters To The Switch dialog box shown in Figure 5.31 allows you to add adapters not only to the list of active adapters but also to the list of standby or unused adapters. Simply change the desired group using the Failover Order Group drop-down list.

6. Click OK to return to the Manage Physical Network Adapters dialog box.

7. Click OK to complete the process and return to the Networking section of the Manage tab for the selected ESXi host. Note that it might take a moment or two for the display to update with the new physical adapter.

After a NIC team is established for a vSwitch, ESXi can then perform load balancing for that vSwitch. The load-balancing feature of NIC teaming does not function like the load-balancing feature of advanced routing protocols. Load balancing across a NIC team is not a product of identifying the amount of traffic transmitted through a network adapter and shifting traffic to equalize data flow through all available adapters. The load-balancing algorithm for NIC teams in a vSwitch is a balance of the number of connections—not the amount of traffic. NIC teams on a vSwitch can be configured with one of the following four load-balancing policies:

◆ vSwitch port-based load balancing (default)

◆ Source MAC-based load balancing

◆ IP hash-based load balancing

◆ Explicit failover order

The last option, explicit failover order, isn't really a "load-balancing" policy; instead, it uses the administrator-assigned failover order whereby the highest order uplink from the list of active adapters that passes failover detection criteria is used. More information on the failover order is provided in the section "Configuring Failover Detection and Failover Policy." Also, note that the list we've supplied here applies only to vSphere Standard Switches; vSphere Distributed Switches, which we cover later in this chapter in the section "Working with vSphere Distributed Switches," have additional options for load balancing and failover.

OUTBOUND LOAD BALANCING

The load-balancing feature of NIC teams on a vSwitch applies only to the outbound traffic.

REVIEWING VIRTUAL SWITCH PORT-BASED LOAD BALANCING

The vSwitch port-based load-balancing policy that is used by default uses an algorithm that ties (or pins) each virtual switch port to a specific uplink associated with the vSwitch. The algorithm attempts to maintain an equal number of port-to-uplink assignments across all uplinks to achieve load balancing. As shown in Figure 5.32, this policy setting ensures that traffic from a specific virtual network adapter connected to a virtual switch port will consistently use the same physical network adapter. In the event that one of the uplinks fails, the traffic from the failed uplink will fail over to another physical network adapter.

FIGURE 5.32

The vSwitch port-
based load-
balancing policy
assigns each vir-
tual switch port to
a specific uplink.
Failover to another
uplink occurs when
one of the physical
network adapters
experiences failure.

You can see how this policy does not provide dynamic load balancing but does provide redundancy. Because the port for a VM does not change, each VM is tied to a physical network adapter until failover occurs regardless of the amount of network traffic. Looking at Figure 5.32, imagine that the Linux VM and the Windows VM on the far left are the two most network-intensive VMs. In this case, the vSwitch port-based policy has assigned both ports for these VMs to the same physical network adapter. In this case, one physical network adapter could be much more heavily utilized than other network adapters in the NIC team.

The physical switch passing the traffic learns the port association and therefore sends replies back through the same physical network adapter from which the request initiated. The vSwitch port-based policy is best used when you have more virtual network adapters than physical network adapters. When there are fewer virtual network adapters, then some physical adapters will not be used. For example, if five VMs are connected to a vSwitch with six uplinks, only five vSwitch ports will be assigned to exactly five uplinks, leaving one uplink with no traffic to process.

REVIEWING SOURCE MAC-BASED LOAD BALANCING

The second load-balancing policy available for a NIC team is the source MAC-based policy, shown in Figure 5.33. This policy is susceptible to the same pitfalls as the vSwitch port-based policy simply because the static nature of the source MAC address is the same as the static nature of a vSwitch port assignment. The source MAC-based policy is also best used when you have more virtual network adapters than physical network adapters. In addition, VMs still cannot use multiple physical adapters unless configured with multiple virtual network adapters. Multiple virtual network adapters inside the guest OS of a VM will provide multiple source MAC addresses and allow multiple physical network adapters.

FIGURE 5.33
The source MAC-based load-balancing policy, as the name suggests, ties a virtual network adapter to a physical network adapter based on the MAC address.

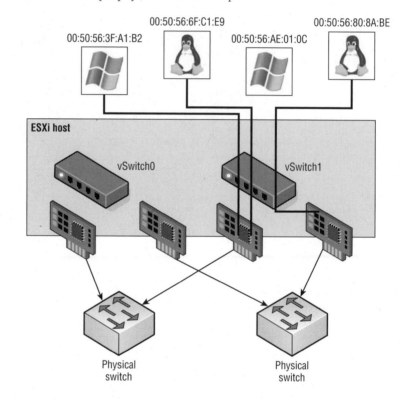

VIRTUAL SWITCH TO PHYSICAL SWITCH

To eliminate a single point of failure, you can connect the physical network adapters in NIC teams set to use the vSwitch port-based or source MAC-based load-balancing policies to different physical switches; however, the physical switches must belong to the same layer 2 broadcast domain. Link aggregation using 802.3ad teaming is not supported with either of these load-balancing policies.

REVIEWING IP HASH-BASED LOAD BALANCING

The third load-balancing policy available for NIC teams is the IP hash-based policy, also called the *out-IP* policy. This policy, shown in Figure 5.34, addresses the limitation of the other two policies. The IP hash-based policy uses the source and destination IP addresses to calculate a hash.

The hash determines the physical network adapter to use for communication. Different combinations of source and destination IP addresses will, quite naturally, produce different hashes. Based on the hash, then, this algorithm could allow a single VM to communicate over different physical network adapters when communicating with different destinations, assuming that the calculated hashes select a different physical NIC.

FIGURE 5.34

The IP hash-based policy is a more scalable load-balancing policy that allows VMs to use more than one physical network adapter when communicating with multiple destination hosts.

Unless the physical hardware supports it, a vSwitch with the NIC teaming load-balancing policy set to use the IP-based hash must have all physical network adapters connected to the same physical switch. Some newer switches support link aggregation across physical switches, but otherwise all the physical network adapters will need to connect to the same switch. In addition, the switch must be configured for link aggregation. ESXi configured to use a vSphere Standard Switch supports standard 802.3ad teaming in static (manual) mode—sometimes referred to as EtherChannel in Cisco networking environments—but does not support the Link Aggregation Control Protocol (LACP) or Port Aggregation Protocol (PAgP) commonly found on switch devices. Link aggregation will increase overall aggregate throughput by potentially combining the bandwidth of multiple physical network adapters for use by a single virtual network adapter of a VM.

Another consideration to point out when using the IP hash-based load-balancing policy is that all physical NICs must be set to active instead of some configured as active and some as passive. This is because of the way IP hash-based load balancing works between the virtual switch and the physical switch.

Figure 5.35 shows a snippet of the configuration of a Cisco switch configured for link aggregation. Keep in mind that other switch manufacturers will have their own ways of configuring link aggregation, so refer to your specific vendor's documentation.

FIGURE 5.35
The physical switches must be configured to support the IP hash-based load-balancing policy.

```
!
interface Port-channel2
 description Link aggregate for ESX server
 switchport trunk encapsulation dot1q
 switchport trunk native vlan 999
 switchport mode trunk
!
interface GigabitEthernet0/1
 switchport trunk encapsulation dot1q
 switchport trunk native vlan 999
 switchport mode trunk
 channel-group 2 mode on
 spanning-tree portfast trunk
!
```

Perform the following steps to alter the NIC teaming load-balancing policy of a vSwitch:

1. Use the vSphere Web Client to establish a connection to a vCenter Server instance.

2. Using your method of choice, navigate to the specific ESXi host that has the vSwitch whose NIC teaming configuration you wish to modify.

3. With an ESXi host selected, go to the Manage tab, select Networking, and then make sure that Virtual Switches is highlighted.

4. Select the name of the virtual switch from the list of virtual switches, and then click the Edit icon (it looks like a pencil).

5. In the Edit Settings dialog box, select Teaming And Failover, and then select the desired load-balancing strategy from the Load Balancing drop-down list, as shown in Figure 5.36.

6. Click OK to save the changes.

Now that we've explained the load-balancing policies—and before we explain explicit failover order—let's take a deeper look at the failover and failback of uplinks in a NIC team. There are two parts to consider: failover detection and failover policy. We'll cover both of these in the next section.

FIGURE 5.36
Select the load-
balancing policy
for a vSwitch in
the Teaming And
Failover section.

CONFIGURING FAILOVER DETECTION AND FAILOVER POLICY

Failover detection with NIC teaming can be configured to use either a link status method or a beacon-probing method.

The link status failover-detection method works just as the name suggests. The link status of the physical network adapter identifies the failure of an uplink. In this case, failure is identified for events like removed cables or power failures on a physical switch. The downside to the setting for link status failover-detection is its inability to identify misconfigurations or pulled cables that connect the switch to other networking devices (for example, a cable connecting one switch to an upstream switch.)

OTHER WAYS OF DETECTING UPSTREAM FAILURES

Some network switch manufacturers have also added features into their network switches that assist in detecting upstream network failures. In the Cisco product line, for example, there is a feature known as *link state tracking* that enables the switch to detect when an upstream port has gone down and react accordingly. This feature can reduce or even eliminate the need for beacon probing.

The beacon-probing failover-detection setting, which includes link status as well, sends Ethernet broadcast frames across all physical network adapters in the NIC team. These broadcast frames allow the vSwitch to detect upstream network connection failures and will force failover when Spanning Tree Protocol blocks ports, when ports are configured with the wrong VLAN, or when a switch-to-switch connection has failed. When a beacon is not returned on a physical network adapter, the vSwitch triggers the failover notice and reroutes the traffic from the failed network adapter through another available network adapter based on the failover policy.

Consider a vSwitch with a NIC team consisting of three physical network adapters, where each adapter is connected to a different physical switch and each physical switch is connected to a single physical switch, which is then connected to an upstream switch, as shown in Figure 5.37. When the NIC team is set to the beacon-probing failover-detection method, a beacon will be sent out over all three uplinks.

FIGURE 5.37

The beacon-probing failover-detection policy sends beacons out across the physical network adapters of a NIC team to identify upstream network failures or switch misconfigurations.

After a failure is detected, either via link status or beacon probing, a failover will occur. Traffic from any VMs or VMkernel ports is rerouted to another member of the NIC team. Exactly which member that might be, though, depends primarily on the configured failover order.

Figure 5.38 shows the failover order configuration for a vSwitch with two adapters in a NIC team. In this configuration, both adapters are configured as active adapters, and either adapter or both adapters may be used at any given time to handle traffic for this vSwitch and all its associated ports or port groups.

Now look at Figure 5.39. This figure shows a vSwitch with three physical network adapters in a NIC team. In this configuration, one of the adapters is configured as a standby adapter. Any adapters listed as standby adapters will not be used until a failure occurs on one of the active adapters, at which time the standby adapters activate in the order listed.

It should go without saying, but adapters that are listed in the Unused Adapters section will not be used in the event of a failure.

Now take a quick look back at Figure 5.36. You'll see an option there labeled Use Explicit Failover Order. This is the explicit failover order policy that we mentioned toward the beginning of the section "Configuring NIC Teaming." If you select that option instead of one of the other load-balancing options, then traffic will move to the next available uplink in the list of active adapters. If no active adapters are available, then traffic will move down the list to the standby adapters. Just as the name of the option implies, ESXi will use the order of the adapters in the failover order to determine how traffic will be placed on the physical network adapters. Because this option does not perform any sort of load balancing whatsoever, it's generally not recommended and one of the other options is used instead.

FIGURE 5.38
The failover order helps determine how adapters in a NIC team are used when a failover occurs.

FIGURE 5.39
Standby adapters automatically activate when an active adapter fails.

The Failback option controls how ESXi will handle a failed network adapter when it recovers from failure. The default setting, Yes, as shown in Figure 5.38 and Figure 5.39, indicates that the adapter will be returned to active duty immediately upon recovery, and it will replace any standby adapter that may have taken its place during the failure. Setting Failback to No means that the recovered adapter remains inactive until another adapter fails, triggering the replacement of the newly failed adapter.

USING FAILBACK WITH VMKERNEL PORTS AND IP-BASED STORAGE

We recommend setting Failback to No for VMkernel ports you've configured for IP-based storage. Otherwise, in the event of a "port-flapping" issue—a situation in which a link may repeatedly go up and down quickly—performance is negatively impacted. Setting Failback to No in this case protects performance in the event of port flapping.

Perform the following steps to configure the Failover Order policy for a NIC team:

1. Use the vSphere Web Client to establish a connection to a vCenter Server instance.

2. Navigate to the ESXi host that has the vSwitch for which you'd like to change the failover order. With an ESXi host selected, select the Manage tab, then click Networking.

3. With Virtual Switches highlighted on the left, select the virtual switch you want to edit, then click the Edit Settings icon.

4. Select Teaming And Failover.

5. Use the Move Up and Move Down buttons to adjust the order of the network adapters and their location within the Active Adapters, Standby Adapters, and Unused Adapters lists, as shown in Figure 5.40.

FIGURE 5.40
Failover order for a NIC team is determined by the order of network adapters as listed in the Active Adapters, Standby Adapters, and Unused Adapters lists.

6. Click OK to save the changes.

When a failover event occurs on a vSwitch with a NIC team, the vSwitch is obviously aware of the event. The physical switch that the vSwitch is connected to, however, will not know immediately. As you can see in Figure 5.40, a vSwitch includes a Notify Switches configuration setting, which, when set to Yes, will allow the physical switch to immediately learn of any of the following changes:

◆ A VM is powered on (or any other time a client registers itself with the vSwitch).

◆ A vMotion occurs.

◆ A MAC address is changed.

◆ A NIC team failover or failback has occurred.

TURNING OFF NOTIFY SWITCHES

The Notify Switches option should be set to No when the port group has VMs using Microsoft Network Load Balancing (NLB) in Unicast mode.

In any of these events, the physical switch is notified of the change using the Reverse Address Resolution Protocol (RARP). RARP updates the lookup tables on the physical switches and offers the shortest latency when a failover event occurs.

Although the VMkernel works proactively to keep traffic flowing from the virtual networking components to the physical networking components, VMware recommends taking the following actions to minimize networking delays:

◆ Disable Port Aggregation Protocol (PAgP) and Link Aggregation Control Protocol (LACP) on the physical switches.

◆ Disable Dynamic Trunking Protocol (DTP) or trunk negotiation.

◆ Disable Spanning Tree Protocol (STP).

VIRTUAL SWITCHES WITH CISCO SWITCHES

VMware recommends configuring Cisco devices to use PortFast mode for access ports or PortFast trunk mode for trunk ports.

Using and Configuring Traffic Shaping

By default, all virtual network adapters connected to a vSwitch have access to the full amount of bandwidth on the physical network adapter with which the vSwitch is associated. In other words, if a vSwitch is assigned a 1 Gbps network adapter, then each VM configured to use the vSwitch has access to 1 Gbps of bandwidth. Naturally, if contention becomes a bottleneck hindering VM performance, NIC teaming will help. However, as a complement to NIC teaming, you can also enable and configure traffic shaping. Traffic shaping establishes hard-coded limits for peak bandwidth, average bandwidth, and burst size to reduce a VM's outbound bandwidth capability.

As shown in Figure 5.41, the Peak Bandwidth value and the Average Bandwidth value are specified in kilobits per second, and the Burst Size value is configured in units of kilobytes. The value entered for Average Bandwidth dictates the data transfer per second across the virtual vSwitch. The Peak Bandwidth value identifies the maximum amount of bandwidth a vSwitch can pass without dropping packets. Finally, the Burst Size value defines the maximum amount of data included in a burst. The burst size is a calculation of bandwidth multiplied by time. During periods of high utilization, if a burst exceeds the configured value, packets are dropped in favor of other traffic; however, if the queue for network traffic processing is not full, the packets are retained for transmission at a later time.

FIGURE 5.41
Traffic shaping
reduces the out-
bound bandwidth
available to a port
group.

TRAFFIC SHAPING AS A LAST RESORT

Use the traffic-shaping feature sparingly. Traffic shaping should be reserved for situations where VMs are competing for bandwidth and the opportunity to add physical network adapters isn't available because you don't have enough expansion slots on the physical chassis. With the low cost of network adapters, it is more worthwhile to spend time building vSwitch devices with NIC teams as opposed to cutting the bandwidth available to a set of VMs.

Perform the following steps to configure traffic shaping:

1. Use the vSphere Web Client to establish a connection to a vCenter Server instance.

2. Navigate to the ESXi host on which you'd like to configure traffic shaping. With an ESXi host selected, go to the Networking section of the Manage tab.

3. Make sure Virtual Switches is selected, click the virtual switch on which traffic shaping should be enabled, and then click the Edit Settings icon.

4. Select Traffic Shaping.

5. Select the Enabled option from the Status drop-down list.

6. Adjust the Average Bandwidth value to the desired number of kilobits per second.

7. Adjust the Peak Bandwidth value to the desired number of kilobits per second.

8. Adjust the Burst Size value to the desired number of kilobytes.

Keep in mind that traffic shaping on a vSphere Standard Switch applies only to outbound traffic.

Bringing It All Together

By now you've seen how all the various components of ESXi virtual networking interact with each other—vSwitches, ports and port groups, uplinks and NIC teams, and VLANs. But how do you assemble all these pieces into a usable whole?

The number and the configuration of the vSwitches and port groups depend on several factors, including the number of network adapters in the ESXi host, the number of IP subnets, the existence of VLANs, and the number of physical networks. With respect to the configuration of the vSwitches and VM port groups, no single correct configuration will satisfy every scenario. However, the greater the number of physical network adapters in an ESXi host, the more flexibility you will have in your virtual networking architecture.

Later in the chapter we'll discuss some advanced design factors, but for now let's stick with some basic design considerations. If the vSwitches created in the VMkernel will not be configured with multiple port groups or VLANs, you will be required to create a separate vSwitch for every IP subnet or physical network to which you need to connect. This was illustrated previously in Figure 5.24 in our discussion about VLANs. To really understand this concept, let's look at two more examples.

Figure 5.42 shows a scenario in which there are five IP subnets that your virtual infrastructure components need to reach. The VMs in the production environment must reach the production LAN, the VMs in the test environment must reach the test LAN, the VMkernel needs to access the IP storage and vMotion LANs, and finally, the ESXi host must have access to the management LAN. In this scenario, without the use of VLANs and port groups, the ESXi host must have five different vSwitches and five different physical network adapters. (Of course, this doesn't account for redundancy or NIC teaming for the vSwitches.)

FIGURE 5.42
Without the use of port groups and VLANs in the vSwitches, each IP subnet will require a separate vSwitch with the appropriate connection type.

Real World Scenario

WHY DESIGN IT THAT WAY?

During the virtual network design process we are often asked questions such as why virtual switches should not be created with the largest number of ports to leave room to grow or why multiple vSwitches should be used instead of a single vSwitch (or vice versa). Some of these questions are easy to answer; the answers to others are a matter of experience and, to be honest, personal preference.

Consider the question about why vSwitches should not be created with the largest number of ports. As you'll see in Table 5.1, the maximum number of virtual network switch ports per host is 4096. This means that if virtual switches are created with 1024 ports, only 4 virtual switches can be created. Calculate 1024 x 4, and you'll arrive at the per-host maximum of 4096 ports. (Keep in mind that virtual switches actually have 8 reserved ports, so a 1016-port switch actually has 1024 ports.)

Other questions aren't necessarily so clear cut. We have found that using multiple vSwitches can make it easier to shift certain networks to dedicated physical networks; for example, if a customer wants to move their management network to a dedicated physical network for greater security, this is more easily accomplished when using multiple vSwitches instead of a single vSwitch. The same can be said for using VLANs.

In the end, though, many areas of virtual networking design are simply areas of personal preference and not technical necessity. Learning to determine which areas are which will go a long way to helping you understand your virtualized networking environment.

Figure 5.43 shows the same configuration, but this time using VLANs for the Management, vMotion, Production, and Test/Dev networks. The IP storage network is still a physically separate network (a common configuration in many environments).

The configuration in Figure 5.43 still uses five network adapters, but this time you're able to provide NIC teaming for all the networks except for the IP storage network.

If the IP storage network had been configured as a VLAN, the number of vSwitches and uplinks could have been even further reduced. Figure 5.44 shows a possible configuration that would support this sort of scenario.

FIGURE 5.43
The use of the physically separate IP storage network limits the reduction in the number of vSwitches and uplinks.

FIGURE 5.44

With the use of port groups and VLANs in the vSwitches, even fewer vSwitches and uplinks are required.

This time, you're able to provide NIC teaming to all the traffic types involved—Management, vMotion, IP storage, and VM traffic—using only a single vSwitch with multiple uplinks.

Clearly, there is a tremendous amount of flexibility in how vSwitches, uplinks, and port groups are assembled to create a virtual network capable of supporting your infrastructure. Even given all this flexibility, though, there are limits. Table 5.1 lists some of the limits of ESXi networking.

VIRTUAL SWITCH CONFIGURATIONS: DON'T GO TOO BIG OR TOO SMALL

Although you can create a vSwitch with a maximum of 4088 ports (really 4096), it is not recommended if you anticipate growth. Because ESXi hosts cannot have more than 4096 ports, if you create a vSwitch with 4088 ports, then you are limited to a single vSwitch on that host. With only a single vSwitch, you may not be able to connect to all the networks that you need. In the event you do run out of ports on an ESXi host and need to create a new vSwitch, you can reduce the number of ports on an existing vSwitch. That change requires a reboot to take effect, but vMotion allows you to move the VMs to a different host to prevent VM downtime.

You also want to be sure that you account for scenarios such as a host failure, when VMs will be restarted on other hosts using vSphere HA (described in more detail in Chapter 7, "Ensuring High Availability and Business Continuity"). In this case, if you make your vSwitch too small (for example, not enough ports), then you could run into an issue there also.

Our key takeaway: Virtual switch sizing is the factor of multiple variables that you need to consider, so plan carefully! We recommend creating virtual switches with enough ports to cover existing needs, projected growth, and failover capacity.

TABLE 5.1: Configuration maximums for ESXi networking components (vSphere Standard Switches)

CONFIGURATION ITEM	MAXIMUM
Ports per vSwitch	4088
Maximum ports per host (vSS/vDS)	4096
Port groups per vSwitch	512
Uplinks per vSwitch	32
Maximum active ports per host (vSS/vDS)	1016

With all the flexibility provided by the different virtual networking components, you can be assured that whatever the physical network configuration might hold in store, there are several ways to integrate the virtual networking. What you configure today may change as the infrastructure changes or as the hardware changes. ESXi provides enough tools and options to ensure a successful communication scheme between the virtual and physical networks.

Working with vSphere Distributed Switches

So far our discussion has focused solely on vSphere Standard Switches (just vSwitches). Starting with vSphere 4.0 and continuing with vSphere 5.0 and the current release, there is another option: vSphere Distributed Switches.

Whereas vSwitches are managed per host, a vSphere Distributed Switch functions as a single virtual switch across all the associated ESXi hosts. There are a number of similarities between a vSphere Distributed Switch and a Standard vSwitch:

◆ A vSphere Distributed Switch provides connectivity for VMs and VMkernel interfaces.

◆ A vSphere Distributed Switch leverages physical network adapters as uplinks to provide connectivity to the external physical network.

◆ A vSphere Distributed Switch can leverage VLANs for logical network segmentation.

Of course, there are differences as well, but the biggest of these is that a vSphere Distributed Switch spans multiple hosts in a cluster instead of each host having its own set of independent vSwitches and port groups. This greatly reduces complexity in clustered ESXi environments and simplifies the addition of new servers to an ESXi cluster.

VMware's official abbreviation for a vSphere Distributed Switch is VDS. In this chapter, we'll use the full name (vSphere Distributed Switch), VDS, or sometimes just distributed switch to refer to this feature.

Creating a vSphere Distributed Switch

The process of creating and configuring a distributed switch is twofold. First, you create the distributed switch and then you add ESXi hosts to it. To help simplify the process, vSphere automatically includes the option to add an ESXi host to the distributed switch during the process of creating it.

Perform the following steps to create a new vSphere Distributed Switch:

1. Launch the vSphere Web Client and connect to a vCenter Server instance.

2. On the vSphere Web Client home screen, select the vCenter object from the list on the left, then select Distributed Switches from the Inventory Lists area.

3. On the right side of the vSphere Web Client, click the Create A New Distributed Switch icon (it looks like a switch with a green plus mark in the corner).

   This launches the New Distributed Switch wizard.

4. Supply a name for the new distributed switch, and select a location within the vCenter inventory (a datacenter object or a folder) where you'd like to store the new distributed switch. Click Next.

5. Next, select the version of the VDS you'd like to create. Figure 5.45 shows the options for distributed switch versions.

FIGURE 5.45
If you want to support all the features included in vSphere 5.5, you must use a Version 5.5.0 distributed switch.

Five options are available:

◆ Distributed Switch: 4.0: This type of distributed switch is compatible back to vSphere 4.0 and limits the distributed switch to features supported only by vSphere 4.0.

◆ Distributed Switch: 4.1.0: This version adds support for Load-Based Teaming and Network I/O Control. This version is supported by vSphere 4.1 and later.

◆ Distributed Switch: 5.0.0: This version is compatible only with vSphere 5.0 and later and adds support for features such as user-defined network resource pools in Network I/O Control, NetFlow, and port mirroring.

◆ Distributed Switch: 5.1.0: Compatible with vSphere 5.1 or later, this version of the distributed switch adds support for Network Rollback and Recovery, Health Check, Enhanced Port Mirroring, and LACP.

◆ Distributed Switch: 5.5.0: This is the latest version, and it's supported on only vSphere 5.5 or later. This distributed switch adds Traffic Filtering and Marking and enhanced support for LACP.

In this case, select vSphere Distributed Switch Version 5.5.0 and click Next.

6. Specify the number of uplink ports, as illustrated in Figure 5.46.

FIGURE 5.46
The number of uplinks controls how many physical adapters from each host can serve as uplinks for the distributed switch.

7. On the same screen shown in Figure 5.46, select whether you want Network I/O Control enabled or disabled. Also select whether you want to create a default port group and, if so, what the name of that default port group should be. For this example, leave Network I/O Control enabled, and create a default port group with the name of your choosing. Click Next.

8. Review the settings for your new distributed switch. If everything looks correct, click Finish; otherwise, use the Back button to go back and change settings as needed.

After you complete the New Distributed Switch wizard, a new distributed switch will appear in the list of distributed switches in the vSphere Web Client. You can click the new distributed switch to see the ESXi hosts connected to it (none yet), the VMs hosted on it (none yet), the distributed ports groups on (only one—the one you created during the wizard), and the uplink port groups (of which there is also only one).

All this information is also available using the vSphere CLI or vSphere Management Assistant, but due to the nature of how the esxcli command is structured, you'll need to have an ESXi host added to the distributed switch first. Let's look at how that's done.

---

vSphere Distributed Switches Require vCenter Server

This may seem obvious, but it's important to point out that because of the shared nature of a vSphere Distributed Switch, vCenter Server is required. That is, you cannot have a vSphere Distributed Switch in an environment that is not being managed by vCenter Server.

Once you've created a distributed switch, it is relatively easy to add an ESXi host. When the ESXi host is created, all of the distributed port groups will automatically be propagated to the new host with the correct configuration. This is the distributed nature of the distributed switch—as configuration changes are made via the vSphere Web Client, vCenter Server pushes those changes out to all participating ESXi hosts. VMware administrators who are used to managing large ESXi clusters and having to repeatedly create vSwitches and port groups across all the servers individually will be very pleased with the reduction in administrative overhead that distributed switches offer.

Perform the following steps to add an ESXi host to an existing distributed switch:

1. Launch the vSphere Web Client, and connect to a vCenter Server instance.

2. Navigate to the list of distributed switches. One way of getting there is to start at the vCenter home screen, then click Distributed Switches in the Inventory Lists area.

3. Select an existing distributed switch in the list of objects on the right, and select Add And Manage Hosts from the Actions menu.

   This launches the Add And Manage Hosts wizard, shown in Figure 5.47.

FIGURE 5.47
When you're working with distributed switches, the vSphere Web Client offers a single wizard to add hosts, remove hosts, or manage host networking.

4. Select the Add Hosts radio button and click Next.

5. Click the green plus icon to add an ESXi host. This opens the Select New Host dialog box.

6. From the list of new hosts to add, place a check mark next to the name of each ESXi host you'd like to add to the distributed switch. Click OK when you're done, and then click Next to continue.

7. The next screen offers four different adapter-related tasks to perform, as shown in Figure 5.48. In this case, make sure only Manage Physical Adapters is selected. Click Next to continue.

FIGURE 5.48
All adapter-related changes to distributed switches are consolidated into a single wizard.

The Manage Virtual Adapters option allows you to add, migrate, edit, or remove virtual adapters (VMkernel ports) from this distributed switch.

The Migrate Virtual Machine Networking option enables you to migrate VM network adapters to this distributed switch.

The Manage Advanced Host Settings option lets you set the number of ports per legacy host proxy switch.

8. The next screen lets you choose the physical adapters on the new host that should be connected to the uplinks port group for the distributed switch. For each physical adapter you'd like to add, click the adapter and then click Assign Uplink. You'll be prompted to confirm the uplink to which this physical adapter should be connected. Repeat this process to add as many physical adapters as you have uplinks configured for the distributed switch.

9. Repeat step 8 for each ESXi host you're adding to the distributed switch. Click Next when you're finished adding uplinks for all ESXi hosts.

10. The Analyze Impact screen displays the potential affects of the changes proposed by the wizard. If everything looks OK, click Next; otherwise, click Back to go back and change the settings.

11. Click Finish to complete the wizard.

You'll have an opportunity to see this wizard again in later sections. For example, we'll discuss the options for managing physical and virtual adapters in more detail in the section "Managing Adapters" later in this chapter.

We mentioned earlier in this section that you could use the vSphere CLI or vSphere Management Assistant to see distributed switch information once you'd added a host to the distributed switch. The following command will show you a list of the distributed switches to which a particular ESXi host has been joined:

```
esxcli --server=<vCenter host name> --vihost=<ESXi host name>
--username=<vCenter administrative user> network vswitch dvs vmware list
```

The output will look similar to the output shown in Figure 5.49.

FIGURE 5.49

The esxcli command shows full details on the configuration of a distributed switch.

```
○ ○ ○                           2. ssh
vi-admin@vma:~> esxcli --server=172.16.1.235 --vihost=172.16.1.21 --username=roo
t network vswitch dvs vmware list
Enter password:
DSwitch01
   Name: DSwitch01
   VDS ID: 7c d2 00 50 bc aa 4c 8d-28 94 d3 89 fc 05 29 d0
   Class: etherswitch
   Num Ports: 1536
   Used Ports: 10
   Configured Ports: 512
   MTU: 1500
   CDP Status: listen
   Beacon Timeout: -1
   Uplinks: vmnic1, vmnic3, vmnic4, vmnic5
   VMware Branded: true
   DVPort:
         Client: vmnic1
         DVPortgroup ID: dvportgroup-27
         In Use: true
         Port ID: 12

         Client: vmnic3
         DVPortgroup ID: dvportgroup-27
         In Use: true
         Port ID: 13
```

Use the `--help` parameter with the `network vswitch dvs vmware namespace` command to see some of the other tasks that you can perform with the vSphere CLI or vSphere Management Assistant related to vSphere Distributed Switches.

Now, let's take a look at a few other tasks related to distributed switches. We'll start with removing an ESXi host from a distributed switch.

Removing an ESXi Host from a Distributed Switch

Naturally, you can also remove ESXi hosts from a distributed switch. You can't remove a host from a distributed switch if it still has VMs connected to a distributed port group on that switch. This is analogous to trying to delete a standard vSwitch or a port group while a VM is still connected; this, too, is prevented. To allow the host to be removed from the distributed switch, you must move all VMs to a standard vSwitch or a different distributed switch.

Perform the following steps to remove an individual ESXi host from a distributed switch:

1. Launch the vSphere Web Client, and connect to a vCenter Server instance.

2. Navigate to the list of distributed switches and select the specific distributed switch from which you'd like to remove an individual ESXi host.

3. From the Actions menu, select Add And Manage Hosts. This will bring up the Add And Manage Hosts dialog box, shown earlier in Figure 5.47.

4. Select the Remove Hosts radio button. Click Next.

5. Click the green plus icon to select hosts to be removed from the distributed switch.

ADDING HOSTS TO BE REMOVED

It might seem a bit counterintuitive to use the green plus icon when selecting the hosts to be removed from the distributed switch. The easiest way to think about it is to remember that you're adding hosts to the list of hosts that will be removed.

---

6. In the Select Member Hosts dialog box, place a check mark next to each ESXi host you'd like to remove from the distributed switch. Click OK when you're done selecting hosts.

7. Click Finish to remove the selected ESXi hosts.

8. If any VMs are still connected to the distributed switch, the vSphere Web Client will display an error similar to the one shown in Figure 5.50.

FIGURE 5.50
The vSphere Web Client won't allow a host to be removed from a distributed switch if a VM is still attached.

Notification   ⊗

Task Name: Reconfigure vSphere Distributed Switch

Target: DSwitch01

Status: The resource '0' is in use.
             vDS DSwitch01 port 0 is still on host
             adamant.lowehome.net connected to ubuntu-01
             nic=4000 type=vmVnic

More Tasks

To correct this error, reconfigure the VM(s) to use a different distributed switch or vSwitch, or migrate the VMs to a different host using vMotion. Then proceed with removing the host from the distributed switch.

9. If there were no VMs attached to the distributed switch, or after all VMs are reconfigured to use a different vSwitch or distributed switch, the host is removed.

In addition to removing individual ESXi hosts from a distributed switch, you can remove the entire distributed switch.

Removing a Distributed Switch

Removing the last ESXi host from a distributed switch does not remove the distributed switch itself. Even if all the VMs and/or ESXi hosts have been removed from the distributed switch, the distributed switch still exists in the vCenter inventory. You must still remove the distributed switch object itself.

Removing a distributed switch is possible only if no VMs have been assigned to a distributed port group on the distributed switch. Otherwise, the removal of the distributed switch is blocked with an error message similar to the one displayed previously in Figure 5.50. Again, you'll need to reconfigure the VM(s) to use a different vSwitch or distributed switch before the operation can proceed. Refer to Chapter 9, "Creating and Managing Virtual Machines," for more information on modifying a VM's network settings.

Perform the following steps to remove the distributed switch if no VMs are using it or any of the distributed port groups on it:

1. Launch the vSphere Web Client, and connect to a vCenter Server instance.

2. From the vSphere Web Client home screen, navigate to the Distributed Switches inventory list.

3. Select an existing vSphere Distributed Switch in the inventory pane on the left.

4. From the Actions menu, select All vCenter Actions ➤ Remove From Inventory.

5. The distributed switch and all associated distributed port groups are removed from the inventory and from any connected hosts.

The bulk of the configuration for a distributed switch isn't performed for the distributed switch itself but rather for the distributed port groups on that distributed switch. Nevertheless, let's first take a look at managing distributed switches themselves.

Managing Distributed Switches

As we stated earlier, the vast majority of the things that a VMware administrator will need to do with a distributed switch involve working with distributed port groups. We'll discuss distributed port groups later, but now we want to point out a few things involved with managing the distributed switch. We'll focus primarily on the functionality found on the Monitor, Manage, and Related Objects tabs of a distributed switch in the vSphere Web Client.

We'll start with the Related Objects tab, where you can see ESXi hosts, VMs, templates, distributed port groups, and uplink groups that are connected to the selected distributed switch.

This is a great way to explore the relationships between the distributed switch and other components in the environment.

The Manage tab is an area you've already seen and will see again throughout this chapter; in particular, you've been working in the Settings section of the Manage tab quite a bit, and you'll continue to do so as you start creating distributed port groups. The Manage tab also includes the following sections:

◆ In the Alarm Definitions section, you'll be able to create custom alarms for monitoring. This topic is covered in more depth in Chapter 13, "Monitoring VMware vSphere Performance."

◆ The Tags section allows VMware administrators to assign *tags* to objects within the vSphere Web Client and then use the search functionality to quickly and easily find all the objects with a certain tag.

◆ The Permissions section shows you the roles that have been assigned to various users or groups for the selected distributed switch. Note that in order to change these permissions, though, you'll have to work with the datacenter object or folder in which the distributed switch is stored.

◆ The Network Protocol Profiles section allows you to create profiles that are associated with a distributed port group. These profiles help shape how IPv4 and/or IPv6 are configured for VMs attached to a distributed port group with an associated profile.

◆ The Ports section provides a list of all the ports on the distributed switch and their current status.

◆ Finally, the Resource Allocation section is where you'll create network resource pools for use with Network I/O Control, a topic we'll discuss later in Chapter 11, "Managing Resource Allocation."

On the Monitor tab, there are four sections:

◆ The Issues section shows issues and/or alarms pertaining to a distributed switch.

◆ The Tasks and Events sections provide insight into recently performed tasks and a list of events. You could use these sections to see which user performed a certain task or to review various events pertaining to the selected distributed switch.

◆ The Health section centralizes health information for the distributed switch, such as VLAN checks, MTU checks, and other health checks.

The Health section contains some rather important functionality, so let's dig a little deeper into that section in particular.

USING HEALTH CHECKS AND NETWORK ROLLBACK

The vSphere Distributed Switch Health Check feature was added in vSphere 5.1 and is available only when you're using a version 5.1.0 or version 5.5.0 distributed switch. The idea behind the health check feature is to help VMware administrators identify mismatched VLAN configurations, mismatched MTU configurations, and mismatched NIC teaming policies—all of which are common sources of connectivity issues.

There are a few requirements to using the health check feature that you should know:

◆ As we mentioned earlier, you must be using a version 5.1.0 or version 5.5.0 distributed switch.

◆ VLAN and MTU checks require at least two NICs with active links.

◆ The teaming policy check requires at least two NICs with active links and at least two hosts.

By default, vSphere Distributed Switch Health Check is turned off; you must enable it in order to perform checks.

To enable vSphere Distributed Switch Health Check, perform these steps:

1. Connect to a vCenter Server instance using the vSphere Web Client.

2. Navigate to a distributed switch object in the vSphere Web Client, and select the distributed switch for which you want to enable health checks.

3. Click the Manage tab, choose Settings, and then select Health Check.

4. Click the Edit button.

5. In the Edit Health Check Settings dialog box, you can independently enable checks for VLAN and MTU, teaming and failover, or both. Click OK when finished.

Once the health checks are enabled, you can view the health check information on the Monitor tab of the distributed switch. Figure 5.51 shows the health check information for a distributed switch once health checks have been enabled.

Closely related to the health check functionality is a feature added in vSphere 5.1 called vSphere Network Rollback. The idea behind network rollback is to automatically protect environments against changes that would disconnect ESXi hosts from vCenter Server by rolling back changes if they are invalid. For example, changes to the speed or duplex of a physical NIC, updating teaming and failover policies for a switch that contains the ESXi host's management interface, or changing the IP settings of a host's management interface are all examples of changes that are validated when they occur. If the change would result in a loss of management connectivity to the host, the change is reverted—or rolled back—automatically.

Rollbacks can occur at two levels: at the host networking level or distributed switch level. Rollback is enabled by default, but you can enable or disable the feature at the vCenter level (doing so requires editing the vCenter Server configuration file; there is no GUI setting).

In addition to automatic rollbacks, VMware administrators have the option of performing manual rollbacks. We showed you how to do a manual rollback at the host level earlier in the section titled "Configuring Management Networking," when we discussed the Network Restore Options area of an ESXi host's DCUI. To perform a manual rollback of a distributed switch, you use the same process as restoring from a saved configuration, which is what we're going to discuss in the next section.

FIGURE 5.51

The vSphere Distributed Switch Health Check helps identify potential problems in configuration.

IMPORTING AND EXPORTING DISTRIBUTED SWITCH CONFIGURATION

vSphere 5.1 added the ability to export (save) and import (load) the configuration of a distributed switch. This functionality can serve a number of purposes; one purpose that we just mentioned is to manually "roll back" to a previously saved configuration.

To export (save) the configuration of a distributed switch to a file, perform these steps:

1. Log into a vCenter Server instance using the vSphere Web Client.

2. Navigate to the distributed switch whose configuration you'd like to save.

3. From the Actions menu, select All vCenter Actions ➢ Export Configuration. This opens the Export Configuration dialog box.

4. Select the appropriate radio button to export either the configuration of the distributed switch and all the distributed ports groups or just the configuration of the distributed switch.

5. Optionally, supply a description of the exported (saved) configuration, then click OK.

6. When prompted if you want to save the exported configuration file, click Yes.

7. Use your operating system's File Save dialog box to select the location where the exported configuration file (named backup.zip) should be saved.

Once you have the configuration exported to a file, you can then import this configuration back into your vSphere environment at a later date to restore the saved configuration. You can also import the configuration into a different vSphere environment, such as an environment being managed by a separate vCenter Server instance.

To import a saved configuration, perform these steps:

1. Log into a vCenter Server instance using the vSphere Web Client.

2. Navigate to the distributed switch whose configuration you'd like to restore.

3. From the Actions menu, select All vCenter Actions ➢ Restore Configuration. This opens the Restore Configuration wizard.

4. Use the Browse button to select the saved configuration file created earlier by exporting the configuration.

5. Select the appropriate radio button to restore either the distributed switch and all distributed port groups or just the distributed switch configuration.

6. Note that if vSphere automatically saved a previous version of the configuration (to protect against loss of management connectivity), this dialog box will also have the option of restoring the previous configuration. In this case, you do not need to select the saved backup file.

7. Click Next.

8. Review the settings that the wizard will import. If everything is correct, click Finish; otherwise, use Back to go back and make changes.

Both vSphere Network Rollback and the ability to manually export or import the configuration of a distributed switch are major steps forward in managing distributed switches in a vSphere environment.

Most of the work that a VMware administrator needs to perform will revolve around distributed port groups, so let's turn our attention to working with them.

Working With Distributed Port Groups

With vSphere Standard Switches, port groups are the key to connectivity for the VMkernel and for VMs. Without ports and port groups on a vSwitch, nothing can be connected to that vSwitch. The same is true for vSphere Distributed Switches. Without a distributed port group, nothing can be connected to a distributed switch, and the distributed switch is, therefore, unusable. In the following sections, you'll take a closer look at creating, configuring, and removing distributed port groups.

CREATING A DISTRIBUTED PORT GROUP

Perform the following steps to create a new distributed port group:

1. Launch the vSphere Web Client, and connect to a vCenter Server instance.

2. On the vSphere Web Client home screen, navigate to the Distributed Switches inventory list.

3. Select an existing vSphere Distributed Switch in the inventory pane on the left, and then click the Create A New Distributed Port Group icon on the right. This launches the New Distributed Port Group wizard.

4. Supply a name for the new distributed port group. Click Next to continue.

5. The Configure Setting screen, shown in Figure 5.52, allows you to specify a number of settings for the new distributed port group.

FIGURE 5.52
The New Distributed Port Group wizard gives you extensive access to customize the new distributed port group's settings.

The Port Binding and Port Allocation options allow you more fine-grained control over how ports in the distributed port group are allocated to VMs.

◆ With Port Binding set to Static Binding, ports are statically assigned to a VM when a VM is connected to the distributed switch. You may also set the Port Allocation to be either Elastic (in which case the distributed port group starts with 8 ports and adds more in 8-port increments as needed) or Fixed (in which case it defaults to 128 ports).

◆ With Port Binding set to Dynamic Binding, you specify how many ports the distributed port group should have (the default is 128). Note that this option is deprecated; the vSphere Web Client will post a warning to that effect if you select this option.

◆ With Port Binding set to Ephemeral Binding, you can't specify the number of ports or the Port Allocation method.

The Network Resource Pool option allows you to connect this distributed port group to a Network I/O Control custom resource pool. Network I/O Control and network resource pools are described in more detail in Chapter 11.

Finally, the options for VLAN Type might also need a bit more explanation:

♦ With VLAN Type set to None, the distributed port group will receive only untagged traffic. In this case, the uplinks must connect to physical switch ports configured as access ports or they will receive only untagged/native VLAN traffic.

♦ With VLAN Type set to VLAN, you'll need to specify a VLAN ID. The distributed port group will receive traffic tagged with that VLAN ID. The uplinks must connect to physical switch ports configured as VLAN trunks.

♦ With VLAN Type set to VLAN Trunking, you'll need to specify the range of allowed VLANs. The distributed port group will pass the VLAN tags up to the guest OSes on any connected VMs.

♦ With VLAN Type set to Private VLAN, you'll need to specify a Private VLAN entry. Private VLANs are described in detail later in the section "Setting Up Private VLANs."

Select the desired port binding settings (and port allocation, if necessary), the desired network resource pool, and the desired VLAN type, and then click Next.

6. On the summary screen, review the settings, and click Finish if everything is correct. If you need to make changes, use the Back button to go back and make the necessary edits.

After a distributed port group has been created, you can select that distributed port group in the VM configuration as a possible network connection, as shown in Figure 5.53.

After you create a distributed port group, it will appear in the Topology View for the distributed switch that hosts it. In the vSphere Web Client, this view is accessible from the Settings area of the Manage tab for the distributed switch. From there, clicking the Info icon (the small *i* in the blue circle) will provide more information about the distributed port group and its current state. Figure 5.54 shows some of the information shown by the vSphere Web Client about a distributed port group.

EDITING A DISTRIBUTED PORT GROUP

To edit the configuration of a distributed port group, use the Edit Distributed Port Group Settings link in the Topology View for the distributed switch. In the vSphere Web Client, you can locate this area by selecting a distributed switch in the inventory list and then going to the Settings area of the Manage tab. Finally, select Topology to produce the Topology view shown in Figure 5.55.

FIGURE 5.53
A distributed port group is selected as a network connection for VMs, just like port groups on a vSphere Standard vSwitch.

FIGURE 5.54
The vSphere Web Client provides a summary of the distributed port group's configuration.

FIGURE 5.55

The Topology view for a distributed switch provides easy access to view and edit distributed port groups.

For now, let's focus on modifying VLAN settings, traffic shaping, and NIC teaming for the distributed port group. Policy settings for security and monitoring follow later in this chapter.

DIFFERENT OPTIONS ARE AVAILABLE DEPENDING ON THE VSPHERE DISTRIBUTED SWITCH VERSION

Recall that you can create different versions of distributed switches in the vSphere Web Client. Certain configuration options are available only with a version 5.1.0 or version 5.5.0 vSphere Distributed Switch.

Perform the following steps to modify the VLAN settings for a distributed port group:

1. Connect to a vCenter Server instance using the vSphere Web Client.

2. Navigate to the Topology view for the distributed switch containing the distributed port group you want to edit.

3. Select a distributed port group by clicking its name, which acts like a hyperlink in the vSphere Web Client, and then click the Edit Distributed Port Group Settings icon in the row of icons just above the switch topology.

4. In the Edit Settings dialog box, select the VLAN option from the list of options on the left.

5. Modify the VLAN settings by changing the VLAN ID or by changing the VLAN Type setting to VLAN Trunking or Private VLAN.

   Refer to Figure 5.52 for the different VLAN configuration options.

6. Click OK when you have finished making changes.

Perform the following steps to modify the traffic-shaping policy for a distributed port group:

1. Using a supported web browser, connect to a vCenter Server instance to launch the vSphere Web Client.

2. Navigate to the Topology view for the distributed switch containing the distributed port group you want to edit.

3. Select a distributed port group by clicking its name, which acts like a hyperlink in the vSphere Web Client, and then click the Edit Distributed Port Group Settings icon in the row of icons just above the switch topology.

4. Select the Traffic Shaping option from the list of options on the left of the distributed port group settings dialog box, as illustrated in Figure 5.56.

   Traffic shaping was described in detail earlier in this chapter in the section "Using and Configuring Traffic Shaping." The big difference here is that with a distributed switch, you can apply traffic-shaping policies to both ingress and egress traffic. With vSphere Standard Switches, you could apply traffic-shaping policies only to egress (outbound) traffic. Otherwise, the settings here are for a distributed port group function as described earlier.

FIGURE 5.56
You can apply both ingress and egress traffic-shaping policies to a distributed port group on a distributed switch.

5. Click OK when you have finished making changes.

Perform the following steps to modify the NIC teaming and failover policies for a distributed port group:

1. Launch the vSphere Web Client by connecting to a vCenter Server instance with a supported web browser.

2. Navigate to the Topology view for the distributed switch containing the distributed port group you want to edit.

3. Select a distributed port group by clicking its name, which acts like a hyperlink in the vSphere Web Client, and then click the Edit Distributed Port Group Settings icon in the row of icons just above the switch topology.

4. Select the Teaming And Failover option from the list of options on the left of the Edit Settings dialog box, as illustrated in Figure 5.57.

FIGURE 5.57

The Teaming And
Failover item in the
distributed port
group Edit Settings
dialog box provides
options for modify-
ing how a distrib-
uted port group
uses uplinks.

These settings were described in detail in the section "Configuring NIC Teaming," with
one notable exception—version 4.1 and higher distributed switches support a new load-
balancing type, Route Based On Physical NIC Load. When this load-balancing policy is
selected, ESXi checks the utilization of the uplinks every 30 seconds for congestion. In
this case, congestion is defined as either transmit or receive traffic greater than 75 percent
mean utilization over a 30-second period. If congestion is detected on an uplink, ESXi
will dynamically reassign the VM to a different uplink.

REQUIREMENTS FOR LOAD-BASED TEAMING

Load-Based Teaming (LBT) requires that all upstream physical switches be part of the same layer
2 (broadcast) domain. In addition, VMware recommends that you enable the PortFast or PortFast
Trunk option on all physical switch ports connected to a distributed switch that is using Load-
Based Teaming.

---

5. Click OK when you have finished making changes.

Later in this chapter in the section titled "Configuring LACP," we'll provide more detail on
vSphere's support for Link Aggregation Control Protocol (LACP), including how you would
configure a distributed switch for use with LACP. In that section, we'll also refer back to some of
this information on modifying NIC teaming and failover.

If you browse through the available settings, you might notice a Blocked policy option. This
is the equivalent of disabling a group of ports in the distributed port group. Figure 5.58 shows
that the Block All Ports setting is set to either Yes or No. If you set the Block policy to Yes, then
all traffic to and from that distributed port group is dropped. Don't set the Block policy to Yes
unless you are prepared for network downtime for all VMs attached to that distributed port
group!

FIGURE 5.58

The Block policy is set to either Yes or No. Setting the Block policy to Yes disables all the ports in that distributed port group.

IS THERE A FEATURE THAT COULD HELP HERE?

Suppose you accidentally set Block to Yes on a distributed port group that contains the management interface. Is there a feature that we've discussed that might help here? That's right—vSphere Network Rollback would help here.

REMOVING A DISTRIBUTED PORT GROUP

The easiest way to delete a distributed port group is to use the Topology view of the distributed switch itself. This view is found in the Settings area of the Manage tab for the distributed switch.

To delete a distributed port group, first select the distributed port group by clicking its name in the Topology view. Then, click the Remove The Distributed Port Group icon, which looks like a red *X*. Finally, click Yes to confirm that you do want to remove the distributed port group.

If any VMs are still attached to that distributed port group, the vSphere Web Client prevents the deletion of it and logs an error notification.

To delete the distributed port group to which a VM is attached, you first have to reconfigure the VM to use a different distributed port group on the same distributed switch, a distributed port group on a different distributed switch, or a vSwitch. You can either use the Migrate VM To Another Network command on the Actions menu, or you can just reconfigure the VM's network settings directly.

Once all VMs have been moved off of a distributed port group, you can remove the distributed port group using the process described in the previous paragraphs.

In the next section, we'll turn our attention to managing adapters, both physical and virtual, when working with a vSphere Distributed Switch.

Managing Adapters

With a distributed switch, managing virtual and physical adapters is handled quite differently than with a standard vSwitch. Virtual adapters are VMkernel interfaces, so by managing virtual adapters, we're really talking about managing VMkernel traffic—management, vMotion, IP-based storage, and Fault Tolerance logging—on a distributed switch. Physical adapters are, of course, the physical network adapters that serve as uplinks for the distributed switch. Managing physical adapters means adding or removing physical adapters connected to ports in the uplinks distributed port group on the distributed switch.

Perform the following steps to add a virtual adapter to a distributed switch:

1. Launch a supported web browser and connect to a vCenter Server instance to start the vSphere Web Client. Log in as a user with administrative permissions.

2. From the vSphere Web Client home screen, navigate to the distributed switch you'd like to edit. One way of doing this is to select vCenter, then choose Distributed Switches from the inventory lists (not the inventory tree).

3. Select a distributed switch from the inventory list on the left, click the Manage tab in the details pane on the right, select Settings, and make sure Topology is selected.

4. Click the second icon in the row across the top; the pop-up tooltip reads "Add hosts to this distributed switch and add or migrate physical or virtual network adapters." This launches the Add And Manage Hosts wizard.

5. Select the Manage Host Networking radio button, and then click Next.

6. At the Select Hosts screen, use the green plus icon to add hosts to the list of hosts that will be modified during this process. It might seem like the wizard is asking you to add hosts to the distributed switch, but what you're really doing here is adding hosts to the list of hosts that will be modified. Click Next when you're ready to move to the next step.

7. In this case, we're modifying virtual adapters, so make sure only the Manage Virtual Adapters check box is selected. Click Next.

8. With an ESXi host selected, click the New Adapter link near the top of the Manage Virtual Network Adapters screen, shown in Figure 5.59. This opens the Add Networking wizard.

FIGURE 5.59
The Manage Virtual Network Adapters screen of the wizard allows you to add new adapters as well as migrate existing adapters.

CREATE THE DISTRIBUTED PORT GROUP FIRST

When you are adding new virtual adapters to a distributed switch, make sure you've created the distributed port group you'd like this new virtual adapter to use first. The wizard for adding a new virtual adapter does not provide a way to create a distributed port group as part of the process.

9. In the Add Networking wizard, click the Browse button to select the existing distributed port group to which this new virtual adapter should be added. (Refer to the sidebar "Create the Distributed Port Group First" for an important note.) Click OK once you've selected an existing distributed port group, and then click Next.

10. On the Port Properties screen, select whether you want to enable IPv4 only, IPv6 only, or both protocols.

11. Enable the desired services—like vMotion or Fault Tolerance logging—that should be enabled on this new virtual adapter. Click Next.

12. Depending on whether you selected IPv4, IPv6, or IPv4 and IPv6, the next couple of screens ask you to configure the appropriate network settings.

   If you selected only IPv4, then supply the desired IPv4 settings.

   If you selected only IPv6, then supply the correct IPv6 settings for your network.

   If you selected both IPv4 and IPv6, then there will be two configuration screens in the wizard, one for IPv4 and a separate screen for IPv6.

13. Once you've entered the correct network protocol settings, the final screen of the wizard presents the settings that will be applied. If everything is correct, click Finish; otherwise, use the Back button to go back and change settings as necessary.

14. This returns you to the Add And Manage Hosts wizard, where you'll now see the new virtual adapter that will be added. Repeat steps 8 through 13 if you need to add a virtual adapter for another ESXi host at the same time; otherwise, click Next.

15. The Analyze Impact screen will show you the potential impact of the changes you're making. If necessary, use the Back button to go back and make changes to mitigate any negative impacts. When you're ready to proceed, click Next.

16. Click Finish to commit the changes to the selected distributed switch and ESXi hosts.

Migrating an existing virtual adapter—such as a VMkernel port on an existing vSwitch—is done in exactly the same way. The only real difference is that in step 8, you'll select an existing virtual adapter, then click the Assign Port Group link across the top. Select an existing port group and click OK to return to the wizard, where the screen will look similar to what's shown in Figure 5.60.

FIGURE 5.60
Migrating a virtual adapter involves assigning it to an existing distributed port group.

After a virtual adapter has been created or migrated, the same wizard allows for changes to the virtual port, such as modifying the IP address, changing the distributed port group to which the adapter is assigned, or enabling features such as vMotion or Fault Tolerance logging. To edit an existing virtual adapter, you'd select the Edit Adapter link seen in Figure 5.60. You would remove virtual adapters using this same wizard as well, using the Remove link on the Manage Virtual Network Adapters screen of the Add And Manage Hosts wizard.

Not surprisingly, the vSphere Web Client also allows you to add or remove physical adapters connected to ports in the uplinks port group on the distributed switch. Although you can specify physical adapters during the process of adding a host to a distributed switch, as shown earlier, it might be necessary at times to connect a physical NIC to the distributed switch after the host is already participating in it.

Perform the following steps to add a physical network adapter in an ESXi host to a distributed switch:

1. Start the vSphere Web Client by launching a supported web browser and connecting to a vCenter Server instance.

2. From the vSphere Web Client home screen, navigate to the distributed switch you'd like to modify.

3. Make sure the distributed switch is selected in the inventory list on the left, then go to the Manage tab, select Settings, and click Topology.

4. From the Actions menu, select Add And Manage Hosts. This opens the Add And Manage Hosts wizard.

5. Select the Manage Host Networking radio button, and then click Next.

6. Use the green plus icon to add ESXi hosts to the list of hosts that will be affected by the changes in the wizard. Click Next when you're finished adding ESXi hosts to the list.

7. Make sure only the Manage Physical Adapters option is selected, as shown in Figure 5.61, and click Next.

FIGURE 5.61
To manage uplinks on a distributed switch, make sure only the Manage Physical Adapters option is selected.

8. At the Manage Physical Network Adapters screen, you can add or remove physical network adapters to the selected distributed switch.

To add a physical adapter as an uplink, select an unassigned adapter from the list and click the Assign Uplink link. You can also use the Assign Uplink link to change the uplink to which a given physical adapter is assigned (for example, to move it from uplink 2 to uplink 3).

To remove a physical adapter as an uplink, select an assigned adapter from the list and click the Unassign Adapter link.

To migrate a physical adapter from another switch to this distributed switch, select the already-assigned adapter and use the Assign Uplink link. This will automatically remove it from the other switch and assign it to the selected switch.

Repeat this process for each host in the list. Click Next when you're ready to proceed.

9. At the Analyze Impact screen, the vSphere Web Client will provide feedback on the anticipated impact of the changes. If the impact of the changes is undesirable, use the Back button to go back and make any necessary changes. Otherwise, click Next.

10. Click Finish to complete the wizard and commit the changes.

In addition to migrating virtual adapters and modifying the physical adapters, you can use vCenter Server to assist in migrating VM adapters—that is, migrating a VM's networking between vSphere Standard Switches and vSphere Distributed Switches, as shown in Figure 5.62.

FIGURE 5.62
The Migrate
Virtual Machine
Networking wizard
automates the pro-
cess of migrating
VMs between a
source and destina-
tion network.

FIGURE 5.62
The Migrate
Virtual Machine
Networking wizard
automates the pro-
cess of migrating
VMs between a
source and destina-
tion network.

This tool, accessed using the Actions menu when a distributed switch is selected in the inventory lists, will reconfigure all selected VMs to use the selected destination network. This is a lot easier than individually reconfiguring a bunch of VMs! In addition, this tool allows you to easily migrate VMs both *to* a distributed switch and *from* a distributed switch. Let's walk through the process so that you can see how it works.

Perform the following steps to migrate VMs from a vSphere Standard Switch to a vSphere Distributed Switch:

1. From within a supported web browser, connect to a vCenter Server instance to launch the vSphere Web Client.

2. Navigate to a distributed switch in the inventory lists.

3. Select a distributed switch from the inventory tree on the left, and then select Migrate VM To Another Network from the Actions menu. This launches the Migrate Virtual Machine Networking wizard.

4. Use the Browse button to select the source network that contains the VMs you'd like to migrate. You can use the Filter and Find search boxes to limit the results if you need to. Click OK once you've selected the source network.

5. Use the Browse button to select the destination network to which you'd like the VMs to be migrated. Again, use the Filter and Find search boxes, where needed, to make it easier to locate the desired destination network. Click OK to return to the wizard once you've selected the destination network.

6. Click Next after you've finished selecting the source and destination networks.

7. A list of matching VMs is generated, and each VM is analyzed to determine if the destination network is accessible or inaccessible to the VM.

   Figure 5.63 shows a list with both accessible and inaccessible destination networks. A destination network might show up as inaccessible if the ESXi host on which that VM is running isn't part of the distributed switch (as is the case in this instance). Select the VMs you want to migrate; then click Next.

FIGURE 5.63

You cannot migrate VMs matching your source network selection if the destination network is listed as inaccessible.

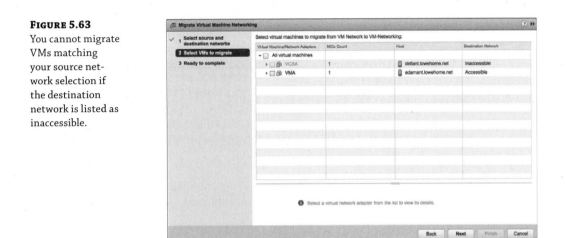

8. Click Finish to start the migration of the selected VMs from the specified source network to the selected destination network.

   You'll see a Reconfigure Virtual Machine task spawn in the Tasks pane for each VM that needs to be migrated.

Keep in mind that this tool can migrate VMs from a vSwitch to a distributed switch or from a distributed switch to a vSwitch—you only need to specify the source and destination networks accordingly.

Now that we've covered the basics of distributed switches, we'd like to delve into a few advanced topics. First up is network monitoring using NetFlow.

Using NetFlow on vSphere Distributed Switches

NetFlow is a mechanism for efficiently reporting IP-based traffic information as a series of *traffic flows*. Traffic flows are defined as the combination of source and destination IP address, source and destination TCP or UDP ports, IP, and IP Type of Service (ToS). Network devices that support NetFlow will track and report information on the traffic flows, typically sending this information to a NetFlow collector. Using the data collected, network administrators gain detailed insight into the types and amount of traffic flows across the network.

In vSphere 5.0, VMware introduced support for NetFlow with vSphere Distributed Switches (only on distributed switches that are version 5.0.0 or higher). This allows ESXi hosts to gather detailed per-flow information and report that information to a NetFlow collector.

Configuring NetFlow is a two-step process:

1. Configure the NetFlow properties on the distributed switch.

2. Enable or disable NetFlow (the default is disabled) on a per–distributed port group basis.

Let's take a closer look at these steps.

To configure the NetFlow properties for a distributed switch, perform these steps:

1. Connect to a vCenter Server instance using a supported web browser; this starts the vSphere Web Client.

2. Navigate to the list of distributed switches from the vSphere Web Client's inventory lists, and select the distributed switch where you want to enable NetFlow.

3. With the desired distributed switch selected, from the Actions menu, select All vCenter Actions ➤ Edit NetFlow.

   This opens the Edit NetFlow Settings dialog box.

4. As shown in Figure 5.64, specify the IP address of the NetFlow collector, the port on the NetFlow collector, and an IP address to identify the distributed switch.

5. You can modify the Advanced Settings if advised to do so by your networking team.

6. If you want the distributed switch to process only internal traffic flows—that is, traffic flows from VM to VM on that host—set Process Internal Flows Only to Enabled.

7. Click OK to commit the changes and return to the vSphere Web Client.

FIGURE 5.64
You'll need the IP address and port number for the NetFlow collector in order to send flow information from a distributed switch.

After you configure the NetFlow properties for the distributed switch, you then enable NetFlow on a per–distributed port group basis. The default setting is Disabled. Perform these steps to enable NetFlow on a specific distributed port group:

1. In the vSphere Web Client, navigate to the distributed switch hosting the distributed port group where you want to enable NetFlow. You must have already performed the previous procedure to configure NetFlow on that distributed switch.

2. From the Actions menu, select Manage Distributed Port Groups. This opens the Manage Distributed Port Groups wizard.

3. Place a check mark next to Monitoring, and then click Next.

4. From the list of distributed port groups on that distributed switch, select the distributed port group(s) that you want to edit. You can select multiple distributed port groups, if you desire. For Windows users, this usually means pressing the Ctrl key while selecting the second and subsequent distributed port groups; on OS X, you would use the Command key.

   Click Next once you've selected the desired distributed port groups.

5. At the Monitoring screen, shown in Figure 5.65, set NetFlow to enabled; then click Next.

6. Click Finish to save the changes to the distributed port group.

This distributed port group will start capturing NetFlow statistics and reporting that information to the specified NetFlow collector.

Another feature that is quite useful is vSphere's support for switch discovery protocols, like Cisco Discovery Protocol (CDP) and Link Layer Discovery Protocol (LLDP). The next section shows you how to enable these protocols in vSphere.

FIGURE 5.65
NetFlow is disabled by default. You enable NetFlow on a per–distributed port group basis.

Enabling Switch Discovery Protocols

Previous versions of vSphere supported Cisco Discovery Protocol (CDP), a protocol for exchanging information between network devices. However, it required using the command line to enable and configure CDP.

In vSphere 5.0, VMware added support for Link Layer Discovery Protocol (LLDP), an industry-standardized form of CDP, and provided a location within the vSphere Client where CDP/LLDP support can be configured.

Perform the following steps to configure switch discovery support:

1. In the vSphere Web Client, navigate to a specific distributed switch in the vSphere Web Client's inventory lists.

2. With the distributed switch selected on the left, select Edit Settings from the Actions menu.

3. In the Edit Settings dialog box, select Advanced.

4. Configure the distributed switch for CDP or LLDP support, as shown in Figure 5.66.

FIGURE 5.66
LLDP support
enables distrib-
uted switches to
exchange discovery
information with
other LLDP-enabled
devices over the
network.

This figure shows the distributed switch configured for LLDP support, both listening (receiving LLDP information from other connected devices) and advertising (sending LLDP information to other connected devices).

5. Click OK to save your changes.

Once the ESXi hosts participating in this distributed switch start exchanging discovery information, you can view that information from the physical switch(es). For example, on most Cisco switches, the show cdp neighbor command will display information about CDP-enabled network devices, including ESXi hosts. Entries for ESXi hosts will include information on the physical NIC used and the vSwitch/distributed switch involved.

vSphere Standard Switches also support CDP (not LLDP), but there is no GUI for configuring this support; you must use esxcli. This command will set CDP to Both (listen and advertise) on vSwitch0:

```
esxcli --server=<vCenter IP address> --vihost=<ESXi host IP address>
--username=<vCenter administrative user> network vswitch standard set
--cdp-status=both --vswitch-name=vSwitch0
```

The next advanced networking topic we'll review is private VLANs.

Setting Up Private VLANs

Private VLANs (PVLANs) are an advanced networking feature of vSphere that build on the functionality of vSphere Distributed Switches. Within the vSphere environment, PVLANs are possible only when using distributed switches and are not available to use with vSphere Standard Switches. Further, you must ensure that the upstream physical switches to which your vSphere environment is connected also support PVLANs.

We'll provide a quick overview of private VLANs. PVLANs are a way to further isolate ports within a given VLAN (some refer to this as micro-segmentation). For example, consider the scenario of hosts within a demilitarized zone (DMZ). Hosts within a DMZ rarely need to communicate with each other, but using a VLAN for each host quickly becomes unwieldy for a number of reasons. By using PVLANs, you can isolate hosts from each other while keeping them on the same IP subnet. Figure 5.67 provides a graphical overview of how PVLANs work.

PVLANs are configured in pairs: the primary VLAN and any secondary VLANs. The primary VLAN is considered the *downstream* VLAN; that is, traffic to the host travels along the primary VLAN. The secondary VLAN is considered the *upstream* VLAN; that is, traffic from the host travels along the secondary VLAN.

To use PVLANs, first configure the PVLANs on the physical switches connecting to the ESXi hosts, and then add the PVLAN entries to the distributed switch in vCenter Server.

Perform the following steps to define PVLAN entries on a distributed switch:

1. Launch the vSphere Web Client by connecting to a vCenter Server instance.

2. On the vSphere Web Client home screen, select vCenter, then select Distributed Switches from the inventory lists on the left.

3. Select an existing distributed switch in the inventory pane on the left, select the Manage tab in the details pane on the right, and select Settings.

4. Select Private VLAN, then click the Edit button.

FIGURE 5.67
Private VLANs can help isolate ports on the same IP subnet.

5. In the Edit Private VLAN Settings dialog box, click Add to add a primary VLAN ID to the list on the left.

6. For each primary VLAN ID in the list on the left, add one or more secondary VLANs to the list on the right, as shown in Figure 5.68.

FIGURE 5.68
Private VLAN entries consist of a primary VLAN and one or more secondary VLAN entries.

Secondary VLANs are classified as one of the two following types:

- Isolated: Ports placed in secondary PVLANs configured as isolated are allowed to communicate only with promiscuous ports in the same secondary VLAN. We'll explain promiscuous ports shortly.

- Community: Ports in a secondary PVLAN are allowed to communicate with other ports in the same secondary PVLAN as well as with promiscuous ports.

Only one isolated secondary VLAN is permitted for each primary VLAN. Multiple secondary VLANs configured as community VLANs are allowed.

7. When you finish adding all the PVLAN pairs, click OK to save the changes and return to the vSphere Web Client.

After you enter the PVLAN IDs for a distributed switch, you must create a distributed port group that takes advantage of the PVLAN configuration. The process for creating a distributed port group was described previously. Figure 5.69 shows the New Distributed Port Group wizard for a distributed port group that uses PVLANs.

In Figure 5.69 you can see the term *promiscuous* again. In PVLAN parlance, a promiscuous port is allowed to send and receive layer 2 frames to any other port in the VLAN. This type of port is typically reserved for the default gateway for an IP subnet—for example, a layer 3 router.

PVLANs are a powerful configuration tool but also a complex configuration topic and one that can be difficult to understand. For additional information on PVLANs, we recommend visiting Cisco's website at www.cisco.com and searching for *private VLANs*.

As with vSphere Standard Switches, vSphere Distributed Switches provide a tremendous amount of flexibility in designing and configuring a virtual network. But, as with all things, there are limits to the flexibility. Table 5.2 lists some of the configuration maximums for vSphere Distributed Switches.

FIGURE 5.69

When a distributed port group is created with PVLANs, the distributed port group is associated with both the primary VLAN ID and a secondary VLAN ID.

TABLE 5.2:   Configuration maximums for ESXi networking components (vSphere Distributed Switches)

CONFIGURATION ITEM	MAXIMUM
Switches per vCenter Server	128
Maximum ports per host (vSS/vDS)	4096
vDS ports per vCenter instance	60000
ESXi hosts per vDS	1000
Static port groups per vCenter instance	10000
Ephemeral port groups per vCenter instance	1016

VMware vSphere also lets you use compatible third-party distributed switches in your vSphere environment. Before we move into some options available for third-party distributed virtual switches in your environment, we'd like to first discuss one final advanced networking feature in vSphere: support for Link Aggregation Control Protocol (LACP).

Configuring LACP

Link Aggregation Control Protocol (LACP) is a standardized protocol for supporting the aggregation, or joining, of multiple individual network links into a single, logical network link.

LACP support was first added in vSphere 5.1, and the LACP support in vSphere 5.5 has been enhanced. Note that LACP support is available only when you are using a vSphere Distributed Switch; vSphere Standard Switches do not support LACP.

IS LACP THE ONLY WAY?

Note that it's possible to use link aggregation without LACP. When you use either a vSphere Standard Switch or a vSphere Distributed Switch, setting the NIC teaming policy to Route Based On IP Hash enables link aggregation. Although it enables link aggregation, this configuration does not use LACP. This is the only way to use link aggregation with a vSphere Standard Switch.

We'll start with a review of how to configure basic LACP support on a version 5.1.0 vSphere Distributed Switch; then we'll show you how the LACP support has been enhanced in vSphere 5.5.

Using a version 5.1.0 vSphere Distributed Switch, you must configure the following four areas:

◆ Enable LACP in the properties for the distributed switch's uplink group.

◆ Set the NIC teaming policy for all distributed port groups to Route Based On IP Hash.

◆ Set the network detection policy for all distributed port groups to link status only.

◆ Configure all distributed port groups so that all uplinks are active, not standby or unused.

Figure 5.70 shows the Edit Settings dialog box for the uplink group on a version 5.1.0 vSphere Distributed Switch. You can see here the setting for enabling LACP as well as the reminder of the other settings that are required.

FIGURE 5.70
Basic LACP support in a version 5.1.0 vSphere Distributed Switch is enabled in the uplink group but requires other settings as well.

GETTING TO THE EDIT SETTINGS DIALOG BOX FOR THE UPLINKS GROUP

Getting to the Edit Settings dialog box for a distributed switch's uplink group, like the one shown in Figure 5.70, might seem a bit unintuitive at first. The trick is to select (or highlight) the uplink group in Topology view and then click the Edit Distributed Port Group Settings icon. As far as we know, this is the only way in the vSphere Web Client to get to this dialog box—it's not accessible from the Actions menu, nor is it available through any right-click menu.

You must configure LACP on the physical switch to which the ESXi host is connected; the exact way you enable LACP will vary from vendor to vendor. The Mode setting shown in Figure 5.70—which is set to either Active or Passive—helps dictate how the ESXi host will communicate with the physical switch to establish the link aggregate:

♦ When LACP Mode is set to Passive, the ESXi host won't initiate any communications to the physical switch; the switch must initiate the negotiation.

♦ When LACP Mode is set to Active, the ESXi host will actively initiate the negotiation of the link aggregation with the physical switch.

You can probably gather from this discussion of using LACP with a version 5.1.0 vSphere Distributed Switch that only a single link aggregate (a single bundle of LACP-negotiated links) is supported and LACP is enabled or disabled for the entire vSphere Distributed Switch.

When you upgrade to a version 5.5.0 vSphere Distributed Switch, though, the LACP support is enhanced to eliminate these limitations. Version 5.5.0 distributed switches support multiple LACP bundles, and how those LACP bundles are used (or not used) can be configured on a per–distributed port group basis. Let's take a look at how you'd configure LACP support with a version 5.5.0 distributed switch.

With a version 5.5.0 distributed switch, a new LACP section appears in the Settings area of the Manage tab, as you can see in Figure 5.71. From this area, you'll define one or more link aggregation groups (LAGs), each of which will appear as a logical uplink to the distributed port groups on that distributed switch. vSphere 5.5 supports multiple LAGs on a single distributed switch, which allows administrators to dual-home distributed switches (connect distributed switches to multiple upstream physical switches) while still using LACP. (There are a few limitations, which we'll describe near the end of this section.)

FIGURE 5.71
vSphere 5.5's enhanced LACP support eliminates many of the limitations of the support found in vSphere 5.1.

To use LACP with a version 5.5.0 distributed switch, three basic steps are required:

1. Define one or more LAGs in the LACP section of the Settings area of the Manage tab.

2. Add physical adapters into the LAG(s) you've created.

3. Modify the distributed port groups to use those LAGs as uplinks in the distributed port groups' teaming and failover configuration.

Let's take a look at each of these steps in a bit more detail.
To create a LAG, perform these steps:

1. Connect to a vCenter Server instance using a supported web browser and log in with administrative credentials.

2. Navigate to the specific distributed switch for which you want to configure a LACP link aggregation group.

3. With the distributed switch selected in the inventory list on the left, click the Manage tab, then click Settings, and then click LACP. This displays the screen shown earlier in Figure 5.71.

4. Click the green plus symbol to add a LAG. This displays the New Link Aggregation Group dialog box, shown in Figure 5.72.

FIGURE 5.72
With a version 5.5.0 distributed switch, the LACP properties are configured on a per-LAG basis instead of for the entire distributed switch.

5. In the New Link Aggregation Group dialog box, specify a name for the new LAG.

6. Specify the number of physical ports that will be included in the LAG.

7. Specify the LACP mode—either Active or Passive, as we described earlier—that this LAG should use.

8. Select a load-balancing mode. Note that this load-balancing mode affects only outbound traffic; inbound traffic will be load balanced according to the load-balancing mode configured on the physical switch. (For best results and ease of troubleshooting, the configuration here should match the configuration on the physical switch where possible.)

9. If you need to override port policies for this LAG, you can do so at the bottom of this dialog box.

10. Click OK to create the new LAG and return to the LACP area of the vSphere Web Client.

Now that at least one LAG has been created, you need to assign physical adapters to it. To do this, you'll follow the process we outlined earlier for managing physical adapters (see the section titled "Managing Adapters" for the specific details). The one change you'll note is that when you click the Assign Uplink link for a selected physical adapter, you'll now see an option to assign that adapter to one of the available uplink ports in the LAG(s) that you created. Figure 5.73 shows the dialog box for assigning an uplink for a distributed switch with two LAGs.

FIGURE 5.73
Once a LAG has been created, physical adapters can be added to it.

Uplink	Assigned Adapter
Uplink 1	vmnic1
Uplink 2	vmnic3
Uplink 3	—
Uplink 4	—
▼ lag1 ports	
lag1-0	—
lag1-1	—
▼ lag2 ports	
lag2-0	—
lag2-1	—
(Auto-assign)	

Once you've added physical adapters to the LAG(s), you can proceed with the final step: configuring the LAG(s) as uplinks for the distributed port groups on that distributed switch. Specific instructions for this process were given earlier in the section titled "Editing a Distributed Port Group." Note that the LAG(s) will appear as physical uplinks in the teaming and failover configuration, as you can see in Figure 5.74. You can assign the LAG as an active uplink, a standby uplink, or an unused uplink.

FIGURE 5.74
LAGs appear as
physical uplinks to
the distributed port
groups.

When using LAGs, you should be aware of a the following limitations:

◆ You can't mix LAGs and physical uplinks for a given distributed port group. Any physical uplinks must be listed as unused adapters.

◆ You can't use multiple active LAGs on a single distributed port group. Place one LAG in the active uplinks list; place any other LAGs in the list of unused uplinks.

Note that these limitations are per distributed port group; you can use different active LAGs or standalone uplinks with other distributed port groups because the teaming and failover configuration is set for each individual distributed port group.

IGNORE THE LOAD BALANCING SETTING WITH LAGS

When using LACP and LAGs with a version 5.5.0 distributed switch, you can ignore the Load Balancing setting seen earlier in Figure 5.74. It is overridden by the load-balancing policy set on the LAG(s).

As you can see, the enhanced LACP support present in vSphere 5.5 and version 5.5.0 distributed switches offers VMware administrators and their counterparts in the networking team a great deal of functionality and flexibility.

We'd like to now turn our attention to some of the options available for using third-party distributed switches in your vSphere environment.

Examining Third-Party Distributed Virtual Switches

When VMware first introduced distributed switches with vSphere 4.0 in 2009, it also enabled third-party developers to produce their own distributed switches that would "plug in" to vSphere's distributed switch APIs. This would allow VMware partners to extend the functionality available within vSphere environments through third-party distributed switches. At the time this functionality was introduced, only a single VMware partner had a product ready: Cisco with its Nexus 1000V. Since then, at least two other VMware partners have created their own distributed switches, and now VMware customers have a few different options.

At the time of this writing, three third-party distributed switches were available for use with vSphere 5.5:

- Cisco Nexus 1000V

- IBM Distributed Virtual Switch 5000V

- HP FlexFabric Virtual Switch 5900v

In the following sections, we'll take a quick look at each of these options.

Cisco Nexus 1000V

The first third-party distributed switch, the Cisco Nexus 1000V, leverages Cisco NX-OS in a virtual environment to allow network administrators to use a familiar, CLI-based network management environment in the vSphere environment as well as in the physical environment.

The Cisco Nexus 1000V has the following two major components:

- The Virtual Ethernet Module (VEM), which executes inside the ESXi hypervisor and replaces the standard vSwitch functionality. The VEM leverages the vSphere Distributed Switch APIs to enable features like quality of service (QoS), private VLANs, access control lists, NetFlow, and SPAN.

- The Virtual Supervisor Module (VSM), which is a Cisco NX-OS instance running as a VM (note that Cisco also sells a hardware appliance, called the Nexus 1010, that can provide a Nexus 1000V VSM). The VSM controls multiple VEMs as one logical modular switch. All configuration is performed through the VSM and propagated to the VEMs automatically through a management link with vCenter Server. The Nexus 1000V supports redundant VSMs, a configuration with both a primary VSM and a secondary VSM.

Although the Nexus 1000V uses the Cisco "Nexus" brand name, it is interoperable with any upstream physical switch from any vendor; it does not require physical Cisco Nexus switches. Of course, the features that are supported will vary based on the upstream physical switches, so keep in mind that some Nexus 1000V features may not work with all physical switches.

For more detailed information on the Cisco Nexus 1000V, please refer to Cisco's website at www.cisco.com/en/US/products/ps9902/index.html.

IBM Distributed Virtual Switch 5000V

The IBM Distributed Virtual Switch (DVS) 5000V was the second third-party distributed switch to become available for vSphere environments.

Like the Cisco Nexus 1000V, the IBM DVS 5000V employs a two-part architecture:

- The DVS 5000V Data Path Module (DPM) is embedded in the ESXi hypervisor and replaces the standard virtual switching functionality found there. The DPM supports features like QoS, sFlow v5, RADIUS, TACACS+, private VLANs, local VM-to-VM traffic control using access control lists (ACLs), local port mirroring (SPAN), remote port mirroring (ERSPAN), and advanced VM troubleshooting and visibility.

◆ The DVS 5000V Controller performs the central management and configuration of the DPMs that exist on a number of ESXi hosts, communicating with vCenter Server so that the 5000V looks like a distributed switch to the VMware environment.

One point of difference between the Cisco 1000V and the IBM 5000V is that the IBM 5000V supports newer Ethernet technologies such as Edge Virtual Bridging (EVB), Virtual Ethernet Port Aggregation (VEPA), and Virtual Station Interface (VSI) Discovery and Configuration Protocol (VDP). These technologies are intended to enable greater integration between the virtual switches in a vSphere environment and the physical switches upstream. For more details about the IBM DVS 5000V, please refer to IBM's website at

`www-03.ibm.com/systems/networking/switches/virtual/dvs5000v/index.html`

HP FlexFabric Virtual Switch 5900v

In May 2013, HP unveiled its third-party distributed virtual switch, the HP FlexFabric Virtual Switch 5900v, initially expected to be available in the fourth quarter of 2013. Because of the dates of announcement and availability, information about the HP FlexFabric 5900v was fairly limited at the time of writing.

HP took a slightly different approach with the 5900v than IBM and Cisco did with their virtual switches. Whereas both IBM and Cisco support multiple types and brands of upstream physical switches, the HP 5900v is designed to work only with HP's FlexFabric 5900AF top-of-rack (ToR) switches through the use of EVB, VEPA, and VDP. In this arrangement, all traffic—even VM-to-VM traffic on the same ESXi host—flows through the HP 5900AF ToR switch, giving the networking teams full visibility and full control over the traffic. This enables HP to support a full range of networking features like QoS, ACLs, and hardware-based sFlow. The HP 5900v is also designed to integrate with HP Intelligent Management Center (IMC) to simplify creating and applying policies that control features like ACLs and QoS to traffic flowing through the HP 5900v and HP 5900AF ToR switches.

For more details about the HP 5900v, please contact HP. (There was no public URL for the HP FlexFabric Virtual Switch 5900v available at the time of writing.)

Before we wrap up this chapter on networking with a quick look toward the future, we'd like to discuss some security-related settings and features available in vSphere environments.

Configuring Virtual Switch Security

Even though vSwitches and distributed switches are considered to be "dumb switches," you can configure them with security policies to enhance or ensure layer 2 security. For vSphere Standard Switches, you can apply security policies at the vSwitch or at the port group level. For vSphere Distributed Switches, you apply security policies only at the distributed port group level. The security settings include the following three options:

◆ Promiscuous mode

◆ MAC address changes

◆ Forged transmits

Applying a security policy to a vSwitch is effective, by default, for all connection types within the switch. However, if a port group on that vSwitch is configured with a competing security policy, it will override the policy set at the vSwitch. For example, if a vSwitch is configured with a security policy that rejects MAC address changes but a port group on the switch is configured to accept MAC address changes, then any VMs connected to that port group will be allowed to communicate even though it is using a MAC address that differs from what is configured in its VMX file.

The default security profile for a vSwitch, shown in Figure 5.75, is set to reject Promiscuous mode and to accept MAC address changes and forged transmits. Similarly, Figure 5.76 shows the default security profile for a distributed port group on a distributed switch.

FIGURE 5.75

The default security profile for a vSwitch prevents Promiscuous mode but allows MAC address changes and forged transmits.

FIGURE 5.76

The default security profile for a distributed port group on a distributed switch also denies MAC address changes and forged transmits.

Each of these security options is explored in more detail in the following sections.

Understanding and Using Promiscuous Mode

The Promiscuous Mode option is set to Reject by default to prevent virtual network adapters from observing any of the traffic submitted through a vSwitch or distributed switch. For enhanced security, allowing Promiscuous mode is not recommended because it is an insecure mode of operation that allows a virtual adapter to access traffic other than its own. Despite the security concerns, there are valid reasons for permitting a switch to operate in Promiscuous mode. An intrusion-detection system (IDS) must be able to identify all traffic to scan for anomalies and malicious patterns of traffic, for example.

Previously in this chapter, we talked about how port groups and VLANs did not have a one-to-one relationship and that occasions may arise when you have multiple port groups on a vSwitch/distributed switch configured with the same VLAN ID. This is exactly one of those situations—you need a system, the IDS, to see traffic intended for other virtual network adapters. Rather than granting that ability to all the systems on a port group, you can create a dedicated port group for just the IDS system. It will have the same VLAN ID and other settings but will allow Promiscuous mode instead of rejecting it. This allows you, the administrator, to carefully control which systems are allowed to use this powerful and potentially security-threatening feature.

As shown in Figure 5.77, the virtual switch security policy will remain at the default setting of Reject for the Promiscuous Mode option, while the VM port group for the IDS will be set to Accept. This setting will override the virtual switch, allowing the IDS to monitor all traffic for that VLAN.

Allowing MAC Address Changes and Forged Transmits

When a VM is created with one or more virtual network adapters, a MAC address is generated for each virtual adapter. Just as Intel, Broadcom, and others manufacture network adapters that include unique MAC address strings, VMware is a network adapter manufacturer that has its own MAC prefix to ensure uniqueness. Of course, VMware doesn't actually manufacture anything because the product exists as a virtual NIC in a VM. You can see the 6-byte, randomly generated MAC addresses for a VM in the configuration file (.vmx) of the VM as well as in the Settings area for a VM within the vSphere Web Client, shown in Figure 5.78. A VMware-assigned MAC address begins with the prefix 00:50:56 or 00:0C:29. In previous versions of ESXi, the value of the fourth set (XX) would not exceed 3F to prevent conflicts with other VMware products, but this appears to have changed in vSphere 5.0. The fifth and sixth sets (YY:ZZ) are generated randomly based on the universally unique identifier (UUID) of the VM that is tied to the location of the VM. For this reason, when a VM location is changed, a prompt appears prior to successful boot. The prompt inquires about keeping the UUID or generating a new UUID, which helps prevent MAC address conflicts.

FIGURE 5.77
Promiscuous mode, though it reduces security, is required when using an intrusion-detection system.

MANUALLY SETTING THE MAC ADDRESS

Manually configuring a MAC address in the configuration file of a VM does not work unless the first three bytes are VMware-provided prefixes and the last three bytes are unique. If a non-VMware MAC prefix is entered in the configuration file, the VM will not power on.

FIGURE 5.78
A VM's initial
MAC address is
automatically
generated and
listed in the
configuration file
for the VM and
displayed within
the vSphere Web
Client.

VM Hardware		Edit...
▸ CPU	1 CPU(s), 0 MHz used	
▸ Memory	1024 MB, 10 MB used	
▸ Hard disk 1	8 GB	
💿 CD/DVD drive 1	Disconnected	🔧▾
💾 Floppy drive 1	Disconnected	🔧▾
▸ Video card	4 MB	
▸ Other	Additional Hardware	
▾ Network adapter 1		
MAC Address	00:50:56:80:dc:c3	
DirectPath I/O	Inactive 🛈	
Network	VM-Networking (connected)	
Compatibility	ESXi 5.5 and later (VM version 10)	

All VMs have two MAC addresses: the initial MAC and the effective MAC. The initial MAC address is the MAC address discussed in the previous paragraph that is generated automatically and that resides in the configuration file. The guest OS has no control over the initial MAC address. The effective MAC address is the MAC address configured by the guest OS that is used during communication with other systems. The effective MAC address is included in network communication as the source MAC of the VM. By default, these two addresses are identical. To force a non-VMware-assigned MAC address to a guest operating system, change the effective MAC address from within the guest OS, as shown in Figure 5.79.

FIGURE 5.79
A VM's source MAC
address is the effec-
tive MAC address,
which by default
matches the ini-
tial MAC address
configured in the
VMX file. The guest
OS, however, may
change the effective
MAC address.

The ability to alter the effective MAC address cannot be removed from the guest OS. However, the ability to let the system function with this altered MAC address is easily addressable through the security policy of a vSwitch or distributed switch. The remaining two settings of a virtual switch security policy are MAC Address Changes and Forged Transmits. These security policies allow or deny differences between the initial MAC address in the configuration file and the effective MAC address in the guest OS. As noted earlier, the default security policy is to accept the differences and process traffic as needed.

The difference between the MAC Address Changes and Forged Transmits security settings involves the direction of the traffic. MAC Address Changes is concerned with the integrity of incoming traffic, while Forged Transmits oversees the integrity of outgoing traffic. If the MAC Address Changes option is set to Reject, traffic will not be passed through the vSwitch to the VM (incoming) if the initial and the effective MAC addresses do not match. If the Forged Transmits option is set to Reject, traffic will not be passed from the VM to the vSwitch (outgoing) if the initial and the effective MAC addresses do not match. Figure 5.80 highlights the security restrictions implemented when MAC Address Changes and Forged Transmits are set to Reject.

FIGURE 5.80
The MAC Address Changes and Forged Transmits security options deal with incoming and outgoing traffic, respectively.

For the highest level of security, VMware recommends setting MAC Address Changes, Forged Transmits, and Promiscuous Mode on each vSwitch or distributed switch/distributed port group to Reject. When warranted or necessary, use port groups to loosen the security for a subset of VMs to connect to the port group.

VIRTUAL SWITCH POLICIES FOR MICROSOFT NETWORK LOAD BALANCING

As with anything, there are, of course, exceptions to the general recommendations for how a virtual switch should be configured. The recommendations for allowing MAC address changes and forged transmits is one great example. For VMs that will be configured as part of a Microsoft Network Load Balancing (NLB) cluster set in Unicast mode, the VM port group must allow MAC address changes and forged transmits. Systems that are part of an NLB cluster will share a common IP address and virtual MAC address.

The shared virtual MAC address is generated by using an algorithm that includes a static component based on the NLB cluster's configuration of Unicast or Multicast mode plus a hexadecimal representation of the four octets that make up the IP address. This shared MAC address will certainly differ from the MAC address defined in the VMX file of the VM. If the VM port group does not allow for differences between the MAC addresses in the VMX and guest OS, NLB will not function as expected. VMware recommends running NLB clusters in Multicast mode because of these issues with NLB clusters in Unicast mode.

Perform the following steps to edit the security profile of a vSwitch:

1. Use a supported web browser to establish a connection to a vCenter Server instance; this launches the vSphere Web Client.

2. Navigate to the specific ESXi host that has the vSwitch you'd like to edit. One way to get there from the vSphere Web Client home screen is to click vCenter, then select Hosts from the Inventory Lists, then select the specific ESXi host from the list of objects on the right.

3. With an ESXi host selected in the inventory list on the left, click the Manage tab, select Settings, and then click Virtual Switches.

4. From the list of virtual switches, select the vSphere Standard Switch you'd like to edit, then click the Edit link (looks like a pencil). This brings up the Edit Settings dialog box for the selected vSwitch.

5. Click Security on the list on the left side of the dialog box, and make the necessary adjustments.

6. Click OK.

Perform the following steps to edit the security profile of a port group on a vSwitch:

1. Connect to a vCenter Server instance using the vSphere Web Client.

2. Navigate to the specific ESXi host and vSphere Standard Switch that contains the port group you wish to edit. You'll find vSwitches in the Virtual Switches section of the Settings area under the Manage tab for a selected ESXi host.

3. Click the name of the port group under the graphical representation of the virtual switch, and then click the Edit link.

4. Click Security, and make the necessary adjustments. You'll need to place a check mark in the Override box to allow the port group to use a different setting than its parent virtual switch.

5. Click OK to save your changes.

Perform the following steps to edit the security profile of a distributed port group on a vSphere Distributed Switch:

1. Use the vSphere Web Client to connection to an instance of vCenter Server.

2. Using the vSphere Web Client, navigate to the Distributed Switches inventory list; you can get there from the vSphere Web Client home page by clicking vCenter, then selecting Distributed Switches from the Inventory Lists area on the left.

3. With a distributed switch selected on the left, click the Manage tab, select Settings, and then click Topology. This will display a graphical representation of the distributed switch.

4. Select an existing distributed port group by clicking its name in the Topology view, and then click the Edit Distributed Port Group Settings icon.

5. Select Security from the list of policy options on the left side of the dialog box.

6. Make the necessary adjustments to the security policy.

7. Click OK to save the changes.

If you need to make the same security-related change to multiple distributed port groups, you can use the Manage Distributed Port Groups command on the Actions menu to perform the same configuration task to multiple distributed port groups at the same time.

Managing the security of a virtual network architecture is much the same as managing the security for any other portion of your information systems. Security policy should dictate that settings be configured as secure as possible to err on the side of caution. Only with proper authorization, documentation, and change-management processes should security be reduced. In addition, the reduction in security should be as controlled as possible to affect the least number of systems if not just the systems requiring the adjustments.

We'll close out this chapter on networking with a quick look ahead at the future of networking in a VMware vSphere environment.

Looking Ahead

The past few years have been fairly tumultuous for the networking industry, which is undergoing a revolution comparable to the revolution of some years ago when server virtualization started seeing broader adoption. A number of forces are driving this revolution: increased use of open-source software in various industries; increased competition among hardware manufacturers, including very low-cost overseas manufacturers; expanded use of x86-based systems and compute virtualization for providing network services (often referred to as network functions virtualization, or NFV); and the rise of control plane protocols like OpenFlow. This latter force has given rise to an entirely new term within networking: *software-defined networking* (SDN).

In March 2013, VMware described its vision for *network virtualization*, which harnesses a number of these macro trends together to enable organizations to provision network services more quickly and in a more automated fashion than before. VMware intends to bring network virtualization to the market in the form of VMware NSX, a product that integrates technologies together from Nicira's Network Virtualization Platform and VMware's own vCloud Networking and Security product suite.

VMware NSX will leverage a number of technologies to enable organizations to create virtual networks—networks that exist entirely in software but that faithfully re-create physical networks. The following technologies are among those that will be found in VMware NSX:

♦ Network overlay protocols like VXLAN, STT, and GRE, to enable isolation of network traffic

♦ Separation of the control plane and data plane using protocols like OpenFlow

◆ Virtualization of network services like load balancing, firewalling, NAT, and dynamic routing (aka NFV)

◆ Centralized controllers that automatically compute and program the virtual network topologies across ESXi hosts

Network virtualization will dramatically change the networking landscape moving forward, but many of the basic principles outlined in this chapter are still going to be applicable as this vision evolves. Getting started with virtual networking in vSphere 5.5 environments is a great first step to moving toward full network virtualization in VMware NSX.

In the next chapter, we'll dive deep into storage in VMware vSphere, a critical component of your vSphere environment.

The Bottom Line

Identify the components of virtual networking.   Virtual networking is a blend of virtual switches, physical switches, VLANs, physical network adapters, virtual adapters, uplinks, NIC teaming, VMs, and port groups.

> **Master It**   What factors contribute to the design of a virtual network and the components involved?

Create virtual switches and distributed virtual switches.   vSphere supports both vSphere Standard Switches and vSphere Distributed Switches. vSphere Distributed Switches bring new functionality to the vSphere networking environment, including private VLANs and a centralized point of management for ESXi clusters.

> **Master It**   You've asked a fellow vSphere administrator to create a vSphere Distributed Switch for you, but the administrator is having problems completing the task because he can't find out how to do this with an ESXi host selected in the vSphere Web Client. What should you tell this administrator?

> **Master It**   As a joint project between the networking and server teams, you are going to implement LACP in your VMware vSphere 5.5 environment. What are some limitations you need to know about?

Create and manage NIC teaming, VLANs, and private VLANs.   NIC teaming allows virtual switches to have redundant network connections to the rest of the network. Virtual switches also provide support for VLANs, which provide logical segmentation of the network, and private VLANs, which provide added security to existing VLANs while allowing systems to share the same IP subnet.

> **Master It**   You'd like to use NIC teaming to bond multiple physical uplinks together for greater redundancy and improved throughput. When selecting the NIC teaming policy, you select Route Based On IP Hash, but then the vSwitch seems to lose connectivity. What could be wrong?

> **Master It**   How do you configure both a vSphere Standard Switch and a vSphere Distributed Switch to pass VLAN tags all the way up to a guest OS?

Examine the options for third-party virtual switches in your environment. In addition to the vSphere Standard Switch and the vSphere Distributed Switch, vSphere also supports a number of third-party virtual switches. These third-party virtual switches support a range of features.

Master It What three third-party virtual switches are, at the time of this book's writing, available for vSphere environments?

Configure virtual switch security policies. Virtual switches support security policies for allowing or rejecting Promiscuous mode, allowing or rejecting MAC address changes, and allowing or rejecting forged transmits. All of the security options can help increase layer 2 security.

Master It You have a networking application that needs to see traffic on the virtual network that is intended for other production systems on the same VLAN. The networking application accomplishes this by using Promiscuous mode. How can you accommodate the needs of this networking application without sacrificing the security of the entire virtual switch?

Master It Another vSphere administrator on your team is trying to configure the security policies on a distributed switch but is having some difficulty. What could be the problem?

Chapter 6

Creating and Configuring Storage Devices

Storage has always been a critical element for any environment, and the storage infrastructure supporting vSphere is no different. This chapter will help you with all the elements required for a proper storage subsystem design, starting with vSphere storage fundamentals at the datastore and VM level and extending to best practices for configuring the storage array. Good storage design is critical for anyone building a virtual datacenter.

In this chapter, you will learn to

◆ Differentiate and understand the fundamentals of shared storage, including SANs and NAS

◆ Understand vSphere storage options

◆ Configure storage at the vSphere layer

◆ Configure storage at the VM layer

◆ Leverage best practices for SAN and NAS storage with vSphere

Reviewing the Importance of Storage Design

Storage design has always been important, but it becomes more so as vSphere is used for larger workloads, for mission-critical applications, for larger clusters, and as the basis for offerings based on Infrastructure as a Service (IaaS) in a nearly 100 percent virtualized datacenter. You can probably imagine why this is the case:

Advanced Capabilities Many of vSphere's advanced features depend on shared storage; vSphere High Availability (HA), vSphere Distributed Resource Scheduler (DRS), vSphere Fault Tolerance (FT), and VMware vCenter Site Recovery Manager all have a critical dependency on shared storage.

Performance People understand the benefits that virtualization brings—consolidation, higher utilization, more flexibility, and higher efficiency. But often, people have initial questions about how vSphere can deliver performance for individual applications when it is inherently consolidated and oversubscribed. Likewise, the overall performance of the VMs and the entire vSphere cluster both depend on shared storage, which is also highly consolidated and oversubscribed.

Availability   The overall availability of your virtualized infrastructure—and by extension, the VMs running on that infrastructure—depend on the shared storage infrastructure. Designing high availability into this infrastructure element is paramount. If the storage is not available, vSphere HA will not be able to recover and the aggregate community of VMs can be affected. (We discuss vSphere HA in detail in Chapter 7, "Ensuring High Availability and Business Continuity.")

While design choices at the server layer can make the vSphere environment relatively more or less optimal, design choices for shared resources such as networking and storage can sometimes make the difference between virtualization success and failure. This is especially true for storage because of its critical role. The importance of storage design and storage design choices remains true regardless of whether you are using storage area networks (SANs), which present shared storage as disks or logical units (LUNs); network attached storage (NAS), which presents shared storage as remotely accessed file systems; or a mix of both. Done correctly, you can create a shared storage design that lowers the cost and increases the efficiency, performance, availability, and flexibility of your vSphere environment.

This chapter breaks down these topics into the following main sections:

◆   "Examining Shared Storage Fundamentals" covers broad topics of shared storage that are critical with vSphere, including hardware architectures, protocol choices, and key terminology. Although these topics apply to any environment that uses shared storage, understanding these core technologies is a prerequisite to understanding how to apply storage technology in a vSphere implementation.

◆   "Implementing vSphere Storage Fundamentals" covers how storage technologies covered in the previous main section are applied and used in vSphere environments. This main section is broken down into a section on VMFS datastores ("Working with VMFS Datastores"), raw device mappings ("Working with Raw Device Mappings"), NFS datastores ("Working with NFS Datastores"), and VM-level storage configurations ("Working with VM-Level Storage Configuration").

◆   "Leveraging SAN and NAS Best Practices" covers how to pull together all the topics discussed to move forward with a design that will support a broad set of vSphere environments.

Examining Shared Storage Fundamentals

vSphere 5.5 offers numerous storage choices and configuration options relative to previous versions of vSphere or to nonvirtualized environments. These choices and configuration options apply at two fundamental levels: the virtualization layer and the VM layer. The storage requirements for a vSphere environment and the VMs it supports are unique, making broad generalizations impossible. The requirements for any given vSphere environment span use cases ranging from virtual servers and desktops to templates and virtual CD/DVD (ISO) images. The virtual server use cases vary from light utility VMs with few storage performance considerations to the largest database workloads possible, with incredibly important storage layout considerations.

Let's start by examining this at a fundamental level. Figure 6.1 shows a simple three-host vSphere environment attached to shared storage.

It's immediately apparent that the ESXi hosts and the VMs will be contending for the shared storage asset. In a way similar to how ESXi can consolidate many VMs onto a single ESXi host, the shared storage consolidates the storage needs of all the VMs.

FIGURE 6.1
When ESXi hosts are connected to that same shared storage, they share its capabilities.

When sizing or designing the storage solution, you focus on attributes like capacity (gigabytes or terabytes) and performance, which is measured in bandwidth (megabytes per second, or MBps), throughput (I/O operations per second, or IOPS), and latency (in milliseconds). It goes sometimes without saying, but designing for availability, redundancy, and fault tolerance is also of paramount importance.

DETERMINING PERFORMANCE REQUIREMENTS

How do you determine the storage performance requirements of an application that will be virtualized, a single ESXi host, or even a complete vSphere environment? There are many rules of thumb for key applications, and the best practices for every application could fill a book. Here are some quick considerations:

◆ Online transaction processing (OLTP) databases need low latency (as low as you can get, but a few milliseconds is a good target). They are also sensitive to input/output operations per second (IOPS), because their I/O size is small (4 KB to 8 KB). TPC-C and TPC-E benchmarks generate this kind of I/O pattern.

◆ Decision support system/business intelligence databases and SQL Server instances that support Microsoft Office SharePoint Server need high bandwidth, which can be hundreds of megabytes per second because their I/O size is large (64 KB to 1 MB). They are not particularly sensitive to latency; TPC-H benchmarks generate the kind of I/O pattern used by these use cases.

◆ Copying files, deploying from templates, using Storage vMotion, and backing up VMs (within the guest or from a proxy server via vSphere Storage APIs) without using array-based approaches generally all need high bandwidth. In fact, the more, the better.

So, what does vSphere need? The answer is basic—the needs of the vSphere environment are the aggregate sum of all the use cases across all the VMs, which can cover a broad set of requirements. If the VMs are *all* small-block workloads and you don't do backups inside guests (which generate large-block workloads), then it's all about IOPS. If the VMs are *all* large-block workloads, then it's all about MBps. More often than not, a virtual datacenter has a mix, so the storage design should be flexible enough to deliver a broad range of capabilities and capacity—but without overbuilding.

How can you best determine what you will need? With small workloads, too much planning can result in overbuilding. You can use simple tools, including VMware Capacity Planner, Windows Perfmon, and top in Linux, to determine the I/O pattern of the applications and OSes that will be virtualized.

Also, if you have many VMs, consider the aggregate performance requirements, and don't just look at capacity requirements. After all, 1000 VMs with 10 IOPS each need an aggregate of 10000 IOPS, which is 50 to 80 fast spindle's worth, regardless of the capacity (in gigabytes or terabytes) needed.

Use large pool designs for generic, light workload VMs.

Conversely, focused, larger VM I/O workloads (such as virtualized SQL Server instances, SharePoint, Exchange, and other use cases) should be where you spend some time planning and thinking about layout. There are numerous VMware published best practices and a great deal of VMware partner reference architecture documentation that can help with virtualizing Exchange, SQL Server, Oracle, and SAP workloads. We have listed a few resources for you:

◆ Exchange

www.vmware.com/solutions/business-critical-apps/exchange/index.html

◆ SQL Server

www.vmware.com/solutions/business-critical-apps/sql-virtualization/overview.html

◆ Oracle

www.vmware.com/solutions/business-critical-apps/oracle-virtualization/index.html

◆ SAP

www.vmware.com/solutions/business-critical-apps/sap-virtualization/index.html

As with performance, the overall availability of the vSphere environment and the VMs depends on the same shared storage infrastructure, so a robust design is paramount. If the storage is not available, vSphere HA will not be able to recover and the consolidated community of VMs will be affected.

Note that we said the "consolidated community of VMs." That statement underscores the need to put more care and focus on the availability of the configuration than on the performance or capacity requirements. In virtual configurations, the availability impact of storage issues is more pronounced, so you must use greater care in an availability design than in the physical world. It's not just one workload being affected—it's multiple workloads.

At the same time, advanced vSphere options such as Storage vMotion and advanced array techniques allow you to add, move, or change storage configurations nondisruptively, making it unlikely that you'll create a design where you can't nondisruptively fix performance issues.

Before going too much further, it's important to cover several basics of storage:

◆ Local storage versus shared storage

◆ Common storage array architectures

◆ RAID technologies

◆ Midrange and enterprise storage array design

◆ Protocol choices

We'll start with a brief discussion of local storage versus shared storage.

Comparing Local Storage with Shared Storage

An ESXi host can have one or more storage options actively configured, including the following:

◆ Local SAS/SATA/SCSI storage

◆ Fibre Channel

◆ Fibre Channel over Ethernet (FCoE)

◆ iSCSI using software and hardware initiators

◆ NAS (specifically, NFS)

◆ InfiniBand

Traditionally, local storage has been used in a limited fashion with vSphere because so many of vSphere's advanced features—such as vMotion, vSphere HA, vSphere DRS, and vSphere FT—required shared external storage. With vSphere Auto Deploy and the ability to deploy ESXi images directly to RAM at boot time coupled with host profiles to automate the configuration, in *some* environments local storage from vSphere 5.0 serves even less of a function than it did in previous versions.

With vSphere 5.0, VMware introduced a way to utilize local storage though the installation of a virtual appliance called the vSphere Storage Appliance, or simply VSA. At a high level, the VSA takes local storage and presents it back to ESXi hosts as a shared NFS mount. There are some limitations however. It can be configured with only two or three hosts, there are strict rules around the hardware that can run the VSA, and on top of this, it is licensed as a separate product. While it does utilize the underused local storage of servers, the use case for the VSA simply is not valid for many organizations.

vSphere 5.5, however, has two new features that are significantly more relevant to organizations than the VSA. vSphere Flash Read Cache and VSAN both take advantage of local storage, in particular, local *flash* storage. vSphere Flash Read Cache takes flash-based storage and allows administrators to allocate portions of it as a read cache for VM read I/O. VSAN extends on the idea behind the VSA and presents the local storage as a distributed datastore across many hosts. While this concept is similar to the VSA, the use of a virtual appliance is not required, nor are NFS mounts; it's entirely built into the ESXi hypervisor. Think of this as shared *internal* storage. Later in this chapter we'll explain how VSAN works and you can find information on vSphere Flash Read Cache in Chapter 11, "Managing Resource Allocation."

So, how carefully do you need to design your local storage? The answer is simple—generally speaking, careful planning is not necessary for storage local to the ESXi installation. ESXi stores very little locally, and by using host profiles and distributed virtual switches, it can be easy and fast to replace a failed ESXi host. During this time, vSphere HA will make sure the VMs are running on the other ESXi hosts in the cluster. However, taking advantage of new features within vSphere 5.5 such as VSAN will certainly require careful consideration. Storage underpins your entire vSphere environment. Make the effort to ensure that your shared storage design is robust, taking into consideration internal- and external-based shared storage choices.

Real World Scenario

NO LOCAL STORAGE? NO PROBLEM!

What if you don't *have* local storage? (Perhaps you have a diskless blade system, for example.) There are many options for diskless systems, including booting from Fibre Channel/iSCSI SAN and network-based boot methods like vSphere Auto Deploy (discussed in Chapter 2, "Planning and Installing VMware ESXi"). There is also the option of using USB boot, a technique that we've employed on numerous occasions in lab and production environments. Both Auto Deploy and USB boot give you some flexibility in quickly reprovisioning hardware or deploying updated versions of vSphere, but there are some quirks, so plan accordingly. Refer to Chapter 2 for more details on selecting the configuration of your ESXi hosts.

Shared storage is the basis for most vSphere environments because it supports the VMs themselves and because it is a requirement for many of vSphere's features. Shared *external* storage in SAN configurations (which encompasses Fibre Channel, FCoE, and iSCSI) and NAS (NFS) is always highly consolidated. This makes it efficient. SAN/NAS or VSAN can take the direct attached storage in physical servers that are 10 percent utilized and consolidate them to 80 percent utilization.

As you can see, shared storage is a key design point. Whether it's shared external storage or you're planning to share the local storage system out, it's important to understand some of the array architectures that vendors use to provide shared storage to vSphere environments. The high-level overview in the following section is neutral on specific storage array vendors because the internal architectures vary tremendously.

Defining Common Storage Array Architectures

This section is remedial for anyone with basic storage experience, but it's needed for vSphere administrators with no storage knowledge. For people unfamiliar with storage, the topic can be a bit disorienting at first. Servers across vendors tend to be relatively similar, but the same logic can't be applied to the storage layer because core architectural differences between storage vendor architectures are vast. In spite of that, storage arrays have several core architectural elements that are consistent across vendors, across implementations, and even across protocols.

The elements that make up a shared storage array consist of external connectivity, storage processors, array software, cache memory, disks, and bandwidth:

External Connectivity The external (physical) connectivity between the storage array and the hosts (in this case, the ESXi hosts) is generally Fibre Channel or Ethernet, though InfiniBand and other rare protocols exist. The characteristics of this connectivity define the maximum bandwidth (given no other constraints, and there usually are other constraints) of the communication between the ESXi host and the shared storage array.

Storage Processors Different vendors have different names for storage processors, which are considered the brains of the array. They handle the I/O and run the array software. In most modern arrays, the storage processors are not purpose-built application-specific integrated circuits (ASICs) but instead are general-purpose CPUs. Some arrays use PowerPC, some use specific ASICs, and some use custom ASICs for specific purposes. But in general, if you cracked open an array, you would most likely find an Intel or AMD CPU.

Array Software Although hardware specifications are important and can define the scaling limits of the array, just as important are the functional capabilities the array software provides. The capabilities of modern storage arrays are vast—similar in scope to vSphere itself—and vary wildly among vendors. At a high level, the following list includes some examples of these array capabilities and key functions:

- Remote storage replication for disaster recovery. These technologies come in many flavors with features that deliver varying capabilities. These include varying recovery point objectives (RPOs)—which reflect how current the remote replica is at any time, ranging from synchronous to asynchronous and continuous. Asynchronous RPOs can range from less than minutes to more than hours, and continuous is a constant remote journal that can recover to varying RPOs. Other examples of remote replication technologies are technologies that drive synchronicity across storage objects (or "consistency technology"), compression, and many other attributes, such as integration with VMware vCenter Site Recovery Manager.

- Snapshot and clone capabilities for instant point-in-time local copies for test and development and local recovery. These also share some of the ideas of the remote replication technologies like "consistency technology," and some variations of point-in-time protection and replicas also have TiVo-like continuous journaling locally and remotely where you can recover/copy any point in time.

- Capacity-reduction techniques such as archiving and deduplication.

- Automated data movement between performance/cost storage tiers at varying levels of granularity.

- LUN/file system expansion and mobility, which means reconfiguring storage properties dynamically and nondisruptively to add capacity or performance as needed.

- Thin provisioning, which typically involves allocating storage on demand as applications and workloads require it.

- Storage quality of service (QoS), which means prioritizing I/O to deliver a given MBps, IOPS, or latency.

The array software defines the "persona" of the array, which in turn impacts core concepts and behavior. Arrays generally have a "file server" persona (sometimes with the ability to do some block storage by presenting a file as a LUN) or a "block" persona (generally with no ability to act as a file server). In some cases, arrays are combinations of file servers and block devices.

Cache Memory Every array differs as to how cache memory is implemented, but all have some degree of nonvolatile memory used for various caching functions—delivering lower latency and higher IOPS throughput by buffering I/O using write caches and storing commonly read data to deliver a faster response time using read caches. Nonvolatility (meaning ability to survive a power loss) is critical for write caches because the data is not yet committed to disk, but it's not critical for read caches. Cached performance is often used when describing shared storage array performance maximums (in IOPS, MBps, or latency) in specification sheets. These results generally do not reflect real-world scenarios. In most real-world scenarios, performance tends to be dominated by the disk performance (the type and number of disks) and is helped by write caches in most cases, but only marginally by read caches (with the exception of large relational database management systems, which depend heavily on read-ahead cache algorithms). One vSphere use case that is helped by read caches is a situation where many boot images are stored only once (through the use of vSphere or storage array technology), but this is also a small subset of the overall VM I/O pattern.

Disks   Arrays differ as to which type of disks (often called *spindles*) they support and how many they can scale to support. Drives are described according to two different attributes. First, drives are often separated by the drive interface they use: Fibre Channel, serial-attached SCSI (SAS), and serial ATA (SATA). In addition, drives—with the exception of enterprise flash drives (EFDs)—are described by their rotational speed, noted in revolutions per minute (RPM). Fibre Channel drives typically come in 15K RPM and 10K RPM variants, SATA drives are usually found in 5400 RPM and 7200 RPM variants, and SAS drives are usually 15K RPM or 10K RPM variants. Second, EFDs, which are now mainstream, are solid state and have no moving parts; therefore rotational speed does not apply. The type and number of disks are very important. Coupled with how they are configured, this determines how a storage object (either a LUN for a block device or a file system for a NAS device) performs. Shared storage vendors generally use disks from the same disk vendors, so this is an area of commonality across shared storage vendors. The following list is a quick reference on what to expect under a random read/write workload from a given disk drive:

- 7,200 RPM SATA: 80 IOPS

- 10K RPM SATA/SAS/Fibre Channel: 120 IOPS

- 15K RPM SAS/Fibre Channel: 180 IOPS

- A commercial solid-state drive (SSD) based on Multi-Level Cell (MLC) technology: 1,000–2,000 IOPS

- An Enterprise Flash Drive (EFD) based on Single-Level Cell (SLC) technology and much deeper, very high-speed memory buffers: 6,000–30,000 IOPS

Bandwidth (Megabytes per Second)   Performance tends to be more consistent across drive types when large-block, sequential workloads are used (such as single-purpose workloads like archiving or backup to disk), so in these cases, large SATA drives deliver strong performance at a low cost.

Explaining RAID

Redundant Array of Inexpensive (sometimes "Independent") Disks (RAID) is a fundamental and critical method of storing the same data several times. RAID is used to increase data availability (by protecting against the failure of a drive) and to scale performance beyond that of a single drive. Every array implements various RAID schemes (even if it is largely invisible in file server persona arrays where RAID is done below the file system, which is the primary management element).

Think of it this way: Disks are mechanical, spinning, rust-colored surfaces. The read/write heads are flying microns above the surface while reading minute magnetic field variations and writing data by affecting surface areas also only microns in size.

THE "MAGIC" OF DISK DRIVE TECHNOLOGY

It really is a technological miracle that magnetic disks work at all. What a disk does all day long is analogous to a pilot flying a 747 at 600 miles per hour 6 inches off the ground and reading pages in a book while doing it!

In spite of the technological wonder of hard disks, they have unbelievable reliability statistics. But they do fail—and fail predictably, unlike other elements of a system. RAID schemes address this by leveraging multiple disks together and using copies of data to support I/O until the drive can be replaced and the RAID protection can be rebuilt. Each RAID configuration tends to have different performance characteristics and different capacity overhead impact.

We recommend that you view RAID choices as a significant factor in your design. Most arrays layer additional constructs on top of the basic RAID protection. (These constructs have many different names, but common ones are *metas, virtual pools, aggregates,* and *volumes.*)

Remember, all the RAID protection in the world won't protect you from an outage if the connectivity to your host is lost, if you don't monitor and replace failed drives and allocate drives as hot spares to automatically replace failed drives, or if the entire array is lost. It's for these reasons that it's important to design the storage network properly, to configure hot spares as advised by the storage vendor, and to monitor for and replace failed elements. Always consider a disaster-recovery plan and remote replication to protect from complete array failure.

Let's examine the RAID choices:

RAID 0   This RAID level offers no redundancy and no protection against drive failure (see Figure 6.2). In fact, it has a *higher* aggregate risk than a single disk because any single disk failing affects the whole RAID group. Data is spread across all the disks in the RAID group, which is often called a *stripe*. Although it delivers fast performance, this is the only RAID type that is usually not appropriate for any production vSphere use because of the availability profile.

FIGURE 6.2
In a RAID 0 configuration, the data is striped across all the disks in the RAID set, providing very good performance but very poor availability.

RAID 1, 1+0, 0+1   These mirrored RAID levels offer high degrees of protection but at the cost of 50 percent loss of usable capacity (see Figure 6.3). This is versus the raw aggregate capacity of the sum of the capacity of the drives. RAID 1 simply writes every I/O to two drives and can balance reads across both drives (because there are two copies). This can be coupled with RAID 0 to form RAID 1+0 (or RAID 10), which mirrors a stripe set, or to form RAID 0+1, which stripes data across pairs of mirrors. This has the benefit of being able to withstand multiple drives failing, but only if the drives fail on different elements of a stripe on different mirrors, thus making RAID 1+0 more fault tolerant than RAID 0+1. The other benefit of a mirrored RAID configuration is that, in the case of a failed drive, rebuild times can be very rapid, which shortens periods of exposure.

FIGURE 6.3
This RAID 10 2+2 configuration provides good performance and good availability, but at the cost of 50 percent of the usable capacity.

Data: 1011

Write: 10   Write: 11   Write: 10   Write: 11

Parity RAID (RAID 5, RAID 6)   These RAID levels use a mathematical calculation (an XOR parity calculation) to represent the data across several drives. This tends to be a good compromise between the availability of RAID 1 and the capacity efficiency of RAID 0. RAID 5 calculates the parity across the drives in the set and writes the parity to another drive. This parity block calculation with RAID 5 is rotated among the arrays in the RAID 5 set.

Parity RAID schemes can deliver very good performance, but there is always some degree of write penalty. For a full-stripe write, the only penalty is the parity calculation and the parity write, but in a partial-stripe write, the old block contents need to be read, a new parity calculation needs to be made, and all the blocks need to be updated. However, generally modern arrays have various methods to minimize this effect.

Read performance, on the other hand, is generally excellent because a larger number of drives can be read from than with mirrored RAID schemes. RAID 5 nomenclature refers to the number of drives in the RAID group, so Figure 6.4 would be referred to as a RAID 5 4+1 set. In the figure, the storage efficiency (in terms of usable to raw capacity) is 80 percent, which is much better than RAID 1 or 10.

FIGURE 6.4
A RAID 5 4+1 configuration offers a balance between performance and efficiency.

Data: 1011

Write: 1   Write: 0   Write: 1   Write: 1   Write: Parity

RAID 5 can be coupled with stripes, so RAID 50 is a pair of RAID 5 sets with data striped across them.

When a drive fails in a RAID 5 set, I/O can be fulfilled using the remaining drives and the parity drive, and when the failed drive is replaced, the data can be reconstructed using the remaining data and parity.

A Key RAID 5 Consideration

One downside to RAID 5 is that only one drive can fail in the RAID set. If another drive fails before the failed drive is replaced and rebuilt using the parity data, data loss occurs. The period of exposure to data loss because of the second drive failing should be mitigated.

The period of time that a RAID 5 set is rebuilding should be as short as possible to minimize the risk. The following designs aggravate this situation by creating longer rebuild periods:

◆ Very large RAID groups (think 8+1 and larger), which require more reads to reconstruct the failed drive.

◆ Very large drives (think 1 TB SATA and 500 GB Fibre Channel drives), which cause more data to be rebuilt.

◆ Slower drives that struggle heavily during the period when they are providing the data to rebuild the replaced drive and simultaneously support production I/O (think SATA drives, which tend to be slower during the random I/O that characterizes a RAID rebuild). The period of a RAID rebuild is actually one of the most stressful parts of a disk's life. Not only must it service the production I/O workload, but it must also provide data to support the rebuild, and it is known that drives are statistically more likely to fail during a rebuild than during normal duty cycles.

The following technologies all mitigate the risk of a dual drive failure (and most arrays do various degrees of each of these items):

◆ Using proactive hot sparing, which shortens the rebuild period substantially by automatically starting the hot spare *before* the drive fails. The failure of a disk is generally preceded with read errors (which are recoverable; they are detected and corrected using on-disk parity information) or write errors, both of which are noncatastrophic. When a threshold of these errors occurs *before* the disk itself fails, the failing drive is replaced by a hot spare by the array. This is much faster than the rebuild after the failure, because the bulk of the failing drive can be used for the copy and because only the portions of the drive that are failing need to use parity information from other disks.

◆ Using smaller RAID 5 sets (for faster rebuild) and striping the data across them using a higher-level construct.

◆ Using a second parity calculation and storing this on another disk.

As described in the sidebar "A Key RAID 5 Consideration," one way to protect against data loss in the event of a single drive failure in a RAID 5 set is to use another parity calculation. This type of RAID is called RAID 6 (RAID-DP is a RAID 6 variant that uses two dedicated parity drives, analogous to RAID 4). This is a good choice when large RAID groups and SATA are used.

Figure 6.5 shows an example of a RAID 6 4+2 configuration. The data is striped across four disks, and a parity calculation is stored on the fifth disk. A second parity calculation is stored on another disk. RAID 6 rotates the parity location with I/O, and RAID-DP uses a pair of dedicated parity disks. This provides good performance and good availability but a loss in capacity efficiency. The purpose of the second parity bit is to withstand a second drive failure during RAID rebuild periods. It is important to use RAID 6 in place of RAID 5 if you meet the conditions noted in the previous sidebar and are unable to otherwise use the mitigation methods noted.

FIGURE 6.5

A RAID 6 4+2 configuration offers protection against double drive failures.

While this is a reasonably detailed discussion of RAID levels, what you should take from it is that you shouldn't worry about it too much. Just don't use RAID 0 unless you have a proper use case for it. Use hot spare drives and follow the vendor best practices on hot spare density. EMC, for example, generally recommends one hot spare for every 30 drives in its arrays, whereas Compellent recommends one hot spare per drive type and per drive shelf. Just be sure to check with your storage vendor for their specific recommendations.

For most vSphere implementations, RAID 5 is a good balance of capacity efficiency, performance, and availability. Use RAID 6 if you have to use large SATA RAID groups or don't have proactive hot spares. RAID 10 schemes still make sense when you need significant write performance. Remember that for your vSphere environment it doesn't all have to be one RAID type; in fact, mixing different RAID types can be very useful to deliver different tiers of performance/availability.

For example, you can use most datastores with RAID 5 as the default LUN configuration, sparingly use RAID 10 schemes where needed, and use storage-based policy management, which we'll discuss later in this chapter, to ensure that the VMs are located on the storage that suits their requirements.

You should definitely make sure that you have enough spindles in the RAID group to meet the aggregate workload of the LUNs you create in that RAID group. The RAID type will affect the ability of the RAID group to support the workload, so keep RAID overhead (like the RAID 5 write penalty) in mind. Fortunately, some storage arrays can nondisruptively add spindles to a RAID group to add performance as needed, so if you find that you need more performance, you can correct it. Storage vMotion can also help you manually balance workloads.

Now let's take a closer look at some specific storage array design architectures that will impact your vSphere storage environment.

Understanding VSAN

vSphere 5.5 introduces a brand-new storage feature, virtual SAN, or simply VSAN. At a high level, VSAN pools the locally attached storage from members of a VSAN–enabled cluster and presents the aggregated pool back to all hosts within the cluster. This could be considered an "array" of sorts because just like a normal SAN, it has multiple disks presented to multiple hosts, but we would take it one step further and consider it an "internal array." While VMware has announced VSAN as a new feature in vSphere 5.5, there are a few caveats. During the first few months of its availability it will be considered "beta only" and therefore not for production use. Also note that VSAN is licensed separately from vSphere itself.

As we mentioned earlier, in the section "Comparing Local Storage with Shared Storage," VSAN does not require any additional software installations. It is built directly into ESXi. Managed from vCenter Server, VSAN is compatible with all the other cluster features that vSphere offers, such as vMotion, HA, and DRS. You can even use Storage DRS to migrate VMs on or off a VSAN datastore.

VSAN uses the disks directly attached to the ESXi hosts and is simple to set up, but there are a few specific requirements. Listed here is what you'll need to get VSAN up and running:

◆ ESXi 5.5 hosts

◆ vCenter 5.5

◆ One or more SSDs per host

◆ One or more HDDs per host

◆ Minimum of three hosts per VSAN cluster

◆ Maximum of eight hosts per VSAN cluster

◆ 1 Gbps network between hosts (10 Gbps recommended)

As you can see from the list, VSAN requires at least one flash-based device in each host. What may not be apparent from the requirements list is that the capacity of the SSD is not actually added to the overall usable space of the VSAN datastore. VSANs use the SSD as a read and write cache just as some external SANs do. When blocks are written to the underlying datastore, they are written to the SSDs first, and later the data can be relocated to the (spinning) HDDs if it's not considered to be frequently accessed.

VSAN doesn't use the traditional RAID concepts that we explained in the previous section; it uses what VMware is calling RAIN, or Reliable Array of Independent Nodes. So, if there's no RAID, how do you achieve the expected reliability when using VSAN? VSAN uses a combination of VASA and Storage Service Policies to ensure that VMs are located on more than one disk and/or host to achieve their performance and availability requirements. This is why VMware recommends 10 Gbps networking between ESXi hosts when using VSAN. A VM's virtual disk could be located on one physical host but could be running on another host's CPU and memory. The storage system is fully abstracted from the compute resources, as you can see in Figure 6.6. In all likelihood the VMs virtual disk files could be located on multiple hosts in the cluster to ensure a level of redundancy.

FIGURE 6.6
VSAN abstracts the ESXi host's local disks and presents them to the entire VSAN cluster to consume.

Understanding Midrange and External Enterprise Storage Array Design

There are some major differences in physical array design that can be pertinent in a vSphere design.

Traditional external midrange storage arrays are generally arrays with dual-storage processor cache designs where the cache is localized to one storage processor or another but commonly mirrored between them. (Remember that all vendors call storage processors something slightly different; sometimes they are called *controllers*, *heads*, *engines*, or *nodes*.) In cases where one of the storage processors fails, the array remains available, but in general, performance is degraded (unless you drive the storage processors to only 50 percent storage processor utilization during normal operation).

External enterprise storage arrays are generally considered to be those that scale to many more controllers and a much larger global cache (memory can be accessed through some common shared model). In these cases, multiple elements can fail while the array is being used at a very high degree of utilization—without any significant performance degradation. Enterprise arrays can also include support for mainframes, and there are other characteristics that are beyond the scope of this book.

Hybrid designs exist as well, such as scale-out designs where they can scale out to more than two storage processors but without the features otherwise associated with enterprise storage arrays. Often these are iSCSI-only arrays and leverage iSCSI redirection techniques (which are not options of the Fibre Channel or NAS protocol stacks) as a core part of their scale-out design.

Design can be confusing, however, because VMware and storage vendors use the same words to express different things. To most storage vendors, an *active-active* storage array is an array that can service I/O on all storage processor units at once, and an *active-passive* design is a system where one storage processor is idle until it takes over for the failed unit. VMware has specific nomenclature for these terms that is focused on the model for a *specific LUN*. VMware defines active-active and active-passive arrays in the following way (this information is taken from the *vSphere Storage Guide*):

Active-Active Storage System   An active-active storage system provides access to LUNs simultaneously through all available storage ports without significant performance degradation. Barring a path failure, all paths are active at all times.

Active-Passive Storage System   In an active-passive storage system, one storage processor is actively providing access to a given LUN. Other processors act as backup for the LUN and can be actively servicing I/O to other LUNs. In the event of the failure of an active storage port, one of the passive storage processors can be activated to handle I/O.

Asymmetrical Storage System   An asymmetrical storage system supports Asymmetric Logical Unit Access (ALUA), which allows storage systems to provide different levels of access per port. This permits the hosts to determine the states of target ports and establish priority for paths. (See the sidebar "The Fine Line between Active-Active and Active-Passive" for more details on ALUA.)

Virtual Port Storage System   Access to all LUNs is provided through a single virtual port. These are active-active devices where the multiple connections are disguised behind the single virtual port. Virtual port storage systems handle failover and connection balancing transparently, which is often referred to as "transparent failover."

This distinction between array types is important because VMware's definition is based on the multipathing mechanics, not whether you can use both storage processors at once. The active-active and active-passive definitions apply equally to Fibre Channel (and FCoE) and iSCSI arrays, and the virtual port definition applies to only iSCSI (because it uses an iSCSI redirection mechanism that is not possible on Fibre Channel/FCoE).

THE FINE LINE BETWEEN ACTIVE-ACTIVE AND ACTIVE-PASSIVE

Wondering why VMware specifies "without significant performance degradation" in the active-active definition? The reason is found within ALUA, a standard supported by many midrange arrays. vSphere supports ALUA with arrays that implement ALUA compliant with the SPC-3 standard.

Midrange arrays usually have an internal interconnect between the two storage processors used for write cache mirroring and other management purposes. ALUA was an addition to the SCSI standard that enables a LUN to be presented on its primary path and on an asymmetrical (significantly slower) path via the secondary storage processor, transferring the data over this internal interconnect.

The key is that the "non-optimized path" generally comes with a significant performance degradation. The midrange arrays don't have the internal interconnection bandwidth to deliver the same response on both storage processors because there is usually a relatively small, or higher-latency, internal interconnect used for cache mirroring that is used for ALUA versus enterprise arrays that have a very-high-bandwidth internal model.

Without ALUA, on an array with an active-passive LUN ownership model, paths to a LUN are shown as active, standby (designates that the port is reachable but is on a processor that does not have the LUN), and dead. When the failover mode is set to ALUA, a new state is possible: active non-optimized. This is not shown distinctly in the vSphere Web Client GUI, but it looks instead like a normal active path. The difference is that it is not used for any I/O.

So, should you configure your midrange array to use ALUA? Follow your storage vendor's best practice. For some arrays this is more important than others. Remember, however, that the non-optimized paths will not be used (by default) even if you select the Round Robin policy. An active-passive array using ALUA is not functionally equivalent to an active-passive array where all paths are used. This behavior can be different if using a third-party multipathing module—see the section "Reviewing Multipathing" later in this chapter.

By definition, all enterprise arrays are active-active arrays (by VMware's definition), but not all midrange arrays are active-passive. To make things even more confusing, not all active-active arrays (again, by VMware's definition) are enterprise arrays!

So, what do you do? What kind of array architecture is the right one for VMware? The answer is simple: All of them on VMware's Hardware Compatibility List (HCL) work; you just need to understand how the one *you* have works.

Most customers' needs are well met by midrange arrays, regardless of whether they have an active-active, active-passive, or virtual port (iSCSI-only) design or whether they are NAS devices. Generally, only the most mission-critical virtual workloads at the highest scale require the characteristics of enterprise-class storage arrays. In these cases, *scale* refers to VMs that number in the thousands, datastores that number in the hundreds, local and remote replicas that number in the hundreds, and the highest possible workloads—all that perform consistently even after component failures.

The most important considerations are as follows:

◆ If you have a midrange array, recognize that it is possible to oversubscribe the storage processors significantly. In such a situation, if a storage processor fails, performance will be degraded. For some customers, that is acceptable because storage processor failure is rare. For others, it is not, in which case you should limit the workload on either storage processor to less than 50 percent or consider an enterprise array.

◆ Understand the failover behavior of your array. Active-active arrays use the fixed-path selection policy by default, and active-passive arrays use the most recently used (MRU) policy by default. (See the section "Reviewing Multipathing" for more information.)

◆ Do you need specific advanced features? For example, if you want disaster recovery, make sure your array has integrated support on the VMware vCenter Site Recovery Manager HCL. Or, do you need array-integrated VMware snapshots? Do they have integrated management tools? More generally, do they support the vSphere Storage APIs? Ask your array vendor to illustrate its VMware integration and the use cases it supports.

We're now left with the last major area of storage fundamentals before we move on to discussing storage in a vSphere-specific context. The last remaining area deals with choosing a storage protocol.

Choosing a Storage Protocol

vSphere offers several shared storage protocol choices, including Fibre Channel, FCoE, iSCSI, and Network File System (NFS), which is a form of NAS. A little understanding of each goes a long way in designing the storage for your vSphere environment.

REVIEWING FIBRE CHANNEL

SANs are most commonly associated with Fibre Channel storage because Fibre Channel was the first protocol type used with SANs. However, *SAN* refers to a network topology, not a connection protocol. Although people often use the acronym *SAN* to refer to a Fibre Channel SAN, you can create a SAN topology using different types of protocols, including iSCSI, FCoE, and InfiniBand.

SANs were initially deployed to mimic the characteristics of local or direct attached SCSI devices. A SAN is a network where storage devices (logical units—or LUNs—just as on a SCSI or SAS controller) are presented from a storage target (one or more ports on an array) to one or more initiators. An initiator is usually a host bus adapter (HBA) or converged network adapter (CNA), though software-based initiators are available for iSCSI and FCoE. See Figure 6.7.

Today, Fibre Channel HBAs have roughly the same cost as high-end multiported Ethernet interfaces or local SAS controllers, and the per-port cost of a Fibre Channel switch is about twice that of a high-end managed Ethernet switch.

Fibre Channel uses an optical interconnect (though there are copper variants), which is used since the Fibre Channel protocol assumes a very high-bandwidth, low-latency, and lossless physical layer. Standard Fibre Channel HBAs today support very-high-throughput, 4 Gbps,

8 Gbps, and even 16 Gbps connectivity in single-, dual-, or quad-ported options. Older, obsolete HBAs supported up to only 2 Gbps. Some HBAs supported by ESXi are the QLogic QLE2462 and Emulex LP10000. You can find the authoritative list of supported HBAs on the VMware HCL at www.vmware.com/resources/compatibility/search.php. For end-to-end compatibility (in other words, from host to HBA to switch to array), every storage vendor maintains a similar compatibility matrix.

FIGURE 6.7
A Fibre Channel SAN presents LUNs from a target array (in this case an EMC VNX) to a series of initiators (in this case a Cisco Virtual Interface Controller).

Although in the early days of Fibre Channel there were many types of cables and interoperability of various Fibre Channel initiators, firmware revisions, switches, and targets (arrays) were not guaranteed, today interoperability is broad. Still, it is always a best practice to maintain your environment with the vendor interoperability matrix. From a connectivity standpoint, almost all cases use a common OM2 (orange-colored cables) multimode duplex LC/LC cable. The newer OM3 and OM4 (aqua-colored cables) are used for longer distances and are generally used for 10 Gbps Ethernet and 8/16 Gbps Fibre Channel (which otherwise have shorter distances using OM2). They all plug into standard optical interfaces.

The Fibre Channel protocol can operate in three modes: point-to-point (FC-P2P), arbitrated loop (FC-AL), and switched (FC-SW). Point-to-point and arbitrated loop are rarely used today. FC-AL is commonly used by some array architectures to connect their backend spindle enclosures (vendors give different hardware names to them, but they're the hardware elements that contain and support the physical disks) to the storage processors, but even in these cases, most modern array designs are moving to switched designs, which have higher bandwidth per disk enclosure.

As Figure 6.8 shows, each ESXi host has a minimum of two HBA ports, and each is physically connected to two Fibre Channel switches. Each switch has a minimum of two connections to two redundant front-end array ports (across storage processors).

FIGURE 6.8

The most common Fibre Channel configuration: a switched Fibre Channel (FC-SW) SAN. This enables the Fibre Channel LUN to be easily presented to all the hosts while creating a redundant network design.

Each ESXi host has a minimum of two HBA ports, and each is physically connected to two FC switches.

Each switch has a minimum of two connections to two redundant front-end array ports (across storage processors).

Switched Fibre Channel

HOW DIFFERENT IS FCoE?

Aside from discussions of the physical media and topologies, the concepts for FCoE are almost identical to those of Fibre Channel. This is because FCoE was designed to be seamlessly interoperable with existing Fibre Channel–based SANs.

All the objects (initiators, targets, and LUNs) on a Fibre Channel SAN are identified by a unique 64-bit identifier called a *worldwide name* (WWN). WWNs can be worldwide port names (a port on a switch) or node names (a port on an endpoint). For anyone unfamiliar with Fibre Channel, this concept is simple. It's the same technique as Media Access Control (MAC) addresses on Ethernet. Figure 6.8 shows an ESXi host with FCoE CNAs, where the highlighted CNA has the following worldwide node name: worldwide port name (WWnN: WWpN) in the identifier column:

20:00:00:25:b5:10:00:2c 20:00:00:25:b5:a0:01:2f

Like Ethernet MAC addresses, WWNs have a structure. The most significant two bytes are used by the vendor (the four hexadecimal characters starting on the left) and are unique to the vendor, so there is a pattern for QLogic or Emulex HBAs or array vendors. In the previous example, these are Cisco CNAs connected to an EMC VNX storage array.

Fibre Channel and FCoE SANs also have a critical concept of zoning. Fibre Channel switches implement zoning to restrict which initiators and targets can see each other as if they were on a common bus. If you have Ethernet networking experience, the idea is somewhat analogous to non-routable VLANs with Ethernet.

IS THERE A FIBRE CHANNEL EQUIVALENT TO VLANS?

Actually, yes, there is. Virtual storage area networks (VSANs) were adopted as a standard in 2004. Like VLANs, VSANs provide isolation between multiple logical SANs that exist on a common physical platform. This enables SAN administrators greater flexibility and another layer of separation in addition to zoning. These are not to be confused with VMware's new VSAN feature described earlier in this chapter.

Zoning is used for the following two purposes:

♦ To ensure that a LUN that is required to be visible to multiple hosts in a cluster (for example in a vSphere cluster, a Microsoft cluster, or an Oracle RAC cluster) has common visibility to the underlying LUN while ensuring that hosts that should *not* have visibility to that LUN do not. For example, it's used to ensure that VMFS volumes aren't visible to Windows servers (with the exception of backup proxy servers using software that leverages the vSphere Storage APIs for Data Protection).

♦ To create fault and error domains on the SAN fabric, where noise, chatter, and errors are not transmitted to all the initiators/targets attached to the switch. Again, it's somewhat analogous to one of the uses of VLANs to partition very dense Ethernet switches into broadcast domains.

Zoning is configured on the Fibre Channel switches via simple GUIs or CLI tools and can be configured by port or by WWN:

♦ Using port-based zoning, you would zone by configuring your Fibre Channel switch to "put port 5 and port 10 into a zone that we'll call zone_5_10." Any device (and therefore any WWN) you physically plug into port 5 could communicate only to a device (or WWN) physically plugged into port 10.

♦ Using WWN-based zoning, you would zone by configuring your Fibre Channel switch to "put WWN from this HBA and these array port WWNs into a zone we'll call ESXi_55_host1_CX_SPA_0." In this case, if you moved the cables, the zones would move to the ports with the matching WWNs.

The ESXi configuration shown in Figure 6.9 shows the LUN by its runtime or "shorthand" name. Masked behind this name is an unbelievably long name that that combines the initiator WWN, the Fibre Channel switch ports, and the Network Address Authority (NAA) identifier. This provides an explicit name that uniquely identifies not only the storage device but also the full end-to-end path.

We'll give you more details on storage object naming later in this chapter, in the sidebar titled "What Is All the Stuff in the Storage Device Details List?"

Zoning should not be confused with LUN masking. *Masking* is the ability of a host or an array to intentionally ignore WWNs that it *can* actively see (in other words, that are zoned to it). Masking is used to further limit what LUNs are presented to a host (commonly used with test and development replicas of LUNs).

You can put many initiators and targets into a zone and group zones together, as illustrated in Figure 6.10. For features like vSphere HA and vSphere DRS, ESXi hosts must have shared storage to which all applicable hosts have access. Generally, this means that every ESXi host in a vSphere environment must be zoned such that it can see each LUN. Also, every initiator (HBA or CNA) needs to be zoned to all the front-end array ports that *could* present the LUN. So, what's the best configuration practice? The answer is single initiator/single target zoning. This creates smaller zones, creates less cross talk, and makes it more difficult to administratively make an error that removes a LUN from all paths to a host or many hosts at once with a switch configuration error.

FIGURE 6.9
The Edit Multipathing Policies dialog box shows the storage runtime (short-hand) name.

| 172.16.68.251 - Edit Multipathing Policies for naa.600601602f6131002e3ad1cd89e9e211 | | | | | ? |

Path selection policy:

Fixed (VMware) ▾

Select the preferred path for this policy:

🔍 Filter ▾

Runtime Name	Status	Target	LUN	Preferred
vmhba1:C0:T1:L1	◆ Active (I/O)	50:06:01:60:be:a0:6e:60 50:06:01:6e...	1	
vmhba2:C0:T1:L1	◆ Active (I/O)	50:06:01:60:be:a0:6e:60 50:06:01:6f...	1	

OK   Cancel

FIGURE 6.10
There are many ways to configure zoning. From left to right: multi-initiator/multi-target zoning, single-initiator/multi-target zoning, and single-initiator/single-target zoning.

Remember that the goal is to ensure that every LUN is visible to all the nodes in the vSphere cluster. The left side of the figure is how most people who are not familiar with Fibre Channel start—multi-initiator zoning, with all array ports and all the ESXi Fibre Channel initiators in one massive zone. The middle is better—with two zones, one for each side of the dual-fabric Fibre Channel SAN design, and each zone includes all possible storage processors' front-end ports (critically, at least one from each storage processor!). The right one is the best and recommended zoning configuration—single-initiator/single-target zoning—however this method requires more administrative overhead to initially create all the zones.

When you're using single-initiator/single-target zoning as shown in the figure, each zone consists of a single initiator and a single target array port. This means you'll end up with multiple zones for each ESXi host, so that each ESXi host can see all applicable target array ports (again, at least one from each storage processor/controller!). This reduces the risk of administrative error and eliminates HBA issues affecting adjacent zones, but it takes a little more time to configure and results in a larger number of zones overall. It is always critical to ensure that each HBA is zoned to at least one front-end port on each storage processor.

REVIEWING FIBRE CHANNEL OVER ETHERNET

We mentioned in the sidebar titled "How Different Is FCoE?" that FCoE was designed to be interoperable and compatible with Fibre Channel. In fact, the FCoE standard is maintained by the same T11 body as Fibre Channel (the current standard is FC-BB-5). At the upper layers of the protocol stacks, Fibre Channel and FCoE look identical.

It's at the lower levels of the stack that the protocols diverge. Fibre Channel as a protocol doesn't specify the physical transport it runs over. However, unlike TCP, which has retransmission mechanics to deal with a lossy transport, Fibre Channel has far fewer mechanisms for dealing with loss and retransmission, which is why it requires a lossless, low-jitter, high-bandwidth physical layer connection. It's for this reason that Fibre Channel traditionally is run over relatively short optical cables rather than the unshielded twisted-pair (UTP) cables that Ethernet uses.

To address the need for lossless Ethernet, the IEEE created a series of standards—all of which had been approved and finalized at the time of this writing—that make 10 GbE lossless for FCoE traffic. Three key standards, all part of the Data Center Bridging (DCB) effort, make this possible:

♦ Priority Flow Control (PFC, also called Per-Priority Pause)

♦ Enhanced Transmission Selection (ETS)

♦ Datacenter Bridging Exchange (DCBX)

Used together, these three protocols allow Fibre Channel frames to be encapsulated into Ethernet frames, as illustrated in Figure 6.11, and transmitted in a lossless manner. Thus, FCoE uses whatever physical cable plant that 10 Gb Ethernet uses. Today, 10 GbE connectivity is generally optical (same cables as Fibre Channel) and Twinax (which is a pair of coaxial copper cables), InfiniBand-like CX cables, and some emerging 10 Gb unshielded twisted pair (UTP) use cases via the new 10GBase-T standard. Each has its specific distance-based use cases and varying interface cost, size, and power consumption.

FIGURE 6.11
FCoE simply encapsulates Fibre Channel frames into Ethernet frames for transmission over a lossless Ethernet transport.

Ethernet

Fibre Channel Traffic

WHAT ABOUT DATACENTER ETHERNET OR CONVERGED ENHANCED ETHERNET?

Datacenter Ethernet (DCE) and *Converged Enhanced Ethernet* (CEE) are prestandard terms used to describe a lossless Ethernet network. DCE describes Cisco's prestandard implementation of the DCB standards; CEE was a multivendor effort of the same nature.

Because FCoE uses Ethernet, why use FCoE instead of NFS or iSCSI over 10 Gb Ethernet? The answer is usually driven by the following two factors:

♦ There are existing infrastructure, processes, and tools in large enterprises that are designed for Fibre Channel, and they expect WWN addressing, not IP addresses. This provides an option for a converged network and greater efficiency, without a "rip and replace" model. In fact, early prestandard FCoE implementations did not include elements required to cross multiple Ethernet switches. These elements, part of something called FCoE Initialization Protocol (FIP), are part of the official FC-BB-5 standard and are required in order to comply with the final standard. This means that most FCoE switches in use today function as FCoE/LAN/Fibre Channel bridges. This makes them excellent choices to integrate and extend existing 10 GbE/1 GbE LANs and Fibre Channel SAN networks. The largest cost savings, power savings, cable and port reduction, and impact on management simplification are on this layer from the ESXi host to the first switch.

♦ Certain applications require a lossless, extremely low-latency transport network model—something that cannot be achieved using a transport where dropped frames are normal and long-window TCP retransmit mechanisms are the protection mechanism. Now, this is a very high-end set of applications, and those historically were not virtualized. However, in the era of vSphere 5.5, the goal is to virtualize every workload, so I/O models that can deliver those performance envelopes while still supporting a converged network become more important.

In practice, the debate of iSCSI versus FCoE versus NFS on 10 Gb Ethernet infrastructure is not material. All FCoE adapters are converged adapters, referred to as converged network adapters (CNAs). They support native 10 GbE (and therefore also NFS and iSCSI) as well as FCoE simultaneously, and they appear in the ESXi host as multiple 10 GbE network adapters and multiple Fibre Channel adapters. If you have FCoE support, in effect you have it all. All protocol options are yours.

A list of FCoE CNAs supported by vSphere can be found in the I/O section of the VMware compatibility guide.

UNDERSTANDING iSCSI

iSCSI brings the idea of a block storage SAN to customers with no Fibre Channel infrastructure. iSCSI is an Internet Engineering Task Force (IETF) standard for encapsulating SCSI control and data in TCP/IP packets, which in turn are encapsulated in Ethernet frames. Figure 6.12 shows how iSCSI is encapsulated in TCP/IP and Ethernet frames. TCP retransmission is used to handle dropped Ethernet frames or significant transmission errors. Storage traffic can be intense relative to most LAN traffic. This makes it important that you minimize retransmits, minimize dropped frames, and ensure that you have "bet-the-business" Ethernet infrastructure when using iSCSI.

FIGURE 6.12

Using iSCSI, SCSI control and data are encapsulated in both TCP/IP and Ethernet frames.

Ethernet frame	IP packet	TCP packet	**iSCSI payload data unit (PDU)**

Although Fibre Channel is often viewed as having higher performance than iSCSI, in many cases iSCSI can more than meet the requirements for many customers, and a carefully planned and scaled-up iSCSI infrastructure can, for the most part, match the performance of a moderate Fibre Channel SAN.

Also, iSCSI and Fibre Channel SANs are roughly comparable in complexity and share many of the same core concepts. Arguably, getting the first iSCSI LUN visible to an ESXi host is simpler than getting the first Fibre Channel LUN visible for people with expertise with Ethernet but not Fibre Channel because understanding worldwide names and zoning is not needed. In practice, designing a scalable, robust iSCSI network requires the same degree of diligence that is applied to Fibre Channel. You should use VLAN (or physical) isolation techniques similarly to Fibre Channel zoning, and you need to scale up connections to achieve comparable bandwidth. Look at Figure 6.13, and compare it to the switched Fibre Channel network diagram in Figure 6.8.

FIGURE 6.13

Notice how the topology of an iSCSI SAN is the same as a switched Fibre Channel SAN.

Each ESXi host has a minimum of two VMkernel ports, and each is physically connected to two Ethernet switches. (Recall from Chapter 5, "Creating and Configuring Virtual Networks," that VMkernel ports are used by the hypervisor for network traffic such as IP-based storage traffic, like iSCSI or NFS.) Storage and LAN are isolated—physically or via VLANs. Each switch has a minimum of two connections to two redundant front-end array network interfaces (across storage processors).

The one additional concept to focus on with iSCSI is the concept of *fan-in ratio*. This applies to all shared storage networks, including Fibre Channel, but the effect is often most pronounced with Gigabit Ethernet (GbE) networks. Across all shared networks, there is almost always a higher amount of bandwidth available across all the host nodes than there is on the egress of the switches and front-end connectivity of the array. It's important to remember that the host bandwidth is gated by congestion wherever it occurs. Don't minimize the array port-to-switch configuration. If you connect only four GbE interfaces on your array and you have 100 hosts with two GbE interfaces each, then expect contention, because your fan-in ratio is too large.

Also, when iSCSI and iSCSI SANs are examined, many core ideas are similar to Fibre Channel and Fibre Channel SANs, but in some cases there are material differences. Let's look at the terminology:

iSCSI Initiator   An iSCSI initiator is a logical host-side device that serves the same function as a physical host bus adapter in Fibre Channel/FCoE or SCSI/SAS. iSCSI initiators can be software initiators (which use host CPU cycles to load/unload SCSI payloads into standard TCP/IP packets and perform error checking) or hardware initiators (the iSCSI equivalent of a Fibre Channel HBA or FCoE CNA). Examples of software initiators that are pertinent to vSphere administrators are the native ESXi software initiator and the guest software initiators available in Windows XP and later and in most current Linux distributions. Examples of iSCSI hardware initiators are add-in cards like the QLogic QLA 405x and QLE 406x host bus adapters. These cards perform all the iSCSI functions in hardware. An iSCSI initiator is identified by an iSCSI qualified name (referred to as an IQN). An iSCSI initiator uses an iSCSI network portal that consists of one or more IP addresses. An iSCSI initiator "logs in" to an iSCSI target.

iSCSI Target   An iSCSI target is a logical target-side device that serves the same function as a target in Fibre Channel SANs. It is the device that hosts iSCSI LUNs and masks to specific iSCSI initiators. Different arrays use iSCSI targets differently—some use hardware, some use software implementations—but largely this is unimportant. More important is that an iSCSI target doesn't necessarily map to a physical port as is the case with Fibre Channel; each array does this differently. Some have one iSCSI target per physical Ethernet port; some have one iSCSI target per iSCSI LUN, which is visible across multiple physical ports; and some have logical iSCSI targets that map to physical ports and LUNs in any relationship the administrator configures within the array. An iSCSI target is identified by an iSCSI qualified name (an IQN). An iSCSI target uses an iSCSI network portal that consists of one or more IP addresses.

iSCSI Logical Unit   An iSCSI LUN is a LUN hosted by an iSCSI target. There can be one or more LUNs behind a single iSCSI target.

iSCSI Network Portal   An iSCSI network portal is one or more IP addresses that are used by an iSCSI initiator or iSCSI target.

iSCSI Qualified Name   An iSCSI qualified name (IQN) serves the purpose of the WWN in Fibre Channel SANs; it is the unique identifier for an iSCSI initiator, target, or LUN. The format of the IQN is based on the iSCSI IETF standard.

Challenge Authentication Protocol   CHAP is a widely used basic authentication protocol, where a password exchange is used to authenticate the source or target of communication.

Unidirectional CHAP is one-way; the source authenticates to the destination, or, in the case of iSCSI, the iSCSI initiator authenticates to the iSCSI target. Bidirectional CHAP is two-way; the iSCSI initiator authenticates to the iSCSI target, and vice versa, before communication is established. Although Fibre Channel SANs are viewed as intrinsically secure because they are physically isolated from the Ethernet network, and although initiators not zoned to targets cannot communicate, this is not by definition true of iSCSI. With iSCSI, it is possible (but not recommended) to use the same Ethernet segment as general LAN traffic, and there is no intrinsic zoning model. Because the storage and general networking traffic could share networking infrastructure, CHAP is an optional mechanism to authenticate the source and destination of iSCSI traffic for some additional security. In practice, Fibre Channel and iSCSI SANs have the same security and same degree of isolation (logical or physical).

IP Security   IPsec is an IETF standard that uses public-key encryption techniques to secure the iSCSI payloads so that they are not susceptible to man-in-the-middle security attacks. Like CHAP for authentication, this higher level of optional security is part of the iSCSI standards because it is possible (but not recommended) to use a general-purpose IP network for iSCSI transport—and in these cases, not encrypting data exposes a security risk (for example, a man-in-the-middle attack could determine data on a host it can't authenticate to by simply reconstructing the data from the iSCSI packets). IPsec is relatively rarely used because it has a heavy CPU impact on the initiator and the target.

Static/Dynamic Discovery   iSCSI uses a method of discovery where the iSCSI initiator can query an iSCSI target for the available LUNs. Static discovery involves a manual configuration, whereas dynamic discovery issues an iSCSI-standard SendTargets command to one of the iSCSI targets on the array. This target then reports all the available targets and LUNs to that particular initiator.

iSCSI Naming Service   The iSCSI Naming Service (iSNS) is analogous to the Domain Name System (DNS); it's where an iSNS server stores all the available iSCSI targets for a very large iSCSI deployment. iSNS is rarely used.

Figure 6.14 shows the key iSCSI elements in an example logical diagram. This diagram shows iSCSI in the broadest sense.

In general, the iSCSI session can be multiple TCP connections, called *Multiple Connections Per Session*. Note that this cannot be done in VMware. An iSCSI initiator and iSCSI target can communicate on an iSCSI network portal that can consist of one or more IP addresses. The concept of network portals is done differently on each array; some arrays always have one IP address per target port, while some arrays use network portals extensively. The iSCSI initiator logs into the iSCSI target, creating an iSCSI session. You can have many iSCSI sessions for a single target, and each session can have multiple TCP connections (Multiple Connections Per Session, which isn't currently supported by vSphere). There can be varied numbers of iSCSI LUNs behind an iSCSI target—many or just one. Every array does this differently. We'll discuss the particulars of the vSphere software iSCSI initiator implementation in detail in the section "Adding a LUN via iSCSI."

What about the debate regarding hardware iSCSI initiators (iSCSI HBAs) versus software iSCSI initiators? Figure 6.15 shows the differences among software iSCSI on generic network interfaces, network interfaces that do TCP/IP offload, and full iSCSI HBAs. Clearly there are more things the ESXi host needs to process with software iSCSI initiators, but the additional CPU is relatively light. Fully saturating several GbE links will use only roughly one core of a modern CPU, and the cost of iSCSI HBAs is usually less than the cost of slightly more CPU. Keep the CPU overhead in mind as you craft your storage design, but don't let it be your sole criterion.

FIGURE 6.14
The iSCSI IETF standard has several different elements.

FIGURE 6.15
Some parts of the stack are handled by the adapter card versus the ESXi host CPU in various implementations.

Also note the difference between a dependent hardware iSCSI adapter and an independent hardware iSCSI adapter. As the name suggests, the former depends on vSphere networking and iSCSI configuration, whereas the latter uses its own networking and iSCSI configuration.

Prior to vSphere 5.0, one thing that remained the exclusive domain of the iSCSI HBAs was booting from an iSCSI SAN. From version 5.0, vSphere includes support for iSCSI Boot Firmware Table (iBFT), a mechanism that enables booting from iSCSI SAN with a software iSCSI initiator.

You must have appropriate support for iBFT in the hardware. One might argue that using Auto Deploy would provide much of the same benefit as booting from an iSCSI SAN, but each approach has its advantages and disadvantages.

iSCSI is the last of the block-based shared storage options available in vSphere; now we move on to the Network File System (NFS), the only NAS protocol that vSphere supports.

JUMBO FRAMES ARE SUPPORTED

VMware ESXi does support jumbo frames for all VMkernel traffic, including both iSCSI and NFS, and they should be used when needed. However, it is then critical to configure a consistent, larger maximum transfer unit (MTU) size on *all* devices in all the possible networking paths; otherwise, Ethernet frame fragmentation will cause communication problems. Depending on the network hardware and traffic type, jumbo frames may or may not yield significant benefits. As always, you will need to weigh the benefits against the operational overhead of supporting this configuration.

UNDERSTANDING THE NETWORK FILE SYSTEM

NFS protocol is a standard originally developed by Sun Microsystems to enable remote systems to access a file system on another host as if it were locally attached. vSphere implements a client compliant with NFSv3 using TCP.

When NFS datastores are used by vSphere, no local file system (such as VMFS) is used. The file system is on the remote NFS server. This means that NFS datastores need to handle the same access control and file-locking requirements that vSphere delivers on block storage using the vSphere Virtual Machine File System, or VMFS (we'll describe VMFS in more detail later in this chapter in the section "Examining the vSphere Virtual Machine File System"). NFS servers accomplish this through traditional NFS file locks.

The movement of the file system from the ESXi host to the NFS server also means that you don't need to handle zoning/masking tasks. This makes an NFS datastore one of the easiest storage options to simply get up and running. On the other hand, it also means that all of the high availability and multipathing functionality that is normally part of a Fibre Channel, FCoE, or iSCSI storage stack is replaced by the networking stack. We'll discuss the implications of this in the section titled "Crafting a Highly Available NFS Design."

Figure 6.16 shows the topology of an NFS configuration. Note the similarities to the topologies in Figure 6.8 and Figure 6.13.

Technically, any NFS server that complies with NFSv3 over TCP will work with vSphere (vSphere does not support NFS over UDP), but similar to the considerations for Fibre Channel and iSCSI, the infrastructure needs to support your entire vSphere environment. Therefore, we recommend you use only NFS servers that are explicitly on the VMware HCL.

Using NFS datastores moves the elements of storage design associated with LUNs from the ESXi hosts to the NFS server. Instead of exposing block storage—which uses the RAID techniques described earlier for data protection—and allowing the ESXi hosts to create a file system (VMFS) on those block devices, the NFS server uses its block storage—protected using RAID—and creates its own file systems on that block storage. These file systems are then exported via NFS and mounted on your ESXi hosts.

FIGURE 6.16
The topology of an
NFS configuration
is similar to iSCSI
from a connectiv-
ity standpoint but
very different from
a configuration
standpoint.

In the early days of using NFS with VMware, NFS was categorized as being a lower-performance option for use with ISOs and templates but not production VMs. If production VMs were used on NFS datastores, the historical recommendation would have been to relocate the VM swap to block storage. Although it is true that NAS and block architectures are different and, likewise, their scaling models and bottlenecks are generally different, this perception is mostly rooted in how people have used NAS historically.

The reality is that it's absolutely possible to build an enterprise-class NAS infrastructure. NFS datastores can support a broad range of virtualized workloads and do not require you to relocate the VM swap. However, in cases where NFS will be supporting a broad set of production VM workloads, you will need to pay attention to the NFS server backend design and network infrastructure. You need to apply the same degree of care to bet-the-business NAS as you would if you were using block storage via Fibre Channel, FCoE, or iSCSI. With vSphere, your NFS server isn't being used as a traditional file server, where performance and availability requirements are relatively low. Rather, it's being used as an NFS server supporting a mission-critical application—in this case the vSphere environment and all the VMs on those NFS datastores.

We mentioned previously that vSphere implements an NFSv3 client using TCP. This is important to note because it directly impacts your connectivity options. Each NFS datastore uses two TCP sessions to the NFS server: one for NFS control traffic and the other for NFS data traffic. In effect, this means that the vast majority of the NFS traffic for a single datastore will use a single TCP session. Consequently, this means that link aggregation (which works on a per-flow basis from one source to one target) will use only one Ethernet link per datastore, regardless of how many links are included in the link aggregation group. To use the aggregate throughput of multiple Ethernet interfaces, you need multiple datastores, and no single datastore will be able to use more than one link's worth of bandwidth. The approach available to iSCSI (multiple iSCSI sessions per iSCSI target) is not available in the NFS use case. We'll discuss techniques for designing high-performance NFS datastores in the section titled "Crafting a Highly Available NFS Design."

As in the previous sections that covered the common storage array architectures, the protocol choices available to the vSphere administrator are broad. You can make most vSphere deployments work well on all protocols, and each has advantages and disadvantages. The key is to understand and determine what will work best for you. In the following section, we'll summarize how to make these basic storage choices.

Making Basic Storage Choices

Most vSphere workloads can be met by midrange array architectures (regardless of active-active, active-passive, asymmetrical, or virtual port design). Use enterprise array designs when mission-critical and very large-scale virtual datacenter workloads demand uncompromising availability and performance linearity.

As shown in Table 6.1, each storage choice can support most use cases. It's not about one versus the other but rather about understanding and leveraging their differences and applying them to deliver maximum flexibility.

TABLE 6.1:   Storage choices

FEATURE	FIBRE CHANNEL SAN	ISCSI SAN	NFS	VSAN
ESXi boot (boot from SAN)	Yes	Hardware initiator or software initiator with iBFT support	No	No
VM boot	Yes	Yes	Yes	Yes
Raw device mapping	Yes	Yes	No	No
Dynamic extension	Yes	Yes	Yes	Yes
Availability and scaling model	Storage stack (PSA), ESXi LUN queues, array configuration	Storage stack (PSA), ESXi LUN queues, array configuration	Network Stage (NIC teaming and routing), network and NFS server configuration	Storage stack (local), Network Stage (NIC teaming and routing)
VMware feature support (vSphere HA, vMotion, Storage vMotion, vSphere FT)	Yes	Yes	Yes	Yes

Picking a protocol type has historically been focused on the following criteria:

vSphere Feature Support   Although major VMware features such as vSphere HA and vMotion initially required VMFS, they are now supported on all storage types, including raw device mappings (RDMs) and NFS datastores. vSphere feature support is generally not a protocol-selection criterion, and there are only a few features that lag on RDMs and NFS, such as native vSphere snapshots on physical compatibility mode RDMs or the ability to create RDMs on NFS.

Storage Capacity Efficiency   Thin provisioning behavior at the vSphere layer, universally and properly applied, drives a very high efficiency, regardless of protocol choice. Applying thin provisioning at the storage array (on both block and NFS objects) delivers a higher overall efficiency than applying it only at the virtualization layer. Emerging techniques for extra array capacity efficiency (such as detecting and reducing storage consumed when there is information in common using compression and data deduplication) are currently most effectively used on NFS datastores but are expanding to include block use cases. One common error is to look at storage capacity (GB) as the sole vector of efficiency—in many cases, the performance envelope requires a fixed number of spindles even with advanced caching techniques. Often in these cases, efficiency is measured in spindle density, not in GB. For most vSphere customers, efficiency tends to be a function of operational process rather than protocol or platform choice.

Performance   Many vSphere customers see similar performance regardless of a given protocol choice. Properly designed iSCSI and NFS over Gigabit Ethernet can support very large VMware deployments, particularly with small-block (4 KB–64 KB) I/O patterns that characterize most general Windows workloads and don't need more than roughly 80 MBps of 100 percent read or write I/O bandwidth or 160 MBps of mixed I/O bandwidth. This difference in the throughput limit is due to the 1 Gbps/2 Gbps bidirectional nature of 1GbE—pure read or pure write workloads are unidirectional, but mixed workloads are bidirectional.

Fibre Channel (and by extension, FCoE) generally delivers a better performance envelope with very large-block I/O (VMs supporting DSS database workloads or SharePoint), which tends to demand a high degree of throughput. Less important generally but still important for some workloads, Fibre Channel delivers a lower-latency model and also tends to have a faster failover behavior because iSCSI and NFS always depend on some degree of TCP retransmission for loss and, in some iSCSI cases, ARP—all of which drive failover handling into tens of seconds versus seconds with Fibre Channel or FCoE. Load balancing and scale-out with IP storage using multiple Gigabit Ethernet links with IP storage can work for iSCSI to drive up throughput. Link aggregation techniques can help, but they work only when you have many TCP sessions. Because the NFS client in vSphere uses a single TCP session for data transmission, link aggregation won't improve the throughput of individual NFS datastores. Broad availability of 10 Gb Ethernet brings higher-throughput options to NFS datastores.

You can make every protocol configuration work in almost all use cases; the key is in the details (covered in this chapter). In practice, the most important thing is what you know and feel comfortable with.

The most flexible vSphere configurations tend to use a combination of both VMFS (which requires block storage) and NFS datastores (which require NAS), as well as RDMs on a selective basis (block storage).

The choice of which block protocol should be used to support the VMFS and RDM use cases depends on the enterprise more than the technologies and tends to follow this pattern:

◆ iSCSI for customers who have never used and have no existing Fibre Channel SAN infrastructure

◆ Fibre Channel for those with existing Fibre Channel SAN infrastructure that meets their needs

◆ FCoE for those upgrading existing Fibre Channel SAN infrastructure

vSphere can be applied to a very broad set of use cases—from the desktop/laptop to the server and on the server workloads—ranging from test and development to heavy workloads and mission-critical applications. A simple one-size-fits-all model can work, but only for the simplest deployments. The advantage of vSphere is that all protocols and all models are supported. Becoming fixated on one model means that not everything is virtualized that can be and the enterprise isn't as flexible and efficient as it can be.

Now that you've learned about the basic principles of shared storage and determined how to make the basic storage choices for your environment, it's time to see how these are applied in vSphere.

Implementing vSphere Storage Fundamentals

This part of the chapter examines how the shared storage technologies covered previously are applied in vSphere. We will cover these elements in a logical sequence, starting with core vSphere storage concepts. Next, we'll cover the storage options in vSphere for datastores to contain groups of VMs (VMFS datastores and NFS datastores). We'll follow that discussion with options for presenting disk devices directly into VMs (raw device mappings). Finally, we'll examine VM-level storage configuration details.

Reviewing Core vSphere Storage Concepts

One of the core concepts of virtualization is encapsulation. What used to be a physical system is encapsulated by vSphere, resulting in VMs that are represented by a set of files. Chapter 9, "Creating and Managing Virtual Machines," provides more detail on the specific files that compose a VM and their purpose. For reasons we've described already, these VM files reside on the shared storage infrastructure (with the exception of a raw device mapping, or RDM, which we'll discuss shortly).

In general, vSphere uses a shared-everything storage model. All ESXi hosts in a vSphere environment use commonly accessed storage objects using block storage protocols (Fibre Channel, FCoE, or iSCSI, in which case the storage objects are LUNs) or network attached storage protocols (NFS, in which case the storage objects are NFS exports). Depending on the environment, these storage objects will be exposed to the majority of your ESXi hosts, although not necessarily to all ESXi hosts in the environment. In Chapter 7, we'll again review the concept of a cluster, which is a key part of features like vSphere HA and vSphere DRS. Within a cluster, you'll want to ensure that all ESXi hosts have visibility and access to the same set of storage objects.

Before we get into the details of how to configure the various storage objects in vSphere, we need to first review some core vSphere storage technologies, concepts, and terminology. This information will provide a foundation upon which we will build later in the chapter. We'll start with a look at the vSphere Virtual Machine File System, a key technology found in practically every vSphere deployment.

EXAMINING THE vSPHERE VIRTUAL MACHINE FILE SYSTEM

The vSphere Virtual Machine File System (VMFS) is a common configuration option for many vSphere deployments. It's similar to NTFS for Windows Server and ext3 for Linux. Like these file systems, it is native; it's included with vSphere and operates on top of block storage objects. If you're leveraging any form of block storage, you're using VMFS.

The purpose of VMFS is to simplify the storage environment. It would clearly be difficult to scale a virtual environment if each VM directly accessed its own storage rather than storing the set of files on a shared volume. VMFS creates a shared storage pool that is used for one or more VMs.

While similar to NTFS and ext3, VMFS differs from these common file systems in several important ways:

◆ It was designed to be a clustered file system from its inception; neither NTFS nor ext3 is a clustered file system. Unlike many clustered file systems, it is simple and easy to use.

◆ VMFS's simplicity is derived from its simple and transparent distributed locking mechanism. This is generally much simpler than traditional clustered file systems with network cluster lock managers.

◆ VMFS enables simple direct-to-disk, steady-state I/O that results in high throughput at a low CPU overhead for the ESXi hosts.

◆ Locking is handled using metadata in a hidden section of the file system, as illustrated in Figure 6.17. The metadata portion of the file system contains critical information in the form of on-disk lock structures (files), such as which ESXi host is the current owner of a given VM, ensuring that there is no contention or corruption of the VM.

◆ Depending on the storage array's support for VAAI, when these on-disk lock structures are updated, the ESXi host performing the update momentarily locks the LUN using a nonpersistent SCSI lock (SCSI Reserve/Reset commands). This operation is completely transparent to the vSphere administrator.

◆ These metadata updates do *not* occur during normal read/write I/O operations and do not represent a fundamental scaling limit when compared with more traditional file systems.

◆ During the metadata updates, there is minimal impact to the production I/O (covered in a VMware white paper at www.vmware.com/resources/techresources/1059). This impact is negligible to the ESXi host holding the SCSI lock but more pronounced on the other hosts accessing the same VMFS datastore.

◆ These metadata updates include, but are not limited to the following:

   ◆ The creation of a file in the VMFS datastore (powering on a VM, creating/deleting a VM, or taking a snapshot, for example)

   ◆ Actions that change the ESXi host that owns a VM (vMotion and vSphere HA)

◆ Changes to the VMFS file system itself (extending the file system or adding a file system extent)

FIGURE 6.17
VMFS stores metadata in a hidden area of the first extent.

Simple, single extent VMFS datastore

Spanned, multi-extent VMFS datastore

VSPHERE 5.5 AND SCSI-3 DEPENDENCY

In vSphere 5.5, like previous vSphere versions, only SCSI-3–compliant block storage objects are supported. Most major storage arrays have, or can be upgraded via their array software to, full SCSI-3 support, but check with your storage vendor before upgrading. If your storage array doesn't support SCSI-3, the storage details shown on the Configuration tab for the vSphere host will not display correctly.

In spite of this requirement, vSphere still uses SCSI-2 reservations for general ESXi-level SCSI reservations (not to be confused with guest-level reservations). This is important for Asymmetrical Logical Unit Access (ALUA) support, covered in the section "Reviewing Multipathing."

Earlier versions of vSphere exclusively used VMFS version 3 (VMFS-3), and vSphere 5.0, 5.1, and 5.5 continue to provide support for VMFS-3. In addition to supporting VMFS-3, vSphere 5.0 introduced VMFS version 5 (VMFS-5) with further enhancements in vSphere 5.5. Only hosts running ESXi 5.0 or later support VMFS-5; hosts running ESX/ESXi 4.x will not be able to see or access VMFS-5 datastores. VMFS-5 offers a number of advantages:

◆ VMFS-5 datastores can now grow up to 64 TB in size using only a single extent. Datastores built on multiple extents are still limited to 64 TB as well.

◆ VMFS-5 datastores use a single block size of 1 MB, but you can now create files of up to 62 TB on VMFS-5 datastores.

◆ VMFS-5 uses a more efficient sub-block allocation size of only 8 KB, compared to 64 KB for VMFS-3.

◆ VMFS-5 lets you create virtual-mode RDMs for devices up to 62 TB in size. (VMFS-3 limits RDMs to 2 TB in size. We'll cover RDMs later in the section "Working with Raw Device Mappings.")

Even better than the improvements in VMFS-5 is the fact that you can upgrade VMFS-3 datastores to VMFS-5 in place and online—without any disruption to the VMs running on that datastore. You're also not required to upgrade VMFS-3 datastores to VMFS-5, which further simplifies the migration from earlier versions.

Later in this chapter in the section "Working with VMFS Datastores," we'll provide more details on how to create, expand, delete, and upgrade VMFS datastores.

Closely related to VMFS is the idea of multipathing, a topic that we will discuss in the next section.

REVIEWING MULTIPATHING

Multipathing is the term used to describe how a host, such as an ESXi host, manages storage devices that have multiple ways (or paths) to access them. Multipathing is extremely common in Fibre Channel and FCoE environments and is also found in iSCSI environments. We won't go so far as to say that multipathing is strictly for block-based storage environments, but we will say that multipathing for NFS is generally handled much differently than for block storage.

In vSphere 4, VMware and VMware technology partners spent considerable effort overhauling how the elements of the vSphere storage stack that deal with multipathing work. This architecture, known as the Pluggable Storage Architecture (PSA), is still present in vSphere 5.5 as well. Figure 6.18 shows an overview of the PSA.

FIGURE 6.18
vSphere's
Pluggable Storage
Architecture is
highly modular and
extensible.

One of the key goals in the development of the PSA was to make vSphere multipathing much more flexible. Pre–vSphere 4 versions of VMware ESX/ESXi had a rigid set of lists that determined failover policy and multipathing policy, and this architecture was updated only with major VMware releases. With the PSA's modular architecture, vSphere administrators have a much more flexible approach.

Four different modules compose the PSA:

♦ Native multipathing plug-in (NMP)

♦ Storage array type plug-in (SATP)

♦ Path selection plug-in (PSP)

♦ Multipathing plug-in (MPP)

Any given ESXi host can have multiple modules in use at any point and can be connected to multiple arrays, and you can configure the combination of modules used (an NMP/SATP/PSP combination or an MPP) on a LUN-by-LUN basis.

Let's see how they work together.

Understanding the NMP Module

The NMP module handles overall MPIO (multipath I/O) behavior and array identification. The NMP leverages the SATP and PSP modules and isn't generally configured in any way.

Understanding SATP Modules

SATP modules handle path failover for a given storage array and determine the failover type for a LUN.

vSphere ships with SATPs for a broad set of arrays, with generic SATPs for nonspecified arrays and a local SATP for local storage. The SATP modules contain the rules on how to handle array-specific actions or behavior as well as any specific operations needed to manage array paths. This is part of what makes the NMP modular (unlike the NMP in prior versions); it doesn't need to contain the array-specific logic, and additional modules for new arrays can be added without changing the NMP. Using the SCSI Array ID reported by the array via a SCSI query, the NMP selects the appropriate SATP to use. After that, the SATP monitors, deactivates, and activates paths (and when a manual rescan occurs, detects new paths)—providing information up to the NMP. The SATP also performs array-specific tasks such as activating passive paths on active-passive arrays.

To see what array SATP modules exist, enter the following command from the vCLI (we ran this from the ESXi shell):

```
esxcli storage nmp satp list
```

Figure 6.19 shows the results this command returns (note that the default PSP for a given SATP is also shown).

Understanding PSP Modules

The PSP module handles the actual path used for every given I/O.

The NMP assigns a default PSP, which can be overridden manually for every LUN based on the SATP associated with that device. This command (and the output captured in Figure 6.20) shows you the three PSPs vSphere includes by default:

```
esxcli storage nmp psp list
```

FIGURE 6.19
Only the SATPs for
the arrays to which
an ESXi host is con-
nected are loaded.

FIGURE 6.20
vSphere ships with
three default PSPs.

Each of these PSPs performs path selection slightly differently:

◆ Most Recently Used (noted as VMW_PSP_MRU) selects the path it used most recently. If this
path becomes unavailable, the ESXi host switches to an alternative path and continues to
use the new path while it is available. This is the default for active-passive array types.

◆ Fixed (noted as VMW_PSP_FIXED) uses the designated preferred path, if it has been configured. Otherwise, it uses the first working path discovered at system boot time. If the ESXi
host cannot use the preferred path, it selects a random alternative available path. The ESXi
host automatically reverts to the preferred path as soon as the path becomes available. This
is the default for active-active array types (or active-passive arrays that use ALUA with
SCSI-2 reservation mechanisms—in these cases, they appear as active-active).

◆ Round Robin (noted as VMW_PSP_RR) rotates the path selection among all available optimized paths and enables basic load balancing across the paths and fabrics. This is not a

weighted algorithm, nor is it responsive to queue depth, but it is a significant improvement. In prior ESXi versions, there was no way to load balance a LUN, and customers needed to statically distribute LUNs across paths, which was a poor proxy for true load balancing.

WHICH PSP IS RIGHT IF YOU'RE USING ALUA?

What do you do if your array can be configured to use ALUA—and therefore could use the Fixed, MRU, or Round Robin policy? See the section "Understanding Midrange and External Enterprise Storage Array Design" for information on ALUA.

The Fixed and MRU path failover policies deliver failover only and work fine with active-active and active-passive designs, regardless of whether ALUA is used. Of course, they both drive workloads down a single path. Ensure that you manually select active I/O paths that are the "good" ports, which are the ones where the port is on the storage processor owning the LUN. You don't want to select the "bad" ports, which are the higher-latency, lower-throughput ones that transit the internal interconnect to get to the LUN.

The out-of-the-box load-balancing policy in vSphere (Round Robin) doesn't use the non-optimized paths (though they are noted as active in the vSphere Web Client). Third-party multipathing plug-ins that are aware of the difference between the asymmetrical path choices can optimize an ALUA configuration.

Perform the following steps to see what SATP (and PSP) is being used for a given LUN in the vSphere Web Client:

1. In the vSphere Web Client, navigate to the Hosts And Clusters view.

2. Select a host from the list on the left; then select the Manage tab on the right.

3. Click the Storage subsection.

4. Finally, click the Storage Devices selection on the left.

   This opens the Storage Devices area. When a LUN or disk is selected from the list, an SATP will be listed near the bottom, as shown in Figure 6.21.

In this example, the array is an EMC VNX and the generic VMW_SATP_ALUA_CX is selected. The default PSP is Round Robin (VMware). A change in the PSP takes place *immediately* when you change it. There is no confirmation. Note that the PSP is configurable on a LUN-by-LUN basis.

WHAT IS ALL THE STUFF IN THE STORAGE DEVICE DETAILS LIST?

In the runtime name, the *C* is the channel identifier, the *T* is the target identifier, and the *L* is the LUN.

And that long text string starting with *naa*? This is the Network Address Authority ID, which is a unique identifier for the target and a LUN. This ID is guaranteed to be persistent through reboots and is used throughout vSphere.

FIGURE 6.21
The SATP for this
datastore is VMW_
SATP_ALUA_CX,
which is the default
SATP for EMC VNX
arrays.

Understanding MPP Modules

The MPP module can add significantly enhanced multipathing to vSphere, and for the given LUNs it supports, it replaces the NMP, SATP, and PSP. The MPP claim policy (the LUNs that it manages) is defined on a LUN-by-LUN and array-by-array basis, and MPPs can coexist with NMP.

Because it replaces the NMP, SATP, and PSP, the MPP can change the path selection normally handled by the PSP. This allows the MPP to provide more sophisticated path selection than the VMware-supplied PSPs can—including selecting by host queue depth and, in some cases, the array target port state. As a result of this more sophisticated path selection, an MPP could offer notable performance increases or other new functionality not present in vSphere by default.

The PSA was written not only to be modular but also to support third-party extensibility; third-party SATPs, PSPs, and MPPs are technically possible. At the time of this writing, only a few MPPs were generally available, though other vendors are likely to create third-party SATPs, PSPs, and potentially full MPPs. Once the MPP is loaded on an ESXi host via the vSphere Web Client's host update tools, all multipathing for LUNs managed by that MPP become fully automated.

AN EXAMPLE OF A THIRD-PARTY MPP

EMC PowerPath/VE is a third-party multipathing plug-in that supports a broad set of EMC and non-EMC array types. PowerPath/VE enhances load balancing, performance, and availability using the following techniques:

Better availability:

◆ Through active management of intermittent path behavior

◆ Through more rapid path state detection

◆ Through automated path discovery behavior without manual rescan

Better performance:

◆ Through better path selection using weighted algorithms, which is critical in cases where the paths are unequal (ALUA).

◆ Through monitoring and adjusting the ESXi host queue depth to select the path for a given I/O, shifting the workload from heavily used paths to lightly used paths.

◆ With some arrays by predictive optimization based on the array port queues. (The array port queues are generally the first point of contention and tend to affect all the ESXi hosts simultaneously; without predictive advance handling, they tend to cause simultaneous path choice across the ESXi cluster.)

Previously in this chapter, in the section on VMFS, we mentioned that one potential advantage to having a VMFS datastore spanned across multiple extents on multiple LUNs would be to increase the parallelism of the LUN queues. In addition, in this section you've heard us mention how a third-party MPP might make multipathing decisions based on host or target queues. Why is queuing so important? We'll review queuing in the next section.

THE IMPORTANCE OF LUN QUEUES

Queues are an important construct in block storage environments (across all protocols, including Fibre Channel, FCoE, and iSCSI). Think of a queue as a line at the supermarket checkout. Queues exist on the server (in this case the ESXi host), generally at both the HBA and LUN levels. They also exist on the storage array. Every array does this differently, but they all have the same concept. Block-centric storage arrays generally have these queues at the target ports, array-wide, at the array LUN levels, and finally at the spindles themselves. File-centric storage arrays generally have queues at the target ports and array-wide, but abstract the array LUN queues because the LUNs actually exist as files in the file system. However, file-centric designs have internal LUN queues underneath the file systems themselves and then ultimately at the spindle level—in other words, it's internal to how the file server accesses its own storage.

The queue depth is a function of how fast things are being loaded into the queue and how fast the queue is being drained. How fast the queue is being drained is a function of the amount of time needed for the array to service the I/O requests. This is called the *service time*, and in the supermarket checkout it is the speed of the person behind the checkout counter (ergo, the array service time).

CAN I VIEW THE QUEUE?

To determine how many outstanding items are in the queue, use resxtop, press U to get to the storage screen, and look at the QUED column.

The array service time itself is a function of many things, predominantly the workload, then the spindle configuration, then the write cache (for writes only), then the storage processors, and finally, with certain rare workloads, the read caches.

So why is all this important? Well, for most customers it will never come up, and all queuing will be happening behind the scenes. However, for some customers, LUN queues determine whether your VMs are happy or not from a storage performance perspective.

When a queue overflows (either because the storage configuration cannot handle the steady-state workload or because the storage configuration cannot absorb a burst), it causes many upstream effects to slow down the I/O. For IP-focused people, this effect is analogous to TCP windowing, which should be avoided for storage just as queue overflow should be avoided.

You can change the default queue depths for your HBAs and for each LUN/device. (See www .vmware.com for HBA-specific steps.) After changing the queue depths on the HBAs, you need to perform a second step at the VMkernel layer. You must change the amount of outstanding disk requests from the VMs to VMFS to match the HBA setting. You can do this in the ESXi advanced settings, as shown in Figure 6.22 or by using ESXCLI. In general, the default settings for queues and Disk.* are the best. We don't recommend changing these values unless instructed to do so by VMware or your storage vendor.

FIGURE 6.22
It is possible to adjust the advanced properties for advanced use cases, increasing the number of consecutive requests allowed to match adjusted queues.

If the queue overflow is not a case of dealing with short bursts but rather that you are under-configured for the steady state workload, making the queues deeper can have a downside: higher latency. Then it overflows anyway. This is the predominant case, so before increasing your LUN queues, check the array service time. If it's taking more than 10 milliseconds to service I/O requests, you need to improve the service time, usually by adding more spindles to the LUN or by moving the LUN to a faster-performing tier.

The last topic we'll cover before moving on to more hands-on topics is the vSphere Storage APIs.

UNCOVERING THE VSPHERE STORAGE APIS

Formerly known as the vStorage APIs, the vSphere Storage APIs aren't necessarily application programming interfaces (APIs) in the truest sense of the word. In some cases, yes, but in other cases, they are simply storage commands that vSphere leverages.

There are several broad families of storage APIs that vSphere offers:

- vSphere Storage APIs for Array Integration
- vSphere APIs for Storage Awareness
- vSphere Storage APIs for Site Recovery
- vSphere Storage APIs for Multipathing
- vSphere Storage APIs for Data Protection

Because of the previous naming convention (vStorage APIs), some of these technologies are more popularly known by their acronyms. Table 6.2 maps the well-known acronyms to their new official names.

TABLE 6.2: vSphere Storage API acronyms

WELL-KNOWN ACRONYM	OFFICIAL NAME
VAAI	vSphere Storage APIs for Array Integration
VASA	vSphere APIs for Storage Awareness
VADP	vSphere Storage APIs for Data Protection

In this book, for consistency with the community and the marketplace, we'll use the well-known acronyms to refer to these technologies.

As we mentioned previously, some of these technologies are truly APIs. The Storage APIs for Multipathing are the APIs that VMware partners can use to create third-party MPPs, SATPs, and PSPs for use in the PSA. Similarly, the Storage APIs for Site Recovery encompass the actual programming interfaces that enable array vendors to make their storage arrays work with VMware's Site Recovery Manager product, and the Storage APIs for Data Protection (VADP) are the APIs that third-party companies can use to build virtualization-aware and virtualization-friendly backup solutions.

There are two sets remaining that we haven't yet mentioned, and that's because we'd like to delve into those a bit more deeply. We'll start with the Storage APIs for Array Integration.

Exploring the vSphere Storage APIs for Array Integration

The vSphere Storage APIs for Array Integration (more popularly known as VAAI) were first introduced in vSphere 4.1 as a means of offloading storage-related operations from the ESXi hosts to the storage array. Although VAAI is largely based on SCSI commands ratified by the

T10 committee in charge of the SCSI standards, it does require appropriate support from storage vendors, so you'll want to check with your storage vendor to see what is required in order to support VAAI. In addition to the VAAI features introduced in vSphere 4.1 and 5.0, vSphere 5.5 introduces even more storage offloads. Here's a quick rundown of the storage offloads available in vSphere 5.5:

Hardware-Assisted Locking   Also called atomic test and set (ATS), this feature supports discrete VM locking without the use of LUN level SCSI reservations. In the section titled "Examining the vSphere Virtual Machine File System," we briefly described how vSphere uses SCSI reservations when VMFS metadata needs to be updated. Hardware-assisted locking allows for disk locking per sector instead of locking the entire LUN. This offers a dramatic increase in performance when lots of metadata updates are necessary (such as when powering on many VMs at the same time).

Hardware-Accelerated Full Copy   Support for hardware-accelerated full copy allows storage arrays to make full copies of data completely internal to the array instead of requiring the ESXi host to read and write the data. This causes a significant reduction in the storage traffic between the host and the array and can reduce the time required to perform operations like cloning VMs or deploying new VMs from templates.

Hardware-Accelerated Block Zeroing   Sometimes called write same, this functionality allows storage arrays to zero out large numbers of blocks to provide newly allocated storage without any previously written data. This can speed up operations like creating VMs and formatting virtual disks.

Thin Provisioning   vSphere 5.0 added an additional set of hardware offloads around thin provisioning. First, vSphere is thin-provisioning aware, meaning that it will recognize when a LUN presented by an array is thin provisioned. In addition, vSphere 5.0 added and vSphere 5.5 improves on the ability to reclaim dead space (space no longer used) via the T10 UNMAP command; this will help keep space utilization in thin-provisioned environments in check. Finally, vSphere also has support for providing advance warning of thin-provisioned out-of-space conditions and provides better handling for true out-of-space conditions.

STANDARDS-BASED OR PROPRIETARY?

So is the functionality of VAAI standards based or proprietary? Well, the answer is a little of both. In vSphere 4.1, the hardware-accelerated block zeroing was fully T10 compliant, but the hardware-assisted locking and hardware-accelerated full copy were not fully T10 compliant and required specific support from the array vendors. In vSphere 5.5, all three of these features are fully T10 compliant, as is the thin-provisioning support, and will work with any array that is also T10 compliant.

The NAS offloads, however, are not standards based, and will require specific plug-ins from the NAS vendors to take advantage of these offloads.

Like previous versions, vSphere 5.5 includes hardware offloads for NAS:

Reserve Space   This functionality lets you create thick-provisioned VMDKs on NFS datastores, much like what is possible on VMFS datastores.

Full File Clone   The Full File Clone functionality allows offline VMDKs to be cloned (copied) by the NAS device.

Lazy File Clone   This feature allows NAS devices to create native snapshots for the purpose of space-conservative VMDKs for virtual desktop infrastructure (VDI) environments. It's specifically targeted at emulating the Linked Clone functionality vSphere offers on VMFS datastores.

Extended Statistics   When you're leveraging the Lazy File Clone feature, this feature allows more accurate space reporting.

In all cases, support for VAAI requires that the storage vendor's array be fully T10 compliant (for block-level VAAI commands) or support VMware's file-level NAS offloads via a vendor-supplied plug-in. Check with your storage vendor to determine what firmware revisions, software levels, or other requirements are necessary to support VAAI/VAAIv2 with vSphere 5.5.

The vSphere Web Client reports VAAI support, so it's easy to determine if your array has been recognized as VAAI capable by vSphere. Figure 6.23 shows a series of datastores; note the status of the Hardware Acceleration column. You can see that some datastores clearly report Supported in that column.

FIGURE 6.23
If all hardware offload features are supported, the Hardware Acceleration status is listed as Supported.

vSphere determines the hardware acceleration status for VMFS datastores and NFS datastores differently. For VMFS datastores, if at least one of the various SCSI commands is unsupported but others are supported, then the status will be listed as Unknown. If all the commands are unsupported, it will list Not Supported; if all the commands are supported, it will list Supported. You can gather a bit more detail about which commands are supported or not supported using the esxcli command-line utility from the vSphere Management Assistant. Run this command:

```
esxcli -s vcenter-01 -h esxi-05.lab.local storage core device vaai status get
```

You'll get output that looks something like Figure 6.24; note that on some LUNS the commands are listed as unsupported. When there is at least one supported and one unsupported per LUN, vSphere reports the status as Unknown.

FIGURE 6.24

The VAAI support detail is more granular when using ESXCLI compared with the Web Client.

For the inquisitive types who are interested in just a bit more detail on how VAAI works and fits into the vSphere PSA, try running this command from the vSphere Management Assistant:

```
esxcli -s vcenter-01 -h esxi-05.lab.local storage core claimrules list -c all
```

The output will look something like Figure 6.25.

FIGURE 6.25

VAAI works hand in hand with claimrules that are used by the PSA for assigning an SATP and PSP for detected storage devices.

This output shows you that VAAI works in conjunction with the claimrules that the PSA uses when determining the SATP and PSP for a given storage device.

> ### You Can Disable VAAI if Necessary
>
> There might be situations where disabling VAAI is required. Some advanced SAN fabric features, for example, aren't currently compatible with VAAI. To disable VAAI, set the value of the following advanced settings to zero:
>
> ◆ /VMFS3/HardwareAcceleratedLocking
>
> ◆ /DataMoverHardwareAcceleratedMove
>
> ◆ /DataMover/HardwareAcceleratedInit
>
> No reboot is necessary for this change to take effect. To re-enable VAAI, change the value for these advanced settings back to 1.

VAAI is not the only mechanism for advanced storage integration with vSphere; with vSphere 5, VMware also introduced the Storage APIs for Storage Awareness. We'll describe those in the next section.

Exploring the vSphere Storage APIs for Storage Awareness

The vSphere APIs for Storage Awareness, more commonly known as VASA (from its previous name, the vStorage APIs for Storage Awareness), enables more advanced out-of-band communication between storage arrays and the virtualization layer. At a high level, VASA operates in the following manner:

◆ The storage array communicates its capabilities to the VASA provider. These capabilities could be just about anything: replication status, snapshot capabilities, storage tier, drive type, or IOPS capacity. Exactly what capabilities are communicated to the VASA provider are strictly determined by the storage vendor.

◆ The VASA provider communicates these capabilities to vCenter Server. This allows vSphere administrators to, for the very first time, see storage capabilities within vCenter Server.

To enable this communication, you must have a VASA provider supplied by your storage vendor. This VASA provider might be a separate VM supplied by the storage vendor, or it might be an additional service provided by the software on the array. The one restriction that VMware does place on the VASA provider is that it can't run on the same operating system as vCenter Server. Once you have this VASA provider, you'll then add it to vCenter Server using the Storage Providers area found under vCenter Server ➤ Manage ➤ Storage Providers, shown in Figure 6.26.

FIGURE 6.26

The Storage Providers area is where you go to enable communication between the VASA provider and vCenter Server.

Once the storage provider has been added to vCenter Server, it will communicate storage capabilities up to vCenter Server.

However, the presence of these storage capabilities is only half the picture. The other half of the picture is what the vSphere administrator does with these capabilities: build policy-driven VM storage policies, as we describe in the next section.

EXAMINING POLICY-DRIVEN STORAGE

Working in conjunction with VASA, the principle behind policy-driven storage is simple: Allow vSphere administrators to build VM storage policies that describe the specific storage attributes that a VM requires. Then, allow vSphere administrators to place VMs on datastores that are compliant with that storage policy, thus ensuring that the needs of the VM are properly serviced by the underlying storage. Once a VM is up and running, vCenter monitors and will send an alert if a VM happens to be in breach of the assigned storage policy.

Working with policy-driven storage involves the following three steps:

1. Use VASA to populate system storage capabilities and/or create user-defined storage capabilities. System capabilities are automatically propagated to datastores; user-defined capabilities must be manually assigned.

2. Create VM storage policies that define the specific features a VM requires from the underlying storage.

3. Assign a VM storage policy to a VM and then check its compliance (or noncompliance) with the assigned VM storage policy.

We'll provide the details on how to accomplish step 2 and step 3 later in the section "Creating and Assigning VM Storage Policy." In the section "Assigning a Storage Capability to a Datastore," we'll show you how to assign a user-defined storage capability to a datastore.

In the section "Creating and Assigning VM Storage Policies," we'll show you how to create a VM storage policy and then determine the compliance or noncompliance of a VM with that storage policy.

For now, we'd like to show you how to create a user-defined storage capability. Keep in mind that the bulk of the power of policy-driven storage comes from the interaction with VASA to automatically gather storage capabilities from the underlying array. However, you might find it necessary or useful to define one or more additional storage capabilities that you can use in building your VM storage policies.

Before you can create a custom storage policy, you must have a tag to associate with it. Tags are explained in more detail in Chapter 3, "Installing and Configuring vCenter Server." The following steps outline how to create tags:

1. In the vSphere Web Client, navigate to the Home screen and select Tags from the Navigator list.

2. Once in the Tags area, click the New Tag icon.

3. Name the tag Gold Storage and select New Category from the drop-down list.

4. The New Tag dialog box will expand so you can also create a category. Name this category Storage Types.

5. Change Cardinality to Many Tags Per Object.

6. Select the check boxes next to Datastore and Datastore Cluster as shown in Figure 6.27.

7. Finally, click OK.

FIGURE 6.27
The New Tag dialog box can be expanded to also create a tag category.

8. Repeat steps 2 and 3 but select the Storage Types category you just created for additional silver and bronze tags.

Now that the preparation work is complete, you can perform the following steps to create a user-defined storage capability:

1. In the vSphere Web Client, navigate to the Home screen and click the VM Storage Policies icon, shown in Figure 6.28.

FIGURE 6.28
The VM Storage Policies area in the vSphere Web Client is one place to create user-defined storage capabilities. You can also create them from the Datastores And Datastore Clusters view.

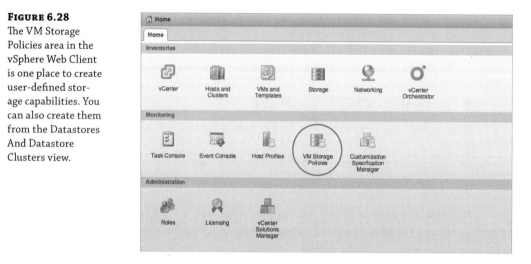

2. In the VM Storage Policies screen, click the Create A New VM Storage Policy icon.

This will bring up the Create A New VM Storage Policy dialog box.

3. Provide a name and description for the new VM storage policy and click Next.

4. The Rule-Sets explanation is displayed, Click Next to go to the rule creation page.

5. Click the Add Tag-Based Rule button, and choose the tag category and the tag associated with the datastores; then click OK.

Multiple tags can be added to a single rule-set and multiple rule-sets can be added to a storage policy.

6. Click Next to finish the rule-set creation and verify the matching resources on the following page.

7. Finally, click Next and Finish to exit the Create New VM Storage Policy dialog box.

Figure 6.29 shows a number of a user-defined storage policies.

Any system-provided storage capabilities supplied by VASA will also show up in the Rule-Set page on the Create New VM Storage Policy dialog box. These can be substituted by user-created tags as needed.

You'll come back to the VM Storage Policies area of the vSphere Web Client later in this chapter when we show you how to create a VM storage policy and assign it to a VM.

Now that we've covered some vSphere-specific storage basics, let's move on to working with VMFS datastores.

FIGURE 6.29
VM storage policies
can match user-
defined tags or
vendor-specific
capabilities.

Working with VMFS Datastores

It's time to shift the focus away from concepts and into practice. Next, we'll take a look at working with VMFS datastores. As you have learned, VMFS is the file system that vSphere uses for all block-based storage, so it's common. Working with VMFS datastores will be a daily task that you, as a vSphere administrator, will be responsible for accomplishing.

Let's start with adding a VMFS datastore. Every VMFS datastore is backed by a LUN, so first we'll need to review the process for adding a LUN to your ESXi hosts. The process for adding a LUN will vary based on the block storage protocol, so the next three sections will describe adding a LUN via Fibre Channel, adding a LUN via FCoE (these are essentially the same), and adding a LUN via iSCSI.

ADDING A LUN VIA FIBRE CHANNEL

Adding a LUN to vSphere via Fibre Channel is really more of a task for the storage administrator (who might also be the vSphere administrator in some environments!). As we mentioned previously in the section "Reviewing Fibre Channel," making a LUN visible over a Fibre Channel SAN involves a few steps, only one of which is done in the vSphere environment:

1. Zone the Fibre Channel SAN so that the ESXi host(s) can see the target port(s) on the storage array.

2. On the storage array, present the LUN to the ESXi host(s). This procedure varies from vendor to vendor. In a NetApp environment, this involves adding the host's WWNs to an initiator group (or *igroup*); in an EMC environment, it involves creating a storage group. Refer to your specific storage vendor's instructions.

3. Rescan for new storage devices on the ESXi host.

That last step is the only step that involves the vSphere environment. There are two ways to rescan for new storage devices: You can rescan a specific storage adapter, or you can rescan all storage adapters.

Perform the following steps to rescan only a specific storage adapter:

1. In the vSphere Web Client, navigate to the Manage tab for a specific ESXi host in the Hosts And Clusters view.

2. In the Storage subsection, select Storage Adapters from the left.

This will display the storage adapters recognized in the selected ESXi host.

3. Click the Rescan All icon.

4. If you want to scan only for new LUNs that have been zoned or presented to the ESXi host, select Scan For New Storage Devices and deselect Scan For New VMFS Volumes.

5. If you want to scan only for new VMFS datastores, deselect Scan For New Storage Devices and select Scan For New VMFS Volumes.

6. If you want to do both, simply click OK (both are selected by default). You'll see the appropriate tasks appear in the Tasks pane of the vSphere Web Client.

You'll note that two tasks appear in the Recent Tasks pane of the vSphere Web Client: a task for rescanning all the HBAs and a task for rescanning VMFS.

The task for rescanning the HBAs is pretty straightforward; this is a query to the host HBAs to see if new storage is available. If new storage is available to an adapter, it will appear in the details pane of the Storage Adapters area in the vSphere Web Client.

The second task is a bit different. The VMFS rescan is triggered automatically, and it scans available storage devices for an existing VMFS datastore. If it finds an existing VMFS datastore, it will attempt to mount the VMFS datastore and make it available to the ESXi host. Automatically triggering the VMFS rescan simplifies the process of making new VMFS datastores available to ESXi hosts.

In addition to rescanning just all HBAs or CNAs, you can rescan a single storage adapter. Perform the following steps to rescan a single storage adapter:

1. In the vSphere Web Client, navigate to the Manage tab for a specific ESXi host in the Hosts And Clusters view.

2. From the Storage subsection, select Storage Adapters on the left.

3. Select one of the adapters in the list and then click the Rescan icon above the list (fourth from the left).

YOU CAN ALSO RESCAN AN ENTIRE CLUSTER

If you right-click a cluster object in the Hosts And Clusters view, you can also rescan an entire cluster for new storage objects by clicking All vCenter Actions ➤ Rescan Storage.

Assuming that the zoning of your Fibre Channel SAN is correct and that the storage has been presented to the ESXi host properly, your new LUN should appear in the details pane.

Once the LUN is visible, you're ready to create a new VMFS datastore on it, but before we get to that, we need to cover the processes for adding a LUN via FCoE and via iSCSI.

ADDING A LUN VIA FCOE

The process for adding a LUN via FCoE really depends on one key question: Are you using a CNA where the FCoE is handled in hardware, or are you using vSphere's software-based FCoE initiator?

In previous versions of vSphere, FCoE was supported strictly in hardware, meaning that you could use FCoE only if you had an FCoE CNA installed in your ESXi host. In this configuration, the CNA drivers presented the CNAs to the ESXi host as if they were Fibre Channel HBAs. Therefore, the process of adding a LUN to an ESXi host using hardware-based FCoE was virtually identical to the process we described previously in the section "Adding a LUN via Fibre Channel." Because it's so similar, we won't repeat those steps here.

However, vSphere 5.0 added the ability to perform FCoE in software via an FCoE software initiator. There is still an element of hardware support required, though; only certain network interface cards that support partial FCoE offload are supported. Refer to the *vSphere Compatibility Guide* or the vSphere HCL.

Assuming you have a supported NIC, the process for configuring the software FCoE initiator is twofold: Configure the FCoE networking and then activate the software FCoE adapter. In Chapter 5 we explained in much greater detail the networking components, including virtual switches and VMkernel ports, that will be used in the next few sections.

Perform the following steps to configure the networking for software FCoE:

1. Log in to the vSphere Web Client, and connect to an ESXi host or to a vCenter Server instance.

2. Navigate to the Hosts And Clusters view.

3. Select a host from the Navigator panel and then click the Manage tab.

4. Select the Network subsection.

5. Use the Add Host Networking icon to create a new vSphere Standard Switch with a VMkernel port.

    When selecting uplinks for the new vSwitch, be sure to select the NIC that supports partial FCoE offload. You can add multiple NICs to a single vSwitch, or you can add each FCoE offload-capable NIC to a separate vSwitch. However, once you add the NICs to a vSwitch, don't remove them or you'll disrupt the FCoE traffic.

    For more information on creating a vSphere Standard Switch, creating a VMkernel port, or selecting uplinks for a vSwitch, refer to Chapter 5.

6. Once you've configured the network, select the Storage subsection in the ESXi host ➢ Manage tab.

    (You should still be on this tab after completing the network configuration.)

7. Click Add New Storage Adapter icon, select Software FCoE adapter, and click OK.

8. On the Add Software FCoE Adapter dialog box, select the appropriate NIC (one that supports partial FCoE offload and that was used as an uplink for the vSwitch you created previously) from the drop-down list of physical adapters.

9. Click OK.

OTHER NETWORKING LIMITATIONS FOR SOFTWARE FCoE

Don't move a network adapter port from one vSwitch to another when FCoE traffic is active or you'll run into problems. If you made this change, moving the network adapter port back to the original vSwitch will correct the problem. Reboot your ESXi host if you need to move the network adapter port permanently.

Also, be sure to use a VLAN for FCoE that is not used for any other form of networking on your ESXi host.

Double-check that you've disabled Spanning Tree Protocol (STP) on the ports that will support software FCoE from your ESXi host. Otherwise, the FCoE Initialization Protocol (FIP) exchange might be delayed and cause the software adapter not to function properly.

---

vSphere will create a new adapter in the list of storage adapters. Once the adapter is created, you can select it to view its properties, such as getting the WWN assigned to the software adapter. You'll use that WWN in the zoning and LUN presentation as described in the section on adding a LUN via Fibre Channel. After you've completed the zoning and LUN presentation, you can rescan the adapter to see the new LUN appear.

The next procedure we'll review is adding a LUN with iSCSI.

ADDING A LUN VIA iSCSI

As with FCoE, the procedure for adding a LUN via iSCSI depends on whether you are using hardware-based iSCSI (using an iSCSI HBA) or leveraging vSphere's software iSCSI initiator.

With a hardware iSCSI solution, the configuration takes place in the iSCSI HBA itself. The instructions for configuring your iSCSI HBA will vary from vendor to vendor; so refer to your specific vendor's documentation on how to configure it to properly connect to your iSCSI SAN. After the iSCSI HBA is configured, then the process for adding a LUN via hardware-based iSCSI is much like the process we described for Fibre Channel, so we won't repeat the steps here.

If you instead choose to use vSphere's software iSCSI initiator, then you can take advantage of iSCSI connectivity without the need for iSCSI hardware installed in your server.

As with the software FCoE adapter, there are a few of different steps involved in setting up the software iSCSI initiator:

1. Configure networking for the software iSCSI initiator.

2. Activate and configure the software iSCSI initiator.

The following sections describe these steps in more detail.

Configuring Networking for the Software iSCSI Initiator

With iSCSI, although the Ethernet stack can technically be used to perform some multipathing and load balancing, this is not how iSCSI is generally designed. iSCSI uses the same multipath I/O (MPIO) storage framework as Fibre Channel and FCoE SANs. As a result, a specific networking configuration is required to support this framework. In particular, you'll need to configure the networking so that each path through the network uses only a single physical NIC. The MPIO framework can then use each NIC as a path and perform the appropriate multipathing functions. This configuration also allows iSCSI connections to scale across multiple NICs; using Ethernet-based techniques like link aggregation will increase overall throughput but will not increase throughput for any single iSCSI target.

Perform the following steps to configure the virtual networking properly for the software iSCSI initiator:

1. In the vSphere Web Client, navigate to the Hosts And Clusters view and select an ESXi host from the inventory panel.

2. Select the Manage tab and then click Networking.

3. Create a new vSwitch with at least two uplinks. Make sure all uplinks are listed as active NICs in the vSwitch's failover order.

   (You can also use a vSphere Distributed Switch, but for simplicity we'll use a vSwitch in this procedure.)

USING SHARED UPLINKS VS. DEDICATED UPLINKS

Generally, a bet-the-business iSCSI configuration will use a dedicated vSwitch with dedicated uplinks. However, if you are using 10 Gigabit Ethernet, you may have only two uplinks. In this case, you will have to use a shared vSwitch and shared uplinks. If at all possible, we recommend configuring Quality of Service on the vSwitch, either by using a vSphere Distributed Switch with Network I/O Control or by using the Cisco Nexus 1000V and QoS. This will help ensure that iSCSI traffic is granted the appropriate network bandwidth so that your storage performance doesn't suffer.

---

4. Create a VMkernel port for use by iSCSI. Configure the VMkernel port to use only one of the available uplinks on the vSwitch.

5. Repeat step 4 for each uplink on the vSwitch. Ensure that each VMkernel port is assigned only one active uplink and that no uplinks are shared between VMkernel ports.

   Figure 6.30 shows the NIC Teaming tab for an iSCSI VMkernel port; note that only one uplink is listed as an active NIC. All other uplinks must be set to unused in this configuration.

FIGURE 6.30

For proper iSCSI multipathing and scalability, only one uplink can be active for each iSCSI VMkernel port. All others must be set to unused.

WHAT'S THE MAXIMUM NUMBER OF LINKS THAT YOU CAN USE FOR ISCSI?

You can use the method shown previously to drive I/O down eight separate vmnics. Testing has shown that vSphere can drive nine Gbps of iSCSI throughput through a single ESXi host.

For more information on how to create a vSwitch, assign uplinks, create VMkernel ports, and modify the NIC failover order for a vSwitch or VMkernel port, refer to Chapter 5.

When you finish with the networking configuration, you're ready for the next step.

Activating and Configuring the Software iSCSI Initiator

After configuring the network appropriately for iSCSI, perform these steps to activate and configure the software iSCSI initiator:

1. In the vSphere Web Client, navigate to the Hosts And Clusters view and select an ESXi host from the inventory panel.

2. Click the Manage tab and select the Storage subsection.

3. Click the Add New Storage Adapter icon. From the Add Storage Adapter drop-down, select Software iSCSI Adapter and click OK.

4. A dialog box will appear, informing you that a software iSCSI will be added to the list of storage adapters. Click OK.

After a few moments, a new storage adapter under iSCSI Software Adapter will appear, as shown in Figure 6.31.

5. Select the new iSCSI adapter.

FIGURE 6.31

This storage adapter is where you will perform all the configuration for the software iSCSI initiator.

6. Click the Network Port Binding tab.

7. Click the Add button to add a VMkernel port binding.

This will create the link between a VMkernel port used for iSCSI traffic and a physical NIC.

8. From the Bind With VMkernel Network Adapter dialog box, select a compliant port group.

A compliant port group is a port group with a VMkernel port configured with only a single physical uplink. Figure 6.32 shows an example of two compliant port groups you could select to bind to the VMkernel network adapter.

FIGURE 6.32
Only compliant
port groups will be
listed as available
to bind with the
VMkernel adapter.

Click OK after selecting a compliant port group.

9. Repeat step 8 for each VMkernel port and uplink you created previously when configuring the network for iSCSI.

    When you've finished, the iSCSI initiator Properties dialog box will look something like Figure 6.33.

10. Select the Targets tab and under Dynamic Discovery click Add.

11. In the Add Send Target Server dialog box, enter the IP address of the iSCSI target. Click OK when you've finished.

    Configuring discovery tells the iSCSI initiator what iSCSI target it should communicate with to get details about storage that is available to it and actually has the iSCSI initiator log in to the target—which makes it known to the iSCSI target. This also populates all the other known iSCSI targets and populates the Static Discovery entries.

12. Finally, click the Rescan Adapter icon to discover any new storage devices.

FIGURE 6.33
This configuration allows for robust multipathing and greater bandwidth for iSCSI storage configurations.

If you've already performed the necessary masking/presentation tasks on the iSCSI array to make LUNs available, then the LUN should now show up in the list of devices on the software iSCSI adapter, and you can use that LUN to create a VMFS datastore. If you haven't already presented the LUN to the ESXi host, you'll need to do so according to your vendor's instructions (every array vendor is different). After the storage is presented to the host, a rescan of the iSCSI adapter—using the procedure we outlined in the section "Adding a LUN via Fibre Channel"—should cause the device to show up.

TROUBLESHOOTING iSCSI LUNs

If you're having a problem getting the iSCSI LUN to show up on your ESXi host, check the following troubleshooting list:

◆ Can you ping the iSCSI target from the initiator? (Use the Direct Console User Interface [DCUI] to test connectivity from the ESXi host, or enable the ESXi shell and use the vmkping command.)

◆ Is the physical cabling correct? Are the link lights showing a connected state on the physical interfaces on the ESXi host, the Ethernet switches, and the iSCSI arrays?

◆ Are your VLANs configured correctly? If you've configured VLANs, have you properly configured the same VLAN on the host, the switch, and the interface(s) that will be used on the array for the iSCSI target?

◆ Is your IP routing correct and functional? Have you properly configured the IP addresses of the VMkernel port and the interface(s) that will be used on the array for the iSCSI target? Are they on the same subnet? If not, they should be. Although iSCSI can be routed, it's not a good idea because routing adds significant latency and isn't involved in a bet-the-business storage Ethernet network. In addition, it's generally not recommended in vSphere environments.

◆ Is iSCSI traffic being allowed through any firewalls? If the ping succeeds but subsequently the iSCSI initiator can't log into the iSCSI target, check whether TCP port 3620 is being blocked by a firewall somewhere in the path. Again, the general recommendation is to avoid firewalls in the midst of the iSCSI data path wherever possible to avoid introducing additional latency.

◆ Is your CHAP configuration correct? Have you correctly configured authentication on both the iSCSI initiator and the iSCSI target?

Now that you have a LUN presented and visible to the ESXi hosts, you can add (or create) a VMFS datastore on that LUN. We'll cover this process in the next section.

CREATING A VMFS DATASTORE

When you have a LUN available to the ESXi hosts, you can create a VMFS datastore.

Before starting this process, you'll want to double-check that the LUN you will be using for the new VMFS datastore is shown under the configuration's Storage Adapters list. (LUNs appear in the bottom of the vSphere Web Client properties pane associated with a storage adapter.) If you've provisioned a LUN that doesn't appear, rescan for new devices.

Perform the following steps to configure a VMFS datastore on an available LUN:

1. Launch the vSphere Web Client if it isn't already running, and connect to a vCenter Server instance.

2. Navigate to the Hosts And Clusters view, and select an ESXi host from the inventory tree.

3. Click the Related Objects tab.

4. Click the Create New Datastore icon to launch the New Datastore Wizard.

ANOTHER WAY TO OPEN THE NEW DATASTORE WIZARD

You can also access the New Datastore Wizard by right-clicking a datacenter or ESXi host object in the Navigator and selecting New Datastore from the context menu.

---

5. After clicking Next on the first screen of the New Datastore Wizard, you are prompted for the storage type. Select VMFS, and click Next.

   (We'll show you how to use the Add Storage Wizard to create an NFS datastore in the section "Working with NFS Datastores" later in this chapter.)

6. Create a name for the new datastore, and then if prompted, select a host that can access the LUN.

We recommend that you use as descriptive a name as possible. You might also consider using a naming scheme that includes an array identifier, a LUN identifier, a protection detail (RAID type and whether it is replicated remotely for disaster recovery purposes), or other key configuration data. Clear datastore naming can help the vSphere administrator later in determining VM placement and can help streamline troubleshooting if a problem arises.

7. Select the LUN on which you want to create the new VMFS datastore.

    For each visible LUN, you will see the LUN name and identifier information, along with the LUN. Figure 6.34 shows two available LUNs on which to create a VMFS datastore.

FIGURE 6.34
You'll choose from a list of available LUNs when creating a new VMFS datastore.

After you've selected the LUN you want to use, click Next.

8. Select whether you'd like to create a VMFS-5 datastore or a VMFS-3 datastore.

    We described the differences between VMFS-5 and VMFS-3 in the section titled "Examining the vSphere Virtual Machine File System." Click Next after selecting a version.

9. The next screen, displayed for you in Figure 6.35, shows a summary of the details of the LUN selected and the action that will be taken; if it's a new LUN (no preexisting VMFS partition), the wizard will note that a VMFS partition will be created.

FIGURE 6.35
The Current Partition Layout screen provides information on the partitioning action that will be taken to create a VMFS datastore on the selected LUN.

Click Next to continue.

If the selected LUN has an existing VMFS partition, you will be presented with some different options; see the section "Expanding a VMFS Datastore" for more information.

10. If you selected VMFS-3 in step 8, you'll need to select the VMFS allocation size.

For VMFS-5 datastores, you won't need to select a VMFS allocation size (VMFS-5 always uses a 1 MB block size).

Refer back to "Examining the vSphere Virtual Machine File System" for more information on block sizes and their impact.

11. For both VMFS-5 and VMFS-3, in the Capacity section you'll specify how you want to utilize the space on the selected LUN.

Generally speaking, you will select Maximize Available Space to use all the space available on the LUN. If, for whatever reason, you can't or don't want to use all of the space available on the LUN, select Custom Space Setting and specify the size of the VMFS datastore you are creating. Click Next when you are ready to proceed.

12. At the Ready To Complete screen, double-check all the information. If everything is correct, click Finish; otherwise, use the Back button to go back and make any changes.

When you click Finish and finish creating the datastore, vSphere will trigger the remaining hosts in the same cluster to rescan for new devices. This ensures that the other hosts in the cluster will also see the LUN and the VMFS datastore on that LUN. You will still need to rescan for devices (using the process in the sections on adding a LUN) for ESXi hosts that are not in the same cluster.

After you've created a VMFS datastore, you may need to complete a few extra tasks. Although these tasks are storage-related, we've included them in other areas of the book. Here's a quick reference to some of the other tasks you might need to perform on a VMFS datastore:

♦ To enable Storage I/O Control, a mechanism for enforcing prioritized access to storage I/O resources, refer to the section "Controlling Storage I/O Utilization" in Chapter 11.

♦ To create a datastore cluster to enable Storage DRS, refer to "Introducing and Working with Storage DRS" in Chapter 12, "Balancing Resource Utilization."

♦ To create some alarms on this new VMFS datastore, refer to "Using Alarms" in Chapter 13, "Monitoring VMware vSphere Performance."

Creating new VMFS datastores is not the only way to make additional space available to vSphere for use by VMs. Depending on your configuration, you might be able to expand an existing VMFS datastore, as we'll describe in the next section.

EXPANDING A VMFS DATASTORE

Recall from our previous discussion of VMFS (in the section "Examining the vSphere Virtual Machine File System") that we mentioned that VMFS supports multiple extents. In previous versions of vSphere, administrators could use multiple extents as a way of getting past the 2 TB limit for VMFS-3 datastores. By combining multiple extents, vSphere administrators could take VMFS-3 datastores up to 64 TB (32 extents of 2 TB each). VMFS-5 eliminates this need because it now supports single-extent VMFS volumes of up to 64 TB in size. However, adding extents is not the only way to expand a VMFS datastore.

If you have a VMFS datastore (either VMFS-3 or VMFS-5), there are two ways of expanding it to make more space available:

- You can dynamically expand the VMFS datastore.

    VMFS can be easily and dynamically expanded in vSphere without adding extents, as long as the underlying LUN has more capacity than was configured in the VMFS datastore. Many modern storage arrays have the ability to nondisruptively add capacity to a LUN; when combined with the ability to nondisruptively expand a VMFS volume, this gives you a great deal of flexibility as a vSphere administrator. This is true for both VMFS-3 and VMFS-5.

- You can add an extent.

    You can also expand a VMFS datastore by adding an extent. You need to add an extent if the datastore is a VMFS-3 datastore that has already hit its size limit (2 TB minus 512 bytes) or if the underlying LUN on which the datastore resides does not have any additional free space available. This latter condition would apply for VMFS-3 as well as VMFS-5 datastores.

These procedures are extremely similar; many of the steps in both procedures are exactly the same.

Perform these steps to expand a VMFS datastore (either by nondisruptively expanding the datastore on the same LUN or by adding an extent):

1. In the vSphere Web Client, navigate to the Hosts inventory list.

2. Select a host from the Navigator tree on the left, and then click the Related Objects tab in the content area.

3. From the Datastores subsection, select the datastore you wish to expand.

4. Click the green Increase Datastore Capacity icon, shown in Figure 6.36. This will open the Increase Datastore Capacity Wizard.

    You'll note that this wizard looks similar to the Add Storage Wizard you saw previously when creating a new VMFS datastore.

5. If the underlying LUN has free space available, then the Expandable column will report Yes, as shown in Figure 6.37. Select this LUN to nondisruptively expand the VMFS datastore using the free space on the same LUN.

FIGURE 6.36
From the Datastores subsection of the Related Objects tab, you can increase the size of the datastore.

FIGURE 6.37
If the Expandable column reports Yes, the VMFS volume can be expanded into the available free space.

If the underlying LUN has no additional free space available, the Expandable column will report No, and you must expand the VMFS datastore by adding an extent. Select an available LUN.

Click Next when you are ready to proceed.

6. If you are expanding the VMFS datastore using free space on the LUN, the Specify Configuration screen will report that the free space will be used to expand the volume.

If you are adding an extent to the VMFS datastore, the Specify Configuration screen will indicate that a new partition will be created.

Click Next to proceed.

7. Regardless of the method you're using—expanding into free space on the LUN or adding an extent—if you are expanding a VMFS-3 datastore, you'll note that the block size drop-down list is grayed out. You don't have an option to change the VMFS block size when expanding a VMFS-3 datastore.

8. If you didn't want to use or couldn't use all of the free space on the underlying LUN, you could change the capacity from Maximize Available Space to Custom Space Setting and specify the amount. Generally, you will leave the default of Maximize Available Space selected. Click Next.

9. Review the summary information, and if everything is correct, click Finish.

If you added an extent to the datastore, the datastore properties pane in Datastores And Datastore Clusters view will reflect the fact that the datastore now has at least two extents. This is also shown in the Datastore Properties dialog box, as you can see in Figure 6.38.

FIGURE 6.38
This 20 GB datastore actually comprises two 10 GB extents.

Regardless of the procedure used to expand the datastore, it is nondisruptive—there is no need to evacuate VMs or incur downtime.

Another nondisruptive task is upgrading a datastore from VMFS-3 to VMFS-5, a procedure that we describe in the following section.

Upgrading a Datastore from VMFS-3 to VMFS-5

As we described in "Examining the vSphere Virtual Machine File System," vSphere 5.0 introduced a new version of VMFS called VMFS-5. VMFS-5 offers a number of new features. To take advantage of these new features, you'll need to upgrade your VMFS datastores from VMFS-3 to VMFS-5. Keep in mind that upgrading your datastores to VMFS-5 is required only if you need to take advantage of the features available in VMFS-5.

To help vSphere administrators keep clear about which datastores are VMFS-3 and which datastores are VMFS-5, VMware added that information in multiple places through the vSphere Web Client. Figure 6.39 shows the Configuration tab for an ESXi host; note that the datastore listing in the Storage section includes a column for VMFS version.

FIGURE 6.39
The columns in the Datastores list can be rearranged and reordered, and they include a column for VMFS version.

Figure 6.40 shows the details pane for a datastore, found on the Configuration tab for a datastore in Datastores And Datastore Clusters view. Again, note that the VMFS version is included in the information provided about that datastore. This view, by the way, is also a great view to see information about storage capabilities (used by policy-driven storage), the path policy in use, and whether or not Storage I/O Control is enabled for this datastore. The datastore in Figure 6.40 does have a user-defined storage capability assigned and has Storage I/O Control enabled.

FIGURE 6.40
Among the other details listed for a datastore, the VMFS version is also included.

Perform the following steps to upgrade a datastore from VMFS-3 to VMFS-5:

1. Log into the vSphere Web Client, if it isn't already running.

2. Navigate to the Storage view and select a datastore from the Navigator list.

3. Select the Manage tab and the Settings subsection.

4. Under the General area, click the Upgrade To VMFS-5 button.

5. If you are clear to proceed—meaning that all hosts attached are running at least ESXi 5.0 and support VMFS-5—a dialog box will appear to that effect. Click OK to start the upgrade of the datastore.

6. The VMFS-5 upgrade will start. A task will appear in the Tasks pane for the upgrade; when the upgrade is complete, the vSphere Web Client will trigger a VMFS rescan on the attached hosts so that they also recognize that the datastore has been upgraded to VMFS-5.

After a datastore has been upgraded to VMFS-5, you cannot downgrade it back to VMFS-3.

ONE POTENTIAL REASON NOT TO UPGRADE VMFS-3 DATASTORES

Although you can upgrade a VMFS-3 datastore to VMFS-5, the underlying block size of the datastore does not change. This means that you could run into situations where Storage vMotion operations between an upgraded VMFS-3 datastore and a newly created VMFS-5 datastore could be slower than expected. This is because vSphere won't take advantage of hardware offloads when the block sizes are different between the source and destination datastores. For this reason, you might prefer (and we would recommend) to migrate your VMs off the VMFS-3 datastore and re-create it as a native VMFS-5 datastore instead of upgrading it.

We'd like to make one final note about VMFS versions. You'll note in the screen shot in Figure 6.40 that the selected datastore is running VMFS 5.60. vSphere 5.5 uses VMFS version

3.60 and VMFS version 5.60. For datastores running previous versions of VMFS-3 (say, VMFS 3.46), there is no need or any way to upgrade to VMFS 3.60. VMware only provides an upgrade path for moving from VMFS-3 to VMFS-5.

Figure 6.40 shows a datastore that has a user-defined storage capability assigned. As you know already, this is part of the functionality of policy-driven storage. Let's take a look at how to assign a capability to a datastore.

ASSIGNING A STORAGE CAPABILITY TO A DATASTORE

As we explained in "Examining Policy-Driven Storage," you can define your own set of storage capabilities. These user-defined storage capabilities will be used with system-provided storage capabilities (supplied by VASA) in determining the compliance or noncompliance of a VM with its assigned VM storage policy. We'll discuss the creation of VM storage policies and compliance later in this chapter in the section "Assigning VM Storage Policies." In this section, we'll just show you how to assign a user-defined storage capability to a datastore.

Perform these steps to assign a user-defined storage capability to a datastore:

1. Launch the vSphere Web Client if it's not already running, and connect to a vCenter Server instance.

   Policy-driven storage requires vCenter Server.

2. Navigate to VM Storage Policies from the home screen.

3. Click the icon labeled Enable VM Storage Polices.

   This brings up the Enable VM Storage Polices dialog box, captured in Figure 6.41.

FIGURE 6.41
From this dialog box, you can enable or disable storage policies on a per-cluster level.

4. Select the cluster for which you want to use storage polices and click the Enable button.

5. When storage policies are enabled, click the Close button on the dialog box.

After you have created a storage capability (as explained in the section Examining Policy-Driven Storage) and the cluster is enabled for storage polices, you simply assign the tag you associated with the storage policy to the datastore itself. This provides the link between the storage policy and the datastore.

6. From the vSphere Web Client Storage view, right-click a datastore and select Assign Tag.

vCenter Server will assign the selected capability to the datastore, and it will show up in the datastore details view you saw previously in Figure 6.40.

Prior to vSphere 5.5, storage capabilities were directly assigned to a datastore. As you can see from the steps just outlined, the process is slightly different and uses tags to create a link between a datastore and a storage policy.

There are other datastore properties that you might also need to edit or change, such as renaming a datastore. We'll describe that process in the next section.

RENAMING A VMFS DATASTORE

You can rename a VMFS datastore in two ways:

◆ Right-click a datastore object and select Rename.

◆ When a datastore is selected in the Navigator, the Actions drop-down menu next to its name in the content area also has the rename command.

Both methods will produce the same result; the datastore will be renamed. You can use whichever method best suits you.

Modifying the multipathing policy for a VMFS datastore is another important function with which any vSphere administrator should be familiar.

MODIFYING THE MULTIPATHING POLICY FOR A VMFS DATASTORE

In the section "Reviewing Multipathing," we described vSphere's Pluggable Storage Architecture (PSA) and how it manages multipathing for block-based storage devices. VMFS datastores are built on block-based storage devices, and so viewing or changing the multipathing configuration for a VMFS datastore is an integral part of working with VMFS datastores.

Changing the multipathing policy for a VMFS datastore is done using the Manage Paths button under the Datastore Manage tab in the Settings subsection. We've highlighted the Edit Multipathing button in Figure 6.42.

FIGURE 6.42

You'll use the Edit Multipathing button in the Datastore Manage ➤ Settings area to modify the multipathing policy.

When you select Edit Multipathing, the Edit Multipathing Policies dialog box comes up (Figure 6.43). From this screen shot and from the information we've provided in this chapter, you should be able to deduce a few key facts:

FIGURE 6.43

This datastore resides on an active-active array; specifically, an EMC VNX. You can tell this by the currently assigned path selection policy and the storage array type information.

◆ This VMFS datastore is hosted on an active-active storage array; the currently assigned policy is Fixed (VMware), which is the default for an active-active array.

◆ This VMFS datastore resides on the first LUN hosted by an EMC VNX array. This is noted by the LUN column and also the L1 in the runtime name.

To change the multipathing policy, simply select a new policy from the Path Selection Policy drop-down list and click OK. One word of caution: Choosing the wrong path selection policy for your specific storage array can cause problems, so be sure to choose a path selection policy recommended by your storage vendor. In this particular case, the Round Robin policy is also supported by active-active arrays such as the EMC VNX hosting this LUN, so we'll change the path selection to Round Robin (VMware).

Changes to the path selection are immediate and do not require a reboot.

We're nearing the end of the discussion of VMFS datastores, but we do need to cover two more topics. First, we'll discuss managing copies of VMFS datastores, and then we'll wrap up this discussion with a quick review of removing VMFS datastores.

MANAGING VMFS DATASTORE COPIES

Every VMFS datastore has a universally unique identifier (UUID) embedded in the file system. When you clone or replicate a VMFS datastore, the copy of the datastore is a byte-for-byte copy, right down to the UUID. If you attempt to mount the LUN that has the copy of the VMFS data-store, vSphere will see this as a duplicate copy and will require that you do one of two things:

◆ Unmount the original and mount the copy with the same UUID.

◆ Keep the original mounted and write a new signature to the copy.

Other storage operations might also cause this behavior. If you change the LUN ID after creating a VMFS datastore, vSphere will recognize that the UUID is now associated with a new device (vSphere uses the NAA ID to track the devices) and will follow this behavior.

In either case, vSphere provides a GUI in the Add Storage Wizard that allows you to clearly choose which option you'd like to use in these situations:

◆ Choose Keep Existing Signature if you want to mount the datastore copy without writing a new signature. vSphere won't allow UUID collisions, so you can mount without resig-naturing only if the original datastore has been unmounted or no longer exists (this is the case if you change the LUN ID, for example). If you mount a datastore copy without resig-naturing and then later want to mount the original, you'll need to unmount the copy first.

◆ Choose Assign A New Signature if you want to write a new signature onto the VMFS datastore. This will allow you to have both the copy and the original mount as separate and distinct datastores. Keep in mind that this process is irreversible—you can't undo the resignaturing operation. If the resignatured datastore contains any VMs, you will likely need to reregister those VMs in vCenter Server because the paths to the VM's configuration files will have changed. The section "Adding or Registering Existing VMs" in Chapter 9 describes how to reregister a VM.

Let's take a look at removing a VMFS datastore.

REMOVING A VMFS DATASTORE

Removing a VMFS datastore is, fortunately, as straightforward as it seems. To remove a VMFS datastore, simply right-click the datastore object and select All vCenter Actions ➤ Delete Datastore. The vSphere Web Client will prompt for confirmation—reminding you that you will lose all the files associated with all VMs on this datastore—before actually deleting the datastore.

As with many of the other datastore-related tasks we've shown you, the vSphere Web Client will trigger a VMFS rescan for other ESXi hosts so that all hosts are aware that the VMFS datastore has been deleted.

Like resignaturing a datastore, deleting a datastore is irreversible. Once you delete a datastore, you can't recover the datastore or any of the files that were stored in it. Be sure to double-check that you're deleting the right datastore before you proceed!

Let's now shift from working with VMFS datastores to working with another form of block-based storage, albeit one that is far less frequently used: raw device mappings, or RDMs.

Working with Raw Device Mappings

Although the concept of shared pool mechanisms (like VMFS or NFS datastores) for VMs works well for many use cases, there are certain use cases where a storage device must be presented directly to the guest operating system (guest OS) inside a VM.

vSphere provides this functionality via a raw device mapping (RDM). RDMs are presented to your ESXi hosts and then via vCenter Server directly to a VM. Subsequent data I/O bypasses the VMFS and volume manager completely, though management is handled via a mapping file that is stored on a VMFS volume.

IN-GUEST iSCSI AS AN ALTERNATIVE TO RDMs

In addition to using RDMs to present storage devices directly to the guest OS inside a VM, you can use in-guest iSCSI software initiators. We'll provide more information on that scenario in the section "Using In-Guest iSCSI Initiators" later in this chapter.

RDMs should be viewed as a tactical tool in the vSphere administrators' toolkit rather than as a common use case. A common misconception is that RDMs perform better than VMFS. In reality, the performance delta between the storage types is within the margin of error of tests. Although it is possible to oversubscribe a VMFS or NFS datastore (because they are shared resources) and not an RDM (because it is presented to specific VMs only), this is better handled through design and monitoring rather than through the extensive use of RDMs. In other words, if your concerns about oversubscription of a storage resource are driving the choice of an RDM over a shared datastore model, simply choose to not put multiple VMs in the pooled datastore.

You can configure RDMs in two different modes:

Physical Compatibility Mode (pRDM)   In this mode, all I/O passes directly through to the underlying LUN device, and the mapping file is used solely for locking and vSphere management tasks. Generally, when a storage vendor says "RDM" without specifying further, it means physical compatibility mode RDM. You might also see this referred to as a pass-through disk.

Virtual Mode (vRDM)   In this mode, there is still a mapping file, but it enables more (not all) features that are supported with normal VMDKs. Generally, when VMware says "RDM" without specifying further, it means a virtual mode RDM.

Contrary to common misconception, both modes support almost all vSphere advanced functions such as vSphere HA and vMotion, but there is one important difference: virtual mode RDMs can be included in a vSphere snapshot, while physical mode RDMs cannot. This inability to take a native vSphere snapshot of a pRDM also means that features that depend on snapshots don't work with pRDMs. In addition, a virtual mode RDM can go from virtual mode RDM to a virtual disk via Storage vMotion, but a physical mode RDM cannot.

PHYSICAL OR VIRTUAL? BE SURE TO ASK!

When a feature specifies RDM as an option, make sure to check the type: physical compatibility mode or virtual mode.

The most common use case for RDMs are VMs configured as Microsoft Windows clusters. In Windows Server 2008, this is called Windows Failover Clusters (WFC), and in Windows Server 2003, this is called Microsoft Cluster Services (MSCS). In Chapter 7, the section "Introducing Windows Server Failover Clustering" provides full details on how to use RDMs with Windows Server–based clusters.

Another important use case of pRDMs is that they can be presented from a VM to a physical host interchangeably. This gives pRDMs a flexibility that isn't found with virtual mode RDMs or virtual disks. This flexibility is especially useful in cases where an independent software vendor (ISV) hasn't yet embraced virtualization and indicates that virtual configurations are not supported. In this instance, the RDMs can easily be moved to a physical host to reproduce the issue on a physical machine. For example, this is useful in Oracle on vSphere use cases.

In a small set of use cases, storage vendor features and functions depend on the guest directly accessing the LUN and therefore need pRDMs. For example, certain arrays, such as EMC Symmetrix, use in-band communication for management to isolate management from the IP network. This means the management traffic is communicated via the block protocol (most commonly Fibre Channel). In these cases, EMC gatekeeper LUNs are used for host-array communication and, if they are used in a VM (commonly where EMC Solutions Enabler is used), require pRDMs.

Finally, another example of storage features that are associated with RDMs are those related to storage array features such as application-integrated snapshot tools. These are applications that integrate with Microsoft Exchange, SQL Server, SharePoint, Oracle, and other applications to handle recovery modes and actions. Examples include EMC's Replication Manager, NetApp's SnapManager family, and Dell/EqualLogic's Auto Volume Replicator tools. Previous generations of these tools required the use of RDMs, but most of the vendors now can manage these without the use of RDMs and integrate with vCenter Server APIs. Check with your array vendor for the latest details.

In Chapter 7, we show you how to create an RDM, and we briefly discuss RDMs in Chapter 9.

We're now ready to shift away from block-based storage in a vSphere environment and move into a discussion of working with NAS/NFS datastores.

Working with NFS Datastores

NFS datastores are used in much the same way as VMFS datastores: as shared pools of storage for VMs. Although VMFS and NFS are both shared pools of storage for VMs, they are different in other ways. The two most important differences between VMFS and NFS datastores are as follows:

♦ With NFS datastores the file system itself is not managed or controlled by the ESXi host; rather, ESXi is using the NFS protocol via an NFS client to access a remote file system managed by the NFS server.

♦ With NFS datastores all the vSphere elements of high availability and performance scaling design are not part of the storage stack but are part of the networking stack of the ESXi host.

These differences create some unique challenges in properly architecting an NFS-based solution. This is not to say that NFS is in any way inferior to block-based storage protocols; rather, the challenges that NFS presents are simply different challenges that many storage-savvy vSphere administrators have probably not encountered before. Networking-savvy vSphere administrators will be quite familiar with some of these behaviors, which center on the use of link aggregation and its behavior with TCP sessions.

Before going into detail on how to create or remove an NFS datastore, we'd like to first address some of the networking-related considerations.

CRAFTING A HIGHLY AVAILABLE NFS DESIGN

High-availability design for NFS datastores is substantially different from that of block storage devices. Block storage devices use MPIO, which is an end-to-end path model. For Ethernet networking and NFS, the domain of link selection is from one Ethernet MAC to another Ethernet MAC, or one link hop. This is configured from the host to switch, from switch to host, and from NFS server to switch and switch to NFS server; Figure 6.44 shows the comparison. In the figure, "link aggregation" refers to NIC teaming where multiple connections are bonded together for greater aggregate throughput (with some caveats, as we'll explain in a moment).

FIGURE 6.44
NFS uses the networking stack, not the storage stack, for high availability and load balancing.

The mechanisms used to select one link or another are fundamentally the following:

♦ A NIC teaming/link aggregation choice, which is set up per TCP connection and is either static (set up once and permanent for the duration of the TCP session) or dynamic (can be renegotiated while maintaining the TCP connection, but still always on only one link or the other).

♦ A TCP/IP routing choice, where an IP address (and the associated link) is selected based on layer 3 routing—note that this doesn't imply that traffic crosses subnets via a gateway, only that the ESXi host selects the NIC or a given datastore based on the IP subnet.

Figure 6.45 shows the basic decision tree.

FIGURE 6.45
The choices to configure highly available NFS datastores depend on your network infrastructure and configuration.

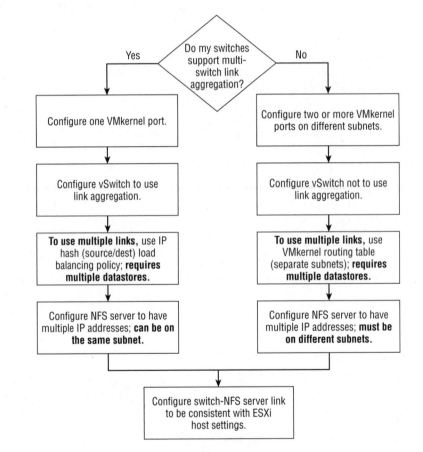

The path on the left has a topology that looks like Figure 6.46. Note that the little arrows mean that link aggregation/static teaming is configured from the ESXi host to the switch and on the switch to the ESXi host; in addition, note that there is the same setup on both sides for the relationship between the switch and the NFS server.

FIGURE 6.46

If you have a network switch that supports multi-switch link aggregation, you can easily create a network team that spans switches.

The path on the right has a topology that looks like Figure 6.47. You can use link aggregation/teaming on the links in addition to the routing mechanism, but this has limited value—remember that it won't help with a single datastore. Routing is the selection mechanism for the outbound NIC for a datastore, and each NFS datastore should be reachable via an alias on both subnets.

FIGURE 6.47

If you have a basic network switch without multiswitch link aggregation or don't have the experience or control of your network infrastructure, you can use VMkernel routing by placing multiple VMkernel network interfaces on separate vSwitches and different subnets.

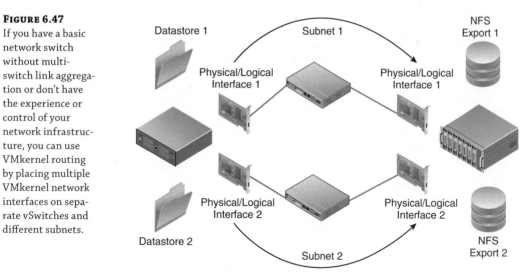

The key to understanding why NIC teaming and link aggregation techniques cannot be used to scale up the bandwidth of a single NFS datastore is how TCP is used in the NFS case. Remember that the MPIO-based multipathing options used for block storage and iSCSI in particular are not options here because NFS datastores use the networking stack, not the storage stack. The VMware NFS client uses two TCP sessions per datastore (as shown in Figure 6.48): one for control traffic and one for data flow. The TCP connection for the data flow is the vast majority of the bandwidth. With all NIC teaming/link aggregation technologies, Ethernet link choice is based on TCP connections. This happens either as a one-time operation when the connection is established with NIC teaming or dynamically, with 802.3ad. Regardless, there's always only one active link per TCP connection and therefore only one active link for all the data flow for a single NFS datastore.

FIGURE 6.48
Every NFS datastore has two TCP connections to the NFS server but only one for data.

This highlights that, as with VMFS, the "one big datastore" model is not a good design principle. In the case of VMFS, it's not a good model because of the extremely large number of VMs and the implications on LUN queues (and to a far lesser extent, SCSI locking impact). In the case of NFS, it is not a good model because the bulk of the bandwidth would be on a single TCP session and therefore would use a single Ethernet link (regardless of network interface teaming, link aggregation, or routing). This has implications for supporting high-bandwidth workloads on NFS, as we'll explore later in this section.

Another consideration of highly available design with NFS datastores is that NAS device failover is generally longer than for a native block device. Block storage devices generally can fail over after a storage processor failure in seconds (or milliseconds). NAS devices, on the other hand, tend to fail over in tens of seconds and can take longer depending on the NAS device and the configuration specifics. There are NFS servers that fail over faster, but these tend to be relatively rare in vSphere use cases. This long failover period should not be considered intrinsically negative but rather a configuration question that determines the fit for NFS datastores, based on the VM service-level agreement (SLA) expectation.

The key questions are these:

♦ How much time elapses before ESXi does something about a datastore being unreachable?

♦ How much time elapses before the guest OS does something about its virtual disk not responding?

FAILOVER IS NOT UNIQUE TO NFS

The concept of failover exists with Fibre Channel and iSCSI, though, as noted in the text, it is generally in shorter time intervals. This time period depends on specifics of the HBA configuration, but typically it is less than 30 seconds for Fibre Channel/FCoE and less than 60 seconds for iSCSI. Depending on your multipathing configuration within vSphere, path failure detection and switching to a different path might be much faster (nearly instantaneous).

The answer to both questions is a single word: time-outs. Time-outs exist at the vSphere layer to determine how much time should pass before a datastore is marked as unreachable, and time-outs exist within the guest OS to control the behavior of the guest OS. Let's look at each of these.

At the time of this writing, both EMC and NetApp recommend the same ESXi failover settings. Because these recommendations change, please be sure to refer to the latest recommendations from your storage vendor to be sure you have the right settings for your environment. Based on your storage vendor's recommendations, you can change the time-out value for NFS datastores by changing the values in the Advanced Settings dialog box, shown in Figure 6.49.

FIGURE 6.49
When configuring NFS datastores, it's important to extend the ESXi host time-outs to match the vendor best practices. This host is not configured with the recommended settings.

The current settings (at the time of this writing) that both EMC and NetApp recommend are as follows:

♦   NFS.HeartbeatDelta: 12

♦   NFS.HeartbeatTimeout: 5

♦   NFS.HeartbeatMaxFailures: 10

You should configure these settings across all ESXi hosts that will be connected to NFS datastores.

Here's how these settings work:

♦   Every NFS.HeartbeatDelta (or 12 seconds), the ESXi host checks to see that the NFS datastore is reachable.

♦   Those heartbeats expire after NFS.HeartbeatTimeout (or 5 seconds), after which another heartbeat is sent.

♦   If NFS.HeartbeatMaxFailures (or 10) heartbeats fail in a row, the datastore is marked as unavailable, and the VMs crash.

This means that the NFS datastore can be unavailable for a maximum of 125 seconds before being marked unavailable, which covers the large majority of failover events (including those for both NetApp and EMC NAS devices serving NFS to a vSphere environment).

What does a guest OS see during this period? It sees a nonresponsive SCSI disk on the vSCSI adapter (similar to the failover behavior of a Fibre Channel or iSCSI device, though the interval is generally shorter). The disk time-out is how long the guest OS will wait while the disk is nonresponsive before throwing an I/O error. This error is a delayed write error, and for a boot volume it will result in the guest OS crashing. Windows Server, for example, has a disk time-out default of 60 seconds. A recommendation is to increase the guest OS disk time-out value to match the NFS datastore time-out value. Otherwise, the VMs can timeout their boot storage (which will cause a crash) while ESXi is still waiting for the NFS datastore within the longer time-out value. Without extending the guest time-out, if vSphere HA is configured for VM monitoring, the VMs will reboot (when the NFS datastore returns), but obviously extending the time-out is preferable to avoid this extra step and the additional delay and extra I/O workload it generates.

Perform the following steps to set operating system time-out for Windows Server to match the 125-second maximum set for the datastore. You'll need to be logged into the Windows Server system as a user who has administrative credentials.

1. Back up your Windows Registry.

2. Select Start ➤ Run, type **regedit.exe**, and click OK.

3. In the left panel hierarchy view, double-click HKEY_LOCAL_MACHINE, then System, then CurrentControlSet, then Services, and then Disk.

4. Select the TimeOutValue value, and set the data value to 125 (decimal).

There are two sub-cases of NFS that we want to examine briefly before we start showing you how to create and manage NFS datastores: large bandwidth workloads and large throughput workloads. Each of these cases deserves a bit of extra attention when planning your highly available design for NFS.

Supporting Large Bandwidth (MBps) Workloads on NFS

Bandwidth for large I/O sizes is generally gated by the transport link (in this case the TCP session used by the NFS datastore being 1 Gbps or 10 Gbps) and overall network design. At larger scales, you should apply the same care and design as you would for iSCSI or Fibre Channel networks. In this case, it means carefully planning the physical network/VLAN, implementing end-to-end jumbo frames, and leveraging enterprise-class Ethernet switches with sufficient buffers to handle significant workload. At 10 GbE speeds, features such as TCP Segment Offload (TSO) and other offload mechanisms, as well as the processing power and I/O architecture of the NFS server, become important for NFS datastore and ESXi performance.

So, what is a reasonable performance expectation for bandwidth on an NFS datastore? From a bandwidth standpoint, where 1 Gbps Ethernet is used (which has 2 Gbps of bandwidth bidirectionally), the reasonable bandwidth limits are 80 MBps (unidirectional 100 percent read or 100 percent write) to 160 MBps (bidirectional mixed read/write workloads) for a single NFS datastore. That limits scale accordingly with 10 Gigabit Ethernet. Because of how TCP connections are handled by the ESXi NFS client, and because of how networking handles link selection in link aggregation or layer 3 routing decisions, almost all the bandwidth for a single NFS datastore will always use only one link. If you therefore need more bandwidth from an NFS datastore than a single Gigabit Ethernet link can provide, you have no other choice than to migrate to 10 Gigabit Ethernet, because link aggregation won't help (as we explained earlier).

Supporting Large Throughput (IOPS) Workloads on NFS

High-throughput (IOPS) workloads are usually gated by the backend configuration (as true of NAS devices as it is with block devices) and not the protocol or transport since they are also generally low bandwidth (MBps). By *backend*, we mean the array target. If the workload is cached, then it's determined by the cache response, which is almost always astronomical. However, in the real world, most often the performance is not determined by cache response; the performance is determined by the spindle configuration that supports the storage object. In the case of NFS datastores, the storage object is the file system, so the considerations that apply at the ESXi host for VMFS (disk configuration and interface queues) apply within the NFS server. Because the internal architecture of an NFS server varies so greatly from vendor to vendor, it's almost impossible to provide recommendations, but here are a few examples. On a NetApp FAS array, the IOPS achieved is primarily determined by the FlexVol/aggregate/RAID group configuration. On an EMC VNX array, it is likewise primarily determined by the Automated Volume Manager/dVol/RAID group configuration. Although there are other considerations (at a certain point, the scale of the interfaces on the array and the host's ability to generate I/Os become limited, but up to the limits that users commonly encounter), performance is far more often constrained by the backend disk configuration that supports the file system. Make sure your file system has sufficient backend spindles in the container to deliver performance for all the VMs that will be contained in the file system exported via NFS.

With these NFS storage design considerations in mind, let's move forward with creating and mounting an NFS datastore.

THERE'S ALWAYS AN EXCEPTION TO THE RULE

Thus far, we've been talking about how NFS always uses only a single link, and how you always need to use multiple VMkernel ports and multiple NFS exports in order to utilize multiple links.

Normally, vSphere requires that you mount an NFS datastore using the same IP address or hostname and path on all hosts. vSphere 5.0 added the ability to use a DNS hostname that resolves to multiple IP addresses. However, each vSphere host will resolve the DNS name only once. This means that it will resolve to only a single IP address and will continue to use only a single link. In this case, there is no exception to the rule. However, this configuration can provide some rudimentary load balancing for multiple hosts accessing a datastore via NFS over multiple links.

CREATING AND MOUNTING AN NFS DATASTORE

In this procedure, we will show you how to create and mount an NFS datastore in vSphere. The term *create* here is a bit of a misnomer; the file system is actually created on the NFS server and just exported. That process we can't really show you, because the procedures vary so greatly from vendor to vendor. What works for one vendor to create an NFS datastore is likely to be different for another vendor.

Before you start, ensure that you've completed the following steps:

1. You created at least one VMkernel port for NFS traffic. If you intend to use multiple VMkernel ports for NFS traffic, ensure that you configure your vSwitches and physical switches appropriately, as described in "Crafting a Highly Available NFS Design."

2. You configured your ESXi host for NFS storage according to the vendor's best practices, including time-out values and any other settings. At the time of this writing, many

storage vendors recommend an important series of advanced ESXi parameter settings to maximize performance (including increasing memory assigned to the networking stack and changing other characteristics). Be sure to refer to your storage vendor's recommendations for using its product with vSphere.

3. You created a file system on your NAS device and exported it via NFS. A key part of this configuration is the specifics of the NFS export itself; the ESXi NFS client must have full root access to the NFS export. If the NFS export was exported with `root squash`, the file system will not be able to mount on the ESXi host. (Root users are downgraded to unprivileged file system access. On a traditional Linux system, when `root squash` is configured on the export, the remote systems are mapped to the "nobody" account.) You have one of two options for NFS exports that are going to be used with ESXi hosts:

   ♦ Use the `no_root_squash` option, and give the ESXi hosts explicit read/write access.

   ♦ Add the ESXi host's IP addresses as root-privileged hosts on the NFS server.

For more information on setting up the VMkernel networking for NFS traffic, refer to Chapter 5; for more information on setting up your NFS export, refer to your storage vendor's documentation.

After you complete these steps, you're ready to mount an NFS datastore.

Perform the following steps to mount an NFS datastore on an ESXi host:

1. Make a note of the IP address on which the NFS export is hosted as well as the name (and full path) of the NFS export; you'll need this information later in this process.

2. Launch the vSphere Web Client and connect to an ESXi host or to a vCenter Server instance.

3. In the vSphere Web Client, navigate to the Storage view.

4. Right-click the datacenter object and select All vCenter Actions ➢ New Datastore. This launches the New Datastore Wizard.

5. At the Storage Type screen, select Network File System. Click Next.

6. At the Name And Configuration screen, you'll need to supply three pieces of information:

   ♦ First, you'll need to supply a datastore name. As with VMFS datastores, we recommend a naming scheme that identifies the NFS server and other pertinent information for easier troubleshooting.

   ♦ You'll need to supply the IP address on which the NFS export is hosted. If you don't know this information, you'll need to go back to your storage array and determine what IP address it is using to host the NFS export. In general, identifying the NFS server by IP addresses is recommended, but it is not recommended to use a hostname because it places an unnecessary dependency on DNS and because generally it is being specified on a relatively small number of hosts. There are, of course, some cases where a hostname may be applicable—for example, where NAS virtualization techniques are used to provide transparent file mobility between NFS servers—but this is relatively rare. Also, refer to the sidebar titled "There's Always an Exception to the Rule"; that sidebar describes another configuration in which you might want to use a hostname that resolves to multiple IP addresses.

◆ You'll need to supply the folder or path to the NFS export. Again, this is determined by the NFS server and the settings on the NFS export.

Figure 6.50 shows an example of the Name And Configuration screen of the New Datastore wizard, where we've supplied the necessary information.

FIGURE 6.50
Mounting an NFS datastore requires that you know the IP address and the export name from the NFS server.

7. If the NFS datastore should be read-only, then select Mount NFS As Read Only.

You might need to mount a read-only NFS datastore if the datastore contains only ISO images, for example.

When you click Next to continue, your server IP and folder path will be validated.

8. On the following screen you can select one or multiple hosts to connect to this datastore.

9. Review the information at the summary screen. If everything is correct, click Finish to continue; otherwise, go back and make the necessary changes.

When you click Finish, the vSphere Web Client will mount the NFS datastore on the selected ESXi host and the new NFS datastore will appear in the list of datastores, as you can see in Figure 6.51.

FIGURE 6.51
NFS datastores are listed in among VMFS datastores, but the information provided for each is different.

TROUBLESHOOTING NFS CONNECTIVITY

If you're having problems getting an NFS datastore to mount, the following list can help you trouble-shoot the problem:

◆ Can you ping the IP address of the NFS export from the ESXi host? (Use the Direct Console User Interface [DCUI] to test connectivity from the ESXi host, or enable the ESXi shell and use the vmkping command.)

◆ Is the physical cabling correct? Are the link lights showing a connected state on the physical interfaces on the ESXi host, the Ethernet switches, and the NFS server?

◆ Are your VLANs configured correctly? If you've configured VLANs, have you properly configured the same VLAN on the host, the switch, and the interface(s) that will be used on your NFS server?

◆ Is your IP routing correct and functional? Have you properly configured the IP addresses of the VMkernel port and the interface(s) that will be used on the NFS server? Are they on the same subnet? If not, they should be. Although you can route NFS traffic, it's not a good idea because routing adds significant latency and isn't involved in a bet-the-business storage Ethernet network. In addition, it's generally not recommended in vSphere environments.

◆ Is the NFS traffic being allowed through any firewalls? If the ping succeeds but you can't mount the NFS export, check to see if NFS is being blocked by a firewall somewhere in the path. Again, the general recommendation is to avoid firewalls in the midst of the data path wherever possible to avoid introducing additional latency.

◆ Are jumbo frames configured correctly? If you're using jumbo frames, have you configured jumbo frames on the VMkernel port, the vSwitch or distributed vSwitch, all physical switches along the data path, and the NFS server?

◆ Are you allowing the ESXi host root access to the NFS export?

Unlike VMFS datastores in vSphere, you need to add the NFS datastore on each host in the vSphere environment. Also, it's important to use consistent NFS properties (for example, a consistent IP/domain name) as well as common datastore names; this is not enforced. VMware provides a helpful reminder on the Name And Configuration screen, which you can see in Figure 6.50. In the vSphere 5.5 Web Client you now have the ability to add additional hosts to an existing NFS datastore without needing the NFS server IP and folder. Simply right-click an NFS datastore and select All vCenter Actions ➤ Mount Datastore To Additional Host.

After the NFS datastore is mounted, you can use it as you would any other datastore—you can select it as a Storage vMotion source or destination, you can create virtual disks on it, or you can map ISO images stored on an NFS datastore into a VM as a virtual CD/DVD drive.

As you can see, using NFS requires a simple series of steps, several fewer than using VMFS. And yet, with the same level of care, planning, and attention to detail, you can create robust NFS infrastructures that provide the same level of support as traditional block-based storage infrastructures.

So far we've examined both block-based storage and NFS-based storage at the hypervisor level. But what if you need a storage device presented directly to a VM, not a shared container, as is the case with VMFS and NFS datastores? The next sections discuss some common VM-level storage configuration options.

Working with VM-Level Storage Configuration

Let's move from ESXi- and vSphere-level storage configuration to the storage configuration details for individual VMs.

First, we'll review virtual disks and the types of virtual disks supported in vSphere. Next we'll review the virtual SCSI controllers. Then we'll move into a discussion of VM storage policies and how to assign them to a VM, and we'll wrap up this discussion with a brief exploration of using an in-guest iSCSI initiator to access storage resources.

INVESTIGATING VIRTUAL DISKS

Virtual disks (referred to as VMDKs because of the filename extension used by vSphere) are how VMs encapsulate their disk devices (if not using RDMs), and they warrant further discussion. Figure 6.52 shows the properties of a VM. Hard disk 1 is a 30 GB thick-provisioned virtual disk on a VMFS datastore. Hard disk 2, conversely, is an RDM.

FIGURE 6.52
This VM has both a virtual disk on a VMFS datastore and an RDM.

We discussed RDMs previously in the section "Working with Raw Device Mappings," and we'll discuss RDMs in a bit more detail in Chapter 7 as well. As you know already, RDMs are used to present a storage device directly to a VM instead of encapsulating the disk into a file on a VMFS datastore.

Virtual disks come in three formats:

Thin-Provisioned Disk   In this format, the size of the VDMK file on the datastore is only as much as is used (or was at some point used) within the VM itself. The top of Figure 6.53 illustrates this concept. For example, if you create a 500 GB virtual disk and place 100 GB of data in it, the VMDK file will be 100 GB in size. As I/O occurs in the guest, the VMkernel zeroes out the space needed right before the guest I/O is committed and grows the VMDK file similarly. Sometimes, this is referred to as a *sparse file*. Note that space deleted from the guest OS's file system won't necessarily be released from the VMDK; if you added 50 GB of data but then turned around and deleted 50 GB of data, the space wouldn't necessarily be released to the hypervisor so that the VMDK can shrink in size. (Some guest OSes support the necessary T10 SCSI commands to address this situation.)

FIGURE 6.53

A thin-provisioned virtual disk uses only as much as the guest OS in the VM uses. A flat disk doesn't pre-zero unused space, so an array with thin provisioning would show only 100 GB used. A thickly provisioned (eager zeroed) virtual disk consumes 500 GB immediately because it is pre-zeroed.

100 GB VMDK file size

500 GB virtual disk

100 GB actual usage (footprint)

500 GB VMDK file size

500 GB virtual disk

400 GB stranded (but not pre-zeroed) storage

100 GB application usage

500 GB VMDK file size

500 GB virtual disk

400 GB stranded (and pre-zeroed)

100 GB application usage

Thick Provisioned Lazy Zeroed   In this format (sometimes referred to as a flat disk), the size of the VDMK file on the datastore is the size of the virtual disk that you create, but within the file, it is not pre-zeroed at the time of initial creation. For example, if you create a 500 GB virtual disk and place 100 GB of data in it, the VMDK will appear to be 500 GB at the datastore file system, but it contains only 100 GB of data on disk. This is shown in center of Figure 6.53. As I/O occurs in the guest, the VMkernel zeroes out the space needed right before the guest I/O is committed, but the VDMK file size does not grow (since it was already 500 GB).

Thick Provisioned Eager Zeroed   Thick provisioned eager zeroed virtual disks, also referred to as eagerly zeroed disks or eagerzeroedthick disks, are truly thick. In this format, the size of the VDMK file on the datastore is the size of the virtual disk that you create, and within the file, it is pre-zeroed, as illustrated at the bottom of Figure 6.53. For example, if you create a 500 GB virtual disk and place 100 GB of data in it, the VMDK will appear to be 500 GB at the datastore file system, and it contains 100 GB of data and 400 GB of zeros on disk. As I/O occurs in the guest, the VMkernel does not need to zero the blocks prior to the I/O occurring. This results in slightly improved I/O latency and fewer backend storage I/O operations during initial I/O operations to new allocations in the guest OS, but it results in significantly more backend storage I/O operation up front during the creation of the VM. If the array supports VAAI, vSphere can offload the up-front task of zeroing all the blocks and reduce the initial I/O and time requirements.

This third type of virtual disk occupies more space than the first two, but it is required if you are going to use vSphere FT. (If they are thin-provisioned or flat virtual disks, conversion occurs automatically when the vSphere FT feature is enabled.)

As you'll see in Chapter 12 when we discuss Storage vMotion, you can convert between these virtual disk types using Storage vMotion.

ALIGNING VIRTUAL DISKS

Do you need to align the virtual disks? The answer is it depends on the guest operating system. Although not absolutely mandatory, it's recommended that you follow VMware's recommended best practices for aligning the volumes of guest OSes—and do so across all vendor platforms and all storage types. These are the same as the very mature standard techniques for aligning the partitions in standard physical configurations from most storage vendors.

Why do this? Aligning a partition aligns the I/O along the underlying RAID stripes of the array, which is particularly important in Windows environments (Windows Server from 2008 onward automatically aligns partitions). This alignment step minimizes the extra I/Os by aligning the I/Os with the array RAID stripe boundaries. Extra I/O work is generated when the I/Os cross the stripe boundary with all RAID schemes as opposed to a full stripe write. Aligning the partition provides a more efficient use of what is usually the most constrained storage array resource—IOPS. If you align a template and then deploy from a template, you maintain the correct alignment.

Why is it important to do this across vendors and across protocols? Changing the alignment of the guest OS partition is a difficult operation once data has been put in the partition—so it is best done up front when creating a VM or when creating a template.

Some of these types of virtual disks are supported in certain environments and others are not. VMFS datastores support all three types of virtual disks (thin, flat, and thick), but NFS datastores support only thin unless the NFS server supports the VAAIv2 NAS extensions and vSphere has been configured with the vendor-supplied plug-in. Figure 6.54 shows the screen for creating a new virtual disk for a VM (a procedure we'll describe in full detail in Chapter 9) on a

VMFS datastore; the two thick provisioning options are not available if you are provisioning to an NFS datastore that does not have VAAIv2 support.

FIGURE 6.54
VMFS datastores support all three virtual disk types.

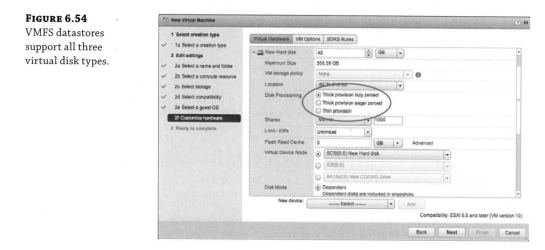

Is there a way to tell which type of virtual disk a VM is using? Certainly. In all three cases, the free space indication within the guest OS is always going to indicate the maximum size of the virtual disk, so you won't be able to use that. Fortunately, VMware provides several other ways to determine the disk type:

◆ In the Datastore Storage Reports subsection, vSphere includes columns for virtual disk space, uncommitted space, provisioned space, and space used. As you can see in Figure 6.55, the columns break out these statistics on a per-VM basis. This allows you to clearly see things like the maximum size of a thin-provisioned VM as well as the current space usage. By right-clicking on the columns, you can select other columns that are not shown in this screen shot, such as these:

◆ Cluster

◆ Resource Pool

◆ Multipathing Status

◆ % Space Used

◆ % Snapshot Space

◆ % Virtual Disk Space

◆ Swap Space

◆ % Swap Space

◆ Other VM Space

- ◆ % Other VM Space

- ◆ % Shared Space

FIGURE 6.55
The Space Used and
Provisioned Space
columns tell you the
current and maximum
space allocations for a
thin-provisioned disk.

- ◆ On the Summary tab of a VM, the vSphere Web Client provides statistics on currently provisioned space, and used space. Figure 6.56 shows the statistics for a deployed instance of the vCenter Server virtual appliance.

FIGURE 6.56
The Summary tab of
a VM will report the
total provisioned
space as well as the
used space.

- ◆ Finally, the Edit Settings dialog box will also display the virtual disk type for a selected virtual disk in a VM. Using the same deployed instance of the vCenter virtual appliance as an example, Figure 6.57 shows the information supplied in this dialog box. You can't determine current space usage, but you can at least determine what type of disk is configured.

FIGURE 6.57
The Edit Settings dialog box tells you what kind of disk is configured, but doesn't provide current space usage statistics.

Closely related to virtual disks are the virtual SCSI adapters that are present within every VM.

EXPLORING VIRTUAL STORAGE ADAPTERS

You configure virtual storage adapters in your VMs, and you will attach these adapters to virtual disks and RDMs, just as a physical server needs an adapter to connect physical hard disks to. In the guest OS, each virtual storage adapter has its own HBA queue, so for intense storage workloads, there are advantages to configuring multiple virtual SCSI adapters within a single guest.

There are a number of different virtual storage adapters in ESXi, as shown in Figure 6.58.

FIGURE 6.58
There are various
virtual SCSI adapt-
ers that a VM can
use. You can config-
ure up to four vir-
tual SCSI adapters
for each VM.

Table 6.3 summarizes the information about the five types of virtual storage adapters available for you to use.

TABLE 6.3:   Virtual SCSi and SATA storage adapters in vSphere 5.5

VIRTUAL STORAGE ADAPTER	VM HARDWARE VERSIONS SUPPORTED	DESCRIPTION
AHCI (SATA)	10	The AHCI is the only non-SCSI storage adapter. Introduced in vSphere 5.5, this virtual SATA adapter is compatible with newer Windows and Linux OSes and supports all Mac OS X versions. It supports a maximum of four adapters per VM and 30 virtual drives per adapter. Typically it's used for virtual CD-ROM devices.
BusLogic parallel	4, 7, 8, 9, 10	This virtual SCSI adapter emulates the BusLogic parallel SCSI adapter. The BusLogic adapter is well supported for older guest OSes but doesn't perform as well as some other virtual SCSI adapters.

TABLE 6.3: Virtual SCSi and SATA storage adapters in vSphere 5.5 *(CONTINUED)*

VIRTUAL STORAGE ADAPTER	VM HARDWARE VERSIONS SUPPORTED	DESCRIPTION
LSI Logic parallel	4, 7, 8, 9, 10	The LSI Logic parallel SCSI virtual adapter is well suited for and well supported by newer guest OSes. Both LSI Logic controllers provide equivalent performance.
LSI Logic SAS	7, 8, 9, 10	The LSI Logic SAS controller is a better choice than LSI Logic parallel when the guest OS is phasing out support for parallel SCSI in favor of SAS. Performance between the two controllers is equivalent.
VMware Paravirtual	7, 8, 9, 10	The VMware Paravirtual SCSI adapter is a virtualization-optimized controller that provides higher throughput with lower CPU overhead but at the cost of guest OS compatibility.

As you can see from Table 6.3, two of these adapters—the LSI Logic SAS and VMware Paravirtual—are available only for VM hardware version 7 or higher. The LSI Logic SAS controller is the default SCSI adapter suggested for VMs running Windows Server 2008 and 2008 R2, while the LSI Logic parallel SCSI controller is the default for Windows Server 2003. Many of the various Linux flavors default to the BusLogic parallel SCSI adapters.

The BusLogic and LSI Logic controllers are pretty straightforward; they emulate a known SCSI controller. The AHCI adapter is a SATA-based controller to replace the older IDE adapter. Typically this would only be used to support guest virtual CD-ROM drives. The VMware Paravirtual SCSI adapter, though, is a different kind of controller.

In short, paravirtualized devices (and their corresponding drivers) are specifically optimized to communicate more directly with the underlying VM Monitor (VMM); they deliver higher throughput and lower latency, and they usually significantly lower the CPU impact of the I/O operations. This is the case with the VMware Paravirtual SCSI adapter in vSphere. We'll discuss paravirtualized drivers in greater detail in Chapter 9.

Compared to other virtual SCSI adapters, the paravirtualized SCSI adapter shows improvements in performance for virtual disks as well as improvements in the number of IOPS delivered at any given CPU utilization. The paravirtualized SCSI adapter also shows improvements (decreases) in storage latency as observed from the guest OS.

If the paravirtualized SCSI adapter works so well, why not use it for everything? Well, for one, this is an adapter type that exists only in vSphere environments, so you won't find the drivers for the paravirtualized SCSI adapter on the install disk for most guest OSes. In general, we recommend using the virtual SCSI adapter suggested by vSphere for the boot disk and the paravirtualized SCSI adapter for any other virtual disks, especially other virtual disks with active workloads.

As you can see, there are lots of options for configuring VM-level storage. When you factor in different datastores and different protocol options, how can you ensure that VMs are placed on the right storage? This is where VM storage policies come into play.

ASSIGNING VM STORAGE POLICIES

VM storage policies are a key component of policy-driven storage. By leveraging system-provided storage capabilities supplied by a VASA provider (which is provided by the storage vendor), as well as user-defined storage capabilities, you can build VM storage policies that help shape and control how VMs are allocated to storage.

We have already shown you in various places in this chapter how to configure the various components to configure end-to-end storage policies, but let's recap the requirements before we move onto the final step. In the section "Examining Policy-Driven Storage," we explained how to configure tags and tag categories to assign to datastores storage policy rule sets. We also showed you how to create rule sets based on those tags and capabilities discovered by VASA, as shown in Figure 6.59. In the section "Assigning a Storage Capability to a Datastore," we showed you how to enable storage policies for use within a cluster, as shown in Figure 6.60, and how to assign tags to a datastore. The last component to configure is linking the VM to the storage policy itself.

FIGURE 6.59
This VM storage policy requires a specific user-defined storage capability.

	VM Storage Policies	
Objects		

Name	Description	VC
Tier 1	Specifies a Tier 1 datastore. Backed by flash drives.	VC
Tier 2	Specifies a Tier 2 datastore. Backed by 15k drives.	VC
Tier 3	Specifies a Tier 3 datastore. Backed by 7.2k-10k drives.	VC
NAS	Specifies a datastore that is a file-based datastore	VC
Block	Specifies a datastore that is a block-based datastore	VC

After the VM Storage Policy feature is enabled, a new area appears on the Summary tab for a VM that shows compliance or noncompliance with the assigned VM storage policy. For a VM that does not have a storage policy assigned—and we'll show you how to assign one shortly—the box is empty, like the one shown in Figure 6.61.

Perform these steps to assign a VM storage policy to a VM:

1. In the vSphere Web Client, navigate to either the Hosts And Clusters view or the VMs And Templates view.

2. Right-click a VM from the inventory panel and select Edit Settings.

3. In the Edit Settings dialog box, click the arrow next to the virtual hard disk(s).

4. From the drop-down list under VM Storage Policy, select the VM storage policy you want to assign to the VM's configuration and configuration-related files.

5. For each virtual disk listed, select the VM storage policy you want associated with it.

Figure 6.62 shows a VM with a VM storage policy assigned to virtual hard disk 1.

FIGURE 6.60
The Enable VM
Storage Policies
dialog box shows
the current status
of VM policies and
licensing compli-
ance for the feature.

FIGURE 6.61
This VM does not
have a VM storage
policy assigned yet.

6. Click OK to save the changes to the VM and apply the storage policy.

After a VM storage policy is assigned, this area will show the compliance (or noncompliance) of the VM's current storage with the assigned storage policy, as in Figure 6.63 and Figure 6.64.

FIGURE 6.62
Each virtual disk can have its own VM storage policy, so you tailor VM storage capabilities on a per-virtual disk basis.

FIGURE 6.63
The storage capabilities specified in this VM storage policy don't match the capabilities of the VM's current storage location.

FIGURE 6.64
This VM's current storage is compliant with its assigned VM storage policy.

Figure 6.63 and Figure 6.64 also show the date and time of the last compliance check. Note that you can force a compliance check by clicking the Refresh hyperlink.

When we discuss creating VMs and adding virtual disks to a VM in Chapter 9, we'll revisit the concept of policy-driven storage and VM storage policies.

In addition to the various methods we've shown you so far for accessing storage from a VM, there's still one method left: using an in-guest iSCSI initiator.

Using In-Guest iSCSI Initiators

We mentioned in the section "Working with Raw Device Mappings" that RDMs were not the only way to present storage devices directly to a VM. You can also use an in-guest iSCSI initiator to bypass the hypervisor and access storage directly.

The decision whether to use in-guest iSCSI initiators will depend on numerous factors, including, but not limited to, your storage configuration (does your array support iSCSI?), your networking configuration and policy (do you have enough network bandwidth to support the additional iSCSI traffic on the VM-facing networks?), your application needs (do you have applications that need or are specifically designed to work with in-guest iSCSI initiators, or applications that need RDMs that could work with in-guest iSCSI initiators instead?), consolidation target (can you afford the extra CPU and memory overhead in the VMs as a result of using an in-guest iSCSI initiator?), and your guest OS (is there a software iSCSI initiator for your particular guest OS?).

Should you decide to use an in-guest iSCSI initiator, keep in mind the following tips:

◆ The storage that you access via the in-guest initiator will be separate from the NFS and VMFS datastores you'll use for virtual disks. Keep this in mind so that you can plan your storage configuration accordingly.

◆ You will be placing more load and more visibility on the VM networks because all iSCSI traffic will bypass the hypervisor. You'll also be responsible for configuring and supplying redundant connections and multipathing separately from the configuration you might have supplied for iSCSI at the hypervisor level. This could result in a need for more physical NICs in your server than you had planned.

◆ If you are using 10 Gigabit Ethernet, you might need to create a more complex QoS/Network I/O Control configuration to ensure that the in-guest iSCSI traffic is appropriately prioritized.

◆ You'll lose Storage vMotion functionality for storage accessed via the in-guest iSCSI initiator because the hypervisor is not involved.

◆ For the same reason, vSphere snapshots would not be supported for in-guest iSCSI initiator–access storage.

As with so many different areas in vSphere, there is no absolute wrong or right choice, only the correct choice for your environment. Review the impact of using iSCSI initiators in the guest OSes, and if it makes sense for your environment, proceed as needed.

THIN PROVISIONING: SHOULD YOU DO IT IN THE ARRAY OR IN VMWARE?

The general answer is that *both* are right.

If your array supports thin provisioning, it's generally more efficient to use array-level thin provisioning in most operational models. If you thick provision at the LUN or file system level, there will always be large amounts of unused space until you start to get it highly utilized, unless you start small and keep extending the datastore, which operationally is heavyweight.

Also, when you use thin-provisioning techniques at the array level using NFS or block storage, you always benefit. In vSphere, the common default virtual disk types—both thin and flat (with the exception of thick provisioned, which in vSphere is used far more rarely)—are friendly to storage-array-level thin provisioning since they don't pre-zero the files.

Thin provisioning also tends to be more efficient the larger the scale of the thin pool. On an array, this construct (often called a *pool*) tends to be larger than a single datastore and therefore more efficient because thin provisioning is more efficient at larger scales of thinly provisioned objects in the oversubscribed pool.

One other benefit of thin provisioning on the array, which is sometimes overlooked, is the extra capacity available for nonvirtual storage. When you're thin provisioning within vSphere only, the VMFS datastore takes the entire datastore capacity on the array, even if the datastore itself has no VMs stored within it.

Is there a downside to thin on thin? Not really, if you are able and willing to carefully monitor usage at both the vSphere layer and the storage layer. Use vSphere or third-party usage reports in conjunction with array-level reports, and set thresholds with notification and automated action on both the vSphere layer and the array level, if your array supports that. (See Chapter 13 for more information on creating alarms to monitor datastores.) Why? Even though vSphere 5.0 added thin-provisioning awareness and support, thin provisioning still needs to be carefully managed for out-of-space conditions because you are oversubscribing an asset that has no backdoor. Unlike the way VMware oversubscribes guest memory that can use VM swap if needed, if you run out of actual capacity for a datastore, the VMs on that datastore will be affected. When you use thin on thin, it can be marginally more efficient but can accelerate the transition to oversubscription and an outage.

An example here is instructive. If the total amount of provisioned space at the virtual disk layer in a datastore is 500 GB with thick virtual disks, then the datastore needs to be at least 500 GB in size, and therefore the LUN or NFS exported file system would need to look as if it were at least 500 GB in size. Now, those thick virtual disks are not actually using 500 GB; imagine that they have 100 GB of used space, and the remainder is empty. If you use thin provisioning at the storage array level, you provision a LUN or file system that is 500 GB, but only 100 GB in the pool is used. The space used cannot exceed 500 GB, so monitoring is needed only at the storage layer.

Conversely, if you use thin virtual disks, technically the datastore needs to be only 100 GB in size. The exact same amount of storage is being used (100 GB), but clearly there is a possibility of quickly needing more than 100 GB since the virtual disks could grow up to 500 GB without any administrative action—with only the VMs writing more data in their guest OSes. Therefore, the datastore *and* the underlying storage LUN/file system must be monitored closely, and the administrator must be ready to respond with more storage on the array and grow the datastore if needed.

There are only two exceptions to the "always thin provision at the array level if you can" guideline. The first is in the most extreme performance use cases, because the thin-provisioning architectures generally have a performance impact (usually marginal—and this varies from array to array) compared to a traditional thick-storage configuration. The second is large, high-performance RDBMS storage objects when the amount of array cache is significantly smaller than the database; ergo, the actual backend spindles are tightly coupled to the host I/O. These database structures have internal logic that generally expects I/O locality, which is a fancy way of saying that they structure data expecting the on-disk structure to reflect their internal structure. With very large array caches, the host and the backend spindles with RDBMS-type workloads can be decoupled, and this consideration is irrelevant. These two cases are important but rare. "Always thin provision at the array level if you can" is a good general guiding principle.

In the last section of this chapter, we'll pull together everything you've learned in the previous sections and summarize with some recommended practices.

Leveraging SAN and NAS Best Practices

After all the discussion of configuring and managing storage in vSphere environments, these are the core principles:

◆ Pick a storage architecture for your immediate and midterm scaling goals. Don't design for extreme growth scenarios. You can always use Storage vMotion to migrate up to larger arrays.

◆ Consider using VMFS and NFS together; the combination provides a great deal of flexibility.

◆ When sizing your initial array design for your entire vSphere environment, think about availability, performance (IOPS, MBps, latency), and then capacity—always together and generally in that order.

The last point in the previous list cannot be overstated. People who are new to storage tend to think primarily in the dimension of storage capacity (TB) and neglect availability and performance. Capacity is generally not the limit for a proper storage configuration. With modern large-capacity disks (300 GB+ per disk is common) and capacity reduction techniques such as thin provisioning, deduplication, and compression, you can fit a *lot* on a very small number of disks. Therefore, capacity is not always the driver of efficiency.

To make this clear, an example scenario will help. First, let's work through the capacity-centered planning dynamic:

◆ You determine you will have 150 VMs that are each 50 GB in size.

◆ This means that at a minimum, if you don't apply any special techniques, you will need 7.5 TB (150 × 50 GB). Because of extra space for vSphere snapshots and VM swap, you assume 25 percent overhead, so you plan 10 TB of storage for your vSphere environment.

◆ With 10 TB, you could fit that on approximately 13 large 1 TB SATA drives (assuming a 10+2 RAID 6 and one hot spare).

◆ Thinking about this further and trying to be more efficient, you determine that while the virtual disks will be configured to be 50 GB, on average they will need only 20 TB, and the rest will be empty, so you can use thin provisioning at the vSphere or storage array layer. Using this would reduce the requirement to 3 TB, and you decide that with good use of vSphere managed datastore objects and alerts, you can cut the extra space down from 25 percent to 20 percent. This reduces the requirement down to 3.6 TB.

◆ Also, depending on your array, you may be able to deduplicate the storage itself, which has a high degree of commonality. Assuming a conservative 2:1 deduplication ratio, you would then need only 1.5 TB of capacity—and with an additional 20 percent for various things, that's 1.8 TB.

◆ With only 1.8 TB needed, you could fit that on a very small 3+1 RAID 5 using 750 GB drives, which would net 2.25 TB.

This would be much cheaper, right? Much more efficient, right? After all, we've gone from 13 1 TB spindles to 4 750 GB spindles.

It's not that simple. This will be clear going through this a second time, but this time work through the same design with a performance-centered planning dynamic:

◆ You determine you will have 150 VMs (the same as before).

◆ You look at their workloads, and although they spike at 200 IOPS, they average at 50 IOPS, and the duty cycle across all the VMs doesn't seem to spike at the same time, so you decide to use the average.

◆ You look at the throughput requirements and see that although they spike at 200 MBps during a backup, for the most part, they drive only 3 MBps. (For perspective, copying a file to a USB 2 memory stick can drive 12 MBps—so this is a small amount of bandwidth for a server.) The I/O size is generally small—in the 4 KB size.

◆ Among the 150 virtual purpose machines, while most are general-purpose servers, there are 10 that are "big hosts" (for example, Exchange servers and some SharePoint backend SQL Server machines) that require specific planning, so you put them aside to design separately using the reference architecture approach. The remaining 140 VMs can be characterized as needing an average of 7,000 IOPS (140 × 50 IOPS) and 420 MBps of average throughput (140 × 3 MBps).

◆ Assuming no RAID losses or cache gains, 7,000 IOPS translates to the following:

   ◆ 39 15K RPM Fibre Channel/SAS drives (7,000 IOPS/180 IOPS per drive)

   ◆ 59 10K RPM Fibre Channel/SAS drives (7,000 IOPS/120 IOPS per drive)

   ◆ 87 5,400 RPM SATA drives (7,000 IOPS/80 IOPS per drive)

   ◆ 7 enterprise flash drives (7,000 IOPS/1000 IOPS per drive)

◆ Assuming no RAID losses or cache gains, 420 MBps translates into 3,360 Mbps. At the array and the ESXi hosts layers, this will require the following:

   ◆ Two 4 Gbps Fibre Channel array ports (although it could fit on one, you need two for high availability).

   ◆ Two 10 GbE ports (though it could fit on one, you need two for high availability).

- ◆ Four 1 GbE ports for iSCSI or NFS. NFS will require careful multi-datastore planning to hit the throughput goal because of how it works in link aggregation configurations. iSCSI will require careful multipathing configuration to hit the throughput goal.

- ◆ If using block devices, you'll need to distribute VMs across datastores to design the datastores and backing LUNs themselves to ensure that they can support the IOPS of the VMs they contain so the queues don't overflow.

- ◆ It's immediately apparent that the SATA drives are not ideal in this case (they would require 87 spindles!). Using 300 GB 15K RPM drives (without using enterprise flash drives), at a minimum you will have 11.7 TB of raw capacity, assuming 10 percent RAID 6 capacity loss (10.6 TB usable). This is more than enough to store the thickly provisioned VMs, not to mention their thinly provisioned and then deduplicated variations.

- ◆ Will thin provisioning and deduplication techniques save capacity? Yes. Could you use that saved capacity? Maybe, but probably not. Remember, we've sized the configuration to meet the IOPS workload—unless the workload is lighter than we measured or the additional workloads you would like to load on those spindles generate no I/O during the periods the VMs need it. The spindles will all be busy servicing the existing VMs, and additional workloads will increase the I/O service time.

What's the moral of the story? That thin provisioning and data deduplication have no usefulness? That performance is all that matters?

No. The moral of the story is that to be efficient you need to think about efficiency in multiple dimensions: performance, capacity, power, operational simplicity, and flexibility. Here is a simple five-step sequence you can use to guide the process:

1. Look at your workload, and examine the IOPS, MBps, and latency requirements.

2. Put the outliers to one side, and plan for the average.

3. Use reference architectures and a focused plan to design a virtualized configuration for the outlier heavy workloads.

4. Plan first on the most efficient way to meet the aggregate performance workloads.

5. Then, by using the performance configuration developed in step 4, back into the most efficient capacity configuration to hit that mark. Some workloads are performance bound (ergo, step 4 is the constraint), and some are capacity bound (ergo, step 5 is the constraint).

Let's quantify all this learning into applicable best practices:

When thinking about performance

- ◆ Do a little engineering by simple planning or estimation. Measure sample hosts, or use VMware Capacity Planner to profile the IOPS and bandwidth workload of each host that will be virtualized onto the infrastructure. If you can't measure, at least estimate. For virtual desktops, estimate between 5 and 20 IOPS. For light servers, estimate 50 to 100 IOPS. Usually, most configurations are IOPS bound, not throughput bound, but if you can, measure the average I/O size of the hosts (or again, use Capacity Planner). Although estimation can work for light server use cases, for heavy servers, don't ever estimate—measure them. It's so easy to measure, it's absolutely a "measure twice, cut once" case, particularly for VMs you know will have a heavy workload.

◆ For large applications (Exchange, SQL Server, SharePoint, Oracle, MySQL, and so on), the sizing, layout, and best practices for storage for large database workloads are not dissimilar to physical deployments and can be a good choice for RDMs or VMFS volumes with no other virtual disks. Also, leverage joint-reference architectures available from VMware and the storage vendors.

◆ Remember that the datastore will need to have enough IOPS and capacity for the total of all the VMs. Just remember 80 to 180 IOPS per spindle, depending on spindle type (refer to the Disks item in the list of elements that make up a shared storage array in the section "Defining Common Storage Array Architectures" earlier in this chapter), to support the aggregate of all the VMs in it. If you just add up all the aggregate IOPS needed by the sum of the VMs that will be in a datastore, you have a good approximation of the total. Additional I/Os are generated by the zeroing activity that occurs for thin and flat (but not thick, which is pre-zeroed up front), but this tends to be negligible. You lose some IOPS because of the RAID protection, but you know you're in the ballpark if the number of spindles supporting the datastore (via a file system and NFS or a LUN and VMFS) times the number of IOPS per spindle is more than the total number of IOPS needed for the aggregate workload. Keep your storage vendor honest and you'll have a much more successful virtualization project!

◆ Cache benefits are difficult to predict; they vary a great deal. If you can't do a test, assume they will have a large effect in terms of improving VM boot times with RDBMS environments on VMware but almost no effect otherwise, so plan your spindle count cautiously.

When thinking about capacity

◆ Consider not only the VM disks in the datastores but also their snapshots, their swap, and their suspended state and memory. A good rule of thumb is to assume 25 percent more than from the virtual disks alone. If you use thin provisioning at the array level, oversizing the datastore has no downside because only what is necessary is actually used.

◆ There is no exact best practice datastore-sizing model. Historically, people have recommended one fixed size or another. A simple model is to select a standard guideline for the number of VMs you feel comfortable with in a datastore, multiply that number by the average size of the virtual disks of each VM, add the overall 25 percent extra space, and use that as a standardized building block. Remember, VMFS and NFS datastores don't have an effective limit on the number of VMs—with VMFS you need to consider disk queuing and, to a much lesser extent, SCSI reservations; with NFS you need to consider the bandwidth to a single datastore.

◆ Be flexible and efficient. Use thin provisioning at the array level if possible, and if your array doesn't support it, use it at the VMware layer. It never hurts (so long as you monitor), but don't count on it resulting in needing fewer spindles (because of performance requirements).

◆ If your array doesn't support thin provisioning but does support extending LUNs, use thin provisioning at the vSphere layer, but start with smaller VMFS volumes to avoid oversizing and being inefficient.

◆ In general, don't oversize. Every modern array can add capacity dynamically, and you can use Storage vMotion to redistribute workloads. Use the new managed datastore function to set thresholds and actions, and then extend LUNs and the VMFS datastores using the new vSphere VMFS extension capability, or grow NFS datastores.

When thinking about availability

◆ Spend the bulk of your storage planning and configuration time to ensure that your design has high availability. Check that array configuration, storage fabric (whether Fibre Channel or Ethernet), and NMP/MPP multipathing configuration (or NIC teaming/link aggregation and routing for NFS) are properly configured. Spend the effort to stay up to date with the interoperability matrices of your vendors and the firmware update processes.

◆ Remember, you can deal with performance and capacity issues as they come up nondisruptively (VMFS expansion/extends, array tools to add performance, and Storage vMotion). Something that affects the overall storage availability will be an emergency.

When deciding on a VM datastore placement philosophy, there are two common models: the predictive scheme and the adaptive scheme.

Predictive scheme

◆ Create several datastores (VMFS or NFS) with different storage characteristics, and label each datastore according to its characteristics.

◆ Locate each application in the appropriate RAID for its requirements by measuring the requirements in advance.

◆ Run the applications, and see whether VM performance is acceptable (or monitor the HBA queues as they approach the queue-full threshold).

◆ Use RDMs sparingly as needed.

Adaptive scheme

◆ Create a standardized datastore building-block model (VMFS or NFS).

◆ Place virtual disks on the datastore. Remember, regardless of what you hear, there's no practical datastore maximum number. The question is the performance scaling of the datastore.

◆ Run the applications and see whether disk performance is acceptable (on a VMFS datastore, monitor the HBA queues as they approach the queue-full threshold).

◆ If performance is acceptable, you can place additional virtual disks on the datastore. If it is not, create a new datastore and use Storage vMotion to distribute the workload.

◆ Use RDMs sparingly.

Our preference is a hybrid. Specifically, you can use the adaptive scheme coupled with (starting with) two wildly divergent datastore performance profiles (the idea from the predictive scheme), one for utility VMs and one for priority VMs.

Always read, follow, and leverage the key documentation:

◆ VMware's Fibre Channel and iSCSI SAN configuration guides

◆ VMware's HCL

♦ Your storage vendor's best practices/solutions guides

Sometimes the documents go out of date. Don't just ignore the guidance if you think it's incorrect; use the online community or reach out to VMware or your storage vendor to get the latest information.

Most important, have no fear!

Physical host and storage configurations have historically been extremely static, and the penalty of error in storage configuration from a performance or capacity standpoint was steep. The errors of misconfiguration would inevitably lead not only to application issues but to complex work and downtime to resolve. This pain of error has ingrained in administrators a tendency to overplan when it comes to performance and capacity.

Between the capabilities of modern arrays to modify many storage attributes dynamically and Storage vMotion (the ultimate "get out of jail free card"—including complete array replacement!), the penalty and risk are less about misconfiguration, and now the risk is more about oversizing or overbuying. You cannot be trapped with an underperforming configuration you can't change nondisruptively.

More important than any storage configuration or feature per se is to design a highly available configuration that meets your immediate needs and is as flexible to change as VMware makes the rest of the IT stack.

The Bottom Line

Differentiate and understand the fundamentals of shared storage, including SANs and NAS. vSphere depends on shared storage for advanced functions, cluster-wide availability, and the aggregate performance of all the VMs in a cluster. Designing a high-performance and highly available shared storage infrastructure is possible on Fibre Channel, FCoE, and iSCSI SANs and is possible using NAS; in addition, it's available for midrange to enterprise storage architectures. Always design the storage architecture to meet the performance requirements first, and then ensure that capacity requirements are met as a corollary.

> **Master It**   Identify examples where each of the protocol choices would be ideal for different vSphere deployments.

> **Master It**   Identify the three storage performance parameters and the primary determinant of storage performance and how to quickly estimate it for a given storage configuration.

Understand vSphere storage options. vSphere has three fundamental storage presentation models: VMFS on block, RDM, and NFS. The most flexible configurations use all three, predominantly via a shared-container model and selective use of RDMs.

> **Master It**   Characterize use cases for VMFS datastores, NFS datastores, and RDMs.

> **Master It**   If you're using VMFS and there's one performance metric to track, what would it be? Configure a monitor for that metric.

Configure storage at the vSphere layer. After a shared storage platform is selected, vSphere needs a storage network configured. The network (whether Fibre Channel or Ethernet based) must be designed to meet availability and throughput requirements, which are influenced by protocol choice and vSphere fundamental storage stack (and in the case of NFS, the network stack) architecture. Proper network design involves physical redundancy and physical or logical isolation mechanisms (SAN zoning and network VLANs). With connectivity in place, configure LUNs and VMFS datastores and/or NFS exports/NFS datastores using the predictive or adaptive model (or a hybrid model). Use Storage vMotion to resolve hot spots and other non-optimal VM placement.

Master It   What would best identify an oversubscribed VMFS datastore from a performance standpoint? How would you identify the issue? What is it most likely to be? What would be two possible corrective actions you could take?

Master It   A VMFS volume is filling up. What are three possible nondisruptive corrective actions you could take?

Master It   What would best identify an oversubscribed NFS volume from a performance standpoint? How would you identify the issue? What is it most likely to be? What are two possible corrective actions you could take?

Configure storage at the VM layer.   With datastores in place, create VMs. During the creation of the VMs, place VMs in the appropriate datastores, and employ selective use of RDMs but only where required. Leverage in-guest iSCSI where it makes sense, but understand the impact to your vSphere environment.

Master It   Without turning the machine off, convert the virtual disks on a VMFS volume from thin to thick (eagerzeroedthick) and back to thin.

Master It   Identify where you would use a physical compatibility mode RDM, and configure that use case.

Leverage best practices for SAN and NAS storage with vSphere.   Read, follow, and leverage key VMware and storage vendors' best practices/solutions guide documentation. Don't oversize up front, but instead learn to leverage VMware and storage array features to monitor performance, queues, and backend load—and then nondisruptively adapt. Plan for performance first and capacity second. (Usually capacity is a given for performance requirements to be met.) Spend design time on availability design and on the large, heavy I/O VMs, and use flexible pool design for the general-purpose VMFS and NFS datastores.

Master It   Quickly estimate the minimum usable capacity needed for 200 VMs with an average VM size of 40 GB. Make some assumptions about vSphere snapshots. What would be the raw capacity needed in the array if you used RAID 10? RAID 5 (4+1)? RAID 6 (10+2)? What would you do to nondisruptively cope if you ran out of capacity?

Master It   Using the configurations in the previous question, what would the minimum amount of raw capacity need to be if the VMs are actually only 20 GB of data in each VM, even though they are provisioning 40 GB and you used thick on an array that didn't support thin provisioning? What if the array did support thin provisioning? What if you used Storage vMotion to convert from thick to thin (both in the case where the array supports thin provisioning and in the case where it doesn't)?

Master It   Estimate the number of spindles needed for 100 VMs that drive 200 IOPS each and are 40 GB in size. Assume no RAID loss or cache gain. How many if you use 500 GB SATA 7200 RPM? 300 GB 10K Fibre Channel/SAS? 300 GB 15K Fibre Channel/SAS? 160 GB consumer-grade SSD? 200 GB Enterprise Flash?

Chapter 7

Ensuring High Availability and Business Continuity

Ensuring high availability and business continuity is a key part of virtualization that is often overlooked or considered after the fact. It is equally as important as configuring storage devices and setting up virtual networking. Virtualization and VMware vSphere in particular enable new ways to provide high availability and business continuity. There are multiple layers where vSphere administrators can help provide high availability in a variety of ways depending on the needs of the business and the unique requirements of the organization. This chapter discusses some of the tools and techniques available for ensuring high availability and business continuity.

In this chapter, you will learn to

◆ Understand Windows clustering and the different types of clusters

◆ Use vSphere's built-in high-availability functionality

◆ Recognize differences between different high-availability solutions

◆ Understand additional components of business continuity

Understanding the Layers of High Availability

Even in nonvirtualized environments, there are multiple ways to achieve high availability for OS instances and applications. When you introduce virtualization into the mix with vSphere, you gain additional methods of providing high availability. Figure 7.1 shows these different layers.

FIGURE 7.1
Each layer has its
own forms of high
availability.

At each layer, there are tools and techniques for providing high availability and business continuity:

◆ At the Application layer, options include Oracle Real Application Clusters (RAC).

◆ At the OS layer, solutions include OS clustering functionality, such as Windows Server Failover Clustering (WSFC).

◆ The Virtualization layer offers a number of features for high availability, including vSphere High Availability (HA) and vSphere Fault Tolerance (FT).

◆ At the Physical layer high availability is achieved through redundant hardware—multiple network interface cards (NICs) or host bus adapters (HBAs), multiple storage area network (SAN) switches and fabrics, multiple paths to storage, multiple controllers in storage arrays, redundant power supplies, and so forth.

Each of these various technologies or techniques has its own strengths and weaknesses. For example, providing redundancy at the Physical layer is great, but it doesn't help with failures at the Application layer. Conversely, protecting against application failures is great but won't help much if the underlying hardware isn't redundant. As you set forth to establish high availability for your virtualized workloads, keep in mind that there is no "one size fits all" solution. Use the right tool for the job based on your specific requirements.

Given that this is a book on vSphere, we can cover only some of the various possibilities for ensuring high availability, so we'll focus out efforts on three key technologies or techniques that help provide high availability:

◆ OS clustering in Microsoft Windows

◆ ESXi host clustering using vSphere HA

◆ VM mirroring using vSphere FT

After a discussion of these three broad areas, we discuss some areas relating to business continuity. You can find details relating to High Availability at the physical layer in other chapters of this book, such as Chapter 5, "Creating and Configuring Virtual Networks," and Chapter 6, "Creating and Configuring Storage Devices."

First, though, let's start with a well-known technique for achieving high availability at the OS level: OS clustering, specifically clustering Microsoft Windows Server instances.

Clustering VMs

Because Windows Server is widely used in corporate and enterprise datacenters today, it's quite likely that at one point or another you've been asked to create or support a Windows-based cluster. There are two primary ways to use clustering to provide high availability for Windows Server:

♦ Network Load Balancing (NLB) clustering

♦ Windows Server Failover Clustering (WSFC)

While both of these methods are described as clustering, they each target very different purposes. NLB typically provides scalable performance, while WSFC usually focuses on providing redundancy and high availability in the form of active/passive workload clustering.

Some experts say that vSphere HA eliminates the need for WSFC because—as you'll see later in this chapter in the section "Implementing vSphere High Availability"—vSphere HA can provide failover in the event of a physical host failure. That's true, but it's important to understand that these high-availability mechanisms operate at different layers (refer back to Figure 7.1). WSFC operates at the OS layer, providing redundancy in the event that one of the OS instances in the cluster fails. That OS failure could be the result of hardware failure. vSphere HA (and vSphere FT) operate at a layer beneath the OS and don't operate in exactly the same way. As we'll reiterate throughout this chapter, each of the high-availability mechanisms described in this chapter has advantages and disadvantages. You'll want to be sure you understand these so that you can choose the right approach for your specific environment.

Table 7.1 provides a quick overview of the clustering support provided by the various versions of Windows Server.

TABLE 7.1:   Windows Server 2003/2008 clustering support

OPERATING SYSTEM	NETWORK LOAD BALANCING	WINDOWS FAILOVER CLUSTERING
Windows Server 2003/2008 Web Edition	Yes (up to 32 nodes)	No
Windows Server 2003/2008 Standard Edition	Yes (up to 32 nodes)	No
Windows Server 2003/2008 Enterprise Edition	Yes (up to 32 nodes)	Yes (up to 8 nodes in 2003 and 16 nodes in 2008)
Windows Server 2003/2008 Datacenter Edition	Yes (up to 32 nodes)	Yes (up to 8 nodes in 2003 and 16 nodes in 2008)
Windows Server 2012	Yes (up to 32 nodes)	Yes (up to 64 nodes)

We'll start with a quick review of NLB clustering and how you can use it in your vSphere environment.

Introducing Network Load Balancing Clustering

The Network Load Balancing configuration involves an aggregation of stateless servers that balances the requests for applications or services. In a typical NLB cluster, all nodes are active participants in the cluster and are consistently responding to requests for services. If one of the nodes in the NLB cluster goes down, client connections are simply redirected to another available node in the NLB cluster. NLB clusters are most commonly deployed to enhance performance and availability. Because client connections could be directed to any available node within the cluster, NLB clusters are best suited for scenarios involving stateless connections and protocols, such as environments using Microsoft Internet Information Services (IIS), virtual private networking (VPN), or Microsoft Internet Security and Acceleration (ISA) Server, to name a few. Figure 7.2 summarizes the architecture of an NLB cluster made up of Windows-based VMs (the architecture is the same for physical systems).

FIGURE 7.2
An NLB cluster can contain up to 32 active nodes (only 5 are shown here), and traffic is distributed equally across each available node. The NLB software allows the nodes to share a common name and IP address that is referenced by clients.

Load-balanced identity: www.lab.local (10.1.1.10)

NETWORK LOAD-BALANCING SUPPORT FROM VMWARE

As of this writing, VMware supports NLB, but you will need to run NLB in Multicast mode to support vMotion and VMs on different physical hosts. You will also need to configure static Address Resolution Protocol (ARP) entries on the physical switch to achieve this, which greatly limits the scalability of the solution. If NLB is running in Unicast mode, then the VMs will all need to be running on the same host, which is generally not a good idea if you want high availability! Another option to consider would be third-party load balancers to achieve the same results.

NLB clusters aren't the right fit for every application or workload. For applications and workloads that aren't a good fit for NLB, Microsoft offers Windows Server Failover Clustering.

Introducing Windows Server Failover Clustering

Unlike NLB clusters, Windows Server Failover Clustering (WSFC) clusters (which we'll refer to as server clusters, failover clusters, or simply WSFC from here on) are used solely for the sake of availability. Server clusters do not enhance performance outside of high availability. In a typical server cluster, multiple stateful nodes are configured to be able to own a service or application resource, but only one node owns the resource at a given time. Server clusters are most often used for applications like Microsoft SQL Server and DHCP services, in which each share the need for a common datastore. The common datastore houses the information accessible by the node that is online and currently owns the resource as well as the other possible owners that could assume ownership in the event of failure. Each node requires at least two network connections: one for the production network and one for the cluster service heartbeat between nodes. Figure 7.3 details the structure of a server cluster built using physical systems (we'll illustrate several ways server clusters are built with VMs later in the next section, "Reviewing VM Clustering Configurations").

FIGURE 7.3
Server clusters are best suited for applications and services like SQL Server, DHCP, and so on, which use a common dataset.

Public network
Shared identity: sql.lab.local (10.1.1.20)

Private (heartbeat) network

Shared datastore

Server clusters, when constructed properly, provide automatic failover of services and applications hosted across multiple cluster nodes. When multiple nodes are configured as a cluster for a service or application resource, only one node owns the resource at any given time. When the current resource owner experiences failure, causing a loss in the heartbeat between the cluster nodes, another node assumes ownership of the resource to allow continued access with minimal data loss. Windows Server has multiple ways of configuring Windows Server Failover Clustering, or Microsoft Cluster Server (MSCS). Because this is a VMware book and not a Windows Server book, we'll concentrate examples on the most popular Windows Server version, 2008 R2. To configure multiple Windows Server 2008 nodes into a Microsoft cluster, the following requirements must be met:

◆ Nodes must be running either Enterprise Edition or Datacenter Edition of Windows Server 2008.

◆ All nodes should have access to the same storage device(s). The specific details of the storage device(s) and how they are shared will depend on how the cluster is built.

◆ All nodes should have two similarly connected and configured network adapters: one for the production (or public) network and one for the heartbeat (or private) network.

◆ All nodes should have Microsoft Cluster Services for the version of Windows that you are using.

Earlier versions of Microsoft Exchange used to align to the shared storage based on the cluster model that we've just explained. However, Exchange 2010 introduced a new concept, the database availability groups (DAGs). While Exchange can still be installed with an application-based cluster configuration, it has departed from the common requirement of shared storage and uses local storage on each node instead. Because of the I/O profile that Exchange can require, local storage is seen to be a better fit for this application. Before we can provide you with the details on how to build a server cluster running Microsoft Windows Server 2008 on vSphere, we first need to discuss the different scenarios of how server clusters can be built.

REVIEWING VM CLUSTERING CONFIGURATIONS

Building a server cluster with Windows Server 2008 VMs requires one of three different configurations, as follows:

Cluster in a Box   The clustering of VMs on the same ESXi host is also known as a *cluster in a box*. This is the easiest of the three configurations to set up. Minimal configuration needs to be applied to make this work.

Cluster across Boxes   The clustering of VMs that are running on different ESXi hosts is known as a *cluster across boxes*. VMware had restrictions in place for this configuration in earlier versions: the cluster node's C: drive must be stored on the host's local storage or local VMFS datastore, the cluster shared storage must be stored on Fibre Channel external disks, and you must use raw device mappings on the storage. In vSphere 4 and vSphere 5, this was changed and updated to allow .vmdk files on the SAN and to allow the cluster VM boot drive or C: drive on the SAN, but vMotion and vSphere Distributed Resource Scheduler (DRS) are not supported using Microsoft-clustered VMs.

Physical-to-Virtual Clustering   The clustering of a physical server and a VM together is often referred to as a *physical-to-virtual cluster*. This configuration of using physical and virtual servers together gives you the best of both worlds, and the only other added restriction is that you cannot use Virtual Compatibility mode with the RDMs.

We'll examine all three configurations in more details in the sections that follow.

Building Windows-based server clusters has long been considered an advanced technology practiced only by those with high technical skills in implementing and managing high-availability environments. Although this might be more rumor than truth, it is certainly a more complex solution to set up and maintain, and running on top of a hypervisor can increase this complexity.

Although you might succeed in setting up clustered VMs, you may not receive support for your clustered solution if you violate any of the clustering restrictions put forth by VMware. The following list summarizes and reviews the dos and don'ts of clustering VMs as published by VMware:

◆ 32-bit and 64-bit VMs can be configured as nodes in a server cluster.

◆ Majority node set clusters with application-level replication (for example, Microsoft Exchange 2007 cluster continuous replication) are now supported.

♦ Up to five-node clustering is allowed.

♦ Clustering does not support NIC teaming in the VMs.

♦ VMs configured as cluster nodes must use the LSI Logic SCSI adapter (for Windows Server 2003) or the LSI Logic SAS adapter (for Windows Server 2008) and the vmxnet network adapter.

♦ VMs in a clustered configuration are not valid candidates for vSphere FT or Storage DRS. They can be part of a cluster that has these features enabled, but the features must be disabled for the VMs participating in the server cluster.

♦ VMs in a server cluster cannot use N_Port ID Virtualization.

♦ All the ESXi systems hosting VMs that are part of a server cluster must be running the same version of ESXi.

There is something else that you need to do. You must set the I/O timeout to 60 seconds or more by modifying HKLM\System\CurrentControlSet\Services\Disk\TimeOutValue, and if you re-create a cluster, you'll need to reset the value again. Additionally, it's a good idea to check this value on each node when VMware Tools is installed or upgraded.

So, let's get into some more details on clustering and look at the specific clustering options available in the virtual environment. We will start with the most basic design configuration, the cluster in a box.

EXAMINING CLUSTER-IN-A-BOX SCENARIOS

The cluster-in-a-box scenario involves configuring two VMs hosted by the same ESXi host as nodes in a server cluster. The shared disks of the server cluster can exist as .vmdk files stored on local Virtual Machine File System (VMFS) volumes or on a shared VMFS volume. Figure 7.4 details the configuration of a cluster in a box.

FIGURE 7.4

A cluster-in-a-box configuration does not provide protection against a single point of failure. Therefore, it is not a common or suggested form of deploying Microsoft server clusters in VMs.

After reviewing the diagram of a cluster-in-a-box configuration, you might wonder why you would want to deploy such a thing. The truth is, you would want to deploy a cluster-in-a-box configuration only in certain circumstances because it still maintains a single point of failure. With both VMs running on the same host, if that host fails, both VMs fail. This architecture contradicts the very reason for creating failover clusters. A cluster-in-a-box configuration still contains a single point of failure that can result in downtime of the clustered application. If the ESXi host hosting the two-node cluster-in-a-box configuration fails, then both nodes are lost, and a failover does not occur. It's a relatively simple setup to configure and probably best suited for learning or testing the cluster service configurations. You may also find yourself in a situation where it's needed for planned downtime or patching.

CONFIGURATION OPTIONS FOR VIRTUAL CLUSTERING

As suggested in the first part of this chapter, server clusters are deployed for high availability. In a vSphere-based outage, high availability is not achieved by using a cluster-in-a-box configuration, and therefore you should avoid this configuration for any type of critical production applications and services.

EXAMINING CLUSTER-ACROSS-BOXES CONFIGURATIONS

Although the cluster-in-a-box scenario is more of an experimental or education tool for clustering, the cluster-across-boxes configuration provides a solid solution for critical VMs with stringent uptime requirements—for example, the enterprise-level servers and services like SQL Server and Exchange Server that are heavily relied upon by the bulk of end users. The cluster-across-boxes scenario, as the name applies, draws its high availability from the fact that the two nodes in the cluster are managed on different ESXi hosts. In the event that one of the hosts fails, the second node of the cluster will assume ownership of the cluster group and its resources, and the service or application will continue responding to client requests.

The cluster-across-boxes configuration requires that VMs have access to the same shared storage, which must reside on a Fibre Channel, FCoE, or iSCSI storage device external to the ESXi hosts where the VMs run. The virtual hard drives that make up the operating system volume of the cluster nodes can be a standard VMDK implementation; however, the drives used as the shared storage must be set up as a special kind of drive called a *raw device mapping* (RDM). An RDM is a feature that allows a VM to establish direct access to a LUN on a SAN device. We also discussed RDMs briefly in Chapter 6.

A cluster-across-boxes configuration requires a more complex setup than a cluster-in-a-box configuration. When clustering across boxes, all proper communication between VMs and all proper communication from VMs and storage devices must be configured properly. Figure 7.5 provides details on the setup of a two-node VM cluster-across-box configuration using Windows Server 2008 as the guest operating system (guest OS).

FIGURE 7.5

A Microsoft cluster built on VMs residing on separate ESXi hosts requires shared storage access from each VM using an RDM.

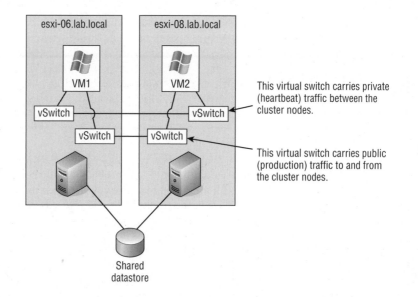

This virtual switch carries private (heartbeat) traffic between the cluster nodes.

This virtual switch carries public (production) traffic to and from the cluster nodes.

USING RAW DEVICE MAPPINGS IN YOUR VIRTUAL CLUSTERS

An RDM is not a direct access to a LUN, and it is not a normal virtual hard disk file. An RDM is a blend of the two. When you're adding a new disk to a VM, as you will soon see, the Add Hardware Wizard presents the RDMs as an option on the Select A Disk page. This page defines the RDM as having the ability to give a VM direct access to the SAN, thereby allowing SAN management. We know this seems like a contradiction to the opening statement of this sidebar; however, we're getting to the part that, oddly enough, makes both statements true.

By selecting an RDM for a new disk, you're forced to select a compatibility mode for the RDM. An RDM can be configured in either Physical Compatibility mode or Virtual Compatibility mode. The Physical Compatibility mode option allows the VM to have direct raw LUN access. The Virtual Compatibility mode, however, is the hybrid configuration that allows raw LUN access but only through a VMDK file acting as a proxy. The following image details the architecture of using an RDM in Virtual Compatibility mode.

So, why choose one over the other if both are ultimately providing raw LUN access? Because the RDM in the Virtual Compatibility mode file offers the advantage of allowing snapshots to be taken. By using the Virtual Compatibility mode, you will gain the ability to use snapshots on top of the raw LUN access in addition to any SAN-level snapshot or mirroring software. Or, of course, in the absence of SAN-level software, the VMware snapshot feature can certainly be a valuable tool. The decision to use Physical Compatibility or Virtual Compatibility is predicated solely on the opportunity and/or need to use VMware snapshot technology or when using physical-to-virtual clustering.

Make sure you document things well when you start using RDMs. Any storage that is presented to ESXi, is not formatted with VMFS, and has not already been allocated as an RDM will show up as available storage. If all the administrators are not on the same page, it used to be very easy to take a LUN that was used for an RDM and reprovision that LUN as a VMFS datastore, effectively blowing away the RDM data in the process. RDMs are now hidden by default when they are allocated, but we have seen this mistake happen firsthand, and let us tell you, the process is very quick to erase any data that is there. We have gone so far as to create a separate column in vCenter Server to list any RDM LUNs that are configured to make sure everyone has a reference point; similarly you might want to use a tag (explained in Chapter 3, "Installing and Configuring vCenter Server").

Let's keep moving and perform the following steps to configure Microsoft Cluster Services on Windows Server 2008 across VMs on separate ESXi hosts.

Creating the First Cluster Node in Windows Server 2008

Perform the following steps to create the first cluster node:

1. Using the vSphere Web Client, create a new VM, and install Windows Server 2008 (or clone an existing VM or template with Windows Server 2008 already installed).

   Refer to Chapter 9, "Creating and Managing Virtual Machines," for more details on creating VMs; refer to Chapter 10, "Using Templates and vApps," for more information on cloning VMs.

2. Configure the VM so that it has two NICs, as shown in Figure 7.6—one for the public (production) network and one for the private (heartbeat) network. Assign IP addresses within Windows Server 2008 as needed. Shut down the VM after you have completed the networking configuration.

3. Right-click the new VM and select Edit Settings.

4. Click the New Device drop-down, select RDM Disk and click Add, as shown in Figure 7.7.

5. Select the appropriate target LUN from the list of available targets, and then click OK.

   We'll remind you again: Make sure you have the correct LUN or you could overwrite important data!

6. Click the arrow next the New Hard Disk item and next to Location choose "Store with the virtual machine to keep the VMDK proxy file on the same datastore as the VM."

7. Select either Physical or Virtual for the RDM compatibility mode.

FIGURE 7.6
A node in a Microsoft Windows Server cluster requires at least two NICs. One adapter must be able to communicate on the production network, and the second adapter is configured for internal cluster heartbeat communication.

FIGURE 7.7
Add a new device of type RDM Disk for the first node in a cluster and Existing Hard Disk for additional nodes.

Different versions have different requirements. In this case, select Physical and then click Next.

RDM REQUIREMENTS FOR WINDOWS SERVER 2003 AND WINDOWS SERVER 2008

When building a cluster across multiple ESXi hosts using Windows Server 2003, you can use Virtual mode RDMs. If you are using Windows Server 2008 to build the cluster across ESXi hosts, you must use Physical Compatibility mode.

---

8. Select the virtual device node to which the RDM should be connected, as shown in Figure 7.8.

   Note that you must select a different SCSI node; you can't put the RDM on SCSI 0.0.

SCSI NODES FOR RDMS

RDMs used for shared storage in a Microsoft server cluster must be configured on a SCSI node that is different from the SCSI to which the hard disk is connected and that holds the operating system. For example, if the operating system's virtual hard drive is configured to use the SCSI0 node, then the RDM should use the SCSI1 node. This rule applies to both virtual and physical clustering.

FIGURE 7.8
The SCSI bus sharing for the new SCSI adapter must be set to Physical to support running a Microsoft cluster across multiple ESXi hosts.

9. Repeat steps 2 through 8 to configure additional RDMs for shared storage locations needed by nodes of a Microsoft server cluster.

   In this case, we're going to present a single RDM.

10. Power on the first node of the cluster. Verify that you've assigned valid IP addresses to the network adapters configured for the production and heartbeat networks. Then format the new drive representing the RDM and assign drive letters, as shown in Figure 7.9.

FIGURE 7.9
The RDM presented to the first cluster node is formatted and assigned a drive letter.

11. Proceed to the next section to configure the second cluster node and the respective ESXi host.

Creating the Second Cluster Node in Windows Server 2008

Perform the following steps to create the second cluster node:

1. Using the vSphere Web Client, create a second VM running Windows Server 2008 that is a member of the same Active Directory domain as the first cluster node. Ensure that the VM has two NICs and that the NICs have appropriate IP addresses assigned for the production (public) and heartbeat (private) networks.

2. Shut down the second VM.

3. Add the same RDMs to the second cluster node.

   This time around, you can't select Raw Device Mappings, because the LUN you selected when setting up the first node won't be listed (it's already been used). Instead, select Existing Virtual Disk, as shown in Figure 7.7, and then navigate to the location of the VMDK proxy file (if you selected Store With The Virtual Machine in step 6 of setting up the first node, you'll find a VMDK file there with the same size as the backing LUN).

Be sure to use the same SCSI node values on the second VM. For example, if the first node used SCSI 1:0 for the first RDM, then configure the second node to use the same configuration. Don't forget to edit the SCSI bus sharing configuration for the new SCSI adapter (Physical SCSI bus sharing).

4. Power on the second VM.

5. Verify that the hard drives corresponding to the RDMs can be seen in Disk Manager. At this point, the drives will show a status of Healthy, but drive letters will not be assigned.

Creating the Failover Cluster in Windows Server 2008

Perform the following steps to create the management cluster:

1. Log into the first node as an administrative user.

2. Launch Server Manager from the Start menu, if it doesn't launch automatically.

3. Click Add Features.

4. From the list of features in the Add Features Wizard, select Failover Clustering and click Next.

5. Click Install. When the install is completed, click Close.

6. Repeat this process on the second node.

With failover clustering installed on both nodes, you can validate the cluster configuration to ensure that everything is configured properly:

1. Log into the first node as an administrative user.

2. From the Start menu, select Administrative Tools ➢ Failover Cluster Management.

3. Click Validate A Configuration. This launches the Validate A Configuration Wizard. Click Next to start the wizard.

4. Enter the names of both the first and second cluster nodes, clicking Add after each server name to add it to the list. Click Next.

5. Leave the default selection (Run All Tests) and click Next.

6. Click Next at the Confirmation step.

7. Review the report. If any errors are reported, follow the guidance to address the errors. Click Finish when you are done.

Now you're ready to create the cluster:

1. While still logged into the first node as an administrative user and still running Failover Cluster Management, click Create A Cluster.

2. At the first screen of the Create Cluster Wizard, click Next.

3. Enter the names of both nodes, and click Add after each server to add it to the list. Click Next to continue.

4. Select the option to not run the validation tests (you've already run them). Click Next.

5. Specify a cluster name and an IP address on the production (public) network. Click Next to continue.

6. Click Next at the Confirmation screen.

7. The Create Cluster Wizard will perform the necessary steps to create the cluster and bring the resources online. When it has completed, review the report and click Finish.

After the cluster is up and running, you can use the Failover Cluster Management application to add resources, applications, and services. Some applications, such as Microsoft SQL Server and Microsoft Exchange Server, not only are cluster-aware applications but also allow you to create a server cluster as part of the standard installation wizard. Other cluster-aware applications and services can be configured into a cluster using the cluster administrator. Refer to the documentation for Microsoft Windows Server 2008 and/or the specific application you want to cluster for more details.

EXAMINING PHYSICAL-TO-VIRTUAL CLUSTERING

The last type of clustering scenario to discuss is physical-to-virtual clustering. As you might have guessed, this involves building a cluster with two nodes where one node is a physical machine and the other node is a VM. Figure 7.10 details the setup of a two-node physical-to-virtual cluster.

FIGURE 7.10
Clustering physical machines with VM counterparts can be a cost-effective way of providing high availability.

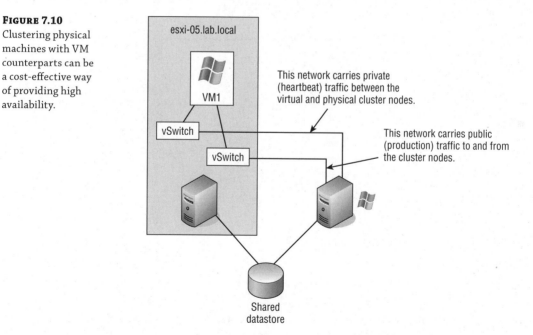

The constraints surrounding the construction of a physical-to-virtual cluster are identical to those noted in the previous configuration. Likewise, the steps to configure the VM acting as a node in the physical-to-virtual cluster are identical to the steps outlined in the previous section, with one addition: You must set up the RDMs in Physical Compatibility mode, regardless of the version of Windows Server you're using. The VM must have access to all the same storage locations as the physical machine. The VM must also have access to the same pair of networks used by the physical machine for production and heartbeat communication, respectively.

The advantage to implementing a physical-to-virtual cluster is the resulting high availability with lower cost. Physical-to-virtual clustering, because of the two-node limitation of VM clustering, ends up as an N+1 clustered solution, where N is the number of physical servers in the environment and the 1 represents one additional physical server to host the VMs. In each case, each physical VM cluster creates a failover pair. With the scope of the cluster design limited to a failover pair, the most important design aspect in a physical-to-virtual cluster is the scale of the host running the ESXi host. As you may have figured, the more powerful the ESXi host, the more failover incidents it can handle. A more powerful ESXi host will handle multiple physical host failures better, whereas a less powerful ESXi host might handle only a single physical host failure before performance levels experience a noticeable decline. Figure 7.11 shows an example of many-to-one physical-to-virtual clustering.

FIGURE 7.11
Using a single powerful ESXi system to host multiple failover clusters is one use case for physical-to-virtual clustering.

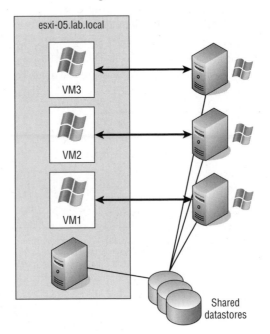

OS CLUSTERING IS NOT LIMITED TO WINDOWS

Although we've discussed only Windows Server–based OS clustering methods in this section, you are not limited to Windows to use OS clustering. Other supported OSes also offer ways to provide high availability within the OS itself.

Now that we've covered OS clustering in Windows Server, let's take a look at VMware's version of high availability. VMware has a built-in option called vSphere High Availability (HA). As you'll see, vSphere HA uses a very different method than OS clustering to provide high availability.

Implementing vSphere High Availability

You've already seen how you can use OS clustering to provide high availability for OSes and applications. In addition to OS clustering, vSphere provides a feature intended to provide high availability at the virtualization layer. vSphere High Availability (HA) is a component of the vSphere product that provides for the automatic failover of VMs. Because the term *high availability* can mean different things to different people, it's important to understand the behavior of vSphere HA to ensure that you are using the right high-availability mechanism to meet the requirements of your organization. Depending on your requirements, one of the other high-availability mechanisms described in this chapter might be more appropriate.

A Complete Rewrite from Previous Versions

The underpinnings of vSphere HA underwent a complete rewrite for vSphere 5.0. If you are familiar with older versions of vSphere, keep this in mind as you look at how vSphere HA behaves in this version.

Understanding vSphere High Availability

The vSphere HA feature is designed to provide an automatic restart of the VMs that were running on an ESXi host at the time it became unavailable, as shown in Figure 7.12.

FIGURE 7.12
vSphere HA provides an automatic restart of VMs that were running on an ESXi host when it failed.

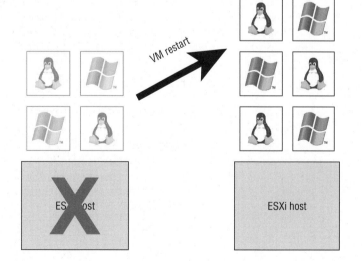

vSphere HA primarily targets ESXi host failures, but it can also be used to protect against VM- and application-level failures. In all cases, vSphere HA uses a restart of the VM as the mechanism for addressing the detected failure. This means there is a period of downtime when a failure occurs. Unfortunately, you can't calculate the exact duration of the downtime because it is unknown ahead of time how long it will take to boot a VM or a series of VMs. From this you can gather that vSphere HA might not provide the same level of high availability found in other high-availability solutions. Further, when a failover occurs between ESXi hosts as a result of the vSphere HA feature, there is a slight potential for data loss and/or filesystem corruption because the VM was immediately powered off when the server failed and then brought back up minutes later on another server. However, given the journaling filesystems in use by Windows and many distributions of Linux, this possibility is relatively slim.

🌐 Real World Scenario

vSphere HA Experience in the Field

Author Nick Marshall says, "I want to mention my own personal experience with vSphere HA and the results I encountered. Your mileage might vary, but this should give you a reasonable expectation of what to expect. I had a VMware ESXi host that was a member of a five-node cluster. This node crashed some time during the night, and when the host went down, it took anywhere from 15 to 20 VMs with it. vSphere HA kicked in and restarted all the VMs as expected.

"What made this an interesting experience is that the crash must have happened right after the polling of the monitoring and alerting server. All the VMs that were on the general alerting schedule were restarted without triggering any alerts. Some of the VMs with more aggressive monitoring that tripped off alerts that were recovered before anyone was able to log into the system and investigate. I tried to argue the point that if an alert never fired, did the downtime really happen? I did not get too far with that argument, but I was pleased with the results.

"In another case, during testing I had a VM running on a two-node cluster. I pulled the power cords on the host that the VM was running to create the failure. My time to recovery from pull to ping was between 5 and 6 minutes. That's not too bad for general use but not good enough for all cases. vSphere Fault Tolerance can now fill that gap for even the most important and critical servers in your environment. We'll talk more about vSphere FT in a bit."

Understanding vSphere HA's Underpinnings

On the surface, the functionality of vSphere HA is similar to the functionality provided in previous versions of vSphere. Under the covers, though, from vSphere 5.0 HA uses a new VMware-developed tool known as Fault Domain Manager (FDM). FDM was developed from the ground up to replace Automated Availability Manager (AAM), which powered vSphere HA in earlier versions of vSphere. AAM had a number of notable limitations, including a strong dependence on name resolution and scalability limits. FDM was developed to address these limitations while still providing all the same functionality from earlier versions of vSphere. FDM also offers a few significant improvements over AAM:

◆ FDM uses a master/slave architecture that does not rely on primary/secondary host designations.

◆ FDM uses both the management network and storage devices for communication.

◆ FDM introduces support for IPv6.

◆ FDM addresses the issues of both network partition and network isolation.

FDM uses the concept of an agent that runs on each ESXi host. This agent is separate and decoupled from the vCenter management agents that vCenter uses to communicate with ESXi hosts (this management agent is known as vpxa). This agent gets installed into the ESXi hosts at /opt/vmware/fdm and stores its configuration files at /etc/opt/vmware/fdm (note that you must enable SSH and the ESXi shell in order to view these directories).

Although FDM is markedly different from AAM, as an end user you will notice very little difference in how vSphere HA operates. Therefore, we generally won't refer to FDM directly, but instead we'll refer to vSphere HA. We did want to bring it to your attention, though, so that you are aware of the underlying differences.

When vSphere HA is enabled, the vSphere HA agents participate in an election to pick a vSphere HA master. The vSphere HA master is responsible for the following key tasks within a vSphere HA–enabled cluster:

◆ Monitors slave hosts and will restart VMs in the event of a slave host failure.

◆ Monitors the power state of all protected VMs. If a protected VM fails, the vSphere HA master will restart the VM.

◆ Manages the list of hosts that are members of the cluster and manages the process of adding and removing hosts from the cluster.

◆ Manages the list of protected VMs. It updates this list after each user-initiated power-on or power-off operation. These updates are at the request of vCenter Server, which requests the master to protect or unprotect VMs.

◆ Caches the cluster configuration. The master notifies and informs slave hosts of changes in the cluster configuration.

◆ The vSphere HA master host sends heartbeat messages to the slave hosts so that the slave hosts know the master is alive.

◆ Reports state information to vCenter Server. vCenter Server typically communicates only with the master.

As you can see, the role of the vSphere HA master is quite important. For this reason, if the existing master fails, a new vSphere HA master is automatically elected. The new master will then take over the responsibilities listed here, including communication with vCenter Server.

DOES vCENTER SERVER TALK TO vSPHERE HA SLAVE HOSTS?

There are a few instances in which vCenter Server will talk to vSphere HA agents on slave hosts: When it is scanning for a vSphere HA master, when a host is reported as isolated or partitioned, or if the existing master informs vCenter that it cannot reach a slave agent.

Once an ESXi host in a vSphere HA–enabled cluster elects a vSphere HA master, all other hosts become slaves connected to that master. The slave hosts have the following responsibilities:

◆ A slave host watches the runtime state of the VMs running locally on that host. Significant changes in the runtime state of these VMs are forwarded to the vSphere HA master.

◆ vSphere HA slaves monitor the health of the master. If the master fails, slaves will participate in a new master election.

◆ vSphere HA slave hosts implement vSphere HA features that don't require central coordination by the master. This includes VM health monitoring.

The role of any given ESXi host within a vSphere HA–enabled cluster is noted on the Summary tab of the ESXi host within the vSphere Web Client. The composite screenshot in Figure 7.13 shows how the vSphere Web Client presents this information.

FIGURE 7.13
The status of an ESXi host as either master or slave is provided on the host's Summary tab. Here you can see both a master host and a slave host.

We mentioned that vSphere HA uses the management network as well as storage devices to communicate. In the event that the master cannot communicate with a slave across the management network, the master can check its *heartbeat datastores*—selected datastores used by vSphere HA for communication—to see if the slave host is still alive. This functionality is what helps vSphere HA deal with network partition as well as network isolation.

Network partition is the term used to describe the situation in which one or more slave hosts cannot communicate with the master even though they still have network connectivity with each other. In this case, vSphere HA is able to use the heartbeat datastores to detect whether the partitioned hosts are still live and whether action needs to be taken to protect VMs on those hosts or initiate an election for a new master within the network partition.

Network isolation is the situation in which one or more slave hosts have lost all management network connectivity. Isolated hosts can neither communicate with the vSphere HA master nor communicate with other ESXi hosts. In this case, the slave host uses heartbeat datastores to notify the master that it is isolated. The slave host uses a special binary file, the host-*X*-poweron file, to notify the master. The vSphere HA master can then take the appropriate action to ensure that the VMs are protected. We'll discuss network isolation and how an ESXi host reacts to network isolation later in this chapter in the section "vSphere High Availability Isolation Response."

Figure 7.14 shows the files on a VMFS datastore that vSphere HA uses for storage heartbeating between the vSphere HA master and slave hosts.

FIGURE 7.14
vSphere HA uses the host-*X*-poweron files for a slave host to notify the master that it has become isolated from the network.

In the section "Setting vSphere High Availability Datastore Heartbeating," we'll show you how to see which datastores are used as heartbeat datastores as well as how to tell vSphere HA which datastores should or should not be used for heartbeating.

With this overview of the vSphere HA architecture and behavior under your belt, let's move on to enabling vSphere HA to protect your VMs.

Enabling vSphere High Availability

To implement vSphere HA, all of the following requirements should be met:

◆ All hosts in a vSphere HA–enabled cluster must have access to the same shared storage locations used by all VMs on the cluster. This includes any Fibre Channel, FCoE, iSCSI, and NFS datastores used by VMs.

◆ All hosts in a vSphere HA cluster should have an identical virtual networking configuration. If a new switch is added to one host, the same new switch should be added to all hosts in the cluster. If you are using a vSphere Distributed Switch (vDS), all hosts should be participating in the same vDS.

A TEST FOR vSPHERE HA

An easy and simple test for identifying vSphere HA capability for a VM is to perform a vMotion. The requirements of vMotion are actually more stringent than those for performing a vSphere HA failover, though some of the requirements are identical. In short, if a VM can successfully perform a vMotion across the hosts in a cluster, then it is safe to assume that vSphere HA will be able to power on that VM from any of the hosts. To perform a full test of a VM on a cluster with four nodes, perform a vMotion from node 1 to node 2, node 2 to node 3, node 3 to node 4, and finally node 4 back to node 1. If it works, then the VM has passed the test!

As with earlier versions, vSphere HA is a cluster-level configuration. In order to use vSphere HA to protect VMs, you must first place your ESXi hosts into a cluster. Remember, a VMware cluster represents a logical aggregation of CPU and memory resources. With vSphere HA, a cluster also represents a logical protection boundary. VMs can be protected by vSphere HA only if they are running on an ESXi host in a vSphere HA–enabled cluster. By editing the cluster settings, you can enable the vSphere HA feature for a cluster, as you can see in Figure 7.15.

FIGURE 7.15
vSphere HA is enabled or disabled for an entire cluster.

When vSphere HA is enabled for a cluster, it will elect a master as described in the previous section. The other hosts in the cluster will become slave hosts connected to that master host. You can observe this process by watching the Tasks pane of the vSphere Web Client when you enable vSphere HA. Figure 7.16 shows an example of the tasks that are generated when you enable vSphere HA for a cluster.

FIGURE 7.16
As you can see in the Tasks pane, vSphere HA elects a master host when it is enabled on a cluster of ESXi hosts.

After vSphere HA is enabled, you may occasionally need to temporarily halt it, such as during network maintenance windows. Previously we discussed the behavior of vSphere HA when a network partition or network isolation occurs. If you will be performing network maintenance that might trigger one of these events, uncheck Enable Host Monitoring to prevent vSphere HA from triggering isolation response or network partition behaviors. Note the Enable Host Monitoring check box shown in Figure 7.17; this is how you can temporarily disable the host-monitoring function of vSphere HA during network maintenance so as not to trigger network partition or network isolation behaviors.

FIGURE 7.17

Deselecting Enable Host Monitoring when performing network maintenance will prevent vSphere HA from unnecessarily triggering network isolation or network partition responses.

Configuring vSphere High Availability

After vSphere HA is enabled, configuring vSphere HA revolves around several key areas:

◆ Admission control and admission control policy

◆ VM options

◆ VM monitoring

◆ Datastore heartbeating

Each of these configuration areas is described in detail in the following sections.

CONFIGURING VSPHERE HA ADMISSION CONTROL

The vSphere HA Admission Control and Admission Control Policy settings control the behavior of the vSphere HA–enabled cluster with regard to cluster capacity. Specifically, should vSphere HA allow the user to power on more VMs than it has capacity to support in the event of a failure? Or should the cluster prevent more VMs from being powered on than it can actually protect? That is the basis for the Admission Control—and by extension, the Admission Control Policy—settings.

Admission Control has two settings:

◆ Enable: Disallow VM power-on operations that violate availability constraints.

◆ Disable: Allow VM power-on operations that violate availability constraints.

These options go hand in hand with the Admission Control Policy settings, which we'll explain in a moment. First, though, let's take a closer look at the Admission Control settings.

Consider for a moment that you have a cluster of four identical ESXi hosts. Running on these four ESXi hosts are a bunch of identically configured VMs. These VMs consume a total of 75 percent of the resources in the cluster. This cluster is configured for a single ESXi host failure (we'll go into more detail on these settings in a bit). Further, let's say now you want to power on one more VM, and the resource consumption by that VM will push you past the 75 percent resource usage mark. It is at this point that the Admission Control settings will come into play.

If Admission Control is set to Enabled, then vSphere HA would block the power-on operation of this additional VM. Why? Because the cluster is already at the limit of the capacity it could support if one of the ESXi hosts in the cluster failed (one host out of our four identical hosts is equal to 25 percent of the cluster's capacity). Because you've told vSphere HA to prevent power-on operations that violate availability constraints, vSphere HA will prevent you from starting more VMs than it has resources to protect. In effect, vSphere HA is guaranteeing you that you'll always have enough resources to restart all the protected VMs in the event of a failure.

If, on the other hand, Admission Control is set to Disabled, then vSphere HA will let you power on VMs until all of the cluster's resources are allocated. If there is an ESXi host failure at that point, it's possible that some of the VMs would not be able to be restarted because there are not sufficient resources to power on all the VMs. vSphere HA allowed you to exceed the availability constraints of the cluster.

OVERCOMMITMENT IN A vSPHERE HA–ENABLED CLUSTER

When the Admission Control setting is set to allow VMs to be powered on even if they violate availability constraints, you could find yourself in a position where there is more physical memory allocated to VMs than actually exists.

This situation, called *overcommitment*, can lead to poor performance on VMs that become forced to page information from fast RAM out to the slower disk-based swap file. Yes, your VMs will start, but after the host gets maxed out, the whole system and all VMs will slow down dramatically. This will increase the amount of time that HA will need to recover the VMs. What should have been a 20- to 30-minute recovery could end up being an hour or even more. Refer to Chapter 11, "Managing Resource Allocation," for more details on resource allocation and how vSphere handles memory overcommitment.

You should be able to see now how integral the Admission Control Policy settings are to the behavior of Admission Control. When Admission Control is enabled, the Admission Control Policy settings control its behavior by determining how many resources need to be reserved and the limit that the cluster can handle and still be able to tolerate failure.

The Admission Control Policy settings are illustrated in Figure 7.18.

There are three options for the Admission Control Policy:

- The first option, Define Failover Capacity By Static Number Of Hosts, allows you to specify how many host failures the cluster should be configured to withstand. Because the ESXi hosts may have different amounts of RAM and/or CPU capacity, and because the VMs in the cluster may have different levels of resource allocation, vSphere HA uses the idea of a slot to calculate the capacity of the cluster. This option also gives you the flexibility to specify the slot size of the cluster. We'll discuss slots in more detail in just a moment.

- The second option, Define Failover Capacity By Reserving A Percentage Of The Cluster Resources, allows you to specify a percentage of the cluster's total resources that should be used for spare capacity in the event of a failure. You can specify different percentages for CPU and memory. The availability constraints are established by simply calculating the specified percentage of the cluster's total available resources.

◆   The third option, Use Dedicated Failover Hosts, allows you to specify one or more ESXi hosts as failover hosts. These hosts are used as spare capacity, and in the event of a failure, vSphere HA will use these hosts to restart VMs.

FIGURE 7.18
The Admission Control Policy settings will determine how a vSphere HA–enabled cluster determines availability constraints.

BE CAREFUL ABOUT USING FAILOVER HOSTS

When you select an ESXi host as a vSphere HA failover host, it's almost like putting that host into Maintenance mode. vSphere DRS, which we'll describe in more detail in Chapter 12, "Balancing Resource Utilization," won't place VMs here at startup and won't consider these hosts in its load-balancing calculations. You can't manually power on VMs on the failover host(s) either. These hosts are truly set aside as spare capacity.

For the most part, the Admission Control Policy settings are pretty easy to understand. One area that can be confusing, however, involve slots and slot sizes, which are used by vSphere HA when Admission Control Policy is set to failover capacity by a static number of hosts.

Why slots and slot sizes? vSphere HA uses slots and slot sizes because the ESXi hosts in the cluster might have different configurations: One host might have 8 CPU cores and 24 GB of RAM, while another host might have 12 CPU cores and 48 GB of RAM. Similarly, the VMs in the cluster are likely to have different resource configurations. One VM might need 4 GB of RAM, but another VM might require 8 GB of RAM. Some VMs will have 1 vCPU and other VMs will have 2 or even 4 vCPUs. Because vSphere doesn't know in advance which host will fail and which VMs will be affected by that failure (naturally), vSphere HA needed a way to establish a "least common denominator" to express the overall capacity of the cluster. Once that overall capacity of the cluster can be expressed, vSphere HA can set aside the appropriate amount of resources to protect against the configured number of host failures.

Here's how slots and slot sizes work. First, vSphere HA examines all the VMs in the cluster to determine the largest values for reserved memory and reserved CPU. For example, if one of the VMs in the cluster has a 2 GB memory reservation but all others do not have a memory reservation, vSphere HA will use 2 GB as the value for calculating slots based on memory. In the same fashion, if one VM has a reservation for 2 GHz of CPU capacity but all the other VMs don't have any reservation value, it will use 2 GHz as the value. Basically, vSphere HA constructs the least common denominator as a VM with the largest memory reservation and the largest CPU reservation.

WHAT IF THERE ARE NO RESERVATIONS?

vSphere HA uses reservations, described in Chapter 11, to calculate the slot size. If no VMs have reservations for CPU or memory, vSphere will use the default value of 32 MHz for CPU to calculate slot size. For memory, vSphere HA will use the largest memory overhead value when calculating the slot size. These settings can be seen, grayed out, in Figure 7.18.

Once it has constructed the least common denominator, vSphere HA then calculates the total number of slots that each ESXi host in the cluster could support. Then it determines how many slots the cluster could support if the host with the largest number of slots were to fail (a worst-case scenario). vSphere HA performs these calculations and comparisons for both CPU and memory and then uses the most restrictive result. If vSphere HA calculated 50 slots for memory and 100 slots for CPU, then 50 is the number vSphere HA uses. VMs are then assigned to the slots to determine how many slots are used and how many slots are free, and Admission Control uses this to determine whether additional VMs can be powered on (enough slots remain) or cannot be powered on (not enough slots are available).

The slot-size calculation algorithm just described can result in unexpected settings when you have an unbalanced cluster. An *unbalanced cluster* is a cluster with dramatically different ESXi hosts, such as a host with 12 GB of RAM along with an ESXi host with 96 GB of RAM in the same cluster. You might also have an unbalanced cluster if you have dramatically different resource reservations assigned to VMs in the cluster (for example, one VM with an 8 GB memory reservation while all the other VMs use much less than that). While you can fine-tune the behavior of the vSphere HA slot-calculation mechanism using advanced settings, it's generally not recommended. For these situations, you have a couple of options:

◆ You could place similarly sized VMs (or similarly sized hosts) in their own cluster.

◆ You could use percentage-based availability constraints (via the Percentage Of Cluster Resources Reserved As Failover Spare Capacity setting) instead of host failures or failover hosts.

Using reservations on resource pools might be another way to help alleviate the impact to slot size calculations, if the reservations are necessary. Refer to Chapter 11 for more details on both reservations and resource pools.

The next major area of configuration for vSphere HA is VM options.

CONFIGURING VSPHERE HIGH AVAILABILITY VM OPTIONS

Figure 7.19 shows the VM options that are available to control the behavior of VMs for vSphere HA. Two VM options are available for administrators to configure: VM Restart Priority and Host Isolation Response. Both options are configurable as a cluster default setting as well as a per-VM setting.

FIGURE 7.19

You can define cluster default VM options to customize the behavior of vSphere HA.

vSphere High Availability VM Restart Priority

Not all VMs are equal. Some VMs are more important or more critical and require higher priority when ensuring availability. When an ESXi host experiences failure and the remaining cluster nodes are tasked by vSphere HA with bringing VMs back online, they have a finite amount of resources before there are no more resources to allocate to VMs that need to be powered on. This is especially true when Admission Control is set to Disabled, allowing more VMs to be powered on than the cluster could support given a failure. Rather than leave important VMs to chance, a vSphere HA–enabled cluster allows you to prioritize VMs through VM Restart Priority.

The VM Restart Priority options for VMs in a vSphere HA–enabled cluster include Low, Medium, High, and Disabled. For VMs that should be brought up first, the restart priority should be set to High. For VMs that should be brought up if resources are available, the restart priority can be set to Medium or Low. For VMs that will not be missed for a period of time and should not be brought online when available resources are low, the restart priority should be set to Disabled. You can define a default restart priority for the entire cluster, as shown in Figure 7.19, but what if there is a VM that is more (or less) important? The VM Overrides section allows you to define a per-VM restart priority. Figure 7.20 shows VM Restart Priority set to Medium for the cluster and set to low for another VM based on their importance to the organization.

The restart priority is put into place only for the VMs running on the ESXi hosts that experience an unexpected failure. VMs running on hosts that have not failed are not affected by the restart priority. It is possible then that VMs configured with a restart priority of High might not be powered on by vSphere HA because of limited resources, which is in part because of lower-priority VMs that continue to run (again, only if Admission Control was set to Disabled). For example, as shown in Figure 7.21, the ESXi host esxi-05 hosts four VMs with a priority of High and four other VMs with priority values of Medium or Low. Meanwhile, esxi-06 and esxi-07 together hold 13 VMs, but of those VMs only two are considered of High priority. When esxi-05 fails, the FDM master host in the cluster will begin powering the VMs with a High priority. If vSphere DRS is enabled, the VMs will be automatically placed on one of the surviving hosts. However, assume there were only enough resources to power on three of the four VMs with High priority. That leaves a High-priority VM powered off while all other VMs of Medium and Low priorities continue to run on the remaining hosts.

FIGURE 7.20

Use the VM Overrides setting to specify which VMs should be restarted first or ignored entirely.

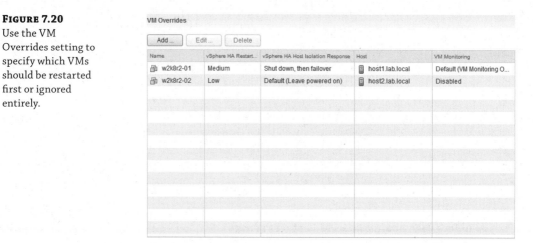

FIGURE 7.21

High-priority VMs from a failed ESXi host might not be powered on because of a lack of resources— resources consumed by VMs with a lower priority that are running on the other hosts in a vSphere HA– enabled cluster.

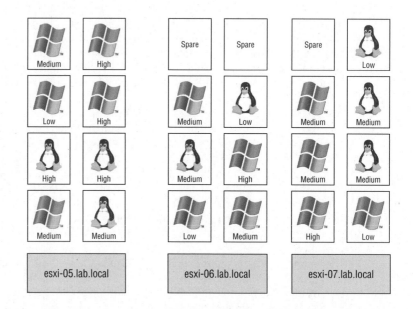

At this point, you can still manually remedy this imbalance. Any business continuity plan in a virtual environment built on vSphere should include a contingency plan that identifies VMs to be powered off to make resources available for those VMs with higher priority because of the network services they provide. If the budget allows, construct the vSphere HA cluster to ensure that there are ample resources to cover the needs of the critical VMs, even in times of reduced computing capacity. You can enforce guaranteed resource availability for restarting VMs by setting Admission Control to Enabled, as described previously in the section "Configuring vSphere HA Admission Control."

vSphere High Availability Isolation Response

Previously, we introduced FDM as the underpinning for vSphere HA and how it uses the ESXi management network to communicate between the master host and all connected slave hosts. When the vSphere HA master is no longer receiving status updates from a slave host, then the master assumes that host has failed and instructs the other connected slave hosts to spring into action to power on all the VMs that the missing node was running.

But what if the node with the missing heartbeat was not really missing? What if the heartbeat was missing but the node was still running? This is the scenario described in the section "Understanding vSphere HA's Underpinnings" when we discussed the idea of *network isolation*. When an ESXi host in a vSphere HA–enabled cluster is isolated—that is, it cannot communicate with the master host nor can it communicate with any other ESXi hosts or any other network devices—then the ESXi host triggers the isolation response configured in the dialog box shown in Figure 7.19. As you can see, for the entire cluster the default isolation response is Leave Powered On. You can change this setting (generally not recommended) either for the entire cluster here or for one or more specific VMs in the VM Overrides section.

Because vSphere HA uses the ESXi management network as well as connected datastores (via datastore heartbeating) to communicate, network isolation is handled a bit differently starting with vSphere 5.0 than in previous versions of vSphere. In previous versions of vSphere, when a host was isolated it would automatically trigger the configured isolation response. A host considered itself isolated when it was not receiving heartbeats from any other hosts and when it could not reach the *isolation address* (by default, the default gateway on the management network).

From vSphere 5.0, the process for determining if a host is isolated is only slightly different. A host that is the master is looking for communication from its slave hosts; a host that is running as a slave is looking for updates from the master host. In either case, if the master or slave is not receiving any vSphere HA network heartbeat information, it will then attempt to contact the isolation address (by default, the default gateway on the management network). If it can reach the default gateway or an additional configured isolation address(es), then the ESXi host considers itself to be in a network partition state and reacts as described in the section titled "Understanding vSphere HA's Underpinnings." If the host can't reach the isolation address, then it considers itself isolated. Here is where this behavior diverges from the behavior of previous versions.

At this point, an ESXi host that has determined it is network-isolated will modify a special bit in the binary host-X-poweron file on all datastores that are configured for datastore heartbeating (more on that in the section titled "Setting vSphere High Availability Datastore Heartbeating"). The master sees that this bit, used to denote isolation, has been set and is therefore notified that this slave host has been isolated. When a master sees that a slave has been isolated, the master locks another file used by vSphere HA on the heartbeat datastore. When the isolated node sees that this file has been locked by a master, it knows that the master is assuming responsibility for restarting the VMs—remember that only a master can restart VMs—and the isolated host is then free to execute the configured isolation response. Therefore, even if the isolation response is set to Shut Down or Power Off, that action won't take place until the isolated slave has confirmed, via the datastore heartbeating structures, that a master has assumed responsibility for restarting the VMs.

The question still remains, though: Should I change the Host Isolation Response setting?

The answer to this question is highly dependent on the virtual and physical network infrastructures in place. Let's look at a couple of examples.

Let's say we have a host in which both the ESXi management network and the VM networks are connected to the same virtual switch bound to a single network adapter (clearly not a generally recommended configuration). In this case, when the cable for the uplink on this vSwitch is unplugged, communication to the ESXi management network and every VM on that computer is lost. The solution, then, should be to shut down the VMs. When an ESXi host determines it is isolated and has confirmed that a master host has assumed responsibility for restarting the VMs, it can execute the isolation response so that the VMs can be restarted on another host with full network connectivity.

A more realistic example might be a situation in which a single vSwitch has two uplinks, but both uplinks go to the same physical switch. If this vSwitch hosts both the ESXi management and VM networks, then the loss of that physical switch means that both management traffic and VM traffic have been interrupted. Setting Host Isolation Response to Shut Down would allow vSphere HA to restart those VMs on another ESXi host and restore connectivity to the VMs.

However, a network configuration that employs multiple uplinks, multiple vSwitches, and multiple physical switches, as shown in Figure 7.22, should probably leave Host Isolation Response set to Leave Powered On because it's unlikely that a network isolation event would also leave the VMs on that host inaccessible.

FIGURE 7.22
The option to leave VMs running when a host is isolated should be set only when the virtual and the physical networking infrastructures support high availability.

CONFIGURING THE ISOLATION RESPONSE ADDRESS

In some highly secure virtual environments, management access is limited to a single, non-routed management network. In these cases, the security plan calls for the elimination of the default gateway on the ESXi management network. The idea is to lock the ESXi management network onto the local subnet, thus preventing any type of remote network access to the management interfaces. The disadvantage, as you might have guessed, is that without a default gateway IP address configured for the management network, there is no isolation address to ping as a determination of network isolation status.

It is possible, however, to customize the isolation response address for scenarios just like this. The IP address can be any IP address but should be an IP address that is not going to be unavailable or taken from the network at any time.

Perform the following steps to define a custom isolation response address:

1. Use the vSphere Web Client to connect to a vCenter Server instance.

2. Open the Hosts And Clusters View, right-click an existing cluster, and select the Settings option.

3. Ensure that vSphere HA is selected in the left column and click the Edit button.

4. Expand the Advanced Options section and click the Add button.

5. Enter **das.isolationaddress** in the Option column in the Advanced Options (HA) dialog box.

6. Enter the IP address to be used as the isolation response address for ESXi hosts that cannot communicate with the FDM master host.

7. Click the OK button.

This interface can also be configured with the following options:

◆ das.isolationaddress1: to specify the first address to try

◆ das.isolationaddress2: to specify the second address to try

◆ das.AllowNetwork: to specify a different port group to use for HA heartbeat

So far, you've only seen how vSphere HA handles ESXi host failures. In the next section, we'll show you how you can use vSphere HA to help protect against guest OS and application failures as well.

CONFIGURING VSPHERE HIGH AVAILABILITY VM MONITORING

In addition to monitoring for ESXi host failures and reacting accordingly, vSphere HA has the ability to look for guest OS and application failures. When a failure is detected, vSphere HA can restart the VM. Figure 7.23 shows the area of the Edit Cluster Settings dialog box where you configure this behavior.

The foundation for this functionality is built into VMware Tools, which we'll describe in greater detail in Chapter 9. VMware Tools provides a series of heartbeats from the guest OS up to the ESXi host on which that VM is running. By monitoring these heartbeats in conjunction with disk and network I/O activity, vSphere HA can attempt to determine if the guest OS has failed. If there are no VMware Tools heartbeats, no disk I/O, and no network I/O for a period of time, then vSphere HA—if VM Monitoring is enabled—will restart the VM under the assumption that the guest OS has failed. To help with troubleshooting, vSphere also takes a screen shot of the VM's console right before vSphere HA restarts the VM. This might help capture any sort of diagnostic information, such as a kernel dump or blue-screen STOP error for Windows-based systems.

FIGURE 7.23

You can configure vSphere HA to monitor for guest OS and application heartbeats and restart a VM when a failure occurs.

vSphere HA also has application monitoring. This functionality requires third-party software to take advantage of APIs built into VMware Tools to provide application-specific heartbeats to vSphere HA. By leveraging these APIs, third-party software developers can further extend the functionality of vSphere HA to protect against the failure of specific applications. To enable VM or application monitoring, simply select the desired level of protection from the VM Monitoring Status drop-down list shown in Figure 7.23.

If you have enabled VM or application monitoring, you can then adjust the monitoring sensitivity. This slider bar controls how often vSphere HA will restart a VM based on a loss of VMware Tools heartbeats and a lack of disk and network I/O traffic. The slider bar also controls the failure window before which vSphere HA will restart a VM again after a maximum number of failures. Table 7.2 shows the values set by each position on the slider.

TABLE 7.2:   VM monitoring sensitivity settings

MONITORING SENSITIVITY SETTING	FAILURE INTERVAL	MINIMUM UPTIME	MAXIMUM FAILURES	FAILURE WINDOW
Low	2 minutes	8 minutes	3	7 days
Medium	1 minute	4 minutes	3	24 hours
High	30 seconds	2 minutes	3	1 hour

Here's how to read this information:

◆ Failure Interval: If vSphere HA doesn't detect any VMware Tools heartbeats, disk I/O, or network I/O within this time frame, it will consider the VM failed and will restart the VM.

◆ Minimum Uptime: vSphere will wait for a set amount of time after the VM has been powered on before starting to monitor VMware Tools heartbeats. This is to ensure that the OS has time to boot and heartbeats stabilize.

◆ Maximum Failures: This is the maximum number of times vSphere HA will restart a VM within the specified failure window. If Maximum Failures is set at 3 and a VM is marked as failed a fourth time within the specified failure window, it will not be automatically restarted. This prevents vSphere HA from endlessly restarting problematic VMs.

◆ Failure Window: vSphere will restart the VM only a maximum number of times (Maximum Failures) within this time frame. If more failures occur within this period of time, the VM is not restarted.

If these predefined options aren't sufficient, you can select Custom and specify your own values for Failure Interval, Minimum Uptime, Maximum Per-VM Resets (Maximum Failures), and Maximum Resets Time Window (Failure Window). Figure 7.24 shows a custom VM Monitoring sensitivity configuration.

FIGURE 7.24
The Custom option provides specific control over how vSphere HA monitors VMs for guest OS failure.

As with other areas of vSphere HA, you also have the option of configuring per-VM monitoring settings. This allows you, on a per-VM basis, to enable or disable VM monitoring and application monitoring sensitivity levels. Thus, if you need VM monitoring for only a few VMs, you can define a default cluster setting and then configure the exceptions accordingly.

The last configuration area for vSphere HA is datastore heartbeating.

SETTING VSPHERE HIGH AVAILABILITY DATASTORE HEARTBEATING

Datastore heartbeating is part of the functionality found in vSphere HA from vSphere 5.0. By communicating through shared datastores when the ESXi management network is not available, vSphere HA provides greater protection against outages due to network partition or network isolation.

This part of the vSphere HA configuration allows you to specify which datastores should be used by vSphere HA for heartbeating. Figure 7.25 shows the Datastore Heartbeating section of the Edit Cluster dialog box.

FIGURE 7.25
Select the shared datastores that vSphere HA should use for datastore heartbeating.

vSphere HA provides three different settings for how the administrator can influence the selection of datastores for heartbeating:

♦ The first option, Automatically Select Datastores Accessible From The Host, disables the manual selection of datastores from the list. With this option, any cluster datastore could be used by vSphere HA for heartbeating.

♦ The second option, Use Datastores Only From The Specified List, constrains vSphere HA to using only those datastores selected from the list of datastores. If one of those datastores becomes unavailable for whatever reason, vSphere HA will not perform heartbeating through a different datastore.

♦ The last option is Use Datastores From The Specified List And Complement Automatically If Needed. This is a bit of a blend of the previous two options. With this option, the administrator selects the preferred datastores that vSphere HA should use. vSphere HA chooses from among the datastores in that list. If one of the datastores becomes unavailable, vSphere HA will choose a different datastore, until none of the preferred datastores are available. At that point it will choose any available cluster datastore.

The last option is probably the most flexible, but how would you know which datastores were being used by vSphere HA? In the next section, "Managing vSphere High Availability," we'll show you how to tell which datastores vSphere HA is actually using for datastore heartbeating as well as how to determine the slot size, see any cluster configuration issues, and gather information on the total number of protected and unprotected VMs.

Managing vSphere High Availability

Much of what vSphere HA does is calculated automatically: things like slot size, total number of slots, selection of hosts for datastore heartbeating, and the selection of the master/slave roles by FDM are just a few examples. Without proper exposure of these values, it would be difficult for administrators to properly manage vSphere HA and its operation. Fortunately, VMware included information about vSphere HA in the vSphere Web Client to help make it easier to manage vSphere HA.

Some of the information is pretty easy to find. For example, the Summary tab of an ESXi host in a vSphere HA–enabled cluster will show the master/slave status, as shown earlier in Figure 7.13.

Similarly, the protected/unprotected status of a VM—indicating that the vSphere HA master has recognized that the VM has been powered on and has taken responsibility for restarting it in the event of a failure—is also noted on the Summary tab of a VM. You can see this in Figure 7.26.

FIGURE 7.26
This blended figure shows the difference between a VM currently listed as Unprotected by vSphere HA and one that is Protected by vSphere HA. VMs may be Unprotected because the master has not yet been notified by vCenter Server that the VM has been powered on and needs to be protected.

However, other pieces of information are found under Cluster ➤ Monitor ➤ vSphere HA, as shown in Figure 7.27.

The Summary Area

The summary area outlines all the relevant details for vSphere HA-enabled clusters. Divided into three sections, in this area you will find:

◆ Hosts lists the current vSphere HA master and the number of slave hosts connected to the master host. Although the vSphere HA master status is also displayed on the Summary tab for an ESXi host, using this dialog box might be easier and faster for clusters with a large number of hosts.

◆ Virtual Machines shows the current number of protected and unprotected VMs. This gives you a quick "at a glance" protection summary and is a fast way to determine how many, if any, VMs are unprotected by vSphere HA.

◆ Advanced Runtime Info exposes the vSphere HA calculations for slot size, total slots in cluster, used slots, available slots, and failover slots. This is very useful information to have. If you have Admission Control set to Enabled and aren't able to power on VMs that you think you should be able to power on, checking this dialog box for the slot size might reveal that the slot size is different than what you were expecting.

FIGURE 7.27
The vSphere HA Summary tab holds a wealth of information about vSphere HA and its operation. The current vSphere HA master, the number of protected and unprotected VMs, and the datastores used for heartbeating is all found here.

▼ Hosts	
Master	esxi-01a.lab.local
Hosts connected to master	1
Hosts not connected to master	0
vSphere HA agent not reachable	0
vSphere HA agent configuration error	0
Hosts failed	0
Network isolated	0
Network partitioned	0
vSphere HA agent initializing	0
Disconnected from vCenter	0
Standby mode	0
Maintenance mode	0
vSphere HA agent unconfiguration failures	0

▼ Advanced Runtime Info	
Slot size	32 MHz 31 MB
Total slots in cluster	118
Used slots	4
Available slots	55
Failover slots	59
Total powered-on virtual machines in cluster	4
Total hosts in cluster	2
Total good hosts in cluster	2
	Refresh

▼ Virtual Machines	
Protected	2
Unprotected	2

HEARTBEAT DATASTORES AREA

The Heartbeat Datastores area shows which datastores are currently being used by vSphere HA for heartbeating. If you haven't explicitly defined which datastore can or should be used, this is where you can tell which datastores were selected by vSphere HA for heartbeating.

CONFIGURATION ISSUES AREA

In the Configuration Issues area, vSphere HA will display any configuration issues, for example, if the cluster has exceeded the configured failover capacity. You might also see warnings about management network redundancy (if the ESXi management network isn't redundant and protected against single points of failure). Based on the issues displayed here, you can take the appropriate action to correct the problem or potential problem.

vSphere HA is a powerful feature, and we highly recommend its use in every vSphere implementation. However, vSphere HA does rely on restarting VMs in order to provide that level of high availability. What if there are applications for which you need a higher level of availability? vSphere offers that functionality with vSphere Fault Tolerance (FT). Based on VMware's vLockstep technology, vSphere FT provides zero downtime, zero data loss, and continuous availability for your applications.

That sounds pretty impressive, doesn't it? But how does it work? That's the focus of the next section.

Implementing vSphere Fault Tolerance

vSphere Fault Tolerance (FT) is the evolution of "continuous availability" that works by utilizing VMware vLockstep technology to keep a primary machine and a secondary machine in a virtual lockstep. This virtual lockstep is based on the record/playback technology that VMware introduced in VMware Workstation in 2006. vSphere FT will stream data that will be recorded (only nondeterministic events are recorded), and the replay will occur deterministically. By doing it this way, VMware has created a process that matches instruction for instruction and memory for memory to get identical results.

Deterministic means that the computer processor will execute the same instruction stream on the secondary VM so it ends up in the same state as the primary VM. On the other hand, nondeterministic events are functions, such as network, disk, and keyboard I/O, as well as hardware interrupts. So, the record process will take the data stream, and the playback will perform all the keyboard actions and mouse clicks. It is pretty slick to move the mouse on the primary VM and see it also move on the secondary VM.

Before we show you how to enable vSphere FT for a VM, we need to cover some requirements for using vSphere FT. Because vSphere FT is matching instruction for instruction and memory for memory to create two identical VMs running on two different ESXi hosts, there are some fairly stringent requirements for vSphere FT. These requirements exist at three levels: at a cluster level, at a host level, and finally, at a VM level.

vSphere FT has the following requirements at a cluster level:

◆ Host certificate checking must be enabled. This is the default for vCenter Server 4.1 and later.

◆ The cluster must have at least two ESXi hosts running the same FT version or build number. The FT version is displayed in the Fault Tolerance section of the ESXi host's Summary tab.

◆ vSphere HA must be enabled on the cluster. vSphere HA must be enabled before you can power on vSphere FT–enabled VMs.

◆ VMware EVC must be enabled if you want to use vSphere FT in conjunction with vSphere DRS. Otherwise, vSphere DRS will be disabled on any vSphere FT–enabled VMs.

In addition, vSphere FT has the following requirements on each ESXi host:

◆ The ESXi hosts must have access to the same datastores and networks.

◆ The ESXi hosts must have a Fault Tolerance logging network connection configured. This vSphere FT logging network requires at least Gigabit Ethernet connectivity, and 10 Gigabit Ethernet is recommended. Although VMware calls for dedicated vSphere FT logging NICs, NICs can be shared with other functions if necessary.

◆ The hosts must have CPUs that are vSphere FT compatible.

◆ Hosts must be licensed for vSphere FT.

◆ Hardware Virtualization (HV) must be enabled in the ESXi host's BIOS in order to enable CPU support for vSphere FT.

Finally, vSphere FT has the following requirements on any VM that is to be protected using vSphere FT:

◆ Only VMs with a single vCPU are supported with vSphere FT. VMs with more than one vCPU are not compatible with vSphere FT.

◆ VMs must be running a supported guest OS.

◆ VM files must be stored on shared storage that is accessible to all applicable ESXi hosts. vSphere FT supports Fibre Channel, FCoE, iSCSI, and NFS for shared storage.

◆ A VM's virtual disks must be in thick provisioned (eagerzeroedthick) format or a Virtual mode RDM. Physical mode RDMs are not supported.

◆ The VM must not have any snapshots. You must remove or commit snapshots before you can enable vSphere FT for a VM.

◆ The VM must not be a linked clone.

◆ The VM cannot have any USB devices, sound devices, serial ports, or parallel ports in its configuration. Remove these items from the VM configuration before attempting to enable vSphere FT.

◆ The VM cannot use N_Port ID Virtualization (NPIV).

◆ Nested page tables/extended page tables (NPT/EPT) are not supported. vSphere FT will disable NPTs/EPTs on VMs for which vSphere FT is enabled.

◆ The VM cannot use NIC passthrough or the older vlance network drivers. Turn off NIC passthrough and update the networking drivers to vmxnet2, vmxnet3, or E1000.

◆ The VM cannot have CD-ROM or floppy devices backed by a physical or remote device. You'll need to disconnect these devices or configure them to point to an ISO or FLP image on a shared datastore.

◆ The VM cannot use a paravirtualized kernel. Turn off paravirtualization in order to use vSphere FT.

As you can see, vSphere FT has some fairly stringent requirements in order to be properly supported.

vSphere FT also introduces some operational changes that must be taken into account as well:

◆ It is recommended that power management (also known as *power capping*) be turned off in the BIOS of any ESXi host that will participate in vSphere FT. This helps ensure uniformity in the CPU speeds of the ESXi hosts in the cluster.

◆ While you can use vMotion with a vSphere FT–protected VM, you cannot use Storage vMotion. By extension, this means that vSphere FT–protected VMs cannot take advantage of Storage DRS. To use Storage vMotion, you must first turn off vSphere FT.

◆ Hot-plugging devices is not supported, so you cannot make any virtual hardware changes when a vSphere FT–protected VM is powered on.

No Hardware Changes Includes No Network Changes

Changing the settings of a virtual network card while a VM is running requires that the network card be unplugged and then plugged back in. As a result, you can't make changes to virtual network cards while vSphere FT is running.

◆ Because snapshots aren't supported with vSphere FT, you can't back up VMs using any backup methodology that relies on snapshots. This includes any backup solution that leverages the vSphere Storage API for Data Protection as well as VMware Data Protection. To back up a vSphere FT–enabled VM with one of these tools, you must first disable vSphere FT. Chapter 3 explains how you can set a scheduled task to perform a "Disable FT" and "Enable FT" at a set time frame to suit your backup window.

Be sure to keep these operational constraints in mind when deciding where and how to use vSphere FT in your environment.

Now you're ready to actually enable vSphere FT on a VM. Perform the following steps to enable vSphere FT:

1. If the vSphere Web Client is not already running, launch it and connect to a vCenter Server instance. vSphere FT is available only when using vCenter Server.

2. Navigate to the Hosts And Clusters or VMs And Templates view. Right-click a running VM and then select Fault Tolerance ➢ Turn On Fault Tolerance, as shown in Figure 7.28.

FIGURE 7.28
You can turn on vSphere FT from the context menu for a VM.

ERROR MESSAGE ABOUT "INCORRECT MONITOR MODE" WHEN ENABLING vSPHERE FAULT TOLERANCE

If you receive an error message when attempting to enable vSphere FT for a running VM and the error message mentions an "incorrect monitor mode," this is probably because your specific CPU family can enable vSphere FT for VMs only when they are powered down. Certain CPU families—most notably, the Intel "Nehalem" or Xeon 55xx series of CPUs—aren't able to enable vSphere FT when the VM is powered on. The workaround is to power the VM off and then enable vSphere FT.

---

3. A pop-up message appears to warn you that enabling vSphere FT will result in several changes. First, all virtual disks will be converted to Thick Provision Eager Zeroed disks, also called eagerzeroedthick disks (virtual disks with all blocks zeroed out ahead of time). Second, vSphere DRS will be disabled for this VM if VMware EVC is not enabled on the cluster. Third, the memory reservation for this VM will be set equal to the configured memory of the VM, as shown in Figure 7.29. Click Yes to turn on vSphere FT for the selected VM.

FIGURE 7.29
Several other configuration changes are enforced when you activate vSphere FT on a VM.

Turn On Fault Tolerance

Turning Fault Tolerance On will take thin-provisioned disks and disks witth blocks zeroed out when written to and convert them to disks with all blocks zeroed out. This disk conversion requires that a virtual machine use more disk space and requires some processing time.

The memory reservation of this VM will be changed to the memory size of the VM and maintained equal to it until Fault Tolerance is turned off.

Do you want to turn On Fault Tolerance?

[Yes] [No]

WILL vSPHERE FAULT TOLERANCE DISABLE vSPHERE DISTRIBUTED RESOURCE SCHEDULER FOR A VM?

If VMware EVC is not enabled on the cluster, then vSphere FT will disable DRS for the selected VM when vSphere FT is enabled. If VMware EVC is enabled, then vSphere 5.5 supports the use of vSphere DRS in conjunction with vSphere FT.

---

4. After you have selected to enable vSphere FT, the creation task begins, as shown in Figure 7.30.

If the VM's virtual disks were not already in the Thick Provision Eager Zeroed format, those disks will be converted. Depending on the size of the virtual disks, this might take quite some time.

FIGURE 7.30

vSphere FT must convert existing virtual disks to Thick Provision (eagerzeroedthick) format as it's powering on for the first time.

5. Once the process is complete, the VM's icon in the Navigator tree will change. Figure 7.31 shows a VM that has been enabled for vSphere FT.

FIGURE 7.31

The darker VM icon indicates that vSphere FT is enabled for this VM.

And that's it. It is literally that simple—at least on the surface.

Behind the scenes, after vSphere FT is turned on, vCenter Server will initiate the creation of the secondary VM by using a special type of vMotion. Both the primary and secondary VMs will share a common disk between them, and using VMware vLockstep, vSphere FT will then be able to keep the VMs in sync. vSphere FT uses a network connection between the ESXi hosts to keep the primary and secondary VMs in sync (recall from our earlier discussion of requirements that the ESXi hosts must have a Fault Tolerance logging connection established; Chapter 5 provides more detail on how to configure this network connection). Only the primary VM will respond to other systems across the network, which leaves the secondary VM a silent partner. You can almost compare this to active/passive cluster configuration in that only one node owns the shared network at a time. When the ESXi host supporting the primary VM fails, the secondary VM takes over immediately with no break in network connection. A reverse ARP is sent to the physical switch to notify the network of the new location of the VM. Does that sound familiar? It is exactly what vMotion does when the VM switches to a new host. Once the secondary VM becomes the primary, the creation of the new secondary VM is repeated until the sync is locked. After the sync is locked, as shown in Figure 7.32, you'll see green icons.

FIGURE 7.32

The vSphere Web Client shows vSphere FT status information in the Fault Tolerance area on the Summary tab of a VM.

Once you've met the requirements, there isn't any configuration to vSphere FT after you've enabled it.

Before wrapping up this discussion of vSphere FT, we want to discuss using vSphere FT in conjunction with vSphere HA and vSphere DRS. We'll start with vSphere FT and vSphere HA together.

Using vSphere Fault Tolerance with vSphere High Availability

vSphere FT works in conjunction with vSphere HA. Recall that vSphere HA must be enabled on both the cluster and the VM in order to enable vSphere FT. As mentioned previously, if the ESXi host where the primary VM is running fails, the secondary VM takes over and a new secondary VM is created automatically to ensure protection. But what happens if there are multiple host failures?

In the event of multiple host failures, vSphere HA will restart the primary VM. vSphere FT will then re-create the secondary VM on another host to ensure protection.

In the case of a guest OS failure, vSphere FT will take no action because, as far as FT is concerned, the VMs are in sync. Both VMs will fail at the same time and place. vSphere HA VM monitoring—if enabled—can detect the failure in the primary and restart it, and the secondary creation process will start again. Have you noticed a pattern about the secondary VMs? After the sync has failed, the secondary machine is always re-created. This helps avoid any potential split-brain issues with vSphere FT.

ONE OS IMAGE VS. TWO OS IMAGES

Many people misunderstand vSphere FT's behavior when it comes to guest OS failure. If the guest OS in the primary VM crashes, the guest OS in the secondary VM is also going to crash. While these appear to be two separate guest OS instances, they are really one synchronized guest OS instance running in lockstep on two different ESXi hosts. A failure in one will mean a failure in both.

This is markedly different from traditional guest OS clustering solutions, which rely on two separate and distinct guest OS instances. If one of the guest OS instances fails, the other instance is still up and running and can take over for the failed instance. Microsoft Windows Server Failover Clustering (WSFC) is one example of this sort of configuration.

Understanding these differences between guest OS clustering and vSphere FT will help you choose the right high-availability mechanism for your particular application and needs.

Using vSphere Fault Tolerance with vSphere Distributed Resource Scheduler

vSphere FT can also interoperate and integrate with vSphere DRS. However, you must enable VMware EVC for this interoperability and integration to function properly.

When VMware EVC is enabled at the cluster level, vSphere FT can also take advantage of vSphere DRS. When both VMware EVC and vSphere DRS are enabled and set to fully automated, vSphere DRS makes the initial placement recommendations for the fault-tolerant VMs, includes the fault-tolerant VMs during cluster rebalancing calculations and operations, and lets you assign a vSphere DRS automation level to the primary VM (the secondary VM assumes the same setting as the primary VM).

Without EVC, vSphere DRS is set to Disabled for the fault-tolerant VMs, initial placement is provided only for the secondary VM, and neither of the fault-tolerant VMs is included in cluster rebalancing calculations or operations.

Examining vSphere Fault Tolerance Use Cases

vSphere FT is not designed or meant to be run on all your VMs. You should use this service sparingly and take this form of fault tolerance only for your most important VMs. The documentation for VMware's configuration maximums states that there should be no more than four vSphere FT–protected VMs (primary or secondary) on any single ESXi host. Remember, once you have primary and secondary VMs locked and in sync, you will be using double the resources for a protected VM.

Now that we have looked at a couple of high-availability options, let's move on to planning and designing for disaster recovery.

Planning for Business Continuity

High availability is only part of the solution, one component in the bigger picture of business continuity. Business continuity is about ensuring that the business can continue operating in the face of some significant event. High availability deals with business continuity from a fairly narrow perspective: ensuring that the business can continue operating in the event of a physical server failure, an OS or application failure, or a network component failure. There are many more types of failures that you must account for and protect against, but we'll mention two primary ones here:

♦ First, you'll need to protect against the loss of data due to equipment failure, software malfunction, or simple user error (ever deleted something by mistake?).

♦ Second, you'll want to ensure that you've done the necessary work around planning for disaster recovery in the event your entire datacenter is rendered unusable or unavailable.

Most organizations have a policy or a set of policies that define the processes, procedures, tools, and technologies that help address these failure scenarios. As you review the information provided in the following sections, you'll want to be sure that any solution you are considering complies with your company's policy for business continuity. If your company doesn't yet have a policy for business continuity, now is a great time to create one!

In the next two sections, we'll look at both of these failure scenarios, along with some of the products and technologies that are applicable. Let's start with data protection.

Providing Data Protection

Backups are an essential part of every IT department's responsibilities, yet they're often the source of the greatest conflict and frustration. Many organizations hoped that virtualizing would make backups easier, and in some ways it has. In other ways, it has made backups more difficult as well. We'll examine the basic methods for backing up VMs and then provide an overview of VMware Data Recovery, a backup solution provided by VMware to help with smaller implementations of vSphere.

EXAMINING VM BACKUP METHODS

There are three high-level methods of backing up VMs in a VMware vSphere environment:

◆ Running a backup agent of some sort in the guest OS

◆ Leveraging vSphere snapshots and the vSphere Storage APIs for Data Protection (more popularly known as VADP)

◆ Using array-based snapshot integration

While various backup applications might have slight variations, the basic methods remain the same. Each of these methods has its own advantages and disadvantages, and no one solution will be the right fit for all customers.

Figure 7.33 illustrates the flow of information when using backup agents inside the guest OS.

FIGURE 7.33
Running backup agents inside the guest OS can provide application- and OS-level integration, but not without some drawbacks.

As you can see from Figure 7.33, running a backup agent within the guest OS affords you OS-level and application-level awareness and integration. The backup agent can leverage the APIs of the guest OS to integrate with the OS and applications running in the OS (for example, by leveraging the Volume Shadow Copy Service in Microsoft Windows). This allows the backup agent to perform very granular backups, such as specific tables within an SQL database, particular mailboxes in Microsoft Exchange, or a subset of files within a Linux filesystem.

However, running backup agents within the guest OS has its drawbacks too:

◆ The network traffic typically runs across the network, which can create network bottlenecks. This is especially true if the backup traffic runs across the same network as end user–facing traffic.

◆ To avoid bottlenecks with end user–facing traffic, organizations introduced dedicated backup networks. This means more NICs in the ESXi hosts, separate vSwitches, separate physical switches, additional vNICs in the VMs, and additional complexity in the guest OS and the solution as a whole. Separate backup networks can also complicate troubleshooting and operations.

◆ The backup agents are individually running in each guest OS instance, so as more and more VMs (and guest OS instances) are consolidated onto physical servers, this creates additional overhead. Given that the overall utilization of the physical hosts was higher anyway because of consolidation, this leaves little headroom for the backup process, which in turn often translates to longer backup windows.

♦ Some backup vendors charged a separate license for every installation of the backup agent, which has decreased the financial benefits of virtualization and consolidation.

Despite these drawbacks, the tight OS- and application-level integration they offer make backup agents the preferred choice in areas where granularity and application integration are paramount.

The second significant way that you perform backups in the vSphere environment is to operate outside the guest OS. Instead, leverage the snapshot functionality of VMware vSphere to unlock the VM's virtual disks and then back up the virtual disks directly. When the backup of the virtual disk is complete, commit the snapshot and you're finished. The framework for driving this process in an automated fashion—so that backup vendors can make it easier to use—is the vSphere Storage APIs for Data Protection.

The overall process looks something like this:

1. The backup software requests a snapshot of the virtual disks for the VM to be backed up.

2. VMware vSphere creates a snapshot, and all writes to the virtual disks for that VM now start flowing into the delta disks. The base VMDK files are unlocked.

3. The backup application backs up the base VMDK files.

4. When the backup of the base VMDK files is complete, the backup software requests vSphere to commit the snapshot.

5. The writes in the delta disk are committed to the base VMDK, and the snapshot is removed.

6. The process repeats itself for the next VM.

VADP helps provide a standard interface for backup vendors to interact with vSphere for backing up VMs, and it introduces a few other useful features. Changed Block Tracking (CBT), for example, allows vSphere and backup applications to track which blocks in a VMDK have changed and back up only those changed blocks. You can consider CBT the VMDK block equivalent to the archive flag in DOS and NTFS.

Like in-guest backups, VADP-based backups also have advantages and disadvantages:

♦ There is generally less processor and memory overhead because there's no need to run a backup agent inside every guest OS instance. Depending on the environment, this might allow you to achieve a higher consolidation ratio or provide better performance for your workloads.

♦ Because there is generally little to no coordination with applications running in the guest OS instances, VADP-based backups typically cannot provide the same level of backup/restore granularity as in-guest backups. There may also be issues ensuring application consistency.

♦ Depending on how you implement the VADP-based backup solution, file-level restores may be difficult. Some of these solutions require that you restore the entire VM and then manually pull out the individual file or files that need to be restored. Be sure to consider this operational issue in your evaluation.

Numerous backup vendors leverage VADP to perform VM backups. In fact, VMware itself provides an entry-level backup solution that leverages VADP. That solution is called VMware Data Recovery.

IMPLEMENTING VMWARE DATA PROTECTION

VMware Data Protection (VDP) is a disk-based backup and recovery solution. This solution fully integrates with vCenter Server to enable centralized and efficient management backup jobs, and it also includes data deduplication. VDP leverages VADP to streamline the process of backing up VMs.

So, how does VDP work? VDP is composed of three main components. The first component is the VDP virtual backup appliance that will manage the backup and recovery process. The second component is the user interface plug-in for vSphere Web Client. The third and last component is the deduplicated destination storage, which is a predetermined sized VMDK within the VDP virtual backup appliance, with the available sizes being 0.5 TB, 1.0 TB, or 2.0 TB.

Once the VDP virtual backup appliance has been installed, using the vSphere Web Client, select the Backup tab on the VMs that you want to protect. You can then schedule the backup job and configure the data-retention policy. vCenter Server will then send the job information to the VDP virtual backup appliance to start the backup process by initiating the point-in-time snapshots of the protected VM. Like its predecessors, VDP frees up network traffic on the LAN by mounting the snapshot directly to the VDP virtual backup appliance. After the snapshot is mounted, the virtual appliance begins streaming the block-level data directly to the destination storage. It is during this streaming process, before the data gets to the destination disks, that the VDP appliance will deduplicate the data to ensure that the redundant data is eliminated. After all the data has been written to the destination disk, the VDP appliance will then dismount the snapshot and apply the snapshot to the VM.

Backups are no good if you can't recover the data, naturally. With VDP, the recovery process is a point-in-time file-level or complete system restoration. The VDP virtual backup appliance will retrieve and stream the specific blocks of data that are needed for the restore. The virtual appliance will efficiently transfer only data that has changed. This speeds up and streamlines the process. When restoring a single file, or performing a file-level restore, the process is initiated from inside the VM console.

In the end, the method you use to provide data protection isn't what's important. What's important is that you do provide data protection for your virtualized datacenter.

USING YOUR STORAGE ARRAY TO PROTECT DATA

Many of the storage vendors have started adding the ability to do point-in-time snapshots of data on the array. The specifics of how the snapshots work will vary from vendor to vendor, and—as with so many other aspects of IT—there are advantages and disadvantages to each approach. The result of this functionality is the ability to hold point-in-time views of your company's information for a predetermined amount of time. This time frame could be hours, days, weeks, or months depending on the amount of disk space you have provided for this. These snapshots can serve as a "first line of defense" in data protection. Here's an example. Let's say a VM was deleted by accident. With point-in-time restore, you can dial back in time to right before the VM was deleted. Mount the LUN from that specific moment in time, and restore your VM. While not traditionally thought of as a suitable replacement for other backup solutions, array-based snapshots and even array replication are starting to make a lot more sense. As data footprints continue to grow and businesses demand more aggressive recovery point objectives (RPOs) and recovery time objectives (RTOs), traditional backup solutions can struggle to meet business needs. Array capabilities have continued to mature and now offer a number of different business continuity and disaster recovery options such as offsite replication and offloading to lower storage tiers.

Recovering from Disasters

High availability makes up only half of the ability to keep your application/systems up in day-to-day operation. The other half is disaster recovery, which is the ability to recover from a catastrophic failure. The risks posed by hurricanes, earthquakes and other natural (and man-made) disasters underscore how important it is to establish a thoughtfully designed plan that you can execute with certainty. Entire datacenters can be destroyed by one of these events, and even the datacenters that survive and keep functioning do not stay operational for long when generators run out of gas. When real events like Hurricane Katrina occur, the aftermath drives the point home that businesses need to be prepared.

Before virtualization, the disaster recovery (DR) team showed up, and the remote recovery site was slated with the task of recovering the enterprise in a timely manner. A timely manner back then was at least a few days to build and install the recovery servers and then restore the enterprise from the backup media.

Sounds simple, right? Well, in theory, it is supposed to be, but problems always occur during the process. First, during the recovery process, you can rarely restore your environment at the remote datacenter location to the same make and model that you run in your current environment. Thus, after you restore your data from your backup media, you are greeted with the pretty blue screen that announces that the drivers are different. For the most part, after the restore completes, you can rerun the installation of the drivers for the recovery servers, but Murphy tends to show up and lay down his law.

Second, the restore process itself is another form of literal contention. If your backup strategy does not consider which servers you want to recover first, then during a disaster, when you try to restore and bring up systems based on importance, you waste a lot of time waiting for tape machines to become available. This contention becomes even worse if your backups span more than one tape. Speaking of tapes, it is not uncommon for tapes to become corrupt and unreadable. Backups are completed and the tapes are sent off site but not tested until they are needed. If all goes well, you might finish your backup in a few days, but success can be elusive.

Today, a majority of data is kept on the SAN, and the data is replicated to another SAN at your remote disaster recovery co-location site. So, your data is waiting for you when you need to perform a recovery, which really speeds up the process. At first this remote replication was an expensive undertaking because only the high-dollar enterprise SANs had this capability. Over the years, though, this approach has become the standard, and software solutions have started enabling similar functionality without the need for matching hardware at each endpoint.

To set up SAN replication, a company purchases two SANs to be set up at different locations, and the data is replicated between the two sites. Many vendors offer replication solutions, and the particulars of these replication solutions vary. Some replication solutions use Fibre Channel (or Fibre Channel over IP, FCIP); others use standard TCP/IP connections. Some replication solutions support only that vendor's storage arrays (like EMC SRDF or NetApp SnapMirror), while other replication solutions support heterogeneous storage environments. Some replication solutions allow for replicated data to be "split off" for other purposes (might be good for backups); others don't have that functionality.

In spite of these differences, all replication solutions fall into one of two very broad buckets:

◆ Synchronous replication solutions

◆ Asynchronous replication solutions

In synchronous replication solutions, the primary array waits until the secondary array has acknowledged each write before sending a write acknowledgement back to the host, ensuring that the replicated copy of the data is always as current as the primary. In this situation latency comes into play, and it increases significantly with distance. Therefore, you must limit the distance between synchronous replication solutions to keep latency to a minimum.

Asynchronous replication solutions transfer data to the secondary array in chunks and do not wait for a write acknowledgement from the remote array before acknowledging the write to the host. Using this method, the remote copy of the data will never be as current as the primary copy, but this method can replicate data over very long distances and with reduced bandwidth requirements.

In a vSphere environment, you can combine SAN- and/or host-based replication—synchronous or asynchronous—with VMware Site Recovery Manager (SRM), a workflow automation tool that helps administrators with the task of orchestrating the startup of all the VMs in a datacenter. SRM is a great product but well outside the scope of this book. However, you can refer to the VMware SRM website at www.vmware.com/products/site-recovery-manager/ for more information.

---

vSphere High Availability Failover with Synchronous Replication?

Earlier in this chapter we told you that you could not perform HA failover to another site. As a general rule, this is true—even with synchronous SAN replication. Although synchronous SAN replication ensures that the data in the remote site is always up-to-date, every traditional replication product on the market today marks the replication target as read only. This means that you can't fail over via vSphere HA because the target datastore is read-only. As new solutions are brought to market that enable read/write access to storage in multiple locations at the same time, this ability becomes a reality.

While SAN-based replication is great, there may be times when it's just not feasible. For smaller businesses or remote offices, the size and cost of the infrastructure cannot be justified. Inevitably, DR is still a requirement, and for this reason, VMware has an IP-based replication engine simply called vSphere Replication.

Using vSphere Replication

The ability to make a copy of your important data and workloads at a remote location is often one of the top priorities for business management. They realize that recovering important workloads and data is crucial to keeping the business operating, and the quicker they can be up and running, the less productivity they potentially lose. As discussed in the previous section, "Recovering from Disasters," replicating data from your primary location to a secondary location can be performed using SAN-based replication, but this can be a costly solution. The other option available to VMware administrators is the built-in vSphere Replication.

vSphere Replication was introduced in SRM 5.0 and decoupled as a new feature in vSphere version 5.1, and it has been further improved in version 5.5. It provides VM-based replication and recovery at the hypervisor level. This means that there are no external requirements to provide the replication, apart from network connectivity between two locations. Available for every license level above Essentials Plus, vSphere Replication can copy VMs within the same cluster or to a different cluster, which means your target and source could be either the same vCenter or a completely different vCenter on the other side of the country! Before we show you how to configure vSphere Replication, let us explain the architecture and limitations around this feature.

As mentioned earlier, vSphere Replication can be configured regardless of the underlying storage system or protocol. It will work with locally attached SATA, Fibre Channel SANs, or IP-based NASs. vSphere Replication has no preference of type and is even flexible enough for the source and destination to differ in storage configuration, as shown in Figure 7.34.

FIGURE 7.34
vSphere Replication can work between datacenters, as long as there is a network joining them.

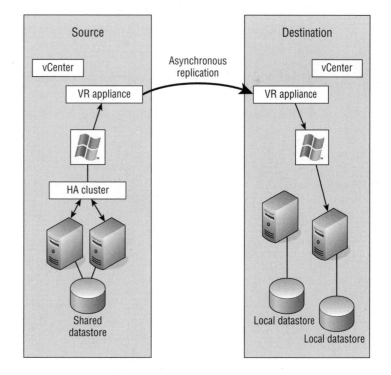

The following constraints affect how vSphere Replication can be configured:

◆ Maximum replication time (RPO): 24 hours

◆ Minimum replication time (RPO): 15 minutes

◆ Maximum protected VMs: 500/instance

◆ Maximum instances: 10/vCenter Server

vSphere Replication is installed by deploying a virtual appliance to extend the feature set within vSphere. The installation is much like that of vCenter Operations Manager or the vSphere Management Assistant. Let's step through the installation process, and then we'll show you how to configure a VM to replicate to a different cluster under a single vCenter Server instance.

1. If the vSphere Web Client is not already running, launch it and connect to a vCenter Server instance.

2. Right-click a cluster or datacenter object, and select Deploy OVF Template.

3. Browse to the local file where you downloaded the vSphere Replication appliance OVF file. Click Next to proceed to the next screen.

4. Review the details to ensure that they are correct. Click Next to move onto the EULA screen.

5. Click the Accept button, and then click Next to continue.

6. Choose a name and location for the appliance, then click Next.

7. Decide on the storage format, remembering that the appliance doesn't hold any of the replication data itself.

8. Choose the appropriate network configuration. As you can see in Figure 7.35, we have selected a static IP assignment.

FIGURE 7.35
The network configuration for the vSphere Replication appliance happens before it is deployed.

9. Configure the appliance password and static IP (if selected previously) on this page. Click Next to continue.

10. On the second to last screen you will be asked to choose a vCenter service for the vSphere Replication appliance. In this case, we only have one. Click Next to continue.

11. Review the selections and then click the Finish button to commence the deployment.

12. Once the vSphere Replication appliance has finished deploying, power it on as you would any VM.

On the main vSphere Web Client home page, a new icon has been created labeled vSphere Replication. Within this section you can monitor existing replication jobs and configure target sites. Most of the actual configuration happens when you want to set up a VM for replication. Adding additional sites is as simple as deploying another vSphere Replication Virtual Appliance and then adding it into Target Sites. For simplicity, let's assume we only have a single site and we want to configure a local replication of a VM:

1. If the vSphere Web Client is not already running, launch it and connect to a vCenter Server instance.

2. Open the Hosts And Clusters or VMs And Templates view.

3. When you right-click a VM, there is now an additional menu at the bottom labeled vSphere Replication. Within this menu, select Configure Replication as shown in Figure 7.36.

FIGURE 7.36
New menus are often added in the vSphere Web Client when virtual appliances that add functionality are deployed.

4. When the Configure Replication dialog box appears, select the target site. In this case, the only site is the local one.

5. The next screen allows you to choose a replication server appliance. Select Auto-Assign and click Next.

6. On the Target location screen, you are able to pick the datastore that you wish the replica to reside on. Choose this wisely because you could fill this datastore with replication data, depending on your RPO schedule. Click Next to continue.

7. The Replication options let you pick a guest OS quiescing method, with Microsoft Shadow Copy Services (VSS) as the only available option. Quiescing will ensure that the VSS-aware applications running on the VM have flushed all their cached data to disk before taking a copy.

8. The Recovery Settings page is the most important settings page because this is where you set the frequency of replication and how many copies to keep. Set your RPO to 8 hours and the point-in-time instances to 3/day for 5 days, as shown in Figure 7.37.

FIGURE 7.37
Always config-
ure the recovery
settings within
vSphere Replication
to match (or exceed)
your application's
RPO requirements.

9. On the final page, review all the settings and click Finish.

Your VM will now be replicated to the site and datastore as per the replication settings. If at some stage you need to recover the VM, simply click the vSphere Replication icon on the vCenter home screen, find the VM in the Replications lists, and select Recover. You will then be asked for a destination to recover to. Keep in mind that when recovering VMs, initially they are powered on without being connected to any port groups. This ensures that if they are recovered while another copy exists on the network, there will not be any conflicts.

In this chapter, we explained that high availability is for increasing uptime and business continuity is about ensuring that a business can continue in the event of a significant adverse event. The bottom line, to be blunt, is that you'd better have both in place in your environment. High availability is an important part of any IT shop, and you should design and create a solution with proper care. However, you cannot stop there; you absolutely must test, test, and test again any solution to make sure that your solution works as designed and, most important, that it will work when you need it.

The Bottom Line

Understand Windows clustering and the different types of clusters.   Windows clustering plays a central role in the design of any high-availability solution for both virtual and physical servers. Microsoft Windows clustering gives us the ability to have application failover to the secondary server when the primary server fails.

> **Master It**   Specifically with regard to Windows clustering in a virtual environment, what are three different types of cluster configurations that you can have?

> **Master It**   What is the key difference between NLB clusters and Windows failover clusters?

Use vSphere's built-in high-availability functionality.   VMware Virtual Infrastructure has high-availability options built in and available to you out of the box: vSphere High Availability (HA) and vSphere Fault Tolerance (FT). These options help you provide better uptime for your critical applications.

> **Master It**   What are the two types of high-availability options that VMware provides in vSphere, and how are they different?

Recognize differences between different high-availability solutions.   A high-availability solution that operates at the application layer, like Oracle Real Application Cluster (RAC), is different in architecture and operation from an OS-level clustering solution like Windows failover clustering. Similarly, OS-level clustering solutions are very different from hypervisor-based solutions such as vSphere HA or vSphere FT. Each approach has advantages and disadvantages, and today's administrators will likely need to use multiple approaches in their datacenter.

> **Master It**   Name one advantage of a hypervisor-based high-availability solution over an OS-level solution.

Understand additional components of business continuity.   There are other components of ensuring business continuity for your organization. Data protection (backups) and replication of your data to a secondary location are two areas that can help ensure that business continuity needs are satisfied, even in the event of a disaster.

> **Master It**   What are three methods to replicate your data to a secondary location and what is the golden rule for any continuity plan?

Chapter 8

Securing VMware vSphere

On a scale of 1 to 10 in importance, security always rates close to a 10 in setting up and managing a vSphere environment. Well, maybe not—but it should. Even though VMware has increased the capabilities and features that come with its products, these same products and features must fit within the security policies applied to other servers. Most of the time, ESXi and vCenter Server fit easily and nicely within those security policies, but sometimes the process is a bit of a challenge. This chapter examines the tools and techniques that will help you ensure that your vSphere environment appropriately follows the security policies of your organization.

In this chapter, you will learn to

- ◆ Configure and control authentication to vSphere

- ◆ Manage roles and access controls

- ◆ Control network access to services on ESXi hosts

- ◆ Integrate with Active Directory

Overview of vSphere Security

As with most other areas of security within information technology, securing a vSphere environment means securing all the different components of vSphere. Specifically, securing vSphere means securing the following components:

- ◆ The ESXi hosts

- ◆ vCenter Server

- ◆ The VMs, specifically the guest operating systems (guest OSes) running inside the VMs

- ◆ The applications running in the VMs

In this chapter we'll discuss the security considerations for the vSphere components: the ESXi hosts, Single Sign-On, vCenter Server, and the guest OSes running in your VMs. Each of these components has its own unique set of security challenges, and each has different ways of addressing those security challenges. For example, ESXi has a different set of security challenges than the Windows-based vCenter Server or the Linux-based vCenter Server virtual appliance. We won't address how to secure the applications within your VMs because that task falls well outside the scope of this book. We do encourage you, however, to be sure to keep application-level security in mind as you work toward securing your vSphere environment.

When considering how to secure the various components involved in a vSphere environment, you must consider the following three aspects to security:

◆ Authentication

◆ Authorization

◆ Accounting

This model—often referred to as the AAA model—describes the way in which a user must be authenticated (properly identified as who they claim to be), authorized (enabled or permitted to perform a task, which also includes network access controls), and accounted for (all actions are tracked and logged for future reference). In using this AAA model, you can ensure that you've covered the key aspects of securing the different components of a vSphere environment. We'll use the AAA model as a rough guideline to structure the discussion of securing vSphere in this chapter.

As you work your way through this chapter, keep in mind that some of the recommendations we make here have absolutely nothing to do with virtualization. Because virtualizing with vSphere affects many areas of the datacenter, you must also consider those areas when you look at security. Further, some of the recommendations we make are made elsewhere in the book, so you might see some duplicate information. Security should be woven into every aspect of your vSphere design and implementation, so it's completely natural that you'll see some of the same tips during this focused discussion on security.

The first components we discuss securing are the ESXi hosts.

Securing ESXi Hosts

VMware ESXi sits at the heart of vSphere, so any discussion of how to secure vSphere includes a discussion on how to secure ESXi. In the following sections, we'll discuss securing your ESXi hosts using the AAA model as a guiding framework, starting with the concept of authentication.

Working with ESXi Authentication

The majority of what you need to do as a vSphere administrator involves working with vCenter Server. Even so, it's still necessary to discuss how ESXi handles user authentication, because the mechanism vCenter Server uses to manage ESXi hosts also relies on ESXi authentication. Additionally, there are occasions where it might be necessary to connect directly to an ESXi host. Although using vCenter Server eliminates the largest part of the need to connect directly to an ESXi host, the need does not go away entirely. There are instances when a task cannot be accomplished through vCenter Server, such as, for example, in the following situations:

◆ vCenter Server is not available or is down.

◆ You are troubleshooting ESXi boot and configuration problems.

Because the need to authenticate to ESXi still exists (even if you are authenticating indirectly through vCenter Server), you need to understand the options for managing users and groups on ESXi hosts. There are two basic options: managing users and groups locally on each host or integrating with Active Directory. We'll cover each of these options in the following sections.

Managing Users and Groups Locally

In most cases, the number and frequency of local user accounts on an ESXi host have both diminished considerably. Usually, you need only two or three accounts for access to an ESXi host. Why two or three and not just one? You need at least two accounts in case one account is unavailable during situations such as when a user is on vacation or is sick or an accident occurs. As you already know, users and groups on ESXi hosts are, by default, managed independently per ESXi host. Because you need fewer local accounts, many organizations find that the administrative overhead of managing only a few accounts across multiple ESXi hosts is an acceptable burden.

If this is the case in your environment, you have two ways of managing users and groups locally. You can use command-line tools, or you can use the vSphere Client. The method that is right for you will largely depend on your experience and preferences. For example, we feel very comfortable using the command line, so using the command-line interface (CLI) would be our first choice. However, if you are more comfortable with a Windows-based application, then the vSphere Client is the best option for you. We'll describe both methods so you can choose the method that works best for you.

Perform the following steps to view local users and groups with the vSphere Client:

1. Launch the traditional vSphere Client if it is not already running, and connect to an ESXi host.

   Remember, the vSphere Web Client cannot directly manage ESXi hosts and you cannot manage ESXi local users and groups in either client while connected to a vCenter Server instance.

2. Select the ESXi host from the inventory list on the left.

3. Click the Local Users & Groups tab in the content pane on the right.

On the Local Users & Groups tab, you can create new users or groups, edit existing users or groups (including changing the password), and delete users and groups. We'll walk through each of these tasks shortly.

You can also use the CLI to manage local users and groups. Although ESXi offers a local shell (covered in a bit more detail in the section "Controlling Local CLI Access"), the preferred way of using the CLI to work with ESXi is via the vSphere CLI (also referred to as the vCLI). We find using the vSphere Management Assistant (vMA) is the best way of working with the vSphere CLI. As we show you the process for creating, editing, and deleting local users or groups in the next few sections, the CLI environment we'll use and describe is the vMA.

Let's take a look at creating a user or group, editing a user or group, and deleting a user or group.

Creating a Local User or Group

Perform the following steps (these steps assume you're already viewing the Local Users & Groups tab in the vSphere Client) to create a local user or group using the vSphere Client:

1. Right-click a blank area of the Local Users & Groups tab and select Add.

   This opens the Add New User dialog box.

2. Supply a login and (optionally) a UID and username.

   If you do not supply a UID, the system will assign the next available UID, starting at 500. If the ESXi host is being managed by vCenter Server, UID 500 might already be taken by the vpxuser account, which we'll explain later in this chapter in the section "Understanding the vpxuser Account."

3. Enter and confirm the password for the new user account.

4. If you want this user to be able to use the ESXi Shell, check Grant Shell Access To This User.

5. Under Group Membership, select a group from the drop-down and click Add.

6. Click OK to create the user with the specified values.

   The new user appears in the list of users.
   In the section "Managing ESXi Host Permissions," we'll show you how to assign a role to this user to control what actions the user is allowed to perform.

ADDING "ROOT" USERS TO VSPHERE

Prior to vSphere 5.1, no functionality existed to create additional accounts with the same privileges as the built-in root account; everyone had to share the root account. This meant that whenever an escalated task was performed, it was impossible to relate that action back to a particular person. From vSphere 5.1 onward, the local ESXi "root" group gives actual "root" permissions.

Perform these steps to create a local group using the vSphere Client:

1. Click the Groups button near the top of the Local Users & Groups tab.

2. Right-click a blank area of the tab and select Add.

   This opens the Create New Group dialog box.

3. Specify a group name and, optionally, a group ID.

   If you do not specify a group ID, the system will assign one automatically, starting with 500.

4. From the drop-down list, select the user you'd like to add to this group and click Add. Repeat the process for each user you want to add.

5. Click OK to create the group and return to the vSphere Client.

   The new group will appear in the list of groups on the Local Users & Groups tab.
   You can also use the CLI to create users and groups. From the vMA, you can use the `vicfg-user` command to create users and groups on a specific ESXi host.
   Perform these steps to create a user or group using the CLI:

1. Establish an SSH session to the vMA.

2. From the vMA command prompt, enter this command to create a new user account on a specific ESXi host:

   ```
   vicfg-user --server server.domain.com --username root --entity user --login
   LoginName --operation add
   ```

To create a new group, replace the `--entity` and `--login` parameters, like this:

```
vicfg-user --server server.domain.com --username root --entity group --group
GroupName --operation add
```

3. Depending on your vMA configuration, you might be prompted for a password to execute the command. Enter the password for the user specified in the previous command (`root`, in this example).

4. If you are creating a new user account, you will be prompted for the password for the new user. Enter the password you want assigned to the new user account you are creating, and then confirm that password when prompted again.

Figure 8.1 shows the vMA prompting for a password to perform the command as well as the password for the new user account.

FIGURE 8.1

The `vicfg-user` command prompts for a password to execute the command and then prompts for a password for the new user you are creating.

```
NMARSHALL-MBP:~ nmarshall$ ssh vi-admin@192.168.0.206
Welcome to vSphere Management Assistant
vi-admin@192.168.0.206's password:
Last login: Mon May 27 21:35:02 2013 from 192.168.0.13
vi-admin@vma:~> vicfg-user --server 192.168.0.113 --username root --entity user
--login Valkyrie --operation add
Enter password:
Enter password for the user:
Enter password for the user again:
Created user Valkyrie successfully.
vi-admin@vma:~>
```

As we mentioned previously, creating a new user or group is only part of the process; in order to use that account with the vSphere Client, you also need to assign a role. We'll cover roles and permissions in the section "Managing ESXi Host Permissions" later in this chapter.

Now let's take a look at editing a user or group both from the vSphere Client and from the CLI.

Editing a Local User or Group

Perform the following steps to edit a local user or group using the vSphere Client:

1. Assuming you've already launched the vSphere Client and connected to an ESXi host, select the ESXi host from the inventory and click the Local Users & Groups tab.

2. Right-click the user you want to modify and select Edit.

This opens the Edit User dialog box.

3. From the Edit User dialog box, make any necessary changes to the user account.

As you can see from Figure 8.2, the Login field cannot be changed.

FIGURE 8.2

For a user, you can change the UID, username, password, and group membership, but you can't change the Login field.

4. Click OK to make the changes to the selected user account.

To edit a group using the vSphere Client, the steps are almost identical to the preceding steps. However, when you're editing a group, the context menu won't show an Edit command; you'll use Properties instead. Also, when editing a group, you can't change any properties of the group except its members.

Perform the following steps to edit a local user or group using the CLI:

1. Using PuTTY.exe (Windows) or a terminal window (Mac OS X or Linux), establish an SSH session to the vMA instance.

2. Use this command to modify a user account on a specific ESXi host:

   ```
   vicfg-user --server esxi-03.lab.local --username root --entity user
   --login LoginName --newusername "New Full Name" --operation modify
   ```

   To modify a group, change the --entity and --login parameters, like this:

   ```
   Vicfg-user --server esxi-03.lab.local --username root --entity group
   --operation modify --group TestGroup --adduser testuser --removeuser bob
   ```

   As with the vSphere Client, editing a group via vicfg-user is limited to adding users to or removing users from the group.

3. If prompted for the password to execute the command (this will depend on your vMA configuration), enter the password for the user specified with the --username parameter.

Let's wrap up this discussion of managing local users and groups with a review of how to delete local users and groups from an ESXi host.

Deleting a Local User or Group

Perform the following steps to delete a local user or group from a specific ESXi host using the vSphere Client:

1. After you've connected to the desired ESXi host using the vSphere Client, select the ESXi host from the inventory and click the Local Users & Groups tab.

2. To delete a user, click the Users button. To delete a group, click the Groups button.

3. Right-click the user or group you want to remove, and select Remove from the context menu. When prompted for confirmation, select Yes.

Perform these steps to delete a local user or group using the vCLI:

1. Log into the vMA via SSH using PuTTY.exe (Windows) or a terminal window (Mac OS X or Linux).

2. Use the following command to remove a user:

```
vicfg-user --server esxi-03.lab.local --username root --entity user
--operation delete --login UserName
```

To remove a group, change the --entity and --login parameters:

```
vicfg-user --server esxi-03.lab.local --username root --entity group
--operation delete --group GroupName
```

Note that you cannot delete a group from the CLI without first removing all of its members. This limitation does not apply when deleting a group from the vSphere Client.

TO VC OR NOT TO VC

The best way to administer your vSphere environment is to connect the vSphere Web Client to a vCenter Server instance. Although you can connect the legacy vSphere Client to an ESXi host directly, you lose a great deal of functionality. If you didn't purchase vCenter Server, you may have no other choice than to connect to the ESXi hosts. In such instances, you'd have to create user accounts locally on the ESXi hosts for VM administration as outlined in this section.

Now that you have an idea of the specific steps used to manage users and groups locally on each ESXi host, what are the security challenges involved in doing so? And how can those security challenges be addressed? Here are just a couple of examples:

◆ You must manually manage users and groups separately on each and every ESXi host. If you forget to delete a user account for a departing employee on a specific ESXi host, you've just created a potential security problem.

◆ There is no way to centrally enforce password policies. Although you can set password policies on each ESXi host, you have to do this separately on every ESXi host in your environment. If you ever need to change the password policy, you must do so on each ESXi host individually.

You can address both of these particular security challenges by leveraging functionality provided by VMware with ESXi to integrate authentication into Active Directory, as you'll see in the next section.

ENABLING ACTIVE DIRECTORY INTEGRATION

You've already seen how, by default, ESXi uses local users and groups to assign permissions to directories and files. The presence of these local users and groups is the key to the ESXi security model, as you'll see in the section "Managing ESXi Host Permissions." Although these local users and groups form the foundation of the ESXi security model, managing them locally on every ESXi host in the enterprise can create a great deal of administrative overhead and has some security challenges, as we've already described.

What if you were able to continue to accommodate the need for local access to an ESXi host but in a way that avoided some of the security challenges of managing users and groups locally?

One answer to these security challenges is to use a centralized security authority. In vSphere you can use Microsoft Active Directory, a widely deployed directory service, as the centralized security authority for ESXi hosts. As you'll see in the section "Authenticating Users with Single Sign-On," the Windows-based version of vCenter Server can already leverage Active Directory, so allowing your ESXi hosts to leverage the same security authority makes sense.

Before you can join your ESXi hosts into Active Directory, you need to satisfy four prerequisites:

◆ You must ensure that the time on your ESXi hosts is synchronized with the time on the Active Directory domain controllers. ESXi supports NTP, and in Chapter 2, "Planning and Installing VMware ESXi," we showed you how to configure NTP on your ESXi hosts.

◆ You must ensure that your ESXi hosts can resolve the Active Directory domain name and locate the domain controllers via DNS. Typically, this means configuring the ESXi hosts to use the same DNS servers as the Active Directory domain controllers, and just like NTP, this is covered in Chapter 2.

◆ The fully qualified domain name (FQDN) of the ESXi host must use the same domain suffix as the Active Directory domain.

◆ You must create an ESX Admins group in Active Directory. Put the user accounts that should be permitted to connect to an ESXi host in this group. You can't use any other group name; it must be named ESX Admins.

Once you've satisfied these prerequisites, you can configure your ESXi host to authenticate to Active Directory.

Perform these steps to configure your ESXi host to use Active Directory as its centralized security authority:

1. Log into the ESXi host using the vSphere Client and authenticating with the root account (or an equivalent account).

2. Select the ESXi host from the inventory and click the Configuration tab.

3. From the Software section, select Authentication Services.

4. Click Properties in the upper-right corner.

5. From the Directory Services Configuration dialog box, select Active Directory from the Select Directory Service Type drop-down list.

6. Supply the DNS domain name of the Active Directory domain this ESXi host will use for authentication.

7. Click the Join Domain button.

8. Specify a username and password that has permission to allow the host to join the domain.

Once the ESXi host is joined to Active Directory, users will be able to authenticate to an ESXi host using their Active Directory credentials. Using the vSphere Client or the vCLI, users can use either the domain\username or username@domain syntax. From the vCLI, users must enclose the domain\username syntax in double quotes, as in this example:

```
vicfg-users --server esxi-03.lab.local --username "lab\administrator"
--entity group --operation list
```

To further simplify the use of the vMA, you can also configure the vMA to use Active Directory authentication.

Although managing how users authenticate is important, it's also important to control how users access ESXi hosts. In the next section, we'll examine how you can control access to your ESXi hosts.

Controlling Access to ESXi Hosts

The second part of the AAA model is authorization, which encompasses access control mechanisms that affect local access or network access. In the following sections, we'll describe the mechanisms available to you to control access to your ESXi hosts.

CONTROLLING LOCAL ACCESS

ESXi offers direct access via the server console through the Direct Console User Interface, or DCUI. We've shown you screen shots of the DCUI in various other parts of this book, such as Chapter 2.

Access to the DCUI on an ESXi host is limited to users who have the Administrator role on it. We haven't discussed the concept of roles yet (see "Managing ESXi Host Permissions" later in this chapter for more details), but this limitation on the DCUI allows you to control who is permitted to access the DCUI. As with other forms of security, it's important to secure access to the host via the physical server console, and limiting DCUI access to users with the Administrator role helps accomplish that goal.

CONTROLLING LOCAL CLI ACCESS

ESXi has a CLI environment that is accessible from the server's physical console. However, by default, this CLI environment—known as the ESXi Shell—is disabled. If you need CLI access to

ESXi, you must first enable the ESXi Shell. You can enable the ESXi Shell via the DCUI or via the vSphere Client.

Perform these steps to enable the ESXi Shell via the DCUI:

1. Access the console of the ESXi host using the physical server console or some KVM mechanism (many server vendors provide remote console functionality).

2. Press F2 to log into the DCUI. When prompted for username and password, supply a username and password with permission to access the DCUI (this user must have the Administrator role for this ESXi host).

3. Navigate down to Troubleshooting Options and press Enter.

4. Select Enable ESXi Shell.

   This enables the CLI environment on the ESXi host.

5. Press Esc until you return to the main DCUI screen.

6. Press Alt+F1 to access the CLI environment on that ESXi host.

   If your host is using local authentication, you can authenticate using a user account defined locally on that host. If your host is using Active Directory authentication as described in the previous section, you can log in using Active Directory credentials (using either the domain\username or username@domain syntax).

Perform the following steps to enable the ESXi Shell via the vSphere Client:

1. Connect to the ESXi host using the vSphere Client.

2. Select the ESXi host in the inventory, and click the Configuration tab.

3. From the Software section, select Security Profile.

4. Click the Properties hyperlink near Services.

   This opens the Services Properties dialog box.

5. Select ESXi Shell from the list of services and then click Options.

6. Click Start.

7. Click OK to return to the Services Properties dialog box.

   The status for the ESXi Shell should now be listed as Running.

8. Click OK to return to the vSphere Client.

   The ESXi Shell is now available.

You can now use the local CLI at the ESXi host's console. It's important to note, though, that VMware doesn't recommend regular, routine use of the ESXi Shell as your primary means of managing and maintaining ESXi. Instead, you should use the vSphere Client and/or the vMA and resort to the ESXi Shell only when absolutely necessary.

While following these steps gets you local CLI access, it doesn't get you remote CLI access. For remote CLI access, another step is required, as you'll see in the next section.

Controlling Remote CLI Access via SSH

Secure Shell, often referred to just as SSH, is a widely known and widely used encrypted remote console protocol. SSH was originally developed in 1995 to replace other protocols, such as tel-net, rsh, and rlogin, that did not provide strong authentication and did not protect against password-sniffing attacks on the network. SSH gained rapid adoption, and the SSH-2 protocol is now a proposed Internet standard with the Internet Engineering Task Force (IETF).

ESXi includes SSH as a method of remote console access. This allows vSphere administrators to use an SSH client, such as PuTTY.exe on Windows or OpenSSH on Linux or Mac OS X, to remotely access the CLI of an ESXi host in order to perform management tasks. However, as with the ESXi Shell, SSH access to an ESXi host is disabled by default. To gain remote CLI access to an ESXi host via SSH, you must first enable the ESXi Shell and enable SSH. You've already seen how to enable the ESXi Shell; now we'll show you how to enable SSH, both via the DCUI and via the vSphere Client.

Perform the following steps to enable SSH via the DCUI:

1. Access the console of the ESXi host using the physical server console or some KVM mechanism (many server vendors provide remote console functionality).

2. Press F2 to log into the DCUI. When prompted for username and password, supply a username and password with permission to access the DCUI (this user must have the Administrator role for this ESXi host).

3. Navigate down to Troubleshooting Options and press Enter.

4. Select Enable SSH. This enables the SSH server (or daemon) on the ESXi host.

5. Press Esc until you return to the main DCUI screen.

Perform these steps to enable SSH via the vSphere Client:

1. Connect to the ESXi host using the vSphere Client.

2. Select the ESXi host in the inventory and click the Configuration tab.

3. From the Software section, select Security Profile.

4. Click the Properties hyperlink near Services.

   This opens the Services Properties dialog box.

5. Select SSH from the list of services; then click Options.

6. Click Start.

7. Click OK to return to the Services Properties dialog box.

   The status for SSH should now be listed as Running.

8. Click OK to return to the vSphere Client. You can now use PuTTY.exe (Windows) or OpenSSH (Mac OS X, Linux, and other Unix variants) to establish an SSH session to the ESXi host.

As with local CLI access, VMware recommends against using SSH as a means of routinely managing your ESXi hosts. In fact, in previous versions of vSphere, SSH access to ESXi was unsupported. It is supported in this version of vSphere, but VMware still recommends against its regular use. If you want to use a CLI environment, we recommend getting familiar with the vMA as your primary CLI environment.

ROOT LOGIN VIA SSH IS ENABLED BY DEFAULT

Generally speaking, allowing the root user to log into a host via SSH is considered a violation of security best practices. However, in vSphere 5.0, when SSH and the ESXi Shell are enabled, the root user is allowed to log in via SSH. This is yet one more reason to keep SSH and the ESXi Shell disabled during the normal course of operation.

Although VMware provides SSH as a means of accessing the CLI environment on an ESXi host, this version of SSH does not provide all the same flexibility as a "full" SSH installation. This further underscores the need to use SSH on an as-needed basis as well as the need for additional access controls for your ESXi hosts, such as a network firewall.

CONTROLLING NETWORK ACCESS VIA THE ESXI FIREWALL

ESXi ships with a firewall that controls network traffic into or out of the host. This firewall gives the vSphere administrator an additional level of control over what types of network traffic are allowed to enter or leave the ESXi hosts.

By default, the ESXi firewall allows only incoming and outgoing connections necessary for managing the VMs and the ESXi host. The following default ports are among those that are open:

◆ TCP 443 and 902: vSphere Client, vCenter Agent

◆ UDP 53: Domain Name System (DNS) client

◆ TCP and UDP 427: Common Information Model (CIM) Service Location Protocol (SLP)

◆ TCP 8000: vMotion

◆ TCP 22: SSH

To see the full list of ports that are open on an ESXi host, you can use the vSphere Client connected directly to an ESXi host, as illustrated in Figure 8.3, or use the vSphere Web Client connected to a vCenter server, select a host, and navigate to Manage ➤ Settings ➤ Security Profile.

From this same area of the vSphere Client, you can also enable additional ports through the firewall or disable ports that are currently open. There are a number of predefined ports and related services listed here that can be configured.

Perform the following steps to enable or disable traffic through the ESXi firewall:

1. Launch the traditional vSphere Client and connect to an ESXi host.

2. Select an ESXi host from the inventory view and select the Configuration tab.

3. From the Software section, select Security Profile.

4. Click the Properties hyperlink to the right of the Firewall heading.

This opens the Firewall Properties dialog box.

5. To enable a particular type of traffic through the ESXi firewall, select the check box next to that traffic type. To disable a type of traffic, deselect the check box for that traffic type.

6. Click OK to return to the client.

FIGURE 8.3

The Security Profile area of the Configuration tab in the traditional vSphere Client shows the current ESXi firewall configuration.

The ESXi firewall also allows you to configure more fine-grained controls over network access by specifying particular source addresses from which traffic should be allowed. This gives you the ability to enable certain types of traffic through the ESXi firewall but restrict access to specific IP addresses or groups of IP addresses.

Perform these steps to limit access to a network service to a specific source:

1. Launch the Web Client and connect to a vCenter Server instance.

2. Select an ESXi host from the inventory view and select the Manage tab.

   You might need to navigate to the Hosts And Clusters view first if you are connected to a vCenter Server instance.

3. From the Settings section, select Security Profile.

4. Click the Edit button to the right of the content area.

   This opens the Firewall Properties dialog box.

5. Select a particular port that is currently enabled through the firewall.

6. To restrict access to a particular source, toward the bottom of the dialog box, deselect the check box labeled Allow Connections From Any IP Address.

You can then specify the allowed source address or addresses in three different formats:

◆ 192.168.1.24: A specific source IPv4 address

◆ 192.168.1.0/24: A specific subnet of source IPv4 addresses

◆ 2001::1/64: A subnet of source IPv6 addresses

Figure 8.4 shows a source subnet of 10.0.0.0/8 configured for the selected network traffic.

FIGURE 8.4
Traffic to the selected network traffic on this ESXi host will be limited to addresses from the specified subnet.

7. Click OK to close the Firewall Settings dialog box and return to the Firewall Properties dialog box.

8. Click OK to close the Firewall Properties dialog box and return to the vSphere Client.

This feature of the ESXi firewall gives you much more flexibility in not only defining what services are allowed into or out of your ESXi hosts but also in defining the source of the traffic into or out of the host. The two previous examples outline how to perform firewall tasks with both the traditional vSphere Client and the vSphere Web Client. There may be the odd occasion when you need to configure your own ports and services through the firewall, and this needs to be performed through the ESXi shell or via SSH.

The following steps will guide you through creating your own custom firewall rules.

1. Log on to the ESXi shell via SSH.

2. To display the current firewall rules run the following command:

```
esxcli network firewall ruleset list
```

3. Make a backup of the firewall configuration file:

```
cp /etc/vmware/firewall/service.xml /etc/vmware/firewall/service.xml.bak
```

4. Allow the firewall configuration file to be changed with the following:

```
chmod 644 /etc/vmware/firewall/service.xml
```

5. Toggle the sticky bit flag using the following command:

```
chmod +t /etc/vmware/firewall/service.xml
```

6. Open the firewall configuration file with a text editor; in this example Vi is used:

```
vi /etc/vmware/firewall/service.xml
```

7. As per Figure 8.5, add a service following the same syntax as those that already exist in the file:

```
<service id='0101'>
  <id>lab.local</id>
  <rule id='0000'>
    <direction>inbound</direction>
    <protocol>udp</protocol>
    <porttype>dst</porttype>
    <port>1337</port>
  </rule>
  <rule id='0001'>
    <direction>outbound</direction>
    <protocol>udp</protocol>
    <porttype>src</porttype>
    <port>1337</port>
  </rule>
  <enabled>true</enabled>
  <required>false</required>
</service>
```

FIGURE 8.5
Adding the correct XML to the `services.xml` file allows you to customize the ESXi host firewall ports.

8. Change the firewall configuration permissions back to their original value:

```
chmod 444 /etc/vmware/firewall/service.xml
```

9. Update the firewall configuration by running the following command:

```
esxcli network firewall refresh
```

10. Finally, list the firewall rules again to ensure that the changes are active:

```
esxcli network firewall ruleset list
```

Maintaining the ESXi firewall configuration is an important part of ESXi host security.

Another recommended security practice is to isolate the ESXi management network to control network access to the management interfaces of your ESXi hosts. You can accomplish this using a network firewall, a technique we describe in the next section.

CONTROLLING NETWORK ACCESS TO THE ESXI MANAGEMENT INTERFACES

The ESXi firewall allows you to control access to specific TCP/IP ports on an ESXi host, but an additional step to consider is a network firewall to control access to the management interfaces of the ESXi host. Using a network firewall to enforce access control lists (ACLs) that govern which systems are allowed to make connections to the management interfaces of your ESXi hosts is a complementary step to using the ESXi firewall, and it follows the well-known recommended practice of using "defense in depth."

Should you choose to isolate the management interfaces of your ESXi hosts on a separate network segment, keep in mind the following two important considerations:

◆ Be sure to allow proper access from vCenter Server to the ESXi hosts. You can handle this by allowing the appropriate ports through the firewall or by adding an extra network interface on the isolated management segment to the vCenter Server system. Personally, we prefer the latter approach, but both approaches are perfectly valid.

◆ Don't forget to allow access from the vMA or from systems on which you will run PowerCLI scripts if you'll be accessing the ESXi hosts directly. If the vMA or the PowerCLI scripts will be connecting to vCenter Server, then you just need to allow access to vCenter Server.

⊕ Real World Scenario

USING A JUMP BOX

One technique that we've seen, and used, in a fair number of installations is a *jump box*. This is a system—typically a Windows Server–based system—that has network interfaces to the isolated management network as well as the rest of your network segments. You'll connect to the jump box and then connect from there to your vSphere environment using the vSphere Client, PowerCLI, vMA, or other tools. This neatly sidesteps the issue of having to create firewall rules to allow traffic into or out of the isolated management network but still provides access to manage the environment. If you are considering isolating the management interfaces of your ESXi hosts, a jump box might be an approach to consider for your environment.

Controlling network access to your ESXi hosts is an important part of your overall security strategy, but it's also important to keep your ESXi hosts patched against security vulnerabilities.

Keeping ESXi Hosts Patched

Another key component in maintaining the security of your vSphere environment is keeping your ESXi hosts fully patched and up-to-date. On an as-needed basis, VMware releases security patches for ESXi. Failing to apply these security patches could expose your vSphere environment to potential security risks.

vSphere Update Manager (VUM) is the tool VMware supplies with vSphere to address this need. We discussed the VUM extensively in Chapter 4, "vSphere Update Manager and the vCenter Support Tools." In order to keep your vSphere environment as secure as possible, you should strongly consider using VUM in your environment to keep your ESXi hosts patched.

In the next section, we'll move on to another aspect of authorization: access controls to manage what a user is allowed to do on an ESXi host after being authenticated.

Managing ESXi Host Permissions

We've shown you how to manage users and groups, both locally and through Active Directory integration. Another key aspect of ESXi host security is the concept of *roles*.

Both vCenter Server and ESXi hosts use the same structured security model to allow users to manage portions of the virtual infrastructure. This model consists of users, groups, roles, privileges, and permissions, as shown in Figure 8.6.

FIGURE 8.6
vCenter Server and ESXi share a common security model for assigning access control.

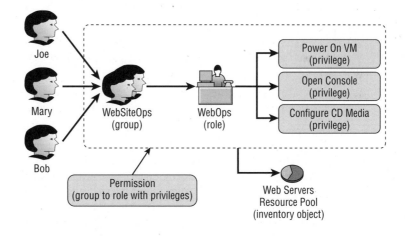

The items that differ between the non–vCenter Server environment and the vCenter Server environment are predominantly in the following two areas:

◆ The location of the user and group objects created

◆ The level of granularity of the roles and privileges available in each environment

You've already seen how ESXi can either use users and groups defined locally on each ESXi host or leverage Microsoft Active Directory as a centralized security authority. As you'll see later in the section "Authenticating Users with Single Sign-On," vCenter can also leverage a directory such as Active Directory as a centralized security authority. Prior to vSphere 5.1, the Windows-based vCenter Server itself was a member of Active Directory, and permissions were leveraged through this connection. From vSphere 5.1 onward, the architecture has significantly changed with the introduction of vCenter Single Sign-On (SSO). We'll explain more about SSO later in this chapter. This is the first key difference in managing permissions for environments that don't use vCenter Server versus environments that do.

The second key difference is the level of granularity of the roles and privileges available in each environment. To explain this difference, we must first discuss and define roles and privileges.

For environments that don't have vCenter Server, or where the administrator chooses to have users authenticate directly to the ESXi hosts to perform management tasks, it is important to start with a discussion of the security model.

In the vCenter Server/ESXi security model's most basic format, users or groups are assigned to a role that has privileges. The user-role-privilege combination is then associated with an object in the inventory as a permission. This means there are four basic components to the vCenter Server/ESXi security model:

User or Group A user is an authentication mechanism; a group is a way of collecting users. In earlier sections of this chapter, we showed you how to manage users and groups and how ESXi can leverage either local users and groups or users and groups from Active Directory. Users and groups form a basic building block of the security model.

Privilege A privilege is an action that you can perform on an inventory object. This would include allocating space in a datastore, powering on a VM, configuring the network, or attaching a virtual CD/DVD to a VM.

Role A role is a collection of privileges. ESXi comes with some built-in roles, as we'll show you shortly, and you also have the ability to create your own custom roles.

Permission A permission allows a user or group to perform the activities specified by a role assigned to an inventory object. For example, you might assign a role that has all privileges to a particular inventory object. Attaching the role to the inventory object creates a permission.

This modular security model provides a great deal of flexibility. vSphere administrators can either use the built-in roles provided with ESXi or create custom roles with custom sets of privileges and assign those custom roles to inventory objects in order to properly re-create the correct set of abilities in the virtual infrastructure. By associating roles with users or groups, vSphere administrators need to define the role only once; then, anytime someone needs those privileges, all the administrator needs to do is associate the appropriate user or group with the appropriate role. This can really help simplify the management of permissions.

An ESXi host has the following three default roles:

No Access The No Access role works as the name suggests. This role prevents access to an object or objects in the inventory. The No Access role can be used if a user was granted access higher up in the inventory. The No Access role can also be used at lower-level objects to prevent object access. For example, if a user is granted permissions on the ESXi host but should be prevented from accessing a specific VM, you could use the No Access role on that specific VM.

Read-Only Read-Only allows a user to see the objects within the vSphere Client inventory. It does not allow the user to interact with any of the visible objects in any way. For example, a user with the Read-Only permission would be able to see a list of VMs in the inventory but could not act on any of them.

Administrator The Administrator role has the utmost authority, but it is only a role, and it needs to be assigned using a combination of a user or a group object and an inventory object such as a VM.

With only three built-in roles on ESXi hosts, the defaults don't leave room for much flexibility. In addition, the default roles just described can't be modified, so you can't customize them. However, don't let that slow you down. Any limits created by the default roles are easily overcome by creating custom roles. You can create custom roles that will better suit your needs, or you can clone existing roles to make additional roles to modify for your own purposes.

Let's take a closer look at how to create a custom role.

CREATING CUSTOM ROLES

If you find that the default roles provided with ESXi don't suit your organization's needs with regard to permissions and management, then you should create custom roles to better map to your business needs. For example, assume that a set of users needs to interact with the console of a VM and also needs to change the CD and floppy media of those VMs. These needs aren't properly reflected in any of the default roles, so a custom role is necessary.

Perform the following steps to create a custom role named Operator:

1. Launch the traditional vSphere Client if it is not already running, and connect to an ESXi host.

2. Navigate to the Administration area by using the navigation bar or by selecting View ➢ Administration ➢ Roles.

   You can also press the Ctrl+Shift+R keyboard shortcut.

3. Click the Add Role button.

4. Type the name of the new role in the Name text box (in this example, **Operator**), and then select the privileges that will be required by members of the role, as shown in Figure 8.7.

   The privileges shown in Figure 8.7 allow users or groups assigned to the Operator role to interact with the console of a VM, change the CD and floppy media, and change the power state of a VM.

PERMISSIONS FOR CHANGING VIRTUAL MEDIA

To change floppy and CD media using floppy disk images (files with a `.flp` filename extension) and CD/DVD disk images (files with a `.iso` filename extension) that are stored on a SAN volume, you will also need to grant that group Browse Datastore privileges at the root of the hierarchy—in this case, at the ESXi host itself.

---

5. Click OK to complete the custom role creation.

The new Operator role is now defined, but it's not operational yet. You must still assign users or groups to the role and apply the role to the ESXi host and/or individual VM(s).

GRANTING PERMISSIONS

As simple and useful as roles are, they are not functional until a user or group is assigned to the role and the role is then assigned to an inventory object as a permission. Assume that a group of users exists that needs to interact with all VMs that are web servers. If access control is managed through the ESXi host, then you have to create a user account on that host (or leverage an Active Directory user account) together with a new group—for example, WebServerOps. Once these users and groups exist, you can execute the security model.

FIGURE 8.7
Custom roles strengthen management capabilities and add flexibility to permission delegations.

Perform the following steps to grant VM access control to a user or group:

1. Launch the traditional vSphere Client if it is not already running, and connect to an ESXi host.

2. Right-click the object in the inventory tree on the left to which permission should be assigned, and click the Add Permission option. In this case, right-click the ESXi host.

3. Click the Add button in the Assign Permissions dialog box.

4. In the Select Users And Groups dialog box, select the appropriate user or group (for example, WinESXOps).

Use the Domain drop-down box to show users and groups from Active Directory if you've configured your ESXi host to integrate with Active Directory.

Once you've found the user or group you want, click the Add button, and then click OK. This returns you to the Assign Permissions dialog box, where the user or group is listed on the left side.

5. From the Assigned Role drop-down list, choose the role to which the selected users or groups should be assigned. In this case, select Operator—the role you defined earlier— from the drop-down list to assign that role to the selected user or group.

What if you have an ESXi host that will host 30 VMs and only 10 of those are the web server VMs? If you assign the permission at the ESXi host level, as we just demonstrated, then you'll assign that role to all 30 VMs, not just the 10 web server VMs. This is because when you assign a permission, an option named Propagate To Child Objects is enabled by default. Figure 8.8 shows the Assign Permissions dialog box; note the option to propagate permissions in the lower-right corner of the dialog box.

FIGURE 8.8
By default, assigning a permission to an object will propagate that permission to all child objects.

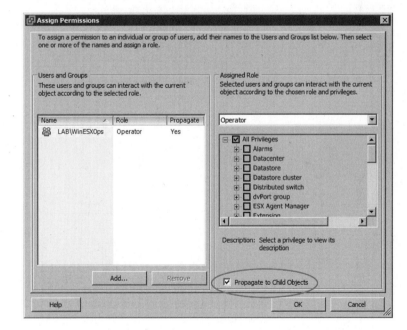

This option works like the security inheritance settings in a Windows filesystem. It allows the privileges assigned in this role to be applied to objects beneath the selected object. For example, if the Operator role is applied as a permission on the ESXi host in the inventory panel and the Propagate To Child Objects option is enabled, all members of the Operator role will be able to interact with *all* the VMs hosted on the ESXi host. Although this certainly simplifies access control implementation, it adds another problem: The permissions of the Operator role have been overextended and now apply to all VMs and not just the web servers. With access control granted at the host level, members of the Operator role will be able to change floppy and CD media and use the console of the web server VMs, but they will also be able to do that on any other VM in the inventory.

To make this work as you would expect, you would have to assign permissions on each of the 10 web server VMs individually. Clearly, this is not an efficient process. Further growth resulting in more web server VMs would require additional administrative effort to ensure access control.

Alternatively, you could use the No Access role on the non-web-server VMs to prevent access, but this method also does not scale well and requires administrative overhead.

This issue presents one of the drawbacks of managing access control on an individual ESXi host. Keep in mind as well that all of the steps we have discussed so far would have to be performed on each ESXi host in the virtual infrastructure. What if there were a way to organize the inventory of VMs? In other words, what if you could create a "container object" for the web server VMs, such as a folder, and put all the web server VMs into it? Then you could assign the group to the role at the parent object level and let inheritance take over. As shown in Figure 8.9, the problem is that folder objects are not possible on a single ESXi host. That means your only option is a resource pool.

FIGURE 8.9
Folder objects cannot be added to an individual ESXi host, leaving resource pools as the only viable option to group VMs.

USING RESOURCE POOLS TO ASSIGN PERMISSIONS

A *resource pool* is actually a special object. Think of it as a folder of sorts. We'll discuss resource pools in much greater detail in Chapter 11, "Managing Resource Allocation"; we strongly urge you to read that chapter and understand the purpose behind resource pools and how they work before attempting to use them to organize your VMs. The focus here is on how resource pools can help you organize your VMs, but it's important to understand that using resource pools in this manner might have unintended side effects.

Perform the following steps to create a resource pool:

1. Launch the vSphere Client if it is not already running, and connect to an ESXi host.

2. Navigate to the inventory view by using the navigation bar, by using the Ctrl+Shift+H keyboard shortcut, or by selecting View ➤ Inventory ➤ Inventory from the menu.

3. Right-click the ESXi host, and select New Resource Pool, as shown previously in Figure 8.9.

4. Type a resource pool name in the Name text box, in this case **WebServers**.

5. Configure the resource allocations, if desired, to establish limits and reservations for the resource pool.

> The limit establishes a hard cap on the resource usage, while the reservations establish a resource guarantee.

6. Click OK.

So now that you've created the WebServers resource pool, you can place VMs into it, as shown in Figure 8.10. Putting VMs into a resource pool is simply a matter of creating new VMs in it (refer to Chapter 9, "Creating and Managing Virtual Machines") or dragging and dropping existing VMs into it.

FIGURE 8.10

As objects in the inventory, resource pools are potential levels of infrastructure management.

Additionally, resource pools become inventory objects to which you can assign permissions. The same process you followed earlier, described in the section "Granting Permissions," applies here as well. Simply assign permission to the resource pool, and ensure that the Propagate To Child Objects check box is selected. Those permissions will also apply to all the VMs in the resource pool.

Using resource pools helps you accomplish a couple of key goals: better organization for your VMs and better control over permissions assigned to those VMs.

However, having said all of this, we must point out that we generally *do not recommend using resource pools in this way*. Although you can certainly use resource pools to organize VMs and assign permissions, resource pools are intended to help control resource allocation and consumption; they are not intended as a means of organizing VMs. In Chapter 11, we'll discuss resource allocation and why using resource pools solely for VM organization is generally not a good idea; we highly recommend reading that chapter and gaining a firm understanding of how resource pools affect resource allocation.

Now that we've shown you how to assign permissions, we need to show you how to remove permissions. Let's look at that next.

REMOVING PERMISSIONS

When your management needs change or if you've made some improper permissions assignments, you can remove permissions. In the section "Granting Permissions," you walked through the process of assigning the Operator role permission on the ESXi host. Now that you have a resource group in place to give you more granular control over permissions, you should remove the permissions you previously applied to the host.

Perform the following steps to remove permissions on an object in the inventory:

1. Launch the traditional vSphere Client if it is not already running, and connect to an ESXi host.

2. Navigate to the inventory view using the navigation bar, the menu, or the keyboard shortcut.

3. Select the object in the inventory, and then select the Permissions tab.

   In this case, you need to remove the permissions from the ESXi host, so select the host from the inventory.

4. Right-click the permissions entry to be deleted from the list of existing permissions, and then click the Delete option.

You should see a warning indicating that users may retain their permissions because of assignments on parent objects higher in the hierarchy. In this case, you want to remove the objects on the parent object (the ESXi host) because those permissions have been applied to the child object (the resource pool). In other cases, though, it might be necessary to keep permissions on the parent object.

After you assign permissions throughout the inventory, it is easy to lose track of what you have previously done. Of course, if your company mandates documentation, there might already be a solid audit trail. However, it is easy to see existing role usage from within the vSphere Client.

IDENTIFYING PERMISSION USAGE

As the inventory of VMs and resource pools grows larger and more complex, it's very likely that the permissions granted to these various objects will also become complex. In addition, as company needs and management strategies change over time, these permissions need to change as well. Combined, these factors can create an environment where the permissions usage is quite complex and hard to decipher.

To help combat this issue, the roles view for the vSphere Client helps administrators identify where roles have been assigned and what permissions have been granted in the inventory.

Perform the following steps to identify where a role has been assigned as a permission:

1. Launch the traditional vSphere Client if it is not already running, and connect to an ESXi host.

2. Navigate to the roles view using the navigation bar, the Ctrl+Shift+R keyboard shortcut, or the View ➢ Administration ➢ Roles menu item.

3. Click the role whose usage you want to identify.

The details pane identifies where in the inventory hierarchy the role is used, as you can see illustrated in Figure 8.11.

Using the vSphere Client's roles view allows you, the administrator, to track down where permissions have been assigned so that you can edit or remove permissions when necessary. But it's not only permissions that need to be removed—sometimes roles need to be removed too.

FIGURE 8.11

The vSphere Client provides a break-down of where roles are currently in use.

EDITING AND REMOVING ROLES

Over time, it is almost inevitable that management needs will change. At times, you might have to create new roles, edit an existing role, or even delete a role. If the privileges assigned to a role are no longer applicable in your environment, you should edit the role to add or remove the necessary privileges.

Perform the following steps to edit a role:

1. Launch the vSphere Client if it is not already running, and connect to an ESXi host.

2. Navigate to the roles view using the navigation bar, the Ctrl+Shift+R keyboard shortcut, or the View ➤ Administration ➤ Roles menu item.

3. Right-click the role you want to edit, and select Edit Role.

4. Make the desired changes by adding or removing privileges in the Edit Role dialog box. Click OK when you finish.

As we mentioned earlier in this chapter, ESXi won't allow you to edit the default roles.

If a role is no longer used, it should be removed to minimize the number of objects to be viewed and managed.

Perform the following steps to delete a role:

1. Launch the vSphere Client if it is not already running, and connect to an ESXi host.

2. Navigate to the roles view using the navigation bar, the Ctrl+Shift+R keyboard shortcut, or the View ➤ Administration ➤ Roles menu item.

3. Right-click the role to be deleted, and select Remove.

When a role is in use and is selected for removal, the ESXi host offers the opportunity to transfer the existing role members to a new role or to simply drop all members from the role. This eliminates the chance of accidentally deleting roles that are being used in the inventory.

Now that you understand how to work with local users, groups, roles, and permissions on an individual ESXi host, be aware that you are unlikely to do much of this. Managing local user accounts is administratively more cumbersome because of the lack of centralized management and authentication. Active Directory integration addresses a great deal of this, allowing you to collapse your user and group management into one centralized directory. However, you will still find that you perform most, if not all, of your access control work within vCenter Server.

As you'll see in the section "Managing vCenter Server Permissions," vCenter Server offers greater flexibility than managing individual ESXi hosts.

The last area of ESXi host security we'll discuss pertains to the third A in the AAA model: accounting—in other words, logging. Let's take a closer look at how to handle logs for your ESXi hosts.

Configuring ESXi Host Logging

Capturing information in the system logs is an important aspect of computer and network security. The system logs provide a record, or an accounting, of the actions performed, the events encountered, the errors experienced, and the state of the ESXi host and the VMs on that host.

Every ESXi host runs a syslog daemon (service) that captures events and logs them for future reference. Assuming that you've installed ESXi onto some local disks, the default location for the logs is a 4 GB scratch partition that the ESXi installer creates. Although this provides long-term storage for the ESXi host logs, there is no centralized location for them, making analysis of the logs more difficult than it should be. An administrator would have to connect to each host individually to review the logs for that host.

Further, if you are booting from SAN or if you are using vSphere Auto Deploy, there is no local scratch partition, and logs are stored in memory on the ESXi host—which means they disappear when the ESXi host is restarted. Clearly, this is not an ideal configuration. Not only does it lack centralized access to the logs, but it also lacks long-term storage for the logs.

The typical solution to both of these issues is a third-party syslog server, a server that runs a syslog daemon and is prepared to accept the log entries from the various ESXi hosts. To make things easier, VMware supplies a syslog collector with vSphere 5 in three different forms:

♦ As a service you can install onto a Windows Server–based computer

♦ As a service preinstalled on the vCenter Server virtual appliance

♦ As part of the vMA's built-in syslog daemon

In Chapter 4 we show you how to install the VMware Syslog Collector on a Windows Server–based computer and how to configure your ESXi hosts to send their logs to this centralized syslog service.

Reviewing Other ESXi Security Recommendations

In addition to all the security recommendations we've made so far with regard to ESXi hosts, there are some other recommended practices that you should follow:

♦ Set a root password for the ESXi host. You can set the root password, if it has not already been set, via the server's console by pressing F2. More information on working with the ESXi console is available in Chapter 2.

♦ Use host profiles in vCenter Server. Host profiles can help ensure that the configuration of the ESXi hosts does not drift or change from the settings specified in the host profile. We discussed host profiles in Chapter 3, "Installing and Configuring vCenter Server."

♦ Enable lockdown mode for your ESXi hosts. Enabling lockdown mode disables console-based user access and direct access via the vSphere Client. Root access via the vMA is also restricted.

Now that you've looked at the various ways to secure your ESXi hosts, it's time to move on to securing vCenter Server, the second major component in your vSphere environment.

Securing vCenter Server

For the most part, discussing how to secure vCenter Server entails discussing how to secure the underlying OS. For environments that have deployed the Windows Server–based version of vCenter Server, this means securing Windows Server. For environments using the Linux-based vCenter Server virtual appliance, it means securing SuSE Linux. Because it's a virtual appliance, though, there isn't a lot that you can do to secure the preinstalled SuSE Linux instance.

Securing Windows Server—for those environments running the Windows Server–based version of vCenter Server—is a topic that has been discussed many, many times, so we won't go into great detail here. The following security recommendations are among the more common ones:

◆ Stay current on all Windows Server patches and updates. This helps protect you against potential security exploits.

◆ Harden the Windows Server installation using published best practices and guidelines from Microsoft.

In addition to these standard security recommendations, we can offer a few other security recommendations that are specific to vCenter Server and its components such as SSO, the Inventory Service, and the Web Client:

◆ Be sure to stay current on vCenter Server patches and updates.

◆ Place the vCenter Server backend database on a separate system (physical or VM), if possible, and follow recommended practices to secure the separate system.

◆ If you are using Windows authentication with SQL Server, use a dedicated service account for vCenter Server—don't allow vCenter Server to share a Windows account with other services or applications.

◆ Be sure to secure the separate database server and backend database using published security practices from the appropriate vendor. This includes securing the database server itself (Microsoft SQL Server, or Oracle) as well as the underlying OS for that database server (Windows Server, Linux, or other).

◆ Replace the default self-signed SSL certificates with a valid SSL certificate from a trusted root authority for vCenter Server and all of its components.

SSL Certificate Replacement

With the separation of vCenter components for vSphere version 5.1 and above, the complexity for replacing the default SSL certificates has increased. VMware has addressed this complexity by creating tools to assist the process and also by providing extensive Knowledge Base articles on the topic. It would take a dedicated chapter to explain the entire process step-by-step, so if you're interested we recommend you read the Knowledge Base located at `kb.vmware.com/kb/2034833`.

In addition to these recommendations, there are other steps you should take to ensure that vCenter Server—and the infrastructure being managed by vCenter Server—is appropriately secured and protected.

Once again using the AAA model as a rough structure for the security discussion, we'll start with a review of vCenter Server authentication.

Authenticating Users with Single Sign-On

As with ESXi, users will need to authenticate to get access to vCenter Server in order to perform any tasks, but the process for how this authentication works changed significantly from vSphere 5.1 with the introduction of vCenter Single Sign-On. How you handle that authentication depends on your environment. Both the Windows Server–based version of vCenter Server and the Linux-based vCenter Server virtual appliance offer the same authentication mechanisms. Generally you will probably authenticate against Active Directory, although you could manage users and groups locally within Single Sign-On itself or even connect it to OpenLDAP. Because using Active Directory and using local SSO users are the most common methods of authentication, we'll focus on these for this discussion.

In the following sections, we'll cover these three topics:

◆ Configuring Single Sign-On for authentication against Active Directory

◆ Configuring Single Sign-On for authentication against local users

◆ Understanding how vCenter Server authenticates against ESXi with vpxuser

CONFIGURING SSO ON WINDOWS SERVER FOR ACTIVE DIRECTORY

In previous version of vSphere, when vCenter is installed on a Windows Server computer, leveraging Active Directory is pretty simple: Join the computer to an Active Directory domain before installing vCenter, and vCenter would—by virtue of how Windows integrates with Active Directory—automatically be able to take advantage of users and groups stored within Active Directory. If you choose not to join Active Directory, then the Windows-based version of vCenter will need to be configured for use with an external directory service.

vSphere 5.1 introduced SSO for the first time, and VMware has made some additional changes in vSphere 5.5. The key to SSO and Active Directory integration is the SSO administrator, or "master," account. This account can be used to configure all additional directory services post installation.

When installing vCenter, you will be asked which user or group should be added as a vCenter administrator. By default, the built-in SSO administrator@vsphere.local user account will be used. These default settings in SSO do not by default extend permissions to users within Active Directory. This is a good thing; we don't want to add users who aren't necessarily involved in the administration of the vSphere environment. Generally speaking, you want to assign a permission to only those users who actually need it; this is part of the *principle of least privilege*, a key concept in computer security.

The issue is this: Prior to vSphere .5.5, by default, the domain Administrators group—this is the Active Directory Administrators group—was given the Administrator role in vCenter Server (we'll discuss vCenter Server roles in more detail in the section "Managing vCenter Server Permissions" later in this chapter). This permission assignment happened at the vCenter Server object and was propagated down to all child objects. It has been our experience that in many organizations there are members of the Administrators group who don't have anything to do with the virtualization infrastructure. Granting those users privileges inside vCenter Server is a violation of security best practices; not having the domain group Administrators in SSO Server is, therefore, a good idea.

Perform the following steps to add Active Directory to be used as a source for vCenter Server users:

1. Log on to the vCenter Web Client as the SSO administrator. Unless you have created another account, the username is administrator@vsphere.local.

2. Click Administration in the Navigator pane.

3. Under the Single Sign-On section, click Configuration.

4. Select the middle tab, labeled Identity Sources.

5. Click the green plus icon to add a new identity source.

6. In the Add Identity Source dialog box, you have four options:

   ◆ Active Directory (Integrated Windows Authentication)

   ◆ Active Directory As A LDAP Server

   ◆ Open LDAP

   ◆ Local OS

   The first two options relate to Active Directory, but their connection method is slightly different. Using Windows authentication requires a user or computer account with the relevant rights to traverse the entire directory and Kerberos is used to authenticate.

   The second Active Directory option uses LDAP to connect instead of Kerberos.

   The third option, Open LDAP, is quite simply a way to integrate with OpenLDAP. This could be a connection to a Windows- or Linux-based OpenLDAP system.

   The final option is Local OS. This relates to the operating system on which SSO is installed, in our case a Windows Server 2008 R2 system. This integrates SSO with the local users that are configured within the operating system itself.

   In this example, we'll connect to Active Directory using Windows authentication and a machine account. This is the simplest way to get SSO to integrate with Active Directory as it prepopulates the Active Directory domain name that the SSO server belongs to and can therefore use the machine account for authentication.

   With these options selected, click OK to close the dialog box.

vCenter Server, more specifically Single Sign-On, is now linked with Active Directory. You now have the capability to add users and groups from your domain to specific roles within your vSphere environment. We will explain this in detail later in the chapter.

CONFIGURING SSO ON WINDOWS SERVER FOR LOCAL ACCOUNTS

In the previous sections we configured SSO to use Active Directory as a source for users and groups. Similarly, we can also configure SSO to use the local machine's users and groups as an identity source. One of the great things about SSO is that you can have multiple identity sources at the same time. This is especially helpful in situations with split operational roles as in outsourced IT environments. Adding the local OS is very similar to adding Active Directory; however, you may find that it's already configured by the SSO installer. In the event that you need to configure it manually, simply follow these steps:

1. Log on to the vCenter Web Client as the SSO administrator. Unless you have created another account, the username is administrator@vsphere.local.

2. Click Administration in the Navigator pane.

3. Under the Single Sign-On section, click Configuration.

4. Select the middle tab, labeled Identity Sources.

5. Click the green plus icon to add a new identity source.

6. Select the Local OS radio button.

7. Type in a name for this identity source and click OK.

As we already mentioned, the local OS identity source is added by default as part of the SSO installation. This source can be removed in the Identity Sources tab. Simply highlight the source and click the red cross icon to delete it. The only identity source you cannot delete (or edit) is the vsphere.local (or SSO built-in) source.

In the next section, we'll cover how to configure the vCenter Server virtual appliance for use with Active Directory.

CONFIGURING THE VCENTER SERVER VIRTUAL APPLIANCE FOR ACTIVE DIRECTORY

Two steps are required to leverage Active Directory with the Linux-based vCenter Server virtual appliance:

1. Enable Active Directory integration on the virtual appliance itself.

2. Add appropriate permissions to the vCenter Server hierarchy to allow Active Directory accounts to log in and manage the inventory objects.

Let's look at each of these steps.

Enabling Active Directory Integration on the Virtual Appliance

To enable the Active Directory integration of the virtual appliance, use the management interface of the virtual appliance. The vCenter Server virtual appliance offers a web-based management interface accessible on port 5480 of the IP address assigned to the virtual appliance. For example, if you assigned the IP address 10.1.1.100 to the virtual appliance, you could access the web-based management interface at https://10.1.1.100:5480. At this point, you'll be prompted to log into the virtual appliance. The default login credentials are username root and password vmware.

Perform these steps to enable Active Directory integration after you've logged into the management interface:

1. From the main web-based management screen, click the Authentication tab.

2. Select Active Directory.

3. Select Active Directory Enabled.

4. Supply the name of the Active Directory domain and the username and password of an account that has permission to join the virtual appliance to the domain.

5. Click Save Settings.

This screen notes that any change to the Active Directory configuration will require a restart of the virtual appliance, so the next step is to reboot the virtual appliance.

6. Select the System tab.

7. Click the Reboot button. When prompted for confirmation, select Reboot.

The virtual appliance will reboot.

You can monitor the progress of the reboot using the VM console within the vSphere Client. Once the virtual appliance has rebooted successfully, you can test the Active Directory integration by logging into the virtual appliance's web-based management interface using Active Directory credentials. You can use either the domain\username or the username@domain syntax to log in.

If the login is successful, you're ready to proceed to the next step. If not, you'll need to troubleshoot the Active Directory integration. The vCenter Server virtual appliance supports SSH logins, so you can log in via SSH and review the logs to see what errors were logged during the configuration.

If you're having problems with Active Directory integration, refer to the following list:

◆ Verify that the time on the virtual appliance is synchronized with the time on the Active Directory domain controllers.

◆ Ensure that the virtual appliance is able, via DNS, to resolve the domain name and locate the Active Directory domain controllers. This typically means using the same DNS servers that Active Directory uses.

◆ Verify that there is no firewall between the virtual appliance and the Active Directory domain controllers or that all necessary traffic is permitted through any firewalls that are present.

Once you've verified that the Active Directory integration is working, you're ready to proceed with the second step in configuring the vCenter Server virtual appliance for Active Directory.

Adding Permissions for Active Directory Users or Groups

Although you've successfully configured the Active Directory integration for the vCenter Server virtual appliance, you still can't use any Active Directory credentials to log in using the vSphere Client. To log in via the vSphere Client, you must first grant access to one or more Active Directory users or groups within the vCenter Server hierarchy.

Perform these steps to grant permissions to an Active Directory user or group in order to log into the vCenter Server virtual appliance via the vSphere Client:

1. Launch the vSphere Client, if it is not already running.

2. Specify the DNS name or IP address of the vCenter Server virtual appliance in the IP Address/Name field.

3. Specify the username **root** and the password **vmware**, and click Login to log in to the vCenter Server virtual appliance.

4. Select the vCenter Server object from the inventory pane; then click the Permissions tab.

5. Right-click a blank area of the Permissions tab and select Add Permission.

6. In the Assign Permissions dialog box, click the Add button.

7. From the Domain drop-down box, select the Active Directory domain.

8. Find the user or group to add, click the Add button, and then click OK.

    We do not recommend using a specific user account here; instead, leverage a security group within Active Directory. Recall that ESXi integration into Active Directory requires a security group called ESX Admins; you might want to leverage that group here as well.

9. In the Assign Permissions dialog box, select Administrator from the Assigned Role drop-down list, and make sure that Propagate To Child Objects is selected.

    This ensures that the selected Active Directory users and/or groups have the Administrator role within the vCenter Server virtual appliance. By default, only the predefined root account has this role.

10. Click OK to return to the vSphere Client.

After completing this process, you'll be able to log into the vCenter Server virtual appliance with the vSphere Client using an Active Directory username and password. You're all set—the vCenter Server virtual appliance is configured to use Active Directory.

Before we move on to the topic of managing permissions within vCenter Server, one quick item that we'd like to discuss pertains to how vCenter Server interacts with ESXi hosts. It's important to understand how vCenter Server uses a special user account as a proxy account for managing your ESXi hosts.

Understanding the vpxuser Account

At the beginning of this chapter, we showed you how the ESXi security model employs users, groups, roles, privileges, and permissions. We also showed you how to manage local users and groups and to integrate your ESXi hosts with Active Directory.

As you'll see in the section "Managing vCenter Server Permissions," vCenter Server uses the same user/group-role-privilege-permission security model. When vCenter Server is present, all activities are funneled through vCenter Server using SSO accounts that have been assigned a role that has, in turn, been assigned to one or more inventory objects as a permission. This combination of SSO account, role, and inventory object creates a permission that allows (or disallows) the user to perform certain functions. The user accounts exist in Active Directory or OpenLDAP or on the SSO Server computer itself, not on the ESXi hosts, and the permissions and roles are defined within vCenter Server, not on the ESXi hosts. Because the user doesn't log into the ESXi host directly, this minimizes the need for many local user accounts on the ESXi host and thus provides better security. Alas, there still is a need, however small or infrequent, for local accounts on an ESXi host used primarily for administration, which is why we talked earlier about managing local users and groups and integrating ESXi authentication into Active Directory.

Because the user accounts exist outside the ESXi hosts, and because the roles, privileges, and permissions are defined outside the ESXi hosts, when you use vCenter Server to manage your virtual infrastructure, you are really only creating a task and not directly interacting with the ESXi hosts or the VMs. This is true for any user using vCenter Server to manage hosts or VMs. For instance, Shane, an administrator, wants to log into vCenter Server and create a new VM. Shane first needs the proper role—perhaps a custom role you created specifically for the purpose of creating new VMs—assigned to the proper inventory object or objects within vCenter Server.

Assuming the correct role has been assigned to the correct inventory objects—let's say it's a resource pool—Shane has what he needs to create, modify, and monitor VMs. But does Shane's user account have direct access to the ESXi hosts when he's logged into vCenter Server? No, it does not. In fact, a proxy account is used to communicate Shane's tasks to the appropriate ESXi host or VM. This account, vpxuser, is the only account that vCenter Server stores and tracks in its backend database.

VPXUSER SECURITY

The vpxuser account and password are stored in the vCenter Server database and on the ESXi hosts; it is used to communicate from a vCenter Server computer to an ESXi host. The vpxuser password consists of 32 (randomly selected) characters, is encrypted using SHA1 on an ESXi host, and is obfuscated on vCenter Server. Each vpxuser password is unique to the ESXi host being managed by vCenter Server.

No direct administrator intervention is warranted or advised for this account because that would break vCenter Server functions needing this account. The account and password are never used by humans, and they do not have shell access on any ESXi hosts. Thus, it isn't necessary to manage this account or include it with normal administrative and regular user account security policies.

Anytime vCenter Server polls an ESXi host or an administrator creates a task that needs to be communicated to an ESXi host, the vpxuser account is used. On the ESXi hosts that are managed by vCenter Server, the vpxuser account exists (it's created automatically by vCenter Server; this is why vCenter Server asks you for the root password when adding a host to the inventory) and is assigned the Administrator role. This gives the vpxuser account the ability to perform whatever tasks are necessary on the individual ESXi hosts managed by vCenter Server. When a user logs into vCenter Server, vCenter Server applies its security model (roles, privileges, and permissions) to that user, ensuring that the user is permitted to perform only the tasks for which they are authorized. On the backend, though, all these tasks are proxied onto the individual ESXi hosts as vpxuser.

You should now have a good idea of what's involved in vCenter Server authentication. We'd like to focus now on vCenter Server permissions, which control what users are allowed to do after they've authenticated to vCenter Server.

Managing vCenter Server Permissions

The security model for vCenter Server is identical to that explained in the previous section for an ESXi host: Take a user or group and assign them to a role (which has one or more privileges assigned) for a specific inventory object. The key difference is that vCenter Server enables new objects in the inventory hierarchy that aren't possible with individual ESXi hosts. This would include objects like clusters and folders (both of which we discussed in Chapter 3). vCenter Server also supports resource pools (which we introduced in the section "Using Resource Pools to Assign Permissions" and which we'll discuss in greater detail in Chapter 11). vCenter Server also allows you to assign permissions in different ways; for example, an ESXi host has only one inventory view, while vCenter Server has the Hosts And Clusters view, VMs And Templates view, Storage view, and Networking view. Permissions—the assignment of a role to one or more inventory objects—can occur in any of these views.

As you can see, this means that vCenter Server allows vSphere administrators to create much more complex permissions hierarchies than you could create using only ESXi hosts.

Recall that a key part of the security model is the role—the grouping of privileges that you assign to a user or group in a permission. Let's take a closer look at the predefined roles that come with vCenter Server.

REVIEWING VCENTER SERVER'S ROLES

Where the ESXi host is quite limited in its default roles, vCenter Server provides more, thereby offering a much greater degree of flexibility in constructing access control. Although both security models offer the flexibility of creating custom roles, ESXi includes three default roles, while vCenter Server provides nine, including the same three offered in ESXi. Figure 8.12 details the default vCenter Server roles. These roles are visible from within the vSphere Web Client by selecting Home ➤ Roles.

FIGURE 8.12
The vCenter Server default roles offer much more flexibility than an individual ESXi host offers.

As you can see, VMware provides a large number of roles in a default vCenter Server installation. Remember, just as with the default ESXi roles, vCenter Server will prevent you from modifying the No Access, Read-Only, and Administrator roles—you must clone them in order to customize them. Once you clone one of the built-in roles, you can customize the privileges assigned to that role to meet your specific needs.

The key to using these roles effectively is to understand the functions of each:

No Access   This role is just what it sounds like—it prevents a user or group from gaining access. But why do you need it? The idea behind this role is to prevent a user or group that has permissions at some point higher in the hierarchy from having permissions on the object to which this role is assigned. For instance, you may have granted Eileen the Virtual Machine User role at the datacenter level, which would allow her to administer all of the VMs in the datacenter, but there is a security concern about her having access to one of the accounting VMs in that datacenter. You could assign Eileen to the No Access role on the Accounting VM, which would effectively supersede her Virtual Machine User privileges.

Read-Only   Read-Only allows users to see the vCenter Server inventory. It does not allow them to interact with any of the VMs in any way through the vSphere Client or the web client except to see the power status of each VM in the inventory where they have the Read-Only role applied.

Administrator   A user assigned to an object with the Administrator role will have full administrative capabilities over that object in vCenter Server. Note that this does *not* grant *any* privileges within the guest OSes installed inside the VMs. For instance, a user assigned the Administrator role for a VM may be able to change the RAM assigned to the VM and alter its performance parameters (Shares, Reservations, and Limits) but may not even have the permissions to log into that VM unless they have been granted that right from within the guest OS.

The Administrator role can be granted at any object level in the hierarchy, and the user or group that is assigned the role at that level will have vCenter Server administrative privileges over that object and (if the inheritance box is selected) any child objects in the hierarchy.

Aside from the No Access, Read-Only, and Administrator roles, the rest of the roles are sample roles. These are intended to provide vSphere administrators with an idea of how to organize roles and permissions to model the appropriate administrative structure.

Virtual Machine Power User (Sample)   The Virtual Machine Power User sample role assigns permissions to allow a user to perform most functions on VMs. This includes tasks such as configuring CD and floppy media, changing the power state, taking and deleting snapshots, and modifying the configuration. These permissions apply only to VMs. The idea here is, as an example, if users are granted this role at a datacenter level, they would be able to manage only VMs in that datacenter and would not be able to change settings on objects such as resource pools in that datacenter.

Virtual Machine User (Sample)   The Virtual Machine User sample role grants the user the ability to interact with a VM but not the ability to change its configuration. Users can operate the VM's power controls and change the media in the virtual CD-ROM drive or floppy drive as long as they also have access to the media they want to change. For instance, a user who is assigned this role for a VM will be able to change the CD media from an ISO image on a shared storage volume to their own client system's physical CD-ROM drive. If you want them to be able to change from one ISO file to another (both stored on a Virtual Machine File System [VMFS] volume or Network File System [NFS] volume), they will also need to be granted the Browse Datastore permission at the parent of the datastore object in the vCenter Server hierarchy—usually the datacenter in which the ESX/ESXi host is located.

Resource Pool Administrator (Sample) The Resource Pool Administrator sample role grants the user the ability to manage and configure resources with a resource pool, including VMs, child pools, scheduled tasks, and alarms.

VMware Consolidated Backup User (Sample) As the role name suggests, the VMware Consolidated Backup User sample role grants the user the privileges required for performing a backup of a VM using VCB.

Datastore Consumer (Sample) The Datastore Consumer sample role is targeted at users who need only a single permission: the permission to allocate space from a datastore. Clearly, this role is very limited.

Network Administrator (Sample) Similar to the Datastore Consumer role, the Network Administrator sample role has only a single permission, and that is the permission to assign networks.

These default roles provide a good starting point, but they won't meet every company's needs. If you need something more than what is provided by default, you'll need to create a custom role. We describe this process in the next section.

WORKING WITH vCENTER SERVER ROLES

What if the default roles supplied with vCenter Server don't provide you with the necessary functionality for a particular grouping of users? Well, it depends on what the problem is. Let's take the most basic problem. You've chosen a best-fit role to assign a user privileges, but the role you've selected lacks a key permission, or perhaps the role you've selected grants a few permissions that you don't want included. To get the exact fit you need, you can simply clone the role and then customize it.

Perform the following steps to clone a role in vCenter Server:

1. Launch the vSphere Web Client if it is not already running, and connect to a vCenter Server instance.

2. Navigate to the Roles area from the Home screen.

3. Right-click the role that you want to clone, and select Clone from the context menu or select the role and click the clone icon above the list.

After you've cloned the role, you can add or remove privileges as needed. We described the process of editing a role in the section "Editing and Removing Roles."

LEAVE THE BUILT-IN SAMPLE ROLES INTACT

We recommend leaving all of the built-in sample roles intact and unmodified. vCenter Server prevents you from modifying the No Access, Read-Only, and Administrator roles but does not prevent you from modifying the rest of the roles. To help avoid confusion among multiple administrators, we recommend leaving the built-in sample roles intact and cloning them to a new custom role instead.

To assign a permission to an object within vCenter, you use the same principles as with ESXi hosts. Assign a user to a role and then the role to an object within the vCenter Web Client. Before we delve into what privileges will be assigned to a role, let's run through an example of how to assign a permission to an object within the vSphere Web Client:

1. Log on to the vCenter Web Client as a vCenter administrator. Unless you have created another account, the account is administrator@vsphere.local.

2. Navigate to the object for which you wish to change the permissions. In this example, locate the vCenter Server object.

3. Select the Manage tab and then click the Permissions subsection.

4. Click the green plus arrow to bring up the Add Permission dialog box.

5. In the left column, click the Add button.

6. The Select Users/Groups dialog box allows you to select from a Domain drop-down list. This list is populated with your identity sources previously configured within SSO. Select your Active Directory identity source.

7. Find the Active Directory user from the list. Click the Add button and then the OK button.

8. With the user now specified in the list, it's time to assign a role. Select Administrator from the Assigned Role drop-down list and then click the OK button.

9. The Active Directory user can now log in using the vSphere Web Client and can manage vCenter.

By default, just as with the vSphere Client, the Propagate To Children check box is selected. All objects that are children of the currently selected object will also receive the permission you are granting. By assigning permissions at a vCenter object and leaving Propagate To Children selected, we are giving this user permissions over every object this vCenter Server instance manages. This includes ESXi hosts, VMs, networks, and datastores, to name a few. Keep this in mind when assigning permissions and only ever give the minimum required access.

UNDERSTANDING VCENTER SERVER PRIVILEGES

Roles are very useful, but now that you've started to peek into the properties of the roles and how to edit roles, you also need to understand each of the privileges and what they do for you in terms of customizing roles. Remember that privileges are individual tasks that are assigned to roles. Without privileges assigned, roles are useless, so it's important to understand the privileges available within vCenter Server.

The list of privileges is rather long, but it's broken down into some general categories, so let's look at what each of the categories means in general terms:

Alarms   Controls the ability to create, modify, delete, disable, and acknowledge vCenter Server alarms.

Auto Deploy   Controls the ability to use vSphere Auto Deploy for dynamically provisioning ESXi hosts at boot time.

Datacenter Controls the ability to create, delete, move, and rename datacenters inside vCenter Server. The privilege for working with an IP pool is also found in the Datacenter category.

Datastore Controls who can access files stored on an ESXi attached volume. These privileges need to be assigned at the parent object of the ESXi host itself—for instance, a datacenter, an ESXi cluster, or a folder that contains ESXi hosts.

Datastore Cluster Controls who is permitted to configure a datastore cluster (used with profile-based storage and Storage DRS).

Distributed Switch Controls who can create, delete, or modify distributed virtual switches.

ESX Agent Manager Controls the ability to view, configure, or modify ESX host agents.

Extension Controls the ability to register, update, or unregister extensions in vCenter Server. An example of an extension is vSphere Update Manager (VUM).

Folder Controls the creation, deletion, and general manipulation of folders in the vCenter Server hierarchy.

Global Includes the ability to manage vCenter Server license settings and server settings such as SNMP and SMTP.

Host Controls what users can do with ESXi hosts in the inventory. This includes tasks such as adding and removing ESXi hosts from the inventory, changing the host's memory configuration, and changing the firewall settings.

Host Profile Controls creating, editing, deleting, and viewing host profiles.

Network Controls the configuration or removal of networks from the vCenter Server inventory.

Performance Controls the ability of users to modify the intervals at which the performance chart information is displayed on the Performance tab of an object.

Permissions Controls who has the ability to modify the permissions assigned to a role and who can manipulate a role/user combination for a particular object.

Profile-Driven Storage Controls who can view and update profile-driven storage.

Resource Controls resource pool manipulation, including creating, deleting, or renaming the pool; also controls migration by using vMotion and applying DRS recommendations.

Scheduled Task Controls the configuration of tasks and the ability to run a task that is scheduled inside vCenter Server.

Sessions Controls the ability to view and disconnect vSphere Client sessions connected to vCenter Server and to send a global message to connected vSphere Client users.

Storage Views Controls changing the server configuration and looking at storage views.

Tasks Controls the ability to create or update tasks.

VRMPolicy Controls settings around virtual rights management (VRM). VRM centers on the management of security policies and access controls for VMs.

Virtual Machine Controls the manipulation of VMs in the vCenter Server inventory, including the ability to create, delete, or connect to the remote console of a VM; controls the power state of a VM; controls the ability to change floppy and CD media and to manipulate templates, among other privileges.

Distributed Virtual Port (dvPort) Group Controls who can create, delete, and modify distributed virtual port groups on distributed virtual switches.

vApp Controls the configuration and management of vApps, such as the ability to add VMs to a vApp; clone, create, delete, export, or import a vApp; power on or power off the vApp; and view the Open Virtualization Format (OVF) environment.

Inventory Service Controls who can access the tagging capabilities of the vCenter Inventory Service.

vService Controls the ability to create, remove, and modify vService dependencies with vApps.

How these various privileges are assigned to roles is what really matters. As you saw earlier, vCenter Server ships with some default roles already defined. Some of these—namely, the No Access, Read-Only, and Administrator roles—are fairly well understood and cannot be modified. The other predefined roles are listed in Table 8.1 along with the privileges that are assigned to each role by default.

TABLE 8.1:   Table of privileges for default roles

PREDEFINED ROLE	ASSIGNED PRIVILEGES
Virtual Machine Power User	Datastore ➤ Browse Datastore
	Global ➤ Cancel Task
	Scheduled Task ➤ Create Tasks, Modify Task, Remove Task, Run Task
	Virtual Machine ➤ Configuration ➤ Add Existing Disk, Add New Disk, Add or Remove Device, Advanced, Change CPU Count, Change Resource, Disk Lease, Memory, Modify Device Settings, Remove Disk, Rename, Reset Guest Information, Settings, Upgrade Virtual Hardware
	Virtual Machine ➤ Interaction ➤ Acquire Guest Control Ticket, Answer Question, Configure CD Media, Configure Floppy Media, Console Interaction, Device Connection, Power Off, Power On, Reset, Suspend, VMware Tools Install
	Virtual Machine ➤ State ➤ Create Snapshot, Remove Snapshot, Rename Snapshot, Revert To Snapshot
Virtual Machine User	Global ➤ Cancel Task
	Scheduled Task ➤ Create Tasks, Modify Task, Remove Task, Run Task
	Virtual Machine ➤ Interaction ➤ Answer Question, Configure CD Media, Configure Floppy Media, Console Interaction, Device Connection, Power Off, Power On, Reset, Suspend, VMware Tools Install

TABLE 8.1: Table of privileges for default roles *(CONTINUED)*

PREDEFINED ROLE	ASSIGNED PRIVILEGES
Resource Pool Administrator	Alarms ➤ Create Alarm, Modify Alarm, Remove Alarm
	Datastore ➤ Browse Datastore
	Folder ➤ Create Folder, Delete Folder, Move Folder, Rename Folder
	Global ➤ Cancel Task, Log Event, Set Custom Attribute
	Permissions ➤ Modify Permissions
	Resource ➤ Assign Virtual Machine To Resource Pool, Create Resource Pool, Migrate, Modify Resource Pool, Move Resource Pool, Query vMotion, Relocate, Remove Resource Pool, Rename Resource Pool
	Scheduled Task ➤ Create Tasks, Modify Task, Remove Task, Run Task
	Virtual Machine ➤ Configuration ➤ Add Existing Disk, Add New Disk, Add Or Remove Device, Advanced, Change CPU Count, Change Resource, Disk Lease, Memory, Modify Device Settings, Raw Device, Remove Disk, Rename, Reset Guest Information, Settings, Upgrade Virtual Hardware
	Virtual Machine ➤ Interaction ➤ Answer Question, Configure CD Media, Configure Floppy Media, Console Interaction, Device Connection, Power Off, Power On, Reset, Suspend, VMware Tools Install
	Virtual Machine ➤ Inventory ➤ Create From Existing, Create New, Move, Register, Remove, Unregister
	Virtual Machine ➤ Provisioning ➤ Allow Disk Access, Allow Read-Only Disk Access, Allow Virtual Machine Download, Allow Virtual Machine Files Upload, Clone Template, Clone Virtual Machine, Create Template From Virtual Machine, Customize, Deploy Template, Mark As Template, Mark As Virtual Machine, Modify Customization Specification, Read Customization Specifications
	Virtual Machine ➤ State ➤ Create Snapshot, Remove Snapshot, Rename Snapshot, Revert To Snapshot
VMware Consolidated Backup User	Virtual Machine ➤ Configuration ➤ Disk Lease
	Virtual Machine ➤ Provisioning ➤ Allow Read-Only Disk Access, Allow Virtual Machine Download
	Virtual Machine ➤ State ➤ Create Snapshot, Remove Snapshot
Datastore Consumer	Datastore ➤ Allocate Space
Network Administrator	Network ➤ Assign Network

As you can see, vCenter Server is very specific about the privileges you can assign to roles. Because these privileges are specific, this can sometimes complicate the process of granting users the ability to perform seemingly simple tasks within vCenter Server. Let's review a couple of examples of how privileges, roles, and permissions combine in vCenter Server.

DELEGATING THE ABILITY TO CREATE VIRTUAL MACHINES AND INSTALL A GUEST OS

One common access control delegation in a virtual infrastructure is to give a group of users (for example, a provisioning or deployment team) the rights to create VMs. After just browsing through the list of available privileges, it might seem simple to accomplish this. It is, however, more complex than meets the eye. Providing a user with the ability to create a VM involves assigning a combination of privileges at multiple levels throughout the vCenter Server inventory.

COMBINING PRIVILEGES, ROLES, AND PERMISSIONS IN VCENTER SERVER

So far, we've shown you all the pieces you need to know in order to structure vCenter Server to support your company's management and operational requirements. How these pieces fit together, though, can sometimes be more complex than you might expect. In the next few paragraphs, we will walk you through an example.

Here's the scenario: Within your IT department, one group handles building all Windows servers. Once the servers are built, operational control of the servers is handed off to a separate group. Now that you have virtualized your datacenter, this same separation of duties needs to be re-created within vCenter Server. Sounds simple, right? You just need to configure vCenter Server so that this group has the ability to create VMs. This group is represented within Active Directory with a group object (this Active Directory group is named IT-Provisioning), and you'd like to leverage the Active Directory group membership to control who is granted these permissions within vCenter Server.

In the following steps, we've deliberately kept some of the items at a high level. For example, we don't go into how to create a role or how to assign that role to an inventory object as a permission because those tasks are covered elsewhere in this chapter.

Perform the following steps to allow a Windows-based group to create VMs:

1. Use the vSphere Web Client to connect to a vCenter Server instance. Log in with a user account that has been assigned the Administrator role within vCenter Server.

2. On the Home screen, click on the Roles icon.

3. Create a new role called **VMCreator**.

4. Assign the following privileges to the VMCreator role:

   Datastore ➤ Allocate Space

   Virtual Machine ➤ Inventory ➤ Create New

   Virtual Machine ➤ Configuration ➤ Add New Disk

   Virtual Machine ➤ Configuration ➤ Add Existing Disk

Virtual Machine ➤ Configuration ➤ Raw Device

Resource ➤ Assign Virtual Machine To Resource Pool

These permissions allow the VMCreator role to only create new VMs, not clone existing VMs or deploy from templates. Those actions would require additional privileges. For example, to allow this role to create new VMs from existing VMs, you would add the following privileges to the VMCreator role:

Virtual Machine ➤ Inventory ➤ Create From Existing

Virtual Machine ➤ Provisioning ➤ Clone Virtual Machine

Virtual Machine ➤ Provisioning ➤ Customize

5. Add a permission on a folder, datacenter, cluster, or host for the Windows-based group (IT-Provisioning in our example) with the VMCreator role.

   If you don't assign the role to a datacenter object, then you'll need to assign it separately to a folder in the VMs And Templates view. Otherwise, you'll run into an error when trying to create the VM.

   Similarly, if you don't assign the role to the datacenter object, then the group won't have permission on any datastore objects. Datastore objects are children of the datacenter object, so permissions applied to a datacenter object will, by default, propagate to the datastores. Without permissions on at least one datastore object (either via propagation or via direct assignment), you'll end up unable to create a new VM because you can't choose a datastore in which to store the VM.

6. If you want or need the Windows-based group to see other objects within the vCenter Server hierarchy, then assign the group the Read-Only role on the applicable objects.

   For example, if the group should see all objects within the datacenter, add the Read-Only role on the datacenter object.

At this point, the privileges for creating a VM are complete; however, the IT-Provisioning group does not have the rights to mount a CD/DVD image and therefore cannot install a guest OS. Therefore, more permissions are required to allow the IT-Provisioning group to not only create the VMs and put them in the right place within vCenter Server but also to install the guest OS within those VMs.

Perform the following steps to allow the Windows-based IT-Provisioning group to install a guest OS from a CD/DVD image file:

1. Use the vSphere Web Client to connect to a vCenter Server instance. Log in with a user account that has been assigned the Administrator role within vCenter Server.

2. On the Home screen, click the Roles icon.

3. Create a new role named **GOS-Installers**.

4. Assign the following privileges to the GOS-Installers role:

Datastore ➤ Browse Datastore

Virtual Machine ➤ Configuration

Virtual Machine ➤ Interaction

5. Assign the desired Windows-based group (IT-Provisioning in our example) the GOS-Installers role on the datacenter, folder, cluster, or host, as applicable.

Keep in mind that you can't have the same user or group with two different roles on the same object.

As you can see, the seemingly simple task of creating a VM actually involves a couple of different roles and a number of permissions. This is only a single example; there are obviously an almost infinite number of other configurations where you can create roles and assign permissions to the various objects within ESXi and vCenter Server.

---

vCenter Server Permissions Interaction

In organizations both large and small, users often belong to multiple groups, and those groups are assigned different levels of permissions on different objects. Let's look at the effects of multiple group memberships and permission assignments in the virtual infrastructure.

In one scenario, let's look at the effective permissions when a user belongs to multiple groups with different permissions on objects at different levels in the inventory. In this example, a user named Rick Avsom is a member of the Res_Pool_Admins and VM_Auditors Windows groups. The Res_Pool_Admins group is assigned membership in the Resource Pool Admins vCenter Server role, and the permission is set at the Production resource pool. The VM_Auditors group is assigned membership in the Read-Only vCenter Server role, and the permission is set at the Win2008-02 VM. The Win2008-02 VM resides within the Production resource pool.

When the user is logged on to the vCenter Server computer as Rick Avsom, the inventory reflects only the objects available to him through his permissions. Based on the permission assignment described, Rick Avsom will be able to manage the Production resource pool and will have full privileges over the Win2008-01 VM to which the Resource Pool Admin privileges are propagating. However, Rick Avsom cannot manage the Win2008-02 VM, for which he is limited to Read-Only privileges. Thus, users in multiple groups with conflicting permissions on objects lower in the inventory are granted only the permissions configured directly on the object.

Another common scenario involves the effective permissions when a user belongs to multiple groups with different permissions on the same objects. In this example, a user named Sue Rindlee is a member of the VM_Admins and VM_Auditors Windows groups. The VM_Admins group has been assigned membership in the Virtual Machine Power User vCenter Server role, and the VM_Auditors group is assigned membership in the Read-Only vCenter Server role. Both of these roles have been assigned permissions on the Production resource pool.

When the user is logged on to the vCenter Server computer as Sue Rindlee, the inventory reflects only the objects available to her through her permissions. Based on the permission assignment described, Sue Rindlee will be able to modify all of the VMs in the Production resource pool. This validates that Sue's Virtual Machine Power User status through membership in the VM_Admin group prevails over the Read-Only status obtained through her membership in the VM_Auditors group.

In this scenario, the effective permission is a cumulative permission when a user belongs to multiple groups with different permissions on the same object. Even if Sue Rindlee belonged to a group assigned to the No Access vCenter Server role, her Virtual Machine Power User role would prevail. However, if Sue Rindlee's user account was added directly to a vCenter Server object and assigned the No Access role, then she would not have access to any of the objects to which that permission has propagated.

Even with a good understanding of permission propagation, you should always proceed with caution and maintain the principle of least privilege to ensure that no user has been extended privileges beyond those necessary as part of a job role.

When delegating authority, it is always better to err on the side of caution. Do not provide more permissions than are necessary for the job at hand. Just as in any other information systems environment, your access-control implementation is a living object that will consistently require consideration and revision. Manage your permissions carefully, be flexible, and expect that users and administrators alike are going to be curious and will push their access levels to the limits. Stay a step ahead, and always remember the principle of least privilege.

We'll conclude the discussion of vCenter Server security with a quick look at vCenter Server logging.

Examining vCenter Server Logging

As we mentioned in the section "Configuring ESXi Host Logging," logging is an important part of security, as well as an extremely useful tool in troubleshooting. You've seen how to handle logging for ESXi; now let's take a quick look at vCenter Server logging.

vCenter Server can forward its logs to a centralized VMware-based log server called vCenter Log Insight. However, this is a separate product and outside the scope of this book. The vSphere Web Client does provide a way to view the logs that vCenter Server generates. From the home screen of the vSphere Web Client, select Log Browser to examine the logs. Figure 8.13 shows this section of the vSphere Web Client.

This screen allows you to review the vCenter Server logs for additional information on tasks performed, actions requested, and configuration changes made.

From this screen, you can also search, filter, and export the system logs, a task we described earlier in Chapter 3.

In the next section of this chapter, we'll shift the focus to securing the third and final component of your vSphere environment: the VMs.

FIGURE 8.13
vCenter Server's logs are visible from within the Log Browser section of the vSphere Web Client.

Securing Virtual Machines

As with vCenter Server, any discussion of how to secure a VM is really a discussion of how to secure the guest OS within that VM. Entire books have been and are being written about how to secure Windows, Linux, Solaris, and the other guest OSes vSphere supports, so we won't attempt to cover that sort of material here. We will provide two recommendations around securing VMs. One of these is specific to the vSphere virtualized environment, whereas the other is broader and more general.

First, we want to call your attention to the vSphere network security policies.

Configuring Network Security Policies

vSphere provides some outstanding virtual networking functionality, particularly with the addition of the vSphere Distributed Switch and third-party distributed virtual switches. These virtual switches provide several different security-related policies you can set to help ensure that the security of your VMs is maintained. We discussed all these settings in Chapter 5, "Creating and Configuring Virtual Networks."

The key security-related network security policies you can set in the vSphere virtual networking environment are as follows:

◆ Promiscuous mode

◆ MAC address changes

◆ Forged transmits

VMware recommends keeping all of these policies set to Reject. If there is a valid business need for one of these features to be allowed, you can use per-port group settings to enable the appropriate feature only for the specific VM or machines that require such functionality. One example we've used before is a network-based intrusion detection/intrusion prevention system (IDS/IPS). Rather than allowing promiscuous mode—required for most IDS/IPS to work—on the entire vSwitch, create a separate port group just for that VM and allow promiscuous mode on that port group only.

When considering the security of your VMs, be sure to keep these network security policies in mind, and be sure that they are configured for the correct balance of functionality versus security.

Our next recommendation with regard to securing VMs is much more general but still a valid recommendation nevertheless.

Keeping VMs Patched

As with your ESXi hosts and your vCenter Server computer, it's imperative to keep the guest OSes in your VMs properly patched. Our experience has shown us that many security problems could have been avoided with a proactive patching strategy for the guest OSes in the VMs.

In vSphere 4.x, you could use vSphere Update Manager (then called vCenter Update Manager) to patch the guest OSes inside your VMs. From vSphere 5.0, this functionality has been removed, and vSphere Update Manager—covered in detail in Chapter 4—focuses on keeping your ESXi hosts patched and up-to-date. It's important, therefore, to deploy some sort of guest OS patching solution that will help you ensure that your guest OSes remain patched and current with all vendor-supplied security fixes and updates. In the next chapter, we'll delve into the process of creating and managing VMs.

The Bottom Line

Configure and control authentication to vSphere. Both ESXi and vCenter Server have authentication mechanisms, and both products can utilize local users and groups or users and groups defined in external directories. Authentication is a basic tenet of security; it's important to verify that users are who they claim to be. You can manage local users and groups on your ESXi hosts using either the traditional vSphere Client or the command-line interface (such as the vSphere Management Assistant). Both the Windows-based and the Linux-based virtual appliance versions of vCenter Server can leverage Active Directory, OpenLDAP, or local SSO accounts for authentication as well.

Master It You've asked an administrator on your team to create some accounts on an ESXi host. The administrator is uncomfortable with the command line and is having a problem figuring out how to create the users. Is there another way for this administrator to perform this task?

Manage roles and access controls. Both ESXi and vCenter Server possess a role-based access control system that combines users, groups, privileges, roles, and permissions. vSphere administrators can use this role-based access control system to define very granular permissions that define what users are allowed to do with the vSphere Client against an ESXi host or the vSphere Web Client against a vCenter Server instance. For example, vSphere administrators can limit users to specific actions on specific types of objects within the vSphere Client. vCenter Server ships with some sample roles that help provide an example of how you can use the role-based access control system.

Master It Describe the differences between a role, a privilege, and a permission in the ESXi/vCenter Server security model.

Control network access to services on ESXi hosts. ESXi provides a network firewall that you can use to control network access to services on your ESXi hosts. This firewall can control both inbound and outbound traffic, and you have the ability to further limit traffic to specific source IP addresses or subnets.

Master It Describe how you can use the ESXi firewall to limit traffic to a specific source IP address.

Integrate with Active Directory. All the major components of vSphere—the ESXi hosts and vCenter Server (both the Windows Server–based version and the Linux-based virtual appliance) as well as the vSphere Management Assistant—support integration into Microsoft Active Directory. This gives vSphere administrators the option of using Active Directory as their centralized directory service for all major components of vSphere 5.5.

Master It You've just installed a new ESXi host into your vSphere environment and you are trying to configure the host to enable integration with your Active Directory environment. For some reason, though, it doesn't seem to work. What could be the problem?

Chapter 9

Creating and Managing Virtual Machines

The VMware ESXi hosts are installed, vCenter Server is running, the networks are blinking, the SAN is carved, and the VMFS volumes are formatted… let the virtualization begin! With the virtual infrastructure in place, you as the administrator must shift your attention to deploying the virtual machines.

In this chapter, you will learn to

- ◆ Create a virtual machine
- ◆ Install a guest operating system
- ◆ Install VMware Tools
- ◆ Manage virtual machines
- ◆ Modify virtual machines

Understanding Virtual Machines

It is common for IT professionals to refer to a Windows or Linux system running on an ESXi host as a *virtual machine* (VM). Strictly speaking, this term is not 100 percent accurate. Just as a physical machine is a physical machine before the installation of an operating system, a VM is a VM before the installation of a guest operating system (the term "guest operating system" is used to denote an operating system instance installed into a VM). From an everyday usage perspective, though, you can go on calling the Windows or Linux system a VM. Any references you see to "guest operating system" (or "guest OS") are references to instances of Windows, Linux, or Solaris—or any other supported operating system—installed in a VM.

If a VM is not an instance of a guest OS running on a hypervisor, then what is a VM? The answer to that question depends on your perspective. Are you "inside" the VM, looking out? Or are you "outside" the VM, looking in?

Examining Virtual Machines from the Inside

From the perspective of software running inside a VM, a VM is really just a collection of virtual hardware pieces selected for the purpose of running a guest OS instance.

So, what kind of virtual hardware makes up a VM? By default, VMware ESXi presents the following fairly generic hardware to the VM:

◆ Phoenix BIOS

◆ Intel motherboard

◆ Intel PCI IDE controller

◆ IDE CD-ROM drive

◆ BusLogic parallel SCSI, LSI Logic parallel SCSI, or LSI Logic SAS controller

◆ AMD or Intel CPU, depending upon the physical hardware

◆ Intel E1000, Intel E1000e, or AMD PCnet NIC

◆ Standard VGA video adapter

VMware selected this generic hardware to provide the broadest level of compatibility across the entire supported guest OSes. As a result, it's possible to use commercial off-the-shelf drivers when installing a guest OS into a VM. Figure 9.1 shows a couple of examples of VMware vSphere providing virtual hardware that looks like standard physical hardware. Both the network adapter and the storage adapter—identified as an Intel(R) 82574L Gigabit Network Connection and an LSI SAS 3000 series adapter, respectively—have corresponding physical counterparts, and drivers for these devices are available in many modern guest OSes.

FIGURE 9.1
VMware ESXi provides both generic and virtualization-optimized hardware for VMs.

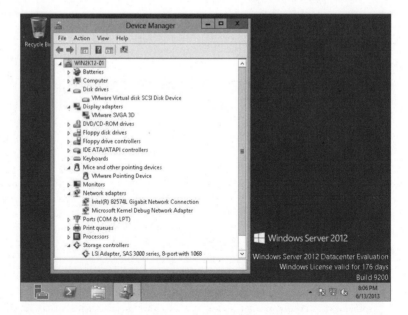

However, VMware vSphere may also present virtual hardware that is unique to the virtualized environment. Look back at the display adapter in Figure 9.1. There is no such physical

card as a VMware SVGA 3D display adapter; this is a device that is unique to the virtualized environment. These virtualization-optimized devices, also known as paravirtualized devices, are designed to operate efficiently within the virtualized environment created by the vSphere hypervisor. Because these devices have no corresponding physical counterpart, guest OS–specific drivers have to be provided. VMware Tools, described later in this chapter in the section titled "Installing VMware Tools," satisfies this function and provides virtualization-optimized drivers to run these devices.

A physical machine might have a certain amount of memory installed, a certain number of network adapters, or a particular number of disk devices, and the same goes for a VM. A VM can include the following types and numbers of virtual hardware devices:

- Processors: Between 1 and 64 processors with vSphere Virtual SMP (the number of processors depends on your vSphere licenses).

- Memory: Maximum of 1 TB of RAM.

- SCSI controller: Maximum of 4 SCSI controllers with 15 devices per controller for a total of 60 SCSI devices per VM; it's possible to boot only from 1 of the first 8.

- SATA controller: Maximum of 4 SATA controllers with 30 devices per controller for a total of 120 SATA devices per VM. Devices can include virtual hard drives or virtual CD/DVD drives.

- Network adapter: Maximum of 10 network adapters.

- Parallel port: Maximum of 3 parallel ports.

- Serial port: Maximum of 4 serial ports.

- Floppy drive: Maximum of 2 floppy disk drives on a single floppy disk controller.

- A single USB controller with up to 20 USB devices connected.

- Keyboard, video card, and mouse.

Hard drives are not included in the previous list because VM hard drives are generally added as SCSI devices. With up to 4 SCSI controllers and 15 SCSI devices per controller, it is possible to attach 60 hard drives to a VM. New in vSphere 5.5, virtual hard drives can now be added as SATA devices as well. Each VM can have a maximum of 4 SATA controllers with 30 devices per controller for a total of 120 possible virtual hard drives. If you are using IDE hard drives, then the VM is subject to the limit of 4 IDE devices per VM, as mentioned previously.

SIZE LIMITS FOR VIRTUAL HARD DRIVES

The maximum size for any virtual hard drive presented to a VM has been raised to 62 TB, up from just shy of 2 TB in previous versions. That's a lot of storage for just one VM and a welcome change for organizations looking to virtualize large-scale business-critical applications.

There's another perspective on VMs besides what the guest OS instance sees. There's also the external perspective—what does the hypervisor see?

Examining Virtual Machines from the Outside

To better understand what a VM is, you must consider more than just how a VM appears from the perspective of the guest OS instance (for example, from the "inside"), as we've just done. You must also consider how a VM appears from the "outside." In other words, you must consider how the VM appears to the ESXi host running the VM.

From the perspective of an ESXi host, a VM consists of several types of files stored on a supported storage device. The two most common files that compose a VM are the configuration file and the virtual hard disk file. The configuration file—hereafter referred to as the VMX file—is a plain-text file identified by a .vmx filename extension, and it functions as the structural definition of the VM. The VMX file defines the virtual hardware that resides in the VM. The number of processors, the amount of RAM, the number of network adapters, the associated MAC addresses, the networks to which the network adapters connect, and the number, names, and locations of all virtual hard drives are stored in the configuration file.

Listing 9.1 shows a sample VMX file for a VM named win2k12-01.

LISTING 9.1:   Example virtual machine configuration (VMX) file

```
.encoding = "UTF-8"
config.version = "8"
virtualHW.version = "10"
nvram = "Win2k12-01.nvram"
pciBridge0.present = "TRUE"
svga.present = "TRUE"
pciBridge4.present = "TRUE"
pciBridge4.virtualDev = "pcieRootPort"
pciBridge4.functions = "8"
pciBridge5.present = "TRUE"
pciBridge5.virtualDev = "pcieRootPort"
pciBridge5.functions = "8"
pciBridge6.present = "TRUE"
pciBridge6.virtualDev = "pcieRootPort"
pciBridge6.functions = "8"
pciBridge7.present = "TRUE"
pciBridge7.virtualDev = "pcieRootPort"
pciBridge7.functions = "8"
vmci0.present = "TRUE"
hpet0.present = "TRUE"
displayName = "Win2k12-01"
extendedConfigFile = "Win2k12-01.vmxf"
virtualHW.productCompatibility = "hosted"
scsi0.present = "TRUE"
disk.EnableUUID = "TRUE"
ide1:0.present = "TRUE"
ethernet0.present = "TRUE"
guestOS = "windows8srv-64"
memSize = "3072"
```

```
toolScripts.afterPowerOn = "TRUE"
toolScripts.afterResume = "TRUE"
toolScripts.beforeSuspend = "TRUE"
toolScripts.beforePowerOff = "TRUE"
uuid.bios = "42 0b c8 94 5e 80 53 23-93 c3 a1 83 e7 eb 3a 3c"
vc.uuid = "50 0b cd 35 8d 65 b5 e8-fa 91 9d 71 1e 4c 96 4b"
scsi0.virtualDev = "lsisas1068"
ide1:0.deviceType = "cdrom-image"
ide1:0.fileName = "/vmfs/volumes/51b386f8-2e41c1dd-cd3f-0050569d341f/9200.16384
.WIN8_RTM.120725-1247_X64FRE_SERVER_EVAL_EN-US-HRM_SSS_X64FREE_EN-US_DV5.ISO"
floppy0.startConnected = "FALSE"
floppy0.clientDevice = "TRUE"
floppy0.fileName = "vmware-null-remote-floppy"
ethernet0.virtualDev = "e1000e"
ethernet0.networkName = "VLAN-25"
ethernet0.addressType = "vpx"
ethernet0.generatedAddress = "00:50:56:8b:7f:44"
scsi0:0.present = "TRUE"
scsi0:0.deviceType = "scsi-hardDisk"
scsi0:0.fileName = "Win2k12-01.vmdk"
scsi0.pciSlotNumber = "160"
ethernet0.pciSlotNumber = "192"
vmci0.id = "-404014532"
vmci0.pciSlotNumber = "32"
uuid.location = "56 4d 63 d4 3c 1a 3b 36-b6 bf e6 a8 32 ce 3e 4e"
cleanShutdown = "FALSE"
replay.supported = "FALSE"
sched.swap.derivedName = "/vmfs/volumes/51b386f8-2e41c1dd-cd3f-0050569d341f/Win2
k12-01/Win2k12-01-9dff3075.vswp"
replay.filename = ""
scsi0:0.redo = ""
pciBridge0.pciSlotNumber = "17"
pciBridge4.pciSlotNumber = "21"
pciBridge5.pciSlotNumber = "22"
pciBridge6.pciSlotNumber = "23"
pciBridge7.pciSlotNumber = "24"
scsi0.sasWWID = "50 05 05 64 5e 80 53 20"
vm.genid = "4785438942692035628"
vm.genidX = "-5102819482874211651"
tools.remindInstall = "FALSE"
vmotion.checkpointFBSize = "4194304"
softPowerOff = "FALSE"
ide1:0.startConnected = "TRUE"
tools.syncTime = "FALSE"
unity.wasCapable = "TRUE"
toolsInstallManager.lastInstallError = "0"
toolsInstallManager.updateCounter = "1"
```

Reading through the `win2k12-01.vmx` file, you can determine the following facts about this VM:

- From the `guestOS` line, you can see that the VM is configured for a guest OS referred to as `"windows8srv-64"`; this corresponds to Windows Server 2012 64-bit.

- Based on the `memsize` line, you know the VM is configured for 3 GB of RAM.

- The `scsi0:0.fileName` line tells you the VM's hard drive is located in the file Win2k12-01.vmdk.

- The VM has a floppy drive configured, based on the presence of the `floppy0` lines, but it does not start connected (see `floppy0.startConnected`).

- The VM has a single network adapter configured to the VLAN-25 port group, based on the `ethernet0` lines.

- Based on the `ethernet0.generatedAddress` line, the VM's single network adapter has an automatically generated MAC address of 00:50:56:8b:7f:44.

While the VMX file is important, it is only the structural definition of the virtual hardware that composes the VM. It does not store any actual data from the guest OS instance running inside the VM. A separate type of file, the virtual hard disk file, performs that role.

The virtual hard disk file, identified by a `.vmdk` filename extension and hereafter referred to as the VMDK file, holds the actual data stored by a VM. Each VMDK file represents a hard drive. For a VM running Windows, the first VMDK file would typically be the storage location for the C: drive. For a Linux system, it would typically be the storage location for the root, boot, and a few other partitions. Additional VMDK files can be added to provide additional storage locations for the VM, and each VMDK file would appear as a physical hard drive to the VM.

While we refer to a virtual hard disk file as "a VMDK file," in reality there are two different files that compose a virtual hard disk. Both of them use the `.vmdk` filename extension, but each performs a very different role. One of these files is the VMDK header file, and the other is the VMDK flat file. There's a good reason why we—and others in the virtualization space—refer to a virtual hard disk file as "a VMDK file," though, and Figure 9.2 helps illustrate why.

FIGURE 9.2
The file browser in the vSphere Web Client shows only a single VMDK file.

Looking closely at Figure 9.2, you'll see only a single VMDK file listed. In actuality, though, there are two files, but to see them you must go to a command-line interface. From there, as shown in Figure 9.3, you'll see the two different VMDK files: the VMDK header (the smaller of the two) and the VMDK flat file (the larger of the two and the one that has -flat in the filename).

FIGURE 9.3
There are actually two different VMDK files for every virtual hard disk in a VM, even though the vSphere Web Client shows only a single file.

Of these two files, the VMDK header file is a plain-text file and is human-readable; the VMDK flat file is a binary file and is not human-readable. The VMDK header file contains only configuration information and pointers to the flat file; the VMDK flat file contains the actual data for the virtual hard disk. Naturally, this means that the VMDK header file is typically very small, while the VMDK flat file could be as large as the configured virtual hard disk in the VMX. So, a 40 GB virtual hard disk could mean a 40 GB VMDK flat file, depending on other configuration settings you'll see later in this chapter.

Listing 9.2 shows the contents of a sample VMDK header file.

LISTING 9.2:   Example VMDK header file

```
# Disk DescriptorFile
version=1
encoding="UTF-8"
CID=1c071021
parentCID=ffffffff
isNativeSnapshot="no"
createType="vmfs"

# Extent description
RW 83886080 VMFS "Win2k12-01-flat.vmdk"

# The Disk Data Base
#DDB
```

```
ddb.adapterType = "lsilogic"
ddb.geometry.cylinders = "5221"
ddb.geometry.heads = "255"
ddb.geometry.sectors = "63"
ddb.longContentID = "328b8afc206187816c4a76061c071021"
ddb.thinProvisioned = "1"
ddb.toolsVersion = "9314"
ddb.uuid = "60 00 C2 94 29 04 46 c9-4c 7f 86 94 c1 ea 41 60"
ddb.virtualHWVersion = "4"
```

There are several other types of files that make up a VM. For example, when the VM is running there will most likely be a VSWP file, which is a VMkernel swap file. You'll learn more about VMkernel swap files in Chapter 11, "Managing Resource Allocation." There will also be an NVRAM file, which stores the VM's BIOS settings.

Now that you have a feel for what makes up a VM, let's get started creating some VMs.

Creating a Virtual Machine

Creating VMs is a core part of using VMware vSphere, and VMware has made the process as easy and straightforward as possible. Let's walk through the process, and we will explain the steps along the way.

---

vSphere Web Client vs. vSphere Client

VMware has decided to move away from the full thick vSphere Client in favor of the multi-platform compatible vSphere Web Client. New features added into vSphere 5.1 and later, including vSphere 5.5, are available only in the vSphere Web Client. Although you can use the vSphere Client to create virtual machines, we recommend that you use the vSphere Web Client whenever possible.

Perform the following steps to create a VM:

1. If it's not already running, launch the vSphere Web Client, and connect to a vCenter Server instance. If a vCenter Server instance is not available, launch the vSphere Client and connect directly to an ESXi host.

2. In the inventory tree, right-click the name of a cluster, a resource pool, or an individual ESXi host, and select the New Virtual Machine option, as shown in Figure 9.4.

FIGURE 9.4
You can launch the New Virtual Machine Wizard from the context menu of an ESXi cluster or an individual ESXi host.

3. When the New Virtual Machine Wizard opens, select Create A New Virtual Machine, shown in Figure 9.5, and then click Next.

FIGURE 9.5
Options for creating a new virtual machine when using the vSphere Web Client.

4. Type a name for the VM, select a location in the inventory where the VM should reside, and click Next.

5. If you selected a cluster without vSphere DRS enabled or you are running vSphere DRS in manual mode, you'll need to select a specific host within the cluster on which to create the VM, as shown in Figure 9.6. Select an ESXi host from the list and then click Next.

LOGICAL INVENTORY AND PHYSICAL INVENTORY

The inventory location you select when you create a new VM, as shown in Figure 9.6, is a logical location. This inventory location does not correspond to the server on which that VM will run or the datastore on which that VM will be stored. This logical inventory displays in the vSphere Web Client when you select VMs And Templates as the inventory view.

FIGURE 9.6
The logical folder structure selected here does not correspond to where the VM files (for example, VMX and VMDK) are located on the selected datastore.

6. Select a datastore where the VM files will be located.

As you can see in Figure 9.7, the vSphere Web Client shows a fair amount of information about the datastores (size, provisioned space, free space, type of datastore). However, the vSphere Web Client doesn't show information such as IOPS capacity or other performance statistics. In Chapter 6, "Creating and Configuring Storage Devices," we discussed storage service levels, which allow you to create VM storage policies based on storage attributes provided to vCenter Server by the storage vendor (as well as user-defined storage attributes created and assigned by the vSphere administrator). In Figure 9.7, you can see the Storage Service Level drop-down list, which lists the currently defined storage service levels. If no service levels are defined or if storage service levels are not enabled, this drop-down list will be disabled.

When you select a storage service level, the datastore listing will separate into two groups: compatible and incompatible. Compatible datastores are datastores whose attributes satisfy the storage service level; incompatible datastores are datastores whose attributes do not meet the criteria specified in the storage service level. Figure 9.8 shows a storage service level selected and a compatible datastore selected for this VM's storage.

FIGURE 9.7
You can use storage service levels to help automate VM storage placement decisions when you create a new VM.

FIGURE 9.8
When using VM storage policies, select a compatible datastore to ensure that the VM's storage needs are properly satisfied.

For more information on VM storage policies, refer to Chapter 6.

After you select a datastore, click Next.

7. Select a VMware VM version. vSphere 5.5 introduces a new VM hardware version, version 10. As with earlier versions of vSphere, previous VM hardware versions are also supported. If the VM you are creating will be shared with ESXi hosts running both version 5.1 and version 5.5, then choose ESXi 5.1 and later (VM version 9). If the VM will be used only with vSphere 5.5, then choose ESXi 5.5 and later (VM version 10). Click Next.

RUNNING VMs FROM PREVIOUS VERSIONS OF ESXi

Unlike previous major versions of ESX/ESXi, version 5.5 allows you to run VMs created in earlier versions of ESXi without any sort of upgrade process. Some readers may recall that the upgrade from ESX 2.*x* to ESX 3.*x*, for example, required a "DMotion" upgrade process or significant downtime for the VMs.

This is not to say that there won't be any downtime for VMs when upgrading from earlier versions to vSphere 5.5, just that the downtime isn't required to occur during the upgrade of the hosts themselves. Instead, the tasks that do require VM downtime—upgrading VMware Tools and upgrading the virtual hardware from version 7 or version 8 to version 10—can be scheduled and performed at a later date.

vSphere supports a Default VM Compatibility level that can be configured at either the datacenter, cluster, or host level. With the Default VM Compatibility setting, you define a default value for the virtual machine version for newly created virtual machines. By setting Default VM Compatibility at a high level within your hierarchy, such as at the cluster level, you can be sure that newly deployed virtual machines will have the correct VM version.

Only the newest VM version, version 11, supports the latest features found in vSphere. If your environment is running only ESXi 5.5, you should consider setting Default VM Compatibility to ESXi 5.5 or later in order to take advantage of all of the new virtual machine features found in vSphere 5.5.

---

8. Select the drop-down box that corresponds to the operating system vendor, select the correct operating system version, and then click Next. As you'll see shortly, this helps the vSphere Web Client provide recommendations for certain values later in the wizard.

9. At this point, you are taken to the Customize Hardware screen where you can customize the virtual hardware that will be presented to your virtual machine. To start, we'll choose how many virtual CPUs will be presented to our virtual machine. Select the number of virtual CPUs by using the drop-down box next to CPU.

You can select between 1 and 64 virtual CPU sockets, depending on your vSphere license. Additionally, you can choose the number of cores per virtual CPU socket. The total number of cores supported per VM with VM hardware version 10 is 64. The number of cores available per virtual CPU socket will change based on the number of virtual CPU sockets selected. For specific information about how many virtual cores are available per virtual CPU socket, refer to the following location: www.vmware.com/support/pubs/.

Keep in mind that the operating system you will install into this VM must support the selected number of virtual CPUs. Also keep in mind that more virtual CPUs doesn't necessarily translate into better performance, and in some cases larger values may negatively impact performance.

When you finish configuring virtual CPUs, click Next to continue.

10. Configure the VM with the determined amount of RAM by typing in the desired memory value, as shown in Figure 9.9. The default memory sizing is listed in megabytes (MB), so it may be easier to change it to gigabytes (GB) so that you do not need to know the precise number of megabytes.

FIGURE 9.9
Based on guest OS selection, the vSphere Web Client provides some basic guidelines on the amount of memory you should configure for the VM.

As shown in Figure 9.9, the vSphere Web Client displays recommendations about the minimum and recommended amounts of RAM based on the earlier selection of operating system and version. This is one of the reasons the selection of the correct guest OS is important when creating a VM.

The amount of RAM configured on this page is the amount of RAM the guest OS reflects in its system properties, and it is the maximum amount that a guest OS will ever be able to use. Think of it as the virtual equivalent of the amount of physical RAM installed in a system. Just as a physical machine cannot use more memory than is physically installed in it, a VM cannot access more memory than it is configured to use.

When you've selected the amount of RAM you want allocated to the VM, click Next.

DO YOU KNOW WHERE YOUR MEMORY IS?

The setting on the Customize Hardware page is not a guarantee that physical memory will be used to achieve the configured value. As we discuss in later chapters, memory for a VM might be physical RAM, VMkernel swap file space, or some combination of the two.

---

11. Select the number of network adapters, the type of each network adapter, and the network to which each adapter will connect. Figure 9.10 shows a screen shot of configuring

virtual NICs, and Table 9.1 provides additional information about the different types of virtual NICs.

FIGURE 9.10
You can configure a VM with up to four network adapters, of the same or different types, that reside on the same or different networks as needed.

MORE INFORMATION ON VIRTUAL NIC ADAPTERS

VMware has detailed descriptions of the virtual NIC adapter types and the support requirements for each on its website at `http://kb.vmware.com/kb/1001805`.

TABLE 9.1:   Virtual NIC types in vSphere 5.5

VIRTUAL NIC TYPE	VM HARDWARE VERSIONS SUPPORTED	DESCRIPTION
E1000	4, 7, 8, 9, 10	This virtual NIC emulates the Intel 82545EM Gigabit Ethernet NIC. The driver for this NIC is found in many modern guest OSes, but some older guest OSes might not have a driver.
E1000e	8, 9, 10	This virtual NIC emulates an Intel 82574L Gigabit Ethernet NIC. This driver is a newer version than the Intel 82545EM NIC found in the E1000 driver. This NIC is the default NIC for Windows Server 2012 and Windows 8 guests.

TABLE 9.1:   Virtual NIC types in vSphere 5.5   *(CONTINUED)*

VIRTUAL NIC TYPE	VM HARDWARE VERSIONS SUPPORTED	DESCRIPTION
Flexible	4, 7, 8, 9, 10	This virtual NIC identifies itself as a Vlance adapter, an emulated form of the AMD 79C970 PCnet32 10 Mbps NIC. Drivers for this NIC are available in most 32-bit guest OSes. Once VMware Tools is installed (we'll discuss VMware Tools later in this chapter), this virtual NIC changes over to the higher-performance VMXNET adapter. The Flexible virtual NIC type is available for use only with certain 32-bit guest OSes. For example, you can't select the Flexible virtual NIC type for VMs running 32-bit versions of Windows Server 2008, but it is an option for 32-bit versions of Windows Server 2003.
VMXNET 2 (Enhanced)	4, 7, 8, 9, 10	This virtual NIC type is based on the VMXNET adapter but provides additional high-performance features like jumbo frames and hardware offload. It's supported only for a limited set of guest OSes.
VMXNET 3	7, 8, 9, 10	The VMXNET 3 virtual NIC type is the latest version of a paravirtualized driver designed for performance. It offers all the features of VMXNET 2 plus additional features like multiqueue support, IPv6 offloads, and MSI/MSI-X interrupt delivery. It's supported only for VM hardware version 7 or later and for a limited set of guest OSes.

12. Select New SCSI Controller to expand the selection area, and then click the drop-down box to choose the appropriate SCSI adapter for the operating system selected on the Select A Guest OS page of the Create New Virtual Machine Wizard.

The correct default driver should already be selected based on the previously selected operating system. For example, the LSI Logic parallel adapter is selected automatically when Windows Server 2003 is selected as the guest OS, but the LSI Logic SAS adapter is selected when Windows Server 2008 is chosen as the guest OS. We provided some additional details on the different virtual SCSI adapters in Chapter 6.

VIRTUAL MACHINE SCSI CONTROLLERS

Windows 2000 has built-in support for the BusLogic parallel SCSI controller, while Windows Server 2003 and later operating systems have built-in support for the LSI Logic parallel SCSI controller. Additionally, Windows Server 2008 has support for the LSI Logic SAS controller. Windows XP doesn't have built-in support for any of these, requiring a driver disk during installation. Choosing the wrong controller will result in an error during the operating system installation. The error states that hard drives cannot be found. Choosing the wrong SCSI controller during a physical-to-virtual (P2V) operation will result in a "blue screen error" for a Windows guest OS inside the VM, and the Windows installation will fail to boot.

13. A virtual hard disk is configured automatically when you create a new virtual machine. If you need to add a new virtual hard disk, select the New Device drop-down box at the bottom of the screen, as shown in Figure 9.11.

FIGURE 9.11
A virtual disk is configured auto-matically when you create a new virtual machine. You can also add additional virtual disks by using the New device option.

You are presented with the following options for adding a virtual disk to your VM.

♦ The New Hard Disk option allows the user to create a new virtual disk (a VMDK file) that will house the guest OS's files and data. Since a virtual hard disk is already added by default when a new virtual machine is created, using this option is useful if the virtual machine needs two disks (such as when an operating system drive and a data drive are required).

♦ The Existing Hard Disk option allows a VM to be created using a virtual disk that is already configured with a guest OS or other data and that resides in an available datastore.

♦ The RDM Disk option allows a VM to have raw SAN LUN access. Raw device map-pings (RDMs) are discussed in a bit more detail in Chapter 6.

Since a virtual hard disk is already configured by default, we'll use it to install our guest OS and we won't need to add another virtual disk.

ADDING EXISTING DISKS

The existing virtual disk doesn't have to contain an instance of the guest OS; it can contain data that perhaps will serve as a secondary drive inside the VM. The ability to add existing disks with data makes virtual hard drives extremely portable, generally allowing users to move them from VM to VM without repercussions. You will obviously need to address any guest OS–specific issues such as partitions, file system type, or permissions.

14. When either adding a new virtual hard disk or using the one provided by default, options are available for the creation of the new virtual disk. Select New Hard Disk to expand the selection area and access these options, as shown in Figure 9.12. First, configure the desired disk size for the VM hard drive. The maximum size will be determined by the format of the datastore on which the virtual disk is stored. Next, select the appropriate Disk Provisioning option:

FIGURE 9.12
vSphere 5.5 offers a
number of different
Disk Provisioning
options when you're
creating new vir-
tual disks.

- To create a virtual disk with all space allocated at creation but not pre-zeroed, select Thick provision lazy zeroed. In this case, the VMDK flat file will be the same size as the specified virtual disk size. A 40 GB virtual disk means a 40 GB VMDK flat file.

- To create a virtual disk with all space allocated at creation and pre-zeroed, select Thick provision eager zeroed. This option is required in order to support vSphere Fault Tolerance. This option also means a "full-size" VMDK flat file that is the same size as the size of the virtual hard disk.

- To create a virtual disk with space allocated on demand, select the Thin provision option. In this case, the VMDK flat file will grow depending on the amount of data actually stored in it, up to the maximum size specified for the virtual hard disk.

Depending on your storage platform, storage type, and storage vendor's support for vSphere's storage integration technologies like VAAI or VASA, some of these options might be grayed out. For example, an NFS datastore that does not support the VAAIv2 extensions will have these options grayed out, as only thin provisioned VMDKs are supported. (VAAI and VASA are discussed in greater detail in Chapter 6.)

There are two options for the location of the new virtual disk. These options are available by selecting the drop-down box next to the Location field. Keep in mind that these options control physical location, not logical location; they will directly affect the datastore and/or directory where files are stored for use by the hypervisor.

- The option Store With The Virtual Machine will place the file in the same subdirectory as the configuration file and the rest of the VM files. This is the most commonly selected option and makes managing the VM files easier.

- The option Browse allows you to browse the available datastores and store the VM file separately from the rest of the files. You'd typically select this option when adding new virtual hard disks to a VM or when you need to separate the operating system virtual disk from a data virtual disk.

You can configure other options, such as shares, limits, or Virtual Flash sizing (discussed in greater detail in Chapter 6) for the virtual machine you are creating, if required.

15. The Virtual Device Node option lets you specify the SCSI node, IDE controller, or SATA controller to which the virtual disk is connected. The Disk Mode option allows you to configure a virtual disk in Independent mode, as shown in Figure 9.13. The disk mode is not normally altered, so you can typically accept the default values provided, as shown in Figure 9.13.

FIGURE 9.13
You can configure the virtual disk on a number of different SCSI adapters and SCSI IDs, and you can configure it as an independent disk.

- The Virtual Device Node drop-down box reflects the 15 different SCSI nodes available on each of the four SCSI adapters a VM supports. When you're using an IDE controller, this drop-down list shows the four different IDE nodes that are available. When you're using a SATA controller, this drop-down shows 30 different SATA nodes that are available.

- By not selecting the Independent mode option, you ensure that the virtual disk remains in the default state that allows VM snapshots to be created. If you select the Independent check box, you can configure the virtual disk as a persistent disk, in which changes are written immediately and permanently to the disk, or as a nonpersistent disk, which discards all changes when the VM is turned off.

When you are done adding or modifying the configuration of the virtual machine, select Next to continue.

16. Complete a final review of the VM configuration. If anything is incorrect, go back and make changes. As you can see in Figure 9.14, the steps on the left side of the wizard are links that allow you to jump directly to an earlier point in the wizard and make changes.

FIGURE 9.14
Reviewing the
configuration of
the New Virtual
Machine Wizard
ensures the correct
settings for the VM
and prevents mis-
takes that require
deleting and
re-creating the VM.

When everything is correct, click Finish.

As you can see, the process for creating a VM is pretty straightforward. What's not so straightforward, though, are some of the values that should be used when creating new VMs. What are the best values to use?

Choosing Values for Your New Virtual Machine

Choosing the right values to use for the number of virtual CPUs, the amount of memory, or the number or types of virtual NICs when creating your new VM can be difficult. Fortunately, there's lots of documentation out there on CPU and RAM sizing as well as networking for VMs, so our only recommendation there will be to right-size the VMs based on your needs (see the sidebar "Provisioning Virtual Machines Is Not the Same as Provisioning Physical Machines" later in this chapter).

VIRTUAL MACHINE SIZING CAN HAVE AN IMPACT

Determining the right size for your VMs is a crucial part of your overall vSphere design, and it can impact a number of different areas. For more information on how right-sizing VMs impacts other areas of your vSphere design, refer to *VMware vSphere Design* by Forbes Guthrie and Scott Lowe (Sybex, 2013).

For other areas besides these, the guidance isn't quite so clear. Out of all the options available during the creation of a new VM, four areas tend to consistently generate questions from both new and experienced users alike:

◆   How can I find out how to size my VMs?

◆   How should I handle naming my VMs?

◆ How big should I make the virtual disks?

◆ Does my virtual machine need high-end graphics?

Let's talk about each of these questions in a bit more detail.

SIZING VIRTUAL MACHINES

You might be hoping that we'll give you specific guidance here about how to size your virtual machines. We wish we could, but unfortunately virtual machine sizing differs greatly depending on the environment, the applications installed on the virtual machines, performance requirements, and many other factors. Instead, it's better to discuss a methodology you can use to understand the resource utilization requirements (CPU, memory, disk, and network) of your physical servers before re-deploying them as virtual machines.

Simply sizing your virtual machines to the same specifications used for physical servers can lead to oversizing (or undersizing) virtual machines unnecessarily. Both oversizing and undersizing a virtual machine can lead to performance problems not only for that virtual machine but potentially other virtual machines on the same ESXi host.

Instead, you can use a process called capacity planning to help you understand how to size your virtual machines. Capacity planning is a process where you learn over time how your current physical servers are utilized and then use that information to size your virtual machines. A typical capacity planning exercise takes place over a two-to-four-week period and uses tools to automatically monitor and report on the performance of physical servers. By monitoring your servers over time, such as over a 30-day period, you can capture normal business cycles such as end of month processing that you might otherwise miss if you monitor for only a short time.

Two of the most common tools used for capacity planning are actually free, though as you'll see, one of them is not available to everyone. Perhaps the most well known is a product by VMware called Capacity Planner. The other product, called Microsoft Assessment and Planning Toolkit, may not be as well known but it's still a powerful tool.

FREE, BUT NOT FOR EVERYONE

VMware Capacity Planner is a free product, but it is not available for everyone to use. Capacity Planner is available only to VMware or VMware's certified partners. If you're an end user of VMware's products, you cannot access Capacity Planner yourself.

Not already working with VMware or a partner? Luckily, you can usually work with your VMware representative to get access to Capacity Planner for servers in your environment.

Microsoft Assessment and Planning Toolkit is a free download on Microsoft's website and is available to everyone. You can download it from the following location:

www.microsoft.com/en-us/download/details.aspx?id=7826

Both tools produce similar results, such as average and maximum utilization values for CPU, memory, disk, network, and other more specific performance counters. Capacity Planner is very customizable, allowing you to add custom performance counters to monitor beyond the standard Windows or application counters. Microsoft Assessment and Planning Toolkit is less customizable, but it includes advanced reporting for Microsoft applications (like SQL Server or SharePoint Server) that are useful if you're looking to virtualize these applications.

The process for using these tools is also similar for both. After running the capacity planning analysis over time, you review the results to understand the actual utilization of your servers. These tools also allow you to produce reports that tell you how many ESXi hosts (or in the case of Microsoft Assessment and Planning Toolkit, Hyper-V hosts, though the results are applicable to ESXi as well) you'll need to support the environment. For example, if you monitor 70 total physical servers, the tools may tell you that, based on the actual utilization of each server, you need only seven total ESXi hosts to support those servers as virtual machines. Your results will vary depending on the actual utilization in your environment.

Capacity planning is such a useful exercise because it tells you the true utilization of your servers before you convert them to virtual machines. Let's say you have a physical server with two CPUs, each with eight cores and 64 GB of RAM, and that server runs Microsoft SQL Server 2012. You might think that because SQL Server is typically an important application, the server must be fully utilized. In reality, many times after a capacity planning exercise you may find that the server really utilizes only two CPU cores and 8 GB of RAM. When you virtualize that server, you can reduce the resources down to what the server actually uses and save resources for other virtual machines.

Whether you're just starting out on your virtualization journey or you're moving on to virtualizing more critical applications, capacity planning will provide valuable information that you can use to properly size your virtual machines. Without performing a capacity planning exercise, you are mostly just guessing at how many ESXi hosts you'll need to support the environment or how to properly size your virtual machines.

NAMING VIRTUAL MACHINES

Choosing the display name for a VM might seem like a trivial assignment, but you must ensure that an appropriate naming strategy is in place. We recommend making the display names of VMs match the hostnames configured in the guest OS being installed. For example, if the intention is to use the name Server1 in the guest OS, then the VM display name should match Server1. If you use spaces in the virtual display name—which is allowed—then using command-line tools to manage VMs becomes a bit tricky because you must quote out the spaces on the command line. In addition, because DNS hostnames cannot include spaces, using spaces in the VM name would create a disparity between the VM name and the guest OS hostname. Ultimately, this means you should avoid using spaces and special characters that are not allowed in standard DNS naming strategies to ensure similar names both inside and outside the VM. Aside from whatever policies might be in place from your organization, this is usually a matter of personal preference.

The display name assigned to a VM also becomes the name of the folder in the VMFS volume where the VM files will live. At the file level, the associated configuration (VMX) and virtual hard drive (VMDK) files will assume the name supplied in the display name text box during VM creation. Refer to Figure 9.15, where you can see that the user-supplied name of win2k12-02 is reused for both the folder name and the filenames for the VM.

FIGURE 9.15
The display name assigned to a VM is used in a variety of places.

SIZING VIRTUAL MACHINE HARD DISKS

The answer to the third question—how big to make the hard disks in your VM—is a bit more complicated. There are many different approaches, but some best practices facilitate the management, scalability, and backup of VMs. First and foremost, you should create VMs with multiple virtual disk files to separate the operating system from the custom user/application data. Separating the system files and the user/application data will make it easier to increase the number of data drives in the future and allow a more practical backup strategy. A system drive of 25 GB to 30 GB, for example, usually provides ample room for installation and continued growth of the operating system. The data drives across different VMs will vary in size because of underlying storage system capacity and functionality, the installed applications, the function of the system, and the number of users who connect to the computer. However, because the extra hard drives are not operating system data, it will be easier to adjust those drives when needed.

Keep in mind that additional virtual hard drives will pick up on the same naming scheme as the original virtual hard drive. For example, a VM named Server1 that has an original virtual hard disk file named win2k12-02.vmdk will name the new virtual hard disk file win2k12-02_1.vmdk. For each additional file, the last number will be incremented, making it easy to identify all virtual disk files related to a particular VM. Figure 9.16 shows a VM with two virtual hard disks so that you can see how vSphere handles the naming for additional virtual hard disks.

In the next chapter, "Using Templates and vApps," you'll revisit the process of creating VMs to see how to use templates to implement and maintain an optimal VM configuration that separates the system data from the user/application data. At this point, though, now that you've created a VM, you're ready to install the guest OS into the VM.

FIGURE 9.16
vSphere automatically appends a number to the filename for additional virtual hard disks.

Real World Scenario

PROVISIONING VIRTUAL MACHINES IS NOT THE SAME AS PROVISIONING PHYSICAL MACHINES

You need to approach provisioning VMs differently from the way you provisioned physical machines in the past. After all, didn't underutilized and overprovisioned servers lead you to use virtualization to consolidate your workloads?

In the physical world, you provision servers based on the maximum you think that server might ever need throughout its lifetime. Because the intended workload for a server might shift over that lifetime, you probably provision the physical server with more CPU resources and more RAM than it really needs.

In the virtual environment, though, VMs should be provisioned only with the resources they really need. Additional resources can be added later should the workload need them, sometimes with no downtime required.

In the event that you don't make this shift in thinking, you'll end up much like our client who had the same problem. During the early phases of the client's consolidation project, they provisioned VMs with the same level of resources given to physical machines. It wasn't until they ran out of resources in the virtual environment and had a far lower consolidation ratio than anticipated that we convinced them to change their provisioning practices. Once the provisioning practices were changed, the client was able to improve their consolidation ratio without negatively impacting the level of service they were able to provide. Right-sizing your VMs is a good thing!

VIRTUAL MACHINE GRAPHICS

Depending on what kind of virtual machines you're deploying in your environment, you may need to think about graphics performance. For backend systems, such as database systems or email platforms, the graphics performance of the virtual machine is not important and is not something you typically have to worry about. If you're deploying a virtual desktop infrastructure (VDI), however, the graphics performance and capabilities of the virtual machine are likely to be a key consideration.

For VDI solutions like VMware Horizon View, end users no longer run a full desktop or laptop but instead connect to their virtual desktop (running on vSphere) from a variety of end-point devices. These devices could be laptops, desktops, thin or zero clients, or even tablets and smartphones. The virtual desktop often acts as a complete desktop replacement for end users, so the desktop needs to perform as well as (or better than) the physical hardware that is being replaced.

In order to provide high-end graphics capabilities to virtual machines, vSphere 5.5 supports vSGA, or Virtual Shared Graphics Acceleration. This technology allows you to install graphics cards into your ESXi host and then offload the processing of 3D rendering to the physical graphics cards instead of the host CPUs. This offloading helps to reduce overall CPU utilization by allowing hardware that is purpose-built for rendering graphics to perform the processing.

Though the 3D rendering settings are configured in the settings of a virtual machine, they are intended only for use with VMware Horizon View. If you are using a VDI solution other than Horizon View, speak to the vendor to understand if 3D rendering on vSphere is supported.

Installing a Guest Operating System

A new VM is analogous to a physical computer with an empty hard drive. All the components are there but without an operating system. After creating the VM, you're ready to install a supported guest OS. The following OSes are some of the more commonly installed guest OSes supported by ESXi (this is not a comprehensive list):

- Windows 8 (32-bit and 64-bit)

- Windows 7 (32-bit and 64-bit)

- Windows Vista (32-bit and 64-bit)

- Windows Server 2012 (64-bit)

- Windows Server 2008 R2 (64-bit)

- Windows Server 2008 (32-bit and 64-bit)

- Windows Server 2003 (32-bit and 64-bit)

- Windows Small Business Server 2003

- Windows XP Professional (32-bit and 64-bit)

- Red Hat Enterprise Linux 3/4/5/6 (32-bit and 64-bit)

- CentOS 4/5 (32-bit and 64-bit)

- SUSE Linux Enterprise Server 8/9/10/11 (32-bit and 64-bit)

- Ubuntu Linux (32-bit and 64-bit)

- NetWare 5.1/6.*x*

◆ Sun Solaris 10 (32-bit and 64-bit)

◆ FreeBSD (32-bit and 64-bit)

VIRTUAL MAC SERVERS?

VMware vSphere 5.0 added support for some new guest OSes. Notably, vSphere 5 added support for Apple Mac OS X Server 10.5 and 10.6. This allows you to run Mac OS X Server VMs on your VMware ESXi hosts. However, it's critically important to note that this is supported only when running ESXi on specific models of the Apple Xserve servers.

Installing any of these supported guest OSes follows the same common order of steps for installation on a physical server, but the nuances and information provided during the install of each guest OS might vary greatly. Because of the differences involved in installing different guest OSes or different versions of a guest OS, we won't go into any detail on the actual guest OS installation process. We'll leave that to the guest OS vendor. Instead, we'll focus on guest OS installation tasks that are specific to a virtualized environment.

Working with Installation Media

One beneficial task in a virtual environment that isn't typically required in a virtual environment concerns guest OS installation media. In the physical world, administrators typically put the OS installation media in the physical server's optical drive, install the OS, and then are done with it. Well, in a virtual world, the process is similar, but here's the issue—where do you put the CD when the server is virtual? There are a couple of different ways to handle it. One way is quick and easy, and the second way takes a bit longer but pays off later.

VMs have a few different ways to access data stored on optical disks. VMs can access optical disks in one of three different ways (Figure 9.17 shows the Datastore ISO File option selected):

Client Device   This option allows an optical drive local to the computer running the vSphere Web Client to be mapped into the VM. For example, if you are using the vSphere Web Client on your corporate-issued HP laptop, you can simply insert a CD/DVD into your local optical drive and map that into the VM with this option. This is the quick-and-easy method that was referenced above.

Host Device   This option maps the ESXi host's optical drive into the VM. VMware administrators would have to insert the CD/DVD into the server's optical drive in order for the VM to have access to the disk.

Datastore ISO File   This last option maps an ISO image (see the sidebar "ISO Image Basics") into the VM. Although using an ISO image typically requires an additional step— creating the ISO image from the physical disk—more and more software is being distributed as an ISO image that can be leveraged directly from within your vSphere environment.

ISO IMAGE BASICS

An ISO image is an archive file of an optical disk. The name is derived from the International Organization for Standardization (ISO) 9660 file system standard used with CD-ROM media, and the ISO format is widely supported by many different software vendors. A variety of software applications can work with ISO images. In fact, most CD-burning software applications for Windows, Linux, and Mac OS X can create ISO images from existing physical disks or burn ISO images to a physical disk.

FIGURE 9.17
VMs can access optical disks physically located on the vSphere Client system, located on the ESXi host, or stored as an ISO image.

ISO images are the recommended way to install a guest OS because they are faster than using an actual optical drive and can be quickly mounted or dismounted with very little effort.

Before you can use an ISO image to install the guest OS, though, you must first put it in a location that ESXi can access. Generally, this means uploading it into a datastore accessible to your ESXi hosts.

Perform these steps to upload an ISO image into a datastore:

1. Use the vSphere Web Client to connect to a vCenter Server instance or launch the vSphere Client to connect to an individual ESXi host.

2. From the vSphere Web Client menu bar, select Storage.

3. Right-click the datastore to which you want to upload the ISO image and select Browse Files from the context menu.

4. Select the destination folder in the datastore where you want to store the ISO image. Use the Create A New Folder button (it looks like a folder with a green plus symbol) if you need to create a new folder in which to store the ISO image.

5. From the toolbar in the Files screen, click the Upload button (it looks like a disk with a green arrow pointing into the disk). From the dialog box that appears, select the ISO image as shown in Figure 9.18 and click Open.

6. The vSphere Web Client uploads the file into the selected folder in that datastore.

After the ISO image is uploaded to an available datastore, you're ready to actually install a guest OS using that ISO image.

FIGURE 9.18
Use the Upload button to upload ISO images for use when installing guest OSes.

Using the Installation Media

Once you have the installation media in place—by using the local CD-ROM drive on the computer where you are running the vSphere Web Client, by using the physical server's optical drive, or by creating and uploading an ISO image into a datastore—you're ready to actually use that installation media to install a guest OS into the VM.

Perform the following steps to install a guest OS using an ISO file on a shared datastore:

1. Use the vSphere Web Client to connect to a vCenter Server instance or use the vSphere Client to connect to an individual ESXi host where a VM has been created.

2. If you're not already in the Hosts And Clusters or VMs And Templates view, use the menu bar to select Home ➢ Hosts And Clusters or Home ➢ VMs And Templates.

3. In the inventory tree, right-click the new VM, and select the Edit Settings menu option. The Virtual Machine Properties window opens.

4. Expand the CD/DVD Drive 1 hardware option to expose the additional properties.

5. Change the drop-down box to Datastore ISO File, and select the Connect At Power On check box. If you fail to select the Connect At Power On check box, the VM will not boot from the selected ISO image.

6. Click the Browse button to browse a datastore for the ISO file of the guest OS.

7. Navigate through the available datastores until you find the ISO file of the guest OS to be installed. After you select the ISO file, the properties page is configured similar to the screen shot shown previously in Figure 9.17.

8. Right-click the virtual machine and select Power On from the menu. Alternatively, you can use the Actions drop-down option on the properties page of the virtual machine. The VM boots from the mounted ISO image and begins the installation of the guest OS.

9. Right-click the VM, and select the Open Console option. Alternatively, you can use the Open Console option from the properties page of the virtual machine.

10. Follow the on-screen instructions to complete the guest OS installation. These will vary depending on the specific guest OS you are installing; refer to the documentation for that guest OS for specific details regarding installation.

VIRTUAL MACHINE GUEST OSES

For a complete list of guest OSes and all respective information regarding installation notes and known issues, refer to the PDF available on the VMware website at www.vmware.com/pdf/GuestOS_guide.pdf (note that this URL is case sensitive).

Working in the Virtual Machine Console

Working within the VM console is like working at the console of a physical system. From here, you can do anything you need to do to the VM: you can access the VM's BIOS and modify settings, you can turn the power to the VM off (and back on again), and you can interact with the guest OS you are installing or have already installed into the VM. We'll describe most of these functions later in this chapter in the sections titled "Managing Virtual Machines" and "Modifying Virtual Machines," but there is one thing that we want to point out now.

The vSphere Web Client must have a way to know if the keystrokes and mouse clicks you're generating go to the VM or if they should be processed by the vSphere Web Client itself. To do this, it uses the concept of *focus*. When you click within a VM console, that VM will have the focus: All of the keystrokes and the mouse clicks will be directed to that VM. Until you have VMware Tools installed—a process we'll describe in the very next section, you'll have to manually tell the vSphere Web Client when you want to shift focus out of the VM. To do this, you use the vSphere Web Client's special keystroke: Ctrl+Alt. When you press Ctrl+Alt, the VM relinquishes control of the mouse and keyboard and returns it to the vSphere Web Client. Keep that in mind when you are trying to use your mouse and it won't travel beyond the confines of the VM console window. Just press Ctrl+Alt, and the VM will release control.

Once you've installed the guest OS, you should then install and configure VMware Tools. I discuss VMware Tools installation and configuration in the next section.

🌐 Real World Scenario

MICROSOFT LICENSING AND WINDOWS ACTIVATION FOR VIRTUAL MACHINES

As the virtualization market has matured, Microsoft has adjusted its licensing practices to reflect that market. In spite of those adjustments—or perhaps because of them—there is still confusion about the virtualization licensing available for the Windows Server operating system. Microsoft has simplified the licensing significantly in Windows Server 2012, reducing the number of versions of the operating system to license. The following list of licensing data is a combination of information from both Microsoft and VMware:

◆ Microsoft Windows Server licenses are attached to the physical machine, not to the VM. Specifically, the Windows Server 2012 license is attached to the CPUs of the physical server.

- A licensed copy of Windows Server 2012 Datacenter Edition entitles a user to install and run an unlimited number of virtual Windows instances on the physical server to which that license is assigned.

- A licensed copy of Windows Server 2012 Standard Edition grants the user the right to install and run up to two Windows instances per physical CPU on the physical server to which the license is assigned.

- Downgrade rights exist so that a physical server licensed with Windows Server 2012 Datacenter Edition can run unlimited VMs running either Datacenter Edition or Standard Edition. This also applies to running previous versions of Windows Server.

- vMotion, which moves a running VM to a new host, does not violate a Microsoft licensing agreement as long as the target ESXi host is licensed for the post-vMotion number of VMs and you maintain active Software Assurance on your Windows licenses. For example, if an ESXi host named ESXi01 with two physical CPUs has four running instances of Windows in VMs, a second ESXi host named ESXi02 with two physical CPUs has three running instances of Windows in VMs, and each of the physical systems has been assigned a Windows Server 2012 Standard Edition license, then it is within the licensing agreement to perform a vMotion move of one VM from ESXi01 to ESXi02. However, a vMotion move from ESXi02 to ESXi01 would violate the licensing agreement because ESXi01 is licensed to run only up to two virtual instances of Windows per CPU at a time.

Because Microsoft requires Windows Server licenses to be attached to physical hardware, many organizations are choosing to license their physical hardware with Windows Server 2012 Datacenter Edition. This gives the organization the ability to run an unlimited number of Windows Server instances on that hardware, and downgrade or previous version rights allow the organization to use the Standard, Enterprise, or Datacenter Edition of Windows Server 2008 or Standard or Datacenter Edition of Windows Server 2012.

Activation is another area requiring a bit of planning. If your licensing structure for a Windows Server guest OS does not fall under the umbrella of a volume licensing agreement, you will be required to activate the operating system with Microsoft within 60 days of installation. Activation can be done automatically over the Internet or by calling the provided regional phone number. With Windows Server operating systems specifically, the activation algorithm takes into account the hardware specifications of the server. In light of this, when enough hardware changes have been made to significantly change the operating system, Windows requires reactivation. To facilitate the activation process and especially to reduce the possibility of reactivation, you should make adjustments to memory and processors and install VMware Tools prior to performing the activation.

Installing VMware Tools

Although VMware Tools is not installed by default, the package is an important part of a VM. VMware Tools offers several great benefits without any detriments. Recall from the beginning of this chapter that VMware vSphere offers certain virtualization-optimized (or *paravirtualized*) devices to VMs in order to improve performance. In many cases, these paravirtualized devices do not have device drivers present in a standard installation of a guest OS. The device drivers for these devices are provided by VMware Tools, which is just one more reason why VMware Tools is an essential part of every VM and guest OS installation.

In other words, installing VMware Tools should be standard practice and not a debatable step in the deployment of a VM. The VMware Tools package provides the following benefits:

- Optimized NIC drivers.

- Optimized SCSI drivers.

- Enhanced video and mouse drivers.

- VM heartbeat.

- VSS support to enable guest quiescing for snapshots and backups. Many VMware and third-party applications and tools rely on the VMware Tools VSS integration.

- Enhanced memory management.

VMware Tools also helps streamline and automate the management of VM focus so that you are able to move into and out of VM consoles easily and seamlessly without having to constantly use the Ctrl+Alt keyboard command.

The VMware Tools package is available for Windows, Linux, NetWare, Solaris, and FreeBSD; however, the installation methods vary because of the differences in the guest OSes. In all cases, the installation of VMware Tools starts when you select the option to install VMware Tools from the vSphere Web Client. Do you recall our discussion earlier about ISO images and how ESXi uses them to present CDs/DVDs to VMs? That's exactly the functionality that is being leveraged in this case. When you select to install VMware Tools, vSphere will mount an ISO as a CD/DVD for the VM, and the guest OS will reflect a mounted CD-ROM that has the installation files for VMware Tools.

WHERE ARE THE VMWARE TOOLS ISOs FOUND?

In the event you're curious, you'll find the VMware Tools ISO images located in the /vmimages/ tools-isoimages directory on an ESXi host. This directory is visible only if you enable the ESX Shell on your ESXi hosts and then open an SSH connection to the host; it is not visible from the vSphere Web Client. The ISO images are placed there automatically during installation; you do not have to download them or obtain them from the installation CD-ROM, and you do not need to do anything to manage or maintain them.

As we mentioned previously, the exact process for installing VMware Tools will depend upon the guest OS. Because Windows and Linux make up the largest portion of VMs deployed on VMware vSphere in most cases, those are the two examples we'll discuss. First, we'll walk you through installing VMware Tools into a Windows-based guest OS.

Installing VMware Tools in Windows

Perform these steps to install VMware Tools into Windows Server 2012 running as a guest OS in a VM (the steps for other versions of Windows are similar):

1. Use the vSphere Web Client to connect to a vCenter Server instance or use the vSphere Client to connect to an individual ESXi host.

2. If you aren't already in the Hosts And Clusters or VMs And Templates inventory view, use Home ➢ Hosts And Clusters or Home ➢ VMs And Templates to navigate to one of these views.

3. Right-click the VM in the inventory tree and select Open Console. You can also use the Open Console option on the properties page of the virtual machine.

4. If you aren't already logged into the guest OS in the VM, select Send Ctrl-Alt-Delete and log into the guest OS.

5. Right-click the virtual machine and select All vCenter Actions ➢ Guest OS ➢ Install VMware Tools. A dialog box providing additional information appears. Click Mount to mount the VMware Tools ISO and dismiss the dialog box.

HOW DO I GET OUT OF HERE AGAIN?

Remember that before VMware Tools is installed into a guest OS, the ability to seamlessly move into and out of the guest OS in the console doesn't exist. Instead, you must click into the VM console in order to interact with the guest OS. When you are finished, you must press Ctrl+Alt to release the mouse and keyboard. After VMware Tools is installed, this happens automatically for you.

---

6. An AutoPlay dialog box appears, prompting the user for action. Select the option Run Setup64.exe.

   If the AutoPlay dialog box does not appear, open Windows Explorer and double-click the CD/DVD drive icon. The AutoPlay dialog box should then appear.

7. Click Next on the Welcome To The Installation Wizard For VMware Tools page.

8. Select the appropriate setup type for the VMware Tools installation, and click Next.

   The Typical radio button will suffice for most situations. The Complete installation option installs all available features, while the Custom installation option allows for the greatest level of feature customization.

9. Click Install.

   During the installation, you may be prompted one or more times to confirm the installation of third-party device drivers; select Install for each of these prompts.

   If the AutoRun dialog box appears again, simply close the dialog box and continue with the installation.

10. After the installation is complete, click Finish.

11. Click Yes to restart the VM immediately, or click No to manually restart the VM at a later time.

Newer versions of Windows, such as Windows Server 2008, use a different mechanism—a different video driver—to improve the graphical performance of a console session.
Perform the following steps to install this different video driver and improve the graphical console performance:

1. From the Start menu, select Run. In the Run dialog box, type **devmgmt.msc** and click OK. This will launch the Device Manager console.

2. Expand the Display Adapters entry.

3. Right-click the Standard VGA Graphics Adapter or VMware SVGA II item, and select Update Driver Software.

4. Click Browse My Computer For Driver Software.

5. Using the Browse button, navigate to

```
C:\Program Files\Common Files\VMware\Drivers\wddm_video
```

and then click Next.

6. After a moment, Windows will report that it has successfully installed the driver for the VMware SVGA 3D (Microsoft Corporation – WDDM) device. Click Close.

7. Restart the VM when prompted.

After Windows restarts in the VM, you should notice improved performance when using the graphical console. Note that this procedure is no longer required in Windows Server 2012. The VMware SVGA 3D driver is automatically installed along with the VMware Tools installation.

For older versions of Windows, such as Windows Server 2003, you can improve the responsiveness of the VM console by configuring the hardware acceleration setting. It is, by default, set to None; setting this to Maximum provides a much smoother console session experience. The VMware Tools installation routine reminds you to set this value at the end of the installation, but if you choose not to set hardware acceleration at that time, it can easily be set later. This is highly recommended to optimize the graphical performance of the VM's console. (Note that Windows XP has this value set to Maximum by default.)

Perform the following steps to adjust the hardware acceleration in a VM running Windows Server 2003 (or Windows XP, in case the value has been changed from the default):

1. Right-click an empty area of the Windows Desktop, and select the Properties option.

2. Select the Settings tab, and click the Advanced button.

3. Select the Troubleshooting tab.

4. Move the Hardware Acceleration slider to the Full setting on the right, as shown in Figure 9.19.

Now that the VMware Tools installation is complete and the VM is rebooted, the system tray displays the VMware Tools icon, the letters *VM* in a small gray box (Windows Taskbar settings might hide the icon). The icon in the system tray indicates that VMware Tools is installed and operational.

In previous versions of vSphere, double-clicking the VMware Tools icon in the system tray would bring up a set of configurable options. As of vSphere 5.1, that interface has been removed and replaced with the informational screen shown in Figure 9.20. Previously you could configure time synchronization, show or hide VMware Tools from the Taskbar, and select scripts to suspend, resume, shut down, or turn on a VM.

VMware now provides a command-line-based tool, called VMwareToolboxCmd.exe, that will allow you to configure these settings. You can access VMwareToolboxCmd.exe by launching a command prompt and browsing to the installation directory of VMware Tools.

As with previous versions of VMware Tools, time synchronization between the guest OS and the host is disabled by default. You'll want to use caution when enabling time synchronization between the guest OS and the ESXi host because Windows domain members rely on Kerberos for authentication and Kerberos is sensitive to time differences between computers. A Windows-based guest OS that belongs to an Active Directory domain is already configured with a native time synchronization process against the domain controller in its domain that holds the PDC Emulator operations master role. If the time on the ESXi host is different from the time on the PDC Emulator operations master domain controller, the guest OS could end up moving outside the 5-minute window allowed by Kerberos. When the 5-minute window is exceeded, Kerberos will experience errors with authentication and replication.

FIGURE 9.19
Changing the hardware acceleration feature of a Windows guest OS is a common and helpful adjustment for improving mouse performance.

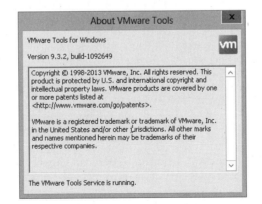

FIGURE 9.20
As of vSphere 5.1, you can no longer configure properties in VMware Tools by interacting with the icon in the system tray.

You can take a few different approaches to managing time synchronizations in a virtual environment. The first approach involves not using VMware Tools time synchronization and relying instead on the W32Time service and a PDC Emulator with a Registry edit that configures synchronization with an external time server. Another approach involves disabling the native time synchronization across the Windows domain and then relying on the VMware Tools feature. A third approach might be to synchronize the VMware ESXi hosts and the PDC Emulator operations master with the same external time server and then to enable the VMware Tools option for synchronization. In this case, both the native W32Time service and VMware Tools should be adjusting the time to the same value.

VMware has a couple of Knowledge Base articles that contain the latest recommendations for timekeeping. For Windows-based guest OS installations, refer to http://kb.vmware.com/kb/1318 or refer to the document "Timekeeping in Virtual Machines" at the following location:

www.vmware.com/files/pdf/Timekeeping-In-VirtualMachines.pdf

CONFIGURING NTP ON ESXI

If you do choose to synchronize the guest OS to the ESXi host using VMware Tools, be sure to synchronize the ESXi host to an authoritative time source using NTP. Refer to Chapter 2, "Planning and Installing VMware ESXi" for more information on how to configure ESXi to synchronize with an NTP-based time server.

We've shown you how to install VMware Tools into a Windows-based guest operation system, so now we'd like to walk through the process for a Linux-based guest OS.

Installing VMware Tools in Linux

There are a number of different versions (or distributions) of Linux available and supported by VMware vSphere, and while they are all called "Linux," they do have subtle differences from one distribution to another that make it difficult to provide a single set of steps that would apply to all Linux distributions. In this section, we'll use Novell SuSE Linux Enterprise Server (SLES) version 11, a popular enterprise-focused distribution of Linux, as the basis for describing how to install VMware Tools in Linux.

Perform the following steps to install VMware Tools into a VM running the 64-bit version of SLES 11 as the guest OS:

1. Use the vSphere Web Client to connect to a vCenter Server instance or use the vSphere Client to connect to an individual ESXi host.

2. You will need access to the console of the VM onto which you're installing VMware Tools. Right-click the VM and select Open Console.

3. Log into the Linux guest OS using an account with appropriate permissions. This will typically be the root account or an equivalent (some Linux distributions, including Ubuntu, disable the root account but provide an administrative account you can use).

4. Right-click the virtual machine and choose All vCenter Actions ➢ Guest OS ➢ Install VMware Tools. Click Mount on the dialog box that pops up.

5. Assuming that you have a graphical user environment running in the Linux VM, a file system browser window will open to display the contents of the VMware Tools ISO that was automatically mounted behind the scenes.

6. Open a Linux terminal window. In many distributions, you can right-click a blank area of the file system browser window and select Open In Terminal.

7. If you are not already in the same directory as the VMware Tools mount point, change directories to the location of the VMware Tools mount point using the following command (the exact path may vary from distribution to distribution and from version to version; this is the path for SLES 11):

```
cd /media/VMware\ Tools
```

8. Extract the compressed TAR file (with the `.tar.gz` filename extension) to a temporary directory, and then change to that temporary directory using the following commands:

```
tar -zxf VMwareTools-9.3.2-1092649.tar.gz -C /tmp
cd /tmp/vmware-tools-distrib
```

9. In the `/tmp/vmware-tools-distrib` directory, use the `sudo` command to run the `vmware-install.pl` Perl script with the following command:

```
sudo ./vmware-install.pl
```

Enter the current account's password when prompted.

10. The installer will provide a series of prompts for information such as where to place the binary files, where the init scripts are located, and where to place the library files. Default answers are provided in brackets; you can just press Enter unless you need to specify a different value that is appropriate for this Linux system.

11. After the installation is complete, the VMware Tools ISO will be unmounted automatically. You can remove the temporary installation directory using these commands:

```
cd
rm -rf /tmp/vmware-tools-distrib
```

12. Reboot the Linux VM for the installation of VMware Tools to take full effect.

The steps described here were performed on a VM running Novell SLES 11 64-bit. Because of variations within different distributions of Linux, the commands you may need to install VMware Tools within another distribution may not match what we've listed here. However, these steps do provide a general guideline of what the procedure looks like.

VMWARE TOOLS FOR LINUX

When installing VMware Tools to a Linux guest OS, the path to the TAR file and the numbers in the TAR filename will vary. Depending upon your Linux distribution, the VMware Tools installer may also provide instructions on replacing the Ethernet driver with an updated VMXNet driver. Typically, these instructions involve unloading the older drivers, scanning for new devices, loading the new VMXNet driver, and then bringing the network interfaces back up.

After VMware Tools is installed, the Summary tab of a VM object identifies the status of VMware Tools as well as other information such as operating system, CPU, memory, DNS (host) name, IP address, and current ESXi host. Figure 9.21 shows a screen shot of this information for the Windows Server 2012 VM into which we installed VMware Tools earlier.

FIGURE 9.21
You can view details about VMware Tools, DNS name, IP address, and so forth from the Summary tab of a VM object.

In the event you are upgrading to vSphere 5.5 from a previous version of VMware vSphere, you will have outdated versions of VMware Tools running in your guest OSes. You'll want to upgrade these in order to get the latest drivers. In Chapter 4, "vSphere Update Manager and the vCenter Support Tools," we discuss the use of vSphere Update Manager to assist in this process, but you can also do it manually.

For Windows-based guest OSes, the process of upgrading VMware Tools is as simple as right-clicking a VM and selecting All vCenter Actions ➤ Guest OS ➤ Upgrade VMware Tools. Select the option labeled Automatic Tools Upgrade, and click OK. vCenter Server will install the updated VMware Tools and automatically reboot the VM, if necessary.

For other guest OSes, upgrading VMware Tools typically means running through the install process again. You can refer to the instructions for installing VMware Tools on SLES previously in this chapter, for example, for information on upgrading VMware Tools in a Linux VM.

Creating VMs is just one aspect of managing VMs. In the next sections we look at some additional VM management tasks.

Managing Virtual Machines

In addition to creating VMs, there is a range of other tasks that vSphere administrators will need to perform. While most of these tasks are relatively easy to figure out, we include them here for completeness.

Adding or Registering Existing VMs

Creating VMs from scratch, as described previously, is only one way of getting VMs into the environment. It's entirely possible that you, as a vSphere administrator, might receive pre-created VMs from another source. Suppose you receive the files that compose a VM—notably, the VMX and VMDK files—from another administrator and you need to put that VM to use in your environment. You've already seen how to use the vSphere Web Client–based file browser to upload files into a datastore, but what needs to happen once it's in the datastore? In this case, you need to register the VM. The process of registering the VM adds it to the vCenter Server (or ESXi host) inventory and allows you to then manage the VM.

Perform the following steps to add (or register) an existing VM into the inventory:

1. Use the vSphere Web Client to connect to a vCenter Server instance or use the vSphere Client to connect to an individual ESXi host.

2. A VM can be registered from a number of different views within the vSphere Web Client. The Storage inventory view, though, is probably the most logical place to do it. Navigate to the Storage inventory view by using the menu bar or the navigation bar.

3. Right-click the datastore containing the VM you want to register. From the context menu, select Register VM as shown in Figure 9.22.

4. Use the file browser to navigate to the folder where the VMX file for the VM resides. Select the correct VMX file and click OK.

Figure 9.22
You invoke the Register Virtual Machine Wizard by right-clicking the datastore and selecting Register VM.

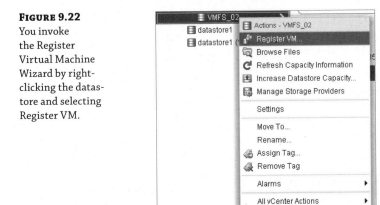

5. The Register Virtual Machine Wizard prepopulates the name of the VM. It does this by reading the contents of the VMX file. Accept the name or type a new one; then select a logical location within the inventory and click Next.

6. Choose the cluster on which you'd like to run this VM and click Next.

7. If you selected a cluster for which VMware DRS is not enabled or is set to Manual, you must also select the specific host on which the VM will run. Choose a specific host and click Next.

8. Review the settings. If everything is correct, click Finish; otherwise, use the hyperlinks on the left side of the wizard or the Back button to go back and make any necessary changes.

When the Register Virtual Machine Wizard is finished, the VM will be added to the vSphere Web Client inventory. From here, you're ready to manipulate the VM in whatever fashion you need, such as powering it on.

Changing VM Power States

There are six different commands involved in changing the power state of a VM. Figure 9.23 shows these six commands on the context menu displayed when you right-click a VM and select All vCenter Actions ➢ Power.

FIGURE 9.23

The Power submenu allows you to power on, power off, suspend, or reset a VM as well as interact with the guest OS if VMware Tools is installed.

By and large, these commands are self-explanatory, but there are a few subtle differences in some of them:

Power On and Power Off   These function exactly as their names suggest. They are equivalent to toggling the virtual power button on the VM without any interaction with the guest OS (if one is installed).

BE CAREFUL WITH POWER OFF

Although the behavior of the Power Off option can be configured in the Virtual Machine Properties dialog box—see the VM Options tab under the settings for each virtual machine—our testing showed that the default value of Power Off (which is Shut Down Guest) still did not behave in the same manner as the actual Shut Down Guest command. Instead, the Power Off command simply turned off power and did not invoke an orderly shutdown of the guest OS.

Suspend   This command suspends the VM. When you resume the VM, it will start back right where it was when you suspended it.

Reset   This command will reset the VM, which is not the same as rebooting the guest OS. This is the virtual equivalent of pressing the Reset button on the front of the computer.

Shut Down Guest OS   This command works only if VMware Tools is installed, and it works through VMware Tools to invoke an orderly shutdown of the guest OS. To avoid file system or data corruption in the guest OS instance, you should use this command whenever possible.

Restart Guest OS   Like the Shut Down Guest command, this command requires VMware Tools and initiates a reboot of the guest OS in an orderly fashion.

Removing VMs

If you have a VM that you need to keep but doesn't need to be listed in the VM inventory, you can remove the VM from the inventory. This keeps the VM files intact, and the VM can be re-added to inventory (i.e., registered) at any time later on using the procedure described earlier in the section titled "Adding or Registering Existing VMs."

To remove a VM, simply right-click a powered-off VM and from the context menu, select All vCenter Actions ➤ Remove From Inventory. Select Yes in the Confirm Remove dialog box and the VM will be removed from the inventory. You can use the vSphere Web Client file browser to verify that the files for the VM are still intact in the same location on the datastore.

Deleting VMs

In the event you have a VM that you no longer need at all—meaning you don't need it listed in the inventory and you don't need the files maintained on the datastore—you can completely remove the VM. Be careful, though; this is not something that you can undo!

To delete a VM entirely, you only need to right-click a powered-off VM and select All vCenter Actions ➤ Delete From Disk from the context menu. The vSphere Web Client will prompt you for confirmation, reminding you that you are deleting the VM and its associated base disks (VMDK files). Click Yes to continue removing the files from both inventory and the datastore. Once the process is done, you can once again use the vSphere Web Client file browser to verify that the VM's files are gone.

Adding existing VMs, removing VMs from inventory, and deleting VMs are all relatively simple tasks. The task of modifying VMs, though, is significant enough to warrant its own section.

Modifying Virtual Machines

Just as physical machines require hardware upgrades or changes, a VM might require virtual hardware upgrades or changes to meet changing performance demands. Perhaps a new memory-intensive client-server application requires an increase in memory, or a new data-mining application requires a second processor or additional network adapters for bandwidth-heavy FTP traffic. In each of these cases, the VM requires a modification of the virtual hardware configured for the guest OS to use. Of course, this is only one task that an administrator charged with managing VMs could be responsible for completing. Other tasks might include leveraging vSphere's snapshot functionality to protect against a potential issue with the guest OS inside a VM. We describe both of these tasks in the following sections, starting with how to change the hardware of a VM.

Changing Virtual Machine Hardware

In most cases, modifying a VM requires that the VM be powered off. There are exceptions to this rule, as shown in Figure 9.24. You can hot-add a USB controller, a SATA controller, an Ethernet adapter, a hard disk, or a SCSI device. Later you'll see that some guest OSes also support the addition of virtual CPUs or RAM while they are powered on as well.

FIGURE 9.24
Users can add some types of hardware while the VM is powered on. If virtual hardware cannot be added while the VM is powered on, the operation will fail.

When you're adding new virtual hardware to a VM using the vSphere Web Client, the screens are similar to the screens used while creating a VM. For example, to add a new virtual hard disk to an existing VM, you would use the New Device drop-down box at the bottom of the Virtual Machine Edit Settings dialog box. You can see in Figure 9.24 that it is possible to add a virtual hard disk to a VM while it is powered on. From there, the vSphere Web Client uses the same steps shown in Figure 9.11, Figure 9.12, and Figure 9.13 earlier in this chapter. The only difference is that now you're adding a new virtual hard disk to an existing VM. As an example, we'll go through the steps to add an Ethernet adapter to a VM (the steps are the same regardless of whether the VM is actually running).

Perform the following steps to add an Ethernet adapter to a VM:

1. Launch the vSphere Web Client, and connect to a vCenter Server instance or use the vSphere Client to connect to an individual ESXi host.

2. If you aren't already in an inventory view that displays VMs, switch to the Hosts And Clusters or VMs And Templates view using the Home ➢ Inventories menu.

3. Right-click the VM to which you want to add the Ethernet adapter, and select Edit Settings.

4. Select the New Device drop-down box at the bottom of the screen and select Network. Click the Add button next to the New Device drop-down box to add the Ethernet adapter to the virtual machine.

5. Expand the New Network option to gain access to additional properties.

6. Select the network adapter type, the network to which it should be connected, and whether the network adapter should be connected at power on, as shown in Figure 9.25.

FIGURE 9.25
To add a new network adapter, you must select the adapter type, the network, and whether it should be connected at power on.

7. Review the settings, and click OK.

Besides adding new virtual hardware, users can make other changes while a VM is powered on. For example, you can mount and unmount CD/DVD drives, ISO images, and floppy disk images while a VM is turned on. We described the process for mounting an ISO image as a virtual CD/DVD drive earlier in this chapter in the section titled "Installing a Guest Operating System." You can also assign and reassign adapters to virtual networks while a VM is running. All of these tasks are performed from the VM Properties dialog box, accessed by selecting Edit Settings from the Context menu for a VM.

DOES ANYONE STILL USE FLOPPY DRIVES?

New VMs created in a vSphere environment automatically come with a floppy drive, although in our experience it is rarely used. In fact, about the only time that it does get used is when a custom storage driver needs to be added during installation of a Windows-based guest OS. Unless you know you will need to use a floppy drive, it's generally safe to remove it from the hardware list.

If you are running Windows Server 2008, Windows Server 2008 R2, or Windows Server 2012 in the VM, then you also gain the ability to add virtual CPUs or RAM to a VM while it is running. To use this functionality, you'll have to first enable it. In a somewhat ironic twist, the VM for which you want to enable hot-add must be powered off.

To enable hot-add of virtual CPUs or RAM, perform these steps:

1. Launch the vSphere Web Client if it is not already running, and connect to a vCenter Server instance or use the vSphere Client to connect to an individual ESXi host.

2. Navigate to either the Hosts And Clusters or VMs And Templates inventory view.

3. If the VM for which you want to enable hot-add is currently running, right-click the VM and select All vCenter Actions ➤ Power ➤ Shut Down Guest. The VM must be shut down in order to enable hot-add functionality.

REMEMBER THE DIFFERENCE BETWEEN POWERING OFF AND SHUTTING DOWN THE GUEST

Recall from earlier in this chapter that the context menu of a VM contains two items that appear to perform the same function.

The Power ➤ Power Off command does exactly that: It powers off the VM. It's like pulling out the power cord unexpectedly. The guest OS has no time to prepare for a shutdown.

The Power ➤ Shut Down Guest OS command issues a shutdown command to the guest OS so that the guest OS can shut down in an orderly fashion. This command requires that VMware Tools be already installed, and it ensures that the guest OS won't be corrupted or damaged by an unexpected shutdown.

In day-to-day operation, use the Shut Down Guest OS option. The Power Off option should be used only when it is absolutely necessary.

---

4. Right-click the VM and select Edit Settings.

5. In the Virtual Hardware tab, select CPU to expand the available options. Select the Enable CPU Hot Add check box in the CPU Hot Plug option.

6. To enable memory hot-add, select Memory to expand the available options. Select the Enable check box in the Memory Hot Plug option to enable hot-plug memory.

7. Click OK to save the changes to the VM.

Once this setting has been configured, you can add RAM or virtual CPUs to the VM when it is powered on. Figure 9.26 shows a powered-on VM that has memory hot-add enabled. Figure 9.27 shows a powered-on VM that has CPU hot-plug enabled; you can change the number of virtual CPU sockets, but you can't change the number of cores per virtual CPU socket.

Aside from the changes described so far, configuration changes to a VM can take place only when the VM is in a powered-off state. When a VM is powered off, all the various configuration options are available to change: RAM, virtual CPUs, or adding or removing other hardware components such as CD/DVD drives or floppy drives.

FIGURE 9.26
The range of memory you can add is restricted when using memory hot-add.

FIGURE 9.27
With CPU hot-plug enabled, more virtual CPU sockets can be configured, but the number of cores per CPU cannot be altered.

ALIGNING VIRTUAL MACHINE FILE SYSTEMS

In Chapter 6, we introduced the concept of aligning VMFS, and we suggested that the VM's file system should also be aligned. If you construct VMs with separate virtual hard drives for the operating system and data, then you are most concerned with the alignment of the file system for the data drive because the greatest amount of I/O occurs on that drive. For example, a VM with Disk 0 (that holds the operating system) and a blank disk called Disk 1 (that holds data that will incur significant I/O) should have Disk 1 aligned. The need to align the guest file system is applicable to almost all distributions of Linux and all but the most recent versions of Windows. For example, Windows 7 and Windows Server 2008 align themselves properly during installation, but earlier versions do not.

Perform the following steps to align Disk 1 of a VM running a version of Windows earlier than Windows Server 2008:

1. Log into the VM using an account with administrative credentials.

2. Open a command prompt, and type **Diskpart**.

3. Type **list disk**, and press Enter.

4. Type **select disk 1**, and press Enter.

5. Type **create partition primary align = 64**, and press Enter.

6. Type **assign letter** =*X*, where *X* is an open letter that can be assigned.

7. Type **list part** to verify the 64 KB offset for the new partition.

8. Format the partition.

Perhaps you are thinking that this seems like a tedious task to perform for all your VMs. It *is* a tedious task; however, the benefit of doing this is realized most when there is a significant I/O requirement.

As you can see, running your operating system in a VM offers advantages when it comes time to reconfigure hardware, even enabling such innovative features as CPU hot-plug. There are other advantages to using VMs too; one of these advantages is a vSphere feature called snapshots.

Using Virtual Machine Snapshots

VM snapshots provide administrators with the ability to create point-in-time checkpoints of a VM. The snapshot captures the state of the VM at a specific point in time. VMware administrators can then revert to their pre-snapshot state in the event the changes made since the snapshot should be discarded. Or, if the changes should be preserved, the administrator can commit the changes and delete the snapshot.

This functionality can be used in a variety of ways. Suppose you'd like to install the latest vendor-supplied patch for the guest OS instance running in a VM but you want to be able to recover in case the patch installation runs amok. By taking a snapshot before installing the patch, you can revert to the snapshot in the event the patch installation doesn't go well. You've just created a safety net for yourself.

OTHER FEATURES LEVERAGE SNAPSHOTS TOO

Snapshots are leveraged by vSphere Update Manager and are also used by various VM backup frameworks.

Before starting to use snapshots, be aware that vSphere FT—discussed in Chapter 7, "Ensuring High Availability and Business Continuity"—does not support snapshots, so you can't take a snapshot of a VM that is protected with vSphere FT. Earlier versions of vSphere did not allow Storage vMotions to occur when a snapshot was present, but this limitation is removed in vSphere 5.

Perform the following steps to create a snapshot of a VM:

1. Use the vSphere Web Client to connect to a vCenter Server instance or use the vSphere Client to connect to an individual ESXi host.

2. Navigate to either the Hosts And Clusters or VMs And Templates inventory view.

3. Right-click the VM in the inventory tree and select Take Snapshot.

4. Provide a name and description for the snapshot, as shown in Figure 9.28, and then click OK.

FIGURE 9.28
Providing names and descriptions for snapshots is an easy way to manage multiple historical snapshots.

As shown in Figure 9.28, there are two options when taking snapshots:

◆ The option labeled Snapshot The Virtual Machine's Memory specifies whether the RAM of the VM should also be included in the snapshot. When this option is selected, the current contents of the VM's RAM are written to a file ending in a `.vmsn` filename extension.

◆ The option labeled Quiesce Guest File System (Needs VMware Tools Installed) controls whether the guest file system will be quiesced—or quieted—so that it is considered consistent. This can help ensure that the data within the guest file system is intact in the snapshot.

When a snapshot is taken, depending on the previous options, some additional files are created on the datastore, as shown in Figure 9.29.

FIGURE 9.29
When a snapshot is taken, some additional files are created on the VM's datastore.

It is a common misconception for administrators to think of snapshots as full copies of VM files. As you can clearly see in Figure 9.29, a snapshot is not a full copy of a VM. VMware's snapshot technology consumes minimal space while still reverting to a previous snapshot by allocating only enough space to store the changes rather than making a full copy.

To demonstrate snapshot technology and illustrate its behavior (for practice only), we performed the following steps:

1. We created a VM with a default installation of Windows Server 2012 with a single hard drive (recognized by the guest OS as drive C:). The virtual hard drive was thin provisioned on a VMFS volume with a maximum size of 40 GB.

2. We took a snapshot named FirstSnap.

3. We added approximately 3 GB of data to drive C:, represented as win2k12-01.vmdk.

4. We took a second snapshot named SecondSnap.

5. We once again added approximately 3 GB of data to drive C:, represented as win2k12-01.vmdk.

Review Table 9.2 for the results we recorded after each step. Note that these results were recorded as part of our example and may differ from your results if you perform a similar test.

TABLE 9.2:   Snapshot demonstration results

	VMDK SIZE	NTFS SIZE	NTFS FREE SPACE
Start (pre-first snapshot)			
win2k12-01.vmdk (C:)	8.6 GB	40 GB	31 GB
First snapshot (pre-data copy)			
win2k12-01.vmdk (C:)	8.6 GB	40 GB	31 GB
win2k12-01-000001.vmdk	17.4 MB		
First snapshot (post-data copy)			
win2k12-01.vmdk (C:)	8.6 GB	40 GB	28.1 GB
win2k12-01-000001.vmdk	3.1 GB		
Second snapshot (pre-data copy)			
win2k12-01.vmdk (C:)	8.6 GB	40 GB	28.1 GB
win2k12-01-000001.vmdk	3.1 GB		
win2k12-01-000002.vmdk	17.4 MB		
Second snapshot (post-data copy)			
win2k12-01.vmdk (C:)	8.6 GB	40 GB	25.2 GB
win2k12-01-000001.vmdk	3.1 GB		
win2k12-01-000002.vmdk	3.1 GB		

As you can see from Table 9.2, the VM is unaware of the presence of the snapshot and the extra VMDK files that are created. ESXi, however, knows to write changes to the VM's virtual disk to the snapshot VMDK, properly known as a *delta disk* (or a *differencing disk*). These delta disks start small and over time grow to accommodate the changes stored within them.

Despite the storage efficiency that snapshots attempt to maintain, over time they can eat up a considerable amount of disk space. Therefore, use them as needed, but be sure to remove older snapshots on a regular basis. Also be aware there are performance ramifications to using snapshots. Because disk space must be allocated to the delta disks on demand, ESXi hosts must update the metadata files (files with the .sf filename extension) every time the differencing disk grows. To update the metadata files, LUNs must be locked, and this might adversely affect the performance of other VMs and hosts using the same LUN.

To view or delete a snapshot or revert to an earlier snapshot, you use the Snapshot Manager. Perform the following steps to access the Snapshot Manager:

1. Use the vSphere Web Client to connect to a vCenter Server instance or use the vSphere Client to connect to an individual ESXi host.

2. In the inventory tree, right-click the name of the VM, and from the context menu select Manage Snapshots.

3. Select the appropriate snapshot to fall back to, as shown in Figure 9.30, and then click the Revert To button.

FIGURE 9.30
The Snapshot Manager can revert to a previous snapshot, but all data written since that snapshot was taken and that hasn't been backed up elsewhere will be lost.

To further illustrate the nature of snapshots, see Figure 9.31 and Figure 9.32. Figure 9.31 shows the file system of a VM running Windows Server 2012 after data has been written into two new folders named temp1 and temp2. Figure 9.32 shows the same VM but after reverting to a snapshot taken before that data was written. As you can see, it's as if the new folders never even existed. (And yes, we can assure you we didn't just delete the folders for these screen shots. Test it yourself!)

FIGURE 9.31
This VM running Windows Server 2012 has had some data placed into two temporary folders.

REVERTING TO A SNAPSHOT

Reverting to a snapshot incurs a loss of data. Any data that was written since the snapshot has occurred will no longer be available, along with any applications that were installed since the snapshot was taken. Therefore, revert to snapshots only if you have determined that the loss of data is acceptable or if the data is backed up elsewhere.

FIGURE 9.32
The same VM, after reverting to a snapshot taken before the temporary folders were created, no longer has any record of the data.

As you can see, snapshots are a great way to protect yourself from unwanted changes to the *data* stored in a VM. Snapshots aren't backups and should not be used in place of backups. However, they can protect you from misbehaving application installations or other processes that might result in data loss or corruption.

There are additional VM management tasks that we'll discuss in other chapters. For example, you might want to migrate a VM from one ESXi host to another ESXi host using vMotion; this is covered in Chapter 12. Changing a VM's resource allocation settings is covered in Chapter 11.

In the next chapter, we'll move from creating and managing VMs to streamlining the VM provisioning process with templates, OVF templates, and vApps. While VMware makes the VM provisioning process pretty easy, we'll show you how using templates can simplify server provisioning even more while bringing some consistency to your VM and guest OS deployments.

The Bottom Line

Create a virtual machine.   A VM is a collection of virtual hardware pieces, like a physical system—one or more virtual CPUs, RAM, video card, SCSI devices, IDE devices, floppy drives, parallel and serial ports, and network adapters. This virtual hardware is virtualized and abstracted from the underlying physical hardware, providing portability to the VM.

Master It   Create two VMs, one intended to run Windows Server 2012 and a second intended to run SLES 11 (64-bit). Make a list of the differences in the configuration that are suggested by the Create New Virtual Machine Wizard.

Install a guest operating system.   Just as a physical machine needs an operating system, a VM also needs an operating system. vSphere supports a broad range of 32-bit and 64-bit operating systems, including all major versions of Windows Server, Windows 7, Windows XP, and Windows 2000 as well as various flavors of Linux, FreeBSD, Novell NetWare, and Solaris.

Master It   What are the three ways in which a guest OS can access data on a CD/DVD, and what are the advantages of each approach?

Install VMware Tools.   For maximum performance of the guest OS, it needs to have virtualization-optimized drivers that are specially written for and designed to work with the ESXi hypervisor. VMware Tools provides these optimized drivers as well as other utilities focused on better operation in virtual environments.

Master It   A fellow administrator contacts you and is having a problem installing VMware Tools. This administrator has selected the Install/Upgrade VMware Tools command, but nothing seems to be happening inside the VM. What could be the cause of the problem?

Manage virtual machines.   Once a VM has been created, the vSphere Web Client makes it easy to manage. Virtual floppy images and CD/DVD drives can be mounted or unmounted as necessary. vSphere provides support for initiating an orderly shutdown of the guest OS in a VM, although this requires that VMware Tools be installed. VM snapshots allow you to take a point-in-time "picture" of a VM so that administrators can roll back changes if needed.

Master It   What are the three different ways an administrator can bring the contents of a CD/DVD into a VM?

Master It   What is the difference between the Shut Down Guest command and the Power Off command?

Modify virtual machines.   vSphere offers a number of features to make it easy to modify VMs after they have been created. Administrators can hot-add certain types of hardware, like virtual hard disks and network adapters, and some guest OSes also support hot-adding virtual CPUs or memory, although this feature must be enabled first.

Master It   Which method is preferred for modifying the configuration of a VM: editing the VMX file or using the vSphere Web Client?

Master It   Name the types of hardware that cannot be added while a VM is running.

Chapter 10

Using Templates and vApps

Creating VMs manually and installing guest operating systems (guest OSes) into those VMs is fine on a small scale, but what if you need to deploy lots of VMs? What if you need to ensure that your VMs are consistent and standardized? Through vCenter Server, VMware vSphere offers a solution: VM cloning and templates. In this chapter, we'll show you how to use cloning, templates, and vApps to help streamline the deployment of VMs in your environment.

In this chapter, you will learn to

◆ Clone a VM

◆ Create a VM template

◆ Deploy new VMs from a template

◆ Deploy a VM from an Open Virtualization Format (OVF) template

◆ Export a VM as an OVF template

◆ Work with vApps

Cloning VMs

If you've ever wished there were a faster way to provision a new server into your environment, then you'll be glad to know that VMware vSphere fulfills that wish in a big way. When you are using vCenter Server in your environment, you have the ability to clone a VM; that is, you can make a copy of the VM, including the VM's virtual disks. How does this help provision new VMs faster? Think about it: What takes the most time when creating a new VM? It's not the creation of the VM itself, because that takes only minutes. It's the installation of the guest OS—whether it is Windows Server, Linux, or some other supported guest OS—that takes up the bulk of the time needed to create a new VM. Using vCenter Server to clone a VM—which means also cloning the VM's virtual disks—keeps you from having to install the guest OS into the cloned VM. By cloning VMs, you eliminate the need to perform a guest OS installation into every new VM.

> ### THE FIRST GUEST OS INSTALLATION IS STILL NEEDED
>
> We mentioned in the text that cloning a VM eliminates the need to perform a guest OS installation into every new VM. That's true—assuming you actually installed the guest OS into the VM that you're cloning. As you consider using VM cloning to help provision new VMs, recognize that you still need to install the guest OS into your source VM. Some things just can't be eliminated!

However, there's a potential problem here: If you are making a clone of a guest OS installation, that means you'll now have two VMs with the same IP address, same computer name, same MAC address, and so forth. Not to worry, though: VMware built the ability to customize the guest OS installation in the cloned VM so that you preserve the guest OS installation but create a new identity in the cloned VM. For Linux-based guest OSes, VMware leverages open-source tools to customize the installation; for Windows-based guest OSes, vCenter Server will leverage Microsoft's well-known Sysprep tool. However, depending on the version of Windows you're cloning, you may need to first install Sysprep on the vCenter Server computer.

Installing Sysprep on the vCenter Server

To customize Windows-based guest OS installations, vCenter Server leverages Microsoft's Sysprep tool. If you aren't familiar with Sysprep, the purpose of the tool is to allow a single Windows installation to be cloned many times over, each time with a unique identity. This ensures that you have to install Windows only once, but you can reuse that Windows installation over and over again, each time using Sysprep to create a new computer name, new IP address, and new security identifier (SID).

In order for vCenter Server to use Sysprep, an administrator must first extract Sysprep and its associated files to a directory created during the installation of vCenter Server. If these files are not extracted before you deploy a VM, the ability to customize the guest OS will be unavailable for all versions of Windows prior to Windows Server 2008. (Windows Server 2008 does not require Sysprep to be installed on the vCenter Server computer). Figure 10.1 shows the Guest Customization page of the Clone Existing Virtual Machine Wizard on a vCenter Server that has not had the Sysprep files extracted.

FIGURE 10.1
If the Sysprep files are not extracted and stored on the vCenter Server system, you might not be able to customize the guest OS when you clone a VM.

Perform these steps to allow guest OS customization of Windows Server 2003 x86 (32-bit) guest OS templates:

1. Insert the Windows Server 2003 x86 CD into the disk drive of the vCenter Server computer.

2. Navigate to the /support/tools/deploy.cab directory on the Windows Server 2003 CD.

3. If the vCenter Server computer is running Windows Server 2003, copy the `sysprep.exe` and `setupcl.exe` files to this directory:

    `C:\Documents and Settings\All Users\Application Data\VMware\VMware`
    `VirtualCenter\sysprep\svr2003`

    If the vCenter Server computer is running Windows Server 2008 or later, then this is the correct path to use:

    `C:\ProgramData\VMware\VMware VirtualCenter\Sysprep\svr2003`

Repeat these steps for other platforms (use the `svr2003-64` folder for customizing 64-bit installations of Windows Server 2003 or the `xp` and `xp-64` folders for customizing installations of Windows XP and Windows XP 64-bit, respectively). As mentioned previously, customizing installations of Windows Server 2008 and later does not require a version of Sysprep to be installed on the vCenter Server computer.

Once you've installed the Sysprep tools for the appropriate versions of Windows (where applicable), you're ready to start cloning and customizing VMs. Before you clone your first VM, though, we recommend that you take the time to create a customization specification, as described in the next section.

Creating a Customization Specification

vCenter Server's customization specification works hand in hand with the tools for customizing VM clones (Sysprep for VMs with a Windows-based guest OS, open-source tools for a VM with a Linux-based guest OS). As you'll see later in this chapter in the section "Cloning a Virtual Machine," the administrator has to provide vCenter Server with the information necessary to give the cloned VM its own unique identity. This includes the IP address, passwords, computer name, and licensing information. With customization specification, an administrator provides all the information only once and then applies it as needed when cloning a VM.

You can create a customization specification in the following two ways:

◆   By creating it during the process of cloning a VM

◆   By using the Customization Specification Manager in vCenter Server

We'll show you how to create a customization specification while cloning a VM in the section "Cloning a Virtual Machine." For now, we'll show you how to use the Customization Specification Manager.

To access the Customization Specification Manager, within the vCenter Web Client select Home ➢ Customization Specification Manager, as you see in Figure 10.2.

After you're in the Customization Specification Manager area of vCenter Server, you can create a new customization specification or edit an existing customization specification. The process is almost identical, and in both cases it involves the New VM Guest Customization Wizard.

Perform the following steps to create a new customization specification:

1. If the vSphere Web Client isn't already running, launch it and connect to a vCenter Server instance. (This functionality is available only when connecting to vCenter Server, not a stand-alone ESXi host.)

2. Navigate to the Customization Specification Manager by selecting Home ➢ Customization Specification Manager.

FIGURE 10.2

The Customization Specification Manager is readily accessible from the home page of the vSphere Web Client in the Management tab.

3. Click the first icon to create a new customization specification. This opens the vSphere Web Client Guest Customization Wizard.

4. From the Target Virtual Machine OS drop-down box, select either Windows or Linux. Windows is the default.

5. Provide a name for the customization specification and, optionally, a description. Click Next to continue.

6. Supply a value for both Name and Organization (you won't be able to proceed until you supply both). Click Next to proceed.

7. Select an option for the computer name within the Windows guest OS installation.

   There are four options from which to select:

   ◆ You can manually supply a name, but this option is useless without also selecting Append A Numeric Value To Ensure Uniqueness.

   ◆ Select Use The Virtual Machine Name to set the computer name within the guest OS installation to the same value as the name of the VM.

   ◆ Choose Enter A Name In The Clone/Deploy Wizard if you want to be prompted for a name when you use this customization specification.

   ◆ The fourth option uses a custom application configured with vCenter Server. Because there is no custom application configured with this instance of vCenter Server, it is currently disabled (grayed out).

We generally recommend selecting Use The Virtual Machine Name. This keeps the guest OS computer name matched up with the VM name, as we recommended when creating new VMs in Chapter 9, "Creating and Managing Virtual Machines." Figure 10.3 shows the four options.

FIGURE 10.3
The Guest Customization Wizard offers several different options for naming a cloned VM.

After you select the option you want to use in this customization specification, click Next.

8. Provide a Windows product key and select the appropriate server licensing mode (Per Seat or Per Server). Click Next.

9. Enter the password for the Windows Administrator account and then confirm the password.

   If you'd like to log on automatically as Administrator (perhaps to help with any auto-mated configuration scripts), select Automatically Log On As The Administrator and specify how many times to log on automatically. Click Next to continue.

10. Select the correct time zone and click Next.

11. If you have any commands you want to run the first time a user logs on, supply those commands at the Run Once screen of the vSphere Web Client Windows Guest Customization Wizard. Click Next if you have no commands to run or when you are fin-ished entering commands to run.

12. Choose the settings you'd like to apply to the network configuration:

    ◆ If you want to use DHCP to assign an IP address to the VM's network interfaces, select Typical Settings.

    ◆ If you want to assign a static IP address to any of the network interfaces, you'll need to select Custom Settings, and the wizard will prompt you to input that information.

Many administrators don't want to use DHCP but still want to ensure that each VM has a unique IP address. To see how this can be done in the customization specification, select Custom Settings and click Next.

13. At the Configure Network screen, click the small pencil above the description field of the NIC1 line. In Figure 10.4 this button is circled for your reference. This will open the Edit Network dialog box shown in Figure 10.5.

FIGURE 10.4
This small button allows you to customize the network interface settings.

FIGURE 10.5
The Edit Network dialog box has an option to prompt the user for an address.

The key to assigning a static IP address to cloned VMs without having to modify the customization specification every time lies in the selection titled Prompt The User For An Address When The Specification Is Used. When you select this option, vCenter Server will prompt the user to supply a unique static IP address every time the specification is used when cloning a VM.

Select Prompt The User For An Address When The Specification Is Used. You must then supply a subnet mask, default gateway, and preferred and alternate DNS servers. Fill in these values, click OK, and then click Next.

14. Select whether you want the Windows-based guest OS to join a workgroup or a domain.

   If the guest OS should join a workgroup, supply the workgroup name. If the guest should join a domain, supply the domain name and credentials to join the domain. Click Next.

15. Generally speaking, you will want to leave Generate New Security ID (SID) selected. Click Next.

16. Review the settings in the final screen of the vSphere Web Client Windows Guest Customization Wizard to ensure that you have the right values supplied.

   If you need to change anything, use the hyperlinks on the left or the Back button to go back and change the values. Otherwise, click Finish to complete the creation of the customization specification.

Because a customization specification for Windows usually contains product keys, you'll probably need to create multiple specifications for different versions or editions of Windows. Repeat the previous steps to create additional specifications.

⊕ Real World Scenario

IMPORTING, EXPORTING, AND CLONING SPECIFICATIONS

When we were helping a customer migrate to a new vSphere environment, they didn't wish to set up their large number of customization specifications from scratch. We used vSphere's ability to export, import, and clone to save all the additional effort.

Within the Customization Specification Manager, there are icons to import from a file, to export to a file, and to clone the selected specification. While you can transfer specifications between environments using these tools, you will lose some of the saved sensitive information such as product keys. You can simply add this information back to the specification after importing it.

Now that you have a customization specification in place and the Sysprep tools installed on the vCenter Server computer (if you are cloning a Windows version earlier than Windows Server 2008), all you need is a source VM with a guest OS installed and you're ready to clone and customize a VM.

CUSTOMIZATION SPECIFICATIONS AREN'T REQUIRED

You aren't required to create customization specifications. However, you will be required to supply the information found in a customization specification when you clone a VM. Because you have to enter the information anyway, why not do it only once by creating a customization specification?

Cloning a Virtual Machine

If you've performed all the steps in the previous two sections, then cloning a VM is actually simple.

Perform the following steps to clone a VM:

1. If the vSphere Web Client isn't already running, launch it and connect to an instance of vCenter Server. Cloning isn't possible when connecting directly to an ESXi host.

2. Navigate to either the Hosts And Clusters or VMs And Templates inventory view.

3. Right-click a VM and select Clone to Virtual Machine. This opens the Clone Existing Virtual Machine Wizard.

4. Supply a name for the VM and select a logical inventory location for the VM. Click Next.

5. Select the host or cluster on which the VM will run. Click Next.

6. If you selected a cluster for which DRS is not enabled or is configured in Manual mode, you must select the specific host on which to run the VM. Click Next.

7. If prompted, select the resource pool in which the VM should be placed. Click Next.

8. Select the desired virtual disk format and select a target datastore or datastore cluster. Use the Advanced button if you want or need to place the VM's configuration files in a different location than the virtual hard disks. Click Next to continue.

9. At this point the Clone Existing Virtual Machine Wizard is prompting you for guest customization options, as shown in Figure 10.6.

   If you want to use a customization specification that you already created, you would select Customize The Operating System. In this case, we want to show you how to create a specification while cloning the VM, so select Customize The Operating System and click Next.

10. Click the Create a Specification icon and the Guest Customization Spec Wizard opens.

    This is the same wizard you used to create the customization specification in the section "Creating a Customization Specification." Refer back to that section for the specific details to use as you walk through the sections of this wizard.

11. At the end of the Guest Customization Spec, as shown in Figure 10.7 the specification is saved for later use.

FIGURE 10.6
The Clone Virtual Machine Wizard offers several options for customizing the guest OS.

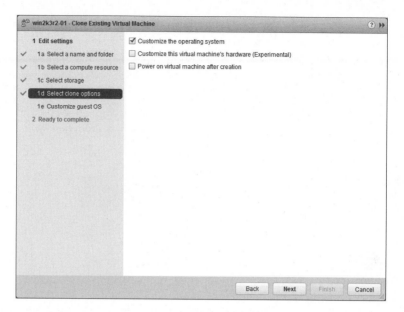

FIGURE 10.7
Your guest OS customizations as a specification are saved for later use, even if created in the middle of the VM cloning wizard.

You've now seen both ways to create a customization specification within the vSphere Web Client.

12. Click Finish to complete the guest customization process and return to the Clone Existing Virtual Machine Wizard, select the newly created specification and then click Next.

13. Review the settings for cloning the VM. If any of the settings are incorrect, use the Back button or the hyperlinks on the left to go back to the appropriate section and make any desired changes. Otherwise, click Finish to start the VM cloning process.

When the VM cloning process kicks off, the vSphere Web Client will show a new active task in the Recent Tasks area, as shown in Figure 10.8. From here, you can monitor the progress of the cloning operation.

FIGURE 10.8
The cloning task in the vSphere Web Client provides feedback on the current status of the VM cloning operation.

Once the cloning is complete, you can power on the VM. Note that the guest OS customization won't begin until you power on the VM. After you power on the VM and the guest OS loads, the vSphere Web Client will kick in and start the guest customization process. Depending on the guest OS, it may take at least one reboot before the customization process is complete.

CLONING RUNNING VMs

It's possible to clone even powered-on VMs! The context menu of a VM provides a Clone option that allows you to make a copy of the VM. The Clone To New Virtual Machine option from the Commands list on a VM summary page accomplishes the same task. These commands are available for VMs that are powered off as well as VMs that are powered on. Keep in mind that unless you customize the guest OS, an exact copy of the original VM will be made. This could be especially useful when you're looking to create a test environment that mirrors a live production environment.

As you can see, cloning VMs—which may take only a few minutes, depending upon the size of the VM and your infrastructure—is a much faster way of deploying new VMs than manually creating the VM and installing the guest OS.

Through VM cloning, administrators can create a library of "gold VM images," master copies of VMs that have certain settings and a particular guest OS installed. The only problem with this approach is that these VMs, which are intended to serve as master copies and not be changed, can still be powered on and modified. This potential shortcoming is addressed through VM templates within vCenter Server. We'll show you how templates work in the next section.

Creating Templates and Deploying Virtual Machines

In a vSphere environment, what would traditionally take several hours to do is now reduced to a matter of minutes. In this chapter, you've already seen how you can quickly and easily spin up new VMs with VM cloning and customization specifications, complete with the guest OS already installed. The templates feature of vCenter Server builds on this functionality to help you roll out new VMs quickly and easily with limited administrative effort while protecting the master VMs from inadvertent changes.

YOU'LL NEED vCENTER SERVER FOR THIS FEATURE

Because templates leverage cloning to deploy new VMs, it's possible to use templates only when you are using vCenter Server to manage your ESXi hosts.

---

vCenter Server offers two different options for creating templates: Clone To Template and Convert To Template. In both cases, you'll start with a VM that already has an instance of a guest OS installed. As the name suggests, the Clone To Template feature copies this initial VM to a template format, leaving the original VM intact. Similarly, the Convert To Template feature takes the initial VM and changes it to template format, thereby removing the ability to perform power operations on the VM without converting back to VM format. Using either approach, once the VM is in template format, that template cannot be powered on or have its settings edited. It's now in a protected format that prevents administrators from inadvertently or unintentionally modifying the "gold image" from which other VMs are deployed.

When considering which VMs you should convert to templates, remember that the idea behind a template is to have a pristine system configuration that can be customized as needed for deployment to the target environment. Any information stored on a VM that becomes a template will become part of the new system that is deployed from that template. If you have VMs that are critical servers for production environments that have applications installed, those are not good candidates for becoming templates. The best VMs to use for templates are VMs that have a new, clean installation of the guest OS and any other base components.

In fact, we recommend creating a new VM specifically for use as a template or creating the template from a VM as soon after creation as possible. This ensures that the template is as pristine as possible and that all VMs cloned from that template will start out the same way.

You can convert a VM to a template using the context menu of the VM or the Convert To Template link in the Commands list. Figure 10.9 shows two ways an existing VM can be changed into a template format. Because templates cannot be modified, to make changes or perform updates to a template you must first convert the template back to a VM, then update it, and finally convert it back to a template. Note that the Convert To Template command is grayed out if the VM is currently powered on. To use the Convert To Template command, the VM must be powered off.

FIGURE 10.9
Users can either convert a VM to a template or clone the VM to a template.

Cloning a Virtual Machine to a Template

The Clone To Template feature provides the same result as the conversion method in creating a template that can be deployed as a new VM, but it differs from the conversion method in that the original VM remains intact. By leaving the original VM in a format that can be turned on, the Clone To Template feature facilitates making updates to the template. This means you don't have to store the template object definition in the same datastore from which the VM was built.

Perform these steps to clone a VM into a template format:

1. Use the vSphere Web Client to connect to a vCenter Server instance. Cloning and templates are not supported when using the vSphere Client to connect directly to an ESXi host.

2. Navigate to the Hosts And Clusters or VMs And Templates inventory view.

   Either view allows you to clone to a template, but you'll only be able to see the template in the VMs And Templates inventory view.

3. Right-click the VM to be used as a template, and select All vCenter Actions ➤ Template ➤ Clone To Template.

4. Type a name for the new template in the Template Name text box, select a logical location in the inventory to store the template, and then click Next.

5. Select the host or cluster where the template should be hosted, and click Next.

6. If you selected a cluster for which DRS is disabled or is configured for Manual operation, you must select a specific host in the cluster. Click Next.

7. At the top of the next screen, shown in Figure 10.10, select the disk format for the template.

FIGURE 10.10

vCenter Server offers four options for storing a template's virtual disks.

Four options are available for the template's disk format:

♦ The Same Format As Source option keeps the template's virtual disks in the same format as the VM that is being cloned.

♦ Thick Provision Lazy Zeroed means that the space is fully allocated when the virtual disk is created but the space is not zeroed out upon creation.

♦ Thick Provision Eager Zeroed also allocates all space on creation and also zeroes all the space out before it can be used. This format is required for use with vSphere FT.

♦ Thin Provision format commits space on demand, meaning that the virtual disks will occupy only as much space as is currently used by the guest OS.

8. If you have defined any VM storage policies, choose the appropriate storage policy from the Storage Service Class drop-down list. If VM storage policies haven't been enabled or none are defined, this drop-down list is disabled (grayed out). Click Next to continue.

9. Review the template configuration information, and click Finish.

YOU DON'T CUSTOMIZE TEMPLATES

You'll note that you didn't have an option to customize the template. The guest OS customization occurs when you deploy VMs from a template, not when you create the template itself. Remember that templates can't be powered on, and guest OS customization requires that the VM be powered on.

Templates have a different icon than the one used to identify a VM in the vCenter Server inventory. The template objects are available by clicking a datacenter object and then selecting the Virtual Machines tab or by adjusting the inventory view to the VMs And Templates view.

Deploying a Virtual Machine from a Template

After you have created a library of templates, provisioning a new VM is as simple as right-clicking the template you'd like to use as the base system image.

Perform these steps to deploy a VM from a template:

1. Use the vSphere Web Client to connect to a vCenter Server instance. Cloning and templates are not supported when using the vSphere Client to connect directly to an ESXi host.

2. Locate the template object to be used as the VM baseline. You will find the template object in the VMs And Templates inventory view.

3. Right-click the template object and select Deploy Virtual Machine From This Template. This launches the Deploy From Template Wizard.

4. Type a name for the new VM in the VM's Name text box, select a logical location in the inventory to store the VM, and then click Next.

5. Select the cluster or host on which the VM should run, and then click Next.

6. If you selected a cluster for which DRS is not enabled or is configured to operate in Manual mode, you must select the specific host on which to run the VM. Click Next.

7. If prompted, select the resource pool in which the VM should be located and click Next.

8. Select the desired virtual disk format for the VM to be created from the template.

9. If you have defined any VM storage policies, choose the appropriate storage policy from the VM Storage policy drop-down list, then select the destination datastore or datastore cluster. Use the Advanced button (shown in Figure 10.11 but not selected) if you need to place VM configuration files and virtual disks in separate locations.

FIGURE 10.11
Select a datastore for a new VM based on the vMotion, DRS, HA, and other constraints of your organization.

10. Select how you want to customize the guest OS.

You can use an existing customization specification by selecting Customize Using An Existing Customization Specification, or you can select Customize Using The Customization Wizard to supply the customization information interactively. We've shown you both options already. In this case, let's use the specification you created earlier, so select Customize Using An Existing Customization Specification and select the specification you created earlier. Click Next.

DON'T SELECT DO NOT CUSTOMIZE

We do not recommend selecting Do Not Customize. This will result in a VM that has the same guest OS and network configuration as the original template. While this might not cause any problems the first time you deploy from this template, it will almost assuredly cause problems for future deployments.

The only instance in which selecting Do Not Customize is applicable is if you have already taken steps within the guest OS installation (such as running Sysprep in a VM with a Windows-based guest OS) before converting it to a template.

---

11. Because the customization specification you created earlier was created with the option to prompt the user for the static IP address to be assigned to the guest OS, the Deploy From Template Wizard now prompts you for the IP address. Enter the IP address you want to assign to this VM and click Next. If the customization had been configured to use DHCP, the wizard would skip this step.

12. Review the template deployment information.

If you need to make changes, use the hyperlinks or the Back button to go back. Otherwise, click Finish to start the VM deployment from the template.

vCenter Server will proceed to copy all the files that compose the template into a new location on the selected datastore. The first time the new VM is powered on, vCenter Server will kick in and perform the customization according to the values stored in the customization specification or the values you entered in the Guest Customization Wizard. Aside from those changes, the new VM will be an exact copy of the original template. By incorporating the latest patches and updates in your templates, you can thus be sure that your cloned VMs are up to date and consistent.

Templates are a great way to help standardize the configuration of your VMs while also speeding up the deployment of new VMs. Unfortunately, vCenter Server doesn't make it possible for you to transport a template between vCenter Server instances or between different installations of VMware vSphere. To help address that limitation, VMware helped develop a new industry standard: the Open Virtualization Format (OVF) standard.

Using OVF Templates

Open Virtualization Format (formerly called Open Virtual Machine Format) is a standard format for describing the configuration of a VM. While originally pioneered by VMware, other virtualization vendors now support OVF as well. VMware vSphere 5 provides OVF support in two different ways:

◆ Deploying new VMs from an OVF template (essentially, importing a VM in OVF format)

◆ Exporting a VM as an OVF template

Let's look first at deploying VMs from an OVF template.

Deploying a VM from an OVF Template

The first way to work with OVF templates is to deploy a VM from an OVF template by simply right-clicking a host, cluster, datacenter, or vCenter Server and selecting Deploy OVF Template. This initiates a wizard that walks you through deploying a new VM from the OVF template. Figure 10.12 shows that vCenter Server can deploy OVF templates stored locally as well as OVF templates that are stored remotely and are accessible with a URL.

FIGURE 10.12
vCenter Server uses a wizard to deploy templates from OVF.

Aside from selecting the source location of the OVF template, the process of deploying a VM from an OVF template is the same regardless of whether you are importing from a local set of files or downloading it across the Internet.

Perform the following steps to deploy a VM from an OVF template:

1. If it is not already running, launch the vSphere Web Client and connect to a vCenter Server instance or an ESXi host.

2. From within the vSphere Web Client Hosts And Clusters view, right-click a host and select Deploy OVF Template.

3. Select the source location of the OVF template—which must be provided in OVF or OVA format—and click Next.

OVF OR OVA?

Later in this chapter, in the section "Examining OVF Templates," we'll provide more information on the difference between OVF and OVA.

4. The OVF Template Details screen summarizes the information about the template. Click Next to continue.

5. Click the Accept button to accept the end user license agreement, and click Next.

6. Supply a name for the new VM you're deploying from the OVF template, and select a location within the vCenter Server inventory.

    This is a logical location, not a physical location; you'll select the physical location (where the new VM will run and where the virtual hard disk files will be stored) in the next step.

7. Select a cluster, an ESXi host, or a resource pool where the new VM will run, and then click Next.

8. If you selected a cluster for which vSphere DRS is not enabled or is set to Manual, you must select a specific host on which to run the VM. Select an ESXi host and click Next.

9. Choose the datastore or datastore cluster where you want to store the new VM.

    If you are unsure of how much space the new VM requires, the OVF Template Details screen, described in step 4, shows how much space the VM requires. Click Next after you've selected the datastore you want to use.

10. Select the virtual disk format you want to use for the new VM.

    Click Next after selecting a disk format.

11. Map each source network defined in the OVF template to a destination network in vCenter Server.

    The destination networks are port groups or dvPort groups, as you can see in Figure 10.13. For more information about port groups, see Chapter 5, "Creating and Configuring Virtual Networks."

FIGURE 10.13
Source networks defined in the OVF template are mapped to port groups and dvPort groups in vCenter Server.

12. Some OVF templates will ask you to confirm how IP addresses should be assigned to the new VM, as you can see in Figure 10.14. Select the option you prefer (Static - Manual or DHCP) and click Next.

FIGURE 10.14
vSphere admin-
istrators have
different options
for controlling
how new VMs are
deployed from
OVF templates
and assigned an IP
address.

SELECTING THE CORRECT IP ALLOCATION POLICY

Generally, you will select either Static - Manual or DHCP from the IP allocation drop-down list. The Transient option requires specific configurations to be enabled within vCenter Server (IP pools cre-ated and configured) as well as support within the guest OS inside the OVF template. This support usually takes the form of a script or an executable application that sets the IP address.

---

13. Some OVF templates will now prompt the user to input certain properties that will be used by the new VM.

For example, if you selected Static - Manual as the IP address allocation mechanism in step 12, you would be prompted to assign an IP address in this step as illustrated in Figure 10.15. Supply the correct value, and then click Next to continue.

14. The Ready To Complete screen summarizes the actions to be taken while deploying the new VM from the OVF template. If everything is correct, click Finish; if anything is incor-rect, use the Back button to go back and make the correct selection.

Once the deployment of the new VM from the OVF template is complete, the new VM is treated like any other VM in the inventory. You can power it on, power it off, clone it, or snap-shot it—refer to Chapter 9 for more details on these tasks.

The other way vCenter Server allows you to work with OVF is to export a VM as an OVF template.

FIGURE 10.15
The Deploy OVF
Template Wizard
provides a warn-
ing if properties
have invalid values
assigned.

Exporting a VM as an OVF Template

In addition to providing the ability to deploy new VMs from an OVF template, vCenter Server lets you export an existing VM as an OVF template. This functionality could be used in a number of different ways:

◆ Creating a template that could be transported between multiple vCenter Server instances

◆ Transporting a VM from one vSphere installation to another vSphere installation

◆ Transporting a VM to or from a different hypervisor that supports the OVF standard

◆ Allowing a software vendor to package its product as a VM and easily distribute it to customers

Whatever your reason for exporting a VM as an OVF template, the process is relatively straightforward.

Perform these steps to export a VM as an OVF template:

1. If it is not already running, launch the vSphere Web Client and connect to a vCenter Server instance or an ESXi host.

2. From within the vSphere Web Client, locate the VM you wish to export.

3. Right-click the VM and select Export OVF Template. This opens the Export OVF Template dialog box.

4. Supply a name for the OVF template, select a directory where the OVF template will be stored, and choose the format:

   ◆ The Folder Of Files (OVF) format puts the separate components of an OVF template—the manifest (MF) file, the structural definition (OVF) file, and the virtual hard disk (VMDK) file—as separate files in a folder.

   ◆ The Single File (OVA) format combines the separate components into a single file. You might find this format easier to transport or distribute.

5. Supply a description for the OVF template.

6. When you are ready to begin the export, click OK.

7. The selected VM is exported to the chosen directory as an OVF template.

   Figure 10.16 shows a VM that was exported as an OVF template in OVF (Folder of Files) format, so that you can see the different components.

FIGURE 10.16
This VM exported as an OVF template shows the different components of the template.

Once the VM has been successfully exported as an OVF template, you can use the steps in "Deploying a VM from an OVF Template" to import that VM back into a VMware vSphere implementation.

Before we move away from the topic of OVF templates, Let's take a quick look at the structure and components that make up an OVF template.

Examining OVF Templates

In Figure 10.16, we showed you the different files that make up an OVF template. In this example, three files make up the OVF template that you exported out of vCenter Server:

   ◆ The name of the manifest file ends in .mf and the file contains SHA-1 digests of the other two files. This allows vCenter Server (and other applications that support the OVF specification) to verify the integrity of the OVF template by computing the SHA-1 digests of the other files in the package and comparing them against the SHA-1 digests in the manifest file. If the digests match, then the contents of the OVF template have not been modified.

WHAT PROTECTS THE MANIFEST?

The manifest contains SHA-1 digests to help an application verify that the components of the OVF template have not been modified. But what protects the manifest? The OVF specification lets you use an optional X.509 digital certificate that can verify the integrity of the manifest file as well.

◆ The OVF descriptor is an XML document, with a filename ending in .ovf, that contains information about the OVF template such as product details, virtual hardware, requirements, licensing, a full list of file references, and a description of the contents of the OVF template. Listing 10.1 shows the partial contents of the OVF descriptor for the VM we exported from vCenter Server in the previous section. (We've added backslashes (\) where a line has been manually wrapped to help with the readability of the OVF descriptor.)

◆ The virtual hard disk file has a filename ending in .vmdk. The OVF specification supports multiple virtual hard disk formats, not just the VMDK files used by VMware vSphere, but obviously vCenter Server and VMware ESXi only natively support virtual hard disks in the VMDK format. Depending on the OVF template, it may contain multiple VMDK files, all of which would need to be referenced in the OVF descriptor file (refer to the <DiskSection> in the OVF descriptor file in Listing 10.1).

LISTING 10.1:   Partial contents of a sample OVF descriptor file

```
<?xml version="1.0" encoding="UTF-8"?>
<!--Generated by VMware VirtualCenter Server, User: Administrator, \
  UTC time: 2013-04-05T00:37:32.238463Z-->
<Envelope vmw:buildId="build-380461" \
xmlns="http://schemas.dmtf.org/ovf/envelope/1" \
xmlns:cim="http://schemas.dmtf.org/wbem/wscim/1/common" \
xmlns:ovf="http://schemas.dmtf.org/ovf/envelope/1" \
xmlns:rasd="http://schemas.dmtf.org/wbem/wscim/1/cim-schema \
/2/CIM_ResourceAllocationSettingData" \
xmlns:vmw="http://www.vmware.com/schema/ovf" \
xmlns:vssd="http://schemas.dmtf.org/wbem/wscim/1/cim-schema \
/2/CIM_VirtualSystemSettingData" \
xmlns:xsi="http://www.w3.org/2001/XMLSchema-instance">
 <References>
   <File ovf:href="core2k8r2-01-disk1.vmdk" ovf:id="file1" \
   ovf:size="1152849920" />
 </References>
 <DiskSection>
```

```
<Info>Virtual disk information</Info>
<Disk ovf:capacity="30" ovf:capacityAllocationUnits="byte * 2^30" \
ovf:diskId="vmdisk1" ovf:fileRef="file1" \
ovf:format="http://www.vmware.com/interfaces/specifications/vmdk.html# \
streamOptimized" ovf:populatedSize="2744057856" />
</DiskSection>
<NetworkSection>
  <Info>The list of logical networks</Info>
  <Network ovf:name="VLAN19">
    <Description>The VLAN19 network</Description>
  </Network>
</NetworkSection>
<VirtualSystem ovf:id="core2k8r2-01">
  <Info>A virtual machine</Info>
  <Name>core2k8r2-01</Name>
  <OperatingSystemSection ovf:id="1" \
  vmw:osType="windows7Server64Guest">
    <Info>The kind of installed guest operating system</Info>
    <Description>Microsoft Windows Server 2008 R2 (64-bit) \
    </Description>
  </OperatingSystemSection>
  <VirtualHardwareSection>
    <Info>Virtual hardware requirements</Info>
    <System>
      <vssd:ElementName>Virtual Hardware Family</vssd:ElementName>
      <vssd:InstanceID>0</vssd:InstanceID>
      <vssd:VirtualSystemIdentifier>core2k8r2-01
      </vssd:VirtualSystemIdentifier>
      <vssd:VirtualSystemType>vmx-08</vssd:VirtualSystemType>
    </System>
  </VirtualHardwareSection>
</VirtualSystem>
</Envelope>
```

The OVF specification allows two different formats for OVF templates, which we've discussed briefly. OVF templates can be distributed as a set of files, like the one we exported from vCenter Server in the previous section. In this case, it's easy to see the different components of the OVF template, but it's a bit more complicated to distribute unless you are distributing the OVF template as a set of files on a web server (keep in mind that vCenter Server and VMware ESXi can deploy VMs from an OVF template stored at a remote URL).

OVF templates can also be distributed as a single file. This single file has a name that ends in .ova and is in TAR format, and the OVF specification has strict requirements about the placement and order of components within the OVA archive. All the components that we've already described are still present, but because everything is stored in a single file, it's more difficult to view them independently of each other. However, using the OVA (single file) format does make it easier to move the OVF template between locations because you work with only a single file.

WANT EVEN MORE DETAIL?

The full OVF specification as approved by the Desktop Management Task Force (DMTF) is available from the DMTF website at www.dmtf.org/standards/ovf. At the time this book was written, the latest version of the specification was version 1.1.0, published in January 2010.

The OVF specification also gives OVF templates another interesting ability: the ability to encapsulate multiple VMs inside a single OVF template. The OVF descriptor contains elements that specify whether the OVF template contains a single VM (noted by the VirtualSystem element, which you can see in Listing 10.1) or multiple VMs (noted by the VirtualSystemCollection element). An OVF template that contains multiple VMs would allow a vSphere administrator to deploy an entire collection of VMs from a single OVF template.

In fact, vSphere leverages this ability of an OVF template to encapsulate multiple VMs in a key feature known as vApps.

Working with vApps

vApps are a way for vSphere administrators to combine multiple VMs into a single unit. Why is this functionality useful? Increasingly, enterprise applications are no longer constrained to a single VM. Instead, they may have components spread across multiple VMs. For example, a typical multitier application might have one or more frontend web servers, an application server, and a backend database server. Although each of these servers is a discrete VM and could be managed as such, they are also part of a larger application that is servicing the organization. Combining these different VMs into a vApp allows the vSphere administrator to manage the different VMs as a single unit.

In the following sections, we'll show you how to work with vApps, including creating vApps and editing vApps. Let's start with creating a vApp.

Creating a vApp

Creating a vApp is a two-step process. First, you create the vApp container and configure any settings. Second, you add one or more VMs to the vApp, by cloning existing VMs, deploying from a template, or creating a new VM from scratch in the vApp. You repeat the process of adding VMs until you have all the necessary VMs contained in the vApp.

Perform these steps to create a vApp:

1. If it is not already running, launch the vSphere Web Client and connect to a vCenter Server instance or launch the traditional vSphere Client and connect to a stand-alone ESXi host.

2. Ensure that you are in an inventory view that will allow you to create a vApp by selecting Hosts And Clusters or VMs And Templates.

3. Right-click an existing host, resource pool, or cluster and select New vApp. This launches the New vApp Wizard.

LIMITATIONS ON CREATING NEW VAPPS

While you can create vApps inside other vApps, you can't create a vApp on a cluster that does not have vSphere DRS enabled.

4. If using the Web Client, you will be asked if you wish to create a new vApp or clone an existing vApp. In this example, we are creating a new vApp, so choose that option and click Next to continue.

5. Supply a name for the new vApp.

   If you are connected to vCenter Server, you must also select a location in the folder hierarchy in which to store the vApp. (This is logical placement, not physical placement.)

6. Click Next. This advances the New vApp Wizard to the Resource Allocation step. If you need to adjust the resource allocation settings for the vApp, you may do so here.

   By default, as shown in Figure 10.17, a new vApp is given normal priority, no reservation, and no limit on CPU or memory usage. It's important to note, however, that these default settings might not fit into your overall resource allocation strategy. Be sure to read Chapter 11, "Managing Resource Allocation," for more information on the impact of these settings on your vApp.

7. Click Next to proceed to the final step in the New vApp Wizard. From here, review the settings for the new vApp. If everything is correct, click Finish; otherwise, go back in the wizard to change what needs to be changed.

After the vApp is created, you can proceed with adding VMs to the vApp. There are a few different ways to add VMs to a vApp:

◆ You can clone an existing VM into a new VM inside the vApp. We described the process of cloning a VM earlier in this chapter in the section "Cloning a Virtual Machine"; that same procedure applies here.

◆ You can deploy a new VM from a vCenter Server template and put the new VM into the vApp.

◆ You can create an entirely new VM from scratch inside the vApp. Because you are creating a new VM from scratch, this means that you will have to install the guest OS into the VM; cloning an existing VM or deploying from a template typically eliminates this task.

◆ You can drag and drop an existing VM and add it to a vApp.

Once the vApp is created and you've added one or more VMs to it, you'll probably need to edit some of the vApp's settings.

FIGURE 10.17
You will want to ensure that these default resource allocation settings are appropriate for your specific environment.

Editing a vApp

Editing a vApp is a bit different because a vApp is a container, of sorts, and the vApp has properties and settings just as the VMs in that vApp have properties and settings. To help avoid confusion about where a setting should be set or edited, VMware has tried to make the vApp container as lean and simple as possible. There are really only a few settings that can be edited at the vApp level.

EDITING A VAPP'S RESOURCE ALLOCATION SETTINGS

To edit a vApp's resource allocation settings, right-click a vApp and select Edit Settings from the context menu. This will bring up the Edit vApp dialog box, shown in Figure 10.18.

FIGURE 10.18

The Edit vApp Settings dialog box is where you can make any changes that need to be made to a vApp's configuration.

Selecting the Options tab and then the Resources option will expose the vApp's resource allocation settings. From here you can assign a higher or lower priority of access to resources, reserve resources for the vApp, or even limit the resources used by the vApp. If you don't understand what these settings mean or how they are used yet, don't worry; Chapter 11 provides complete details on using these settings in your VMware vSphere environment.

EDITING A VAPP'S IP ALLOCATION SCHEME

Within the Edit vApp Settings dialog box, the IP Allocation Policy option allows you to modify how IP addresses will be allocated to VMs contained within the vApp, as shown in Figure 10.19.

The three possible IP allocation settings are Static - Manual, Transient, and DHCP:

♦ When you use the Static-Manual option, the IP addresses must be manually set in the guest OS instance inside the VM.

♦ The Transient option leverages vCenter Server's ability to create and manage IP pools to assign IP addresses to the VMs inside a vApp. When the VMs are powered off, the IP addresses are automatically released.

♦ The DHCP option leverages an external DHCP server to assign IP addresses to the VMs in a vApp.

FIGURE 10.19
There are different options for assigning IP addresses to VMs inside a vApp.

IP POOLS AREN'T THE SAME AS DHCP

You might initially think that using Transient with IP pools means that vCenter Server uses a DHCP-like mechanism to assign IP addresses to VMs inside a vApp without any further interaction from the user. Unfortunately, this is not the case. Using Transient with IP pools requires the guest OSes in the VMs in the vApp to have some sort of support for this functionality. This support is typically in the form of a script, executable, or other mechanism whereby an IP address is obtained from the IP pool, and it is assigned to the guest OS inside the VM. It is not the same as DHCP and it does not replace or supplant DHCP on a network segment.

When you first create a vApp, you will find that the only IP allocation policy that you can select here is Static - Manual. You will need to enable the other two options before you can select them. You enable the other IP allocation options by selecting the OVF Environment check box in the IP Allocation area. This activates the Advanced IP Allocation dialog box shown in Figure 10.20.

EDITING A VAPP'S AUTHORING SETTINGS

The Authoring area of the Edit vApp Settings dialog box is where you can supply some additional metadata about the vApp, such as product name, product version, vendor name, and vendor URL. The values supplied here might be prepopulated, if you have a vApp that you received from a vendor, or you might populate these values yourself. Either way, the values set here show up on the Details area of the Summary tab on the vApp. Figure 10.21 shows a vApp's metadata as it appears in the vSphere Web Client.

EDITING A VAPP'S POWER SETTINGS

One of the value propositions of a vApp is that you can power on or power off all the VMs in a vApp, in the correct order, in one step. We'll show you how that's done in just a moment—although you probably have already figured it out—but first we want to cover the vApp's power settings.

The Start Order section of the Edit vApp Settings dialog box is where you can set the startup order of the VMs and specify how much time will elapse between VMs booting up. Likewise, this is where you can set the shutdown action and timing.

For the most part, the only thing you'll really need to adjust here is the actual startup/shutdown order. Use the up/down arrows to move the order of the VMs so that the VMs boot up in the correct sequence. For example, you may want to ensure that the backend database VM comes up before the middle-tier application server, which should in turn come up before the frontend web server. You can control all this from the Start Order tab. Generally speaking, most of the defaults here are fine.

FIGURE 10.21
The vSphere Web Client displays the metadata in the Details area of the Summary tab of a vApp object.

Note that we said "most of the defaults." There is one default setting that we would recommend you change. Shutdown Action is, by default, set to Power Off. We recommend you change this to Guest Shutdown (which will require VMware Tools to be installed in the guest OS instance). You can set this on a per-VM basis, so if you have a VM that doesn't have the tools installed—not a recommended situation, by the way—then you can leave Shutdown Action set to Power Off.

Figure 10.22 shows the Shutdown Action option for the VM named `win2k8r2-04` set to Guest Shutdown instead of Power Off.

Changing a vApp's Power State

The process for powering on or powering off a vApp is the same as for a standard VM. You can select one of the following three methods to power on a vApp:

◆ The Power On command in the Actions button as shown in Figure 10.23

FIGURE 10.22
Using Guest Shutdown instead of Power Off will provide application and OS consistency and help avoid corruption in the guest OS instance.

FIGURE 10.23
The Actions button for a vApp offers options to change the power state for all VMs within the vApp.

◆ The Power On button on the vSphere Web Client toolbar from within the Related Objects tab

◆ The Power On command from the vApp's context menu, accessible by right-clicking a vApp

The Start Order tab in the vApp's properties controls what happens when the user tells vCenter Server to power on the vApp; you can see this in Figure 10.22. vCenter Server will power on all the VMs in a group, wait the specified period of time, then power on the VMs in the next group, wait the specified period of time, and so on. You can control the order in which VMs should be started as well as the waiting period between the groups by editing the settings shown in the Start Order tab.

Once the vApp is up and running, you can suspend the vApp or power down the vApp just as you would suspend or power down a stand-alone VM. Depending on the settings on the Start Order tab, the VMs within a vApp can be configured in different ways to respond to a Power Off request to the vApp itself. As we recommended in the previous section, it's probably best to set Guest Shutdown as the action to take in response to a request to power off the vApp. Shutdown occurs in the reverse order from startup of the vApp.

Cloning a vApp

In much the same manner as cloning individual VMs, you can also clone a vApp.

Perform the following steps to clone a vApp:

1. If the vSphere Web Client is not already running, launch it and connect to a vCenter Server instance. You must connect to vCenter Server in order to clone a vApp.

2. Navigate to either the Hosts And Clusters or VMs And Templates view; both of them show the vApp objects in the inventory.

3. Right-click the vApp and select All vCenter Actions ➢ Clone.

4. In the Clone vApp Wizard, select a host, cluster, or resource pool on which to run the new vApp. Because vApps require vSphere DRS, you cannot select a cluster on which vSphere DRS is not enabled. Click Next.

5. Supply a name for the new vApp, and select a logical inventory location for the vApp. Click Next to continue.

6. Select a target datastore or datastore cluster, and then click Next. Note that you do not have the option to select a VM storage policy. While member VMs can have VM storage policies assigned, you can't assign a VM storage policy to the vApp itself.

7. Select the target virtual disk format. Click Next.

8. If the vApp has specific properties defined, you will next have the option to edit those properties for the cloned vApp. Click Next when you are ready to continue.

9. Review the settings for the new vApp, and use the Back button or the hyperlinks on the left to go back and make changes if needed. If everything is correct, click Finish.

vCenter Server will clone the vApp container object and all VMs within the vApp. vCenter Server will not, however, customize the guest OS installations inside the VMs in the vApp; the administrator assumes the burden of ensuring that the VMs in the cloned vApp are customized appropriately.

So far in this chapter, you've seen how to clone VMs, customize cloned VMs, create templates, work with OVF templates, and work with vApps. In the last section of this chapter, we'll take a quick look at importing VMs from other environments into your VMware vSphere environment.

Importing Machines from Other Environments

VMware offers a stand-alone free product called VMware Converter to help customers take OS installations on physical hardware and migrate them—using a process called a physical-to-virtual migration, or a P2V migration—into a virtualized environment running vSphere. Not only does VMware Converter provide P2V functionality, but it also provides virtual-to-virtual (V2V) functionality. The V2V functionality allows VMs created on other virtualization platforms to be imported into VMware vSphere. Administrators can also use VMware Converter's V2V functionality to export VMs out of VMware vSphere to other virtualization platforms. This V2V functionality is particularly helpful in moving VMs between VMware's enterprise-class virtualization platform, VMware vSphere, and VMware's hosted virtualization platforms, such as VMware Workstation for Windows or Linux or VMware Fusion for Mac OS X. Although VMware created all these products, slight differences in the architecture of the products require VMware Converter or a similar tool to move VMs between the products.

The Bottom Line

Clone a VM. The ability to clone a VM is a powerful feature that dramatically reduces the amount of time to get a fully functional VM with a guest OS installed and running. vCenter Server provides the ability to clone VMs and to customize VMs, ensuring that each VM is unique. You can save the information to customize a VM as a customization specification and then reuse that information over and over again. vCenter Server can even clone running VMs.

Master It Where and when can customization specifications be created in the vSphere Web Client?

Master It A fellow administrator comes to you and wants you to help streamline the process of deploying Solaris x86 VMs in your VMware vSphere environment. What do you tell him?

Create a VM template. vCenter Server's templates feature is an excellent complement to the cloning functionality. With options to clone or convert an existing VM to a template, vCenter Server makes it easy to create templates. By creating templates, you ensure that your VM master image doesn't get accidentally changed or modified. Then, once a template has been created, vCenter Server can clone VMs from that template, customizing them in the process to ensure that each one is unique.

Master It Of the following tasks, which are appropriate to be performed on a VM running Windows Server 2008 that will eventually be turned into a template?

    a.   Align the guest OS's file system to a 64 KB boundary.

    b.   Join the VM to Active Directory.

    c.   Perform some application-specific configurations and tweaks.

    d.   Install all patches from the operating system vendor.

Deploy new VMs from a template.   By combining templates and cloning, VMware vSphere administrators have a powerful way to standardize the configuration of VMs being deployed, protect the master images from accidental change, and reduce the amount of time it takes to provision new guest OS instances.

> **Master It**   Another VMware vSphere administrator in your environment starts the wizard for deploying a new VM from a template. He has a customization specification he'd like to use, but there is one setting in the specification he wants to change. Does he have to create an all-new customization specification?

Deploy a VM from an OVF template.   Open Virtualization Format (OVF, formerly Open Virtual Machine Format) templates provide a mechanism for moving templates or VMs between different instances of vCenter Server or even entirely different and separate installations of VMware vSphere. OVF templates combine the structural definition of a VM along with the data in the VM's virtual hard disk and can exist either as a folder of files or as a single file. Because OVF templates include the VM's virtual hard disk, OVF templates can contain an installation of a guest OS and are often used by software developers as a way of delivering their software preinstalled into a guest OS inside a VM.

> **Master It**   A vendor has given you a Zip file that contains a VM they are calling a *virtual* appliance. Upon looking inside the Zip file, you see several VMDK files and a VMX file. Will you be able to use vCenter Server's Deploy OVF Template functionality to import this VM? If not, how can you get this VM into your infrastructure?

Export a VM as an OVF template.   To assist in the transport of VMs between VMware vSphere installations, you can use vCenter Server to export a VM as an OVF template. The OVF template will include the configuration of the VM as well as the data found in the VM.

> **Master It**   You are preparing to export a VM to an OVF template. You want to ensure that the OVF template is easy and simple to transport via a USB key or portable hard drive. Which format is most appropriate, OVF or OVA? Why?

Work with vApps.   vSphere vApps leverage OVF as a way to combine multiple VMs into a single administrative unit. When the vApp is powered on, all VMs in it are powered on, in a sequence specified by the administrator. The same goes for shutting down a vApp. vApps also act a bit like resource pools for the VMs contained within them.

> **Master It**   Name two ways to add VMs to a vApp.

Chapter 11

Managing Resource Allocation

The idea that we can take a single physical server and host many VMs has a great deal of value in today's dynamic datacenter environments, but let's face it: There are limits to how many VMs can run on a VMware ESXi host. To make the most of your virtualization platform, you must understand how key resources—memory, processors, disks, and networks—are consumed by the VMs running on the host and how the host itself consumes resources. The method an ESXi host uses to arbitrate access to each of these resources is a bit different. This chapter discusses how an ESXi host allocates these resources and how you can change the way these resources are allocated.

In this chapter, you will learn to

- ◆ Manage VM memory allocation

- ◆ Manage CPU utilization

- ◆ Create and manage resource pools

- ◆ Control network and storage I/O utilization

- ◆ Utilize flash storage

Reviewing Virtual Machine Resource Allocation

One of the most significant advantages of server virtualization is the ability to allocate resources to a VM based on the machine's actual performance needs. In traditional physical server environments, a server is often provided with more resources than it really needs because it was purchased with a specific budget in mind and the server specifications were maximized for the budget provided. For example, does a Dynamic Host Configuration Protocol (DHCP) server really need dual processors, 32 GB of RAM, and 146 GB mirrored hard drives? In most situations, the DHCP server will most certainly underutilize those resources. In the virtual world, you can create a VM better suited for the role of a DHCP server. For this DHCP server, then, you would assemble a VM with a more suitable 2 GB or 4 GB of RAM (depending on the guest OS), access to a single CPU, and 20 GB to 40 GB of disk space, all of which are provided by the ESXi host on which the VM is running. Then, you can create additional VMs with the resources they need to operate effectively without wasting valuable memory, CPU cycles, and disk storage.

Correctly allocating resources based on the anticipated need of the guest OS and the applications inside a VM is the essence of *right-sizing* your VMs, which we discussed in Chapter 9, "Creating and Managing Virtual Machines." Right-sizing your VMs allows you to achieve greater efficiency and higher consolidation ratios (more VMs per physical server).

Even when you right-size your VMs, though, as you add more, each VM places additional demand on the ESXi host, and the host's resources are consumed to support the VMs. At a certain point, the host will run out of resources. What does ESXi do when it runs out of resources? How does ESXi handle it when the VMs are asking for more resources than the physical host can actually provide? How can you guarantee that a guest OS and its applications get the resources they need without being starved by other guest OSes and their applications?

Fortunately, VMware vSphere offers a set of controls that are designed to do exactly that: to guarantee access to resources when necessary, to curb or control the use of resources, and to enable prioritized access to resources when available resources are low. Specifically, vSphere offers three controls for controlling or modifying resource allocation: reservations, limits, and shares.

While the behavior of these mechanisms varies based on the resource, the basic idea behind these mechanisms is as follows:

Reservations   Reservations act as guarantees of a particular resource. You would use reservations when you want to ensure that, no matter what else is going on, a specific VM is absolutely assured to have access to a particular amount of a given resource.

Limits   Limits restrict the amount of a given resource that a VM can use. VMs already have some limits simply by how they are constructed—for example, a VM configured to have a single virtual CPU (vCPU) is limited to using only that single vCPU. The Limit feature within vSphere grants you even greater granularity over how resources are utilized. Depending on the resource to which the limit is being applied, the specific behavior of ESXi will change. This is discussed in detail later in this chapter under each resource's specific section.

Shares   Shares establish priority. When an ESXi host comes under contention and must decide which VM gets access to which resources, shares are used to determine priority. VMs with higher shares assigned will have higher priority, and therefore greater access, to the ESXi host's resources.

Figure 11.1 shows these three mechanisms displayed in the properties of a VM.

Throughout the rest of this chapter, we discuss how one or more of these three mechanisms—reservations, limits, and shares—are applied to control or modify resource allocation across all four major resources in a vSphere environment: memory, CPU, storage, and network.

THE GAME PLAN FOR GROWTH

One of the most challenging aspects of managing a virtual datacenter is managing growth without jeopardizing performance but also without overestimating. For organizations of any size, it is critical to establish a plan for managing VM and ESXi host growth.

The easiest approach is to construct a resource consumption document that details the following:

◆ What is the standard configuration for a new VM to be added to the inventory? Be sure to specify critical configuration points such as the size of the operating system drive, the size of any data drives, and how much RAM is allocated. By establishing standards for VMs, you can increase efficiency and ensure that VMs are right-sized.

◆ What are the decision points for creating a VM with specifications beyond the standard configuration? A standard configuration is great, but it won't address every single need in your organization. There will be exceptions, and you just need to document what drives an exception.

◆ How much of a server's resources can be consumed before availability and performance levels are jeopardized? This both affects and is affected by other design points, like N+1 redundancy.

◆ At the point where the resources for an ESXi host (or an entire cluster) are consumed, do you add a single host or multiple hosts at one time?

◆ What is the maximum size of a cluster for your environment? When does adding another host (or set of hosts) constitute building a new cluster? This could affect operational considerations like how many hosts get added at a time. For example, if you have to start a new cluster, then you'll need at least two hosts, preferably three.

FIGURE 11.1
Reservations, limits, and shares offer more fine-grained control over resource allocation.

The first VM resource we'll examine is memory. In many instances, memory is the first resource to come under constraints, so taking a look at memory first is warranted.

Working with Virtual Machine Memory

Let's start with a discussion of how memory is allocated to a VM. Later we'll discuss how you as an administrator can use reservations, shares, and limits to help control or modify how VMs consume memory.

When you create a new VM through the Web Client, you are asked how much memory the VM should have. The Web Client suggests a default value based on the selected guest OS (the selected guest OS in this case is Windows Server 2008 R2), as shown in Figure 11.2.

The amount of memory you allocate on this screen is the amount the guest OS will see—in this example, it is 4,096 MB. This is the same as when you build a physical system and put a set of four 1,024 MB memory sticks into the system board. If you install Windows Server 2008 R2 in this VM, Windows will report 4,096 MB of RAM installed. Ultimately, this is the amount of memory the VM "thinks" it has and the maximum amount of memory the guest OS will ever be able to access. Like a physical system with four 1,024 MB DIMMs installed, this VM will never be able to use more than 4,096 MB of physical RAM.

Let's assume you have an ESXi host with 16 GB of physical RAM available to run VMs (in other words, the hypervisor is using some RAM and there's 16 GB left over for the VMs). In the case of our new VM, it will comfortably run, leaving approximately 12 GB for other VMs (there is some additional overhead that we discuss later, but for now let's assume that the 12 GB is available to other VMs).

FIGURE 11.2

The memory configuration settings for a VM indicate the amount of RAM the VM "thinks" it has.

What happens when you run three more VMs, each configured with 4 GB of RAM? Each of the additional VMs will request 4 GB of RAM from the ESXi host. At this point, four VMs will be accessing the physical memory, and you will have allocated all 16 GB of memory to the VMs. ESXi has now run out of a critical resource (memory).

What happens when you launch a fifth VM? Will it run? The short answer is yes, and some of the key technologies that enable administrators to overcommit memory—that is, to allocate more memory to VMs than is actually installed in the VMware ESXi host—are quite advanced. Because these technologies are integral to understanding how memory allocation works with VMware ESXi, let's take a look at these technologies and how they work.

Understanding ESXi Advanced Memory Technologies

VMware ESXi supports a number of different technologies for advanced memory management. As a result of these advanced memory management technologies, at the time of this writing, VMware ESXi is the only commercially available hypervisor on the market capable of performing memory overcommitment in a manner that is guest OS agnostic.

ESXi Does Not Require Guest OS Involvement

There are other commercially available hypervisors that offer the ability to overcommit memory, but these products support that functionality only for certain guest OSes.

VMware ESXi employs five different memory-management technologies to make sure the physical server's RAM is utilized as efficiently as possible: idle memory tax, transparent page sharing, ballooning, memory compression, and swapping.

While it doesn't cover everything, for anyone interested in more in-depth and detailed information on some of these memory-management technologies, we strongly recommend reading *Memory Resource Management in VMware ESX Server* by Carl A. Waldspurger, available online at the following location:

```
http://www.waldspurger.org/carl/papers/esx-mem-osdi02.pdf
```

IDLE MEMORY TAX

Before VMware ESXi actively starts making changes to relieve memory pressure, it ensures that VMs do not actively horde memory by "charging" more for the idle memory. Up to 75 percent of the memory allocated to each VM can be borrowed to service another VM by IMT. This setting is configurable on a per-VM basis within the Advanced VM settings (see Chapter 9), although in most cases this is not necessary and not recommended unless there is a specific requirement. Inside the guest OS, VMware Tools will use its balloon driver to understand which memory blocks are allocated but idle and, therefore, available to be used elsewhere. The balloon driver is also used in a more active fashion, which we will explain shortly.

TRANSPARENT PAGE SHARING

The next memory-management technology ESXi uses is *transparent page sharing* (*TPS*), in which identical memory pages are shared among VMs to reduce the total number of memory pages consumed. The hypervisor computes hashes of the contents of memory pages to identify pages that contain identical memory. If it finds a hash match, it compares the matching memory pages to exclude a false positive. Once the pages are confirmed to be identical, the hypervisor will transparently remap the memory pages of the VMs so they are sharing the same physical memory page. This reduces overall host memory consumption. Advanced parameters are available to fine-tune the behavior of the page-sharing mechanisms.

Normally, ESXi works on 4 KB memory pages and will use transparent page sharing on all memory pages. However, when the hypervisor is taking advantage of hardware offloads available in the CPUs—such as Intel Extended Page Tables (EPT) Hardware Assist or AMD Rapid Virtualization Indexing (RVI) Hardware Assist—then the hypervisor uses 2 MB memory pages, also known as large pages. In these cases, ESXi will not share these large pages, but it will compute hashes for the 4 KB pages inside the large pages. In the event that the hypervisor needs to invoke swapping, the large pages will be broken into small pages, and having the hashes already computed allows the hypervisor to invoke page sharing before they are swapped out.

BALLOONING

We mentioned previously that ESXi's memory-management technologies are guest OS agnostic, meaning that the guest OS selection doesn't matter. This is true; any supported guest OS can take advantage of all of ESXi's memory-management functionality. However, these technologies are not necessarily guest OS independent, meaning that they operate without interaction from the guest OS. While transparent page sharing operates independently of the guest OS, ballooning does not.

Ballooning involves the use of a driver—referred to as the balloon driver—installed into the guest OS. This driver is part of VMware Tools and gets installed when VMware Tools is installed. Once installed into the guest OS, the balloon driver can respond to commands from the hypervisor to reclaim memory from that particular guest OS. The balloon driver does this by requesting memory from the guest OS—a process calling *inflating*—and then passing that memory back to the hypervisor for use by other VMs.

Because the guest OS can give up pages it is no longer using when the balloon driver requests memory, it's possible for the hypervisor to reclaim memory without any performance impact on the applications running inside that guest OS. If the guest OS is already under memory pressure—meaning the amount of memory configured for that VM is insufficient for the guest OS and its applications—it's very likely that inflating the balloon driver will invoke guest OS paging (or swapping), which will impair performance.

HOW DOES THE BALLOON DRIVER WORK?

The balloon driver is part of VMware Tools, which were described in detail in Chapter 9. As such, it is specific to the guest OS, meaning that Linux VMs would have a Linux-based balloon driver, Windows VMs would have a Windows-based balloon driver, and so forth.

Regardless of the guest OS, the balloon driver works in the same fashion. When the ESXi host is running low on physical memory, the hypervisor will signal the balloon driver to grow. To do this, the balloon driver will request memory from the guest OS. This causes the balloon driver's memory footprint to grow, or to *inflate*. The memory that is granted to the balloon driver is then passed back to the hypervisor. The hypervisor can use these memory pages to supply memory for other VMs, reducing the need to swap and minimizing the performance impact of the memory constraints. When the memory pressure on the host passes, the balloon driver will *deflate*, or return memory to the guest OS.

The key advantage that ESXi gains from using a guest-OS-specific balloon driver in this fashion is that it allows the guest OS to make the decision about which pages can be given to the balloon driver process (and thus released to the hypervisor). In some cases, the inflation of the balloon driver can release memory back to the hypervisor without any degradation of VM performance because the guest OS is able to give the balloon driver unused or idle pages.

MEMORY COMPRESSION

From vSphere 4.1, VMware added another memory-management technology to the mix: memory compression. When an ESXi host gets to the point that hypervisor swapping is necessary, the VMkernel will attempt to compress memory pages and keep them in RAM in a compressed memory cache. Pages that can be successfully compressed by at least 50 percent are put into the compressed memory cache instead of being written to disk and can then be recovered much more quickly if the guest OS needs that memory page. Memory compression can dramatically reduce the number of pages that must be swapped to disk and thus can dramatically improve the performance of an ESXi host that is under strong memory pressure. There is a configurable amount of VM memory used for the compression cache (by default 10 percent), but this starts at zero and grows as needed when VM memory starts to be swapped out. Compression is invoked only when the ESXi host reaches the point that VMkernel swapping is needed.

SWAPPING

There are two forms of swapping involved when you examine how memory is managed with VMware ESXi. There is *guest OS swapping*, in which the guest OS inside the VM swaps pages out to its virtual disk according to its own memory-management algorithms. This is generally due to memory requirements that are higher than available memory. In a virtualized environment, this would translate into a VM being configured with less memory than the guest OS and its applications require, such as trying to run Windows Server 2008 R2 in only 1 GB of RAM. Guest OS swapping falls strictly under the control of the guest OS and is not controlled by the hypervisor.

The other type of swapping involved is *hypervisor swapping*. In the event that none of the previously described technologies trim guest OS memory usage enough, the ESXi host will be forced to use hypervisor swapping. Hypervisor swapping means that ESXi is going to swap memory pages out to disk in order to reclaim memory that is needed elsewhere. ESXi's swapping takes place without any regard to whether the pages are being actively used by the guest OS. As a result, and due to the fact that disk response times are thousands of times slower than memory response times, guest OS performance is severely impacted if hypervisor swapping is invoked. It is for this reason that ESXi won't invoke swapping unless it is absolutely necessary, as a last resort after all other memory management techniques have been tried.

The key thing to remember about hypervisor swapping is that you want to avoid it if at all possible; there is a significant and noticeable impact to performance. Even swapping to SSD (Solid State Drive) is considerably slower than directly accessing RAM.

Although these advanced memory-management technologies allow ESXi to allocate more memory to VMs than there is actual RAM in the physical server, they do not help guarantee memory or prioritize access to memory. Even with these advanced memory-management technologies, at some point it becomes necessary to exercise some control over how the VMs access and use the memory allocated to them. This is where a VMware vSphere administrator can use reservations, limits, and shares—the three mechanisms described previously—to modify or control how resources are allocated. Next, we'll describe how these mechanisms are used to control memory allocation.

Controlling Memory Allocation

Like all physical resources, memory is a finite resource. The advanced memory-management technologies in ESXi help with the efficient use of this finite resource by making it go farther than it normally would go. For finer-grained control over how ESXi allocates memory, though, administrators must turn to the use of the three mechanisms listed previously: reservations, shares, and limits. Figure 11.3 shows these three settings in the Virtual Machine Properties dialog box for a VM.

The steps for editing a Reservation, Limit, or Shares value for either memory or CPU are the same. Storage I/O and network I/O are handled a bit differently, so we'll discuss those in the appropriate sections later in this chapter. Storage I/O is covered in the section "Controlling Storage I/O Utilization," and network I/O is discussed in the section "Regulating Network I/O Utilization."

Perform the following steps to edit a VM's memory or CPU Reservation, Limit, or Shares value:

1. Use the Web Client to connect to a vCenter Server instance.

2. Navigate to either the Hosts And Clusters or VMs And Templates view, then drill down through the inventory to find the VM to be edited.

3. Select the VM, and select the Edit Settings option in the content area.

4. On the Virtual Hardware tab, click the triangle next to the CPU or Memory item.

5. Adjust the Shares, Reservation, and Limit values as desired.

FIGURE 11.3
vSphere supports the use of reservations, shares, and limits for controlling memory allocation.

Now that you've seen how to adjust the Reservation, Limit, and Shares values, we'll take a detailed look at the specific behaviors of how these mechanisms apply to memory usage and allocation.

USING MEMORY RESERVATIONS

The memory reservation is an optional setting for each VM. You can see in Figure 11.3 that the default memory reservation is 0 MB (the equivalent of no memory reservation at all). You can adjust this value, but what exactly does this value do? What impact does adjusting the memory reservation have?

The memory reservation amount specified in the VM settings is the amount of actual, real physical memory that the ESXi host *must* provide to this VM for the VM to power on. A VM with a memory reservation is guaranteed the amount of RAM configured in its Reservation setting. As mentioned, the default is 0 MB, or no reservation. In the previous example, configuring the VM with 4 GB of RAM and the default reservation of 0 MB means the ESXi host is not required to provide the VM with any physical memory. If the ESXi host is not required to provide actual RAM to the VM, then where will the VM get its memory? In the absence of a reservation, the VMkernel has the option to provide VM memory from *VMkernel swap*.

VMkernel swap is the hypervisor swapping mechanism referred to previously when discussing the various memory-management techniques that ESXi employs. VMkernel swap is implemented as a file with a `.vswp` filename extension that is created when a VM is powered on. These per-VM swapfiles created by the VMkernel reside, by default, in the same datastore location as the VM's configuration file and virtual disk files (although you do have the option of relocating the VMkernel swap, which we'll explain later in the section "Configuring Swap to Host Cache"). In the absence of a memory reservation—the default configuration—this file will be equal in size to the amount of RAM configured for the VM. Thus, a VM configured for 4 GB of RAM will have a VMkernel swapfile that is also 4 GB in size and stored, by default, in the same location as the VM's configuration and virtual disk files.

In theory, this means a VM could get its memory allocation entirely from VMkernel swap—or disk—resulting in VM performance degradation because disk access time is several orders of magnitude slower than RAM access time.

THE SPEED OF RAM

How slow is VMkernel swap compared to RAM? If you make some basic assumptions regarding RAM access times and disk seek times, you can see that both appear fairly fast in terms of human abilities but that in relation to each other, RAM is much faster:

RAM access time = 10 nanoseconds (for example)
SSD seek time = 500 microseconds (for example)
Rotational disk seek time = 8 milliseconds (for example)

The difference between these is calculated as follows:

$$0.008 \div 0.00000001 = 800,000$$
or
$$0.0005 \div 0.00000001 = 50,000$$

RAM is accessed 800,000 times faster than traditional rotational disk or 50,000 times faster than SSD. Or to put it another way, if RAM takes 1 second to access, then disk could take 800,000 seconds to access—or nine and a quarter days. Think having SSD swap cache will help you—it would still take over half a day.

$$((800,000 \div 60 \text{ seconds}) \div 60 \text{ minutes}) \div 24 \text{ hours} = 9.259$$
$$((50,000 \div 60 \text{ seconds}) \div 60 \text{ minutes}) \div 24 \text{ hours} = 0.578$$

As you can see, if VM performance is your goal, it is prudent to spend your money on enough RAM to support the VMs you plan to run. There are other factors, but this is a significant one. This incredible speed difference is also why adding memory compression to ESXi's arsenal of memory-management tools can make a big difference in performance; it helps avoid having to swap pages out to disk and keep them in memory instead. Even compressed pages in RAM are significantly faster than pages swapped out to disk.

Just because a VM without a reservation could potentially get all its memory from VMkernel swap, does this mean that a VM will actually get all of its memory from swap when ESXi host RAM is available? No. ESXi attempts to provide each VM with all the memory it requests, up to the maximum amount configured for that VM. Obviously, a VM configured with only 4,096 MB of RAM cannot request more than 4,096 MB of RAM. However, when an ESXi host doesn't have enough RAM available to satisfy the memory needs of the VMs it is hosting and when technologies such as transparent page sharing, the balloon driver, and memory compression aren't enough, the VMkernel is forced to page some of each VM's memory out to the individual VM's VMkernel swapfile.

Is there a way you can control how much of an individual VM's memory allocation can be provided by swap and how much must be provided by real physical RAM? Yes. This is where a memory reservation comes into play. Recall that we said a memory reservation specifies the amount of real, physical RAM that the ESXi host must provide the VM. By default, a VM has a memory reservation of 0 MB, which means that ESXi is not required to provide any real, physical RAM. This means potentially all of the VM's memory could be paged out to the VMkernel swapfile if necessary.

Let's look at what happens if you decide to set a memory reservation of 1,024 MB for this VM, shown in Figure 11.4. How does this change the way this VM gets memory?

In this example, when this VM is started, the ESXi host must provide at least 1,024 MB of physical RAM to support this VM's memory allocation. In fact, 1,024 MB of RAM is *guaranteed* for this VM. The host can provide the remaining 3,072 MB of RAM from either physical RAM or VMkernel swap, as shown in Figure 11.5. In this case, because some of the VM's RAM is guaranteed to come from physical RAM, ESXi reduces the size of the VMkernel swapfile by the amount of the reservation. Therefore, the VMkernel swapfile is reduced in size by 1,024 MB. This behavior is consistent with what we've shown you so far: With a reservation of 0 MB, the VMkernel swapfile is the same size as the amount of configured memory. As the reservation increases, the size of the VMkernel swapfile decreases in size correspondingly.

FIGURE 11.4

This memory reservation guarantees 1,024 MB of RAM for the VM.

FIGURE 11.5

The memory reservation reduces the potential need for VMkernel swap space by the size of the reservation.

VM with 4,096 MB RAM
and a 1,024 MB reservation

4 GB

Preferentially provided
by physical host RAM
but could be supplied
by VMkernel swap

3 GB

2 GB

1 GB — Reservation

Must be provided by
physical host RAM

0 GB

This behavior ensures that a VM has at least some high-speed memory available to it if the ESXi host is running more VMs than it has actual RAM to support, but there's also a downside. If you assume that each of the VMs you start on this host has a 1,024 MB reservation and you have 8 GB of available RAM in the host to run VMs, then you will be able to launch only eight VMs concurrently (8 × 1,024 MB = 8,192 MB). On a more positive note, if each VM is configured with an initial RAM allocation of 4,096 MB, then you're now running VMs that would need 32 GB of RAM on a host with only 8 GB. ESXi uses the technologies described previously—transparent page sharing, the balloon driver, memory compression, and finally, VMkernel swap—to manage the fact that you, as the administrator, have allocated more RAM than is physically installed in the server.

There's one other side effect from using memory reservations that you must also understand. We mentioned previously that using a memory reservation guarantees physical RAM for the VM. This is true, but only as the guest OS in the VM requests memory. If you have a VM with a 1,024 MB reservation configured, then the ESXi host will allocate RAM to the VM on an as-needed basis, and the first 1,024 MB of RAM allocated to that VM is part of the reservation. RAM is allocated on demand; the presence of a reservation doesn't change that behavior. Once allocated, though, because this RAM is part of the memory reservation, it's locked to this VM—it won't be reclaimed via the balloon driver, and it won't be swapped out to disk or compressed. In a way, that's good; it underscores the fact that this memory is guaranteed to this VM. In a way, it's also bad, though, because the reserved memory, once allocated to a VM, can't be reclaimed for use by other VMs or for use by the hypervisor itself.

RESERVED MEMORY AND TRANSPARENT PAGE SHARING

While reserved memory won't be reclaimed by the hypervisor for use by other purposes—it is, after all, guaranteed for that VM—reserved memory can be shared via transparent page sharing. Transparent page sharing does not affect the availability of reserved memory because the page is still accessible to the VM.

Like all the mechanisms described in this chapter, this means that you'll want to use memory reservations carefully and with a full understanding of the impact on the ESXi host's behavior and operation.

USE MEMORY OVERCOMMITMENT WISELY

Although you can overcommit memory with VMware ESXi, be careful doing so. You must carefully weigh the performance considerations. Although VMware ESXi has advanced memory-management technologies such as transparent page sharing and idle page reclamation that help conserve memory, any workload that actually needs its memory might take a performance hit if that memory isn't available. In our experience, many workloads running in Windows-based VMs utilize only a portion of their configured memory.

In these sorts of environments, it's generally safe to overcommit memory by as much as 50 percent of the physical RAM installed in the server without seeing noticeable performance degradation. This means a server with 32 GB of RAM could potentially host VMs configured to use 48 GB of RAM. Larger overcommitment ratios are certainly very possible, particularly in VDI or virtual desktop environments where a large number of VMs are using the same base OS image. We've seen certain environments where TPS alone provided upwards of 90 percent memory savings. However, the key to wisely using memory overcommitment to maximize the value of your vSphere deployment is knowing the needs of the VMs and how they consume resources.

Using Memory Limits

If you refer back to Figure 11.3, you will also see a setting for a memory limit. By default, all new VMs are created without a limit, which means that the initial RAM you assigned to it during creation is its effective limit. So, what exactly is the purpose of the Limit setting? It sets the actual limit on how much physical RAM may be utilized by that VM.

To see this behavior in action, let's now change the limit on this VM from the default setting of Unlimited to 2,048 MB.

So, what is the effective result of this configuration? Here's how it breaks down:

◆ The VM is configured with 4,096 MB of RAM, so the guest OS running inside that VM believes that it has 4,096 MB of RAM available to use.

◆ The VM has a reservation of 1,024 MB of RAM, which means that the ESXi host *must* allocate 1,024 MB of physical RAM to the VM. This RAM is guaranteed to this VM.

◆ Assuming the ESXi host has enough physical RAM installed and available, the hypervisor will allocate memory to the VM as needed up to 2,048 MB (the limit). Upon reaching 2,048 MB, the balloon driver kicks in to prevent the guest OS from using any more memory beyond 2,048 MB. When the guest OS's memory demands drop below 2,048 MB, the balloon driver deflates and returns memory to the guest. The effective result of this behavior is that the memory the guest OS uses remains below 2,048 MB (the limit).

◆ The 1,024 MB "gap" between the reservation and the limit could be supplied by either physical RAM or VMkernel swap space. ESXi will allocate physical RAM if it is available.

The key problem with memory limits is that they are enforced without any guest OS awareness. If you have a VM configured for 4 GB of RAM, the guest OS inside that VM is going to think it has 4 GB of RAM with which to work, and it will behave accordingly. If you then place a 2 GB limit on that VM, the VMkernel will enforce that the VM only uses 2 GB of RAM. Fine—but it will do so without the knowledge or cooperation of the guest OS inside that VM. The guest OS will continue to behave as if it has 4 GB of RAM, completely unaware of the limit that has been placed on it by the hypervisor. If the working set size of the guest OS and its applications exceeds the memory limit, setting a limit will degrade the performance of the VM because the guest OS will constantly be forced to swap pages to disk (guest OS swapping, not hypervisor swapping).

In general, then, you should consider memory limits a temporary stop-gap measure when you need to reduce physical memory usage on an ESXi host and a negative impact to performance is acceptable. You wouldn't, generally speaking, want to overprovision a VM with RAM and constrain memory usage with a limit on a long-term basis. In that scenario, the VM will typically perform very poorly and would actually perform better with less RAM configured and no limit.

WHY USE MEMORY LIMITS?

You might be asking yourself, "Why should I even use limits? Why not just set the configured limit to whatever I want the VM to use?" That's a good question! Keeping in mind that memory limits are enforced by the VMkernel without any awareness by the guest OS of the configured limit, memory limits can, in many cases, negatively impact the performance of the VM.

However, there are times when you might need to use memory limits as a temporary measure to reduce physical memory usage in your hosts. Perhaps you need to perform maintenance on an ESXi host that is part of a cluster. You plan to use vMotion to migrate VMs to other hosts during the maintenance window, and you want to temporarily push down memory usage on less-important VMs so that you don't overcommit memory too heavily and negatively impact lots of VMs. Limits would help in this situation.

Knowing that memory limits can have negative impacts on performance, be sure to use them only when that negative performance impact is understood and acceptable.

Working together, an initial allocation of memory, a memory reservation, and a memory limit can be powerful tools in efficiently managing the memory available on an ESXi host. But there is still one more tool to examine, and that's memory shares.

USING MEMORY SHARES

In Figure 11.3, there is a third setting called Shares that we have not yet discussed. The two mechanisms described to you already, memory reservations and memory limits, help provide finer-grained controls over how ESXi should or should not allocate memory to a VM. These mechanisms are always in effect; that is, a Limit setting is enforced even if the ESXi host has plenty of physical RAM available for the VM to use.

Memory shares are very different. The share system in VMware is a proportional share system that allows administrators to assign resource priority to VMs, but shares are only used when the ESXi host is experiencing physical RAM contention. In other words, the VMs on an ESXi host are requesting more memory than the host can provide. If an ESXi host has plenty of memory available, shares will not play a role. However, when memory is scarce and ESXi must decide which VM should be given access to memory, shares can establish a priority setting for a VM requesting memory that is greater than the VM's reservation but less than its limit. (Recall that memory under the reservation is guaranteed to the VM, and memory over the limit would not be allocated. Shares, therefore, affect only the allocation of memory between the reservation and the limit.) In other words, if two VMs want more memory than their reservation limit and the ESXi host can't satisfy both of them using RAM, then you can set share values on each VM so that one gets higher-priority access to the RAM in the ESXi host than the other.

Some would say that you should just increase the reservation for that VM. Although that might be a valid technique, it might limit the total number of VMs that a host can run, as indicated previously in this chapter. Increasing the configured amount of RAM also requires a reboot of the VM to become effective (unless you are running a guest OS that supports hot-add of memory and that feature has been enabled for the VM, as described in Chapter 9), but shares can be dynamically adjusted while the VM remains powered on.

One key part we must repeat is that shares come into play only when the ESXi host cannot satisfy the requests for memory. If the ESXi host has enough free memory to satisfy the requests from the VMs for memory, then it doesn't need to prioritize those requests. It has enough to go around. It's only when the ESXi host doesn't have enough to go around that decisions have to be made on how that resource should be allocated.

For the sake of this discussion, let's assume you have two VMs (VM1 and VM2), each with a 1,024 MB reservation and a configured maximum of 4,096 MB, and both are running on an ESXi host with less than 2 GB of RAM available to the VMs. If the two VMs in question have an equal number of shares (let's assume it's 1,000 each; we'll show you actual values shortly), then as each VM requests memory above its reservation value, each VM will receive an equal quantity of RAM from the ESXi host. Furthermore, because the host cannot supply all of the RAM to both VMs, each VM will swap equally to disk (VMkernel swapfile). This is assuming, of course, that ESXi cannot reclaim memory from other running VMs using the balloon driver or other memory-management technologies described previously. If you change VM1's Shares setting to 2,000, then VM1 now has twice the shares VM2 has assigned to it. This also means that when VM1 and VM2 are requesting the RAM above their respective Reservation values, VM1 gets two RAM pages for every one RAM page that VM2 gets. If VM1 has more shares, VM1 has a higher-priority access to available memory in the host. Because VM1 has 2,000 out of 3,000 shares allocated, it will get 67 percent; VM2 has 1,000 out of 3,000 shares allocated and therefore gets only 33 percent. This creates the two-to-one behavior described previously. Each VM is allocated RAM pages based on the proportion of the total number of shares allocated across all VMs. Figure 11.6 illustrates this behavior.

FIGURE 11.6
Shares establish relative priority based on the number of shares assigned out of the total shares allocated.

2,000 shares allocated

VM with 1,000 shares gets 50%

VM with 1,000 shares gets 50%

3,000 shares allocated

VM with 2,000 shares gets 67%

VM with 1,000 shares gets 33%

4,000 shares allocated

VM with 1,500 shares gets 37.5%

VM with 1,500 shares gets 37.5%

VM with 1,000 shares gets 25%

Even if you don't specifically assign shares to a VM, VMware vSphere automatically assigns shares to a VM when it is created. You can see the default Shares value back in Figure 11.3; it is equal to 10 times the configured memory value when the memory allocation is expressed in terms of MB—more accurately, by default 10 shares are granted to every MB assigned to a virtual machine. The VM shown in Figure 11.3 had 4,096 MB of RAM configured; therefore, its default memory Shares value was 40,960. This default allocation ensures that each VM is granted priority to memory on a measure that is directly proportional to the amount of memory configured for it.

It gets more difficult to predict the actual memory utilization and the amount of access each VM gets as more VMs run on the same ESXi host. Later in this chapter, in the section titled "Using Resource Pools," we'll discuss more sophisticated methods of assigning memory limits, reservations, and shares to a group of VMs using resource pools.

We've talked about how VMware ESXi uses some advanced memory management technologies, but there is another aspect of virtualization that you must also consider: overhead. In the next section, we'll provide some information on the memory overhead figures when using ESXi.

EXAMINING MEMORY OVERHEAD

As they say, nothing in this world is free, and in the case of memory on an ESXi host, there is a cost. That cost is memory overhead. Several basic processes on an ESXi host will consume host memory. The VMkernel itself, various daemons (services) running on the ESXi host, and each VM that is running will cause the VMkernel to allocate some memory to host the VM above the initial amount that you assign to it. The amount of RAM allocated to power on each VM depends on the virtual CPU and memory configuration of each VM. VMware has improved the overhead requirements significantly over the last few versions of vSphere. To give you an indication of what they are for version 5.5, see Table 11.1. The values have been rounded to the nearest whole number.

TABLE 11.1: Virtual machine memory overhead

VIRTUAL MEMORY ASSIGNED (MB)	1 VCPU	2 VCPUS	4 VCPUS	8 VCPUS
256	20 MB	20 MB	32 MB	48 MB
1,024	26 MB	30 MB	38 MB	54 MB
4,096	49 MB	53 MB	61 MB	77 MB
16,384	140 MB	144 MB	152 MB	169 MB

Source: VMware vSphere 5.5 documentation from VMware's website at http://pubs.vmware.com/vsphere-51/topic/com.vmware.vsphere.resmgmt.doc/GUID-B42C72C1-F8D5-40DC-93D1-FB31849B1114.html

As you go about planning the allocation of memory to your VMs, be sure to keep these memory overhead figures in mind. You will want to include these overhead values in your calculations of how memory will be assigned and used, especially if you plan on using a number of VMs with large amounts of memory and a large number of virtual CPUs. As you can see in Table 11.1, the memory overhead in that situation could become fairly substantial.

SUMMARIZING HOW RESERVATIONS, LIMITS, AND SHARES WORK WITH MEMORY

Because the specific behavior of reservations, shares, and limits is slightly different for each resource, here's a quick review of their behavior when they are used for controlling memory allocation:

◆ Reservations guarantee memory for a particular VM. Memory isn't allocated until requested by the VM, but the host must have enough free memory to satisfy the entire reservation before the VM can be powered on. Therefore—and this makes sense if you think about it—you cannot reserve more memory than the host physically has installed. Once allocated to a VM, reserved memory is not swapped, nor is it reclaimed by the ESXi host. It is locked to that VM.

◆ Limits enforce an upper ceiling on the usage of memory. Limits are enforced using the balloon driver (if VMware Tools is installed) and—depending on the VM's working set size—could have a dramatic negative impact on performance. As the VM approaches the limit (a limit of which the guest OS is not aware), the balloon driver will inflate to keep VM memory usage under the limit. This will cause the guest OS to swap out to disk, which will typically degrade performance noticeably.

◆ Shares apply only during periods of host RAM contention and serve to establish prioritized access to host RAM. VMs are granted priority based on percentage of shares allocated versus total shares granted. During periods when the host is not experiencing memory contention, shares do not apply and will not affect memory allocation or usage.

We'll provide a similar summary of the behavior of reservations, limits, and shares when they are used to control CPU usage, which is the topic of the next sections.

Managing Virtual Machine CPU Utilization

When creating a new VM using the Web Client, you have two options when configuring the CPU. First, choose how many virtual CPUs you want in the VM and then decide how many cores should be allocated to each socket. Your selection determines how many sockets the VM has. These CPU settings effectively let the guest OS in the VM utilize between 1 and 64 virtual CPUs on the host system, depending upon the guest OS and the vSphere license.

When the VMware engineers designed the virtualization platform, they started with a real system board and modeled the VM after it—in this case it was based on the Intel 440BX chipset. The VM could emulate the PCI bus, which could be mapped to input/output devices through a standard interface, but how could a VM emulate a CPU? The answer was "no emulation." Think about a virtual system board that has a "hole" where the CPU socket goes—and the guest OS simply looks through the hole and sees one of the cores in the host server. This allowed the VMware engineers to avoid writing CPU emulation software that would need to change each time the CPU vendors introduced new instruction sets. If there was an emulation layer, it would also add significant overhead, which would limit the performance of the virtualization platform by adding more computational overhead.

So, how many CPUs should a VM have? A VM that replaces a physical DHCP server that runs at less than 10 percent CPU utilization at its busiest point in the day surely does not need more than one virtual CPU. As a matter of fact, if you give this VM two virtual CPUs (vCPUs), then you might limit the scalability of the entire host. Here's why.

The VMkernel simultaneously schedules CPU cycles for multi-vCPU VMs. This means that when a dual-vCPU VM places a request for CPU cycles, the request goes into a queue for the host to process, and the host has to wait until there are at least two cores or hyperthreads (if hyperthreading is enabled) with concurrent idle cycles to schedule that VM. A *relaxed co-scheduling* algorithm provides a bit of flexibility in allowing the cores to be scheduled on a slightly skewed basis, but even so, it can be more difficult for the hypervisor to find open time slots on at least two cores. This occurs even if the VM needs only a few clock cycles to do some menial task that could be done with a single processor. Here's an example: Have you ever been stuck behind a truck with a wide load that takes up more than one lane? Normally traffic could flow around this slow-moving vehicle, but now traffic is held up because two lanes are occupied.

On the other hand, if a VM needs two vCPUs because of the load it will be processing on a constant basis, then it makes sense to assign two vCPUs to that VM—but only if the host has four or more CPU cores total. If your ESX host is an older-generation dual-processor single-core system, then assigning a VM two vCPUs will mean that the VM owns all of the CPU processing power on that host every time it gets CPU cycles. You will find that the overall performance of the host and any other VMs will be less than stellar. Of course, in today's market of multicore CPUs, this particular consideration is less significant than it was in previous hardware generations, but it is something to keep in mind.

ONE (CPU) FOR ALL—AT LEAST TO BEGIN WITH

Every VM should be created with only a single virtual CPU so as not to create unnecessary contention for physical processor time. Only when a VM's performance level dictates the need for an additional CPU should one be allocated. Remember that multi-CPU VMs should be created only on ESXi hosts that have more cores than the number of virtual CPUs being assigned to the VM. Create a dual-vCPU VM only on a host with two or more cores, a quad-vCPU VM only on a host with four or more cores, and an eight-vCPU VM only on a host with eight or more cores.

Default CPU Allocation

Like the memory settings discussed previously, the Shares, Reservation, and Limit settings can be configured for CPU capacity as well.

When a new VM is created with a single vCPU, the total maximum CPU cycles for that VM equals the clock speed of the host system's core. In other words, if you create a new VM, it can see through the "hole in the system board," and it sees whatever the core is in terms of clock cycles per second—an ESXi host with 3 GHz CPUs in it will allow the VM to see one 3 GHz core.

Figure 11.7 shows the default settings for CPU Reservation, Limits, and Shares.

Figure 11.7

By default, vSphere provides no CPU reservation, no CPU limit, and 1,000 CPU shares.

Setting CPU Affinity

In addition to shares, reservations, and limits, vSphere offers a fourth option for managing CPU usage: CPU affinity. CPU affinity allows an administrator to statically associate a VM to a specific physical CPU core. CPU affinity is generally not recommended; it has a list of rather significant drawbacks:

◆ CPU affinity breaks vMotion.

◆ The hypervisor is unable to load-balance the VM across all the processing cores in the server. This prevents the hypervisor's scheduling engine from making the most efficient use of the host's resources.

◆ Because vMotion is broken, you cannot use CPU affinities in a cluster where vSphere DRS isn't set to Manual operation.

Because of these limitations, most organizations don't use CPU affinity. However, if, for example, you find that you need to use CPU affinity to adhere to licensing requirements, you can configure your VM to use it.

Perform these steps to configure CPU affinity:

1. If it is not already running, launch the Web Client and connect to a vCenter Server instance or a stand-alone ESXi host.

2. Navigate to either the Hosts And Clusters or VMs And Templates view.

3. Right-click the VM for which you'd like to configure CPU affinity and select Edit Settings.

4. On the Virtual Hardware tab, click the triangle next to CPU.

5. In the Scheduling Affinity section, supply a list of the CPU cores this VM is allowed to access.

For example, if you wanted the VM to run on cores 1 through 4, you could type **1–4**.

6. Click OK to save the changes.

Rather than trying to use CPU affinity to guarantee CPU resources, you're far better off using reservations.

Using CPU Reservations

As you saw in Figure 11.7, the default CPU reservation for a new VM is 0 MHz (no reservation). Recall that a reservation is a resource guarantee. Therefore, by default, a VM is not guaranteed any CPU activity by the VMkernel. This means that when the VM has work to be done, it places its CPU request into the CPU queue so that the VMkernel can handle the request in sequence along with all of the other VMs' requests. On a lightly loaded ESXi host, it's unlikely the VM will wait long for CPU time; however, on a heavily loaded host, the time this VM might have to wait could be significant.

If you were to set a 1,024 MHz reservation, as shown in Figure 11.8, this would effectively make that amount of CPU available instantly to this VM if there is a need for CPU cycles.

FIGURE 11.8

A VM configured with a 1,024 MHz reservation for CPU activity is guaranteed that amount of CPU capacity.

Using a CPU reservation has one notable impact on the behavior of the ESXi host, and in this regard CPU reservations and memory reservations behave identically. The ESXi host *must be able to satisfy the reservation* by providing enough resources to meet the reservations. If each VM you create has a 1,024 MHz reservation and your host has 12,000 MHz of CPU capacity, you can power on no more than 11 VMs (1,024 MHz × 11 = 11,264 MHz), even if all of them are idle. Note that we said "power on" and not "create"—resources are allocated only when a VM is powered on, not created.

While a CPU reservation behaves like a memory reservation in this regard, a CPU reservation is very different than a memory reservation when it comes to "sharing" reserved CPU cycles. Recall from the previous section that reserved memory, once allocated to the VM, is never reclaimed, paged out to disk, or shared in any way. The same is not true of CPU reservations. Suppose you have a VM, creatively named VM1, that has a CPU reservation of 1,024 MHz. If VM1 is idle and not using its reserved CPU cycles, those cycles can be given to VM2. If VM1 suddenly needs cycles, VM2 doesn't get them anymore, and they are assigned to VM1.

So using a Reservation setting on CPU is similar to using a Reservation setting with memory, but it is also very different. You saw previously that using a Limit setting with memory had some significant drawbacks; what about CPU limits?

Using CPU Limits

In addition to a CPU reservation, you can set an option to place a limit on the amount of CPU allocated. This effectively limits the VM's ability to utilize a maximum number of clock cycles per second, regardless of what the host has available. Keep in mind that a VM with one single-core virtual CPU hosted on a 3 GHz, quad-processor ESXi host will see only a single 3 GHz core as its maximum, but as administrator you could alter the limit to prevent the VM from using the maximum core speed. For instance, you could set a 500 MHz limit on that DHCP server so that when it re-indexes the DHCP database, it won't try to take all of the 3 GHz on the processor that it can see. The CPU limit lets you throttle the VM with less processing power than is available on a core on the physical host. Not every VM needs to have access to the entire processing capability of the physical processor core.

The key drawback to using a CPU Limit setting is its performance impact on the guest OS and the applications running in that VM. The Limit setting is a true limit; the VM won't be scheduled to run on a physical CPU core more than the limit specifies, even if there are plenty of CPU cycles available. It's important, therefore, to understand the CPU processing needs of your VMs before arbitrarily setting CPU limits or you could find yourself significantly impacting performance.

INCREASING CONTENTION IN THE FACE OF GROWTH

One of the most common problems administrators can encounter occurs when several VMs without limits are deployed on a new virtualized environment. The users get accustomed to stellar performance levels early in the environment life cycle, but as more VMs are deployed and start to compete for CPU cycles, the relative performance of the first VMs deployed will degrade.

One approach to this issue is to set a reservation of approximately 10 to 20 percent of a single core's clock rate and add approximately 20 percent to that value for a limit on the VM. For example, with 3 GHz CPUs in the host, each VM would start with a 300 MHz reservation and a 350 MHz limit. This would ensure that the VM performs similarly on both a lightly loaded ESXi host and a more heavily loaded ESXi host. Consider setting these values on the VM that you use to create a template because these values will pass to any new VMs that were deployed from that template. Note that this is only a starting point. It is possible to limit a VM that really does need more CPU capabilities, and you should always actively monitor the VMs to determine whether they are using all of the CPU you are providing them.

If the numbers seem low, feel free to increase them as needed. The important concept is setting appropriate expectations for VM performance based on your knowledge of the workloads running in those VMs and the anticipated levels of performance.

Using CPU Shares

VMware vSphere's shares model, which lets you prioritize access to resources when resource contention occurs, behaves similarly for both memory and CPU. The shares for CPU will determine how much CPU is provided to a VM in the face of contention with other VMs needing CPU activity. All VMs, by default, start with an equal number of shares, which means that if VMs compete for CPU cycles on an ESXi host, each one gets serviced with equal priority. Keep in mind that this share value affects only those CPU cycles that are greater than the reservation set for the VM, and the share value applies only when the ESXi host has more requests for CPU cycles than it has CPU cycles to allocate. In other words, the VM is granted access to its reservation cycles regardless of what else is happening on the host, but if the VM needs more—and there's competition—then the share values come into play. If there is no CPU contention on the host and it has enough CPU cycles to go around, the CPU Shares value won't affect CPU allocation.

Several conditions have to be met for shares to even be considered for allocating CPU cycles. The best way to determine this is to consider several scenarios. For the scenarios we'll cover, assume the following details about the environment:

◆ The ESXi host includes dual, single-core, 3 GHz CPUs.

◆ The ESXi host has one or more VMs.

Scenario 1   The ESXi host has a single VM running. The shares are set at the defaults for any running VMs. Will the Shares value have any effect in this scenario? No. There's no competition between VMs for CPU time.

Scenario 2   The ESXi host has two idle VMs running. The shares are set at the defaults for the running VMs. Will the Shares values have any effect in this scenario? No. There's no competition between VMs for CPU time because both are idle.

Scenario 3   The ESXi host has two equally busy VMs running (both requesting maximum CPU capacity). The shares are set at the defaults for the running VMs. Will the Shares values have any effect in this scenario? No. Again, there's no competition between VMs for CPU time, this time because each VM is serviced by a different core in the host.

Scenario 4   To force contention, both VMs are configured to use the same CPU by setting the CPU affinity. The ESXi host has two equally busy VMs running (both requesting maximum CPU capacity). This ensures contention between the VMs. The shares are set at the defaults for the running VMs. Will the Shares values have any effect in this scenario? Yes! But in this case, because all VMs have equal Shares values, each VM has equal access to the host's CPU queue, so you do see any effects from the Shares values.

CPU AFFINITY NOT AVAILABLE WITH FULLY AUTOMATED CLUSTERS

If you are using a VSphere Distributed Resource Scheduler–enabled cluster configured in fully automated mode, CPU affinity cannot be set for VMs in that cluster. You must configure the cluster for manual / partially automated mode or set the virtual machine automation mode to manual / partly automated in order to use CPU affinity.

Scenario 5   The ESXi host has two equally busy VMs running (both requesting maximum CPU capacity with CPU affinity set to the same core). The shares are set as follows: VM1 is set to 2,000 CPU shares, and VM2 is set to the default 1,000 CPU shares. Will the Shares values have any effect in this scenario? Yes. In this case, VM1 has double the number of shares that VM2 has. This means that for every clock cycle that VM2 is assigned by the host, VM1 is assigned two clock cycles. Stated another way, out of every three clock cycles assigned to

VMs by the ESXi host, two are assigned to VM1, and one is assigned to VM2. The diagram earlier in Figure 11.6 helps graphically reinforce how shares are allocated based on percentage of the total number of shares assigned to all VMs.

Scenario 6   The ESXi host has three equally busy VMs running (each requesting maximum CPU capabilities with CPU affinity set to the same core). The shares are set as follows: VM1 is set to 2,000 CPU shares, and VM2 and VM3 are set to the default 1,000 CPU shares. Will the Shares values have any effect in this scenario? Yes. In this case, VM1 has double the number of shares that VM2 and VM3 have assigned. This means that for every two clock cycles that VM1 is assigned by the host, VM2 and VM3 are each assigned a single clock cycle. Stated another way, out of every four clock cycles assigned to VMs by the ESXi host, two cycles are assigned to VM1, one is assigned to VM2, and one is assigned to VM3. You can see that this has effectively watered down VM1's CPU capabilities.

Scenario 7   The ESXi host has three VMs running. VM1 is idle while VM2 and VM3 are equally busy (each requesting maximum CPU capabilities, and all three VMs are set with the same CPU affinity). The shares are set as follows: VM1 is set to 2,000 CPU shares, and VM2 and VM3 are set to the default 1,000 CPU shares. Will the Shares values have any effect in this scenario? Yes. But in this case VM1 is idle, which means it isn't requesting any CPU cycles. This means that VM1's Shares value is not considered when apportioning the host CPU to the active VMs. In this case, VM2 and VM3 would equally share the host CPU cycles because their shares are set to an equal value.

AVOID CPU AFFINITY SETTINGS

You should avoid the CPU affinity setting at all costs. Even if a VM is configured to use a single CPU (for example, CPU1), it does not guarantee that it will be the only VM accessing that CPU, unless every other VM is configured not to use that CPU. At this point, vMotion capability will be unavailable for every VM. In short, don't do it. It's not worth losing vMotion. Use shares, limits, and reservations as an alternative.

Given these scenarios, if you were to extrapolate to an eight-core host with 30 or so VMs, it would be difficult to set Shares values on a VM-by-VM basis and to predict how the system will respond. The question then becomes, "Are shares a useful tool?" The answer is yes, but in large enterprise environments, you need to examine resource pools and the ability to set share parameters along with reservations and limits on collections of VMs. We'll introduce resource pools in the section "Using Resource Pools." First, though, we'll summarize the behavior of reservations, limits, and shares when used to control CPU allocation and usage.

Summarizing How Reservations, Limits, and Shares Work with CPUs

The following list includes some key behaviors and facts surrounding the use of reservations, limits, and shares, when applied to controlling or modifying CPU usage:

◆   Reservations set on CPU cycles provide guaranteed processing power for VMs. Unlike memory, reserved CPU cycles can and will be used by ESXi to service other requests when needed. As with memory, the ESXi host must have enough real, physical CPU capacity to satisfy a reservation in order to power on a VM. Therefore, you cannot reserve more CPU cycles than the host is actually capable of delivering.

◆ Limits on CPU usage simply prevent a VM from gaining access to additional CPU cycles even if CPU cycles are available to use. Even if the host has plenty of CPU processing power available to use, a VM with a CPU limit will not be permitted to use more CPU cycles than specified in the limit. Depending on the guest OS and the applications, this might or might not have an adverse effect on performance.

◆ Shares are used to determine CPU allocation when the ESXi host is experiencing CPU contention. Like memory, shares grant CPU access on a percentage basis calculated on the number of shares granted out of the total number of shares assigned. This means that the percentage of CPU cycles granted to a VM based on its Shares value is always relative to the number of other VMs and the total number of shares granted, and it is not an absolute value.

As you can see, there are some key differences as well as a number of similarities between how these mechanisms work for memory when compared to how they work for CPU.

So far we've discussed two of the four major resource types (memory and CPU). Before we can move on to the third resource type—networking—we need to discuss the concept of resource pools.

Using Resource Pools

The settings for VM resource allocation (memory and CPU reservations, limits, and shares) are methods used to modify or control the allocation of resources to individual VMs or to modify the priority of VMs seeking access to resources. In much the same way as you assign users to groups and then assign permissions to the groups, you can leverage resource pools to make allocating resources to collections of VMs a less tedious and more effective process. In other words, instead of configuring reservations, limits, or shares on a per-VM basis, you can use a resource pool to set those values on a group of VMs all at once.

A *resource pool* is a special type of container object, much like a folder, in the Hosts And Clusters view. You can create a resource pool on a stand-alone host or as a management object in a DRS-enabled cluster. Figure 11.9 shows the creation of a resource pool.

If you examine the properties of the resource pool, you'll see two sections: one for CPU settings (Reservation, Limit, and Shares) and another section with similar settings for memory. When you apply resource settings to a resource pool, those settings affect all the VMs found within that resource pool. This provides a scalable way to adjust the resource settings for groups of VMs. Setting CPU and memory shares, reservations, and limits on a resource pool is very much like setting these values on individual VMs. The behavior of these values, however, can be quite different on a resource pool than on an individual VM.

To illustrate how to set shares, reservations, and limits on a resource pool, as well as to explain how these values work when applied to a resource pool, we'll use an example of an ESXi host with two resource pools. The resource pools are named ProductionVMs and

DevelopmentVMs. Figure 11.10 and Figure 11.11 show the values that have been configured for the ProductionVMs and DevelopmentVMs resource pools, respectively.

FIGURE 11.9

You can create resource pools on individual hosts and within clusters. A resource pool provides a management and performance configuration layer in the vCenter Server inventory.

FIGURE 11.10

The ProductionVMs resource pool is guaranteed CPU and memory resources and higher-priority access to resources in the face of contention.

FIGURE 11.11
The Development
VMs resource pool
is configured for
lower-priority
access to CPU and
memory in the
event of resource
contention.

DevelopmentVMs - Edit Resource Settings	? ⏵⏵

▾ CPU

Shares	Low ▾	2000 ▾
Reservation	2925 ▾	MHz ▾

Max reservation: 11,700 MHz

Reservation type	☐ Expandable
Limit	11700 ▾	MHz ▾

Max limit: 63,552 MHz

▾ Memory

Shares	Low ▾	2000 ▾
Reservation	4096 ▾	MB ▾

Max reservation: 24 GB

Reservation type	☐ Expandable
Limit	24576 ▾	MB ▾

Max limit: 40 GB

OK   Cancel

Configuring Resource Pools

Before we can show you how resource pools behave with regard to resource allocation, you must first create and configure the resource pools. Use the resource pools, shown earlier in Figure 11.10 and Figure 11.11, as examples for creating and configuring resource pools.

To create a resource pool, simply right-click either an individual ESXi host or a cluster of ESXi hosts, and select New Resource Pool. In the Create Resource Pool dialog box, you'll need to supply a name for the new resource pool and set the CPU and Memory values as desired.

After you create the resource pool, you must move the VMs into it by clicking the VM in the inventory panel and dragging it onto the appropriate resource pool. The result is a hierarchy similar to that shown in Figure 11.12.

FIGURE 11.12
VMs assigned to
a resource pool
consume resources
allocated to the
resource pool.

In this particular example, you have two classifications of servers, production and development, and you've created a resource pool for each classification. The goal in this example is to ensure that if there's competition for a particular resource, the VMs in production should be assigned higher-priority access to that resource. In addition to that goal, you need to ensure that the VMs in development cannot consume more than 24 GB of physical memory with their running VMs. You don't care how many VMs run concurrently as part of the development group as long as they don't collectively consume more than 24 GB of RAM. Finally, you need to ensure that a minimum amount of resources are guaranteed for both groups of VMs.

To achieve your goal of guaranteeing resources for the production VMs, you will set the ProductionVMs resource pool to use the following settings (refer to Figure 11.10 earlier):

- CPU resources area: Shares value of High.

- CPU resources area: Reservation value of 11,700 MHz.

- CPU resources area: Expandable check box Reservation Type is deselected.

- CPU resources area: No CPU limit (Unlimited option in the Limit drop-down is selected).

- Memory resources area: Reservation value of 16,384 MB.

- Memory resources area: Expandable check box for Reservation Type is deselected.

- Memory resources area: No memory limit (Unlimited option in the Limit drop-down is selected).

Similarly, you will apply the following settings to the DevelopmentVMs resource pool (see Figure 11.11 earlier):

- CPU resources area: Reservation value of 2,925 MHz.

- CPU resources area: Expandable check box for Reservation Type is deselected.

- CPU resources area: Limit value of 11,700 MHz.

- Memory resources area: Reservation value of 4,096 MB.

- Memory resources area: Expandable check box for Reservation Type is deselected.

- Memory resources area: Limit value of 24,576 MB.

Again, setting the values on the DevelopmentVMs resource pool involves right-clicking the resource pool, selecting Edit Settings, and then setting the values you need.

Now that you have an example to work with, we'll explain what these settings will do to the VMs contained in each of the resource pools.

Understanding Resource Allocation with Resource Pools

In the previous section we walked you through creating a couple of resource pools called ProductionVMs and DevelopmentVMs. The values for these resource pools are illustrated in Figure 11.10 and Figure 11.11. The goal behind creating these resource pools and setting the values on them was to ensure that a certain level of resources would always be available to production VMs (those found in the ProductionVMs resource pool) and to limit the resources used by the development VMs (VMs found in the DevelopmentVMs resource pool). In this example, you used all three values—Shares, Reservation, and Limit—in an effort to accomplish your goal. Let's look at the behavior of each of these values when used on a resource pool.

Managing CPU Usage with Resource Pools

First we'll examine the Shares value assigned to the resource pools for CPU usage. As you can see in Figure 11.10, the CPU shares for the ProductionVMs resource pool are set to High (8,000). Figure 11.11 shows the DevelopmentVMs CPU shares set to Low (2,000). The effect of these two settings is similar to that of comparing two VMs' Shares values for CPU—except in this case, if there is any competition for CPU resources between VMs in the ProductionVMs and DevelopmentVMs resource pools, the entire ProductionVMs resource pool and all the VMs in it would have higher priority. Figure 11.13 shows how this would break down with two VMs in each resource pool.

FIGURE 11.13
Two resource pools with different Shares values will be allocated resources proportional to their percentage of share ownership.

As you consider the information presented in Figure 11.13, keep in mind that the resource allocation occurs at each level. There are only two resource pools under the given ESXi host, so the CPU is allocated 80/20 according to its Shares value. This means that the ProductionVMs resource pool gets 80 percent of the CPU time while the DevelopmentVMs resource pool gets only 20 percent of the CPU time.

Now let's expand on Figure 11.13 and add the two VMs in each resource pool to get a more complete view of how Shares values would work with a resource pool. Within the resource pool the CPU Shares values assigned to the VMs, if any at all, come into play. Figure 11.14 shows how this works.

In Figure 11.14, there are no custom CPU shares assigned to the VMs, so they all use the default value of 1,000 CPU shares. With two VMs in the resource pool, this means each VM gets 50 percent of the resources available to the resource pool in which it is located (because each VM has 50 percent of the total number of shares assigned within the pool). In this example, this means 40 percent of the host CPU capacity will go to each of the two VMs in the ProductionVMs resource pool. If there were three VMs in each resource pool, then the CPU allocated to the parent resource pool would be split three ways. Similarly, if there were four VMs, then the CPU would be split four ways. You can verify this breakdown of resource allocation using the Monitor tab on the selected cluster, ESXi host, or resource pool. Figure 11.15 shows the Resource

Allocation subsection for a cluster with the ProductionVMs and DevelopmentVMs resource pools. The CPU button is selected, meaning that the Web Client is showing you the breakdown of CPU allocation for the selected cluster.

FIGURE 11.14

The percentage of resources assigned to a resource pool via its Shares values is further subdivided according to the Shares values of the VMs within the pool.

FIGURE 11.15

The Resource Allocation tab can verify the allocation of resources to objects within the vCenter Server hierarchy.

Name	Reservation (MHz)	Limit (MHz)	Shares	Shares Value	% Shares
DevelopmentVMs	1024	Unlimited	Low	2000	20
ProductionVMs	3072	Unlimited	High	8000	80

Total Capacity	10.55 GHz
Reserved Capacity	4.10 GHz
Available Capacity	6.45 GHz

Note that in the screenshot in Figure 11.15, both resource pools and VMs are directly in the root of the cluster (which, for all intents and purposes, is a resource pool itself). In this case, the sum of all the Shares values—for both resource pools as well as VMs—is used to calculate the percentage of CPU allocated.

SHARES APPLY ONLY DURING ACTUAL RESOURCE CONTENTION

Remember that share allocations come into play only when VMs are fighting one another for a resource—in other words, when an ESXi host is actually unable to satisfy all the requests for a particular resource. If an ESXi host is running only eight VMs on top of two quad-core processors, there won't be contention to manage (assuming these VMs have only a single vCPU) and Shares values won't apply. Be sure to keep this in mind when reviewing the results of Shares allocations like those displayed in Figure 11.15.

Now that we've introduced you to the Resource Allocation tab, we need to discuss an important consideration about the use of resource pools. It's possible to use resource pools as a form of organization, as you would use folders. Some organizations and administrators have taken to using resource pools in this way to help keep VMs organized in a specific fashion. While this is possible, it's not recommended. The Resource Allocation tab helps show why.

Look at Figure 11.16, which shows the Resource Allocation tab for a cluster of ESXi hosts. In the root of this cluster are six VMs assigned a total of 7,000 shares. Because each of these VMs is using the default CPU Shares value (1,000 shares per vCPU), they each get equal access to the host CPU capacity—in this case, 14 percent per vCPU (the VMs with 2,000 shares and 28-percent shares have two vCPUs).

FIGURE 11.16

In the absence of custom CPU shares, CPU capacity is equally allocated to all VMs.

Name	1 ▲	CPU Reservation (MHz)	CPU Limit (MHz)	CPU Allocation Type	CPU Shares	CPU Shares Value
Linux-01		0	Unlimited	N/A	Normal	1000
Linux-02		0	Unlimited	N/A	Normal	1000
Linux-03		0	Unlimited	N/A	Normal	1000
Linux-04		0	Unlimited	N/A	Normal	1000
Win2k8-R2-01		0	Unlimited	N/A	Normal	2000
Win2k8-R2-02		0	Unlimited	N/A	Normal	1000

Now look at Figure 11.17. The only change here is that we've added a resource pool. I did not change any of the default values for the resource pool. Note that the resource pool has a default CPU Shares Value of 4,000, and note how the simple addition of this resource pool changes the default CPU allocation for the individual VMs from 14 percent per vCPU to only 9 percent per vCPU. The resource pool, on the other hand, now gets 36 percent. If you added a single VM to the resource pool, that one VM would get 36 percent of the host CPU capacity while other VMs only received 9 percent (or 18 percent for VMs with two vCPUs).

This unintended change on the resource allocation distribution is why we don't recommend using resource pools strictly for the purposes of organizing VMs. If you do insist on using resource pools in this way, be sure to understand the impact of configuring your environment in this manner. A better way to organize your environment, and one that won't impact the performance, is to use folders or tags within vCenter; for more information, see Chapter 3, "Installing and Configuring vCenter Server."

FIGURE 11.17
The addition of a resource pool will, by default, alter the resource allocation policy even if you don't set any custom values.

The next setting in the resource pool properties to evaluate is CPU Reservation for the CPU. Continuing with the examples shown earlier in Figure 11.10 and Figure 11.11, you can see a CPU Reservation value of 11,700 MHz has been set on the ProductionVM's resource pool. The DevelopmentVMs pool has a CPU Reservation value of 2,925 MHz. (The ESXi hosts in the cluster hosting these resource pools have quad-core 2.93 GHz Intel Xeon CPUs, so this essentially reserves four cores on one server for the ProductionVMs resource pool and one core on one server for the DevelopmentVMs resource pool.) This setting ensures that at least 11,700 MHz of CPU time is available for all the VMs located in the ProductionVMs resource pool (or 2,925 MHz of CPU for VMs in the DevelopmentVMs resource pool). Assuming that the ESXi host has a total of 23,400 MHz CPU (8 × 2,925 MHz = 23,400 MHz), this means 8,775 MHz of CPU time is available on that host for other reservations. If one more resource pool was created with a Reservation value of 8,775 MHz, then the cumulative reservations on the system have reserved all available host CPU capacity (5,850 MHz × 4 = 23400 MHz). This configuration means the administrator will not be able to create any additional resource pools or any individual VMs with Reservation values set. Remember that the ESXi host or cluster has to have enough resource capacity—CPU capacity, in this case—to satisfy all reservations. You can't reserve more capacity than the host actually has.

Part of the CPU Reservation setting is the option to make the reservation expandable. An expandable reservation (noted as such by selecting the Expandable check box next to Reservation Type) allows a resource pool to "borrow" resources from its parent host or parent resource pool in order to satisfy reservations set on individual VMs within the resource pool. Note that a resource pool with an expandable reservation would "borrow" from the parent only to satisfy reservations, not to satisfy requests for resources in excess of the reservations. Neither of the resource pools has expandable reservations, so you will be able to assign only 5,850 MHz of CPU capacity as reservations to individual VMs within each resource pool. Any attempt to reserve more than that amount will result in an error message explaining that you've exceeded the allowed limit.

Deselecting the Expandable check box does not limit the total amount of CPU capacity available to the resource pool; it limits only the total amount of CPU capacity that can be *reserved* within the resource pool. To set an upper limit on actual CPU usage, you'll need to use a CPU Limit setting.

CPU Limit is the third setting on each resource pool. The behavior of the CPU limit on a resource pool is similar to its behavior on individual VMs, except in this case the limit applies to all VMs in the resource pool. All VMs combined are allowed to consume up to this value. In the example, the ProductionVMs resource pool does not have a CPU limit assigned. In this case, the VMs in the ProductionVMs resource pool are allowed to consume as many CPU cycles as the ESXi hosts in the cluster can provide. The DevelopmentVMs resource pool, on the other hand, has a CPU Limit setting of 11,700 MHz, meaning that all the VMs in the DevelopmentVMs resource pool are allowed to consume a maximum of 11,700 MHz of CPU capacity. With 2.93 GHz Intel Xeon CPUs, this is the approximate equivalent of one quad-core CPU.

For the most part, CPU shares, reservations, and limits behave similarly on resource pools and on individual VMs. The same is also true for memory shares, reservations, and limits, as you'll see in the next section.

MANAGING MEMORY USAGE WITH RESOURCE POOLS

In the memory portion of the resource pool settings, the first setting is the Shares value. This setting works in much the same way as memory shares worked on individual VMs. It determines which group of VMs will be the first to give up memory via the balloon driver—or if memory pressure is severe enough, activate memory compression or swap out to disk via hypervisor swapping—in the face of contention. However, this setting sets a priority value for all VMs in the resource pool when they compete for resources with VMs in other pools. Looking at the memory share settings in our example (ProductionVMs = Normal and DevelopmentVMs = Low), this means that if host memory is limited, VMs in the DevelopmentVMs resource pool that need more memory than their reservation would have a lower priority than an equivalent VM in the ProductionVMs resource pool. Figure 11.14, which we used previously to help explain CPU shares on resource pool, applies here as well. As with CPU shares, you can also use the Resource Allocation tab to explore how memory resources are assigned to resource pools or VMs within resource pools.

The second setting is the resource pool's memory reservation. The memory Reservation value will reserve this amount of host RAM for VMs in this resource pool, which effectively ensures that some actual RAM is guaranteed to the VMs. As explained in the discussion on CPU reservations, the Expandable check box next to Reservation Type does not limit how much memory the resource pool can use but rather how much memory you can reserve there.

With the memory Limit value, you set a limit on how much host RAM a particular group of VMs can consume. If administrators have been given the Create Virtual Machines permission, then the memory Limit value would prevent those administrators from running VMs that consume more than that amount of actual host RAM. In our example, the memory Limit value on the DevelopmentVMs resource pool is set to 24,576 MB. How many VMs can administrators in development create? They can create as many as they want.

Although this setting does nothing to limit creating VMs, it places a limit on running VMs. So, how many can they run? The cap placed on memory use is not a per-VM setting but a cumulative setting. Administrators might be able to run only one VM with all the memory or multiple VMs with lower memory configurations. Assuming that each VM is created without an individual memory Reservation value, the administrator can run as many VMs concurrently as they want. However, once the VMs consume 24,576 MB of host RAM, the hypervisor will step in and prevent the VMs in the resource group from using any additional memory. Refer back to the discussion of memory limits in the section titled "Using Memory Limits" for the techniques that the VMkernel uses to enforce the memory limit. If the administrator builds six VMs with 4,096 MB as the initial memory amount, then all four VMs will consume 24,576 MB (assuming no overhead, which we've already shown you isn't the case) and will run in real RAM. If an administrator tried to run 20 VMs configured for 2,048 MB of RAM, then all 20 VMs will share the 24,576 MB of RAM, even though their requirement is for 40,960 MB (20 × 2,048 MB)—the remaining amount of RAM would most likely be provided by VMkernel swap. At this point, performance would be noticeably slow.

If you want to clear a limit, select Unlimited from the Limit drop-down menu. This is true for both CPU limits as well as memory limits. By now you should have a fair idea of how ESXi allocates resources to VMs as well as how you can tweak those settings to meet your specific demands and workloads.

As you can see, if you have groups of VMs with similar resource demands, using resource pools is an excellent way of ensuring consistent resource allocation. As long as you understand the hierarchical nature of resource pools—that resources are allocated first to the pool at its level in the hierarchy, and then the VMs in the pool—then you should be able to use resource pools effectively.

So far you've seen how to control the use of CPU and memory, but those are only two of the four major resources consumed by VMs. In the next section, you'll see how to control network traffic through network resource pools.

Regulating Network I/O Utilization

The resource pools we've shown you so far can only be used to control CPU and memory usage. However, vSphere offers another type of resource pool, a *network resource pool* that allows you to control network utilization. Using network resource pools—to which are assigned shares and limits—you can control incoming and outgoing network traffic. This feature is referred to as vSphere Network I/O Control (NIOC).

ONLY ON A DISTRIBUTED SWITCH

vSphere Network I/O Control applies only to vSphere Distributed Switches (vDS) version 4.1.0 or later and, prior to version 5.1.0, is limited to outbound network traffic only. Refer to Chapter 5, "Creating and Configuring Virtual Networks," for more information on setting up or configuring a vDS.

When you enable vSphere NIOC, vSphere activates eight predefined network resource pools:

◆ NFS Traffic

◆ Management Traffic

◆ vMotion Traffic

◆ vSphere Storage Area Network Traffic

◆ vSphere Replication (VR) Traffic

◆ iSCSI Traffic

◆ Virtual Machine Traffic

◆ Fault Tolerance (FT) Traffic

All of these network resource pools are visible on the Resource Allocation tab of the vDS, as you can see in Figure 11.18.

FIGURE 11.18

Network resource pools on a vDS provide granular control of network traffic.

Two steps are involved in setting up and using NIOC. First, you must enable NIOC on that particular vDS. Second, you must create and configure network resource pools as necessary. The first of these steps is already complete if you create a brand-new vDS with a version set to 5.5.0—NIOC is enabled by default.

Perform the following steps to enable NIOC on an existing vDS:

1. If it is not already running, launch the Web Client and connect to a vCenter Server instance. Because NIOC relies on vDS and vDS is available only with vCenter, NIOC cannot be used when connected directly to an ESXi host.

2. Navigate to the Networking view using the navigation bar or the home screen.

3. Select the vDS for which you want to enable NIOC.

4. Right-click the vDS.

5. Click Edit Settings.

6. Select Enabled in the Network I/O Control drop down box, and then click OK.

This enables NIOC on this vDS. The Resource Allocation tab of the vDS object will note that NIOC is enabled, as shown in Figure 11.19.

Along with actually enabling NIOC, you can also modify existing network resource pools or create new resource pools, if you are using a vDS version 5.0.0 or above. For a version 4.1.0 vDS, you can neither create new network resource pools nor edit the existing network resource pools.

A network resource pool consists of three basic settings:

◆ The first value is *Host Limit*. This value specifies an upper limit on the amount of network traffic, in Mbps, that this network resource pool is allowed to consume. Leaving Unlimited selected means that only the physical adapters themselves limit the network resource pool.

◆ The second value is *Physical Adapter Shares*. Like the shares you used to prioritize access to CPU or RAM when there was contention, physical adapter shares in a network resource pool establish priority for access to the physical network adapters when there is network contention. As with other types of shares, this value does not apply when there is no contention.

You can set this value to one of three predefined values, or you can set a custom value of up to 100. For the predefined values, Low translates to 25 shares, Normal equates to 50 shares, and High equals 100 shares.

◆ The third value is *QoS Tag*. The QoS (Quality of Service) tag is an 802.1p tag that is applied to all outgoing packets. Upstream network switches that are configured to recognize the 802.1p tags can further enhance and enforce the QoS beyond just the ESXi host.

FIGURE 11.19
vCenter Server provides a clear indication that NIOC is enabled for a vDS.

Figure 11.20 shows all three of the values for one of the predefined network resource pools, the Fault Tolerance (FT) Traffic network resource pool.

FIGURE 11.20
vSphere allows an administrator to modify the predefined network resource pools.

Administrators have the option of editing the predefined network resource pools or creating their own network resource pools.

Perform the following steps to edit an existing network resource pool:

1. If it is not already running, launch the Web Client and connect to a vCenter Server instance.

2. Navigate to the Networking view.

3. Select the vDS that contains the network resource pool you want to modify.

4. Click the Resource Allocation tab.

5. Select the network resource pool you want to edit and click the Edit pencil icon.

6. From the Network Resource Pool Settings dialog box, modify the Host Limit, Physical Adapter Shares, or QoS Tag values as desired.

7. Click OK to save the changes to the network resource pool.

You might prefer to leave the predefined network resource pools intact and create your own. Perform the following steps to create a new network resource pool:

1. If it is not already running, launch the Web Client and connect to a vCenter Server instance.

2. Navigate to the Networking view.

3. Select the vDS on which you want to create the new network resource pool.

4. Click the Resource Allocation tab.

5. Click the New Network Resource Pool plus icon. The New Network Resource Pool dialog box appears (Figure 11.21).

FIGURE 11.21
Administrators have the option of creating new network resource pools for custom network traffic control.

6. Supply a name and description for the new network resource pool.

7. For Physical Adapter Shares, select a predefined option (Low, Normal, or High), or select Custom and enter a value from 1 to 100.

8. To set a limit, select the Unlimited check box (to uncheck it) and then enter a value for Host Limit. This value is entered in Mbps (megabits per second).

9. If you want to apply a QoS priority tag, select the value from the drop-down list.

10. Click OK to create the new network resource pool with the values you specified.

After you have at least one user-defined network resource pool, you have the option of mapping port groups to your network resource pool.

CAN'T MAP PORT GROUPS TO SYSTEM POOLS

Port groups can be mapped to only user-defined network resource pools, not system network resource pools. This is to ensure that traffic is appropriately shared within the available bandwidth. For example, it would not be a good idea to have VM traffic in the same resource pool as critical system traffic such as Fault Tolerance or iSCSI.

Perform the following steps to assign a port group to a user-defined network resource pool:

1. Launch the Web Client if it is not already running, and connect to a vCenter Server instance.

2. Switch to the Networking view.

3. Select the vDS that hosts the network resource pool you'd like to map to a port group.

4. Right-click the RPort Group you wish to map and select Edit Settings.

5. Within the settings, select the appropriate network resource pool, as shown in Figure 11.22.

FIGURE 11.22
Users can map a port group to any user-defined network resource pool, and multiple port groups can be associated to a single network resource pool.

6. Click OK to save the changes and return to the Resource Allocation tab.

In large environments with lots of port groups, it might be a bit tedious to try to determine which port groups are mapped to which network resource pools. To help ease this administrative burden, vCenter Server offers an easy way to show all the port groups linked to a particular network resource pool:

♦ With a network resource pool selected, simply click the Distributed Port Groups tab near the bottom of the screen.

♦ The view will shift to show you the specific port groups associated with the selected network resource pool. You can see this displayed in Figure 11.23, which shows the port groups associated with the user-defined network resource pool named Custom Network Resource Pool. You'll notice that a fair amount of networking-specific detail—like VLAN

ID, port binding, number of attached VMs, and so forth—is also included in this display for ease of use.

NIOC offers a powerful way to help ensure that all the various types of converged network traffic present in a VMware vSphere environment will coexist properly, especially as organizations move toward 10 Gigabit Ethernet and away from Gigabit Ethernet. Fewer faster connections means more consolidated traffic and therefore a greater need for controlling how that traffic coexists on the same physical medium.

We've taken you through three of the four major resources and shown you how VMware vSphere offers controls for managing the use of and access to them. Only one resource remains: storage.

Controlling Storage I/O Utilization

For vSphere, controlling memory or CPU allocation and utilization is relatively easy. The hypervisor can easily determine how busy the CPU is and if physical memory has been depleted. When resource contention occurs for these resources, not only is it easy to detect, but it's also easy to correct. If the CPU is too busy and there aren't enough CPU cycles to go around, then you don't schedule cycles for lower-priority VMs and you assign more cycles to higher-priority VMs. And how is this priority determined? Remember that Shares values are the mechanism that vSphere uses to determine priority. Likewise, if RAM becomes constrained, invoke the balloon drivers in the guest OSes and reclaim some memory, or slow down the rate of allocation to lower-priority VMs and increase the rate of allocation to higher-priority VMs. Not only does the hypervisor have complete visibility into the utilization of these resources, it also has complete control over the resources. Nothing gets scheduled on the CPU without going through the hypervisor, and nothing gets stored in RAM without the hypervisor knowing about it. This complete control is what enables vSphere to offer shares as a way of establishing priority and offer reservations (guaranteed access to resources) and also limits (caps on the usage of a resource). You read and learned about these mechanisms in previous parts of this chapter.

When you get to network utilization, things begin to change a little. The hypervisor has some visibility into the network; it can see how many Mbps are being generated and by which VMs. However, the hypervisor does not have complete control over network utilization. It can control inbound and outbound traffic, but traffic generated somewhere else in the network really can't be controlled. Given the nature of networking, it's pretty much a given that other workloads outside the control of VMware vSphere will be present, and vSphere can't control or influence them in any way. Even so, vSphere can offer shares (to establish priority) and limits (to enforce a cap on the amount of network bandwidth a VM can consume). This is Network I/O Control, and we discussed it in the previous section.

With regard to resource allocation and utilization, storage is similar in many ways to networking. Other workloads are likely to be present on the shared storage vSphere requires for so many features. These other workloads will be external to vSphere and can't be controlled or influenced in any way, and therefore vSphere isn't going to have complete control over the resource. It's also generally true that the hypervisor won't have as much visibility into the storage as it does with CPU and memory, making it more difficult to detect and adjust storage resources. There are two metrics, however, that vSphere can use to help determine storage utilization. The first is latency and the second is peak throughput. Using one of these two metrics to detect contention, vSphere can offer shares (to establish priority when contention occurs) as well as limits (to ensure that a VM doesn't consume too many storage resources). The feature that enables this functionality is called Storage I/O Control, or SIOC.

STORAGE I/O CONTROL FIRST APPEARED IN VSPHERE 4.1

Storage I/O Control first appeared in VMware vSphere 4.1 and supported only Fibre Channel and iSCSI datastores. In vSphere 5.0, SIOC added support for NFS as well.

Longtime users of VMware vSphere (and VMware Infrastructure before that) are probably aware that you've been able to assign Shares values to disks for quite some time. The difference between that functionality and what SIOC offers is a matter of scope. Without SIOC, enabling shares on a VM's virtual disk is only effective for that specific host; the ESX/ESXi hosts did not exchange information about how many shares each VM was allocated or how many shares were assigned in total. This meant it was impossible to properly align the Shares values with the correct ratios of access to storage resources across multiple hosts.

SIOC addresses this by extending shares assignments across all hosts accessing a particular datastore. Using vCenter Server as the central information store, SIOC combines all the assigned shares across all the VMs on all the hosts and allocates storage I/O resources in the proper ratios according to the shares assignment.

In order to make this work, SIOC has a few requirements you must meet:

◆ All datastores that are SIOC-enabled must be managed under a single vCenter Server instance. vCenter Server is the "central clearinghouse" for all the shares assignments, so it makes sense that all the datastores and hosts be managed by a single vCenter Server instance.

◆ SIOC is supported on VMFS datastores connected via Fibre Channel (including FCoE) and iSCSI. NFS datastores are also supported. Raw device mappings (RDMs) are not supported.

◆ Datastores must have only a single extent. Datastores with multiple extents are not supported.

STORAGE I/O CONTROL AND ARRAY AUTO-TIERING

If your storage array supports auto-tiering—the ability for the array to seamlessly and transparently migrate data between different tiers (SSD, FC, SAS, SATA) of storage, be sure to double-check the VMware Hardware Compatibility List (HCL) to verify that your array's auto-tiering functionality has been certified to be compatible with SIOC. Also worth checking is your vendor documentation for SIOC best practices. The use of SIOC can undermine the auto-tiering that is built into some storage arrays.

Assuming that your environment meets the requirements, then you can take advantage of SIOC. Configuring SIOC is a two-step process. First, enable SIOC on one or more datastores. Second, assign shares or limits to storage I/O resources on individual VMs.

Let's look first at enabling SIOC for a particular datastore.

Enabling Storage I/O Control

SIOC is enabled on a per-datastore basis. By default, SIOC is disabled for a datastore, meaning that you explicitly enable SIOC to take advantage of its functionality.

DATASTORES VS. DATASTORE CLUSTERS

While SIOC is disabled by default for individual datastores, it is *enabled* by default for Storage DRS–enabled datastore clusters that have I/O metrics enabled for Storage DRS. Refer to "Introducing and Working with Storage DRS" in Chapter 12, "Balancing Resource Utilization," for more information on Storage DRS.

Perform the following steps to enable SIOC for a datastore:

1. Launch the Web Client, if it is not already running, and connect to a vCenter Server instance.

   SIOC is available only when connected to vCenter Server, not when you are connected to an individual ESXi host with the vSphere Client.

2. Navigate to the Storage view.

3. Select the datastore for which you want to enable SIOC.

4. Click the Manage ➢ Settings tab.

5. Select Edit (Figure 11.24).

6. In the Datastore Capabilities dialog box, select Enabled under Storage I/O Control.

7. Click OK.

SIOC is now enabled for the selected datastore; this is reflected in the Datastore Capabilities pane of the Web Client under the datastore manage tab, as you can see in Figure 11.25.

FIGURE 11.24
This dialog box allows you to manage the SIOC configuration of a specific datastore.

FIGURE 11.25
The status of SIOC for a datastore is displayed in the Web Client for easy reference.

Generally speaking, enabling SIOC using these steps is all you need to do to get started using SIOC to control use of storage I/O resources.

However, in some cases, you may need to adjust the configuration of SIOC in order to make it function properly for your specific array and array configuration. Previously in this section, we mentioned that vSphere has two metrics that could be used to detect contention: latency and peak throughput.

SIOC can use latency as the threshold to determine when it should activate and enforce Shares values for access to storage I/O resources. Specifically, when vSphere detects latency in excess of a specific threshold value (measured in milliseconds), SIOC is activated. Because of the vast differences in array architectures and array performance, VMware recognized that users might need to adjust this default congestion threshold value for SIOC. After all, a certain latency measurement might indicate congestion (or contention) on some arrays and configurations but not on others. Making the congestion threshold adjustable allows vSphere administrators to fine-tune the behavior of SIOC to best match their particular array and configuration.

The other metric is the one that's enabled by default in vSphere 5.5—Peak Throughput. SIOC uses a special tool called the IO Injector to test the characteristics of a storage array and perform two main checks. The first check is for overlaps in the underlying disk system of a datastore; this allows Storage DRS to make correct placement decisions for workload balancing, which is explained more in Chapter 12. The other check performed by the IO Injector—more relevant to this section—is a Peak Throughput check. Unlike checking for latency spikes, knowing the maximum capability of a particular datastore can ensure that SIOC kicks in *before* congestion (or contention) occurs. Just like latency, you can adjust this threshold with a percentage setting.

Perform the following steps to adjust the congestion threshold setting for SIOC on a particular datastore:

1. If it is not already running, launch the Web Client and connect to a vCenter Server instance.

2. Navigate to the Storage view.

3. Select the desired datastore from the inventory tree.

4. Select the datastore for which you want to enable SIOC.

5. Click the Manage ➤ Settings tab and click Edit.

6. The Edit Congestion Threshold dialog box appears. Enter the desired congestion threshold setting, in percentage or milliseconds, and then click OK.

WHAT VALUES SHOULD I USE?

When adjusting the congestion threshold setting based on latency, it is imperative that you set it properly based on your specific array, array configuration, and array vendor's recommendations. These recommendations will vary from vendor to vendor and depend on the number of drives in the array, the types of drives in the array, and whether features like array auto-tiering are enabled. In general, though, the following latency settings are considered reasonable guidelines for the congestion threshold:

◆ For datastores composed of SSDs, decrease to 10 ms.

◆ For datastores composed of 10K/15K FC and SAS, leave at 30 ms.

◆ For datastores composed of 7.2K SATA/NL-SAS, increase to 50 ms.

◆ For auto-tiered datastores with multiple drive types, leave at 30 ms.

While these are reasonable guidelines, we strongly urge you to consult your specific vendor's documentation on the recommended values to use as the congestion threshold when using SIOC in conjunction with their products.

Once you have enabled SIOC on one or more datastores and you have (optionally) adjusted the congestion threshold per your storage vendor's recommended values, you can start setting storage I/O resource values on your VMs.

Configuring Storage Resource Settings for a Virtual Machine

SIOC provides two mechanisms for controlling the use of storage I/O by VMs: shares and limits. These mechanisms operate in exactly the same way here as with other resources; the Shares value establishes a relative priority as a ratio of the total number of shares assigned, while the Limit value defines the upper ceiling on the number of I/O operations per second (IOPS) that a given VM may generate. As with memory, CPU, and network I/O, vSphere provides default settings for disk shares and limits. By default, every VM you create is assigned 1,000 disk shares per virtual disk and no IOPS limits.

If you need different settings than the default values, you can easily modify either the assigned storage I/O shares or the assigned storage I/O limit.

ASSIGNING STORAGE I/O SHARES

Modifying the default storage I/O Shares value is done on the VM's Edit Settings dialog box, just as it's done for modifying memory allocation or CPU utilization. Figure 11.26 shows the disk shares for a VM.

FIGURE 11.26
Storage I/O shares are modified from the same area as other resource allocation settings are modified.

Perform the following steps to modify the storage I/O Shares value for a VM:

1. Launch the Web Client, if it is not already running, and connect to a vCenter Server instance.

2. Navigate to either the Hosts And Clusters or VMs And Templates view.

3. Right-click the specific VM for which you'd like to change the storage I/O settings and select Edit Settings from the context menu.

4. Click the triangle next to the hard disk. This displays the dialog box shown previously in Figure 11.26.

5. For each virtual disk, click in the Shares drop-down to change the setting from Normal to Low, High, or Custom, as shown in Figure 11.27.

FIGURE 11.27
You must change the setting to Custom if you want to assign an arbitrary storage I/O Shares value.

6. If you selected Custom in step 5, click in the Shares value drop-down and supply a custom storage I/O Shares value.

7. Repeat steps 4, 5, and 6 for each virtual disk associated with this VM.

8. Click OK to save the changes and return to the Web Client.

The selected virtual disks belonging to this VM will now receive a proportional allocation of storage I/O resources based on the Shares value whenever SIOC detects contention (or congestion) on the datastore. (Keep in mind that vSphere can use latency or peak bandwidth, as specified in the congestion threshold described previously, as the trigger for activating SIOC.) As with all other Shares values, SIOC enforces Shares values only when contention for storage I/O resources is detected. If there is no contention—as indicated by low latency or bandwidth values for that datastore or datastore cluster—then SIOC will not activate.

SHARES ACTIVATE ONLY ON RESOURCE CONTENTION

Shares are applicable only when there is resource contention. This is true for all the different Shares values we've shown you throughout this chapter. Regardless of whether you are setting Shares values for memory, CPU, network, or storage, vSphere will not step in and enforce those shares until the hypervisor detects contention for that particular resource. Shares aren't guarantees or absolute values; they establish relative priority when the hypervisor isn't able to meet all the demands of the VMs.

CONFIGURING STORAGE I/O LIMITS

You can also set a limit on the number of IOPS that a VM is allowed to generate. By default this value is unlimited. However, if you feel that you need to set an IOPS limit, you can set the IOPS limit in the same place you would set storage I/O shares.

Perform these steps to set a storage I/O limit on IOPS:

1. If it is not already running, launch the Web Client and connect to a vCenter Server instance.

2. Navigate to the Hosts And Clusters or VMs And Templates view.

3. Right-click a VM and select Edit Settings.

4. Click the triangle next to the disk on which you'd like to set an IOPS limit.

5. Click in the Limit – IOPS drop-down and type in a value for the maximum number of IOPS that this VM will be allowed to generate against this virtual disk.

6. Repeat steps 4 and step 5 for each virtual disk assigned to this VM.

7. Click OK to save the changes and return to the Web Client.

BE CAREFUL WITH IOPS LIMITS

Setting an improper IOPS limit can have a severe performance impact on a VM. Be sure that you have a clear understanding of the IOPS requirements of the guest OS and the applications installed in that guest OS before assigning an IOPS limit.

Like the limits you apply to memory, CPU, or network I/O, the storage I/O limits are absolute values. The hypervisor will enforce the assigned storage I/O limit, even when there is plenty of storage I/O available.

Setting these storage I/O resource values on a per-VM basis is fine, but what about when you need to have some sort of consolidated view of what settings have been applied to all the VMs on a datastore? Fortunately, vCenter Server and the Web Client provide a way to easily see a summary of the various settings.

VIEWING STORAGE I/O RESOURCE SETTINGS FOR VIRTUAL MACHINES

In the Datastores And Datastore Clusters view, you can view a list of all the datastores managed by a particular vCenter Server instance. You enabled SIOC from this view previously, in the section "Enabling Storage I/O Control," and here you can get a consolidated view of all the storage I/O settings applied to the VMs on a datastore.

On the Virtual Machines tab of a selected datastore in the Datastores And Datastore Clusters view, vCenter Server provides a list of all the VMs on that datastore. If you scroll to the right using the scroll bar at the bottom of the Web Client window, you will see three SIOC-specific columns:

◆ Shares Value

◆ Limit – IOPs

◆ Datastore % Shares

Figure 11.28 shows these three columns on a datastore for which SIOC has been enabled. Note that the default values for the VMs on the selected SIOC-enabled datastore have not been modified.

FIGURE 11.28
The Virtual Machines tab of a datastore provides a useful summary view of storage-related information for all the VMs on that datastore.

As you can see in Figure 11.28, vCenter Server has used the assigned Shares values to establish relative percentages of access to storage I/O resources in the event of contention. This consistent behavior makes the complex task of managing resource allocation a bit easier for vSphere administrators.

STORAGE I/O CONTROL AND EXTERNAL WORKLOADS

Storage I/O Control operates on the basis that only VMware vSphere clusters that support SIOC (4.1 and later) are utilizing the storage I/O resources managed by vCenter Server. However, this is often not the case. Many modern arrays are structured such that many different workloads may all run on the same physical disks that support an SIOC-enabled datastore.

In such cases, SIOC can detect "external workloads" and will automatically stop throttling. However, at the next latency evaluation period (4 seconds), SIOC will again check the latency of the datastore against the congestion threshold and see if it needs to start throttling again, and the cycle starts again.

To resolve this issue, VMware recommends that you avoid sharing physical disks across both virtual and nonvirtual workloads. Because of the architecture of some arrays, this may be difficult, so check with your storage vendor for their recommendations and best practices.

So far we've discussed shared storage where the features and settings are all array agnostic—Fibre Channel, iSCSI, or NFS—it really doesn't matter how it's presented to your ESXi hosts. In the next section, we'll introduce some features that are solely for use with local SSD-based storage.

Utilizing Flash Storage

As physical to virtual ratios increase and environments become denser, the need for faster storage is obvious. Flash storage is quickly becoming an industry standard, and it's not uncommon for both servers and SANs to ship with flash-based storage. Traditionally, SANs have used smaller portions of flash storage as caches to increase the response times to slower spindles, but as SAN sizes increase, so does the need for expensive flash cache. Depending on the scenario, a more cost-effective solution can be to load up servers (either rack mount or blade) with local SSD or PCIe-based flash storage.

vSphere 5.5 offers two completely different ways of using local flash-based host storage, whether it be SSD drives or PCIe cards. vFlash Cache (vFC) is a feature that acts as a buffer for I/O on a per-VM basis. The other feature, Swap to Host Cache, is used to allocate local flash disks as swap space. These features are not mutually exclusive; they can be enabled at the same time and can even be backed by the same SSD, but they work in completely different ways.

FLASH OR SSD?

Although the industry may use different names, all flash-based storage is built on similar NAND technology. SSD, EFD, or just flash is just nonvolatile memory that retains its data even without power. The differentiator between the different products is similar to "regular" hard disks—latency, bandwidth, resiliency, and of course, size. And just as with regular spinning disk drives, there can be very different performance and capacity characteristics depending on the model.

ENABLING vFLASH CACHE FOR VIRTUAL MACHINES

vFlash caching is a resource type that can be allocated on a per-VM basis just like CPU or memory. In fact, it can be allocated down to an individual virtual disk (VMDK) level. However, a VM does not *need* to have vFlash allocated to function. Just like CPU and Memory allocations, no vFlash resources are consumed and the contents of the VM cache are flushed when the VM is powered off. Also just like CPU and Memory allocation, provided you have enough resources configured on each host in a cluster, vFlash Cache is compatible with HA, vMotion, and therefore DRS.

The following instructions outline how to enable vFlash Cache:

1. If it is not already running, launch the Web Client and connect to a vCenter Server instance.

2. Navigate to the Hosts And Clusters or VMs And Templates view.

3. With a host selected, click Manage ➤ Settings ➤ Virtual Flash Resource Management.

4. Within this screen, click the Add Capacity button in the top-right corner of the content area.

5. Select the SSD from the list, as shown in Figure 11.29. Click OK to close the dialog box. The SSD is now allocated to the vFlash Cache resource pool.

FIGURE 11.29
New to vSphere 5.5, you can now add SSDs to the vFlash Cache resource capacity.

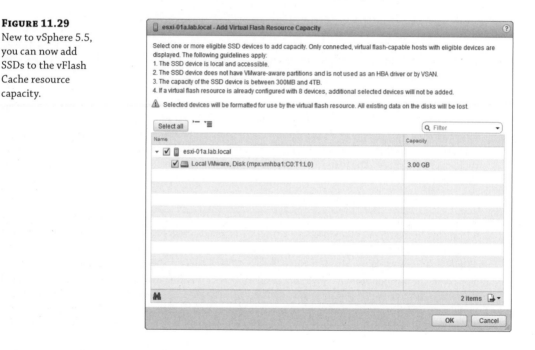

6. Navigate to the VM that you wish to allocate vFlash resources to, select the Actions drop-down menu, and click Edit Settings.

7. From within the Edit Settings dialog box, expand the Hard Disk area of the VM properties and allocate an amount of resources in GB or MB, as shown in Figure 11.30.

8. Click OK to close the dialog box and commit the configuration change to the VM.

FIGURE 11.30
Allocating vFlash
Cache to a VM is as
simple as allocating
it as you would CPU
or memory.

As you can see, configuring and allocating vFlash Cache is a fairly simple task. What won't be so easy is working out which VM hard disks benefit from allocating vFlash Cache and how much to allocate. In Chapter 13, "Monitoring VMware vSphere Performance," we discuss monitoring vSphere Performance in great detail. The use of performance graphs and resxtop will be of great benefit when you start to baseline workloads for vFlash Cache inclusion. Depending on the workloads that your environment runs, you may find that vFlash Cache is of little benefit. In a low I/O but high memory overcommit, you may find that disk I/O is increasing because the hosts need to swap out memory to disk, just as described earlier in this chapter. In this scenario, allocating flash-based resources to swap would be a good idea.

Configuring Swap to Host Cache

Swap to Host Cache, or "Swap to SSD," is a feature that allocates a portion of local SSD storage to be the location of a VMs swapfile. As discussed earlier in this chapter, the VM swapfile is very different from the OS swap/page file.

One very important point to note—this feature is beneficial only within environments that have memory contention to the point that the hypervisor has to swap unreserved VM memory to disk. Based on the figures explained earlier in this chapter, accessing memory swapped to disk (even SSD) is still significantly slower than accessing it from RAM. That being said, if your environment fits within this category, there are significant performance benefits from enabling this feature.

To configure the host for Swap to Cache, a VMFS datastore that has been identified as being backed by an SSD needs to be present. The following steps outline how to enable this feature:

1. If it is not already running, launch the Web Client and connect to a vCenter Server instance.

2. Navigate to the Hosts And Clusters view.

3. Select the appropriate host.

4. Click the Manage ➤ Storage tab.

5. Select Host Cache Configuration as shown in Figure 11.31.

FIGURE 11.31
The Host Cache Configuration feature is designed specifically for SSD datastores.

6. Highlight the appropriate SSD-backed VMFS datastore and click the Edit pencil icon.

7. Finally, ensure the Allocate Space For Host Cache is checked. The size is customizable if you would like to use this datastore for other purposes.

8. Click OK to finalize the configuration.

Once Swap to Host Cache is enabled, the host proceeds to fill the allocated size on the datastore with .vswp files (see Figure 11.32). These .vswp files will be used instead of the "regular" .vswp files that are usually found within the same datastore as the other VM files. Something to keep in mind here is that this setting needs to be enabled on every host within a cluster because it is not cluster aware. If a VM is vMotioned to a host that does not have Swap to Host Cache enabled, the normal datastore-based swapfiles will be used.

FIGURE 11.32
As soon as a datastore has been enabled for Host Cache, it is filled with pre-allocated files.

> ### MAKING BEST USE OF SSDs
>
> Even though both vFlash Cache and Swap to Host Cache can be configured on the same SSD, some thought should go into how to get the best use of this limited resource.
>
> If your VMs have high memory contention and swap to disk often, your SSD datastores would be best allocated to Swap to Host Cache. However, if your VMs are I/O constrained and experience high latency when reading or writing to disk, it would be better to allocate the SSD to vFlash Cache.
>
> In the end, each environment is different. Be sure to think about where your SSDs are allocated and you will be sure to get the most out of your fastest storage device.

Throughout this chapter, we've shown you how to use reservations, shares, and limits to modify the resource allocation and resource utilization behaviors of VMware vSphere. In the next chapter, we'll show you some additional tools for balancing resource utilization across groups of servers.

The Bottom Line

Manage virtual machine memory allocation.   In almost every virtualized datacenter, memory is the resource that typically comes under contention first. Most organizations run out of memory on their VMware ESXi hosts before other resources become constrained. Fortunately, VMware vSphere offers advanced memory-management technologies as well as extensive controls for managing the allocation of memory and utilization of memory by VMs.

> **Master It**   To guarantee certain levels of performance, your IT director believes that all VMs must be configured with at least 8 GB of RAM. However, you know that many of your applications rarely use this much memory. What might be an acceptable compromise to help ensure performance?

> **Master It**   You are configuring a brand-new large-scale VDI environment but you're worried that the cluster hosts won't have enough RAM to handle the expected load. Which advanced memory management technique will ensure that your virtual desktops have enough RAM without having to use the swapfile?

Manage CPU utilization.   In a VMware vSphere environment, the ESXi hosts control VM access to physical CPUs. To effectively manage and scale VMware vSphere, administrators must understand how to allocate CPU resources to VMs, including how to use reservations, limits, and shares. Reservations provide guarantees to resources, limits provide a cap on resource usage, and shares help adjust the allocation of resources in a constrained environment.

> **Master It**   A fellow VMware administrator is a bit concerned about the use of CPU reservations. She is worried that using CPU reservations will "strand" CPU resources, preventing those reserved but unused resources from being used by other VMs. Are this administrator's concerns well founded?

Create and manage resource pools.   Managing resource allocation and usage for large numbers of VMs creates too much administrative overhead. Resource pools provide a mechanism for administrators to apply resource allocation policies to groups of VMs all at the same time. Resource pools use reservations, limits, and shares to control and modify resource allocation behavior, but only for memory and CPU.

Master It Your company runs both test/development workloads and production workloads on the same hardware. How can you help ensure that test/development workloads do not consume too many resources and impact the performance of production workloads?

Control network and storage I/O utilization. Memory, CPU, network I/O, and storage I/O make up the four major resource types that VMware vSphere administrators must effectively manage in order to have an efficient virtualized datacenter. By applying controls to network I/O and storage I/O, administrators can help ensure consistent performance, meet service-level objectives, and prevent one workload from unnecessarily consuming resources at the expense of other workloads.

Master It Name two limitations of Network I/O Control.

Master It What are the requirements for using Storage I/O Control?

Utilize Flash Storage Flash storage is more popular than ever, and vSphere 5.5 has introduced the new vFlash Cache feature to sit alongside the Swap to Host Cache feature. This new resource type benefits environments that need maximum performance.

Master It You have a VM that has a large I/O requirement. Which flash feature should you configure and why?

Chapter 12

Balancing Resource Utilization

Virtualization with VMware vSphere is, among other things, about getting better utilization of your computing resources within a single physical host. vSphere accomplishes this by letting you run multiple instances of a guest operating system on a single physical host. However, it's also about getting better resource utilization across multiple physical hosts, and that means shifting workloads between hosts to balance the resource utilization. vSphere offers a number of powerful tools for helping administrators balance resource utilization.

In this chapter, you will learn to

- ◆ Configure and execute vMotion
- ◆ Ensure vMotion compatibility across processor families
- ◆ Use Storage vMotion
- ◆ Perform Combined vMotion and Storage vMotion
- ◆ Configure and manage vSphere Distributed Resource Scheduler
- ◆ Configure and manage Storage DRS

Comparing Utilization with Allocation

The fundamental but subtle difference between allocation and utilization can be difficult to understand at times. *Allocation* is about how a resource is assigned; so in a vSphere environment, allocation is about how CPU cycles, memory, storage I/O, and network bandwidth are distributed to a particular VM or group of VMs. *Utilization*, on the other hand, is about how resources are used after they are allocated. vSphere provides three mechanisms for allocation: reservations (guaranteed allocations of resources), limits (bounds on the maximum allocation of resources), and shares (prioritized access to resource allocation during periods of resource contention). While these mechanisms are powerful and useful—as you saw in Chapter 11, "Managing Resource Allocation"—they do have their limits (no pun intended). What about situations when a resource is highly utilized on one host and lightly utilized on another host? None of the three mechanisms we've shown you so far will help balance the *utilization* of resources among ESXi hosts; they will only control the *allocation* of resources.

VMware vSphere helps balance the intra-cluster utilization of resources in the following four ways:

vMotion vMotion, also generically known as *live migration*, is used to manually balance compute resource utilization between two ESXi hosts.

Storage vMotion Storage vMotion is the storage equivalent of vMotion, and it is used to manually balance storage utilization between two datastores.

vSphere Distributed Resource Scheduler vSphere Distributed Resource Scheduler (DRS) is used to automatically balance compute resource utilization among two or more ESXi hosts.

Storage DRS Just as Storage vMotion is the storage equivalent of vMotion, Storage DRS is the storage equivalent of DRS, and it is used to automatically balance storage utilization among two or more datastores before and after initial placement of virtual machine files.

As we explain each of these four mechanisms for balancing resource utilization, we'll also introduce or review a few related features of vSphere, such as clusters and VMware Enhanced vMotion Compatibility (EVC).

Let's start with vMotion.

Exploring vMotion

We've defined the vMotion feature as a way to manually balance compute resource utilization between two ESXi hosts. What does that mean, exactly? vMotion can perform a live migration of a VM from one ESXi host to another ESXi host without service interruption. This is a no-downtime operation; network connections are not dropped and applications continue running uninterrupted. In fact, the end users are unaware that the VM has been migrated between physical ESXi hosts. When you use vMotion to migrate a VM from one ESXi host to another, you also migrate the resource allocation—CPU and memory—from one host to another. This makes vMotion an extremely effective tool for manually load-balancing VMs across ESXi hosts and eliminating "hot spots"—heavily utilized ESXi hosts—within your virtualized datacenter.

In addition to manually balancing VM loads among ESXi hosts, vMotion brings other benefits. If an ESXi host needs to be powered off for hardware maintenance or some other function that would take it out of production, you can use vMotion to migrate all active VMs from the host going offline to another host without waiting for a hardware maintenance window. Because vMotion is a live migration—no interruption in service and no downtime—the VMs will remain available to the users who need them.

While it sounds like magic, the basic premise of vMotion is relatively straightforward. vMotion works by copying the contents of VMmemory from one ESXi host to another and then transferring control of the VM's disk files to the target host.

Let's take a closer look. vMotion operates in the following sequence:

1. An administrator initiates a migration of a running VM (VM1) from one ESXi host (esxi-03a) to another (esxi-04a), as shown in Figure 12.1.

2. The source host (esxi-03a) copies the active memory pages VM1 has in host memory to the destination host (esxi-04a) across a VMkernel interface enabled for vMotion. This is called *preCopy*. Meanwhile, the VM still services clients on the source (esxi-04a). As the memory is copied from the source host to the target, pages in memory can be changed. ESXi handles this by keeping a log of changes that occur in the memory of the VM on the source host after that memory address is copied to the target host. This log is called a *memory bitmap*. See Figure 12.2. Note that this process occurs iteratively, repeatedly copying over memory contents that have changed.

FIGURE 12.1
Step 1 in a vMotion migration is invoking a migration while the VM is powered on.

FIGURE 12.2
Step 2 in a vMotion migration is starting the memory copy and adding a memory bitmap.

---

vMotion Can Now Leverage Multiple NICs

As of vSphere 5, vMotion can take advantage of multiple NICs to assist with transferring memory data between hosts.

---

3. After the entire contents of RAM for the migrating VM are transferred to the target host (esxi-04a), then VM1 on the source ESXi host (esxi-03a) is *quiesced*. This means that it is still in memory but is no longer servicing client requests for data. The memory bitmap file is then transferred to the target (esxi-04a). See Figure 12.3.

FIGURE 12.3
Step 3 in a vMotion migration involves quiescing VM1 and transferring the memory bitmap file from the source ESXi host to the destination ESXi host.

THE MEMORY BITMAP

The memory bitmap does not include the contents of the memory address that has changed; it includes only the addresses of that memory—often referred to as the *dirty memory*.

---

4. The target host (esxi-04a) reads the addresses in the memory bitmap file and requests the contents of those addresses from the source (esxi-03a). See Figure 12.4.

FIGURE 12.4
In step 4 in a vMotion migration, the actual memory listed in the bitmap file is fetched from the source to the destination (dirty memory).

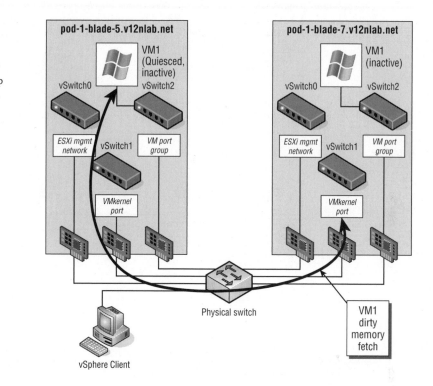

5. After the contents of the memory referred to in the memory bitmap file are transferred to the target host, the VM starts on that host. Note that this is not a reboot—the VM's state is in RAM, so the host simply enables it. At this point a Reverse Address Resolution Protocol (RARP) message is sent by the host to register its MAC address against the physical switch port to which the target ESXi host is connected. This process enables the physical switch infrastructure to send network packets to the appropriate ESXi host from the clients that are attached to the VM that just moved.

6. After the VM is successfully operating on the target host, the memory the VM was using on the source host is deleted. This memory becomes available to the VMkernel to use as appropriate, as shown in Figure 12.5.

FIGURE 12.5
In step 6 in a vMotion migration, vCenter Server deletes the VM from the source ESXi host.

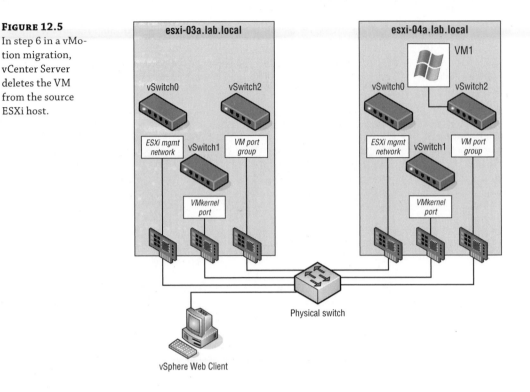

Examining vMotion Requirements

The vMotion migration is pretty amazing, and when users see it work for the first time in a live environment, they are extremely impressed. However, detailed planning is necessary for this procedure to function properly. While vMotion is only available through vCenter Server, the hosts involved in the vMotion process have to meet certain requirements along with the VMs being migrated.

Each of the ESXi hosts involved in vMotion must meet the following requirements:

◆ Shared storage for the VM files (a VMFS or NFS datastore) that is accessible by both the source and target ESXi host.

◆ A Gigabit Ethernet or faster network interface card (NIC) with a VMkernel port defined and enabled for vMotion on each ESXi host.

VMOTION WITHOUT SHARED STORAGE

As you can see in the section "Examining vMotion Requirements," we state that vMotion requires shared storage. vSphere 5.1 introduced the ability to also have "shared nothing" vMotion. This new feature uses both vMotion in conjunction with Storage vMotion, and you will find details later in this chapter in the section "Combining vMotion with Storage vMotion."

This VMkernel port can be on a vSphere Standard Switch, on a vSphere Distributed Switch, or on a third-party distributed virtual switch like the Cisco Nexus 1000V, but it must be enabled for vMotion. The Gigabit Ethernet or faster NIC should be dedicated to vMotion traffic, although you can share this NIC with other traffic types if necessary. In Chapter 5, "Creating and Configuring Virtual Networks," we provided the steps for creating a VMkernel port on a vSwitch. We included instructions for creating a VMkernel port on either a vSphere Standard Switch or a vSphere Distributed Switch. We'll review the steps for creating a VMkernel port on a vSphere Distributed Switch again just for convenience.

Perform the following steps to create a VMkernel port on an existing vSphere Distributed Switch:

1. Launch the Web Client if it is not already running, and connect to an instance of vCenter Server.

2. Navigate to the Hosts And Clusters view.

3. From the inventory list on the left, select an ESXi host that is already participating in the vSphere Distributed Switch.

4. Select the Manage tab from the contents pane on the right.

5. Click Networking to display the host's networking configuration.

6. Click the Virtual Adapters link.

7. In the Virtual Adapters pane, click the link to add a new virtual adapter.

8. Select VMkernel Network Adapter and click Next.

9. Browse to the correct port group, and click Next.

10. Enable the vMotion traffic service and click Next.

11. Specify an IP address and network mask for this VMkernel interface.

12. Review the pending changes to the distributed switch.

    If everything is correct, click Finish to complete adding the VMkernel interface. Otherwise, use the Back button to change the settings accordingly.

Real World Scenario

vMotion Network Security

Whenever we design VMware networks, we always ensure that the vMotion network is separated from all other traffic and, where possible, on a non-routed subnet. The reason behind this design decision is that vMotion traffic is not encrypted. That's right; when a VM's memory is copied between ESXi hosts, the traffic is sent in cleartext. This might not be a concern for a lab or even a development environment, but it certainly needs to be considered within a production or multitenant environment. Let's look at a hypothetical situation involving a large bank.

ABank-ESXi-42a is an ESXi host with a VM running an SQL database. This database holds customers' personal details, including credit card numbers. The VM is secured behind multiple firewalls and is far away from the Internet. Obviously, because of the sensitive nature of the data on this server, it can be accessed by only a select number of senior administration staff to perform tasks and maintenance. Because of these precautions, the bank considers this server to be "secure."

The more junior administration staff have access to the same management network but are specifically denied access to the more sensitive servers, such as this SQL database. One of the junior network admins decides he wants access to the credit card information. He chooses to sniff the network traffic on the management network to see if there's anything interesting going on. In most circumstances, management traffic, such as the vSphere Web Client, is encrypted so the junior admin would get only garbled data.

Unfortunately ABank-ESXi-42a needs to be put into maintenance and the vMotion network is on the same subnet as the management traffic. The vMotion for the SQL VM is initiated and the database that resides in memory is sent in cleartext across the management network for the junior network admin to see.

All the bank needed to do was segment the vMotion network onto an isolated VLAN or subnet that only the vMotion VMkernel ports could access and this situation could have been avoided.

In addition to the configuration requirements just outlined (shared storage and a vMotion-enabled VMkernel port), a successful vMotion migration between two ESXi hosts relies on meeting all of the following conditions:

◆ Both the source and destination hosts must be configured with identical virtual switches that are correctly configured, vMotion-enabled VMkernel ports. If you are using vSphere Distributed Switches, both hosts must be participating in the same vSphere Distributed Switch.

◆ All port groups to which the VM being migrated is attached must exist on both of the ESXi hosts. Port group naming is case sensitive, so create identical port groups on each host, and make sure they plug into the same physical subnets or VLANs. A virtual switch named Production is not the same as a virtual switch named PRODUCTION. Remember that to prevent downtime, the VM is not going to change its network address as it is moved. The VM will retain its MAC address and IP address so clients connected to it don't have to resolve any new information to reconnect.

◆ Processors in both hosts must be compatible. When a VM is transferred between hosts, the VM has already detected the type of processor it is running on when it booted. Because the VM is not rebooted during a vMotion, the guest assumes the CPU instruction set on the target host is the same as on the source host. You can get away with slightly dissimilar processors, but in general the processors in two hosts that perform vMotion must meet the following requirements:

♦ CPUs must be from the same vendor (Intel or AMD).

♦ CPUs must be from the same CPU family (Xeon 55xx, Xeon 56xx, or Opteron).

♦ CPUs must support the same features, such as the presence of SSE2, SSE3, and SSE4 and NX or XD (see the sidebar "Processor Instruction").

♦ For 64-bit VMs, CPUs must have virtualization technology enabled (Intel VT or AMD-v).

We'll talk more about processor compatibility in the section "Ensuring vMotion Compatibility."

PROCESSOR INSTRUCTION

Streaming SIMD Extensions 2 (SSE2) was an enhancement to the original Multimedia Extension (MMX) instruction set found in the PIII processor. The enhancement targeted the floating-point calculation capabilities of the processor by providing 144 new instructions. SSE3 instruction sets are an enhancement to the SSE2 standard targeting multimedia and graphics applications. SSE4 extensions target both the graphics and the application server.

AMD's Execute Disable (XD) and Intel's NoExecute (NX) are features of processors that mark memory pages as data only, which prevents a virus from running executable code at that address. The operating system needs to be written to take advantage of this feature, and in general, versions of Windows starting with Windows 2003 SP1 and Windows XP SP2 support this CPU feature.

The latest processors from Intel and AMD have specialized support for virtualization. The AMD-V and Intel Virtualization Technology (VT) must be enabled in the BIOS in order to create 64-bit VMs.

In addition to the vMotion requirements for the hosts involved, the VM must meet the following requirements to be migrated:

♦ The VM must not be connected to any device physically available to only one ESXi host. This includes disk storage, CD/DVD drives, floppy drives, serial ports, and parallel ports. If the VM to be migrated has one of these mappings, simply deselect the Connected check box beside the offending device. For example, you won't be able to migrate a VM with a CD/DVD drive connected; to disconnect the drive and allow vMotion, deselect the Connected box.

♦ The VM must not be connected to an internal-only virtual switch.

♦ The VM must not have its CPU affinity set to a specific CPU.

♦ The VM must have all disk, configuration, log, and nonvolatile random access memory (NVRAM) files stored on a VMFS or NFS datastore accessible from both the source and the destination ESXi hosts.

If you start a vMotion migration and vCenter Server finds a violation of the vMotion compatibility rules, you will see an error message. In some cases, a warning, not an error, will be issued. In the case of a warning, the vMotion migration will still succeed. For instance, if you have cleared the check box on the host-attached floppy drive, vCenter Server will tell you there is a mapping to a host-only device that is not active. You'll see a prompt asking whether the migration should take place anyway.

VMware states that you need a Gigabit Ethernet NIC for vMotion; however, it does not have to be dedicated to vMotion. When you're designing the ESXi host, dedicate a NIC to vMotion if possible. You thus reduce the contention on the vMotion network, and the vMotion process can happen in a fast and efficient manner.

> **GIGABIT REQUIREMENT FOR VMOTION**
>
> Although the requirements for a vMotion network state the need for 1 Gbps, technically 600 Mbps is the bare minimum. Keep this in mind when using vMotion over long distances because this may be a more achievable requirement.

Now that we've reviewed all the various prerequisites, both for ESXi hosts and VMs, let's actually perform a vMotion migration.

Performing a vMotion Migration

After you've verified the ESXi host requirements as well as the VM requirements, you are ready to perform a vMotion migration.

Perform the following steps to conduct a vMotion migration of a running VM:

1. Launch the Web Client if it is not already running, and connect to a vCenter Server instance.

   vMotion requires vCenter Server.

2. Navigate to either the Hosts And Clusters or VMs And Templates view.

3. Select a powered-on VM in your inventory, right-click the VM, and select Migrate.

4. Select Change Host, and then click Next.

5. If you have any resource pools defined on the target host or target cluster, you'll need to select the target resource pool (or cluster). You can also select a vApp as your target resource pool; we introduced the concept of vApps in Chapter 10, "Using Templates and vApps."

   To select the individual host in a cluster, check Allow Host Selection Within This Cluster.

   Most of the time the same resource pool (or cluster) that the VM currently resides in will suffice, and it is selected by default as the target resource pool. Keep in mind that choosing a different resource pool might change that VM's priority access to resources. Refer to

Chapter 11 for a more in-depth discussion of how resource allocation is affected by placement into a resource pool. If no resource pool is defined on the target host, then vCenter Server skips this step entirely. Click Next.

6. Choose the target host.

Figure 12.6 shows a target host that produces validation errors; that is, vCenter Server has found errors that would prevent a successful vMotion operation. Figure 12.7 shows a compatible and properly configured target host selected.

FIGURE 12.6
vCenter Server will show you errors found during validation of the selected target host in a vMotion operation.

After you've selected the correct target host, click Next.

FIGURE 12.7
If vCenter Server does not show any validation errors, then the vMotion operation is allowed to proceed.

7. Select the priority that the vMotion migration needs to proceed with.

   In vSphere 5.5, this setting controls the share of reserved resources allocated for migrations with vMotion. Migrations marked as Reserve CPU For Optimal vMotion Performance receive a reserved share of CPU resources compared to migrations marked as Perform With Available CPU Resources. Migrations will proceed regardless of the resources reserved. This behavior is different than in earlier versions; see the sidebar "Migration Priority in Earlier Versions of vSphere." Generally, you will select Reserve CPU... (Recommended). Click Next to continue.

MIGRATION PRIORITY IN EARLIER VERSIONS OF VSPHERE

The behavior of the High Priority / Reserved CPU and Standard Priority / Non-Reserved settings for vMotion changed in vSphere 4.1; this behavior carries forward to vSphere 5.5 as described in the text. For vSphere 4, however, the behavior of these options is different. For vSphere 4, high-priority migrations do not proceed if resources are unavailable to be reserved for the migration, whereas standard priority migrations will proceed. However, standard priority migrations might proceed more slowly and might even fail to complete if enough resources are not available.

---

8. Review the settings, and click Finish if all the information is correct.

   If there are any errors, use the Back button or the hyperlinks on the left to go back and correct the errors.

9. The VM should start to migrate. Often, the process will pause at about 14 percent in the progress dialog box and then again at 65 percent.

   The 14 percent pause occurs while the hosts in question establish communications and gather the information for the pages in memory to be migrated; the 65 percent pause occurs when the source VM is quiesced and the dirty memory pages are fetched from the source host, as shown in Figure 12.8.

FIGURE 12.8
The Recent Tasks pane of the Web Client shows the progress of the vMotion operation.

> ### vMotion Is Not a High-Availability Feature
>
> vMotion is a great feature, but it is not a high-availability feature. Yes you can improve uptime by preventing downtime from planned outages, but vMotion will not provide any protection in the event of an unplanned host failure. For that functionality, you'll need vSphere High Availability (HA) and vSphere Fault Tolerance (FT), two features that are discussed in Chapter 7, "Ensuring High Availability and Business Continuity."

vMotion is an invaluable tool for virtual administrators. Once you've managed a datacenter with vMotion, you'll wonder how you managed without it.

Over time, though, you could find yourself in a situation where you are without vMotion. As hardware manufacturers such as Intel and AMD introduce new generations of CPUs, some of your ESXi hosts may have a newer generation of CPUs than others. Remember that one of the requirements for vMotion is compatible CPUs. So what happens when you need to refresh some of your hardware and you have to start using a new generation of CPUs? vSphere addresses this potential problem with a feature called VMware Enhanced vMotion Compatibility (EVC).

Ensuring vMotion Compatibility

In the section "Examining vMotion Requirements," we discussed some of the prerequisites needed to perform a vMotion operation. In particular, I mentioned that vMotion has some fairly strict CPU requirements. Specifically, the CPUs must be from the same vendor, must be in the same family, and must share a common set of CPU instruction sets and features.

In a situation where two physical hosts exist in a cluster and there are CPU differences between the two hosts, vMotion will fail. This is often referred to as a *vMotion boundary*. Until later versions of ESXi 3.*x* and appropriate support from Intel and AMD in their processors, there was no fix for this issue—it was something that virtual datacenter administrators and architects simply had to endure.

However, in later versions of VMware Virtual Infrastructure 3.*x* and continuing into VMware vSphere 4.*x* and 5.*x*, VMware supports hardware extensions from Intel and AMD to help mitigate these CPU differences. In fact, vSphere provides two ways to address this issue, either in part or in whole.

Using Per-Virtual-Machine CPU Masking

vCenter Server offers the ability to create custom CPU masks on a per-VM basis. Although this can offer a tremendous amount of flexibility in enabling vMotion compatibility, it's also important to note that, with one exception, this is *completely unsupported by VMware*.

What is the one exception? On a per-VM basis, you'll find a setting that tells the VM to show or mask the No Execute/Execute Disable (NX/XD) bit in the host CPU, and this specific instance of CPU masking is fully supported by VMware. Masking the NX/XD bit from the VM tells the VM that there's no NX/XD bit present. This is useful if you have two otherwise compatible hosts with an NX/XD bit mismatch. If the VM doesn't know there's an NX or XD bit on one of the hosts, it won't care if the target host has or doesn't have that bit if you migrate that VM using vMotion. The greatest vMotion compatibility is achieved by masking the NX/XD bit. If the NX/XD bit is exposed to the VM, as shown in Figure 12.9, the BIOS setting for NX/XD must match on both the source and destination ESXi hosts.

FIGURE 12.9
The option for masking the NX/XD bit is controlled on a per-VM basis.

For features other than the NX/XD bit, you would have to delve into custom CPU masks. This is where you will step outside the bounds of VMware support. Looking at the dialog box in Figure 12.9, you'll note the Advanced button. Clicking the Advanced button opens the CPU Identification Mask dialog box, shown in Figure 12.10.

In this dialog box, you can create custom CPU masks to mark off specific bits within the CPU ID value. We won't go into great detail here because all of this is unsupported by VMware, and it's generally not needed provided you run hardware that is on the HCL. However, Scott Lowe has two blog articles that provide additional information:

    http://blog.scottlowe.org/2006/09/25/sneaking-around-vmotion-limitations/

    http://blog.scottlowe.org/2007/06/19/more-on-cpu-masking/

Fortunately, there's an easier—and fully supported—way of handling this issue, and it's called VMware Enhanced vMotion Compatibility (EVC).

Using VMware Enhanced vMotion Compatibility

Recognizing that potential compatibility issues with vMotion could be a significant problem, VMware worked closely with both Intel and AMD to craft functionality that would address this issue. On the hardware side, Intel and AMD put functions in their CPUs that would allow them to modify the CPU ID value returned by the CPUs. Intel calls this functionality FlexMigration; AMD simply embedded this functionality into its existing AMD-V virtualization extensions.

On the software side, VMware created software features that would take advantage of this hardware functionality to create a common CPU ID baseline for all the servers within a cluster. This functionality, originally introduced in VMware ESX/ESXi 3.5 Update 2, is called VMware Enhanced vMotion Compatibility.

EVC is enabled at the cluster level. Figure 12.11 shows the EVC controls for a cluster.

FIGURE 12.10
The CPU Identification Mask dialog box allows you to create custom CPU masks.

FIGURE 12.11
VMware EVC is enabled and disabled at the cluster level.

As you can see in Figure 12.11, EVC is enabled on this cluster. This cluster contains servers with AMD Operon processors, so EVC is using an AMD Operon Generation 1 baseline. To change the baseline that EVC is using, follow these steps:

1. Click the Change EVC Mode button.

2. A dialog box opens that allows you to disable EVC or to change the EVC baseline, as illustrated in Figure 12.12.

FIGURE 12.12
You can enable or disable EVC as well as change the processor baseline EVC uses.

vCenter Server performs some validation checks to ensure that the physical hardware can support the selected EVC mode and processor baseline. If you select a setting that the hardware cannot support, the Change EVC Mode dialog box will reflect the incompatibility. Figure 12.13 shows an incompatible EVC mode selected.

When you enable EVC and set the processor baseline, vCenter Server then calculates the correct CPU masks required and communicates that information to the ESXi hosts. The ESXi hypervisor then works with the underlying Intel or AMD processors to create the correct CPU ID values that would match the correct CPU mask. When vCenter Server validates vMotion compatibility by checking CPU compatibility, the underlying CPUs will return compatible CPU masks and CPU ID values. However, vCenter Server and ESXi cannot set CPU masks for VMs that are currently powered on. (You can verify this by opening the properties of a running VM and going to the CPUID Mask area on the Resources tab. You'll find all the controls there are disabled.)

Consequently, if you attempt to change the EVC mode on a cluster that has powered-on VMs, vCenter Server will prevent you from making the change, as you can see in Figure 12.14. You'll have to power down the VMs in order to change the cluster's EVC mode.

FIGURE 12.13
vCenter Server ensures that the selected EVC mode is compatible with the underlying hardware.

FIGURE 12.14
vCenter Server informs the user which ESXi hosts in the cluster have powered-on or suspended VMs that are preventing the change to the cluster's EVC mode.

When setting the EVC mode for a cluster, keep in mind that some CPU-specific features—such as newer multimedia extensions or encryption instructions—could be disabled when vCenter Server and ESXi disable them via EVC. VMs that rely on these advanced extensions might be affected by EVC, so be sure that your workloads won't be adversely affected before setting the cluster's EVC mode.

EVC is a powerful feature that assures vSphere administrators that vMotion compatibility will be maintained over time, even as hardware generations change. With EVC, you won't have to remember what life's like without vMotion.

Traditional vMotion only helps with balancing CPU and memory load. In the next section we'll discuss a method for manually balancing storage load.

Using Storage vMotion

vMotion and Storage vMotion are like two sides of the same coin. Traditional vMotion migrates a running VM from one physical host to another, moving CPU and memory usage between hosts but leaving the VM's storage unchanged. This allows you to manually balance the CPU and memory load by shifting VMs from host to host. Storage vMotion, however, migrates a running VM's virtual disks from one datastore to another datastore but leaves the VM executing—and therefore using CPU and memory resources—on the same ESXi host. This allows you to manually balance the "load" or utilization of a datastore by shifting a VM's storage from one datastore to another. Like vMotion, Storage vMotion is a live migration; the VM does not incur any outage during the migration of its virtual disks from one datastore to another.

So how does Storage vMotion work? The process is relatively straightforward:

1. First, vSphere copies over the nonvolatile files that make up a VM: the configuration file (VMX), VMkernel swap, log files, and snapshots.

2. Next, vSphere starts a ghost or shadow VM on the destination datastore. Because this ghost VM does not yet have a virtual disk (that hasn't been copied over yet), it sits idle waiting for its virtual disk.

3. Storage vMotion first creates the destination disk. Then a mirror device—a new driver that mirrors I/Os between the source and destination—is inserted into the data path between the VM and the underlying storage.

SVM MIRROR DEVICE INFORMATION IN THE LOGS

If you review the vmkernel log files on an ESXi host during and after a Storage vMotion operation, you will see log entries prefixed with *SVM* that show the creation of the mirror device and that provide information about the operation of the mirror device.

---

4. With the I/O mirroring driver in place, vSphere makes a single-pass copy of the virtual disk(s) from the source to the destination. As changes are made to the source, the I/O mirror driver ensures that those changes are also reflected at the destination.

5. When the virtual disk copy is complete, vSphere quickly suspends and resumes in order to transfer control over to the ghost VM created on the destination datastore earlier. This generally happens so quickly that there is no disruption of service, as with vMotion.

6. The files on the source datastore are deleted.

It's important to note that the original files aren't deleted until the migration is confirmed as successful; this allows vSphere to simply fall back to its original location if an error occurs. This helps prevent data loss situations or VM outages because of an error during the Storage vMotion process.

Perform the following steps to migrate a VM's virtual disks using Storage vMotion:

1. Launch the Web Client if it is not already running. Storage vMotion is available only when you are working with vCenter Server.

2. Navigate to the Hosts And Clusters or VMs And Templates view.

3. Right-click the VM whose virtual disks you want to migrate from the inventory tree on the left, and then select Migrate. This is the same dialog box you used to initial a regular vMotion operation.

4. Select Change Datastore and click Next.

5. Select a destination datastore or datastore cluster. (You'll learn more about datastore clusters in the section "Introducing and Working with Storage DRS.")

6. Select the desired virtual disk format (Same Format As Source, Thick Provision Lazy Zeroed, Thick Provision Eager Zeroed, or Thin Provision).

   Storage vMotion lets you change the disk format during the actual disk-migration process, so you can switch from Thick Provision Lazy Zeroed to Thin Provision, for example.

STORAGE VMOTION WITH RAW DEVICE MAPPINGS

Be careful when using Storage vMotion with raw device mappings (RDMs). If you want to migrate only the VMDK mapping file, be sure to select Same Format As Source for the virtual disk format. If you select a different format, virtual mode RDMs will be converted into VMDKs as part of the Storage vMotion operation (physical mode RDMs are not affected). Once an RDM has been converted into a VMDK, it cannot be converted back into an RDM again.

---

7. If you have Storage Service Classes defined in vCenter Server, select the desired class from the Storage Service Class drop-down box.

8. If you need to migrate the VM's configuration file and virtual hard disks separately or to separate destinations, click the Advanced button.

   Figure 12.15 shows the virtual disk format view of the Storage step of the Migrate Virtual Machine Wizard and how you can choose the destination and disk format for the different VM.

FIGURE 12.15
Use the Migrate
Virtual Machine
Wizard to change
a VM's virtual disk
format.

9. When you have finished making selections on the Storage screen, click Next to continue with the Migrate Virtual Machine Wizard.

10. Review the settings for the Storage vMotion to ensure that everything is correct. If you need to make changes, use the hyperlinks on the left or the Back button.

Once you initiate the Storage vMotion operation, the Web Client will show the progress of the migration in the Recent Tasks pane, as you've seen for other tasks (such as vMotion).

There's a notable difference in how Storage vMotion works with vSphere 5.5 when renaming files. In prior versions of vSphere, the feature was enabled, and then in it was disabled in vSphere 5.1. In vSphere 5.5 the renaming feature is back with extra functionality. We won't go into details on how it used to work, but in vSphere 5.5 when you perform a storage vMotion, vSphere will rename the files that reside on datastores to align to the VM name displayed in the vSphere Web Client. This occurs only if the VM in question has been renamed from the vSphere Web Client. If the VM has not been renamed since it was created or from the last Storage vMotion, this process does not occur. Understand, you don't have the choice to *not* rename the files. Storage vMotion renames the underlying files to adhere to the VM display name and the file naming convention that VMware specifies if it needs to.

The following files are renamed when part of a Storage vMotion occurs to the following standard <VM name>.<extension>:

◆ .VMX

◆ .VMXF

◆ .NVRAM

◆ .VMDK

◆ .VMSN

A few notes and caveats: If a VM has two virtual disks (VMDKs) and you only Storage vMotion one of these disks, only the disk and its associated files would potentially be renamed. If (based on the naming standard) there are two files that would receive the same filename, such as a snapshot disk, a numeric suffix is added to resolve conflicts.

Combining vMotion with Storage vMotion

Introduced with vSphere 5.1, vMotion and Storage vMotion can be combined into a single process to produce what is sometimes called *shared nothing* vMotion.

Without the need for (usually) expensive shared storage such as a NAS or a SAN, VMware administrators can move their workloads from host to host, regardless of the storage type. Local storage, mixed shared storage, or standard shared storage are all valid options to use when combining vMotion with Storage vMotion.

Generally speaking, the only requirement for the combined vMotion and Storage vMotion is that both hosts must share the same L2 (layer 2) network. You will however need to be using the vSphere Web Client, as this feature is not enabled in the traditional vSphere Client. Depending on how you want this feature to work, however, you may need to add extra requirements, so we'll explain with the following examples.

Example 1

- ◆ Two hosts on a single vMotion network.
- ◆ Both hosts use local datastores.

The two hosts in Example 1 are connected by a single vMotion network but both hosts only have local datastores, as you can see Figure 12.16. When you're migrating a VM from one to the other, there are two data flows. The first flow initiated is the storage, because this transfer will generally take longer to complete than the memory. After the storage transfer has taken place, the memory copy starts. Although there are two separate data transfers, all data flows over the same vMotion VMkernel network.

FIGURE 12.16
All data flows over the vMotion network when transferring between local datastores.

Example 2

◆ Two hosts on a single vMotion network.

◆ One host uses local datastores.

◆ One host uses SAN datastores.

A single vMotion network connects the two hosts in Example 2. This time, however, one is connected to a SAN for storage. Within this example, not too much changes with the data flows. The only difference is that the second host pushes the received data to the SAN over its storage network instead of a local datastore. You can see this in detail in Figure 12.17. Both hosts are connected to the shared storage, and that leads us to Example 3.

FIGURE 12.17
Data flows over the vMotion network and then the storage network when transferring between local and non-local datastores.

Example 3

◆ Two hosts on a single vMotion network.

◆ Both hosts use a shared Fibre Channel SAN datastore.

The two hosts in Example 3 are more typical of larger enterprise environments. Generally in these situations there is a SAN or NAS connecting all ESXi hosts. In this situation, the data flows are quite different. As usual, the vMotion network carries the memory data flow. The difference in this example involves the shared storage component. Storage vMotion is smart enough to detect when both hosts can see both source and destination datastores. It intelligently uses the storage network instead of the vMotion network to migrate this data even if it's a local datastore at the source! See Figure 12.18.

FIGURE 12.18
Even if the datastores are not the same, Storage vMotion is smart enough to know if both hosts can see the destination datastore. It uses the storage network whenever possible.

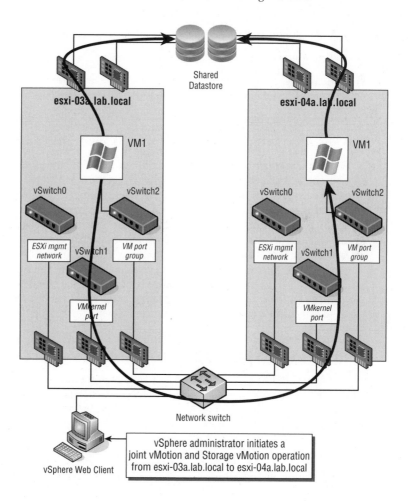

Perform the following steps to migrate a VM to a different host and datastore using the combined vMotion and Storage vMotion:

1. Launch the Web Client if it is not already running.

2. Navigate to the Hosts And Clusters or VMs And Templates view.

3. Right-click the VM whose virtual disks you want to migrate from the inventory tree on the left, and then select Migrate. The same dialog box is used to initiate a vMotion and a Storage vMotion operation opens.

4. Select Change Both Host And Datastore and click Next.

   This option will be grayed out if your cluster hosts are vSphere 5.0 or earlier.

5. Select the destination resource and click Next.

6. Pick the host that you wish to migrate the VM to and click Next.

7. Select a destination datastore or datastore cluster.

8. Select the desired virtual disk format (Same Format As Source, Thick Provision Lazy Zeroed, Thick Provision Eager Zeroed, or Thin Provision). Click Next to continue.

9. Change the vMotion priority if desired, and click Next to review the changes.

10. Finally, review the changes about to be made and click Finish.

When you're combining vMotion and Storage vMotion, the storage is the first migration to take place; the reason behind this is twofold. First, hard disks are both larger and slower than memory; therefore the Storage vMotion will take significantly longer than the vMotion. Second, the rate of change to disk-based storage is usually less than that for memory. If the vMotion operation happened first, the memory bitmap file (discussed earlier in this chapter) would grow much larger while waiting for the Storage vMotion task to complete. That's why it makes a lot more sense for the Storage vMotion operation to happen first.

Like vMotion, Storage vMotion (or a combination of both) is a great approach for manually adjusting the load or utilization of resources, but they are ultimately *reactive* tools. vSphere DRS and Storage DRS leverage vMotion and Storage vMotion to bring a level of automation to help balance utilization across clusters.

Exploring vSphere Distributed Resource Scheduler

When we introduced you to vMotion and Storage vMotion, we stated that they were a way of manually balancing loads across VMware ESXi hosts. vSphere Distributed Resource Scheduler (DRS) builds on this idea by making the load balancing *automatic*. The groups are clusters, which we introduced in Chapter 3, "Installing and Configuring vCenter Server," and discussed again in Chapter 7.

vSphere DRS is a feature of vCenter Server and has the following two main functions:

◆ To decide which node of a cluster should run a VM when it's powered on, or *intelligent placement*

◆ To evaluate the load on the cluster over time and either make recommendations for migrations or use vMotion to automatically move VMs to create a more balanced cluster workload vSphere DRS runs as a process within vCenter Server, which means that you must have vCenter Server in order to use vSphere DRS. By default, DRS checks every 5 minutes (or 300 seconds) to see if the cluster's workload is balanced. DRS is also invoked by certain actions within the cluster, such as adding or removing an ESXi host or changing the resource settings of a VM. When DRS is invoked, it will calculate the imbalance of the cluster, apply any resource controls (such as reservations, shares, and limits), and, if necessary, generate recommendations for migrations of VMs within the cluster. Depending on the configuration of vSphere DRS, these recommendations could be applied automatically, meaning that VMs will automatically be migrated between hosts by DRS in order to maintain cluster balance (or, put another way, to minimize cluster imbalance).

VSPHERE DISTRIBUTED RESOURCE SCHEDULER ENABLES RESOURCE POOLS

DRS enables the use of resource pools when clustering ESXi hosts. If hosts are part of a HA enabled cluster, DRS must also be enabled to allow Resource Pools to be created.

Fortunately, if you like to retain control, you can set how aggressively DRS will automatically move VMs around the cluster.

If you start by looking at the DRS properties—you can view these properties by right-clicking a DRS-enabled cluster, selecting Settings, clicking the vSphere DRS heading on the left, and then clicking Edit—you will see that there are three selections regarding the automation level of the DRS cluster: Manual, Partially Automated, and Fully Automated. If you click the triangle next to DRS Automation, you will find the slider bar that affects the actions of the Fully Automated setting on the cluster. These settings control the initial placement of a VM and the automatic movement of VMs between hosts. We'll examine the behavior of these automation levels in the next three sections.

Understanding Manual Automation Behavior

When a DRS cluster is set to Manual, every time you power on a VM, the cluster prompts you to select the ESXi host where that VM should be hosted. The dialog box rates the available hosts according to suitability at that moment: the lower the priority, the better the choice, as shown in Figure 12.19.

FIGURE 12.19
A DRS cluster set to Manual requires you to specify where the VM should be powered on.

The Manual setting also suggests vMotion migrations when DRS detects an imbalance between ESXi hosts in the cluster. This is an averaging process that works over longer periods of time than many of us are used to in the IT field. It is unusual to see DRS make any recommendations unless an imbalance has existed for longer than 5 minutes. You find the recommended list of migrations by selecting the cluster in the inventory and then selecting the DRS tab.

From the Monitor ➤ DRS tab, the Run DRS Now button allows you to agree with any pending DRS recommendations and initiate a migration. vMotion handles the migration automatically. Figure 12.20 shows some pending recommendations displayed on the DRS recommendations section of a cluster that is set for Manual DRS automation.

FIGURE 12.20
vMotion operations must be approved by an administrator when DRS is set for Manual automation.

Reviewing Partially Automated Behavior

If you select the Partially Automated setting in the DRS Automation settings, DRS will make an automatic decision about which host a VM should run on when it is initially powered on (without prompting the user who is performing the power-on task) but will still prompt for all migrations on the DRS tab. Thus, initial placement is automated, but migrations are still manual.

Examining Fully Automated Behavior

The third setting for DRS is Fully Automated. This setting makes decisions for initial placement without prompting and also makes automatic vMotion decisions based on the selected automation level (the slider bar).

There are five positions for the slider bar for the Fully Automated setting of the DRS cluster. The values of the slider bar range from Conservative to Aggressive. Conservative automatically applies recommendations ranked as priority 1 recommendations. Any other migrations are listed on the DRS tab and require administrator approval. If you move the slider bar from the most conservative setting to the next stop to the right, then all priority 1 and priority 2 recommendations are automatically applied; recommendations higher than priority 2 will wait for administrator approval. With the slider all the way over to the Aggressive setting, any imbalance in the cluster that causes a recommendation is automatically approved (even priority 5 recommendations). Be aware that this can cause additional stress in your ESXi host environment because even a slight imbalance will trigger a migration.

Calculations for migrations can change regularly. Assume that during a period of high activity DRS makes a priority 3 recommendation and the automation level is set so priority 3 recommendations need manual approval, but the recommendation is not noticed (or an administrator is not even in the office). An hour later, the VMs that caused the recommendation in the first place have settled down and are now operating normally. At this point, the DRS tab no longer reflects the recommendation. The recommendation has since been withdrawn. If the migration were still listed, an administrator might approve it and cause an imbalance where one did not exist.

In many cases, priority 1 recommendations have little to do with load on the cluster. Instead, priority 1 recommendations are generally the result of one of two conditions. The first condition that causes a priority 1 recommendation is when you put a host into maintenance mode, as shown in Figure 12.21.

FIGURE 12.21
An ESXi host put into maintenance mode cannot power on new VMs or be a target for vMotion.

Maintenance mode is a host setting that prevents the ESXi host from performing any VM-related functions. VMs running on a host being put into maintenance mode must be shut down or moved to another host before the host will actually enter maintenance mode. That is, an ESXi host in a DRS-enabled cluster will automatically generate priority 1 recommendations to migrate all VMs to other hosts within the cluster. Figure 12.20 shows priority 1 recommendations generated as the result of an ESXi host being placed into maintenance mode.

The second condition that could cause a priority 1 recommendation is when DRS affinity rules come into play. This leads us to a discussion of DRS affinity rules.

A QUICK REVIEW OF DISTRIBUTED RESOURCE SCHEDULER CLUSTER PERFORMANCE

Monitoring the detailed performance of a cluster is an important task for any virtual infrastructure administrator, particularly monitoring the CPU and memory activity of the whole cluster as well as the respective resource utilization of the VMs within the cluster. The Summary tab of the details pane for a cluster object includes information on cluster configuration as well as statistics for the current load distribution. Additionally, the View Resource Distribution Chart shows the current resource distribution of the ESXi hosts in the cluster. While resource allocation and distribution isn't necessarily a direct indicator of performance, it can be a helpful metric nevertheless.

Working with Distributed Resource Scheduler Rules

To further allow an administrator to customize the behavior of vSphere DRS for their specific environment, vSphere lets you create DRS rules. vSphere DRS supports three types of DRS rules:

- ◆ VM affinity rules, referred to as Keep Virtual Machines Together in the Web Client
- ◆ VM anti-affinity rules, referred to as Separate Virtual Machines in the Web Client
- ◆ Host affinity rules, referred to as Virtual Machines To Hosts in the Web Client

Figure 12.22 shows these three types of rules in the dialog box for creating new DRS rules.

FIGURE 12.22
DRS supports VM affinity, VM anti-affinity, and host affinity rules.

Recall from the previous section that DRS rules are the second of two conditions that will trigger a priority 1 recommendation (the other is maintenance mode). When DRS detects that VMs will violate DRS rules, it generates a priority 1 recommendation to migrate one or more VMs in order to satisfy the constraint expressed in the DRS rule.

vSphere's DRS rule functionality gives vSphere administrators the power to model the complex relationships that often exist in today's datacenters. Let's take a closer look at each of these three types of DRS rules.

CREATING VM AFFINITY RULES

Affinity rules keep VMs together on the same host. Consider a multitier application where you have a web application server and a backend database server that frequently communicate with each other and you'd like that communication to take advantage of the high-speed bus within a single server rather than going across the network. In that case, you could define an affinity rule (Keep Virtual Machines Together) that would ensure that these two VMs stay together in the cluster.

Perform the following steps to create a DRS affinity rule:

1. Launch the Web Client if it is not already running, and connect to a vCenter Server instance.

   DRS and DRS rules cannot be managed when connected to a specific ESXi host; you must connect to a vCenter Server instance.

2. Navigate to the Hosts And Clusters view.

3. Right-click the DRS cluster where the rules need to exist, and select the Settings option.

4. Click the DRS Rules option.

5. Click the Add button near the top of the pane.

6. Type a name for the rule, and select Keep Virtual Machines Together for the type of rule to create.

7. Click the Add button to include the necessary VMs in the rule. Simply select the check box for the VMs you want to include in the DRS rule.

8. Click OK.

9. Review the new rule configuration to ensure that it is correct.

10. Click OK.

VM affinity rules let you specify VMs that should always stay together, but what about VMs that should always stay separate? DRS offers that functionality with VM anti-affinity rules.

CREATING VM ANTI-AFFINITY RULES

Consider an environment with two mail server VMs. In all likelihood, administrators would not want both mail servers to reside on the same ESXi host. Instead, the administrators would want the mail servers split onto two different ESXi hosts in the cluster, so that the failure of one host would affect only one of the two mail servers. In this sort of situation, a VM anti-affinity rule is the right tool to use.

Perform the following steps to create a DRS anti-affinity rule:

1. Launch the Web Client if it is not already running, and connect to a vCenter Server instance. Recall that DRS and DRS rules are available only with vCenter Server.

2. Navigate to the Hosts And Clusters view.

3. Right-click the DRS cluster where the rules need to exist, and select the Settings option.

4. Click the DRS Rules option.

5. Click the Add button near the top of the pane.

6. Type a name for the rule, and select Separate Virtual Machines as the type of rule to create.

7. Click the Add button to include the necessary VMs in the rule. Simply select the check box for the VMs you want to include in the DRS rule.

8. Click OK.

9. Review the new rule configuration to ensure that it is correct.

10. Click OK.

With both VM affinity and VM anti-affinity rules, it is possible to create fallible rules, such as building a Separate Virtual Machines rule that has three VMs in it on a DRS cluster that has only two hosts. In this situation, vCenter Server will generate report warnings because DRS cannot satisfy the requirements of the rule.

So far you've seen how to instruct DRS to keep VMs together or to keep VMs separate, but what about situations where you want to constrain VMs to a group of hosts within a cluster? This is where host affinity rules come into play.

HOST AFFINITY RULES FIRST APPEARED IN VSPHERE 4.1

VMware introduced host affinity rules in vSphere 4.1. Host affinity rules were not available in earlier versions.

WORKING WITH HOST AFFINITY RULES

In addition to VM affinity and VM anti-affinity rules, vSphere DRS supports a third type of DRS rule: the host affinity rule. Host affinity rules govern the relationships between VMs and the ESXi hosts in a cluster, letting administrators control which hosts in a cluster can run which VMs. When combined with VM affinity and VM anti-affinity rules, administrators can create very complex rule sets to model the relationships between applications and workloads in their datacenter.

Before you can start creating a host affinity rule, you have to create at least one VM DRS group and at least one host DRS group. Figure 12.23 shows the DRS groups. As you can see, a few groups have already been defined.

FIGURE 12.23

The DRS Groups Manager allows you to create and modify VM DRS groups and host DRS groups.

Perform the following steps to create a VM or host DRS group:

1. Launch the Web Client, if it is not already running, and connect to a vCenter Server instance.

2. Navigate to the Hosts And Clusters view.

3. Right-click the DRS-enabled cluster and select Settings.

4. From the Settings pane, click DRS Groups.

5. To create a DRS group, click the Add button.

6. Supply a name for the new DRS group.

7. Select the type of group from the drop-down list.

8. Depending on the type of group, click add and select the appropriate VMs or hosts to add to the group, use the check box to select each one. If your cluster has a large number of VMs or hosts, there is a filter available in the top right of the dialog box.

   Figure 12.24 shows where we have added four VMs to a new VM DRS group.

9. Click OK when you finish adding or removing VMs or hosts from the DRS group.

10. Click OK in the cluster Settings dialog box to save the DRS groups and return to the Web Client.

FIGURE 12.24
Use the buttons to
add or remove VMs
or hosts from a DRS
group. This screen
shot shows VMs
added to a DRS
group.

FIGURE 12.24
Use the buttons to
add or remove VMs
or hosts from a DRS
group. This screen
shot shows VMs
added to a DRS
group.

The previous steps are the same for both VM DRS groups and host DRS groups, and you'll need to have at least one of each group defined before you can create the rule.

After you've defined your VM DRS groups and host DRS groups, you're ready to actually define the host affinity rule. The host affinity rule brings together a VM DRS group and a host DRS group along with the preferred rule behavior. There are four host affinity rule behaviors:

- Must Run On Hosts In Group

- Should Run On Hosts In Group

- Must Not Run On Hosts In Group

- Should Not Run On Hosts In Group

These rules are, for the most part, self-explanatory. Each rule is either mandatory ("Must") or preferential ("Should") plus affinity ("Run On") or anti-affinity ("Not Run On"). Mandatory host affinity rules—those with "Must"—are honored not only by DRS but also by vSphere HA and vSphere DPM. For example, vSphere HA will not perform a failover if the failover would violate a required host affinity rule. Preferred rules, on the other hand, might be violated. Administrators have the option of creating an event-based alarm to monitor for the violation of preferred host affinity rules. You'll learn about alarms in Chapter 13, "Monitoring VMware vSphere Performance."

Figure 12.25 shows a host affinity rule coming together with a selected VM DRS group, a rule behavior, and a selected host DRS group.

Be careful when defining host affinity rules, especially mandatory host affinity rules like the one shown in Figure 12.25, or you could run into a situation where VMs are severely limited on where they can run; this is illustrated in Figure 12.26.

FIGURE 12.25
This host affinity rule specifies that the selected group of VMs must run on the selected group of ESXi hosts.

> **Resource - Create DRS Rule**
>
> Name: Mandatory Host Affinity Rule
>
> ☑ Enable rule.
>
> Type: Virtual Machines to Hosts ▾
>
> Description:
>
> Virtual machines that are members of the Cluster DRS VM Group Odd-VMs must run on host group Host-Group-1.
>
> VM Group:
>
> Odd-VMs ▾
>
> Must run on hosts in group ▾
>
> Host Group:
>
> Host-Group-1 ▾
>
> OK   Cancel

FIGURE 12.26
Administrators should ensure that using multiple required host affinity rules creates the desired results.

The Windows VM is in a group that is a member of two different host affinity rules. As a result, the VM can only run on hosts that satisfy both rules.

DRS Host Group 1

esxi-02a   esxi-03a   esxi-04a   esxi-05a

DRS Host Group 2

While the different sorts of rules that DRS supports provide lots of flexibility, there might be times when you need an even greater granularity. To satisfy that need for granularity, you can modify or disable DRS on individual VMs in the cluster.

CONFIGURING DRS VM OVERRIDES

Although most VMs should be allowed to take advantage of the DRS balancing act, administrators may be adamant that certain enterprise-critical VMs are not DRS candidates. However, the

VMs should remain in the cluster to take advantage of high-availability features provided by vSphere HA. In other words, VMs will take part in HA but not DRS despite both features being enabled on the cluster. As shown in Figure 12.27, VMs in a cluster can be configured with a VM Override.

FIGURE 12.27
Individual VMs can be prevented from participating in DRS.

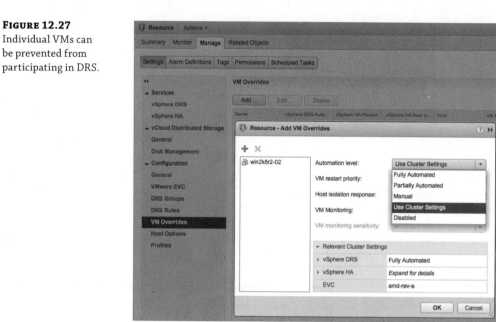

Listed below DRS Groups and DRS Rules in the Cluster Settings pane is VM Overrides. This dialog box allows you to set HA and DRS settings on a per-VM basis that differ from the cluster settings. When you change settings in this way, although you can add them initially in batches of VMs, they are edited individually from then on. If you want more information on VM restart priority, host isolation, and VM monitoring, HA is discussed in Chapter 3 and Chapter 7.

Focusing on DRS, the following automation levels are available:

◆ Fully Automated

◆ Partially Automated

◆ Manual

◆ Use Cluster Settings

◆ Disabled

The first three options work as discussed previously in this chapter, in the sections "Understanding Manual Automation Behavior," "Reviewing Partially Automated Behavior," and "Examining Fully Automated Behavior." The Disabled option turns off DRS, including the automatic host selection at startup and the migration recommendations. The default Use Cluster Settings option does just that; it configures the VM to accept the automation level set at the cluster.

AT LEAST BE OPEN TO CHANGE

Even if you exclude a VM or several VMs from participating in the automation of DRS, it is best not to set VMs to the Disabled option because no recommendations will be provided. A priority 2 recommendation could be provided that suggests moving a VM an administrator thought was best on a specific host to a different host suggested during the migration. For this reason, the Manual option is better. At least be open to the possibility that a VM might perform better on a different host.

VMware vSphere provides a number of tools to make administrators' lives easier, as long as you understand the tools and set them up properly. It might also be prudent to monitor the activities of these tools to see whether a change to the configuration might be warranted over time as your environment grows. Monitoring and alarms are discussed in detail in Chapter 13.

DRS is a valuable and useful part of vSphere, and it builds on vMotion to enable vSphere administrators to be more proactive about managing their environments.

Introducing and Working with Storage DRS

Building on the functionality that VMware introduced in earlier versions—specifically, building on Storage I/O Control and Storage vMotion—SDRS introduces the ability to perform automated balancing of storage utilization. SDRS can perform this automated balancing not only on the basis of space utilization but also on the basis of I/O load balancing.

Like vSphere DRS, SDRS is built on some closely related concepts and terms:

◆ Just as vSphere DRS uses clusters as a collection of hosts on which to act, SDRS uses datastore clusters as a collection of datastores on which it acts.

◆ Just as vSphere DRS can perform both initial placement and manual and ongoing balancing, SDRS also performs initial placement of VMDKs and ongoing balancing of VMDKs. The initial placement functionality of SDRS is especially appealing because it helps simplify the VM provisioning process for vSphere administrators.

◆ Just as vSphere DRS offers affinity and anti-affinity rules to influence recommendations, SDRS offers VMDK affinity and anti-affinity functionality.

As just mentioned, SDRS uses the idea of a *datastore cluster*—a group of datastores treated as shared storage resources—in order to operate. Before you can enable or configure SDRS, you must create a datastore cluster. However, you can't just arbitrarily combine datastores into a datastore cluster; there are some guidelines you need to follow.

Specifically, VMware provides the following guidelines for datastores that are combined into datastore clusters:

◆ Datastores of different sizes and I/O capacities can be combined in a datastore cluster. Although possible, we wouldn't recommend this practice unless you have very specific requirements. Additionally, datastores from different arrays and vendors can be combined into a datastore cluster. However, you cannot combine NFS and VMFS datastores in a datastore cluster.

◆ You cannot combine replicated and nonreplicated datastores into an SDRS-enabled datastore cluster.

◆ All hosts attached to a datastore in a datastore cluster must be running ESXi 5 or later. ESX/ESXi 4.*x* and earlier cannot be connected to a datastore that you want to add to a datastore cluster.

◆ Datastores shared across multiple datacenters are not supported for SDRS.

WHAT ABOUT MIXED HARDWARE ACCELERATION SUPPORT?

Hardware acceleration as a result of support for the vSphere Storage APIs for Array Integration (more commonly known as VAAI) is another factor to consider when creating datastore clusters. As a best practice, VMware recommends against mixing datastores that do support hardware acceleration with datastores that don't support hardware acceleration. All the datastores in a datastore cluster should be homogeneous with regard to hardware acceleration support in the underlying array(s).

Along with these general guidelines from VMware, we recommend you consult your specific storage array vendor for any additional recommendations that are particular to your specific array. Your storage vendors may have recommendations on what array-based features are or are not supported in conjunction with SDRS.

In the next section, we'll show you how to create and work with datastore clusters in preparation for a more in-depth look at configuring SDRS.

Creating and Working with Datastore Clusters

Now you're ready to create a datastore cluster and begin exploring SDRS in greater detail.

Perform these steps to create a datastore cluster:

1. If it is not already running, launch the Web Client.

   Storage DRS and datastore clusters are possible only when you are using vCenter Server in your environment.

2. Navigate to the Storage view.

3. Right-click the datacenter object where you want to create a new datastore cluster. Click New Datastore Cluster; this launches the New Datastore Cluster Wizard.

4. Supply a name for the new datastore cluster.

5. If you want to enable Storage DRS for this datastore, select Turn On Storage DRS. Click Next.

6. Storage DRS can operate in a manual mode, where it will make recommendations only, or in Fully Automated mode, where it will actually perform storage migrations automatically. Select Fully Automated and click Next.

7. If you want Storage DRS to include I/O metrics along with space utilization as part of its recommendations or migrations, select Enable I/O Metric For Storage DRS Recommendations.

Configuring SDRS to include I/O metrics in this manner will automatically enable Storage I/O Control on the datastores that are a part of this cluster.

8. You can adjust the thresholds that Storage DRS uses to control when it recommends or performs migrations (depending on whether Storage DRS is configured for manual or fully automated operation).

   The default utilized space threshold is 80 percent; this means when the datastore reaches 80 percent full, Storage DRS will recommend or perform a storage migration. The default setting for I/O latency is 15 ms; you should adjust this based on recommendations from your storage vendor. Figure 12.28 shows the default settings for the SDRS runtime rules. When you are finished adjusting these values, click Next.

FIGURE 12.28

The default settings for SDRS include I/O metrics and settings for utilized space and I/O latency.

STORAGE I/O CONTROL AND STORAGE DRS LATENCY THRESHOLDS

In Chapter 11 in the section "Enabling Storage I/O Control," we discussed adjusting the threshold for Storage I/O Control (SIOC). You'll note that the default I/O latency threshold for SDRS (15 ms) is well below the default for SIOC (30 ms). The idea behind these default settings is that SDRS can make a migration to balance the load (if fully automated) before throttling becomes necessary.

Just as we recommended you check with your storage vendor for specific recommendations on SIOC latency values, you should also check with your array vendor to see if that vendor offers recommendations for SDRS latency values.

---

9. Place a check in the check box next to the ESXi hosts and/or clusters to which this new datastore cluster should be added; then click Next.

10. Select the available datastores you'd like to add to the new datastore cluster.

    Because of the nature of Storage DRS, you'll want to leave the Show Datastores drop-down box at the default setting of Connected To All Hosts so that any datastores listed here are accessible from the hosts and/or clusters you selected in the previous step. Place a check in the check box next to each datastore you want added to the datastore cluster. Click Next.

11. Review the settings in the final screen of the New Datastore Cluster Wizard.

If any of the settings are incorrect or if you need to make any changes, use the hyperlinks on the left to go back. Otherwise, click Finish.

The newly created datastore cluster will appear in the Storage view. The Summary tab of the datastore cluster, shown in Figure 12.29, will display the aggregate statistics about the datastores in the datastore cluster.

FIGURE 12.29
The Summary tab of a datastore cluster provides overall information about total capacity, total used space, total free space, and largest free space.

Once you've created a datastore cluster, you can add capacity to it by adding more datastores, much in the same way you would add capacity to a vSphere DRS cluster by adding new ESXi hosts.

To add a datastore to a datastore cluster, just right-click an existing datastore cluster and select Move Datastores Into from the pop-up context menu. This opens the Move Datastores Into Cluster dialog box, where you can select additional datastores to add to the datastore cluster. Figure 12.30 shows the Move Datastores Into Datastore Cluster dialog box, where you can see that some datastores cannot be added because all necessary ESXi hosts aren't connected. This ensures that you don't inadvertently add a datastore to a datastore cluster and then find that an SRDS migration renders that VMDK unreachable by one or more ESXi hosts.

FIGURE 12.30

To add a datastore to a datastore cluster, the new datastore must be connected to all the hosts currently connected to the datastore cluster.

SDRS also offers a maintenance mode option for datastores, just as vSphere DRS offers a maintenance mode option for ESXi hosts. To place a datastore into SDRS maintenance mode, right-click the datastore and select All vCenter Actions ➤ Enter Maintenance Mode. If there are any registered VMs currently on that datastore, SDRS will immediately generate migration recommendations, as Figure 12.31 shows. If you select Cancel in the SDRS Maintenance Mode Migration Recommendations dialog box, you will cancel the SDRS maintenance mode request and the datastore will not go into SDRS maintenance mode.

FIGURE 12.31

Putting a datastore into SDRS maintenance mode generates SDRS recommendations to evacuate the datastore.

STORAGE DRS MAINTENANCE MODE DOESN'T AFFECT TEMPLATES AND ISOS

When you enable SDRS maintenance mode for a datastore, recommendations are generated for registered VMs. However, SDRS maintenance mode will not affect templates, unregistered VMs, or ISOs stored on that datastore.

In addition to using the Add Storage dialog box we showed you earlier in this section, you can use drag and drop to add a datastore to an existing datastore cluster. Note, however, that drag and drop won't warn you that you're adding a datastore that doesn't have connections to all the hosts that are currently connected to the datastore cluster, so we generally recommend using the Move Datastores Into Datastore Cluster dialog box shown in Figure 12.30.

Let's now take a more in-depth look at configuring SDRS to work with the datastore cluster(s) that you've created.

Configuring Storage DRS

All of the configuration for SDRS is done from the Manage ➤ Settings pane. You'll open the settings pane box by right-clicking a datastore cluster and selecting Settings or by clicking Settings on the Manage tab of a datastore cluster. Both methods will give you the same result. Within this pane, click the Edit button at the top right of the pane.

From the settings pane, you can accomplish the following tasks:

◆ Enable or disable SDRS

◆ Configure the SDRS automation level

◆ Change or modify the SDRS runtime rules

◆ Configure or modify custom SDRS schedules

◆ Create SDRS rules to influence SDRS behavior

◆ Configure per-VM SDRS settings

The following sections examine each of these areas in more detail.

ENABLING OR DISABLING STORAGE DRS

From the Edit dialog box, you can easily enable or disable SDRS. Figure 12.32 shows this area of the Edit dialog box. From here, you can enable SDRS by selecting Turn ON vSphere Storage DRS. If Storage DRS is already enabled, you can deselect Turn ON vSphere Storage DRS to disable it. If you disable SDRS, the SDRS settings are preserved. If SDRS is later reenabled, the configuration is returned to the point where it was when it was disabled.

FIGURE 12.32
In addition to enabling or disabling Storage DRS, you can enable or disable I/O metrics for SDRS recommendations from this dialog box.

CONFIGURING STORAGE DRS AUTOMATION

SDRS offers two predefined automation levels, as you can see in Figure 12.33: No Automation (Manual Mode) and Fully Automated.

FIGURE 12.33
Storage DRS offers both Manual and Fully Automated modes of operation.

When the SDRS automation level is set to No Automation (Manual Mode), SDRS will generate recommendations for initial placement and for storage migrations based on the configured space and I/O thresholds. Initial placement recommendations occur when you create a new VM (and thus a new virtual disk), add a virtual disk to a VM, or clone a VM or template. The recommendations appear in a pop-up window, like the one shown in Figure 12.34.

FIGURE 12.34
Storage DRS presents a list of initial placement recommendations whenever a new virtual disk is created.

Recommendations for storage migrations are noted in two different ways. First, an alarm is generated to note that an SDRS recommendation is present. You can view this alarm on the Monitor ➤ Issues tab of the datastore cluster in Storage view. The alarm is shown in Figure 12.35.

FIGURE 12.35
This alarm on the datastore cluster indicates that an SDRS recommendation is present.

In addition, the Monitor ➤ Storage DRS tab of the datastore cluster (visible in Storage view, as shown in Figure 12.36) will list the current SDRS recommendations and give you the option to apply those recommendations—that is, initiate the suggested Storage vMotion migrations.

When SDRS is configured for Fully Automated mode, it will automatically initiate Storage vMotion migrations instead of generating recommendations for the administrator to approve. In this instance, you can use the Monitor ➤ Storage DRS tab of the datastore cluster to view the history of SDRS actions by selecting the History button at the top of the Storage DRS tab. Figure 12.37 shows the SDRS history for the selected datastore cluster.

To modify how aggressive SDRS is when running in Fully Automated mode, expand the rules section of the Edit dialog box, described in the next section.

MODIFYING THE STORAGE DRS RUNTIME BEHAVIOR

In the SDRS Edit dialog box, you have several options for modifying the behavior of SDRS.

First, if you'd like to tell SDRS to operate only on the basis of space utilization and not I/O utilization, simply deselect Enable I/O Metric For SDRS Recommendations. This will tell SDRS to recommend or perform (depending on the automation level) migrations based strictly on space utilization.

FIGURE 12.36
Click Apply Recommendations in the Storage DRS tab to initiate the storage migrations suggested by SDRS.

FIGURE 12.37
On the Storage DRS tab of a datastore cluster, use the History button to review the SDRS actions that have taken place when SDRS is running in Fully Automated mode.

Second, the two Storage DRS Thresholds settings allow you to adjust the thresholds that SDRS uses to recommend or perform migrations. By default, the Utilized Space setting is 80 percent, meaning that SDRS will recommend or perform a migration when a datastore reaches 80 percent full. The default I/O Latency setting is 15 ms; when latency measurements exceed 15 ms for a given datastore in a datastore cluster and I/O metrics are enabled, then SDRS will recommend or perform a storage migration to another datastore with a lower latency measurement.

If you click the arrow next to Advanced Options, you can further fine-tune the runtime behavior of SDRS:

◆ Keep VMDKs Together By Default is fairly self-explanatory. By default VM virtual disks (VMDKs) should be kept together unless there is a specific need to always split them between datastores.

◆ The Check Imbalances Every option allows you to control how often SDRS evaluates the I/O or space utilization in order to make a recommendation or perform a migration.

◆ The I/O Imbalance Threshold controls the aggressiveness of the SDRS algorithm. As the slider is moved toward Aggressive and the counter increases, this moves up the priority of the recommendation that will be automatically acted on when SDRS is running in Fully Automated mode.

◆ Minimum Space Utilization Difference is a slider bar that lets you specify how much of an improvement SDRS should look for before making a recommendation or performing a migration. The setting defaults to 5 percent. This means that if the destination's values are 5 percent lower than the source's values, SDRS will make the recommendation or perform the migration.

In addition to the rudimentary schedule control that controls how often SDRS evaluates I/O and space utilization, you can create more complex scheduling settings.

CONFIGURING OR MODIFYING THE STORAGE DRS SCHEDULE

The Schedule Storage DRS button next to the Edit button allows you to create custom schedules. These custom schedules enable vSphere administrators to specify times when the SDRS behavior should be different. For example, are there times when SDRS should be running in No Automation (Manual Mode)? Are there times when the space utilization or I/O latency thresholds should be different? If so, and you need SDRS to adjust to these recurring differences, you can accommodate that through custom SDRS schedules.

Let's look at an example. Let's say that you normally have SDRS running in Fully Automated mode, and it works fine. However, at night, when backups are running, you want SDRS not to automatically perform storage migrations. Using a custom SDRS schedule, you can tell SDRS to switch into manual mode during certain times of the day and days of the week and then return into Fully Automated mode when that day/time period is over.

Perform the following steps to create a custom SDRS schedule:

1. If it's not already running, launch the Web Client.

2. Navigate to the Storage view.

3. Right-click a datastore cluster and select Settings.

4. Select Schedule Storage DRS from the pane on the right. This opens the Edit Storage DRS Settings (scheduled) Wizard.

5. Select the settings that you want to activate for this schedule. Click Scheduling options on the left to continue.

6. Provide a task name and a task description. Now click the Change hyperlink to set the schedule.

7. Specify the time when this custom schedule task should be active.

   For example, if you needed to change SDRS behavior while backups are running in the middle of the night, you could select Setup A Reoccurring Schedule For This Action and set the time to 10:00 PM weekly. Then you select the check box for every weekday and click OK to close the Scheduler.

8. Review the settings. Click OK if they are correct.

After you complete the Schedule Storage DRS Task Wizard, a new set of entries appears in the scheduling list for SDRS, as illustrated in Figure 12.38. Typically, as with this example, you will want to schedule two tasks, one for changing the setting and another for setting it back.

FIGURE 12.38
SDRS scheduling entries allow you to automatically change the settings for SDRS on certain days and at certain times.

The ability to configure SDRS differently at different times or on different days is a powerful feature that will let vSphere administrators customize SDRS behaviors to best suit their environments. SDRS rules are another tool that provide administrators with more control over how SDRS handles VMs and virtual disks, as you'll see in the next section.

CREATING STORAGE DRS RULES

Just as vSphere DRS has affinity and anti-affinity rules, SDRS offers vSphere administrators the ability to create VMDK affinity and anti-affinity rules and VM anti-affinity rules. These rules modify the behavior of SDRS to ensure that specific VMDKs are always kept together (VMDK affinity rule) or separate (VMDK anti-affinity rule) or that all the virtual disks from certain VMs are kept separate (VM anti-affinity rule).

Perform these steps to create an SDRS VMDK affinity or anti-affinity or SDRS VM anti-affinity rule:

1. In the Web Client, navigate to the Hosts And Clusters inventory view.

2. Right-click a VM and select Edit Settings.

3. Select SRDS Rules.

4. Click Add to add a rule.

5. In the Rule dialog box, supply a name for the rule you are creating.

6. From the Type drop-down box, select VMDK affinity, VMDK Anti-Affinity, or VM Anti-Affinity, depending on which type of rule you want to create.

For the purpose of this procedure, select VMDK Anti-Affinity.

7. Select the virtual disks that you want to include in this rule, as shown in Figure 12.39, and then click OK.

FIGURE 12.39
An SDRS VMDK anti-affinity rule allows you to specify particular virtual disks for a VM that should be kept on separate datastores in a datastore cluster.

8. Click OK in the Edit SDRS Rule dialog box to complete the creation of the SDRS anti-affinity rule.

SETTING STORAGE DRS VM OVERRIDES

Just like DRS, Storage DRS can override cluster settings on a per-VM level through the VM Overrides feature. If you need to apply different settings on a particular VM or group of VMs, VM Overrides give you this granular level of control.

Within the Datastore Cluster ➤ Manage ➤ Settings tab, select the VM Overrides option. Here you can add, edit, or delete override rules for individual VMs, as shown in Figure 12.40.

FIGURE 12.40

The per VM Overrides area shows which VMs differ from the SDRS cluster settings.

DRS EVALUATION SCHEDULE

Normally, Storage DRS runs an evaluation every 8 hours (this can be adjusted; refer back to the section "Modifying the Storage DRS Runtime Behavior"). Storage DRS will include the new anti-affinity rule in the next evaluation. If you want to invoke SDRS immediately, the Storage DRS tab of the datastore cluster, shown in Figure 12.41, offers the option to invoke SDRS immediately using the Run Storage DRS link.

FIGURE 12.41

Use the Run Storage DRS link to invoke SDRS on demand.

As you can see, SDRS has a tremendous amount of flexibility built into it to allow vSphere administrators to harness the power of SDRS by tailoring its behavior to best suit their specific environments.

In the next chapter, we'll move into a review and discussion of monitoring and alarms and show what tools or features VMware vSphere offers administrators in the realm of performance monitoring.

The Bottom Line

Configure and execute vMotion.   vMotion is a feature that allows running VMs to be migrated from one physical ESXi host to another physical ESXi host with no downtime to end users. To execute vMotion, you must make sure both the ESXi hosts and the VMs meet specific configuration requirements. In addition, vCenter Server performs validation checks to ensure that vMotion compatibility rules are observed.

Master It   A certain vendor has just released a series of patches for some of the guest OSes in your virtualized infrastructure. You request an outage window from your supervisor, but your supervisor says to just use vMotion to prevent downtime. Is your supervisor correct? Why or why not?

Master It   Is vMotion a solution to prevent unplanned downtime?

Ensure vMotion compatibility across processor families.   vMotion requires compatible CPU families on the source and destination ESXi hosts in order to be successful. To help alleviate any potential problems resulting from changes in processor families over time, vSphere offers Enhanced vMotion Compatibility (EVC), which can mask differences between CPU families to maintain vMotion compatibility.

Master It   Can you change the EVC level for a cluster while there are VMs running on hosts in the cluster?

Use Storage vMotion.   Just as vMotion is used to migrate running VMs from one ESXi host to another, Storage vMotion is used to migrate the virtual disks of a running VM from one datastore to another. You can also use Storage vMotion to convert between thick and thin virtual disk types.

Master It   Name two features of Storage vMotion that would help administrators cope with storage-related changes in their vSphere environment.

Perform combined vMotion and Storage vMotion.   Using vMotion and Storage at the same time gives you greater flexibility when migrating VMs between hosts. Utilizing this feature can also save time when you must evacuate a host for maintenance.

Master It   A fellow administrator is trying to migrate a VM to a different datastore and a different host while it is running and wishes to complete the task as quickly and as simply as possible. Which migration option should she choose?

Configure and manage vSphere Distributed Resource Scheduler.   vSphere Distributed Resource Scheduler enables vCenter Server to automate the process of conducting vMotion migrations to help balance the load across ESXi hosts within a cluster. You can automate DRS as you wish, and vCenter Server has flexible controls for affecting the behavior of DRS and specific VMs within a DRS-enabled cluster.

Master It   You want to take advantage of vSphere DRS to provide some load balancing of virtual workloads within your environment. However, because of business constraints, you have a few workloads that should not be automatically moved to other hosts using vMotion. Can you use DRS? If so, how can you prevent these specific workloads from being affected by DRS?

Configure and manage Storage DRS. Building on Storage vMotion just as vSphere DRS builds on vMotion, Storage DRS automates the process of balancing storage capacity and I/O utilization. Storage DRS uses datastore clusters and can operate in Manual or Fully Automated mode. Numerous customizations exist—such as custom schedules, VM and VMDK anti-affinity rules, and threshold settings—to allow administrators to fine-tune the behavior of Storage DRS for their specific environments.

Master It Name the two ways in which an administrator is notified that a Storage DRS recommendation has been generated.

Master It What is a potential disadvantage of using drag-and-drop to add a datastore to a datastore cluster?

## Chapter 13

Monitoring VMware vSphere Performance

The monitoring of VMware vSphere should be a combination of proactive benchmarking and reactive alarm-based actions. vCenter Server provides both methods to help the administrator keep tabs on each of the VMs and hosts as well as the hierarchical objects in the inventory. Using both methods ensures that the administrator is not caught unaware of performance issues or lack of capacity.

vCenter Server provides some exciting new features for monitoring your VMs and hosts, such as expanded performance views and charts, and it greatly expands the number and types of alarms available by default. Together, these features make it much easier to manage and monitor VMware vSphere performance.

In this chapter, you will learn to

+ Use alarms for proactive monitoring

+ Work with performance charts

+ Integrate vCenter Operations Manager

+ Gather performance information using command-line tools

+ Monitor CPU, memory, network, and disk usage by ESXi hosts and VMs

Overview of Performance Monitoring

Monitoring performance is a key part of every vSphere administrator's job. Fortunately, vCenter Server provides a number of ways to get insight into the behavior of the vSphere environment and the VMs running within that environment.

The first tool vCenter Server provides is its alarms mechanism. Alarm definitions can be attached to just about any object within vCenter Server and provide an ideal way to proactively alert the vSphere administrator or datacenter staff about potential performance concerns or resource usage. We'll discuss alarms in detail in the section "Using Alarms."

Another tool that vCenter Server provides is the content area on the Summary tab of ESXi hosts and VMs. The content area provides quick "at-a-glance" information on resource usage. This information can be useful as a quick barometer of performance, but for more detailed performance information, you will have to dive deeper into the vCenter tools that we'll discuss later in this chapter.

A third tool that provides an at-a-glance performance summary is the Related Objects tab, found on vCenter Server objects, datacenter objects, cluster objects, and ESXi hosts. Figure 13.1 shows the Related Objects ➤ Virtual Machines tab of a cluster object. This tab provides an overview of general performance and resource usage. This information includes CPU utilization, host and guest memory usage, and storage space utilized. As with the Resources pane, this information can be useful, but it is quite limited. However, keep in mind that a quick trip here might help you isolate the one VM that could be causing performance issues for the ESXi host on which it is running.

FIGURE 13.1

The Related Objects ➤ Virtual Machines tab of a cluster object offers a quick look at VM CPU and memory usage.

For ESXi clusters, resource pools, and VMs, another tool you can use is the Resource Allocation tab. The Resource Allocation tab provides a picture of how CPU, memory, and storage resources are being used for the entire pool. This high-level method of looking at resource usage is useful for analyzing overall infrastructure utilization. This tab also provides an easy way of adjusting individual VMs or resource pool reservations, limits, and/or shares without editing each object independently.

vCenter Server offers a powerful, in-depth tool on the Performance tab that lets you create charts that depict the actual resource consumption over time for a given ESXi host or VM. The charts provide historical information and can be used for trend analysis. vCenter Server provides many objects and counters to analyze the performance of a single VM or host for a selected interval. The Performance tab provides powerful tools for isolating performance considerations, and we discuss them in greater detail in the section "Working with Performance Charts."

VMware also allows its enterprise monitoring solution, vCenter Operations Manager Foundation, to be installed alongside vSphere at no charge with the Foundation license. While the default features are limited with the free license, the capabilities are a step up from the standard Performance tab. We'll explain how to install this extra component and what benefits it brings in the section "Understanding vCenter Operations Manager."

VMware also provides `resxtop` for an in-depth view of all the counters available in vSphere to help isolate and identify problems in the hypervisor. `resxtop` runs only inside the vSphere Management Assistant (vMA). We'll take a look at `resxtop` later in this chapter in the section "Working with resxtop."

Finally, we'll take the various tools that we've discussed and show how to use them to monitor the four major resources in a vSphere environment: CPU, memory, network, and storage.

Let's get started with a discussion of alarms.

Using Alarms

In addition to using the charts and high-level information tabs, an administrator can create alarms for VMs, hosts, networks, and datastores based on predefined triggers provided with vCenter Server. Depending on the object, these alarms can monitor resource consumption or the state of the object and alert you when certain conditions have been met, such as high resource usage or even low resource usage. These alarms can then provide an action that informs you of the condition by email or Simple Network Management Protocol (SNMP) trap. An action can also automatically run a script or provide other means to correct the problem the VM or host might be experiencing.

With each revision of vSphere, VMware continues to add to the number of built-in default alarms. As you can see in Figure 13.2, the alarms that come with vCenter Server are defined at the topmost object, the vCenter Server object.

FIGURE 13.2
The default alarms for objects in vCenter Server are defined on the vCenter Server object itself.

These default alarms are usually generic in nature. Some of the predefined alarms alert the administrator if any of the following situations occur:

◆ A host's storage status, CPU status, voltage, temperature, or power status changes.

◆ A cluster experiences a vSphere High Availability (HA) error.

◆ A datastore runs low on free disk space.

◆ A VM's CPU usage, memory usage, disk latency, or even fault tolerance status changes.

In addition to the small sampling of predefined alarms we've just described, there are many more, and VMware has enabled users to create alarms on just about any object within vCenter Server. This greatly increases the ability of vCenter Server to proactively alert administrators to changes within the virtual environment before a problem develops.

Because the default alarms are likely too generic for your administrative needs, creating your own alarms is often necessary. Before showing you how to create an alarm, though, we need to discuss the concept of alarm scopes. Once we've discussed alarm scopes, we'll walk you through creating a few alarms.

Understanding Alarm Scopes

When you create alarms, one thing to keep in mind is the *scope* of the alarm. In Figure 13.2, you saw the default set of alarms available in vCenter Server. These alarms are defined at the vCenter Server object and thus have the greatest scope—they apply to all objects managed by that vCenter Server instance. It's also possible to create alarms at the datacenter level, the cluster level, the host level, or even the VM level. This allows you, the vSphere administrator, to create specific alarms that are limited in scope and are intended to meet specific monitoring needs.

When you define an alarm on an object, that alarm applies to all objects beneath that object in the vCenter Server hierarchy. The default set of alarms that VMware provides with vCenter Server is defined at the vCenter Server object and therefore applies to all objects—datacenters, hosts, clusters, datastores, networks, and VMs—managed by that instance of vCenter Server. If you were to create an alarm on a resource pool, then the alarm would apply only to VMs found in that resource pool. Similarly, if you were to create an alarm on a specific VM, that alarm would apply only to that specific VM.

Alarms are also associated with specific types of objects. For example, some alarms apply only to VMs, while other alarms apply only to ESXi hosts. You'll want to use this filtering mechanism to your advantage when creating alarms. If you needed to monitor a particular condition on all ESXi hosts, for instance, you could define a host alarm on the datacenter or vCenter Server object and it would apply to all ESXi hosts but not to any VMs.

It's important that you keep these scoping effects in mind when defining alarms so that your new alarms work as expected. You don't want to inadvertently exclude some portion of your vSphere environment by creating an alarm at the wrong point in your hierarchy or by creating the wrong type of alarm.

Now you're ready to look at actually creating alarms.

Creating Alarms

As you've already learned, there are many different types of alarms that administrators might want to create. These could be alarms that monitor resource consumption—such as how much CPU time a VM is consuming or how much RAM an ESXi host has allocated—or these alarms could monitor for specific events, such as whenever a specific distributed virtual port group is modified. In addition, you've already learned that alarms can be created on a variety of different objects within vCenter Server. Regardless of the type of alarm or the type of object to which that alarm is attached, the basic steps for creating an alarm are the same. In the following sections, we'll walk you through creating a few different alarms so that you have the opportunity to see the options available to you.

CREATING A RESOURCE CONSUMPTION ALARM

First, let's create an alarm that monitors resource consumption. As discussed in Chapter 9, "Creating and Managing Virtual Machines," vCenter Server supports VM snapshots. These snapshots capture a VM at a specific point in time, allowing you to roll back (or revert) to that state later. However, snapshots require additional space on disk, and monitoring disk space usage by snapshots is an important task. In vSphere, vCenter Server lets you create an alarm that monitors VM snapshot space.

Before you create a custom alarm, though, you should ask yourself a few questions. First, is there an existing alarm that already handles this task for you? Browsing the list of predefined alarms available in vCenter Server shows that although some storage-related alarms are present, there is no alarm that monitors snapshot disk usage. Second, if you're going to create a new alarm, where is the appropriate place within vCenter Server to create that alarm? This refers to the earlier discussion of scope: On what object should you create this alarm so that it is properly scoped and will alert you only under the desired conditions? In this particular case, you'd want to be alerted to any snapshot space usage that exceeds your desired threshold, so a higher-level object such as the datacenter object or even the vCenter Server object would be the best place to create the alarm.

YOU MUST USE vCENTER SERVER FOR ALARMS

You can't create alarms by connecting directly to an ESXi host; vCenter Server provides the alarm functionality. You must connect to a vCenter Server instance in order to work with alarms.

Perform the following steps to create an alarm that monitors VM snapshot disk space usage for all VMs in a datacenter:

1. Launch the vSphere Web Client if it is not already running, and connect to a vCenter Server instance.

2. Navigate to an inventory view, such as Hosts And Clusters or VMs And Templates.

You can use the Navigator or the icon on the home screen.

3. Right-click the datacenter object and select Alarm ➤ New Alarm Definition.

4. On the General tab in the Alarm Settings dialog box, enter an alarm name and alarm description.

5. Select Virtual Machines from the Monitor drop-down list.

6. Be sure that the radio button marked Monitor For Specific Conditions Or State, For Example, CPU Usage is selected. Click Next to move on to the Triggers section.

7. On the Triggers tab, click the add/plus button to add a new trigger.

8. Add the trigger type, VM Snapshot Size (GB). For this alarm, you're interested in snapshot size only, but these other triggers are available:

- VM CPU Demand To Entitlement Ratio
- VM CPU Ready Time
- VM CPU Usage
- VM Disk Aborts
- VM Disk Resets
- VM Disk Usage
- VM Fault Tolerance Latency
- VM Heartbeat
- VM Max Total Disk Latency
- VM Memory Usage
- VM Network Usage
- VM Snapshot Size
- VM State
- VM Total Size on Disk

9. Ensure that the Operator column is set to Is Above.

10. Change the warning and critical conditions to be 1 GB and 2 GB, respectively. Click Next to move to the Actions screen.

Figure 13.3 shows the Triggers tab after changing the Warning and Critical values.

FIGURE 13.3

On the Triggers tab, define the conditions that cause the alarm to activate.

CAUTION: COUNTER VALUES WILL VARY!

The Is Above condition is selected most often for identifying a VM, host, or datastore that exceeds a certain threshold. The administrator decides what that threshold should be and what is considered abnormal behavior (or at least interesting enough behavior to be monitored). For the most part, monitoring across ESXi hosts and datastores will be consistent. For example, administrators will define a threshold that is worthy of notification—such as CPU, memory, or network utilization—and configure an alarm across all hosts for monitoring the corresponding counter. Similarly, administrators may define a threshold for datastores, such as the amount of free space available, and configure an alarm across all datastores to monitor that metric.

However, when looking at VM monitoring, it might be more difficult to come up with a single baseline that works for all VMs. Specifically, think about enterprise applications that must perform well for extended periods of time. For these types of scenarios, administrators will want custom alarms for earlier notifications of performance problems. This way, instead of reacting to a problem, administrators can proactively try to prevent problems from occurring.

For VMs with similar functions like domain controllers and DNS servers, it might be possible to establish baselines and thresholds covering all such infrastructure servers. In the end, the beauty of vCenter Server's alarms is in the flexibility to be as customized and as granular as each individual organization needs.

11. On the Actions tab, specify any additional actions that should be taken when the alarm is triggered.

The following actions are available:

♦ Send a notification email.

♦ Send a notification trap via SNMP.

♦ Change the power state on a VM.

♦ Migrate a VM.

If you leave the Actions tab empty, the alarm will alert administrators only within the vSphere Web Client. For now, leave the Actions tab empty.

CONFIGURING VCENTER SERVER FOR EMAIL AND SNMP NOTIFICATIONS

To have vCenter Server send an email for a triggered alarm, you must configure vCenter Server with an SMTP server. To configure the SMTP server, from the vSphere Web Client choose the vCenter Server from within the Navigator, and then select the Manage ➤ Settings tab. Click the Edit button on the right, then select Mail in the list on the left, and then supply the SMTP server and the sender account. We recommend using a recognizable sender account so that when you receive an email, you know it came from the vCenter Server computer. You might use something like vcenter-alerts@lab.local.

Similarly, to have vCenter Server send an SNMP trap, you must configure the SNMP receivers in the same vCenter Server Settings dialog box under SNMP receivers. You may specify from one to four management receivers to monitor for traps.

---

12. Click Finish to create the alarm.

The alarm is now created. To view the alarm you just created, select the datacenter object from the Navigator on the left, and then click the Manage ➤ Alarm Definitions tab. You'll see your new alarm listed, as shown in Figure 13.4.

USING DURATION AND ACTION FREQUENCY WITH ALARMS

Let's create another alarm. This time you'll create an alarm that takes advantage of the parameters in the Triggers and Actions area. With the VM snapshot alarm, these parameters didn't really make any sense; all you really needed was just to be alerted when the snapshot exceeded a certain size. With other types of alarms, it may make sense to take advantage of these parameters.

Some triggers are simple state checks, like the VM State trigger, while with others you are able to specify a size, like VM Snapshot Size. There is also a third type, which is a combination of size and time (or duration). Triggers such as VM Network Usage will activate only if the size is over (or under) the set threshold for a set period of time.

As you may have noticed when creating the previous example alarm, alarms have two configurable states: Warning, and Critical. When configuring alarm triggers, you can set the level for both warning and critical conditions, anything below these conditions is considered "Normal". The transition between these conditions then "triggers" a set of "actions" that are configured on the Actions screen. You can set actions for both transition directions at both criticality levels:

Normal → Warning

Warning → Critical

Critical → Warning

Warning → Normal

FIGURE 13.4
The Defined In column shows where an alarm was defined.

The Repeat Actions Every parameter controls the period of time during which a triggered alarm is not reported again. Using the built-in VM CPU usage alarm as our example, the Frequency parameter is set, by default, to 5 minutes. This means that a VM whose CPU usage triggers the activation of the alarm won't get reported again—assuming the condition or state is still true—for 5 minutes.

With all this information in mind, let's walk through another example of creating an alarm. This time we'll use a trigger to take advantage of duration and action frequency.

Perform the following steps to create an alarm that is triggered based on VM network usage:

1. Launch the vSphere Web Client if it is not already running, and connect to a vCenter Server instance.

2. Navigate to an inventory view, such as Hosts And Clusters or VMs And Templates.

3. Select the datacenter object from the Navigator on the left.

4. Select the Manage tab from the content area in the middle.

5. Select the Alarm Definitions button just below the tab bar to show alarm definitions.

6. Click the add/plus icon to create a new alarm.

7. Supply an alarm name and description.

8. Set the Monitor drop-down list to Virtual Machines.

9. Select the radio button marked "Monitor For Specific Conditions Or State, For Example, CPU Usage," and click Next.

10. On the Triggers screen of the Alarm Definition dialog box, click the plus/add icon to add a new trigger.

11. Add a Trigger of VM Network Usage (kbps) type.

12. Set Condition to Is Above.

13. Set the value of the Warning column to 500, and leave the Condition Length setting at 5 minutes.

14. Set the value of the Alert column to 1000, and leave the Condition Length setting at 5 minutes.

15. On the Actions tab, click the plus/add icon and add a "Send a notification email" action.

16. For this newly created action, ensure that Normal ➢ Warning is set at Once and Warning ➢ Critical is set to Repeat.

17. Finally, set Repeat Actions Every to 15 minutes.

18. Click Finish to create the alarm.

This alarm will now send email alerts if the VM network usage goes above 500 kbps for more than 5 minutes, but only once. If the VM network usage goes above 1,000 kbps for more than 5 minutes, an email will be sent again and then every 15 minutes advising of this critical state until the alarm is reset to green manually or the usage drops below 1,000 kbps.

ALARMS ON OTHER vCENTER SERVER OBJECTS

Although the two alarms you've created so far have been specific to VMs, the process is similar for other types of objects within vCenter Server.

Alarms can have more than just one trigger condition. The alarms you've created so far had only a single trigger condition. For an example of an alarm that has more than one trigger condition, look at the built-in alarm for monitoring host connection and power state. Figure 13.5 shows the two trigger conditions for this alarm. Note that that *ALL* is selected in the "Trigger if" drop-down menu; it ensures that only powered-on hosts that are not responding will trigger the alarm.

FIGURE 13.5

You can combine multiple triggers to create more complex alarms.

It might seem obvious, but it's important to note that you can have more than one alarm for an object.

As with any new alarm, testing its functionality is crucial to make sure you get the desired results. You might find that the thresholds you configured are not optimized for your environment and either are not activating the alarm when they should or are activating the alarm when they shouldn't. In these cases, edit the alarm to set the thresholds and conditions appropriately. Or, if the alarm is no longer needed, right-click the alarm, and choose Remove to delete it.

You'll be able to edit or delete alarms only if two conditions are met. First, the user account with which you've connected to vCenter Server must have the appropriate permissions granted for you to edit or delete alarms. Second, you must be attempting to edit or delete the alarm from the object on which it was defined. Think back to the discussion on alarm scope and this makes sense. You can't delete an alarm from the datacenter object when that alarm was defined on the vCenter Server object. You must go to the object where the alarm was defined to edit or delete the alarm.

Now that you've seen some examples of creating alarms—and keep in mind that creating alarms for other objects within vCenter Server follows the same basic steps—let's take a look at managing alarms.

Managing Alarms

Several times so far in this chapter we've directed you to the Alarms Definitions tab within the vSphere Web Client. Until now, you've been working with the definitions, looking at defined alarms. There is, however, another view to the alarms, and that's the Triggered Alarms view. Figure 13.6 shows the Triggered Alarms view, which you access by selecting an object within the vCenter Web Client, then clicking the Monitor tab ➤ Issues ➤ Triggered Alarms.

FIGURE 13.6

The Triggered Alarms view shows the alarms that vCenter Server has activated.

The Monitor ➤ Issues ➤ Triggered Alarms area shows all the activated alarms for the selected object and all child objects, while on the right hand pane of the vSphere Web Client in the Global Alarm area, all alarms within vCenter are shown. In Figure 13.6, a Virtual Machine object is selected, so the Triggered Alarms view shows all activated alarms for this VM.

GETTING TO THE TRIGGERED ALARMS VIEW QUICKLY

The vSphere Web Client provides a handy view in the bottom-right corner that displays all the currently triggered alarms. Clicking on these alarms takes you to the Triggered Alarms view of the object on which the alarm is triggered. You can also acknowledge or reset the alarm to green from this panel.

However, if only the VM had been selected, the Triggered Alarms view on the Alarms tab for that VM would show only the two activated alarms for that particular VM. This makes it easy to isolate the specific alarms you need to address.

After you are in Triggered Alarms view for a particular object, a few actions are available to you for each of the activated alarms. For alarms that monitor resource consumption (that is, the alarm definition uses the Monitor For Specific Conditions Or State, For Example, CPU Usage, Power State setting selected under Alarm Type on the General tab), you have the option to acknowledge the alarm. To acknowledge the alarm, right-click the alarm and select Acknowledge.

When an alarm is acknowledged, vCenter Server records the time the alarm was acknowledged and the user account that acknowledged the alarm. As long as the alarm condition persists, the alarm will remain in the Triggered Alarms view but is grayed out. When the alarm condition is resolved, the activated alarm disappears.

For an alarm that monitors events (this would be an alarm that has the "Monitor For Specific Events Occurring On This Object, For Example, VM Powered On" option selected under Alarm Type on the General tab), you can either acknowledge the alarm, as described previously, or reset the alarm status to green. Figure 13.7 illustrates this option.

Resetting an alarm to green removes the activated alarm from the Triggered Alarms view, even if the underlying event that activated the alarm hasn't actually been resolved. This behavior makes sense if you think about it. Alarms that monitor events are merely responding to an event being logged by vCenter Server; whether the underlying condition has been resolved is unknown. So, resetting the alarm to green just tells vCenter Server to act as if the condition has been resolved. Of course, if the event occurs again, the alarm will be triggered again.

Now that we've looked at alarms for proactive performance monitoring, let's move on to using vCenter Server's performance charts to view even more information about the behavior of VMs and ESXi hosts in your vSphere environment.

FIGURE 13.7
For event-based alarms, you also have the option to reset the alarm status to green.

Working with Performance Charts

Alarms are a great tool for alerting administrators of specific conditions or events, but they don't provide the detailed information that administrators sometimes need, such as a resource being used that is still under a warning or critical state. This is where vCenter Server's performance charts come in. vCenter Server has many features for creating and analyzing charts. Without these charts, analyzing the performance of a VM would be nearly impossible. Installing agents inside a VM will not provide accurate details about the server's behavior or resource consumption because a VM is configured with virtual devices. Only the VMkernel knows the exact amount of resource consumption for any of those devices because it acts as the arbitrator between the virtual hardware and the physical hardware. In most virtual environments, the VM's virtual devices can outnumber the actual physical hardware devices, necessitating the complex sharing and scheduling abilities in the VMkernel.

By clicking the Monitor ➤ Performance tab for a datacenter, cluster, host, or VM, you can learn a wealth of information. Before you use these charts to help analyze resource consumption, we need to talk about performance charts and legends. We'll start by covering the two different layouts available in performance charts: the Overview layout and the Advanced layout.

Overview Layout

The Overview layout is the default view when you access the Monitor ➤ Performance tab. Figure 13.8 shows you the Overview layout of the Performance tab for an ESXi host. Note the scroll bars; there's a lot more information here than the vSphere Web Client can fit in a single screen.

FIGURE 13.8
The Overview layout provides information on a range of performance counters.

At the top of the Overview layout are options to change the view and the time range. The contents of the View drop-down list change depending on the object you select in the vSphere Web Client. Table 13.1 lists the different options available for each object.

TABLE 13.1: View options in the Overview area of the Performance tab

SELECTED OBJECT	VIEW OPTIONS
Datacenter	Clusters, Storage
Cluster	Home, Resource Pools & Virtual Machines, Hosts
Resource pool	Home, Resource Pools & Virtual Machines
Host	Home, Virtual Machines
Virtual machine	Home, Storage

Next to the View drop-down list is an option to change the time range for the data currently displayed in the various performance charts. This allows you to set the time range to real time, a day, a week, a month, a year, or a custom value. The Realtime time range setting displays the last hour of data and automatically refreshes every 20 seconds, while the other time range settings do not automatically refresh.

Below these controls are the actual performance charts. The layout and the charts that are included vary based on the object selected and the option chosen in the View drop-down list. While we don't have the room to list all of them, we show you two examples, in Figure 13.9 and Figure 13.10. I encourage you to explore and find the layouts that work best for your environment and, more important, layouts that clearly show you the performance information you require.

FIGURE 13.9

The Virtual Machines view of the Performance tab for an ESXi host in Overview layout offers both per-VM and summary information.

The Overview layout works well if you need a broad overview of the performance data for a datacenter, cluster, resource pool, host, or VM. But what if you need more specific data in a more customizable format? The Advanced layout is the answer, as you'll see in the next section.

Advanced Layout

Although it's called the Advanced layout, to begin with it looks somewhat simpler than the Overview layout. There is only a single chart within this view, but don't let this fool you because there are a significant number of configuration options for this lone performance chart.

Figure 13.11 shows the Advanced layout of the Performance tab for a cluster of ESXi hosts. Here, in the Advanced layout, is where the real power of vCenter Server's performance charts is made available to you.

FIGURE 13.10
The Storage view of the Performance tab for a VM in Overview layout displays a break-down of storage utilization.

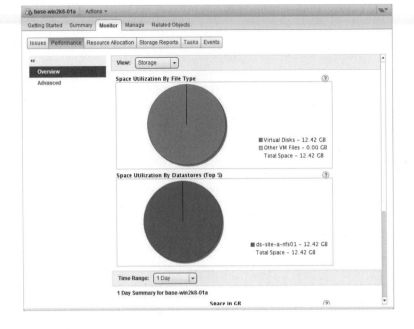

FIGURE 13.11
The Advanced layout of the Performance tab provides extensive controls for viewing performance data.

At the right of the Advanced layout, you'll find a View drop-down list to quickly switch chart settings, followed by buttons to refresh the chart or to export the chart. The Refresh button refreshes the data, while the Export button allows you to export the chart as a JPEG, PNG graphic, or CSV document. We'll discuss this functionality in the section "Exporting Performance Graphs." On each side of the chart are units of measurement. In Figure 13.11, the counters selected are measured in percentages and megahertz. Depending on the counters chosen, there may be only one unit of measurement, but there will be no more than two. Next, on the horizontal axis, is the time interval. Below that, the performance chart legend provides color-coded keys to help the user find a specific object or item of interest. This area also breaks down the chart into the object being measured; the measurement being used; the units of measure; and the Latest, Maximum, Minimum, and Average measurements recorded for that object.

Hovering the mouse pointer over the chart at a particular recorded interval of interest displays the data points at that specific moment in time. Another nice feature of the charts is the ability to emphasize a specific object so that you can more easily select this object from other objects. Clicking the specific item in the chart legend at the bottom will emphasize the object and its representative color .

Now that you have a feel for the Advanced layout, let's take a closer look at the Chart Options link. This link exposes vCenter Server's functionality in creating highly customized performance charts and is where all the nuts and bolts are configured for this feature. Figure 13.12 shows the Chart Options dialog box. This dialog box is the central place where you will come to customize vCenter Server's performance charts; you can also just double-click the chart to display this dialog box. From here, you select the counters to view, the time ranges, and the kind of chart (Line Graph or stacked graph) to display.

FIGURE 13.12
The Chart Options dialog box offers tremendous flexibility to create exactly the performance chart you need.

Because there is so much information available in the Chart Options dialog box, we've grouped the various options and types of information into the sections that follow.

CHOOSING A CHART METRICS AND COUNTERS

On the left side of the Chart Options dialog box (shown in Figure 13.12), you can choose which metric to monitor or analyze. All the available chart metrics are listed here, but only a subset of these are available, depending on the object selected to monitor:

◆ CPU

◆ Cluster Services

◆ Datastore

- Disk

- Memory

- Network

- Power

- Storage Adapter

- Storage Path

- System

- vSphere Flash Module

- Virtual Disk

- Virtual Machine Operations

- vSphere Replication

The actual selections available in this area change depending on the type of object that you have selected within the vCenter Web Client. That is, the options available when viewing the Monitor ➤ Performance tab for an ESXi host are different from the options available when viewing the Monitor ➤ Performance tab of a VM, a cluster, or a datacenter.

Within each of these resources, different objects and counters are available. Be aware that other factors affect what objects and counters are available to view; for example, in some cases the real-time interval shows more objects and counters than other intervals. A description field within the counters list explains what each counter represents. If this description does not fit within the Chart Options dialog box, simply mouse over it to view the full text. The next few sections list the various counters that are available for the different resource types in the Chart Options dialog box.

VIEWING CPU PERFORMANCE INFORMATION

If you select the CPU resource type in the Chart Options dialog box, you can choose what specific objects and counters you'd like to see in the performance chart. Note that the CPU resource type is not available when viewing the Performance tab of a datacenter object (DC). It is available for clusters (CL), ESXi hosts (ESXi), resource pools (RP), and individual virtual machines (VM).

Table 13.2 lists the most important objects and counters available for CPU performance information. A complete list of all CPU performance counters can be found at www.sybex.com/go/masteringvsphere.

TABLE 13.2:   Available CPU performance counters

COUNTER	DC	CL	ESXi	RP	VM
Max Limited					X
Ready			X		X

TABLE 13.2: Available memory performance counters *(CONTINUED)*

COUNTER	DC	CL	ESXI	RP	VM
Run					X
Swap Wait			X		X
System					X
Total		X			
Usage In MHz		X	X	X	X
Used			X		X
Utilization			X		
Wait			X		X

Quite a bit of CPU performance information is available. In the section "Monitoring CPU Usage," we'll discuss how to use these CPU performance objects and counters to monitor CPU usage.

VIEWING MEMORY PERFORMANCE INFORMATION

If you select the Memory resource type in the Chart Options section of the Chart Options dialog box, you can display different objects and counters. The Memory resource type is not available when viewing the Performance tab of a datacenter object. It is available for clusters, ESXi hosts, resource pools, and individual VMs.

Table 13.3 lists the most important objects and counters available for memory performance information. A complete list of all memory performance counters can be found at www.sybex .com/go/masteringvsphere.

TABLE 13.3: Available memory performance counters

COUNTER	DC	CL	ESXI	RP	VM
Active			X		X
Compressed			X		X
Consumed		X	X	X	X
Swap In			X		X
Swap Out			X		X
Swap Used			X		
Usage		X	X		X

TABLE 13.3: Available disk performance counters *(CONTINUED)*

COUNTER	DC	CL	ESXi	RP	VM
Balloon Target					X
Zipped Memory					X
Memory Saved By Zipping					X

In the section "Monitoring Memory Usage," you'll get the opportunity to use these different objects and counters to monitor how ESXi and VMs are using memory.

VIEWING DISK PERFORMANCE INFORMATION

Disk performance is another key area that vSphere administrators need to monitor. Table 13.4 shows you the most important objects and counters available for disk performance information. A complete list of all disk performance counters can be found at www.sybex.com/go/masteringvsphere.

TABLE 13.4: Available disk performance counters

COUNTER	DC	CL	ESXi	RP	VM
Disk Bus Resets			X		X
Disk Commands Terminated			X		X
Disk Kernel Command Latency			X		X
Disk Kernel Read Latency			X		X
Disk Kernel Write Latency			X		X
Disk Maximum Queue Depth			X		X
Disk Command Latency			X		X
Disk Read Latency			X		X
Disk Write Latency			X		X
Disk Queue Command Latency			X		X

Note that these counters aren't supported for datacenters, clusters, and resource pools, but they are supported for ESXi hosts and VMs. Not all counters are visible in all display intervals. You'll use these counters in the section "Monitoring Disk Usage," later in this chapter.

VIEWING NETWORK PERFORMANCE INFORMATION

To monitor network performance, the vCenter Server performance charts cover a wide collection of performance counters. Network performance counters are available only for ESXi hosts and VMs; they are not available for datacenter objects, clusters, or resource pools.

Table 13.5 shows the most important objects and counters available for network performance information. A complete list of all network performance counters can be found at www.sybex .com/go/masteringvsphere.

TABLE 13.5:   Available network performance counters

COUNTER	DC	CL	ESXI	RP	VM
Data Receive Rate			X		X
Data Transmit Rate			X		X
Receive Packets Dropped			X		X
Transmit Packets Dropped			X		X
Packet Receive Errors			X		
Packet Transmit Errors			X		
Packets Received			X		X
Packets Transmitted			X		X
Data Receive Rate			X		X
Data Transmit Rate			X		X
Usage			X		X

You'll use these network performance counters in the section "Monitoring Network Usage" later in this chapter.

VIEWING SYSTEM PERFORMANCE INFORMATION

ESXi hosts and VMs also offer some performance counters in the System resource type. Datacenters, clusters, and resource pools do not support any system performance counters.

Table 13.6 lists the most important objects and counters available for system performance information. A complete list of all system performance counters can be found at www.sybex .com/go/masteringvsphere.

TABLE 13.6: Available system performance counters

COUNTER	DC	CL	ESXI	RP	VM
Resource CPU Active (1 Min Average)			X		
Resource CPU Active (5 Min Average)			X		
Resource CPU Maximum Limited (1 Min)			X		
Resource CPU Maximum Limited (5 Min)			X		
Resource CPU Running (1 Min Average)			X		
Resource CPU Running (5 Min Average)			X		
Resource CPU Usage (Average)			X		
Resource Memory Shared			X		
Resource Memory Swapped			X		
Uptime			X	X	

The majority of these counters are valid only for ESXi hosts, and they all center on how resources are allocated or how the ESXi host itself is consuming CPU resources or memory.

VIEWING DATASTORE PERFORMANCE INFORMATION

Monitoring datastore performance allows you to see the performance of the whole datastore instead of using disk counters per VM. Datastore performance counters are available only for ESXi hosts and VMs; they are not available for datacenter objects, clusters, or resource pools.

Table 13.7 shows the most important objects and counters available for datastore performance information. A complete list of all datastore performance counters can be found at www.sybex .com/go/masteringvsphere.

TABLE 13.7:   Available datastore performance counters

COUNTER	DC	CL	ESXI	RP	VM
Storage I/O Control Aggregated IOPS			X		
Storage I/O Control Datastore Maximum Queue Depth			X		
Storage DRS Datastore Normalized Read Latency			X		
Storage DRS Datastore Normalized write latency			X		
Highest Latency			X		X
Average Read Requests Per Second			X		X
Average Write Requests Per Second			X		X
Storage I/O Control Normalized Latency			X		
Read Latency			X		X
Write Latency			X		X

VIEWING STORAGE PATH PERFORMANCE INFORMATION

Storage Path is one of the new categories of performance counters. As the name suggests, these counters can help you troubleshoot storage path problems. Storage path counters are available only for ESXi; they are not available for datacenter objects, clusters, VMs, or resource pools.

Table 13.8 shows the objects and counters available for storage path performance information.

TABLE 13.8:   Available storage path performance counters

COUNTER	DC	CL	ESXI	RP	VM
Average Commands Issued Per Second			X		
Highest Latency			X		
Average Read Requests Per Second			X		
Average Write Requests Per Second			X		
Read Rate			X		
Storage Path Throughput Usage			X		
Read Latency			X		
Write Latency			X		
Write Rate			X		

VIEWING OTHER PERFORMANCE COUNTERS

The following performance counter types are also available:

◆   ESXi hosts participating in a cluster also have a resource type of Cluster Services, with two performance counters: CPU Fairness and Memory Fairness. Both of these counters show the distribution of resources within a cluster.

◆   The datacenter object contains a resource type marked as Virtual Machine Operations. This resource type contains performance counters that simply monitor the number of times a particular VM operation has occurred. These include VM Power-On Events, VM Power-Off Events, VM Resets, vMotion Operations, and Storage vMotion Operations.

SETTING A CUSTOM INTERVAL

Just as with the Overview layout, within each of the resource types, you have a choice of intervals to view. Some objects offer a Real-Time option; this option shows what is happening with that resource right now, with a historical view over the past hour, and the charts automatically refresh every 20 seconds. The others are self-explanatory in their time span, but note that they do not refresh automatically. The Custom option allows you to specify exactly what you'd like to see on the performance chart. For example, you could specify that you'd like to see performance data for the last 8 hours. Having all of these interval options allows you to choose exactly the right interval necessary to view the precise data you're seeking.

MANAGING CHART SETTINGS

There's one more area of the Chart Options dialog box that we'll discuss, and that's the Chart Options drop-down and Save Options As button along the top.

After you've gone through and selected the resource type, display interval, objects, and performance counters that you'd like to see in the performance chart, you can save that collection of chart settings using the Save Options As button. The vCenter Web Client prompts you to enter a name for the saved chart settings. After a chart setting is saved, you can easily access it again from the drop-down list at the top of the performance chart Advanced layout. Figure 13.13 shows the View drop-down list, where two custom chart settings—CPU-8hr View and MEM - Overhead—are shown. By selecting either of these from the View drop-down list, you can quickly switch to those settings. This allows you to define the performance charts that you need to see and then quickly switch between them.

FIGURE 13.13
You can access saved chart settings from the View drop-down list.

If you have a custom chart saved, the Chart Options dialog box allows you to delete chart settings you've saved but no longer need.

In addition to offering you the option of saving the chart settings, vCenter Server also allows you to save the chart.

EXPORTING PERFORMANCE CHARTS

When we first introduced you to the Advanced layout view of the Performance tab, we briefly mentioned the Export button. This button, found in the upper-right corner of the Advanced layout, allows you to save the results of the performance chart to an external file for long-term archiving, analysis, or reporting.

When you click the Export button, a standard Save dialog box appears. You have the option of choosing where to save the resulting file as well as the option of saving the chart either as a graphic file or as a comma-separated values (CSV) file. If you are going to perform any additional analysis, the option to save the chart data as an Excel spreadsheet is quite useful. The graphics options are useful when you need to put the performance data into a report of some sort.

There's a lot of information exposed via vCenter Server's performance charts. We'll revisit the performance charts again in the sections on monitoring specific types of resources later in this chapter. First we'll show you how vCenter Operations Manager can help you monitor and troubleshoot your vSphere environment.

Understanding vCenter Operations Manager

vCenter Operations (vC Ops) Manager is the primary component of the VMware vCenter Operations Management Suite. This suite is designed to go hand in hand with not just vSphere but VMware's whole vCloud suite of infrastructure products, providing additional management capabilities on the operational side of things. The full enterprise version of vCenter Operations Management Suite includes the following components:

- vCenter Operations Manager
- vCenter Configuration Manager
- vFabric Hyperic
- vCenter Infrastructure Navigator
- vCenter Chargeback Manager

While we could write a whole book on the vC Ops suite, this book is about vSphere, so we will concentrate on just what's available to you for free without the need to purchase anything else.

Installing vC Ops

The vC Ops Manager is a two-VM vApp that comes as a bundled Open Virtualization Format (OVA) package and is a 1.4 GB download from VMware. All customers that have vSphere licensing are able to download and install this product into Foundation mode without the need for a license key. When operating in Foundation mode, vC Ops does not allow a lot of access to the advanced features such as custom dashboards, root cause analysis, and automated workflow triggers or compliance views, but it does extend the functionality of the vSphere Web Client somewhat. Next we'll show you how to install vC Ops, and then later we will explain the features that are available with the Foundation edition.

DEPLOYING THE VC OPS VAPP

This procedure is fairly straightforward and mirrors most appliance-based installs (like the one performed for the vCenter Virtual Appliance in Chapter 3, "Installing and Configuring vCenter Server"), but we'll step you through the process in case you skipped to this section. We will assume that you've already logged on to my.vmware.com and download the 1.4 GB OVA file. Here are the steps:

1. Connect to a vCenter Server instance with the vSphere Web Client.
2. Navigate to the Hosts And Clusters or VMs And Templates view.

3. Right-click the cluster object that you wish to host the vC Ops vApp.

4. Select Deploy OVF Template.

5. Browse and select the downloaded file and then click Next.

6. Review the deployment details, noticing the large disk requirements if thickly provisioned (344 GB). Click Next to continue through the wizard.

7. Accept the license agreement and then click Next.

8. Give your vC Ops installation vApp a name and select the datacenter and then the destination folder.

9. Select the size of the configuration that best suits your environment. Click Next to continue.

---

vCenter Operations Manager Sizing

When installing vC Ops, you have three settings to choose for the environment size: small, medium, or large. While we would normally recommend sticking to VMware's predetermined values, even the smallest installation requires 4 vCPUs and 16 GB of RAM. While you cannot change these values in the installer, you can modify the resources allocated to the VMs after they are deployed. For pilots, testing, or lab work, there is nothing stopping you from lowering the allocation, however, VMware may not support your installation if you deviate from its standard sizings.

---

10. Choose the datastore and provisioning type, keeping in mind the larger requirement if the disk format is set to Thick. Click Next to continue.

11. Ensure that all the relevant networking details are filled in and the vApp is connected to the correct network port group. Once this is complete, click Next to go to the final configuration page.

12. Set the correct time zone for this server and then allocate both the Analytics and UI VMs with their IP addresses. Click Next to go to the review page.

13. Ensure that all the details are correct before clicking Finish to deploy the vC Ops vApp. The vC Ops appliance VMs will now be deployed as a vApp and then can finally be powered on.

REGISTERING WITH vCENTER SERVER

Once the vC Ops appliance is deployed and powered on, you need to register it with the vCenter Server to allow for metric retrieval and also for vSphere Web Client integration. The following steps outline how to register:

1. With the vApp already powered on and finished booting, open a web browser and point it to the IP address of the UI VM.

2. Log in with the username admin and the password admin.

3. Enter the details of your vCenter Server instance and click Next. You may be prompted to accept the SSL certificate; if so, click Yes.

4. The vC Ops admin page will now prompt you to change both the default root and admin passwords. For reference, the default password is admin for the admin account and the default password is vmware for the root account. When they are both changed, click Next to continue.

5. You will now be prompted to enter the details for the vCenter Server instance you wish to register with. Once all your details are entered, click Next to check the connection and then again to continue to the final screen.

6. On the final screen, the vC Ops admin page checks for linked mode vCenter Servers. Click Finish to complete the vC Ops to vCenter registration process; this can take some time depending on the number of objects managed by vCenter.

Now that vC Ops is registered with vCenter, it's time to reload the vCenter Web Client and take a look at the changes that have taken place.

vC Ops Foundation Features

As stated earlier, vC Op has a large number of features, but most of them are disabled with the Foundation version. There are four key features and capabilities that are turned on: Proactive Smart Alerts, Intelligent Operations Groups, vSphere Health Monitoring, and Self-Learning Performance Analytics.

The alerts within Proactive Smart Alerts are different from the standard alerts discussed earlier in this chapter. This feature ties into the Self-learning Performance Analytics feature and will begin to alert you when things are outside their normal operating levels. The Self-Learning Performance Analytics feature will look at all the metrics captured over time and work out what is considered "normal." For example, your environment might have relatively steady workloads during the day, but at 11 p.m., when the backups start, the storage and network utilization peak considerably higher than during the day. With a traditional alert, your threshold would need to take into consideration the peak for your backup window, but with self-learning analysis, vC Ops knows that it is "normal" for high storage and network IO after 11 p.m. and will not alert you. However, if during the day the IO peaked, an alert would still be generated.

Intelligent Operations Groups is a feature that allows you to create a group for monitoring based on a ruleset. You can then apply this ruleset automatically to ensure that all objects are added to the group according to the ruleset. After you add a group of objects to a group, you can monitor them as a whole instead of just individually. The other handy feature with groups is that you can nest groups within groups, allowing you to be as granular as necessary when categorizing objects for reporting.

vSphere Health Monitoring is the most visible feature that you will encounter with vC Ops Foundation, adding a colorful badge to the Summary tab of some objects within the vCenter Web Client. This badge will change color depending on the current health number displayed on the badge, with 100 being the healthiest and 0 being very unhealthy, as shown in Figure 13.14. But what is "health" you ask? Good question!

FIGURE 13.14
vCenter Operations
Manager integrates
with the vSphere
Web Client to show
health information
about the currently
selected object, in
this case the vCen-
ter server itself.

Health is a top-level indicator made up of the subcomponents faults, workload, and anoma-lies. Faults have the most weight when calculating the overall health badge because they are problems that are happening right now. Workload and anomalies are combined to assist with understanding current performance characteristics. As you can probably imagine, all of these components have their own subcomponents too, but how everything is calculated behind the scenes is not relevant for this discussion. The health badge gives an overall view of how an object within vCenter is performing and is calculated every 5 minutes. If the health monitor spots a problem, you can dive in to find out the cause. We'll now explain the last tool in the toolbox, resxtop, and then we'll show you how to combine all of the tools to keep your environ-ment in top condition.

Working with *resxtop*

In addition to alarms and performance charts, VMware provides resxtop to help monitor per-formance and resource usage. In early ESX versions, several tools were available on the service console command line. Later, VMware released ESXi and limited the number of commands avail-able directly on the host but developed a special virtual appliance that provides a command-line interface for managing ESX and ESXi hosts called the vSphere Management Assistant (vMA). You can use the vMA to run commands against the ESXi host as if they were run on the console. In ESXi 3.*x* and ESXi 4.0, access to the console was unsupported. Since ESXi 4.1, VMware has supported the console, but it is locked and therefore inaccessible by default. More commands are available on the console than with previous ESXi versions; however, VMware still advises using the vMA for running commands against ESXi hosts for a few reasons—one of which is to provide yet another means of centralized host management.

Using *resxtop*

You can monitor VM performance using a command-line tool named resxtop. A great reason to use resxtop is the immediate feedback it gives you. Using resxtop, you can monitor all four major resource types (CPU, disk, memory, and network) on a particular ESXi host. Figure 13.15 shows some sample output from resxtop.

FIGURE 13.15
resxtop shows real-time information on CPU, disk, memory, and network utilization.

The resxtop command is included with the vMA, which is deployed like all OVF packaged virtual appliances. Simply download the vMA from the my.vmware.com website and import to your vSphere environment. For more detailed instructions on deploying OVFs, see the Deploying the vC Ops vApp section earlier in this chapter. Before you can actually view real-time performance data, though, you first have to tell resxtop which remote server you want to use. To launch resxtop and connect to a remote server, first connect to the vMA and then enter this command:

```
resxtop --server esxi-03.lab.local
```

You'll want to replace esxi-03.lab.local with the appropriate hostname or IP address of the ESXi host to which you want to connect. When prompted, supply a username and password, and then resxtop will launch. Once resxtop is running, you can use single-letter commands to switch among the various views.

---

esxtop IS ONLY FOR VMWARE ESXI SHELL

It is still possible to run esxtop, which you might know from former ESX versions, in the VMware ESXi shell, but it is highly recommended to use only the VMware vMA.

Upon launch, resxtop defaults to showing CPU utilization, as illustrated in Figure 13.15. At the top of the screen are summary statistics; below that are statistics for specific VMs and VMkernel processes. To show only VMs, press V. Be aware that resxtop, like many Linux commands, is case sensitive, so you'll need to be sure to use an uppercase V in order to toggle the display of VMs only.

Monitoring CPU usage with c   Two CPU counters of interest to view with resxtop are the CPU Used (%USED) and Ready Time (%RDY) counters. You can also see these counters in the VM charts, but with resxtop they are calculated as percentages. The %RDY counter is also helpful in determining whether you have overallocated CPU resources to the VM. This might be the case if, for example, you've allocated two vCPUs to a VM that really needs only a single vCPU. While in CPU mode, you can also press lowercase e to expand a VM's CPU statistics so that you can see the different components that are using CPU time on behalf of a VM. This is quite useful in determining what components of a VM may be taking up CPU capacity.

If you switch away to another resource, press C (uppercase or lowercase) to come back to the CPU counters display. At any time when you are finished with resxtop, you can simply press q (lowercase only) to exit the utility and return to the vMA command prompt.

---

resxtop SHOWS SINGLE HOSTS ONLY

Remember, resxtop shows only a single ESXi host. In an environment where vMotion, vSphere Distributed Resource Scheduler (DRS), and vSphere High Availability (HA) have been deployed, VMs may move around often. It is possible that while you are monitoring a VM, it is suddenly moved off the host by a vMotion action. Also be aware of this when capturing performance in batch mode.

Monitoring Memory Usage with m   Memory is one of the most important components of your ESXi host because this resource is usually one of the first to get exhausted.

To monitor memory usage with resxtop, press m (lowercase only). This gives you real-time statistics about the ESXi host's memory usage in the top portion and the VM's memory usage in the lower section. As with CPU statistics, you can press V (uppercase only) to show only VMs. This helps you weed out VMkernel resources when you are trying to isolate a problem with a VM. The %ACTV counter, which shows current active guest physical memory, is a useful counter, as are the %ACTVS (slow-moving average for long-term estimates), %ACTVF (fast-moving average for short-term estimates), %ACTVN (prediction of %ACTV at next sampling), and SWCUR (current swap usage) counters.

Monitoring Network Statistics with n   Networking in a vSphere environment is often taken for granted, but while your environment grows, you'll learn that keeping an eye on network performance is essential.

To monitor network statistics about the virtual machine network interface cards (vmnics), individual VMs, or VMkernel ports used for iSCSI, VMotion, and NFS, press n (lowercase only). The columns showing network usage include packets transmitted and received and megabytes transmitted and received for each vmnic or port. Also shown in the DNAME column are the vSwitches or dvSwitches and, to the left, what is plugged into them, including VMs, VMkernel, and Service Console ports. If a particular VM is monopolizing the vSwitch, you can look at the amount of network traffic on a specific switch and the individual ports to see which VM is the culprit. Unlike in other `resxtop` views, you can't use V (uppercase only) here to show only VMs.

Monitoring Disk I/O Statistics with d Memory and disk I/O are considered the most important components in your vSphere environment. While memory is important because it gets exhausted first, disk I/O is often overlooked even though bad disk performance will directly impact the VMs performance.

To monitor disk I/O statistics about each of the disk adapters, press d (lowercase only) and press u (lowercase only) for disk devices and v (lowercase only) for disk VM. As with some other views, you can press V (uppercase only) to show only VMs. The columns labeled READS/s, WRITES/s, MBREAD/s, and MBWRTN/s are most often used to determine disk loads. Those columns show loads based on reads and writes per second and megabytes read and written per second.

The `resxtop` command also lets you view CPU interrupts by pressing i. This command will show you the device(s) using the interrupt and is a great way to identify VMkernel devices, such as a vmnic, that might be sharing an interrupt with the Service Console. This sort of interrupt sharing can impede performance.

Capturing and Playing Back Performance Data with *resxtop*

Another great feature of `resxtop` is the ability to capture performance data for a short period of time and then play back that data. Using the command `vm-support`, you can set an interval and duration for the capture.

Perform the following steps to capture data to be played back on `resxtop`:

1. Using PuTTY (Windows) or a terminal window (Mac OS X or Linux), open an SSH session to an ESXi host. Note that this requires enabling the ESXi Shell and SSH, both of which are disabled by default.

2. Enter the **su -** command to assume root privileges.

3. While logged in as root or after switching to the root user, change your working directory to /tmp by issuing the command **cd /tmp**.

4. Enter the command **vm-support -p -i 10 -d 180**. This creates a `resxtop` snapshot, capturing data every 10 seconds, for the duration of 180 seconds.

5. The resulting file is a tarball and is compressed with `gzip`. You must extract it with the command **tar -xzf esx*.tgz**. This creates a `vm-support` directory that is called in the next command.

6. Run **resxtop -R /vm-support*** to replay the data for analysis.

Now that we've shown you the various tools (alarms, performance charts, vC Ops, and `resxtop`) that you will use to monitor performance in a vSphere environment, let's go through the four major resources—CPU, RAM, network, and disk—and see how to monitor the usage of these resources.

Monitoring CPU Usage

When monitoring a VM, it's always a good starting point to keep an eye on CPU consumption. Many VMs started out in life as underperforming physical servers. One of VMware's most successful sales pitches is being able to take all those lackluster physical boxes that are not busy and convert them to VMs. Once they are converted, virtual infrastructure managers tend to think of these VMs as simple, lackluster, and low-utilization servers with nothing to worry over or monitor. The truth, though, is quite the opposite.

When the server was physical, it had an entire box to itself. Now it must share its resources with many other workloads. In aggregate, they represent quite a load, and if some or many of them become somewhat busy, they contend with each other for the finite capabilities of the ESXi host on which they run. Of course, they don't know they are contending for resources because the VMkernel tries to make sure they get the resources they need. Virtual CPUs need to be scheduled, and ESXi does a remarkable job given that there are more VMs than physical processors most of the time. Still, the hypervisor can do only so much with the resources it has, and invariably there comes a time when the applications running in a VM need more CPU time than the host can give.

When this happens, it's usually the application owner who notices first and raises the alarm with the system administrators. Now the vSphere administrators have the task of determining why this VM is underperforming. Fortunately, vCenter Server provides a number of tools that make monitoring and analysis easier. These are the tools you've already seen: alarms, performance charts, vC Ops, and `resxtop`.

Let's begin with a hypothetical scenario. A help desk ticket has been submitted indicating that an application owner isn't getting the expected level of performance on a particular server, which in this case is a VM. As the vSphere administrator, you need to first delve deeper into the problem and ask as many questions as necessary to discover what the application owner needs to be satisfied with performance. Some performance issues are subjective, meaning some users might complain about the slowness of their applications, but they have no objective benchmark for such a claim. Other times, this is reflected in a specific benchmark, such as the number of transactions by a database server or throughput for a web server. In this case, our issue revolves around benchmarking CPU usage, so our application is CPU intensive when it does its job.

ASSESSMENTS, EXPECTATIONS, AND ADJUSTMENTS

If an assessment was done prior to virtualizing a server, there might be hard numbers to look at to give some details as to what was expected with regard to minimum performance or a service-level agreement (SLA). If not, the vSphere administrator needs to work with the application's owner to make more CPU resources available to the VM when needed.

---

vCenter Server's charts, which you have explored in great detail, are the best way to analyze usage, both short and long term. In this case, let's assume the help desk ticket describes a slowness issue in the last hour. As you've already seen, you can easily create a custom performance chart to show CPU usage over the last hour for a particular VM or ESXi host.

Perform the following steps to create a CPU chart that shows data for a VM from the last hour:

1. Connect to a vCenter Server instance with the vSphere Web Client.

2. Navigate to the Hosts And Clusters or VMs And Templates view.

3. In the Navigator, select a virtual machine.

4. Select the Monitor ➤ Performance tab from the contents pane on the right, and then change the view to Advanced.

5. Click the Chart Options link.

6. In the Chart Options dialog box, select CPU from the resource type list. Select the Custom interval for the time span.

7. Change the interval to Last 1 Hour(s).

8. Set the chart type to Line Graph.

9. Select the VM itself from the list of objects.

10. From the list of counters, select CPU Usage In MHz (Average) and CPU Ready.

11. Click OK to apply the chart settings.

CPU READY

CPU Ready shows how long a VM is waiting to be scheduled on a logical processor. A VM waiting many thousands of milliseconds to be scheduled on a processor might indicate that the ESXi host is overloaded, a resource pool has too tight a limit, or the VM has too few CPU shares (or, if no one is complaining, nothing at all). Be sure to work with the server or application owner to determine an acceptable amount of CPU Ready for any CPU-intensive VM.

This chart shows CPU utilization for the selected VM, but it won't necessarily help you get to the bottom of why this particular VM isn't performing as well as expected. In this scenario, we would fully expect the CPU Usage In MHz (Average) counter to be high; this simply tells you that the VM is using all the CPU cycles it can get. Unless the CPU Ready counters are also high, indicating that the VM is waiting on the host to schedule it onto a physical processor, you still haven't uncovered the cause of the slowness that triggered the help desk ticket. Instead, you'll need to move to monitoring host CPU usage.

Monitoring a host's overall CPU usage is fairly straightforward. Keep in mind that other factors usually come into play when looking at spare CPU capacity. Add-ons such as vMotion, vSphere DRS, and vSphere HA directly impact whether there is enough spare capacity on a server or a cluster of servers. Compared to previous versions of ESX, the VMkernel will usually not be as competitive for processor 0 because there are fewer processes to consume CPU time.

VMKERNEL STUCK ON 0

In older ESX versions, the Service Console was stuck to processor 0 only. It wouldn't get migrated to other processors even in the face of heavy contention. In ESXi there is no Service Console anymore, but the VMkernel process is still stuck on processor 0.

Perform the following steps to create a real-time chart for a host's CPU usage:

1. Launch the vSphere Web Client if it is not already running, and connect to a vCenter Server instance.

2. Navigate to the Hosts And Clusters or VMs And Templates view.

3. In the Navigator, select a host. This shows you the Summary tab.

4. Click the Performance tab, and switch to Advanced view.

5. Click the Chart Options link.

6. In the Chart Options dialog box, select the CPU resource type and the Real-Time display interval.

7. Set Chart Type to Stacked Graph (Per VM).

8. Select all objects.

   You should see a separate object for each VM hosted on the selected ESXi host.

9. Select the CPU Usage (Average) performance counter.

10. Click OK to apply the chart settings and return to the Performance tab.

This chart shows the usage of all the VMs on the selected ESXi host in a stacked fashion. From this view, you should be able to determine whether there is a specific VM or group of VMs consuming abnormal amounts of CPU capacity.

VMKERNEL BALANCING ACT

Always remember that on an oversubscribed ESXi host, the VMkernel will load balance the VMs based on current loads, reservations, and shares represented on individual VMs and/or resource pools.

In this scenario, we identified the application within the VM as CPU bound, so these two performance charts should clearly identify why the VM isn't performing well. In all likelihood, the ESXi host on which the VM is running doesn't have enough CPU capacity to satisfy the requests of all the VMs. Your solution, in this case, would be to use the resource allocation tools described in Chapter 11, "Managing Resource Allocation," to ensure that this specific application receives the resources it needs to perform at acceptable levels.

Monitoring Memory Usage

Monitoring memory usage, whether on a host or a VM, can be challenging. The monitoring itself is not difficult; it's the availability of the physical resource that can be a challenge. Of the four resources, memory can be oversubscribed without much effort. Depending on the physical form factor chosen to host VMware ESXi, running out of physical RAM is easy to do. Although the blade form factor creates a very dense consolidation effort, the blades are sometimes constrained by the amount of physical memory and network adapters that can be installed. But even with other regular form factors, having enough memory installed comes down to how much the physical server can accommodate and your budget.

If you suspect that memory usage is a performance issue, the first step is to isolate whether this is a memory shortage affecting the host (you've oversubscribed physical memory and need to add more memory) or whether this is a memory limit affecting only that VM (meaning you need to allocate more memory to this VM or change resource allocation policies). Normally, if the ESXi host is suffering from high memory utilization, the predefined vCenter Server alarm will trigger and alert the vSphere administrator. However, the alarm doesn't allow you to delve deeper into the specifics of how the host is using memory. For that, you'll need a performance chart.

Perform the following steps to create a real-time chart for a host's memory usage:

1. Connect to a vCenter Server instance with the vSphere Web Client.

2. Navigate to Hosts And Clusters view.

3. In the Navigator, click an ESXi host. This shows you the Summary tab.

4. Click the Performance tab, and switch to Advanced view.

5. Click the Chart Options link.

6. In the Chart Options dialog box, select the Memory resource type and the Real-Time display interval.

7. Select Line Graph as the chart type. The host will be selected as the only available object.

8. In the Counters area, select the Memory Usage (Average), Memory Overhead (Average), Memory Active (Average), Memory Consumed (Average), Memory Used by VMkernel, and Memory Swap Used (Average) counters.

    This should give you a fairly clear picture of how much memory the ESXi host is using.

9. Click OK to apply the chart options and return to the Performance tab.

COUNTERS, COUNTERS, AND MORE COUNTERS

As with VMs, you can utilize a plethora of counters with a host to monitor memory usage. Which ones you select will depend on what you're looking for. It is common to monitor straight memory usage, but don't forget that there are other counters that could be helpful, such as Ballooning, Unreserved, VMkernel Swap, and Shared, just to name a few. The ability to assemble the appropriate counters for finding the right information comes with experience and depends on what is being monitored.

These counters, in particular the Memory Swap Used (Average) counter, will give you an idea of whether the ESXi host is under memory pressure. If the ESXi host is not suffering from memory pressure and you still suspect a memory problem, then the issue likely lies with the VM.

Perform the following steps to create a real-time chart for a VM's memory usage:

1. Use the vSphere Web Client to connect to a vCenter Server instance.

2. Navigate to either the Hosts And Clusters or the VMs And Templates view.

3. In the Navigator, click a virtual machine. This shows you the Summary tab.

4. Click the Performance tab, and switch to the Advanced view.

5. Click the Chart Options link.

6. In the Chart Options dialog box, select the Memory resource type and the Real-Time display interval.

7. Select Line Graph as the chart type.

8. In the list of counters, select to show the Memory Usage (Average), Memory Overhead (Average), Memory Consumed (Average), and Memory Granted (Average) counters. This shows memory usage, including usage relative to the amount of memory configured for the VM.

9. Click OK to apply the chart options and return to the Performance tab.

From this performance chart, you will be able to tell how much of the memory configured for the VM is actually being used. This might reveal to you that the applications running inside that VM need more memory than the VM has been assigned and that adding more memory to the VM—assuming that there is sufficient memory at the host level—might improve performance.

Memory, like CPU, is just one of several different factors that can impact VM performance. Network usage is another area that can impact performance, especially perceived performance.

Monitoring Network Usage

vCenter Server's charts provide a wonderful tool for measuring the network usage of a VM or a host.

Monitoring network usage requires a slightly different approach than monitoring CPU or memory. With either CPU or memory, reservations, limits, and shares can dictate how much of these two resources can be consumed by any one VM. Network usage cannot be constrained by these mechanisms. Because VMs plug into a VM port group, which is part of a vSwitch on a single host, how the VM interacts with the vSwitch can be manipulated by the virtual switch's or port group's policy. For instance, if you need to restrict a VM's overall network output, you would configure traffic shaping on the port group to restrict the VM to a specific amount of outbound bandwidth. Unless you are using vSphere Distributed Switches or the Nexus 1000V third-party distributed virtual switch, there is no way to restrict VM inbound bandwidth on ESXi hosts.

VM ISOLATION

Certain VMs may indeed need to be limited to a specific amount of outbound bandwidth. Servers such as FTP, file and print, web and proxy servers, or any server whose main function is to act as a file repository or connection broker may need to be limited or the traffic may need to be shaped to an amount of bandwidth that allows it to meet its service target but not monopolize the host it runs on. Isolating any of these VMs to a vSwitch of its own is more likely a better solution, but it requires the appropriate hardware configuration.

To get an idea of how much network traffic is actually being generated, you can measure outgoing and incoming network traffic from a VM or host using the charts in vCenter Server. The charts can provide accurate information on the actual usage or ample information that a particular VM is monopolizing a virtual switch, especially using the Stacked Graph chart type.

Perform the following steps to create a real-time chart for a stacked graph of transmitted network usage by each VM on an ESXi host:

1. Launch the vSphere Web Client if it is not already running, and connect to a vCenter Server instance.

2. Navigate to either the Hosts And Clusters view or the VMs And Templates view.

3. In the Navigator, click an ESXi host. This shows you the Summary tab.

4. Click the Performance tab, and switch to Advanced view.

5. Click the Chart Options link.

6. From the Chart Options dialog box, select the Network resource type and the Real-Time display interval in the Chart Options area.

7. Select a chart type of Stacked Graph (Per VM).

8. In the objects list, be sure all the VMs are selected.

9. In the list of counters, select the Network Data Transmit Rate counter.

    This gives you an idea of how much network bandwidth each VM is consuming outbound on this ESXi host.

10. Click OK to apply the changes and return to the Performance tab.

What if you wanted a breakdown of traffic on each of the network interface cards (NICs) in the ESXi host instead of by VM? That's fairly easily accomplished by another trip back to the Chart Options dialog box.

Perform the following steps to create a real-time chart for a host's transmitted network usage by NIC:

1. Connect to a vCenter Server instance with the vSphere Web Client.

2. Navigate to the Hosts And Clusters view.

3. In the Navigator, select an ESXi host. This will show you the Summary tab in the content area to the right.

4. Select the Monitor ➤ Performance subsection, and switch to Advanced view.

5. Click the Chart Options link.

6. Under Chart Options in the Chart Options dialog box, select the Network resource type and the Real-Time display interval.

7. Set the chart type to Line Graph.

8. In the objects list, select the ESXi host as well as all the specific NICs.

9. Select the Network Data Transmit Rate and Network Packets Transmitted counters.

10. Click OK to apply the changes and return to the Performance tab.

Very much as with the previous example for a VM, these two counters will give you a window into how much network activity is occurring on this particular host in the outbound direction for each physical NIC. This is especially relevant if you want to see different rates of usage for each physical network interface, which, by definition, represent different virtual switches.

Now that you've examined how to monitor CPU, memory, and network usage, there's only one major area left: monitoring disk usage.

Monitoring Disk Usage

Monitoring a host's controller or VM's virtual disk usage is similar in scope to monitoring network usage. This resource, which represents a controller or the storing of a VM's virtual disk on a type of supported storage, isn't restricted by CPU or memory mechanisms like reservations, limits, or shares. The only way to restrict a VM's disk activity is to assign shares on the individual VM, which in turn may have to compete with other VMs running from the same storage volume. vCenter Server's charts come to our aid again in showing actual usage for both ESXi hosts and VMs.

Perform the following steps to create a host chart showing disk controller utilization:

1. Use the vSphere Web Client to connect to a vCenter Server instance.

2. Navigate to the Hosts And Clusters view.

3. In the Navigator, select an ESXi host.

   This shows you the Summary tab in the Details section on the right.

4. Select the Performance tab, and switch to the Advanced view.

5. Click the Chart Options link. This opens the Chart Options dialog box.

6. Under Chart Options, choose the Real-Time display interval for the Disk resource type.

7. Set the chart type to Line Graph.

8. Selecting an object or objects—in this case a controller—and a counter or counters lets you monitor for activity that is interesting or necessary to meet service levels. Select the objects that represent the ESXi host and one of the disk controllers.

9. In the counters list, select Disk Read Rate, Disk Write Rate, and Disk Usage (Average/Rate) to get an overall view of the activity for the selected controller.

10. Click OK to return to the Performance tab.

This performance chart will give you an idea of the activity on the selected disk controller. But what if you want to see disk activity for the entire host by each VM? In this case, a Stacked Graph view can show you what you need.

STACKED VIEWS

A stacked view is helpful in identifying whether one particular VM is monopolizing a volume. Whichever VM has the tallest stack in the comparison may be degrading the performance of other VMs' virtual disks.

Now let's switch to the virtual machine view. Looking at individual VMs for insight into their disk utilization can lead to some useful conclusions. File and print VMs, or any server that provides print queues or database services, will generate some disk-related I/O that needs to be monitored. In some cases, if the VM is generating too much I/O, it may degrade the performance of other VMs running out of the same volume. Let's take a look at a VM's chart.

Perform the following steps to create a VM chart showing real-time disk controller utilization:

1. Launch the vSphere Web Client if it is not already running, and connect to a vCenter Server instance.

2. Navigate to either the Hosts And Clusters view or the VMs And Templates view.

3. In the Navigator, click a virtual machine.

    This shows you the Summary tab in the Details section on the right.

4. Select the Performance tab, and switch to Advanced view.

5. Click the Chart Options link to open the Chart Options dialog box.

6. Under Chart Options, select the Virtual Disk resource type and the Real-Time display interval.

7. Set the chart type to Line Graph.

8. Set both objects listed in the list of objects.

9. In the list of counters, select Read Rate, Write Rate (Average/Rate).

10. Click OK to apply these changes and return to the Performance tab.

With this chart, you should have an informative picture of this VM's disk I/O behavior. This VM is busy generating reads and writes for its application. Does the chart show enough I/O to meet a service-level agreement, or does this VM need some help? The charts allow administrators to make informed decisions, usually working with the application owners, so that any adjustments to improve I/O will lead to satisfied VM owners.

In addition, by looking at longer intervals of time to gain a historical perspective, you may find that a VM has become busier or fallen off its regular output. If the amount of I/O is just slightly impaired, then adjusting the VM's shares may be a way to prioritize its disk I/O ahead of other VMs sharing the volume. The administrator may be forced to move the VM's virtual disk(s) to another volume or LUN if share adjustments don't achieve the required results. You can use Storage VMotion, described in Chapter 6, "Creating and Configuring Storage Devices," to perform this sort of LUN-based load balancing without any disruption to the end users.

PERFORMANCE MONITORING FROM THE INSIDE AND THE OUTSIDE

It's important to remember that the very nature of how virtualization operates means that it is impossible to use performance metrics from within a guest OS as an indicator of overall resource utilization. Here's why.

In a virtualized environment, each guest OS "sees" only its slice of the hardware as presented by the VMkernel. A guest OS that reports 100 percent CPU utilization isn't reporting that it's using 100 percent of the physical server's CPU but rather that it's using 100 percent of the *CPU capacity given to it by the hypervisor.* A guest OS that is reporting 90 percent RAM utilization is really only using 90 percent of the *RAM made available to it by the hypervisor.*

Does this mean that performance metrics gathered from within a guest OS are useless? No, but these metrics cannot be used to establish overall resource usage—only relative resource usage. You must combine any performance metrics gathered from within a guest OS with matching metrics gathered from outside the guest OS. By combining the metrics from within the guest OS with metrics from outside the guest OS, you can create a more complete view of how a guest OS is using a particular type of resource and therefore get a better idea of what steps to take to resolve any resource constraints.

For example, if a guest OS is reporting high memory utilization but the vCenter Server resource management tools are showing that the physical system has plenty of memory available, this tells you that the guest OS is using everything available to it and might perform better with more memory allocated to it.

Monitoring resources can be tricky, and it requires a good knowledge of the applications running in the VMs in your environment. If you are a new vSphere administrator, it's worth spending some time using vCenter Server's performance charts to establish some baseline behaviors. This helps you become much more familiar with the normal operation of the VMs so that when something unusual or out of the ordinary does occur, you'll be more likely to spot it.

The Bottom Line

Use alarms for proactive monitoring.   vCenter Server offers extensive alarms for alerting vSphere administrators to excessive resource consumption or potentially negative events. You can create alarms on virtually any type of object found within vCenter Server, including datacenters, clusters, ESXi hosts, and VMs. Alarms can monitor for resource consumption or for the occurrence of specific events. Alarms can also trigger actions, such as running a script, migrating a VM, or sending a notification email.

Master It   What are the questions a vSphere administrator should ask before creating a custom alarm?

Work with performance charts.   vCenter Server's detailed performance charts are the key to unlocking the information necessary to determine why an ESXi host or VM is performing poorly. The performance charts expose a large number of performance counters across a variety of resource types, and vCenter Server offers functionality to save customized chart settings, export performance graphs as graphic figures or Excel workbooks, and view performance charts in a separate window.

Master It   You find yourself using the Chart Options link in the Advanced layout of the Performance tab to set up the same chart over and over again. Is there a way to save yourself some time and effort so that you don't have to keep re-creating the custom chart?

Understanding vCenter Operations Manager.   vCenter Operations Manager adds to the functionality of vSphere by assisting in both performance monitoring and troubleshooting. The vC Ops analytics VM collates metrics from hosts and vCenter to calculate badges. The Web UI VM provides a standalone web interface and also integrates with the vSphere Web Client.

Master It   All standard vCenter server licenses come with vCenter Operations Manager Foundation. This version is limited to four main features. What are they?

Gather performance information using command-line tools.   VMware supplies a few command-line tools that are useful in gathering performance information. For VMware ESXi hosts, `resxtop` provides real-time information about CPU, memory, network, or disk utilization. You should run `resxtop` from the VMware vMA. Finally, the `vm-support` tool can gather performance information that can be played back later using `resxtop`.

Master It   Know how to run `resxtop` from the VMware vMA command line.

Monitor CPU, memory, network, and disk usage by ESXi hosts and VMs.   Monitoring usage of the four key resources—CPU, memory, network, and disk—can be difficult at times. Fortunately, the various tools supplied by VMware within vCenter Server can lead the vSphere administrator to the right solution. In particular, using customized performance charts can expose the right information that will help a vSphere administrator uncover the source of performance problems.

Master It   A junior vSphere administrator is trying to resolve a performance problem with a VM. You've asked this administrator to see if it is a CPU problem, and the junior administrator keeps telling you that the VM needs more CPU capacity because the CPU utilization is high within the VM. Is the junior administrator correct, based on the information available to you?

Chapter 14

Automating VMware vSphere

The role of a VMware vSphere administrator has become increasingly more demanding as the features and capabilities of vSphere have increased in both quantity and quality. VMware has done a great job of making these features quickly consumable for an administrator, as you have seen throughout this book. However, these new features lead to additional responsibilities, more opportunities for error and inconsistency, and lower tolerances for outages as more critical and complex workloads can be, and are, virtualized.

As a vSphere administrator, you will need to perform many repetitive tasks with increasingly more touch points. Examples include creating multiple VMs from a template, changing the network configuration on all VMs or ESXi hosts, migrating VMs to new datastores with Storage vMotion, and gathering considerable information about the environment for internal and external audits. Automation can help you complete these task more quickly, provide greater consistency, and ultimately save your organization money through reduced risk of errors and unplanned outages. Clearly, automation is an area that can benefit every administrator and every organization that adopts vSphere in their environment. This benefit can be realized regardless of scale or previous experience.

In this chapter, you will learn to

◆   Identify tools available for automating vSphere

◆   Create a PowerCLI script for automation

◆   Use vCLI to manage ESXi hosts from the command line

◆   Use vCenter in combination with vMA to manage all of your hosts

◆   Employ the Perl toolkit and VMware SDK for virtual server operations from the command line

◆   Configure vCenter Orchestrator

◆   Use a vCenter Orchestrator workflow

Why Use Automation?

This question comes up time and again, and over the years we have narrowed it down to a very simple reason. You are only one person. An individual is capable of performing only a finite amount of work manually in any given hour, day, or week. Automation tools allow the administrator the ability to increase their efficiency, accuracy, and capacity.

Efficiency Automation allows for the completion of repeat tasks with less effort. A phone call or colleague has never distracted a script or workflow, causing it to miss a step or complete its work in a timely manner.

Accuracy Automation allows for the consistent repetition of tasks. Configuration changes, reports, and process workflows can be automated with high confidence that errors will not be made.

Capacity Automation allows for the increased productivity of an administrator. Tasks that would take hours manually can be completed in minutes or seconds with automation.

The benefits of automation are applicable in any environment, especially virtual ones. The increased needs and expectations of businesses mean we must find ways to extend our capabilities and ensure that we deliver consistently. As you are about to see, VMware has invested heavily in tools to automate vSphere environments that are ideal for administrators with a variety of needs and backgrounds.

vSphere Automation Options

VMware has made significant improvements in the automation capabilities and options it offers. This advancement means that VMware vSphere administrators have multiple options to choose from to accomplish their automation goals regardless of their skill level or requirements. In this section, we will briefly outline the different vSphere automation tools and the existing experience that best aligns with them.

> **OTHER AUTOMATION AND ORCHESTRATION PRODUCTS**
>
> This chapter will not cover in any detail non-VMware tools that are available to automate vSphere environments. These tools take advantage of the same VMware vSphere APIs that the VMware automation tools leverage.

The vSphere automation tools discussed in this chapter are PowerCLI, vSphere Management Assistant (vMA), vCenter Orchestrator (vCO), and the vSphere Software Development Kit (SDK) for Perl (Figure 14.1). These tools are covered based on common usage in the virtualization industry and relative learning curve. Our intent is to demonstrate how even those with little or no automation experience can start leveraging these tools to automate tasks in their environment.

FIGURE 14.1
vSphere automation choices

Clearly, you have several options for bringing automation into your vSphere environment—and that is without taking into account any of the numerous third-party solutions available!

In our experience, the most widely adopted automation tool provided by VMware is PowerCLI. It appeals to people with both Windows and Linux backgrounds, as we will discuss in later sections. The vCLI on vMA is also widely used and is an easy draw to those with Linux or general command-line backgrounds. This is especially true for administrators who wish to execute bash scripts against multiple ESXi hosts with minimal effort.

Adoption of vCenter Orchestrator (vCO) is considerably less common, though we highly recommend that anyone reading this book start investing time in understanding how it works. vCO is becoming tightly woven into many VMware products, including the vSphere Web Client and vCloud Automation Center (vCAC).

AUTOMATION AND ESXI FREE VERSION

Testing in production is a bad idea. Because many administrators will want to test and learn the various automation tools outlined in this chapter, it is important to note some limitations when using the free version of ESXi. Unfortunately, remote management tools like PowerCLI, vMA, and vSphere Perl SDK are limited to read-only functionality with the free version of ESXi. Full capabilities are available at no cost by taking advantage of VMware's 60-day trial periods.

Automating with PowerCLI

PowerCLI is VMware's mostly widely adopted and accessible automation tool. Since its inception as the VI Toolkit, it has been unanimously considered the best tool for automating a vSphere environment. This claim is supported by PowerCLI's ability to manage most components in a vSphere environment and its ease of use. People with Windows administration backgrounds generally have some familiarity with PowerShell and find adopting PowerCLI more natural than adopting the other tools. Individuals comfortable with console administration will find PowerCLI very easy to pick up and use.

In the following sections, we'll introduce you to PowerShell, cover the initial configuration of PowerCLI, show you some essential PowerCLI cmdlets to start using and how to build more complicated scripts, demonstrate the complex functionality of PowerCLI, and discuss the new features found in PowerCLI 5.5.

PowerShell and PowerCLI

It is important to understand a little about what Microsoft Windows PowerShell is and how it works. Without PowerShell, PowerCLI would not be possible. PowerShell is Microsoft's standard automation platform that has shipped natively with Microsoft Windows since Windows 7 and Server 2008 but has been available for much longer. Microsoft Exchange and SharePoint administrators have been using PowerShell for many years because those products were among the earliest for which Microsoft made PowerShell the management tool of choice. Built on the .NET framework, PowerShell has tremendous capabilities for managing a wide range of Windows systems and applications. Additionally, many companies—such as VMware, NetApp, and Cisco—have developed modules and snap-ins for PowerShell for managing their applications and hardware. In this section we'll briefly cover some core concepts about PowerShell that will help you get started with PowerCLI.

POWERSHELL V3 NEW FEATURES

PowerShell v3 comes with many new enhancements that can be extremely advantageous when managing vSphere with PowerCLI 5.5. Here are a few:

◆ Workflows and more robust sessions mean long or complex operations are less likely to fail.

◆ Improved cmdlet discovery and automatic module loading are especially useful when adding community resources.

◆ The Show-Command cmdlet provides a visual dialog box, allowing users to identify a cmdlet's parameters.

CMDLETS

The first PowerShell term that needs defining is *cmdlets* (pronounced "command-lets"), which are compiled .NET classes that perform a single action on an object. Their format is <verb> -<singular noun>. For the most part cmdlets are simple to use because they don't attempt to do too much at once. Also, because there is an established naming convention, often you can find the cmdlet you need by simply guessing. For instance, to get all the VMs in vCenter, you run Get-VM—intuitive by design.

OBJECTS

PowerShell is built on the Microsoft .NET Framework, and as such, objects are a critical component to understand in order to be successful with PowerCLI. Put simply, an object is a container of properties and methods. When you execute the PowerCLI cmdlet Get-VM while connected to a Virtual Center server, the information that is returned is a collection of virtual machine objects. Each VM can be treated as its own object that contains unique information for that VM. The information for VM A and VM B will be different, but they will be the same type of object, or container. This means that you can filter or compare properties of each object because they share the same format. To do this, it helps to understand what properties are available. You can do this a variety of ways. We'll show you how to quickly get general and detailed information from an object.

ABOUT THIS SECTION

The information in this section will be more meaningful once you have installed PowerCLI and connected to your virtual environment. We recommend returning to this section at that time and trying out the steps listed next.

General information can be gained by simply entering the cmdlet and reviewing the output. The default output provided has been programmed into PowerCLI to return the most commonly wanted properties of the given object. For instance, running the `Get-VM` cmdlet will return *all* of the VMs in the inventory with the attributes VM name, power state, number of CPUs, and memory (MB). You can specify which information you want to see using the `Select-Object` cmdlet in the pipeline as follows:

```
Get-VM | Select-Object Name, PowerState
```

If you would like to see all information associated with all of the VMs, then you could run the following one-liner with the second option demonstrating the very common `Select-Object` alias `Select`:

```
Get-VM | Select-Object *
OR
Get-VM | Select *
```

We recommend outputting that to a CSV or text file because it's likely to fill up the screen quickly. You can do that by piping to the `Export-CSV` cmdlet:

```
Get-VM | Select * | Export-CSV -Path C:\Test\VMs.csv -NoTypeInformation
```

We mentioned previously that you can get more detailed information about objects. Using `Select *` gives you a full output of all property values, but there is an easier way to identify what properties are available. Using the `Get-Member` cmdlet, you can get a full listing of available properties and methods of a particular object type. Try one of the following where the second option uses GM, the shortened alias for `Get-Member`:

```
Get-VM | Get-Member
OR
Get-VM | GM
```

We have one final tip before moving on to other important PowerShell terms. If you have a large inventory and want things to run faster while you learn, use the capability in the `Select -Object` cmdlet to select only the first couple of returned objects. The following one-liner will return the first three VM objects in your inventory:

```
Get-VM | Select -First 3
```

We'll go over more functionality with objects, but this should give you a taste of how simple it is to select properties that you're interested in and a better understanding of the structure of objects in PowerShell/PowerCLI.

VARIABLES

Variables are not unique to PowerShell; they are used in many programming and scripting languages. In PowerShell, variables begin with a $ followed by alphanumeric characters. There are both global and user-defined variables, and we'll touch on examples of each.

The easiest way to think of a variable is as an empty container where we can store objects within PowerShell. Most common use cases for variables are to collect results of a script or to store information that will be used later in a script. Building on our example in the discussion of objects, let's say we wish to collect all of the VM objects into a variable for later use:

```
$vm = Get-VM | Select-Object Name, PowerState
```

The variable $vm now contains all of the same data that was produced when we ran the one-liner earlier. You can now simply type $vm into the PowerCLI console and you'll see the same results. This means you can do a variety of things with the variable later in your console or in scripts:

```
$vm | Export-CSV -Path C:\Test\VMs.csv -NoTypeInformation
$vm | Where-Object{$_.PowerState -eq "PoweredOn"}
```

Keep in mind that there are also global variables already in use with PowerShell and PowerCLI. You can get a full listing of them with the Get-Variable cmdlet. Most notably, keep in mind that $host is already in use by the system and cannot be set within your scripts. It is common to use $vm and $vmhost instead. You'll also learn about $DefaultVIserver in the section later in this chapter on connecting to your virtual infrastructure with PowerCLI.

You'll see the use of variables throughout this chapter and when you're looking at code examples from both VMware and the community. Always be mindful not to use the same variable twice in your script, and try to name the variable so it's easy to discern what information is located within that container.

PIPELINE

At the base of PowerShell's capability is the *pipeline*. Those coming from a Unix background will be well versed in the concept of a pipeline. However, PowerShell took the traditional pipeline and kicked it up a notch. In the past, pipelines were a means to pass text from one command to another, simplifying the syntax of a given operation. In PowerShell, pipelines are a means to pass whole .NET objects from one cmdlet to another. This ability greatly increased the power of the pipeline while simplifying its ability to accomplish almost any administrative action. In short, this means that as you use PowerCLI cmdlets, you'll be able to pass a Cluster object through the pipeline and retrieve all of the hosts within that single cluster. In this example, we do so and then check each VMhost object so that we return only those that are in maintenance mode.

```
Get-Cluster <cluster name> | Get-VMhost | `
  Where{$_.ConnectionState -eq "Maintenance"}
```

CONTINUING PIPELINE OVER MULTIPLE LINES

When using PowerShell and the pipeline, you may have lines that do not fit cleanly on the screen or your editor. In this book we use the ` symbol to indicate that the code continues onto the next line. This symbol is recognized by PowerShell to continue the current pipeline even though it is written on a separate line. An attempt is made with each use to make the break logical in order to maintain the readability of the code.

Alternatively, you could check all of your clusters for hosts in maintenance mode. Doing so means that you pass a collection of all Cluster objects in inventory through the pipeline and then gather the VMhosts that are in maintenance mode:

```
Get-Cluster | Get-VMhost | Where{$_.ConnectionState -eq "Maintenance"}
```

Note that the `Where-Object` cmdlet, using the alias `Where`, is collecting the VMhost objects to check for the `ConnectionState` property value. This is just a touch of what the pipeline can really provide as you pass objects through. You will see many more examples of the pipeline throughout this chapter, and hopefully the concepts of objects and the pipeline will become second nature to you.

What's New in PowerCLI 5.5

Each version of PowerCLI has included new cmdlets to take advantage of the many new features provided in vSphere. PowerCLI 5.5 provides improvements to existing cmdlets, support for Windows PowerShell 3.0, and the long-awaited Virtual Distributed Switch (VDS) snap-in. The VDS snap-in now provides native capabilities for automating and managing distributed switches and distributed port groups. This gives vSphere administrators the ability to script tasks like adding or removing hosts from a distributed virtual switch, migrating virtual network adapters from standard to distributed port groups, and even import, clone, or roll back the configuration of a distributed virtual switch or distributed port group. We recommend taking some time to review the PowerCLI 5.5 release notes for a full breakdown of the new capabilities, improvements of previous cmdlets, and known issues.

Installing and Configuring PowerCLI

To install PowerCLI 5.5, you must have Microsoft Windows PowerShell v2.0 or v3 as well as .NET Framework 2.0SP2, 3.0, or 3.5 (Figure 14.2). We recommend that you go ahead and upgrade PowerShell to version 3, given that it is now supported with PowerCLI 5.5 and includes several valuable new features, as mentioned previously. At the time of this writing, PowerShell v4 has been announced, but no announcement of PowerCLI support of PowerShell v4 has been made.

FIGURE 14.2
PowerShell 2
required

Installing PowerCLI actually means installing two different components:

◆ PowerShell is a core component of Windows since Windows 7, but if you're running an older version of Windows, you'll need to install the Windows Management Framework, available for download from Microsoft's website at www.microsoft.com/download.

◆ PowerCLI is available for download from VMware's website at www.vmware.com/go/PowerCLI.

Perform the following steps to install PowerCLI:

1. Launch the PowerCLI installer that you downloaded from VMware's website.

2. Click Continue if prompted by Microsoft Windows User Access Control.

3. If the installer displays a dialog box informing you that VMware VIX will be installed at the end of setup, click OK to continue.

4. If a message is displayed warning that the PowerShell execution policy is currently set to Restricted, click Continue. You will change this later.

5. On the first screen of the VMware vSphere PowerCLI Installation Wizard, click Next to start the installation.

6. Select the radio button marked "I Accept The Terms In The License Agreement" (assuming you have read and accept the terms), and click Next.

7. Click Next to accept the default installation location, or change the location where PowerCLI will be installed.

8. Choose the option to install vCloud Director if you plan to use PowerCLI to manage your vCloud Director environment. Then click Next.

9. Click Install.

PowerCLI 64-bit versus PowerCLI 32-bit

If you installed PowerCLI on a 64-bit operating system, you'll notice that you have two icons on your Desktop: one for 64-bit and one for 32-bit. There is only one major functionality difference between the two that you should be aware of. When executing certain PowerCLI cmdlets in environments earlier than vSphere 5.0, you'll need to run PowerCLI 32-bit. Examples include Invoke-VMscript and Copy-VMGuestFile.

Reference the PowerCLI 5.5 release notes for a full list of the 32-bit-only cmdlets.

You have now successfully installed PowerCLI 5.5, and you should see two shortcuts for PowerCLI on your Desktop. However, you're not quite ready to start scripting. Even though you have installed PowerCLI, you still need to modify the script execution policy of PowerShell.

Perform the following steps to set the PowerShell script execution policy:

1. Right-click one of the PowerCLI Desktop shortcuts, and select Run As Administrator.

2. At the PowerShell prompt, enter the following command:

```
Set-ExecutionPolicy RemoteSigned
```

3. Type **Y** and press Enter to validate the change when prompted, or simply press Enter to accept the default Y.

4. To verify the setting, use the `Get-ExecutionPolicy` cmdlet:

`Get-ExecutionPolicy`

The `Get-ExecutionPolicy` cmdlet should return `RemoteSigned`.

5. Type **Exit** and press Enter to close the PowerCLI/PowerShell session.

Now when you relaunch PowerCLI, you are greeted with several excellent starting cmdlets, such as `Connect-VIServer`, `Get-VIcommand`, and `Get-PowerCLIHelp` (Figure 14.3). These suggestions are important, especially since `Connect-VIServer` is a required first cmdlet for connecting to your virtual infrastructure. You're now ready to get started with PowerCLI!

FIGURE 14.3
The PowerCLI startup screen provides quick tips on a few useful commands.

POWERSHELL SCRIPT EXECUTION POLICY

The PowerShell script execution policy allows you to manage which scripts can be run on your computer. By default, PowerShell is run as *Restricted*, which means that no scripts can be run and PowerShell can run only in interactive console mode. This also includes PowerCLI. The recommended setting is *RemoteSigned*, which allows scripts that you write as well as those signed by a trusted publisher, such as VMware. You will likely see recommendations to set the execution policy to *Unrestricted*, which will allow you to run all Windows PowerShell/PowerCLI scripts. This certainly makes things easier for troubleshooting, but you should consider the security of the system before setting the execution policy to Unrestricted. Unrestricted allows even malicious scripts to run.

You can learn more about PowerShell script execution policies by entering the following into a PowerShell/PowerCLI console:

`get-help about_Execution_Policies`

ADDITIONAL POWERCLI CAPABILITIES

VMware has also released a variety of other PowerShell snap-ins to work alongside PowerCLI to manage vSphere environments. Snap-ins for Auto Deploy, Image Builder, Licensing, and the new VDS capabilities are included during the core PowerCLI 5.5 installation. You'll note during the install that there is a custom option to also install and enable the vCloud Director snap-in. Additional snap-ins are available for download to manage VMware View and VMware Update Manager (VUM), and installation of these snap-ins is similar to the PowerCLI installation. The core PowerCLI components include over 370 cmdlets providing considerable capabilities, with more available with the additional snap-ins.

POWERCLI BACKWARD COMPATIBILITY

VMware has done an excellent job making the newest version of PowerCLI backward compatible with previous versions of vSphere. You'll always want to check the release notes of the latest version of PowerCLI to ensure that your scripts will run properly against your environment. PowerCLI 5.5 supports vSphere 4.0 Update 4 and greater.

One exception to backward compatibility with PowerCLI is with the VMware Update Manager (VUM) snap-in. You'll always need to have the version of the snap-in that matches the version of VUM you are running. Keep this in mind when upgrading PowerCLI. In our environments, we would generally have a specific server, sometimes the separate VUM server itself, configured with the correct version so that we could update our core systems more freely.

Getting Started with PowerCLI

The first and most important thing to remember about PowerCLI is that the PowerShell <verb>-<noun> nomenclature for cmdlets makes them easy to read and also makes it easy to find the right cmdlets for the job. In the following sections, we'll go through the basics starting points of PowerCLI. By the end of this discussion, you'll be able to connect PowerCLI to your vSphere resources, locate the cmdlet that you need, get information about how to use that cmdlet, and start creating "one-liner" scripts. These are the first steps to automating vSphere with PowerCLI and skills that you will use frequently as you become a more mature user.

FINDING CMDLETS

VMware has provided a special cmdlet in PowerCLI to aid in finding the cmdlet that you need, Get-VICommand. Get-VICommand is much like Get-Command but is specific to the PowerCLI-provided cmdlets. Let's say that you are looking for available cmdlets for managing your logs. Using the following code, you'll receive a listing of available log cmdlets:

```
Get-VICommand *log*
```

Alternatively, you could also use the Get-Command cmdlet and narrow your search criteria to only the <noun> section of the cmdlet.

```
Get-Command -Noun *log*
```

If you tried these cmdlets, you'll notice that using the Get-Command cmdlet returns more results. Why is this? The Get-Command cmdlet will return all PowerShell cmdlets that contain log in the cmdlet noun section, whereas Get-VICommand will return only those associated with PowerCLI.

If you're using PowerShell version 3, you can then use the Show-Command cmdlet to get a visual of the cmdlet and its parameters.

Also keep in mind that PowerShell provides tab completion for all cmdlets. This means that if you type **Get-VM** and press Tab, PowerShell will start sorting through all of the available cmdlets that begin with Get-VM, starting with Get-VM and then Get-VMGuest. This is not usually the fastest method of finding the cmdlet you're looking for, but it certainly works when you're in a pinch. Tab completion also works within the cmdlet. Pressing the spacebar after a cmdlet and then pressing Tab repeatedly will cycle you through the list of parameters for which you can specify values.

GETTING HELP

It doesn't matter how long you have been working with PowerShell or PowerCLI, there will always be times when you need help. PowerShell provides a very useful cmdlet for just this occasion, Get-Help. Get-Help can provide helpful information about cmdlets or topics within PowerShell. Simply type the cmdlet in your console and press Enter for a breakdown of its capabilities. In the context of PowerCLI, we want to show you how you can get more information from the cmdlets you located previously using Get-VIcommand.

Once you identify the cmdlet you need, you can use Get-Help to find out more about it, like the parameters or parameter sets, description of how it is used, and examples of how to use the it. Try this:

```
Get-Help Get-Log
```

You should notice that it returns a brief synopsis of what Get-Log will do, the syntax for usage, a more detailed description, and links associated with the cmdlet. If you're specifically looking for examples of how to use the cmdlet, simply use the -examples parameter:

```
Get-Help Get-Log -examples
```

There are several other parameters to choose from under the Remarks section, but the most common to use are -full and -examples.

CONNECTING TO vCENTER SERVER AND ESXi HOSTS

The first cmdlet that any PowerCLI user has to know is Connect-VIServer. This cmdlet has many features that make connecting to your vCenter Server or ESXi hosts easy. We'll go over a few of those features in this section. If you'd like to see the full capabilities of Connect-VIServer, you can check the PowerCLI help by entering the following:

```
get-help Connect-VIServer -full
```

Connecting to vCenter Server is the most common use of Connect-VIServer. To connect, you'll need to provide at least the vCenter Server name, a username, and a password:

```
Connect-VIServer -server <vCenter Server Name> `
 -user <username> -password <password>
```

This works well but is certainly not something you'd want to do with someone looking over your shoulder or as part of a script that you may want to share. Including a password in plaintext is simply asking for trouble. PowerCLI will natively use the user's credentials for the system login. If your account has vCenter access, no credentials are required. Many organizations follow the practice of separate administrative accounts, and as such it is important to demonstrate ways to protect credentials. To solve this problem, you can securely prompt for credentials in your scripts and store them encrypted in a variable using the Get-Credential cmdlet. When you call Get-Credential in a script, it will prompt the user for a username and password. It then stores them in the pscredential object, which can then be used by Connect-VIServer as follows:

```
$credential = Get-Credential
Connect-VIServer -server <vCenter Server Name> -Credential $credential
```

The best part of this method, aside from security, is that the $credential variable information remains as long as your PowerCLI session is opened or until you replace it with new information. This means you can have the same variable set to different credentials in different instances of PowerCLI. This is ideal for running multiple scripts simultaneously on the same system and prevents people from seeing your virtual environment credentials if they're not supposed to.

You can also connect to multiple vCenter Server instances or ESXi hosts in the same session by separating them with a comma:

```
Connect-VIServer -server vCenter1,vCenter2 -Credential $credential
```

Here is one final Connect-VIServer tip for vSphere administrators running multiple vCenter Server instances in linked mode. If you have common permissions for an account across vCenter servers in linked mode, you can connect to all of those instances with PowerCLI using the -AllLinked parameter:

```
Connect-VIServer -server vCenter1 -Credential $credential -AllLinked:$true
```

Before we leave the Connect-VIServer cmdlet, it's important to know its counterpart, Disconnect-VIServer. If you run Disconnect-VIServer by itself in the PowerCLI console, you will prompted for verification that you want to disconnect from the server. You can press Enter and it will disconnect from the active server (identified by VIServer). If you are connected to multiple systems, this command will not disconnect from all of them by default. You can accomplish this by specifying the name of the systems you wish to disconnect from or using a wildcard *. Use the -Confirm parameter to prevent being prompted to disconnect:

```
Disconnect-VIServer -Server vCenter1,vCenter2 -Confirm:$false
Disconnect-VIServer * -Confirm:$false
```

You may wish to verify what vCenter servers or ESXi hosts you are connected to. Do this by simply typing in the variable **$DefaultVIServers**. You can also identify the current default system by typing **$DefaultVIServer**. The default server is the one disconnected if no server is specified when using Disconnect-VIServer.

YOUR FIRST ONE-LINER: REPORTING

The most common use of PowerCLI is reporting. A vSphere administrator can gather tremendous amounts of data about their environment in a very short period of time. Previously, in the discussion about the pipeline, we showed you how quickly you can identify the hosts in your environment that are in maintenance mode. That small script is called a one-liner. One-liners are scripts that can be written out and executed in a single line using the pipeline to pass information. Let's now combine a few things we've discussed to show you how you can gener-ate quick reports about your environment.

Since ESXi no longer stores logging information for any extended period of time, it is impor-tant to have all of your ESXi hosts point their syslog data to an external location. Failure to do so would mean that logs would be lost at reboot. How do you know which hosts are configured and which are not? Using PowerCLI, you can find that information very quickly:

```
Get-VMhost | Get-VMHostSyslogServer |`
  Export-CSV E:\Reports\Syslog.csv -NoTypeInformation
```

This one-liner gathers a collection of all of your ESXi hosts in inventory and then collects the syslog server settings for each host. The final pipeline takes that syslog server information for the hosts and exports it to a CSV file. You may note that this script does not tell you *which* host has what configuration!

You can fix this by creating a parameter for the VMHost object in the pipeline. This is an intermediate PowerShell technique but one we want to show you because it is very helpful with cmdlets like Get-VMHostSyslogServer and Get-VMHostNTPServer:

```
Get-VMHost | Select Name, @{N="SyslogServer";E={$_ |Get-VMHostSyslogServer}} |`
  Export-CSV E:\Reports\Syslog.csv -NoTypeInformation
```

Now that you have this information, what do you do if you have multiple ESXi hosts with the incorrect syslog settings? Write a one-liner to update them of course!

YOUR FIRST ONE-LINER: CONFIGURATION CHANGE

PowerCLI is not just for reporting data on the environment. You also have the capability to mod-ify the environment, assuming you have the appropriate privileges. In the preceding section, you identified systems that did not have the correct syslog settings. To change them, you need to identify the supporting cmdlet. In situations like this, where a Get- verb is used in a cmdlet, it is common that a Set- verb is also available. In this instance, you'll want to use the Set-VMHostSyslogServer cmdlet. Get-Help Set-VMHostSyslogServer -full tells you that you'll need to specify the -SyslogServer parameter and perhaps the -SysLogServerPort parameter if the syslog collector is listening on a specific port. Assume in this scenario that you are send-ing your logs to the VMware syslog collector on a server with IP address 192.168.0.100. Go ahead and specify port 514:

```
Get-VMHost | Set-VMHostSyslogServer -SysLogServer`
  192.168.0.100 -SysLogServerPort 514
```

You may have noticed that this one-liner does more than set the correct syslog server settings on the systems that had the incorrect settings. It actually sets the settings on all of the VMHosts collected with Get-VMHost. While this is not necessarily a problem, it could take a long time to run in large environments. Let's assume that you wish to change only those that are not correct.

If you have a small environment, we recommend just running the previous one-liner to update all systems with each pass. If, however, you have a large environment or a strong desire to update only the incorrect settings, let's move forward. We're going to build on what we've gone over previously and use some new PowerShell techniques. Let's identify the hosts with the incorrect setting and update them with a single one-liner:

```
Get-VMHost | Select Name, @{N="SyslogServer";E={$_ |Get-VMHostSyslogServer}} |`
```

```
Where{$_.SyslogServer -notlike "192.168.0.100:514"} |`
Set-VMHostSyslogServer -SysLogServer 192.168.0.100 -SysLogServerPort 514
```

If you are following along, you'll note that this throws up an error. We wanted to show you how this method has changed the VMHost object type, which `Set-VMHostSyslogServer` cannot accept through the pipeline. One way to fix this is by using a ForEach loop (using the common alias %) so that you process each VMHost and changing its object type back to something `Set-VMhostSyslogServer` can use:

```
Get-VMHost | Select Name, @{N="SyslogServer";E={$_ |Get-VMHostSyslogServer}} |`
Where{$_.SyslogServer -notlike "192.168.0.100:514"} |`
%{Set-VMHostSyslogServer -VMhost (Get-VMHost -Name $_.Name)`
-SysLogServer 192.168.0.100 -SysLogServerPort 514}
```

Thanks for following along. We recognize that we had to do a few new things there to accomplish something relatively simple. We wanted to go through this exercise to demonstrate the value of the pipeline, the importance of understanding objects, and how much can be done with a single line of PowerCLI code. You should now have enough exposure to start branching beyond one-liners into multiline PowerCLI scripts.

Building PowerCLI Scripts

You have seen that one-liners are nothing more than a series of PowerCLI cmdlets strung into a series of PowerShell pipelines. Scripts can often be as straightforward as a one-liner saved to a text file with a `.ps1` filename extension for future reuse. Many times, as you have seen, it is necessary to do multiple steps to accomplish your automation goal. This is where you begin to tie all of the topics we've discussed together. With that in mind, we will cover a few more examples of how PowerCLI can make your life easier.

MIGRATING ALL VIRTUAL MACHINES ON A HOST

In the first example, you'll build a simple pipeline using multiple PowerCLI cmdlets. By combining cmdlets in a pipeline, you can build more complex commands, such as the following:

```
Get-VMHost <FirstHost> | Get-VM | Move-VM -destination (Get-VMHost <SecondHost>)
```

This command relocates all VMs on the ESXi host specified by `FirstHost` to the ESXi host represented by `SecondHost`. This includes both running VMs, which are moved with VMotion, as well as powered-off VMs. Notice that we use parentheses when defining the destination VMHost. PowerShell will run the content within the parentheses first and use the result for the -destination parameter. This is similar to the mathematical order of operations.

You could also do this action by storing the source and destination VMHost in a variable:

```
$SourceHost = Get-VMHost <FirstHost>
$DestinationHost = Get-VMHost <SecondHost>
Get-VMHost $SourceHost | Get-VM | Move-VM -destination $DestinationHost
Set-VMHost $SourceHost -State Maintenance
```

Suffice it to say there are always multiple ways to accomplish the same thing.

MANIPULATING VIRTUAL MACHINE SNAPSHOTS

Let's look at a second example of how to use PowerCLI in your VMware vSphere environment. In this example, you'll use PowerCLI to work with VM snapshots.

Let's say that you need to perform an application upgrade for a system with multiple servers. It may be useful to create a snapshot for all the VMs associated with that application, which you have organized in a vCenter inventory folder. This one-liner would accomplish that task for you:

```
Get-Folder <Folder Name> | Get-VM | New-Snapshot -Name "Pre-Upgrade"
```

If you later needed to remove the snapshot you created, you could use the Remove-Snapshot cmdlet to delete it:

```
Get-Folder <Folder Name> | Get-VM | Get-Snapshot -Name "Pre-Upgrade " |`
  Remove-Snapshot
```

Finally, you could use the Get-Snapshot cmdlet to list all snapshots so that you could be sure you had actually created or deleted them:

```
Get-Folder <Folder Name> | Get-VM | Get-Snapshot
```

This command would return a list of any snapshot objects for all the VMs in the specified folder.

RECONFIGURING VIRTUAL MACHINE NETWORKING

In this third example, let's say that you want to move all the VMs currently connected to one port group to an entirely different port group. This is actually possible with a one-line command in PowerCLI:

```
Get-VM | Get-NetworkAdapter | Where-Object {$_.NetworkName -like `
  "OldPortGroupName"} | Set-NetworkAdapter -NetworkName "NewPortGroupName"`
  -Confirm:$false
```

There are a few of the new ideas introduced here, so let us break it down a little bit:

- The Get-VM cmdlet retrieves VM objects.

- These VM objects are passed to the Get-NetworkAdapter cmdlet, which returns virtual NIC objects for all VMs.

- These virtual NIC objects are parsed using the Where-Object cmdlet to include only those virtual NICs whose NetworkName property is like the "OldPortGroupName" string.

- The parsed list of virtual NICs is passed to the Set-NetworkAdapter cmdlet, which sets the NetworkName property to the "NewPortGroupName" value.

- The Confirm parameter instructs PowerShell to not ask the user for confirmation of each operation.

MOVING VIRTUAL MACHINES BETWEEN RESOURCE POOLS

In this last example, you'll use PowerCLI to move a group of VMs from one resource pool to another. However, you want to move only a subset of the VMs in this resource pool. Only the VMs that are running a Microsoft Windows guest operating system (guest OS) should be moved to the new resource pool.

We'll build this example in steps. First, you've probably guessed that you can use the Get-ResourcePool, Get-VM, and Get-VMGuest cmdlets to create a list of VM guest OS objects in the resource pool:

```
Get-ResourcePool <ResourcePoolName> | Get-VM | Get-VMGuest
```

Next, you would need to filter the output to return only those objects identified as Microsoft Windows guest OSes. As you saw in a previous example, you can use the Where-Object cmdlet to filter the output list in a pipeline:

```
Get-ResourcePool <ResourcePoolName> | Get-VM | Get-VMGuest |
Where-Object { $_.OSFullName -match "^Microsoft Windows.*" }
```

This should do it, right? To finish the command, you should be able to add the Move-VM cmdlet and move the VMs to the destination resource pool. Unfortunately, that won't work. You're working with objects with PowerShell, and a VM guest OS object—which is what is being returned by the Get-VMGuest cmdlet—isn't the kind of object that the Move-VM cmdlet will accept as input.

Instead, you'll have to use a multiline script for this, as shown in Listing 14.1.

LISTING 14.1: A PowerCLI script to selectively move VMs to a new resource pool

```
$VMs = Get-VM -Location (Get-ResourcePool Infrastructure)
foreach ($vm in $VMs) {
$vmguest = Get-VMGuest -VM $vm
if ($vmguest.OSFullName -match "^Microsoft Windows.*") {
Move-VM -VM $vm -Destination (Get-ResourcePool "Windows VMs") } }
```

Again, we'll break down the script so that it is easier to understand:

- Line 1 uses the Get-VM and Get-ResourcePool cmdlets to retrieve a list of VM objects in the specified resource pool. That list of VM objects is stored in the $VMs variable.

- Line 2 creates a loop that operates for each of the objects in the $VMs variable. Each individual VM object is stored as $vm.

- Line 3 uses the Get-VMGuest cmdlet with the $vm variable to retrieve the guest OS object for that VM object and store the result in the $vmguest variable.

- Line 4 tests to see whether the OSFullName property of the $vmguest object matches a string starting with Microsoft Windows.

- Line 5 executes only if the test on the fourth line was successful; if it executes, it uses the Move-VM and Get-ResourcePool cmdlets to move the VM object represented by the $vm variable to the resource pool named Windows VMs.

If you were to save the script in Listing 14.1 as MoveWindowsVMs.ps1, then you could run it in PowerCLI like this:

```
<Path to Script>\MoveWindowsVMs.ps1
```

There is so much more that you can do with PowerShell and PowerCLI; these simple examples barely scratch the surface. In the next section, we'll look at some of the advanced capabilities available to automate vSphere with PowerCLI.

PowerCLI Advanced Capabilities

You should now have a fair understanding of the many possibilities for automating a vSphere environment with PowerCLI. We'd like to spend a little time demonstrating some advanced functionality that is available to you to directly leverage the vSphere vCenter API.

PowerCLI users are not limited to just the cmdlets included in PowerCLI 5.5. VMware extends the capabilities of PowerCLI by allowing users to access various methods and information within the vSphere API. The Get-View cmdlet gives PowerCLI users the ability to call these methods as part of their PowerCLI scripts or directly from the PowerShell console.

In Listing 14.2, we share a situation where we recognized functionality in the vCenter server that was not natively available in the PowerCLI cmdlets. Specifically, when attempting to vMotion a VM, we recognized that vCenter would perform checks to verify that the prerequisites for vMotion to that host were met. If something was found to be incorrect, vCenter would notify the administrator that vMotion could not be performed and generally identify the root cause. What we wanted to accomplish was to check every VM in a cluster prior to a scheduled maintenance window, allowing us to identify any issues prior to the scheduled maintenance and address them to minimize delays or the need to roll back.

LISTING 14.2: A PowerCLI function to test vMotion capabilities of VMs

```
Function Test-vMotion{
 param(
  [CmdletBinding()]
  [Parameter(ValueFromPipeline=$true,Position=0,Mandatory=$false,`
    HelpMessage="Enter the Cluster to be checked")]
  [PSObject[]]$Cluster,
  [Parameter(ValueFromPipeline=$false,Position=1,Mandatory=$false,`
    HelpMessage="Enter the VM you wish to migrate")]
  [PSObject[]]$VM,
  [Parameter(ValueFromPipeline=$false,Position=2,Mandatory=$false,`
    HelpMessage="Enter the Destination Host")]
  [PSObject[]]$VMHost,
  [Parameter(ValueFromPipeline=$false,Position=3,Mandatory=$false,`
    HelpMessage="Set to false to Turn off console writing for use in Scheduled Tasks")]
  [Boolean]$Console=$true
 )
$report = @()
#Sets information based on type of work being done.
#Whole cluster or single VM
  If($Cluster -ne $null){
    If($VM -ne $null){
      If($Console = $true){
        Write-Host "VM value $VM cannot be used`
          when using -Cluster paramenter. Value is being set to null"
      }
```

```
                    $VM = $null
            }
        If($VMHost -ne $null){
            $DestHost = Get-VMHost $VMHost
            If(($DestHost.ConnectionState -ne "Connected") -or`
                ($DestHost.PowerState -ne "PoweredOn")){
                Return "You must provide a target host that is Powered on and`
                    not in Maintenance Mode or Disconnected"
            }
        }
        $singlevm = $false
        $targetcluster = Get-Cluster $Cluster
        $vms = $targetcluster | Get-VM | `
          Where{$_.PowerState -eq "PoweredON"} | Sort-Object
        $vmhosts = $targetcluster | Get-VMHost | Where{($_.ConnectionState -eq "Connected")
 -and ($_.PowerState -eq "PoweredOn")}
            If ($vmhosts.Count -lt 2){
                Return "You must provide a target host that is not`
                    the source host $sourcehost"
            }
        $count = $vms.Count
        If($Console = $true){
            Write-Host "Checking $count VMs in cluster $cluster"
        }
    } ELSE {
        $vms = Get-VM $VM
        If($VMHost -eq $null){
            $DestHost = Get-Cluster -VM $vms | Get-VMHost | `
            Where{($_.ConnectionState -eq "Connected") -and `
            ($_.PowerState -eq "PoweredOn")} | Get-Random | Where{$_ -ne $vms.VMhost}
        } ELSE {
            $DestHost = Get-VMHost $VMHost
        }
        $singlevm = $true
    }
    #   Functional Loop
    foreach($v in $vms) {
        If($Console = $true){
            Write-Host "------------------------"
            Write-Host "Checking $v ..."
        }
        $sourcehost = $v.VMhost
        If($singlevm -eq $false){
            While(($DestHost -eq $null) -or ($DestHost -eq $sourcehost)){
                #Select random host from the cluster in the event that Source and Destination
                #are the same or Destination is Null.
                $DestHost = $vmhosts | Get-Random | Where{($_ -ne $sourcehost)`
                  -and ($_ -ne $null)}
```

```
      }
   }
   If($Console = $true){
      Write-Host "from $sourcehost to $DestHost"
   }
   #   Set Variables needed for CheckMigrate Method
   $pool = ($v.ResourcePool).ExtensionData.MoRef
   $vmMoRef = $v.ExtensionData.MoRef
   $hsMoRef = $DestHost.ExtensionData.MoRef

   $si = Get-View ServiceInstance -Server $global:DefaultVIServer
   $VmProvCheck = get-view $si.Content.VmProvisioningChecker
   $result = $VmProvCheck.CheckMigrate( $vmMoRef, $hsMoRef, $pool, $null, $null )

   # Organize Output
   $Output = "" | Select VM, SourceHost, DestinationHost,`
      Error, Warning, CanMigrate
   $Output.VM = $v.Name
   $Output.SourceHost = $sourcehost
   $Output.DestinationHost = $DestHost.Name

   #   Parse Error and Warning messages
   If($result[0].Warning -ne $null){
      $Output.Warning = $result[0].Warning[0].LocalizedMessage
      $Output.CanMigrate = $true
      If($Console = $true){
        Write-Host -ForegroundColor Yellow`
           "$v has warning but can still migrate"
      }
   }
   If($result[0].Error -ne $null){
      $Output.Error = $result[0].Error[0].LocalizedMessage
      $Output.CanMigrate = $False
      If($Console = $true){
        Write-Host -ForegroundColor Red "$v has error and can not migrate"
      }
   }Else {
      $Output.CanMigrate = $true
      If($Console = $true){
        Write-Host -ForegroundColor Green "$v is OK"
      }
   }
   $report += $Output
   #This resets the Destination Host to the preferred host
   #in case it had to be changed.
   If($VMHost -ne $null){
      $DestHost = Get-VMHost $VMHost
   }
```

```
    }
    Return $report
    #    End Function
}
```

To accomplish this, we had to identify the method used in the vSphere API. VMware publishes the vSphere API reference at www.vmware.com/support/pubs/sdk_pubs.html. In that reference we were able to locate the CheckMigrate method. The documentation outlines the required information to invoke the method. You should note in the provided script that we collect those components, the VM, the destination host, and the resource pool as variables in the script prior to calling the CheckMigrate method. The entirety of the script revolves around the small amount of code listed here. Most of the script works on setting the required variables to use the CheckMigrate method and then handling the output of that method:

```
#    Set Variables needed for CheckMigrate Method
     $pool = ($v.ResourcePool).ExtensionData.MoRef
     $vmMoRef = $v.ExtensionData.MoRef
     $hsMoRef = $DestHost.ExtensionData.MoRef

     $si = Get-View ServiceInstance -Server $global:DefaultVIServer
     $VmProvCheck = get-view $si.Content.VmProvisioningChecker
     $result = $VmProvCheck.CheckMigrate($vmMoRef,$hsMoRef,$pool,$null,$null)
```

You should also note that this script is built as a PowerShell function. This means it is designed to be loaded into a PowerShell console session and used like a cmdlet. For example, once you have loaded the function, you can call this command:

```
Get-Cluster "ClusterName" | Test-vMotion
```

LOADING POWERSHELL FUNCTIONS

When you receive functions from trusted sources such as VMware or trusted community contributors, you'll need to make sure you load them into your PowerCLI/PowerShell session. This is done by "dot-sourcing" the function. You simply need to type a period followed by a space followed by the complete path to the function. Unless you add the function to your PowerShell profile, you will need to reload it for each new session of PowerCLI, as in this example:

```
PowerCLI C:> . "C:\Test\Test-vMotion.ps1"
```

You should now have a solid understanding of the vast capabilities of PowerCLI and how to get started. We've tried to provide you with the essential information that we have shared with others to start their journey to automating their VMware environments. Remember to always look to the community forums and bloggers for assistance as you navigate PowerCLI. We also highly recommend the book *VMware vSphere PowerCLI Reference* (Wiley, 2011). It contains a wealth of information and detailed explanations of PowerCLI capabilities.

Using vCLI from vSphere Management Assistant

VMware vSphere 5 saw the retirement of VMware ESX and the traditional Linux-based Service Console. This meant that a lot of vSphere administrators and organizations needed to adapt to not having a Linux environment available on each host. Since administrators still require this type of functionality, VMware released the vSphere CLI (vCLI). The vCLI is built on the vSphere SDK for Perl and implements the familiar console commands from the old ESX Service Console onto Windows and Linux servers. This improves both security and scalability by providing a single managed point of contact for your environment.

VMware took this a step further in introducing the vSphere Management Assistant, most commonly referred to by its acronym, vMA. This 64-bit virtual appliance can be quickly downloaded and implemented into your vSphere environment and comes preloaded with vCLI and the vSphere SDK for Perl. This centrally provides vSphere administrators with the tools they were accustomed to in the service console prior to vSphere 5.0. The vMA can manage vSphere 5.0, 5.1, and vSphere 5.5 environments. Additional features are available in the vMA to make managing multiple ESXi hosts easier. We'll go over a few of those features in the following sections, but let's start with what is new with vCLI and vMA.

What's New in vCLI and vMA for vSphere 5.5

The release of vSphere 5.5 means the inclusion of new features in the vSphere Command Line Interface (vCLI) and the vSphere Management Assistant (vMA). Most notable is the inclusion of commands for managing VSAN configurations, coredump, and vFlash. Check out the vCLI release notes for a full listing of new capabilities. The vMA has not changed significantly with this release outside of the updates to vCLI and SDK for Perl.

Getting Started with vCLI

Whether you are running vCLI from your own deployed server or the vMA, there are a great deal of tasks that you can automate. In this section we'll go over a few examples of using the vCLI.

One common use case for the vCLI that we've used in the past is the manipulation of vSwitches in vSphere. Typically this may be necessary for troubleshooting network connections. Fortunately, the vCLI allows you to do a great deal for reporting and configuring networking on your ESXi hosts. For example, to add a vSwitch to a host with the vCLI, you use the exact same syntax as previously, with an added option to specify the host to which you need to connect:

```
esxcfg-vswitch --server <Hostname> --list
```

Alternatively, you can use the newer vCLI naming convention where the commands use the vicfg- prefix in place of esxcfg-. The esxcfg- prefix is kept for backward compatibility but will be phased out over time. Therefore, you can currently use either format. We suggest you begin adopting vicfg- as soon as you can and update existing scripts accordingly.

```
vicfg-vswitch --server <Hostname> --list
esxcfg-vswitch --server <Hostname> --list
```

By using this set of commands, you can perform common tasks needed for basic host configuration that would previously be done from the bash Service Console. For instance, Listing 14.3 will perform the following:

◆ Create a new vSwitch named vSwitch1.

◆ Add vmnic1 as an uplink to the new vSwitch.

◆ Create a new VM portgroup.

◆ Add a VLAN to the new vSwitch.

LISTING 14.3: Create a new vSwitch from vMA

```
# add a new vSwitch
vi-admin@vma01:~> vicfg-vswitch --server pod-1-blade-6.v12nlab.net -a vSwitch1

# add an uplink to the vSwitch
vi-admin@vma01:~> vicfg-vswitch --server pod-1-blade-6.v12nlab.net`
 -L vmnic1 vSwitch1

# add a VM portgroup to the new vSwitch
vi-admin@vma01:~> vicfg-vswitch --server pod-1-blade-6.v12nlab.net -A "VM-Public"
vSwitch1

# set the VLAN for the new portgroup
vi-admin@vma01:~> vicfg-vswitch --server pod-1-blade-6.v12nlab.net`
 -v 10 -p "VM-Public" vSwitch1
```

Executing these commands, however, becomes tedious very quickly because you must constantly enter the username and password to connect to the server. One workaround would be to wrap the commands in a bash script and pass the username and password as parameters. This is somewhat undesirable, however, because you are leaving credentials to your ESXi hosts available to anyone who can log into your server. This is where the benefit of using vMA over a standard host with the vCLI installed comes into play.

vMA has some additional functionality installed on it called *fastpass*. Fastpass allows you to securely add ESXi hosts, and even vCenter servers, to your vMA once and connect to them without a password during script execution. This allows you to treat the vMA's command line as you would the native host. You must first initialize the host with fastpass to take advantage of this feature. This is easily done:

```
vifp addserver <Hostname>
```

This command then prompts for the ESXi host's root password, connects to the host, and adds two users to the host. These two users are used for executing commands. Should you specify the "adauth" authpolicy, fastpass would use an Active Directory account for authentication to the host.

You can view any hosts that fastpass has been configured for using the `vifp listservers` command:

```
vi-admin@vma01:~> vifp listservers
vSphere01.vSphere.local ESXi
```

You can see that a single host is fastpass enabled, and it is an ESXi host.

Now that fastpass is aware of the host, you set the host as the current target using the `vifptarget` command:

```
vifptarget -s <Hostname>
```

After this you can execute ESXi configuration commands as though you are logged into the console of that host. The list of commands now looks like standard ESX configuration commands from the old Service Console. Note that you can still use the `esxcfg-` prefix for the commands, so existing scripts can be copied into place with minimal changes. For example, Listing 14.4 adds a vSwitch to the vSphere01 host using vMA fastpass.

LISTING 14.4:   Add a vSwitch using vMA fastpass

```
vi-admin@vma01:~>vifptarget -s vSphere01.vSphere.local
vi-admin@vma01:~[vSphere01.vSphere.local]> vicfg-vswitch -a vSwitch1
vi-admin@vma01:~[vSphere01.vSphere.local]> vicfg-vswitch -L vmnic1 vSwitch1
vi-admin@vma01:~[vSphere01.vSphere.local]> vicfg-vswitch -A "VM-Public" ↵
vSwitch1
vi-admin@vma01:~vSphere01.vSphere.local]> vicfg-vswitch -v 10 -p ↵
"VM-Public" vSwitch1
```

By adding additional ESXi servers to fastpass, you can configure multiple hosts quickly using a simple bash loop. For example, Listing 14.5 will connect to each host and add the `vm_nfs01` datastore.

LISTING 14.5:   Add an NFS datastore or multiple hosts by using vMA fastpass

```
for server in "vSphere01 vSphere02 vSphere03 vSphere04 vSphere05"; do
> vifptarget -s $server
> vicfg-nas -a -o FAS3210A.vSphere.local -s /vol/vm_nfs01 vm_nfs01
> vifptarget -c
> done
```

Using vSphere Management Assistant for Automation with vCenter

Leveraging the fastpass technology with vCenter allows you a simple luxury: You no longer have to add each host to fastpass. However, there is a caveat that you must specify an additional command-line parameter for each command.

This has both advantages and disadvantages. It's extremely convenient to no longer be concerned about whether the host you are manipulating has been initialized for fastpass. Scripts that are written can simply use the vCenter credentials to manipulate host settings while still being logged in vCenter's task list. Additionally, all tasks executed through vCenter are logged in vCenter for auditing purposes. The downside is losing the ability to use legacy scripts that assume you are on the console of the host and have not had the additional parameter set.

Connecting vCenter to fastpass is the same as it is for hosts. vMA is kind enough to warn you that storing the vCenter credentials is a security risk, and we do recommend you use vCenter's role-based access to limit the permissions to the minimum needed. That being said, you should always protect your vMA as you would any other server in your environment and ensure that a sufficiently complex password is used for the `vi-admin` user to prevent unauthorized access. Keep in mind that should the vMA become compromised, all of the hosts that are fastpass enabled are also compromised. You should use the same command for vCenter as for your ESXi hosts:

```
vi-admin@vma01:~> vifp addserver vCenter01
Enter username for vCenter01: fp_admin
fp_admin@vCenter01's password:
This will store username and password in credential store which is
a security risk. Do you want to continue?(yes/no): yes
vi-admin@vma01:~> vifp listservers
vCenter01.vSphere.local   vCenter
vi-admin@vma01:~> vifptarget -s vCenter01
vi-admin@vma01:~[vCenter01.vSphere.local]>
```

Notice that you can set the fastpass target server to vCenter just as you can an ESXi host, and you can execute standard host commands against it as well:

```
vi-admin@vma01:~[vCenter01.vSphere.local]> vicfg-vswitch -l
The --vihost option must be specified when connecting to vCenter.
For a summary of command usage, type '/usr/bin/vicfg-vswitch --help'.
For documentation, type 'perldoc /usr/bin/vicfg-vswitch'.
```

But wait! There's an error. Notice that you must specify which ESXi host you want to actually execute the command against now that you are connecting to vCenter. Following the recommendation of the error message, you specify the host using the `--vihost` or `-h` option and execute the command:

```
vi-admin@vma01:~[vCenter01.vSphere.local]> vicfg-vswitch -h vSphere01 -l
Switch Name  Num Ports  Used Ports  Configured Ports  MTU   Uplinks
vSwitch0     128        3           128               1500  vmnic0

    PortGroup Name          VLAN ID  Used Ports       Uplinks
    VM Network              0        0                vmnic0
    Management Network      0        1                vmnic0
```

You can do the same management tasks as before, just using the extra -h switch when executing each one. For example, you can set advanced options and kernel module options on multiple hosts by running the following:

```
vi-admin@vma01:~> vifptarget -s vCenter01
vi-admin@vma01:~[vCenter01.vSphere.local]> for server in "vSphere01 ←
vSphere02 vSphere03 vSphere04 vSphere05"; do
echo "$server is being configured..."
> # see http://kb.vmware.com/kb/1268 for more info on this setting
> vicfg-advcfg -h $server -s 64 Disk.SchedNumReqOutstanding
> # see http://kb.vmware.com/kb/1267 for more info on this setting
> vicfg-module -h $server -s ql2xmaxqdepth=128 qla2xxx
> done
vi-admin@vma01:~[vCenter01.vSphere.local]> vifptarget -c
```

There are lots of ways this script could be improved; for example, there's no error checking to ensure that a matching port group and VMkernel interface are actually found by the first command. Readers already familiar with bash scripting should find utilizing the vCLI and vMA quite comfortable for automating vSphere environments. Make sure you check the vCLI concepts and examples guide from VMware for more examples and instructions on how to utilize vCLI and vMA in your environment.

Leveraging the Perl Toolkit with vSphere Management Assistant

vMA's fastpass with vCenter and the Perl SDK are a powerful combination. With a handful of helper scripts, you can administer a large number of hosts using the vCLI through vCenter.

Listing 14.6 is a Perl script that simply returns the hostnames in a cluster. This can be useful for configuring a cluster of ESXi hosts for a new datastore, a new vSwitch, or other items that you would want to match across all members of the cluster.

LISTING 14.6:   Get all hosts in a cluster by using the Perl SDK

```perl
#!/usr/bin/perl
#
# Script Name: ~/bin/getClusterHosts.pl
# Usage: getClusterHosts.pl --server vCenter.your.domain clusterName
# Result: a newline delimited list of ESXihosts in the cluster
#
use strict;
use warnings;

# include the standard VMware perl SDK modules
use VMware::VIRuntime;

# some additional helper functions
use VMware::VIExt;
```

```perl
# define the options we need for our script
my %opts = (
    # we can use the special _default_ so that we do not have
    # to provide a command line switch when calling our script.
    # The last parameter is assumed to be the clustername
    '_default_' => {
        # this parameter is a string
        type => "=s",

        # what is reported when the user passes the --help option
        help => "Name of the cluster to report hosts for",

        # boolean to determine if the option is mandatory
        required => 1
    }
);

# add the options to the standard VMware options
Opts::add_options(%opts);

# parse the options from the command line
Opts::parse();

# ensure valid input was passed
Opts::validate();

# the user should have passed, or been prompted for, a
# username and password as two of the standard VMware
# options.  connect using them now...
Util::connect();

# search the connected host (should be vCenter) for our cluster
my $clusterName = Opts::get_option('_default_');
my $clusterView = Vim::find_entity_view(
        view_type => 'ClusterComputeResource',
        filter => { name => qr/($clusterName)/i }
    );

# ensure that we found something
if (! $clusterView) {
    VIExt::fail("A cluster with name " . $clusterName . " was not found!");
}

# now we want to search for hosts inside the cluster we just
# retrieved a reference to
my $hostViews = Vim::find_entity_views(
```

```
        view_type => 'HostSystem',
        begin_entity => $clusterView,
        # limit the properties returned for performance
        properties => [ 'name' ]
    );

# print a simple newline delimited list of the found hosts
foreach my $host (@{$hostViews}) {
    print $host->name . "\n";
}

# and destroy the session with the server
Util::disconnect();
```

Executing our script, you see the following results:

```
vi-admin@vma01:~> getClusterHosts.pl --server vCenter01 cluster01
Enter username: administrator
Enter password:
vSphere01.vSphere.local
vSphere02.vSphere.local
```

Notice that we were prompted for the username and password. This is a feature of using the VIRuntime library. VMware has simplified things for developers by providing default options. These are the same as for all of the vCLI scripts, so --username and --password apply regardless of whether you are using a vCLI script or one that you created. If you pass the username and password arguments to the script via the command line, it will not prompt for them. Alternatively, using fastpass will also eliminate the need for a username and password to be supplied.

You can now combine your Perl script with bash and fastpass to configure an entire cluster with a new portgroup quickly and efficiently.

```
vi-admin@vma01:~> vifptarget -s vCenter01
vi-admin@vma01:~[vCenter01.vSphere.local]> for server in ⏎
'getClusterHosts.pl cluster01'; do
> echo "$server is being configured..."
> vicfg-vswitch -h $server -A VLAN100 vSwitch0
> vicfg-vswitch -h $server -v 100 -p VLAN100 vSwitch0
> done
vSphere01.vSphere.local is being configured...
vSphere02.vSphere.local is being configured...
vi-admin@vma01:~[vCenter01.get-admin.com]> vifptarget -c
```

This example is just a tiny portion of what can be done with the Perl toolkit. The vCLI does not include functionality for managing virtual servers; however, you can leverage the Perl toolkit and the SDK to manage VMs just as you can PowerCLI. Using the SDK, you can accomplish any task that can be done through the VI Client or PowerCLI; the difference is the level of effort required to get the same results. Additional sample Perl scripts can be found on vMA at `/usr/lib/vmware-vcli/apps/` and `/usr/share/doc/vmware-vcli/samples/`.

Automating with vCenter Orchestrator

vCenter Orchestrator (vCO) is VMware's process automation tool that comes bundled with vCenter Server. During vCenter Server installations, you may have noticed the inclusion of the vCenter Orchestrator service and installed files. While it is installed by default, it is still up to the administrator to configure vCO for use with vCenter Server. We'll go over that configuration later in this chapter. If you are able to use vCenter's Simple Install, the bulk of vCO configurations are done automatically.

Throughout its evolution vCenter Orchestrator has become an integral component of vCloud Director (vCD) and vCloud Automation Center (vCAC). Conversely though, independent adoption of this tool has been relatively light in comparison to PowerCLI or vMA. In our experience this in large part is due to a couple of factors:

- ◆ vSphere administrators are not yet adopting automation beyond small single-purpose scripts.

- ◆ vSphere administrators find the implementation of tasks and requirements difficult.

- ◆ vSphere administrators find the interface foreign and overwhelming.

No doubt you have seen or heard of vCenter Orchestrator but were probably unclear of how it fit into the vSphere ecosystem.

A few things are unique about vCenter Orchestrator:

- ◆ The ability of the workflow engine to manage many simultaneous processes. It's also able to track and manage pauses or interruptions in the workflow, such as approvals or service restart.

- ◆ Integration into the vSphere Web Client.

- ◆ Open for development of new plug-ins.

New Features in vCenter Orchestrator 5.5

VMware expanded the importance of vCenter Orchestrator as part of vCAC with the release of vSphere v5.1. In vSphere 5.5, its extends vCO by including the following features:

- ◆ Workflow Debugger. Provides a debug mode that workflow developers can use to rerun their workflows and better troubleshoot.

- ◆ vCO Cluster Mode. Provides dynamic scale-up and scale-down of orchestration when used with an external load balancer. This provides application high availability, allowing a workflow to be completed by a different vCO node in the event of a node outage.

- ◆ Security improvements.

- ◆ Improved integration with vSphere Web Client.

Make sure you read over the vCenter Orchestrator 5.5 release notes for the full listing of new features, especially if you're migrating from vCO 4.2.*x* to vCO 5.5.

Understanding vCenter Orchestrator Prerequisites

Because vCO is installed with vCenter Server, many of the prerequisites for vCO are the same as for vCenter Server. Like vCenter Server, vCO runs on any x64 Windows server. Also like vCenter Server, vCO requires a separate backend database. This backend database must be separate from the vCenter Server backend database.

vCO can leverage the following supported databases:

- Microsoft SQL Server Express for small deployments
- Microsoft SQL Server 2003 SP3 (Standard or Enterprise), 32-bit or 64-bit
- Microsoft SQL Server 2008 (SP1 or SP2, Standard or Enterprise), 32-bit or 64-bit
- Oracle 10g (Standard or Enterprise) Release 2 (10.2.0.3.0), 32-bit or 64-bit
- Oracle 11g (Standard or Enterprise) Release 1 (11.1.0.7), 32-bit or 64-bit

MySQL and PostgreSQL are also supported but only for testing and evaluation purposes.

USE A SEPARATE PHYSICAL SERVER FOR THE ORCHESTRATOR DATABASE

Because of CPU and memory usage, VMware recommends placing the vCO database on a separate machine from the vCO server. These machines should reside in the same datacenter for high-speed LAN connectivity.

If you are planning on using an Oracle database, you must download the Oracle drivers and copy them to the appropriate locations; the vCO installer does not do this for you. For more complete information on exactly how this is accomplished, refer to the *vCO Installation and Configuration Guide* available from VMware's website at

```
www.vmware.com/support/pubs/orchestrator_pubs.html
```

vCO also requires a working LDAP server in your environment. Supported LDAP servers include OpenLDAP, Novell eDirectory, Sun Java Directory Server, and Microsoft Active Directory.

If you want to set up vCO cluster mode, you'll need to ensure that the database can accept multiple connections so it can accept connections from each vCO server.

After you verify that you meet all these prerequisites, you are ready to get started configuring vCenter Orchestrator.

Configuring vCenter Orchestrator

vCenter Orchestrator (vCO) is arguably the most versatile and powerful of the automation technologies discussed in this chapter. To take advantage of that functionality, often considerable configurations must be applied. In the following sections, we'll go over the core configurations needed to make use of vCO in your environment. Do not be discouraged by the relatively long list of configuration needs. vCO has many touch points into your environment, and these changes are necessary for vCO to function properly.

STARTING THE VCENTER ORCHESTRATOR CONFIGURATION SERVICE

The first step in configuring vCO is starting the vCO Configuration service. This service allows you to configure settings such as network, database, and server certificate settings for the vCO engine. By default, this service is set to manual startup. It must be running in order to access the web-based configuration interface.

Perform the following steps to start the vCO Configuration service:

1. Log in as an administrative user to the computer running vCenter Server, which will have vCenter Orchestrator also installed automatically.

2. From the Start menu, choose Run.

3. In the Run dialog box, type **services.msc**, and click OK.

4. When the Services window opens, scroll through the list of services in the pane on the right until you see the VMware vCenter Orchestrator Configuration service.

5. Right-click the VMware vCenter Orchestrator Configuration service and select Start.

6. Verify that the service started correctly by ensuring that the Status column for the VMware vCenter Orchestrator Configuration service lists Started.

    After the service starts, you can access the vCO Web Configuration interface.

7. Open a web browser, and go to

    ```
    https://<computer IP address or DNS name>:8283
    ```

8. Log in with default credentials

    User: vmware

    Password: vmware

    You will be prompted to change the default password. This is highly recommended. Make sure you save this password in your records in case you need to make future changes to the vCenter Orchestrator engine. This password must be complex, containing at least eight characters, including one digit, one uppercase letter, and one special character. You will be prompted if any of these conditions are not met.

9. Enter the new password and click Apply Changes.

Once logged in you will see all of your options for configuring the vCenter Orchestrator instance. You'll notice in Figure 14.4 that the default settings have been applied for the vCenter Orchestrator instances that reside on the vCenter Server. This is a marked improvement to setup over previous versions.

FIGURE 14.4
The vCenter
Orchestrator
Configuration
interface

CONFIGURING NETWORKING

Depending on how you choose to deploy vCenter Orchestrator, you may wish to designate a separate IP address for vCO to listen on. This is done easily through the vCenter Orchestrator Configuration page and should be the first thing you set up during your implementation. Follow these steps:

1. Open a web browser, and go to

   `https://<computer IP address or DNS name>:8283`

2. Log in with your credentials:

   User: `vmware`

   Password: `<your password>`

3. Click the Network tab on the left.

4. In the IP Address drop-down, select the IPv4 or IPv6 IP address you wish vCenter Orchestrator to listen on. You'll notice that the DNS and port information populates.

5. Click Apply.

CONFIGURING AUTHENTICATION

vCenter Orchestrator is capable of working with a variety of targets for user authentication. Authentication is critical to get the most out of vCenter Orchestrator while also protecting your vSphere environment from unapproved access. Let's go over the two most common authentication configurations: SSO and LDAP. Follow these steps:

1. Open a web browser, and go to

   `https://<computer IP address or DNS name>:8283`

2. Log in with your credentials:

   User: `vmware`

   Password: `<your password>`

3. Click the Authentication tab on the left.

Configure vCenter Single Sign-On

The default option for vCenter Orchestrator is using SSO. Before completing Single Sign-On authentication, you'll need to import the SSO SSL certificate:

1. Go to the Network tab on the left.

2. Select the SSL Trust Manager tab.

3. Enter the SSO URL under Import From URL:

   `https://<SSO IP address or DNS name>:7444`

4. Click Import.

5. Click the Authentication tab on the left.

6. Enter the vCenter Server hostname with port info:

   `https://<computer IP address or DNS name>:7444`

7. Enter the SSO Admin username and password:

   User: `admin@vsphere-local`

   Password: `<Your SSO Admin Password>`

8. Click the Register Orchestrator button.

Configuring for LDAP – Active Directory

In many cases, you will use Active Directory as your supported LDAP server because vCenter Server also integrates with Active Directory. As mentioned earlier, other LDAP servers are also supported.

Follow these steps to configure Active Directory as your LDAP server:

1. Select your LDAP client. In this example, we use Active Directory.

2. Enter your primary LDAP host and optionally the second LDAP host.

3. Enter the root for your domain. (For example, the `vtesseract.lab` domain would be `dc=vtesseract,dc=lab`.)

4. In the Username and Password text boxes, supply the username and password that vCenter Orchestrator will use to authenticate against Active Directory. Specify the username in DN format (cn=username,cn=Users,dc=domain,dc=com) or universal principal name (UPN) format (username@domain.com).

5. In the User Lookup Base text box, supply the base DN that vCenter Orchestrator should use when searching for user accounts. If you are unsure of what to use, specify the same value as the root DN.

6. In the Group Lookup Base text box, supply the base DN that vCenter Orchestrator should use when searching for groups. If you are unsure of what to use, specify the same value as the root DN.

7. In the vCO Admin Group text box, specify the DN of an Active Directory group that should receive vCenter Orchestrator administration rights. This should look something like cn=Administrators,cn=Builtin,dc=domain,dc=com.

8. Click the Apply Changes button.

Once you have configured vCO for your preferred authentication method, you can test that connection with the Test Connection tab. If you need more advanced LDAP authentication instructions, reference the white paper "Installing and Configuring VMware vCenter Orchestrator."

EXPORT/IMPORT CONFIGURATION

Having a disaster recovery plan for your vCenter and vCO databases is clearly a very good idea. It is also recommended to export your vCO configuration. You can do this, and protect it with a password if desired, through the vCenter Orchestrator Configuration General tab:

1. Open a web browser, and go to

```
https://<computer IP address or DNS name>:8283
```

2. Log in with your credentials:

User: vmware

Password: <your password>

3. Click the General tab on the left.

4. Select the Export Configuration tab.

5. If you would like to password-protect your configuration (recommended), enter that in the Password field.

6. Click Export.

Your configuration file will be stored on the server and the location is displayed on the screen. The file is saved with a .vmoconfig filename extension and the date and time is included in the filename. This file can be imported later if you need to restore your vCO configuration:

1. Open a web browser, and go to
```
https://<computer IP address or DNS name>:8283
```

2. Log in with your credentials:

User: vmware

Password: <your password>

3. Click the General tab on the left.

4. Select the Import Configuration tab.

5. Enter the protection password in the Password field (if required).

6. Browse to the saved configuration file.

7. Select the check box if you wish to override the current internal certificate and networking with the new file.

8. Click Import.

This will restore the configuration settings that you had exported into that file. The Export/ Import capabilities can also make running cluster mode easier to configure.

STARTING vCENTER ORCHESTRATOR SERVICE

Once you have all the configurations you want updated and exported, it is time to start the actual vCenter Orchestrator engine. You can accomplish this two ways. You may wish to use the Windows services console if you'd like to set the service to start automatically. Keep in mind that starting the vCO Server service may take several minutes.

To start the service through the Windows services console, follow these steps:

1. From the Start menu, choose Run.

2. In the Run dialog box, type **services.msc**, and click OK.

3. When the Services window opens, scroll through the list of services in the pane on the right until you see the VMware vCenter Orchestrator Server service.

4. Right-click the VMware vCenter Orchestrator Server service and select Start. Wait patiently.

5. Verify that the service started correctly by ensuring that the Status column for the VMware vCenter Orchestrator Server service lists Started.

6. Set the service to start automatically by right-clicking the service name and choosing Properties.

7. Change the startup type to Automatic.

To start the service through the vCenter Orchestrator Configuration page, follow these steps:

1. Open a web browser, and go to

https://<computer IP address or DNS name>:8283

2. Log in with your credentials:

User: vmware

Password: <your password>

3. Click the Startup Options tab on the left.

4. Click the link on the right that says Start Service. Wait patiently; it is important to give the service several minutes to start.

IMPORTING vCENTER SERVER SSL CERTIFICATE

To connect a standalone instance of vCenter Orchestrator to vCenter Server, you'll need to import the SSL certificate used for that server:

1. Open a web browser, and go to

   `https://<computer IP address or DNS name>:8283`

2. Login with your credentials:

   User: `vmware`

   Password: `<your password>`

3. Click the vCenter Server tab.

4. Click the SSL Certificates link on the right.

5. Under Import From URL, enter the vCenter Server instance's name or IP address and click Import.

6. Review the vCenter certificate information and click Import.

IMPORTING THE vCENTER SERVER LICENSE

vCenter Orchestrator is included and licensed with vCenter Server. The vCenter Server license will be automatically imported when running on vCenter Server. However, most implementations will have vCO running on a different system. You'll need to import the vCenter Server license information. You can do this manually by entering the 25-digit serial number or by importing it from a vCenter Server instance:

1. Open a web browser, and go to

   `https://<computer IP address or DNS name>:8283`

2. Log in with your credentials:

   User: `vmware`

   Password: `<your password>`

3. Click the Licenses tab.

4. Select the Use vCenter Server License radio button.

5. Enter the vCenter Server host name or IP address and login credentials.

6. Click Apply Changes.

Depending on the vCenter Server license that you own, vCenter Orchestrator will operate in one of two modes:

◆ For a vCenter Server Standard license, vCenter Orchestrator operates in Server mode. This provides full access to all Orchestrator elements and the ability to run and edit workflows.

◆ For a vCenter Server Foundation or vCenter Server Essentials license, vCenter Orchestrator runs in Player mode. You are granted read-only permission on Orchestrator elements, and you can run workflows, but you cannot edit them.

CONFIGURING THE PLUG-INS

vCenter Orchestrator uses a plug-in architecture to add functionality and connectivity to the base workflow engine. By default, vCenter Orchestrator comes with a default set of plug-ins, but you'll need to provide the username and password of an account with administrative permissions in vCenter Orchestrator to install them.

Perform the following steps to install the default set of plug-ins:

1. In the vCenter Orchestrator Configuration interface, click the Plug-Ins tab.

2. Specify the username and password of an account that is a member of the vCO Administration group. This is the group you specified previously when you configured the LDAP server.

3. Click Apply Changes.

The Plug-Ins status indicator will change to a green circle, and assuming all the other status indicators are also green circles, the Startup Options status indicator will be as well. You can look for additional plug-ins from VMware's website at

```
www.vmware.com/products/datacenter-virtualization/vcenter-orchestrator/
plugins.html
```

vCenter Orchestrator Appliance

While vCO is provided by default with vCenter Server, VMware highly recommends keeping vCO installed separately and providing it with a separate database as well. You can accomplish this by installing vCO on a Windows server with the standalone installer, separate from the vCenter Server instance, or implementing the vCO appliance. In this section, we'll briefly discuss the steps required to implement the vCO appliance.

Before beginning the implementation of the vCO appliance, you may be asking yourself why you would choose the appliance versus installing vCO on a separate Windows server. You'll see shortly that the primary benefit is ease of implementation. Deploying the vCO appliance is extremely straightforward. The vCO appliance includes the following additional benefits:

◆ Reduced licensing cost

◆ Better scalability

◆ Isolating vCO entirely to minimize impacting other applications

The vCenter Orchestrator appliance comes with the following software installed:

◆ SUSE Linux Enterprise Server 11 Update 1 for VMware, 64-bit

◆ PostgreSQL (suitable for small to medium environments)

◆ OpenLDAP (suitable for experimental and testing purposes)

◆ vCenter Orchestrator 5.5

The vCenter Orchestrator appliance requires the following minimum hardware:

◆ 2 CPU

◆ 3 GB memory

◆ 7 GB hard disk

Implementing the vCenter Orchestrator Appliance

You'll begin implementing the vCO appliance by downloading it from your MyVMware portal where you'll find it listed with the vSphere downloads. Save it to a local directory that the vSphere Client, or vSphere Web Client, has access to since you'll need to deploy with one of vSphere clients. Then follow these steps:

1. Log in to the vSphere Web Client with permissions to deploy OVF files.

2. Select an inventory object that can contain a virtual machine such as a datacenter, folder, cluster, resource pool, or host.

3. Select Actions ➢ All vCenter Actions ➢ Deploy OVF Template.

4. Enter path or URL to the OVF (.ovf) file and click Next.

5. Review the OVF details and click Next.

6. Review and accept the terms in the license agreement and click Next.

7. Specify a name and location for the appliance and click Next.

8. Select the desired destination and click Next.

9. Select the desired disk format and datastore.

10. Specify network settings. Static IP addresses are recommended but DHCP is fully supported. This setting can be changed later through the appliance web console.

11. Review the properties and click Finish. You may also choose to have the virtual machine powered on after deployment.

12. Verify that the appliance is online by browsing to `http:// <appliance address>`.

CHANGING THE DEFAULT ROOT PASSWORD

Once you have established the availability of the vCenter Orchestrator appliance, you will want to change the `root` password. This can be done quickly:

1. Open your supported browser to

   `https://<appliance address>:5480`

2. Enter the default login credentials:

   User: `root`

   Password: `vmware`

3. Click the Admin tab.

4. Enter the current root password, the new administrator password, and retype the new administrator password.

5. Click Change Password.

You will want to log out and log back in with the new credentials.

Accessing vCenter Orchestrator

There are several ways to access vCenter Orchestrator. Previous versions of vCO required connectivity through the web operator or the vCO client. Beginning with the new vSphere Web Client in vSphere 5.1, vCenter Orchestrator provided access through vCenter Server itself. This is a tremendous advantage that was improved greatly in vSphere 5.5. More often than not those building workflows in vCO will find themselves working with the vCO client because it provides the greatest flexibility. If done correctly, it is entirely possible for your infrastructure consumers to take advantage of vCO without logging into any client by utilizing the vSphere Web Client integration.

vCenter Orchestrator and vCenter Server

We mentioned earlier that vCO has been widely integrated into the vSphere Web Client, allowing vSphere administrators the ability to make workflows available to a variety of Web Client users on most objects in vCenter Server. This means that a vCO server can be configured within the vSphere Web Client and then assign workflows to various object types. Role-based access control (RBAC) can then be leveraged to provide Web Client users more opportunity to utilize vCO workflows without leaving the web interface. This functionality has a huge advantage over the other automation options that we have discussed because these workflows are now extremely easy to share and are not limited to those with strong knowledge about the tool or environment. Here are some examples:

- Application owners have the ability to update virtual hardware on their VM (which would include checking that VMware Tools are up to date).

- System owners have the ability to upgrade the virtual hardware of a VM while also including limited options and optional approvals.

- System owners have the ability to launch a report that could provide health and change information about their system, or even the cluster on which the system is located.

KEYS TO vCO SUCCESS

Keep in mind that there are a few things that *must* be in good working order in your environment to take advantage of this feature. First, a vCenter Orchestrator instance needs to be fully configured and ready to begin work. Most of this work is done for you in Simple Install mode, and the steps required are mentioned previously in this chapter for other installs. Second, your authentication must be configured correctly. This is centrally related to Single Sign-On (SSO). If SSO is not working properly, you are going to have great difficulty configuring the integration between vCenter Server and vCO. Finally, you will have to continue with your server certificates. Issues with any of these items can make for challenging vCO-vCenter integration.

ASSIGN vCO INSTANCE TO MANAGE vCENTER

Assigning a vCO server to manage vCenter is actually pretty straightforward once you have validated the required trusts. You'll need to log in to the vSphere Web Client with an account that has administrator privileges, as follows:

1. Verify that the vCenter Orchestrator service is running.

2. Log in to vSphere Web Client.

3. Click the vCenter Orchestrator tab.

4. Click the Manage tab at the right.

5. Select the row with the vCenter Server instance you want managed.

6. Click Edit Configuration.

7. Enter the vCenter Orchestrator name (Figure 14.5).

8. Click Test Connection.

9. Click OK.

FIGURE 14.5
Assigning a vCO instance

Using an Orchestrator Workflow

So far, you've only seen how to configure the vCenter Orchestrator server, but now that the server is up and running, you are ready to launch the client and actually run a workflow. The vCenter Orchestrator client is the application you will use to actually launch a workflow. You can launch the vCenter Orchestrator client from the Start menu and then log in with the Active Directory credentials of an account in the vCO Administrators group (this is the group configured earlier when you set up the LDAP server connection for vCenter Orchestrator).

vCenter Orchestrator comes with a library of preinstalled workflows. To view these workflows in the vCenter Orchestrator client, click the Workflows tab on the left side of the window, and then browse through the tree folder structure to see what workflows are already available for you to use. Figure 14.6 shows some of the preinstalled workflows in the vCenter Orchestrator client.

To run any of the workflows in the vCenter Orchestrator client, you just right-click the workflow and select Execute Workflow. Depending on the workflow, the vCenter Orchestrator client prompts you for the information it needs to complete the workflow, such as the name of a VM or the name of an ESXi host. The information that the vCenter Orchestrator client prompts you to supply will vary based on the workflow you have selected to run.

Real World Scenario

TODAY'S MIRACLES

You return from lunch on Friday to a frantic voicemail from one of the department heads in your company. An initiative has been underway to overhaul a major application that the department depends on. A consultant is coming in on Monday morning to deploy the application in an isolated development environment. There has been discussion about creating this environment but it has not been done yet. Naturally, you protest but agree to work through the weekend to prepare the new environment. That weekend can go dramatically different depending on the amount of automation implemented in your environment.

If you have automated the deployment of new virtual machines, implementation of new VLANs, addition of accounts, and access permissions, you may be able to accomplish the task within a few hours. If you do not have automation you will likely spend many hours implementing the solution manually and missing weekend activities. You are also likely to make mistakes or miss steps that can impact the confidence that the department head and your management have in you. In the end, you know you'll accomplish the task, but the amount of effort required will vary. Regardless of what it takes the department head sees the result and assumes that this is repeatable. As such, you will likely be put on the spot again in the future and doomed to repeat the effort. Today's miracles are tomorrow's expectations.

FIGURE 14.6
The vCenter folder contains all the workflows that automate actions in vCenter Server.

CREATING WORKFLOWS IS MOSTLY A DEVELOPER'S TASK

Unfortunately, creating custom workflows is probably beyond the reach of most vSphere administrators. Creating workflows and actions requires expertise and experience with web development languages like JavaScript. If this is something with which you have some knowledge, then download the *vCenter Orchestrator Developer's Guide* from VMware's website at `www.vmware.com/support/pubs/orchestrator_pubs.html`. This developer's guide provides more detailed information on how to create Orchestrator workflows.

---

vCenter Orchestrator is a powerful tool that is capable of creating some complex and highly interactive workflows. However, it doesn't give up its secrets easily, and creating workflows may be beyond the skills of many vSphere administrators. Fortunately there are more than enough built-in workflows to accomplish the majority of common tasks. With a little practice passing information between existing workflows, you will be able to do increasingly more complex tasks.

The Bottom Line

Identify tools available for automating vSphere.   VMware offers a number of different solutions for automating your vSphere environment, including vCenter Orchestrator, PowerCLI, an SDK for Perl, an SDK for web service developers, and shell scripts in VMware ESXi. Each of these tools has its own advantages and disadvantages.

> **Master It**   VMware offers a number of different automation tools. What are some guidelines for choosing which automation tool to use?

Create a PowerCLI script for automation.   VMware vSphere PowerCLI builds on the object-oriented PowerShell scripting language to provide administrators with a simple yet powerful way to automate tasks within the vSphere environment.

> **Master It**   If you are familiar with other scripting languages, what would be the biggest hurdle in learning to use PowerShell and PowerCLI, other than syntax?

Use vCLI to manage ESXi hosts from the command line.   VMware's command-line interface, or vCLI, is the new way of managing an ESXi host using the familiar `esxcfg-*` command set. By combining the features of fastpass with vCLI, you can seamlessly manage multiple hosts using the same command set from a single login.

> **Master It**   Have you migrated management and configuration operations for which you currently use the ESXi command-line interface to vMA?

Use vCenter in combination with vMA to manage all your hosts.   The new version of vMA can use vCenter as a target. This means that you can manage all of your hosts using vCLI without having to manually add each host to the fastpass target list.

> **Master It**   Use a combination of shell scripting with vCLI commands to execute commands against a number of hosts.

Employ the Perl toolkit and VMware SDK for virtual server operations from the command line.   The vCLI is designed for host management and consequently lacks tools for manipulating virtual servers. With the Perl toolkit, leveraged against the VMware SDK, any task that can be accomplished in the Virtual Infrastructure client can be done from the command line.

Master It Browse the sample scripts and SDK documentation to discover the world of possibilities that are unlocked by using Perl, or any of the other supported languages, to accomplish management tasks.

Configure vCenter Orchestrator vCenter Orchestrator is designed to allow vSphere administrators to run workflows against the vSphere environment and much more. To orchestrate against things like Active Directory and UCS or to run PowerShell scripts, you need the appropriate plug-ins installed and configured.

Master It How can you tell which plug-ins are installed and available for your use?

Use a vCenter Orchestrator workflow After vCenter Orchestrator is configured and running, you can use the vCenter Orchestrator client to run a vCenter Orchestrator workflow. vCenter Orchestrator comes with a number of preinstalled workflows to help automate tasks.

Master It An administrator in your environment configured vCenter Orchestrator and has now asked you to run a couple of workflows. However, when you log into the vCenter Server instance where vCenter Orchestrator is also installed, you don't see the icons for vCenter Orchestrator. Why?

Appendix

The Bottom Line

Each of The Bottom Line sections in the chapters suggest exercises to deepen skills and understanding. Sometimes there is only one possible solution, but often you are encouraged to use your skills and creativity to create something that builds on what you know and lets you explore one of many possible solutions.

Chapter 1: Introducing VMware vSphere 5.5

Identify the role of each product in the vSphere product suite.   The VMware vSphere product suite contains VMware ESXi and vCenter Server. ESXi provides the base virtualization functionality and enables features like Virtual SMP. vCenter Server provides management for ESXi and enables functionality like vMotion, Storage vMotion, vSphere Distributed Resource Scheduler (DRS), vSphere High Availability (HA), and vSphere Fault Tolerance (FT). Storage I/O Control (SIOC) and Network I/O Control (NIOC) provide granular resource controls for VMs. The vStorage APIs for Data Protection (VADP) provide a backup framework that allows for the integration of third-party backup solutions into a vSphere implementation.

Master It   Which products are licensed features within the VMware vSphere suite?

Solution   Licensed features in the VMware vSphere suite are Virtual SMP, vMotion, Storage vMotion, vSphere DRS, vSphere HA, and vSphere FT.

Master It   Which two features of VMware ESXi and VMware vCenter Server together aim to reduce or eliminate downtime due to unplanned hardware failures?

Solution   vSphere HA and vSphere FT are designed to reduce (vSphere HA) and eliminate (vSphere FT) the downtime resulting from unplanned hardware failures.

Master It   Name two storage-related features that are new to vSphere 5.5.

Solution   vSAN and vFlash are both storage-related features that are new to vSphere 5.5 and were not present in earlier releases.

Recognize the interaction and dependencies between the products in the vSphere suite.   VMware ESXi forms the foundation of the vSphere product suite, but some features require the presence of vCenter Server. Features like vMotion, Storage vMotion, vSphere DRS, vSphere HA, vSphere FT, SIOC, and NIOC require ESXi as well as vCenter Server.

Master It   Name three features that are supported only when using vCenter Server along with ESXi.

Solution   All of the following features are available only with vCenter Server: vSphere vMotion, Storage vMotion, vSphere DRS, Storage DRS, vSphere HA, vSphere FT, SIOC, and NIOC.

Master It   Name two features that are supported without vCenter Server but with a licensed installation of ESXi.

Solution   Features that are supported by VMware ESXi without vCenter Server include core virtualization features like virtualized networking, virtualized storage, vSphere vSMP, and resource allocation controls.

Understand how vSphere differs from other virtualization products.   VMware vSphere's hypervisor, ESXi, uses a Type 1 bare-metal hypervisor that handles I/O directly within the hypervisor. This means that a host operating system, like Windows or Linux, is not required in order for ESXi to function. Although other virtualization solutions are listed as "Type 1 bare-metal hypervisors," most other Type 1 hypervisors on the market today require the presence of a "parent partition" or "dom0" through which all VM I/O must travel.

Master It   One of the administrators on your team asked whether he should install Windows Server on the new servers you purchased for ESXi. What should you tell him, and why?

Solution   VMware ESXi is a bare-metal hypervisor that does not require the installation of a general-purpose host operating system. Therefore, it's unnecessary to install Windows Server on the equipment that was purchased for ESXi.

Chapter 2: Planning and Installing VMware ESXi

Understand ESXi compatibility requirements.   Unlike traditional operating systems like Windows or Linux, ESXi has much stricter hardware compatibility requirements. This helps ensure a stable, well-tested product line that is able to support even the most mission-critical applications.

Master It   You have some older servers onto which you'd like to deploy ESXi. They aren't on the Hardware Compatibility Guide. Will they work with ESXi?

Solution   They might, but they won't be supported by VMware. In all likelihood, the CPUs in these older servers don't support some of the hardware virtualization extensions or don't support 64-bit operation, both of which would directly impact the ability of ESXi to run on that hardware. You should choose only hardware that is on the Hardware Compatibility Guide.

Plan an ESXi deployment.   Deploying ESXi will affect many different areas of your organization—not only the server team but also the networking team, the storage team, and the security team. There are many issues to consider, including server hardware, storage hardware, storage protocols or connection types, network topology, and network connections. Failing to plan properly could result in an unstable and unsupported implementation.

Master It   Name three areas of networking that must be considered in a vSphere design.

Solution   Among other things, networking areas that must be considered include VLAN support, link aggregation, network speed (1 Gbps or 10 Gbps), load-balancing algorithms, and the number of NICs and network ports required.

Master It   What are some of the different types of storage that ESXi can be installed on?

Solution   By far the most common way to boot ESXi is the Local/Direct attached disks, but also supported are USB storage, an isolated SAN boot LUN, and utilizing iSCSI.

Deploy ESXi. ESXi can be installed onto any supported and compatible hardware platform. You have three different ways to deploy ESXi: You can install it interactively, you can perform an unattended installation, or you can use vSphere Auto Deploy to provision ESXi as it boots up.

Master It Your manager asks you to provide him with a copy of the unattended installation script that you will be using when you roll out ESXi using vSphere Auto Deploy. Is this something you can give him?

Solution No. When using vSphere Auto Deploy, there is no installation script. The vSphere Auto Deploy server streams an ESXi image to the physical host as it boots up. Redeployment of an ESXi host with vSphere Auto Deploy can be as simple as a reboot.

Master It Name two advantages and two disadvantages of using vSphere Auto Deploy to provision ESXi hosts.

Solution Some advantages include fast provisioning, fast reprovisioning, and the ability to quickly incorporate new ESXi images or updates into the provisioning process. Some disadvantages include additional complexity and dependency on additional infrastructure.

Perform post-installation configuration of ESXi. Following the installation of ESXi, some additional configuration steps may be required. For example, if the wrong NIC is assigned to the management network, then the server won't be accessible across the network. You'll also need to configure time synchronization.

Master It You've installed ESXi on your server, but the welcome web page is inaccessible, and the server doesn't respond to a ping. What could be the problem?

Solution More than likely, the wrong NIC was selected for use with the management network or the incorrect VLAN was selected. You'll need to use the Direct Console User Interface (DCUI) directly at the physical console of the ESXi host in order to reconfigure the management network and restore network connectivity.

Install the vSphere C# Client. ESXi is managed using the vSphere C# Client, a Windows-only application that provides the functionality to manage the virtualization platform. There are a couple different ways to obtain the vSphere Client installer, including running it directly from the VMware vCenter Installer or by downloading it using a web browser connected to the IP address of a vCenter Server instance.

Master It List two ways by which you can install the vSphere Client.

Solution You can download it from the Welcome To vSphere web page on a vCenter Server instance or you can install it from the vCenter Server installation media. You can also download the vSphere Client from VMware's website.

Chapter 3: Installing and Configuring vCenter Server

Understand the components and role of vCenter Server. vCenter Server plays a central role in the management of ESXi hosts and VMs. Key features such as vMotion, Storage vMotion, vSphere DRS, vSphere HA, and vSphere FT are all enabled and made possible by vCenter Server. vCenter Server provides scalable authentication and role-based administration based on integration with Active Directory.

Master It Specifically with regard to authentication, what are three key advantages of using vCenter Server?

Solution First, vCenter Server centralizes the authentication so that user accounts don't have to be managed on a per-host basis. Second, vCenter Server eliminates the need to share the root password for hosts or to use complex configurations to allow administrators to perform tasks on the hosts. Third, vCenter Server brings role-based administration for the granular management of hosts and VMs.

Plan a vCenter Server deployment. Planning a vCenter Server deployment includes selecting a backend database engine, choosing an authentication method, sizing the hardware appropriately, and providing a sufficient level of high availability and business continuity. You must also decide whether you will run vCenter Server as a VM or on a physical system. Finally, you must decide whether you will use the Windows Server–based version of vCenter Server or deploy the vCenter Server virtual appliance.

Master It What are some of the advantages and disadvantages of running vCenter Server as a VM?

Solution Some of the advantages include the ability to easily clone the VM for backup or disaster-recovery purposes, the ability to take snapshots to protect against data loss or data corruption, and the ability to leverage features such as vMotion or Storage vMotion. Some of the disadvantages include the inability to cold clone the vCenter Server VM, cold migrate the vCenter Server VM, or edit the virtual hardware of the vCenter Server VM. It could also add additional recovery complexity if there was an outage on the infrastructure running the vCenter Server VM.

Master It What are some of the advantages and disadvantages of using the vCenter Server virtual appliance?

Solution Some of the advantages include a potentially much easier deployment (just use the Deploy OVF Template option and perform post-deployment configuration instead of installing Windows Server, installing prerequisites, and finally, installing vCenter Server), more services available with a single deployment, and no Windows Server licensing requirements. Disadvantages include a lack of support for linked mode groups and no support for external SQL Server databases.

Install and configure a vCenter Server database. vCenter Server supports several enterprise-grade database engines, including Oracle and Microsoft SQL Server. Depending on the database in use, there are specific configuration steps and specific permissions that must be applied in order for vCenter Server to work properly.

Master It Why is it important to protect the database engine used to support vCenter Server?

Solution Although vCenter Server uses Microsoft Active Directory for authentication, the majority of the information managed by vCenter Server is stored in the backend database. The loss of the backend database would mean the loss of significant amounts of data that are crucial to the operation of vCenter Server. Organizations should take adequate steps to protect the backend database accordingly.

Install and configure the Single Sign On service.   SSO is a major change for the security model of vCenter Server. It allows the vSphere Web Client to present multiple solutions interfaces within a single console provided the authenticated user has access.

> **Master It**   After installing vCenter 5.5 and all the appropriate components, an administrator cannot log into the vCenter Server Web Client with his local credentials and gain access to vCenter. What could be missing from the configuration of SSO?

> **Solution**   SSO does not support local computer user accounts in any form. When configuring SSO, you have the ability to link it to an external directory service such as Active Directory or OpenLDAP. The other option is to manually configure local accounts within SSO itself. These are local to SSO, not local to the server that SSO is installed on.

Install and configure the Inventory Service.   The vCenter Inventory Service is a caching service that sits between the vCenter database and the vSphere Web Client used to reduce the load on the database and the vCenter Server itself.

> **Master It**   A corrupt Inventory database has been discovered in your vCenter server infrastructure and needs to be restored from backup. What data will be lost between when the backup was taken and when the corruption occurred?

> **Solution**   Luckily, the Inventory Service doesn't hold mission-critical data, and the data it does hold does not frequently change. Any custom tags that have been created since the last backup will be the only visible data loss to administrators. All the other data will automatically be flushed and recached from vCenter Server.

Install and configure vCenter Server.   vCenter Server is installed using the VMware vCenter Installer. You can install vCenter Server as a stand-alone instance or join a linked mode group for greater scalability. vCenter Server will use a predefined ODBC DSN to communicate with the separate database server.

> **Master It**   When preparing to install vCenter Server, are there any concerns about which Windows account should be used during the installation?

> **Solution**   From vCenter Server 5.0, no. The account just needs administrative permissions on the computer where vCenter Server is being installed. In previous versions, if you were using Microsoft SQL Server with Windows authentication, you had to log on to the computer that was going to run vCenter Server by using the account previously configured with the appropriate permissions on the SQL Server and SQL database. This is because the earlier versions of the vCenter Server Installer did not provide the ability to choose which account to use; it used the currently logged-on account. This is no longer the case for vCenter Server 5.0 and above.

Install and configure the Web Client Server.   The vSphere Web Client is the next generation of the vSphere client from VMware. Instead of installing a client on every machine used to administer vCenter, simply point a web browser to the Web Server Client Server from any machine.

Master It You have multiple vCenter Server instances within your environment that you wish to manage with the vCenter Web Client. Do you need to install a separate Web Client service for each vCenter server?

Solution No. Each vCenter Server instance can be registered to a single Web Client. When a user logs into the Web Client, only the vCenter objects they have rights to will be visible.

Use vCenter Server's management features. vCenter Server provides a wide range of management features for ESXi hosts and VMs. These features include scheduled tasks, host profiles for consistent configurations, tags for metadata, and event logging.

Master It Your manager has asked you to show him all of the VMs and hosts that belong to the accounts department but is not interested in seeing the test servers. What tools in vCenter Server will help you in this task?

Solution Provided you have vCenter Server configured with the appropriate tags and categories, a simple search on his requirements should provide enough information for your manager.

Chapter 4: vSphere Update Manager and the vCenter Support Tools

Install VUM and integrate it with the vSphere Client. vSphere Update Manager (VUM) is installed from the VMware vCenter installation media and requires that vCenter Server has already been installed. Like vCenter Server, VUM requires the use of a backend database server. Finally, you must install a plug-in into the vSphere Client in order to access, manage, and configure VUM.

Master It You have VUM installed, and you've configured it from the vSphere Client on your laptop. One of the other administrators on your team is saying that she can't access or configure VUM and that there must be something wrong with the installation. What is the most likely cause of the problem?

Solution The most likely cause is that the VUM plug-in hasn't been installed in the other administrator's vSphere Client. The plug-in must be installed on each instance of the vSphere Client in order to be able to manage VUM from that instance.

Determine which ESX/ESXi hosts or VMs need to be patched or upgraded. Baselines are the "measuring sticks" whereby VUM knows whether an ESX/ESXi host or VM instance is up-to-date. VUM compares the ESX/ESXi hosts or VMs to the baselines to determine whether they need to be patched and, if so, what patches need to be applied. VUM also uses baselines to determine which ESX/ESXi hosts need to be upgraded to the latest version or which VMs need to have their VM hardware upgraded. VUM comes with some predefined baselines and allows administrators to create additional baselines specific to their environments. Baselines can be fixed—the contents remain constant—or they can be dynamic, where the contents of the baseline change over time. Baseline groups allow administrators to combine baselines and apply them together.

Master It In addition to ensuring that all your ESX/ESXi hosts have the latest critical and security patches installed, you need to ensure that all your ESX/ESXi hosts have another specific patch installed. This additional patch is noncritical and therefore doesn't get included in the critical patch dynamic baseline. How do you work around this problem?

Solution   Create a baseline group that combines the critical patch dynamic baseline with a fixed baseline that contains the additional patch you want installed on all ESX/ESXi hosts. Attach the baseline group to all your ESX/ESXi hosts. When you perform remediation, VUM will ensure that all the critical patches in the dynamic baseline plus the additional patch in the fixed baseline are applied to the hosts.

Use VUM to upgrade VM hardware or VMware Tools.   VUM can detect VMs with outdated VM hardware versions and guest OSes that have outdated versions of VMware Tools installed. VUM comes with predefined baselines that enable this functionality. In addition, VUM has the ability to upgrade VM hardware versions and upgrade VMware Tools inside guest OSes to ensure that everything is kept up-to-date. This functionality is especially helpful after upgrading your ESX/ESXi hosts to version 5.5 from a previous version.

Master It   You've just finished upgrading your virtual infrastructure to VMware vSphere. What two additional tasks should you complete?

Solution   Upgrade VMware Tools in the guest OSes and then the virtual machine hardware to version 10.

Apply patches to ESX/ESXi hosts.   Like other complex software products, VMware ESX and VMware ESXi need software patches applied from time to time. These patches might be bug fixes or security fixes. To keep your ESX/ESXi hosts up-to-date with the latest patches, VUM can apply patches to your hosts on a schedule of your choosing. In addition, to reduce downtime during the patching process or perhaps to simplify the deployment of patches to remote offices, VUM can stage patches to ESX/ESXi hosts before the patches are applied.

Master It   How can you avoid VM downtime when applying patches (for example, remediating) to your ESX/ESXi hosts?

Solution   VUM automatically leverages advanced VMware vSphere features like Distributed Resource Scheduler (DRS). If you make sure that your ESX/ESXi hosts are in a fully automated DRS cluster, then VUM will leverage vMotion and DRS to move VMs to other ESX/ESXi hosts, avoiding downtime to patch the hosts.

Upgrade hosts and coordinate large-scale datacenter upgrades.   Upgrading hosts manually, each with dozens of VMs on them, is burdensome and doesn't scale well once you have more than a handful to deal with. Short outage windows, host reboots, and VM downtime mean that coordinating upgrades can involve complex planning and careful execution.

Master It   Which VUM functionality can simplify the process of upgrading vSphere across a large number of hosts and their VMs?

Solution   VUM can take care of these interactions in an automated fashion with what is known as an orchestrated upgrade. An orchestrated upgrade combines several baseline groups that include updates for the hosts, then subsequent updates for the VMs' hardware and VMware Tools. Virtual appliance upgrade baselines can also be included. When combined with fully automated DRS clusters and sufficient redundant capacity, potentially an entire vCenter's host inventory can be upgraded in one orchestrated task.

Utilize alternative approaches to VUM updates when required.   VUM presents the simplest and most efficient method to upgrade your vSphere hosts. However, sometimes VUM may not be available. For example, VUM is reliant on vCenter, so if the host isn't connected to a licensed vCenter, then an alternate method to upgrade the host must be used.

Master It   Without using VUM, how else can you upgrade an existing host?

Solution   You can grab the CD install media and run an interactive upgrade on the host. Or you can use the inherent command-line tool on the hosts' themselves: `esxcli software vib update` (see VMware Knowledge Base article 2008939 for full details) or `esxcli software vib install` to patch them with individual VIBs.

Install logging collectors.   vSphere includes two different logging tools for the ESXi hosts. The ESXi Dump Collector takes kernel dumps from the hosts, and the Syslog Collector can centrally store the host's log files.

Master It   You have just started a new job as the vSphere administrator at a company. The company hasn't previously centralized the hosts' logs and you decide you want to collect them, and so you want to install the vSphere Syslog Collector tool and the ESXi Dump Collector tool as well. How do you install them on the company's vCSA instance?

Solution   The Syslog Collector and ESXi Dump Collector are already included in vCSA and enabled by default. You should log into the vCSA console and check that the services are running and adjust the core dump's repository so it's large enough for their environment.

Configure hosts for centralized logging.   To make use of the ESXi Dump Collector or the Syslog Collector tools, you must configure each host to point to the centralized loggers.

Master It   List the ways you can configure your hosts for centralized logging.

Solution   You can send core dumps to the ESXi Dump Collector by using `esxcli system coredump` at each host's command line.

Use the Host Profiles feature in vCenter to propagate the same setting across multiple hosts, or continue to use the CLI on each host.

Use the Web Client to configure each host via its advanced settings under `syslog .global`.

Set each host via the CLI with `esxcli system syslog`.

Use the Host Profiles feature in vCenter to propagate the same setting across multiple hosts, or continue to use one of the previous two methods on each host.

Chapter 5: Creating and Configuring Virtual Networks

Identify the components of virtual networking.   Virtual networking is a blend of virtual switches, physical switches, VLANs, physical network adapters, virtual adapters, uplinks, NIC teaming, VMs, and port groups.

Master It   What factors contribute to the design of a virtual network and the components involved?

Solution   Many factors contribute to a virtual network design. The number of physical network adapters in each ESXi host, using vSphere Standard Switches versus vSphere Distributed Switches, the presence or use of VLANs in the environment, the existing network topology, requirements for the support of LACP or port mirroring, and the connectivity needs of the VMs in the environment are all factors that will play a role in the final network design. These are some common questions to ask while designing the network:

- Do you have or need a dedicated network for management traffic, such as for the management of physical switches?

- Do you have or need a dedicated network for vMotion traffic?

- Are you using 1 Gb Ethernet or 10 Gb Ethernet?

- Do you have an IP storage network? Is this IP storage network a dedicated network? Are you running iSCSI or NAS/NFS?

- Do you need extremely high levels of fault tolerance for VMs?

- Is the existing physical network composed of VLANs?

- Do you want to extend the use of VLANs into the virtual switches?

Create virtual switches and distributed virtual switches.   vSphere supports both vSphere Standard Switches and vSphere Distributed Switches. vSphere Distributed Switches bring new functionality to the vSphere networking environment, including private VLANs and a centralized point of management for ESXi clusters.

Master It   You've asked a fellow vSphere administrator to create a vSphere Distributed Switch for you, but the administrator is having problems completing the task because he can't find out how to do this with an ESXi host selected in the vSphere Web Client. What should you tell this administrator?

Solution   vSphere Distributed Switches aren't created on a per-ESXi-host basis but instead span multiple ESXi hosts at the same time. This is what enables the centralized configuration and management of distributed port groups. Tell the fellow vSphere administrator to navigate to the Distributed Switches area of the vSphere Web Client in order to create a new vSphere Distributed Switch.

Master It   As a joint project between the networking and server teams, you are going to implement LACP in your VMware vSphere 5.5 environment. What are some limitations you need to know about?

Solution   While vSphere 5.5 boasts enhanced LACP support over previous versions of vSphere, there are still limitations. You can't have multiple active link aggregation groups (LAGs) for a particular distributed port group. You also can't have both LAGs and stand-alone uplinks active for a given distributed port group. However, different distributed port groups could potentially use different LAGs, if so desired. The enhanced LACP support also requires the use of a version 5.5.0 vSphere Distributed Switch.

Create and manage NIC teaming, VLANs, and private VLANs.   NIC teaming allows virtual switches to have redundant network connections to the rest of the network. Virtual switches also provide support for VLANs, which provide logical segmentation of the network, and private VLANs, which provide added security to existing VLANs while allowing systems to share the same IP subnet.

Master It   You'd like to use NIC teaming to bond multiple physical uplinks together for greater redundancy and improved throughput. When selecting the NIC teaming policy, you select Route Based On IP Hash, but then the vSwitch seems to lose connectivity. What could be wrong?

Solution   The Route Based On IP Hash load-balancing policy requires that the physical switch be also configured to support this arrangement. This is accomplished through link aggregation, referred to as *EtherChannel* in the Cisco environment. Without an appropriate link aggregation configuration on the physical switch, using the IP hash load-balancing policy will result in a loss of connectivity. One of the other load-balancing policies, such as the default policy titled Route Based On Originating Virtual Port ID, may be more appropriate if the configuration of the physical switch cannot be modified.

Master It   How do you configure both a vSphere Standard Switch and a vSphere Distributed Switch to pass VLAN tags all the way up to a guest OS?

Solution   On a vSphere Standard Switch, you configure Virtual Guest Tagging (VGT, the name of this particular configuration) by setting the VLAN ID for the VM's port group to 4095.

On a vSphere Distributed Switch, you enable VGT by setting the VLAN configuration for a distributed port group to VLAN Trunking and then specifying which specific VLAN IDs should be passed up to the guest OS.

Examine the options for third-party virtual switches in your environment.   In addition to the vSphere Standard Switch and the vSphere Distributed Switch, vSphere also supports a number of third-party virtual switches. These third-party virtual switches support a range of features.

Master It   What three third-party virtual switches are, at the time of this book's writing, available for vSphere environments?

Solution   At the time this book was written, the three third-party virtual switches available for use with vSphere were the Cisco Nexus 1000V, the IBM Distributed Virtual Switch 5000V, and the HP FlexFabric 5900v.

Configure virtual switch security policies.   Virtual switches support security policies for allowing or rejecting Promiscuous mode, allowing or rejecting MAC address changes, and allowing or rejecting forged transmits. All of the security options can help increase layer 2 security.

Master It   You have a networking application that needs to see traffic on the virtual network that is intended for other production systems on the same VLAN. The networking application accomplishes this by using Promiscuous mode. How can you accommodate the needs of this networking application without sacrificing the security of the entire virtual switch?

Solution   Because port groups (or distributed port groups) can override the security policy settings for a virtual switch, and because there can be multiple port groups/distributed port groups that correspond to a VLAN, the best solution involves creating another port group that has all the same settings as the other production port group, including the same VLAN ID. This new port group should allow Promiscuous mode. Assign the VM with the networking application to this new port group, but leave the remainder of the VMs on a port group that rejects Promiscuous mode. This allows the networking application to see the traffic it needs to see without overly compromising the security of the entire virtual switch.

Master It   Another vSphere administrator on your team is trying to configure the security policies on a distributed switch but is having some difficulty. What could be the problem?

Solution   On a vSphere Distributed Switch, all security policies are set at the distributed port group level, not at the distributed switch level. Tell your fellow vSphere administrator to modify the properties of the distributed port group(s), not the distributed switch itself. He or she can also use the Manage Distributed Port Groups command on the Actions menu in the vSphere Web Client to perform the same task on multiple distributed port groups at the same time.

Chapter 6: Creating and Configuring Storage Devices

Differentiate and understand the fundamentals of shared storage, including SANs and NAS.   vSphere depends on shared storage for advanced functions, cluster-wide availability, and the aggregate performance of all the VMs in a cluster. Designing a high-performance and highly available shared storage infrastructure is possible on Fibre Channel, FCoE, and iSCSI SANs and is possible using NAS; in addition, it's available for midrange to enterprise storage architectures. Always design the storage architecture to meet the performance requirements first, and then ensure that capacity requirements are met as a corollary.

Master It   Identify examples where each of the protocol choices would be ideal for different vSphere deployments.

Solution   iSCSI would be a good choice for a customer with no existing Fibre Channel SAN and getting started with vSphere. Fibre Channel would be a good choice for a customer with an existing Fibre Channel infrastructure or for those that have VMs with high-bandwidth (200 MBps+) requirements (not in aggregate but individually). NFS would be a good choice where there are many VMs with a low-bandwidth requirement individually (and in aggregate) that is less than a single link's worth of bandwidth.

Master It   Identify the three storage performance parameters and the primary determinant of storage performance and how to quickly estimate it for a given storage configuration.

Solution   The three factors to consider are bandwidth (MBps), throughput (IOPS), and latency (ms). The maximum bandwidth for a single datastore (or RDM) for Fibre Channel is the HBA speed times the number of HBAs in the system (check the fan-in ratio and number of Fibre Channel ports on the array). The maximum bandwidth for a single datastore (or RDM) for iSCSI is the NIC speed times the number of NICs in the system, up to about 9 Gbps (check the fan-in ratio and number of Ethernet ports on the array). The maximum bandwidth for a single NFS datastore for NFS is the NIC link speed (across multiple datastores, the bandwidth can be balanced across multiple NICs). In all cases, the throughput (IOPS) is primarily a function of the number of spindles (assuming no cache benefit and no RAID loss). A quick rule of thumb is that the total number of

IOPS = IOPS × the number of that type of spindle. Latency is in milliseconds, though it can get to tens of milliseconds in cases where the storage array is overtaxed.

Understand vSphere storage options. vSphere has three fundamental storage presentation models: VMFS on block, RDM, and NFS. The most flexible configurations use all three, predominantly via a shared-container model and selective use of RDMs.

Master It Characterize use cases for VMFS datastores, NFS datastores, and RDMs.

Solution VMFS datastores and NFS datastores are shared-container models; they store virtual disks together. VMFS is governed by the block storage stack, and NFS is governed by the network stack. NFS is generally (without use of 10 GbE LANs) best suited to large numbers of low bandwidth (any throughput) VMs. VMFS is suited for a wide range of workloads. RDMs should be used sparingly for cases where the guest must have direct access to a single LUN.

Master It If you're using VMFS and there's one performance metric to track, what would it be? Configure a monitor for that metric.

Solution The metric to measure is queue depth. Use resxtop to monitor. The datastore-availability or used-capacity managed datastore alerts are good nonperformance metrics to use.

Configure storage at the vSphere layer. After a shared storage platform is selected, vSphere needs a storage network configured. The network (whether Fibre Channel or Ethernet based) must be designed to meet availability and throughput requirements, which are influenced by protocol choice and vSphere fundamental storage stack (and in the case of NFS, the network stack) architecture. Proper network design involves physical redundancy and physical or logical isolation mechanisms (SAN zoning and network VLANs). With connectivity in place, configure LUNs and VMFS datastores and/or NFS exports/NFS datastores using the predictive or adaptive model (or a hybrid model). Use Storage vMotion to resolve hot spots and other non-optimal VM placement.

Master It What would best identify an oversubscribed VMFS datastore from a performance standpoint? How would you identify the issue? What is it most likely to be? What would be two possible corrective actions you could take?

Solution An oversubscribed VMFS datastore is best identified by evaluating the queue depth and would manifest as slow VMs. The best way to track this is with resxtop, using the QUED (the Queue Depth column). If the queue is full, take any or all of these courses of action: Make the queue deeper and increase the Disk.SchedNumReqOutstanding advanced parameter to match; vacate VMs (using Storage vMotion); and add more spindles to the LUN so that it can fulfill the requests more rapidly or move to a faster spindle type.

Master It A VMFS volume is filling up. What are three possible nondisruptive corrective actions you could take?

Solution The actions you could take are as follows:

♦ Use Storage vMotion to migrate some VMs to another datastore.

♦ Grow the backing LUN, and grow the VMFS volume.

♦ Add another backing LUN, and add another VMFS extent.

Master It   What would best identify an oversubscribed NFS volume from a performance standpoint? How would you identify the issue? What is it most likely to be? What are two possible corrective actions you could take?

Solution   The workload in the datastore is reaching the maximum bandwidth of a single link. The easiest way to identify the issue would be using the vCenter performance charts and examining the VMkernel NIC's utilization. If it is at 100 percent, the only options are to upgrade to 10 GbE or to add another NFS datastore, add another VMkernel NIC, follow the load-balancing and high-availability decision tree to determine whether NIC teaming or IP routing would work best, and finally, use Storage vMotion to migrate some VMs to another datastore (remember that the NIC teaming/IP routing works for multiple data stores, not for a single datastore). Remember that using Storage vMotion adds additional work to an already busy datastore, so consider scheduling it during a low I/O period, even though it can be done live.

Configure storage at the VM layer.   With datastores in place, create VMs. During the creation of the VMs, place VMs in the appropriate datastores, and employ selective use of RDMs but only where required. Leverage in-guest iSCSI where it makes sense, but understand the impact to your vSphere environment.

Master It   Without turning the machine off, convert the virtual disks on a VMFS volume from thin to thick (eagerzeroedthick) and back to thin.

Solution   Use Storage vMotion and select the target disk format during the Storage vMotion process.

Master It   Identify where you would use a physical compatibility mode RDM, and configure that use case.

Solution   One use case would be a Microsoft cluster (either W2K3 with MSCS or W2K8 with WFC). You should download the VMware Microsoft clustering guide and follow that use case. Other valid answers are a case where virtual-to-physical mobility of the LUNs is required or one where a Solutions Enabler VM is needed.

Leverage best practices for SAN and NAS storage with vSphere.   Read, follow, and leverage key VMware and storage vendors' best practices/solutions guide documentation. Don't oversize up front, but instead learn to leverage VMware and storage array features to monitor performance, queues, and backend load—and then nondisruptively adapt. Plan for performance first and capacity second. (Usually capacity is a given for performance requirements to be met.) Spend design time on availability design and on the large, heavy I/O VMs, and use flexible pool design for the general-purpose VMFS and NFS datastores.

Master It   Quickly estimate the minimum usable capacity needed for 200 VMs with an average VM size of 40 GB. Make some assumptions about vSphere snapshots. What would be the raw capacity needed in the array if you used RAID 10? RAID 5 (4+1)? RAID 6 (10+2)? What would you do to nondisruptively cope if you ran out of capacity?

Solution   Using rule-of-thumb math, 200 × 40 GB = 8 TB × 25 percent extra space (snapshots, other VMware files) = 10 TB. Using RAID 10, you would need at least 20 TB raw. Using RAID 5 (4+1), you would need 12.5 TB. Using RAID 6 (10+2), you would need 12 TB. If you ran out of capacity, you could add capacity to your array and then add datastores and use Storage vMotion. If your array supports dynamic growth of LUNs, you could grow the VMFS or NFS datastores, and if it doesn't, you could add more VMFS extents.

Master It   Using the configurations in the previous question, what would the minimum amount of raw capacity need to be if the VMs are actually only 20 GB of data in each VM, even though they are provisioning 40 GB and you used thick on an array that didn't support thin provisioning? What if the array *did* support thin provisioning? What if you used Storage vMotion to convert from thick to thin (both in the case where the array supports thin provisioning and in the case where it doesn't)?

Solution   If you use thick virtual disks on an array that doesn't support thin provisioning, the answers are the same as for the previous question. If you use an array that does support thin provisioning, the answers are cut down by 50 percent: 20 TB for RAID 10, 6.25 TB for RAID 5 (4+1), and 6 TB for RAID 6 (10+2). If you use Storage vMotion to convert to thin on the array that doesn't support thin provisioning, the result is the same, just as it is if you do thin on thin.

Master It   Estimate the number of spindles needed for 100 VMs that drive 200 IOPS each and are 40 GB in size. Assume no RAID loss or cache gain. How many if you use 500 GB SATA 7200 RPM? 300 GB 10K Fibre Channel/SAS? 300 GB 15K Fibre Channel/SAS? 160 GB consumer-grade SSD? 200 GB Enterprise Flash?

Solution   This exercise highlights the foolishness of looking just at capacity in the server use case. 100 × 40 GB = 4 TB usable × 200 IOPS = 20,000 IOPS. With 500 GB 7200 RPM, that's 250 drives, which have 125 TB raw (ergo non-optimal). With 300 GB 10K RPM, that's 167 drives, which have 50 TB raw (ergo non-optimal). With 15K RPM, that's 111 drives with 16 TB raw (getting closer). With consumer-grade SSD, that's 20 spindles and 3.2 TB raw (too little). With EFD, that's 4 spindles and 800 GB raw (too little). The moral of the story is that the 15K RPM 146 GB drive is the sweet spot for this workload. Note that the extra space can't be used unless you can find a workload that doesn't need any performance at all; the spindles are working as hard as they can. Also note that the 4 TB requirement was usable, and we were calculating the raw storage capacity. Therefore, in this case, RAID 5, RAID 6, and RAID 10 would all have extra usable capacity in the end. It's unusual to have all VMs with a common workload, and 200 IOPS (as an average) is relatively high. This exercise also shows why it's efficient to have several tiers and several datastores for different classes of VMs (put some on SATA, some on Fibre Channel, some on EFD or SSD)—because you can be more efficient.

Chapter 7: Ensuring High Availability and Business Continuity

Understand Windows clustering and the different types of clusters.   Windows clustering plays a central role in the design of any high-availability solution for both virtual and physical servers. Microsoft Windows clustering gives us the ability to have application failover to the secondary server when the primary server fails.

Master It   Specifically with regard to Windows clustering in a virtual environment, what are three different types of cluster configurations that you can have?

Solution   The first is a cluster in a box, which is mainly used for testing or in a development environment where both nodes of a Windows cluster run on the same ESXi host. The second is the cluster across boxes, which is the most common form of clustering in a virtual environment. In this configuration, you can use Windows clustering on VMs that are running on different physical hosts. The third is the physical-to-virtual configuration, where you have the best of both the physical and virtual worlds by having a Windows clustering node on both a physical server and a virtual server.

Master It   What is the key difference between NLB clusters and Windows failover clusters?

Solution   Network Load Balancing (NLB) clusters are used primarily for scaling performance. Windows failover clusters are primarily used for high availability and redundancy.

Use vSphere's built-in high-availability functionality.   VMware Virtual Infrastructure has high-availability options built in and available to you out of the box: vSphere High Availability (HA) and vSphere Fault Tolerance (FT). These options help you provide better uptime for your critical applications.

Master It   What are the two types of high-availability options that VMware provides in vSphere, and how are they different?

Solution   VMware provides two forms of high availability in vSphere. vSphere HA provides a form of high availability by giving you the ability to restart any VMs that were running on a host that crashes. vSphere Fault Tolerance (FT) uses vLockstep technology to record and replay a running VM on another host in the cluster. Failover from the primary VM to the secondary VM is without any downtime. vSphere HA restarts the VM in the event of failure; vSphere FT does not need to restart the VM because the secondary VM is kept in lockstep with the primary and can take over immediately in the event of a failure.

Recognize differences between different high-availability solutions.   A high-availability solution that operates at the application layer, like Oracle Real Application Cluster (RAC), is different in architecture and operation from an OS-level clustering solution like Windows failover clustering. Similarly, OS-level clustering solutions are very different from hypervisor-based solutions such as vSphere HA or vSphere FT. Each approach has advantages and disadvantages, and today's administrators will likely need to use multiple approaches in their datacenter.

Master It   Name one advantage of a hypervisor-based high-availability solution over an OS-level solution.

Solution   Because a hypervisor-based solution would operate beneath the guest OS level, it would operate independently of the guest OS and could therefore potentially support any number of different guest OSes. Depending on the implementation, hypervisor-based solutions might be simpler than OS-level solutions. For example, vSphere HA is generally less complex and easier to set up or configure than Windows failover clustering.

Understand additional components of business continuity.   There are other components of ensuring business continuity for your organization. Data protection (backups) and replication of your data to a secondary location are two areas that can help ensure that business continuity needs are satisfied, even in the event of a disaster.

Master It   What are three methods to replicate your data to a secondary location and what is the golden rule for any continuity plan?

Solution   First, you have the backup and restore method from tape. It is a best practice to keep backup tapes off site and, when they are needed after a disaster, have them shipped to the secondary site. Second, you can replicate your data by using replication at the SAN level. This gives you the ability to replicate data over both short and long distances. Third, you can use a disk-to-disk backup appliance, such as vSphere Replication, that also offers off-site replication to another location. This method offers shorter backup windows as well as the benefits of off-site backups. Finally, the golden rule for any successful continuity design is to test, test, and test again.

Chapter 8: Securing VMware vSphere

Configure and control authentication to vSphere.   Both ESXi and vCenter Server have authentication mechanisms, and both products can utilize local users and groups or users and groups defined in external directories. Authentication is a basic tenet of security; it's important to verify that users are who they claim to be. You can manage local users and groups on your ESXi hosts using either the traditional vSphere Client or the command-line interface (such as the vSphere Management Assistant). Both the Windows-based and the Linux-based virtual appliance versions of vCenter Server can leverage Active Directory, OpenLDAP, or local SSO accounts for authentication as well.

Master It   You've asked an administrator on your team to create some accounts on an ESXi host. The administrator is uncomfortable with the command line and is having a problem figuring out how to create the users. Is there another way for this administrator to perform this task?

Solution   Yes, the administrator can use the traditional vSphere Client and connect directly to the ESXi hosts on which the accounts need to be created.

Manage roles and access controls.   Both ESXi and vCenter Server possess a role-based access control system that combines users, groups, privileges, roles, and permissions. vSphere administrators can use this role-based access control system to define very granular permissions that define what users are allowed to do with the vSphere Client against an ESXi host or the vSphere Web Client against a vCenter Server instance. For example, vSphere administrators can limit users to specific actions on specific types of objects within the vSphere Client. vCenter Server ships with some sample roles that help provide an example of how you can use the role-based access control system.

Master It   Describe the differences between a role, a privilege, and a permission in the ESXi/vCenter Server security model.

Solution   A role is a combination of privileges; a role is assigned to a user or group. Privileges are specific actions (like power on a VM, power off a VM, configure a VM's CD/DVD drive, and take a snapshot) that a role is allowed to perform. You combine privileges into a role. Permissions are created when you assign a role (with its associated privileges) to an inventory object within ESXi or vCenter Server.

Control network access to services on ESXi hosts. ESXi provides a network firewall that you can use to control network access to services on your ESXi hosts. This firewall can control both inbound and outbound traffic, and you have the ability to further limit traffic to specific source IP addresses or subnets.

Master It Describe how you can use the ESXi firewall to limit traffic to a specific source IP address.

Solution Within the Firewall Properties dialog box, the Firewall button allows you to specify a specific source IP address or source IP subnet.

Integrate with Active Directory. All the major components of vSphere—the ESXi hosts and vCenter Server (both the Windows Server–based version and the Linux-based virtual appliance) as well as the vSphere Management Assistant—support integration into Microsoft Active Directory. This gives vSphere administrators the option of using Active Directory as their centralized directory service for all major components of vSphere 5.5.

Master It You've just installed a new ESXi host into your vSphere environment and you are trying to configure the host to enable integration with your Active Directory environment. For some reason, though, it doesn't seem to work. What could be the problem?

Solution There could be a couple different issues at work here. First, the ESXi host needs to be able to resolve the domain name of the Active Directory domain via DNS. The ESXi host also needs to be able to locate the Active Directory domain controllers via DNS. This usually involves configuring the ESXi host to use the same DNS servers as the domain controllers. Second, there could be network connectivity issues; verify that the ESXi host has connectivity to the Active Directory domain controllers. If there are any firewalls between the ESXi host and the domain controllers, verify that the correct ports are open between the ESXi host and the domain controllers.

Chapter 9: Creating and Managing Virtual Machines

Create a virtual machine. A VM is a collection of virtual hardware pieces, like a physical system—one or more virtual CPUs, RAM, video card, SCSI devices, IDE devices, floppy drives, parallel and serial ports, and network adapters. This virtual hardware is virtualized and abstracted from the underlying physical hardware, providing portability to the VM.

Master It Create two VMs, one intended to run Windows Server 2012 and a second intended to run SLES 11 (64-bit). Make a list of the differences in the configuration that are suggested by the Create New Virtual Machine Wizard.

Solution vCenter Server suggests 1 GB of RAM, an LSI Logic parallel SCSI controller, and a 16 GB virtual disk for 64-bit SLES 11; for Windows Server 2012, the recommendations are 4 GB of RAM, an LSI Logic SAS controller, and a 40 GB virtual disk.

Install a guest operating system. Just as a physical machine needs an operating system, a VM also needs an operating system. vSphere supports a broad range of 32-bit and 64-bit operating systems, including all major versions of Windows Server, Windows 7, Windows XP, and Windows 2000 as well as various flavors of Linux, FreeBSD, Novell NetWare, and Solaris.

Master It What are the three ways in which a guest OS can access data on a CD/DVD, and what are the advantages of each approach?

Solution The three ways to access a CD/DVD are as follows:

◆ Client device: This has the advantage of being very easy to use; VMware administrators can put a CD/DVD into their local workstation and map it into the VM.

◆ Host device: The CD/DVD is physically placed into the optical drive of the ESXi host. This keeps the CD/DVD traffic off the network, which may be advantageous in some situations.

◆ An ISO image on a shared datastore: This is the fastest method and has the advantage of being able to have multiple VMs access the same ISO image at the same time. A bit more work may be required up front to create the ISO image.

Install VMware Tools. For maximum performance of the guest OS, it needs to have virtualization-optimized drivers that are specially written for and designed to work with the ESXi hypervisor. VMware Tools provides these optimized drivers as well as other utilities focused on better operation in virtual environments.

Master It A fellow administrator contacts you and is having a problem installing VMware Tools. This administrator has selected the Install/Upgrade VMware Tools command, but nothing seems to be happening inside the VM. What could be the cause of the problem?

Solution There could be any number of potential issues. First, a guest OS must be installed before VMware Tools can be installed. Second, if the VM is running Windows, AutoPlay may have been disabled. Finally, it's possible—although unlikely—that the source ISO images for VMware Tools installation have been damaged or deleted and need to be replaced on the host.

Manage virtual machines. Once a VM has been created, the vSphere Web Client makes it easy to manage. Virtual floppy images and CD/DVD drives can be mounted or unmounted as necessary. vSphere provides support for initiating an orderly shutdown of the guest OS in a VM, although this requires that VMware Tools be installed. VM snapshots allow you to take a point-in-time "picture" of a VM so that administrators can roll back changes if needed.

Master It What are the three different ways an administrator can bring the contents of a CD/DVD into a VM?

Solution The administrator can insert the CD/DVD into the system running the vSphere Web Client and use the Client Device option in the Virtual Machine Properties dialog box to mount that CD/DVD into the VM. The administrator can also attach the physical CD/DVD drive in the host to the VM and mount the drive, or the administrator can convert the CD/DVD into an ISO image. Once converted, the ISO image can be uploaded into a datastore and mounted into a VM.

Master It What is the difference between the Shut Down Guest command and the Power Off command?

Solution   The Shut Down Guest command uses VMware Tools to initiate an orderly shutdown of the guest OS. This ensures that the guest OS file system is consistent and that applications running in the guest OS are properly terminated. The Power Off command simply "yanks" the power from the VM, much like pulling the power cord out of the back of a physical system.

Modify virtual machines.   vSphere offers a number of features to make it easy to modify VMs after they have been created. Administrators can hot-add certain types of hardware, like virtual hard disks and network adapters, and some guest OSes also support hot-adding virtual CPUs or memory, although this feature must be enabled first.

Master It   Which method is preferred for modifying the configuration of a VM: editing the VMX file or using the vSphere Web Client?

Solution   Although it is possible to edit the VMX file to make changes, that method is error prone and is not recommended. Using the vSphere Web Client is the recommended method.

Master It   Name the types of hardware that cannot be added while a VM is running.

Solution   The following types of virtual hardware cannot be added while a VM is running: serial port, parallel port, floppy drive, CD/DVD drive, and PCI device.

Chapter 10: Using Templates and vApps

Clone a VM.   The ability to clone a VM is a powerful feature that dramatically reduces the amount of time to get a fully functional VM with a guest OS installed and running. vCenter Server provides the ability to clone VMs and to customize VMs, ensuring that each VM is unique. You can save the information to customize a VM as a customization specification and then reuse that information over and over again. vCenter Server can even clone running VMs.

Master It   Where and when can customization specifications be created in the vSphere Web Client?

Solution   Administrators can create customization specifications using the Customization Specification Manager, available from the vSphere Web Client home screen. Administrators can also create customization specifications while cloning VMs or deploying from templates by supplying answers to the Guest Customization Wizard and saving those answers as a customization specification.

Master It   A fellow administrator comes to you and wants you to help streamline the process of deploying Solaris x86 VMs in your VMware vSphere environment. What do you tell him?

Solution   You can use cloning inside vCenter Server to help clone VMs that are running Solaris x86, and that will help speed up the process of deploying new VMs. However, the Solaris administrator(s) will be responsible for customizing the configuration of the cloned VMs because vCenter Server is unable to customize a Solaris guest OS installation as part of the cloning process.

Create a VM template.   vCenter Server's templates feature is an excellent complement to the cloning functionality. With options to clone or convert an existing VM to a template, vCenter Server makes it easy to create templates. By creating templates, you ensure that your VM master image doesn't get accidentally changed or modified. Then, once a template has been created, vCenter Server can clone VMs from that template, customizing them in the process to ensure that each one is unique.

Master It   Of the following tasks, which are appropriate to be performed on a VM running Windows Server 2008 that will eventually be turned into a template?

   a.   Align the guest OS's file system to a 64 KB boundary.

   b.   Join the VM to Active Directory.

   c.   Perform some application-specific configurations and tweaks.

   d.   Install all patches from the operating system vendor.

Solution   The answers are as follows:

   a.   Yes. This is an appropriate task but unnecessary because Windows Server 2008 installs already aligned to a 64 KB boundary. Ensuring alignment ensures that all VMs then cloned from this template will also have their filesystems properly aligned.

   b.   No. This should be done by the vSphere Web Client Guest Customization Wizard or a customization specification.

   c.   No. Templates shouldn't have any application-specific files, tweaks, or configurations unless you are planning on creating multiple application-specific templates.

   d.   Yes. This helps reduce the amount of patching and updating required on any VMs cloned from this template.

Deploy new VMs from a template.   By combining templates and cloning, VMware vSphere administrators have a powerful way to standardize the configuration of VMs being deployed, protect the master images from accidental change, and reduce the amount of time it takes to provision new guest OS instances.

Master It   Another VMware vSphere administrator in your environment starts the wizard for deploying a new VM from a template. He has a customization specification he'd like to use, but there is one setting in the specification he wants to change. Does he have to create an all-new customization specification?

Solution   No. He can select the customization specification he wants to use and then select Use The Customization Wizard To Customize This Specification to supply the alternate values he wants to use for this particular VM deployment. He also has the option of cloning the existing customization specification and then changing the one setting within this new clone.

Deploy a VM from an OVF template.   Open Virtualization Format (OVF, formerly Open Virtual Machine Format) templates provide a mechanism for moving templates or VMs between different instances of vCenter Server or even entirely different and separate installations of VMware vSphere. OVF templates combine the structural definition of a VM along with the data in the VM's virtual hard disk and can exist either as a folder of files or as a single file. Because OVF templates include the VM's virtual hard disk, OVF templates can contain an installation of a guest OS and are often used by software developers as a way of delivering their software preinstalled into a guest OS inside a VM.

Master It A vendor has given you a Zip file that contains a VM they are calling a *virtual appliance*. Upon looking inside the Zip file, you see several VMDK files and a VMX file. Will you be able to use vCenter Server's Deploy OVF Template functionality to import this VM? If not, how can you get this VM into your infrastructure?

Solution You will not be able to use vCenter Server's Deploy OVF Template feature; this requires that the virtual appliance be provided with an OVF file that supplies the information that vCenter Server is expecting to find. However, you can use vCenter Converter to perform a V2V conversion to bring this VM into the VMware vSphere environment, assuming it is coming from a compatible source environment.

Export a VM as an OVF template. To assist in the transport of VMs between VMware vSphere installations, you can use vCenter Server to export a VM as an OVF template. The OVF template will include the configuration of the VM as well as the data found in the VM.

Master It You are preparing to export a VM to an OVF template. You want to ensure that the OVF template is easy and simple to transport via a USB key or portable hard drive. Which format is most appropriate, OVF or OVA? Why?

Solution The OVA format is probably a better option here. OVA distributes the entire OVF template as a single file, making it easy to copy to a USB key or portable hard drive for transport. Using OVF would mean keeping several files together instead of working with only a single file.

Work with vApps. vSphere vApps leverage OVF as a way to combine multiple VMs into a single administrative unit. When the vApp is powered on, all VMs in it are powered on, in a sequence specified by the administrator. The same goes for shutting down a vApp. vApps also act a bit like resource pools for the VMs contained within them.

Master It Name two ways to add VMs to a vApp.

Solution There are four ways to add VMs to a vApp: Create a new VM in the vApp, clone an existing VM into a new VM in the vApp, deploy a VM into the vApp from a template, and drag and drop an existing VM into the vApp.

Chapter 11: Managing Resource Allocation

Manage virtual machine memory allocation. In almost every virtualized datacenter, memory is the resource that typically comes under contention first. Most organizations run out of memory on their VMware ESXi hosts before other resources become constrained. Fortunately, VMware vSphere offers advanced memory-management technologies as well as extensive controls for managing the allocation of memory and utilization of memory by VMs.

Master It To guarantee certain levels of performance, your IT director believes that all VMs must be configured with at least 8 GB of RAM. However, you know that many of your applications rarely use this much memory. What might be an acceptable compromise to help ensure performance?

Solution One way would be to configure the VMs with 8 GB of RAM and specify a reservation of only 2 GB. VMware ESXi will guarantee that every VM will get 2 GB of RAM, including preventing additional VMs from being powered on if there isn't enough RAM to guarantee 2 GB of RAM to that new VM. However, the RAM greater than 2 GB is not guaranteed and, if it is not being used, will be reclaimed by the host for use elsewhere. If plenty of memory is available to the host, the ESXi host will grant what is requested; otherwise, it will arbitrate the allocation of that memory according to the share values of the VMs.

Master It   You are configuring a brand-new large-scale VDI environment but you're worried that the cluster hosts won't have enough RAM to handle the expected load. Which advanced memory management technique will ensure that your virtual desktops have enough RAM without having to use the swapfile?

Solution   Transparent page sharing. TPS ensures that if you have multiple VMs with the same blocks of memory, you allocate it only once. This can almost be thought of as "de-duplication for RAM." Within virtual desktop environments, many VMs are run as "clones" with their operating system and applications all identical—a perfect case for TPS to take advantage of.

Manage CPU utilization.   In a VMware vSphere environment, the ESXi hosts control VM access to physical CPUs. To effectively manage and scale VMware vSphere, administrators must understand how to allocate CPU resources to VMs, including how to use reservations, limits, and shares. Reservations provide guarantees to resources, limits provide a cap on resource usage, and shares help adjust the allocation of resources in a constrained environment.

Master It   A fellow VMware administrator is a bit concerned about the use of CPU reservations. She is worried that using CPU reservations will "strand" CPU resources, preventing those reserved but unused resources from being used by other VMs. Are this administrator's concerns well founded?

Solution   For CPU reservations, no. While it is true that VMware must have enough unreserved CPU capacity to satisfy a CPU reservation when a VM is powered on, reserved CPU capacity is not "locked" to a VM. If a VM has reserved but unused capacity, that capacity can and will be used by other VMs on the same host. The other administrator's concerns could be valid, however, for memory reservations.

Create and manage resource pools.   Managing resource allocation and usage for large numbers of VMs creates too much administrative overhead. Resource pools provide a mechanism for administrators to apply resource allocation policies to groups of VMs all at the same time. Resource pools use reservations, limits, and shares to control and modify resource allocation behavior, but only for memory and CPU.

Master It   Your company runs both test/development workloads and production workloads on the same hardware. How can you help ensure that test/development workloads do not consume too many resources and impact the performance of production workloads?

Solution   Create a resource pool and place all the test/development VMs in that resource pool. Configure the resource pool to have a CPU limit and a lower CPU shares value. This ensures that the test/development will never consume more CPU time than specified in the limit and that, in times of CPU contention, the test/development environment will have a lower priority on the CPU than production workloads.

Control network and storage I/O utilization. Memory, CPU, network I/O, and storage I/O make up the four major resource types that VMware vSphere administrators must effectively manage in order to have an efficient virtualized datacenter. By applying controls to network I/O and storage I/O, administrators can help ensure consistent performance, meet service-level objectives, and prevent one workload from unnecessarily consuming resources at the expense of other workloads.

> **Master It** Name two limitations of Network I/O Control.

> **Solution** Network I/O Control works only with vSphere Distributed Switches and it requires vCenter Server in order to operate. Another limitation is that system network resource pools cannot be assigned to user-created port groups.

> **Master It** What are the requirements for using Storage I/O Control?

> **Solution** All datastores and ESXi hosts that will participate in Storage I/O Control must be managed by the same vCenter Server instance. In addition, raw device mappings (RDMs) are not supported. Datastores must have only a single extent; datastores with multiple extents are not supported.

Utilize Flash Storage Flash storage is more popular than ever, and vSphere 5.5 has introduced the new vFlash Cache feature to sit alongside the Swap to Host Cache feature. This new resource type benefits environments that need maximum performance.

> **Master It** You have a VM that has a large I/O requirement. Which flash feature should you configure and why?

> **Solution** vFlash Cache should be used. This feature acts like a buffer to help accelerate IO for configured disks within individual VMs. The other feature, Swap to Host Cache, is for environments that are memory overcommitted.

Chapter 12: Balancing Resource Utilization

Configure and execute vMotion. vMotion is a feature that allows running VMs to be migrated from one physical ESXi host to another physical ESXi host with no downtime to end users. To execute vMotion, you must make sure both the ESXi hosts and the VMs meet specific configuration requirements. In addition, vCenter Server performs validation checks to ensure that vMotion compatibility rules are observed.

> **Master It** A certain vendor has just released a series of patches for some of the guest OSes in your virtualized infrastructure. You request an outage window from your supervisor, but your supervisor says to just use vMotion to prevent downtime. Is your supervisor correct? Why or why not?

> **Solution** Your supervisor is incorrect. vMotion can be used to move running VMs from one physical host to another, but it does not address outages within a guest OS because of reboots or other malfunctions. If you had been requesting an outage window to apply updates to the host, the supervisor would have been correct—you could use vMotion to move all the VMs to other hosts within the environment and then patch the first host. There would be no end-user downtime in that situation.

> **Master It** Is vMotion a solution to prevent unplanned downtime?

Solution No. vMotion is a solution to address planned downtime of the ESXi hosts on which VMs are running, as well as to manually load balance CPU and memory utilization across multiple ESXi hosts. Both the source and destination ESXi hosts must be up and running and accessible across the network in order for vMotion to succeed.

Ensure vMotion compatibility across processor families. vMotion requires compatible CPU families on the source and destination ESXi hosts in order to be successful. To help alleviate any potential problems resulting from changes in processor families over time, vSphere offers Enhanced vMotion Compatibility (EVC), which can mask differences between CPU families to maintain vMotion compatibility.

Master It Can you change the EVC level for a cluster while there are VMs running on hosts in the cluster?

Solution No, you cannot. Changing the EVC level means that you must calculate and apply new CPU masks. CPU masks can be applied only when VMs are powered off, so you can't change the EVC level on a cluster when there are powered-on VMs in that cluster.

Use Storage vMotion. Just as vMotion is used to migrate running VMs from one ESXi host to another, Storage vMotion is used to migrate the virtual disks of a running VM from one datastore to another. You can also use Storage vMotion to convert between thick and thin virtual disk types.

Master It Name two features of Storage vMotion that would help administrators cope with storage-related changes in their vSphere environment.

Solution You can use Storage vMotion to facilitate no-downtime storage migrations from one storage array to a new storage array, greatly simplifying the migration process. Storage vMotion can also migrate between different types of storage (FC to NFS, iSCSI to FC or FCoE), which helps vSphere administrators cope with changes in how the ESXi hosts access the storage. Finally, Storage vMotion allows administrators to convert VMDKs between thick and thin, to give them the flexibility to use whichever VMDK format is most effective for them.

Perform combined vMotion and Storage vMotion. Using vMotion and Storage at the same time gives you greater flexibility when migrating VMs between hosts. Utilizing this feature can also save time when you must evacuate a host for maintenance.

Master It A fellow administrator is trying to migrate a VM to a different datastore and a different host while it is running and wishes to complete the task as quickly and as simply as possible. Which migration option should she choose?

Solution Storage vMotion, like vMotion, can operate while a VM is running. However, choosing to perform both migration together will not only allow the VM to stay powered on, it turns what is regularly a two-step process into a single step.

Configure and manage vSphere Distributed Resource Scheduler. vSphere Distributed Resource Scheduler enables vCenter Server to automate the process of conducting vMotion migrations to help balance the load across ESXi hosts within a cluster. You can automate DRS as you wish, and vCenter Server has flexible controls for affecting the behavior of DRS and specific VMs within a DRS-enabled cluster.

Master It You want to take advantage of vSphere DRS to provide some load balancing of virtual workloads within your environment. However, because of business constraints, you have a few workloads that should not be automatically moved to other hosts using vMotion. Can you use DRS? If so, how can you prevent these specific workloads from being affected by DRS?

Solution   Yes, you can use DRS. Enable DRS on the cluster, and set the DRS automation level appropriately. For those VMs that should not be automatically migrated by DRS, configure a VM Override set to Manual. This will allow DRS to make recommendations on migrations for these workloads but it will not actually perform the migrations.

Configure and manage Storage DRS.   Building on Storage vMotion just as vSphere DRS builds on vMotion, Storage DRS automates the process of balancing storage capacity and I/O utilization. Storage DRS uses datastore clusters and can operate in Manual or Fully Automated mode. Numerous customizations exist—such as custom schedules, VM and VMDK anti-affinity rules, and threshold settings—to allow administrators to fine-tune the behavior of Storage DRS for their specific environments.

Master It   Name the two ways in which an administrator is notified that a Storage DRS recommendation has been generated.

Solution   On the Storage DRS tab of a datastore cluster, the recommendation(s) will be listed with an option to apply the recommendations. In addition, on the Alarms tab of the datastore cluster, an alarm will be triggered to indicate that a Storage DRS recommendation exists.

Master It   What is a potential disadvantage of using drag-and-drop to add a datastore to a datastore cluster?

Solution   When you use drag-and-drop to add a datastore to a datastore cluster, the user is not notified if the datastore isn't accessible to all the hosts that are currently connected to the datastore cluster. This introduces the possibility that one or more ESXi hosts could be "stranded" from a VM's virtual disks if Storage DRS migrates them onto a datastore that is not accessible from that host.

Chapter 13: Monitoring VMware vSphere Performance

Use alarms for proactive monitoring.   vCenter Server offers extensive alarms for alerting vSphere administrators to excessive resource consumption or potentially negative events. You can create alarms on virtually any type of object found within vCenter Server, including datacenters, clusters, ESXi hosts, and VMs. Alarms can monitor for resource consumption or for the occurrence of specific events. Alarms can also trigger actions, such as running a script, migrating a VM, or sending a notification email.

Master It   What are the questions a vSphere administrator should ask before creating a custom alarm?

Solution   You should ask yourself several questions before you create a custom alarm:

◆   Does an existing alarm meet my needs?

◆   Will vC Ops alert me without needing a custom alarm?

◆   What is the proper scope for this alarm? Do I need to create it at the datacenter level so that it affects all objects of a particular type within the datacenter or at some lower point?

◆ What are the values this alarm needs to use?

◆ What actions, if any, should this alarm take when it is triggered? Does it need to send an email or trigger an SNMP trap?

Work with performance charts. vCenter Server's detailed performance charts are the key to unlocking the information necessary to determine why an ESXi host or VM is performing poorly. The performance charts expose a large number of performance counters across a variety of resource types, and vCenter Server offers functionality to save customized chart settings, export performance graphs as graphic figures or Excel workbooks, and view performance charts in a separate window.

Master It You find yourself using the Chart Options link in the Advanced layout of the Performance tab to set up the same chart over and over again. Is there a way to save yourself some time and effort so that you don't have to keep re-creating the custom chart?

Solution Yes. After using the Chart Options dialog box to configure the performance chart to show the desired counters, use the Save Chart Settings button to save these settings for future use. The next time you need to access these same settings, they will be available from the Switch To drop-down list on the Advanced view of the Performance tab.

Understanding vCenter Operations Manager. vCenter Operations Manager adds to the functionality of vSphere by assisting in both performance monitoring and troubleshooting. The vC Ops analytics VM collates metrics from hosts and vCenter to calculate badges. The Web UI VM provides a standalone web interface and also integrates with the vSphere Web Client.

Master It All standard vCenter server licenses come with vCenter Operations Manager Foundation. This version is limited to four main features. What are they?

Solution The four main features within the Foundation version of vC Ops are Proactive Smart Alerts, Intelligent Operations Groups, vSphere Health Monitoring, and Self-Learning Performance Analytics.

Gather performance information using command-line tools. VMware supplies a few command-line tools that are useful in gathering performance information. For VMware ESXi hosts, resxtop provides real-time information about CPU, memory, network, or disk utilization. You should run resxtop from the VMware vMA. Finally, the vm-support tool can gather performance information that can be played back later using resxtop.

Master It Know how to run resxtop from the VMware vMA command line.

Solution Enter the command **vm-support -p -i 10 -d 180**. This creates a resxtop snapshot, capturing data every 10 seconds, for the duration of 180 seconds.

Monitor CPU, memory, network, and disk usage by ESXi hosts and VMs. Monitoring usage of the four key resources—CPU, memory, network, and disk—can be difficult at times. Fortunately, the various tools supplied by VMware within vCenter Server can lead the vSphere administrator to the right solution. In particular, using customized performance charts can expose the right information that will help a vSphere administrator uncover the source of performance problems.

Master It A junior vSphere administrator is trying to resolve a performance problem with a VM. You've asked this administrator to see if it is a CPU problem, and the junior administrator keeps telling you that the VM needs more CPU capacity because the CPU utilization is high within the VM. Is the junior administrator correct, based on the information available to you?

Solution Based on the available information, not necessarily. A VM may be using all of the cycles being given to it, but because the overall ESXi host is CPU constrained, the VM isn't getting enough cycles to perform acceptably. In this case, adding CPU capacity to the VM wouldn't necessarily fix the problem. If the host is indeed constrained, then migrating VMs to other hosts or changing the shares or the CPU limits for the VMs on this host may help alleviate the problem.

Chapter 14: Automating VMware vSphere

Identify tools available for automating vSphere. VMware offers a number of different solutions for automating your vSphere environment, including vCenter Orchestrator, PowerCLI, an SDK for Perl, an SDK for web service developers, and shell scripts in VMware ESXi. Each of these tools has its own advantages and disadvantages.

Master It VMware offers a number of different automation tools. What are some guidelines for choosing which automation tool to use?

Solution Two primary factors should dictate which tool you choose: your prior experience and the task you wish to complete. If you have experience with creating scripts using Perl, then you will likely be most effective in using the vSphere SDK for Perl to create automation tools. Similarly, having prior experience or knowledge of PowerShell will mean you will likely be most effective using PowerCLI. Recall that the most common tool used is PowerCLI because it is easy to adopt by administrators from the widest range of backgrounds. If you're looking for end-to-end process automation, then vCenter Orchestrator is your tool.

Create a PowerCLI script for automation. VMware vSphere PowerCLI builds on the object-oriented PowerShell scripting language to provide administrators with a simple yet powerful way to automate tasks within the vSphere environment.

Master It If you are familiar with other scripting languages, what would be the biggest hurdle in learning to use PowerShell and PowerCLI, other than syntax?

Solution Everything in PowerShell and PowerCLI is object based. Thus, when a command outputs results, those results are objects. This means you have to be careful to properly match object types between the output of one command and the input of the next command.

Use vCLI to manage ESXi hosts from the command line. VMware's command-line interface, or vCLI, is the new way of managing an ESXi host using the familiar `esxcfg-*` command set. By combining the features of fastpass with vCLI, you can seamlessly manage multiple hosts using the same command set from a single login.

Master It Have you migrated management and configuration operations for which you currently use the ESXi command-line interface to vMA?

Solution Migrating to vMA and the vCLI is extremely simple and can be done quickly using vMA's fastpass technology. Once a host has been configured for fastpass, you can execute the same scripts that were previously used by setting the fastpass target to transparently pass the commands to the host.

Use vCenter in combination with vMA to manage all your hosts. The new version of vMA can use vCenter as a target. This means that you can manage all of your hosts using vCLI without having to manually add each host to the fastpass target list.

Master It Use a combination of shell scripting with vCLI commands to execute commands against a number of hosts.

Solution Bash, the default shell for the vi-admin user, has a full-featured scripting environment capable of using functions, arrays, loops, and other control logic structures. Using these capabilities, in combination with the vCLI command set and fastpass, hosts in clusters can be efficiently configured to match.

Employ the Perl toolkit and VMware SDK for virtual server operations from the command line. The vCLI is designed for host management and consequently lacks tools for manipulating virtual servers. With the Perl toolkit, leveraged against the VMware SDK, any task that can be accomplished in the Virtual Infrastructure client can be done from the command line.

Master It Browse the sample scripts and SDK documentation to discover the world of possibilities that are unlocked by using Perl, or any of the other supported languages, to accomplish management tasks.

Solution Sample scripts are provided with the Perl toolkit on vMA at /usr/share/doc/vmware-viperl/samples. Additional utility scripts for assisting development of Perl applications can be found at /usr/lib/vmware-viperl/apps in the vMA's file structure. Refer to the documentation for their location when you install the Perl toolkit on a Windows server or desktop. SDK documentation can be found at www.vmware.com/sdk.

Configure vCenter Orchestrator vCenter Orchestrator is designed to allow vSphere administrators to run workflows against the vSphere environment and much more. To orchestrate against things like Active Directory and UCS or to run PowerShell scripts, you need the appropriate plug-ins installed and configured.

Master It How can you tell which plug-ins are installed and available for your use?

Solution The Plug-Ins tab of the vCenter Orchestrator Configuration page will list all of the plug-ins installed for vCenter Server. This requires the vCenter Orchestrator Configuration Service to be running and accessing it through your web browser at https://<computer IP address> or the DNS name 8283.

Use a vCenter Orchestrator workflow After vCenter Orchestrator is configured and running, you can use the vCenter Orchestrator client to run a vCenter Orchestrator workflow. vCenter Orchestrator comes with a number of preinstalled workflows to help automate tasks.

Master It An administrator in your environment configured vCenter Orchestrator and has now asked you to run a couple of workflows. However, when you log into the vCenter Server instance where vCenter Orchestrator is also installed, you don't see the icons for vCenter Orchestrator. Why?

Solution The vCenter Server installer creates the vCenter Orchestrator Start menu icons in the user-specific side of the Start menu, so they are visible only to the user who was logged on when vCenter Server was installed. Other users will not see the icons on the Start menu unless they are moved to the All Users portion of the Start menu.

Index